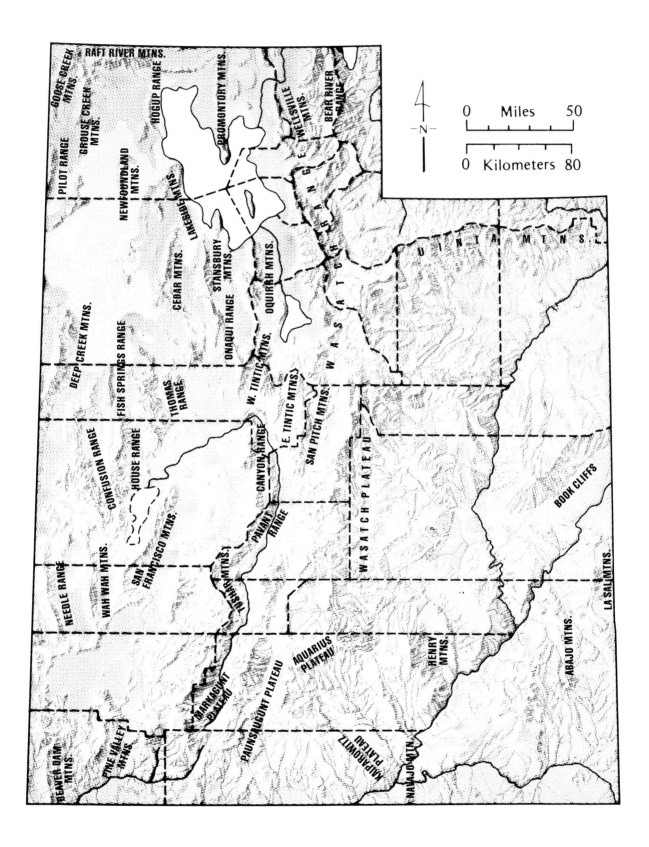

RAFT RIVER MTNS.
GOOSE CREEK MTNS.
PILOT RANGE
GROUSE CREEK MTNS.
HOGUP RANGE
PROMONTORY MTNS.
WELLSVILLE MTNS.
BEAR RIVER RANGE
NEWFOUNDLAND MTNS.
LAKESIDE MTNS.
CEDAR MTNS.
STANSBURY MTNS.
ONAQUI RANGE
OQUIRRH MTNS.
W A S A T C H   R A N G E
U I N T A   M T N S.
DEEP CREEK MTNS.
FISH SPRINGS RANGE
THOMAS RANGE
W. TINTIC MTNS.
E. TINTIC MTNS.
SAN PITCH MTNS.
WASATCH PLATEAU
BOOK CLIFFS
CONFUSION RANGE
HOUSE RANGE
SAN FRANCISCO MTNS.
CANYON RANGE
PAVANT RANGE
NEEDLE RANGE
WAH WAH MTNS.
TUSHAR MTNS.
LA SAL MTNS.
MARKAGUNT PLATEAU
PAUNSAUGUNT PLATEAU
AQUARIUS PLATEAU
HENRY MTNS.
ABAJO MTNS.
BEAVER DAM MTNS.
PINE VALLEY MTNS.
KAIPAROWITZ PLATEAU
NAVAJO MTN.

N

0   Miles   50

0   Kilometers   80

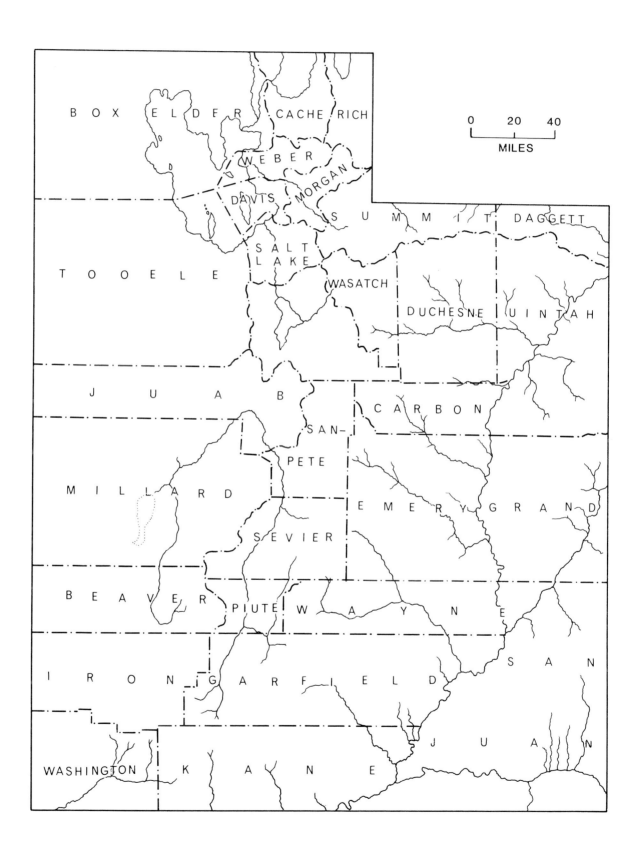

BOX ELDER CACHE RICH
WEBER
MORGAN
DAVIS SUMMIT DAGGETT
SALT LAKE
TOOELE WASATCH
DUCHESNE UINTAH
JUAB CARBON
SAN-
PETE
MILLARD EMERY GRAND
SEVIER
BEAVER PIUTE WAYNE
IRON GARFIELD SAN
JUAN
WASHINGTON KANE

0   20   40
MILES

Atlas of the

Vascular Plants of Utah

Beverly J. Albee

Leila M. Shultz

Sherel Goodrich

Published by

The Utah Museum of Natural History, Salt Lake City
with the aid of a grant from
The Ecology Center, Utah State University, Logan

1988
Utah Museum of Natural History
Occasional Publication No. 7

Published by the Utah Museum of Natural History,
    University of Utah, Salt Lake City, Utah,
    84112
International Standard Book Number :
    0-940378-09-4
Library of Congress Card Catalog Number:
    88-050778
Printed in the United States of America

*Publication of this book was made possible by
contributions from the Utah Museum of Natural
History; the Ecology Center, Utah State University, Logan, Utah; G. Michael Alder, Vice
Chairman, Native Plants, Inc., Salt Lake City;
the U.S. Forest Service, Ogden, Utah; and the
U.S. Bureau of Land Management, Salt Lake City.*

This work is dedicated to Lois Arnow, Curator of the Garrett Herbarium, who provided the vision for the beginning of the project as well as countless hours of labor needed for its completion.

PUBLISHER'S PREFACE

The Utah Museum of Natural History is pleased, as part of its Occasional Publications Series, to expand into another important aspect of natural history in the publishing of this book, *The Atlas of the Vascular Plants of Utah.* Previous numbers in the series have included works on ornithology, anthropology and geology.

It is not coincidence that the Museum's publication program makes this entry into the field of botany. The Garrett Herbarium, founded in 1870 and an integral part of the Museum since 1985 under the aegis of the University of Utah, provided a substantial part of the data from its collections. Support for the work of Beverly Albee, Associate Curator of the Herbarium, was provided by the University of Utah. The timely support of other organizations and individuals, acknowledged elsewhere, have made the publication possible.

Users of this book will find it to be carefully researched and thoughtfully written, the maps constituting the bulk of the work. Its depth is further enhanced by an extensive bibliography adding to its value as an important reference work on Utah's vascular plants.

Donald V. Hague, Director
Utah Museum of Natural History

CONTENTS

FOREWORD

During the past quarter century, knowledge about the Utah flora has grown at an uprecedented pace. That growth has been driven in part by an ever expanding force of trained botanists in high schools, colleges, universities, and natural resource agencies. In addition, governmental requirements that responsible environmental impact statements precede all significant alterations of the nation's environments were vigorously policed during the 1970s and early 1980s. That concern resulted in far more financial support for plant collections and for synthesis of knowledge about our flora than had been available in any previous period of comparable length. Plants of restricted distribution received special attention in connection with the Endangered Species Act. In combination, these factors have resulted in publication of many significant floristic and systematic reports that may not otherwise have appeared for many years. Numerous other reports were produced during the past score of years that exist only in the files of individual workers and the governmental agencies for which the work was done. Such reports are unknown to most students of our flora, but the specimens on which the reports were based have been deposited in the herbaria of one or more of the state's universities (Brigham Young University, University of Utah, and Utah State University). This atlas considers all specimens in the herbaria of those universities and is thus a synthesis of all past botanical collections in Utah.

Plant specimens are the most basic and the least arguable data points available for any flora. All systematic nomenclature is based upon them, and all scholarly conclusions concerning the taxa of a flora must be consistent with the morphological and distributional data inherent in the pool of available specimens. Most specimens convey phenological information that is of critical importance for many kinds of studies. The specimens also reveal evidence concerning morphological characteristics that may vary in predictable ways along environmental gradients such as elevation, latitude, or amount (or seasonality) of precipitation.

Much of the useful information inherent in correctly identifed specimens requires knowledge about where individual collections were made in horizontal and vertical space. Thus, descriptions of the geographical distribution of taxa are important syntheses of valuable information, not only for systematists but also for students of ecology, evolution, morphology, physiology, and reproductive biology.

Range distributions can be reported either in written form or as graphic representations in which collections are shown as dots on a detailed base map (as in this atlas). Such maps have a decided advantage over written accounts in that one sees at a glance the overall pattern of known distribution. Distribution maps that accurately report collection sites of available specimens of a particular taxon are of immense value to foresters, range scientists, horticulturists, agronomists, and sundry others searching for genetic sources adapted to specific geologic substrates or climatic zones. Fortunately, the format of this atlas will greatly facilitate such searches.

Authors of a work such as this atlas face a difficult dilemma relative to time of publication. Premature publication results in range maps that are so incomplete for a high percentage of the flora that distributional limits cannot be discerned with any degree of certainty. On the other hand, there is not likely to be a time in the foreseeable future when knowledgeable and determined collectors will not extend the known distribution of some taxa in a flora. Fortunately, all indications are that publication of the atlas is fully justified at this time. Its publication will almost certainly provide valid impressions of distributional limits for the vast majority of Utah's plant species. Perhaps more importantly, the maps will greatly enhance the efficiency of collectors' field efforts. Collectors who intelligently use the atlas can be more selective of where, when, and what they collect. As a result, solutions to genuinely critical problems facing students of the Utah flora should appear with ever increasing rapidity. In fact, time may well demonstrate that this atlas has stimulated more significant publications about our flora than any other single publication in history!

As significant new collections are made, it is hoped that collectors will make them known to the authors of the atlas and will deposit duplicate collections in the herbaria of the universities of the state. Periodic reports of significant new collections will undoubtedly be welcomed in a number of botanical journals that serve the professional community of the region.

KIMBALL T. HARPER
Professor
Department of Botany and Range Science
Brigham Young Universty

ix

PREFACE

The Atlas of the Vascular Plants of Utah provides distributional information for all native and introduced species growing in the state without benefit of cultivation. Data were obtained chiefly from collections housed in the Herbarium of Brigham Young University, Provo; the Garrett Herbarium of the University of Utah, Salt Lake City; the Intermountain Herbarium of Utah State University, Logan; the U.S. Bureau of Land Management Herbarium, St. George; Headquarters of the U.S. Park Service, Zion National Park; and the U.S. Forest Service Herbarium, Ogden. During the past ten years, Stanley Welsh, his associates and graduate students, have added some 215,000 Utah specimens to the collections at Brigham Young University. These large acquisitions, combined with accelerated collecting by curatorial staff members of the other major herbaria in the state during the same period, make this a propitious time to undertake publication of an atlas.

Beverly J. Albee, Associate Curator of the Garrett Herbarium, University of Utah, is responsible for the treatment accorded all families not covered by the other authors. Leila M. Shultz, Curator of the Intermountain Herbarium, Utah State University, is responsible for the treatment of Asteraceae; Sherel Goodrich, Range Conservationist, U.S. Forest Service, for treatments accorded Apiaceae, Cyperaceae, Grossulariaceae, Juncaceae, Salicaceae, and Saxifragaceae. The authors relied on the contribution of various specialists for the identification of plants in critical groups: specimens of *Mentzelia* were identified by Kay Thorne, Curator of the Herbarium, Brigham Young University; those of Poaceae by Lois Arnow, Curator of the Garrett Herbarium, University of Utah; of Polypodiaceae by Ralph Seiler, fern specialist; and of Viscaceae by Delbert Wiens, Professor of Biology, University of Utah. Whereas general agreement exists among taxonomists concerning species alignments, the treatment accorded some plant groups in the atlas provides an alternative, intentionally conservative view relative to that of other published works.

Approximately 400,000 specimens were critically examined during the seven-year course of the project. As with any floristic work, the value of the product is wholly dependent upon accurate determination of the taxonomic entities involved. Curators are well aware that herbarium specimens are not always correctly identified. For this reason, the authors and their collaborators carefully evaluated each specimen and take full responsibility for their determinations.

The distribution of species reported from more than one location is indicated by dots on a relief map, each dot representing from one to many collections. Species reported in the literature, but not seen by the authors, are represented by triangles. In order to keep the size of the book within reasonable bounds, we did not map subspecies or varieties, or species restricted to an area so small as to have been represented by a single dot on a map. The latter are listed alphabetically in the appendix by family and within the family by genus, with location data provided chiefly in terms of habitat and county. Additional distribution data for a few species were obtained after the maps were completed. In such instances, we added the new data to the appendix, with the result that the list now includes some species with two (rarely three) more or less distant populations.

The scientific name, colloquial name or (in a few instances) names, flowering time, status (whether native or introduced; annual or perennial; herb, shrub or tree), customary habitat, and altitudinal range for each species is provided below each map. Plants described as introduced have originated outside the North American continent; those described as native may be circumboreal, variously distributed in North America, locally endemic, adventive from neighboring states, or (rarely) representative of a disjunct population from the eastern half of the United States. Altitudinal data, usually provided on herbarium specimen labels in feet, have been transposed to the nearest 10 meters. For those unfamiliar with the metric system, a conversion chart to feet is provided. Although the altitudinal range occupied by each plant includes the extremes as specified on specimen labels, the habitat cited for each is that in which it most commonly grows.

Contemporary treatments consulted in assessing each specimen are listed in the bibliography. When multiple taxa currently recognized within a species complex could not be distinguished with certainty, the taxa in question were plotted as a single entity under the oldest name. All names thus excluded are listed in italics in the index, accompanied by the family and map number of the taxon with which they are synonymous. Names favored by other authors and names recently dropped from current use are similarly listed, thus the map for each species can be readily located by means of more than one name.

To the best of our knowledge, the Utah atlas is one of very few publications that provides a precise topographic locality for individual collections of the vascular plants of any sizeable area. Owing to the large size of most Utah counties and to the altitudinal variation within each, we decided early in the project that the usual one-dot-per-county maps would be of limited value. We also decided not to indicate on the base map the outlines of floristic provinces according to traditionally held precepts, in the hope that a more accurate assessment of such areas would evolve from analysis of the actual distribution of species as depicted in the atlas. We hope the information the atlas provides will be useful in various ways to those engaged in systematic and ecological research in this floristically rich and topographically complex area.

Our knowledge of the flora is inevitably incomplete. Natural vegetation is dynamic with new species constantly being introduced while others, for a variety of reasons, pass from the scene. The atlas maps reflect present knowledge based on current collections. Common species, however, are often ignored by collectors with the result that the maps do not necessarily reflect their true distribution. Moreover, areas infrequently visited are obviously not as well sampled as more accessible sites, thus the absence of a dot does not preclude the possibility that the plant occurs there. Range extensions verified by collections would be welcomed as a means of continuing the effort to increase our knowledge of the flora.

We are most grateful to the directors and curators of the various herbaria in Utah for permission to survey Utah collections. Stanley Welsh, Director, and Kay Thorne, Curator, of the Herbarium of Brigham Young University, and Mont Lewis, Curator of the U.S. Forest Service Herbarium in Ogden, were especially gracious in permitting us to invade their respective herbaria.

We wish to thank the following for providing access to unpublished manuscripts: Rupert Barneby (Fabaceae); Arthur Cronquist (Celastraceae, Cornaceae, Elaeagnaceae, Euphorbiaceae, Garryaceae, Haloragaceae, Linaceae, Lythraceae, Onagraceae, Santalaceae, Viscaceae, Zygophyllaceae, and *Rosa*); Elizabeth Neese (*Penstemon*); and Stanley Welsh (Cactaceae, Caryophyllaceae, Geraniaceae, Nyctaginaceae, Polygonaceae, Ranunculaceae, and Rhamnaceae). For access to unpublished distribution data, we thank Theodore Crovello (*Cardamine*), Barbara Ertter (*Ivesia*), and Stanley Welsh (Fabaceae and a number of smaller families).

The contributions of the following are also gratefully acknowledged: Pam Poulson and members of the Department of Geography of the University of Utah provided the base map; Gary Baird, Merton Franklin, and Robert Warrick, graduate students at Brigham Young University, supplied information concerning new additions to the flora of the Beaver Dam, La Sal, and Pine Valley Mountains; Tyrone Harrison, Larry Higgins, Kay Thorne, and Marvin and Pam Poulson reported new (1988) records for Utah; Jay Nielson, Supervisor of Exhibits, Utah Museum of Natural History, provided able assistance in guiding the book through the publication process; and last but by no means least, Marjorie Rasmussen, Herbarium Assistant, helped us through every phase of manuscript preparation.

Responsibility for typographical errors is shared by Lois Arnow, who prepared the camera-ready copy, and by Ted Arnow, who helped to proof the final manuscript.

HOW TO USE THE ATLAS

Maps depicting species distribution are arranged alphabetically according to family and within the family alphabetically according to genus and species. The family name appears on each page above the map depicting the first species in a family and also on the first map at the top of the left hand page if a continuation. Each family and the map for each species within a family is numbered. Those plants restricted in distribution (as explained above) are listed alphabetically in the appendix under the family number assigned therein.

Names recently dropped from current use or currently preferred by other authors (alternate names) are given in italics in the index, followed by the family and map number of the taxon with which they are synonymous. A page index to the families is provided on the inside back cover.

An asterisk precedes the names of species currently listed by the U.S. Fish and Wildlife Service (1987, addendum 1988) as endangered or threatened.

METER-FOOT COMPARATIVE CHART

(For conversion of meters to an approximate number of feet, multiply meters by 3.3)

606 m = ca 2000 ft	2424 m = ca 8000 ft
757 m = ca 2500 ft	2575 m = ca 8500 ft
909 m = ca 3000 ft	2727 m = ca 9000 ft
1060 m = ca 3500 ft	2878 m = ca 9500 ft
1212 m = ca 4000 ft	3030 m = ca 10,000 ft
1363 m = ca 4500 ft	3181 m = ca 10,500 ft
1515 m = ca 5000 ft	3333 m = ca 11,000 ft
1666 m = ca 5500 ft	3484 m = ca 11,500 ft
1818 m = ca 6000 ft	3636 m = ca 12,000 ft
1969 m = ca 6500 ft	3787 m = ca 12,500 ft
2121 m = ca 7000 ft	3939 m = ca 13,000 ft
2272 m = ca 7500 ft	4090 m = ca 13,500 ft

INTRODUCTION

VEGETATION OF UTAH

James A. MacMahon
Department of Biology
Utah State University

Utah is a diverse land of strong contrasts. Elevations throughout the state's 219,932 sq km (84,916 sq mi) range from 670 m (2,200 ft) along the Beaver Dam Wash, Washington Co., to 4,123 m (13,528 ft) on King's Peak in the Uinta Mountains. In places, one can view black basaltic flows overriding bright red sandstones. It is in the context of this environmental variation of both substrate and climate that the state's approximately 2,500 indigenous vascular plant species form recognizable vegetational units.

The structure of these plant admixtures differs in detail from place to place and from time to time. Nonetheless, a variety of workers have attempted to classify groupings of plants into an ecological hierarchy of community types or assemblages. Had this atlas been available to them, scientists would surely have developed more quantitative and informative classifications than those that have emerged. To give some sense of the different attempts at vegetation classification for the state, three examples are provided. The first (Fig. 1) is adapted from Holmgren (1972). This simple presentation of six vegetation zones includes little detail, but it is sufficiently appealing that with minor changes (Fig. 2) it is often used to depict the state's natural resources, e. g., Murphy (1981). Figure 3 uses data derived from climatic variables to predict where major vegetation boundaries should occur (MacMahon and Wieboldt, 1978). A surprising correspondence exists between this predictive system and the empirical system depicted in Figs. 1 and 2. The latter were developed on the basis of botanists' views of where natural "breaks" in vegetation types occur, whereas Fig. 3 relies on the development of life zone boundaries that are predicted on the basis of combinations of three environmental factors (potential evaporation, annual precipitation, and mean annual biotemperature). Figure 4 is based on specific plant species' distributions and a scheme that is of higher resolution than the others (Küchler, 1964). These subdivisions will be used to summarize Utah's vegetation, even though some of them are not familiar. In this limited space, I cannot exhaustively discuss the various vegetation types. Rather, a brief description of each is given, and additional information may be obtained from the references provided.

VEGETATION TYPES

WARM DESERT SHRUBLANDS

Only one warm desert shrubland occurs in Utah, although its species composition varies greatly from place to place. This is especially obvious where soils vary; for example, along the length of a bajada, or where loose sand abuts more stabilized soils, whether they are sandy or not.

Creosote Bush.—This vegetation type corresponds to the northern extension of the Mojave Desert into Utah. The extent of the vegetation type coincides almost exactly with the distribution of creosote bush (*Larrea tridentata*). On lower and mid-slopes of the Beaver Dam Mountains, significant stands of the stately Joshua tree (*Yucca brevifolia*) dominate the view, often mixed with a variety of Great Basin desert species. Many plant species enter the boundaries of the state only in the Mojave Desert section (MacMahon and Wagner, 1985).

COOL DESERTS, SHRUB STEPPES, AND WOODLANDS

These vegetation types dominate in dry areas of valleys and lower slopes of mountains and plateaus in Utah (West, 1988). The dominant shrubs, grasses, and short trees are adapted to the temperate climates of the state's moderate elevations (above 1,000 m but generally below 2,000 m).

Sagebrush Steppe.—Big sagebrush (*Artemisia tridentata*) dominates this vegetation type along with bunch grasses such as *Agropyron, Festuca,* and *Elymus.* This vegetation barely enters Utah in the north and is more characteristic of Wyoming, Idaho, and Oregon (Tisdale and Hironaka, 1981).

Great Basin Sagebrush.—This vegetation type differs from the Sagebrush Steppe by its impoverished flora. Three subspecies of sagebrush occur in this type (Shultz, 1986), which occupies about 15 per cent of Utah's land area. Depending on the elevation, soil depth, and grazing history, codominants include *Tetradymia, Chrysothamnus, Grayia, Atriplex, Ephedra,* and *Ceratoides.* Surprisingly few native forbs occur. The examples of Great Basin Sagebrush in the western part of the state, coupled with the next type, comprise our portion of the Great Basin or Cool Desert.

Saltbush-Greasewood Shrublands.—Nearly 30 per cent of Utah is dominated by valleys that have moderately to highly saline soils and support this mixture of species. Drier, drained sites contain *Atriplex*, especially shadscale (*A. confertifolia*), in association with *Kochia* and *Ceratoides*. Areas where the water table is near the surface often support nearly pure stands of greasewood (*Sarcobatus vermiculatus*) and other salt-tolerant plants such as *Salicornia, Suaeda,* and *Allenrolfea.*

Blackbrush.—This vegetation type is defined by the presence of blackbrush (*Coleogyne ramosissima*), a species occurring in a band straddling the Utah-Arizona border and northeastward along the Colorado River area. This species prefers shallow soils, often with a caliche layer; and it is not unusual for it to occur in nearly pure stands. When it does mix with other species, these often include Mojave Desert forms such as *Krameria, Thamnosma, Lycium,* or *Prunus fasciculata*. Many blackbrush sites are transitional between the Mojave Desert and the deserts of the Great Basin, containing indicators of both. As soils deepen, grasses such as *Hilaria* increase in abundance. In very deep soils, blackbrush loses its dominance to *Bouteloua* and *Muhlenbergia* (Bowns and West, 1976; West, 1983).

Galleta-Three Awn Shrubsteppe.—This vegetation is nearly confined to southeastern Utah on deep soils of the Canyonlands area. Sites are dominated by a variety of bunch and sod-forming grasses. Grazing causes rapid deterioration of stands. Dominants include *Hilaria jamesii, Stipa comata, Oryzopsis hymenoides,* and *Sporobolus cryptandrus*. Interestingly, one of the supposed indicators, *Aristida*, is short-lived and often weedy (Kleiner and Harper, 1972, 1977).

Pinyon-juniper Woodlands.—These pygmy conifer forests cover vast areas of the West. Nearly 30 percent of Utah's land area supports one of the variants of this woodland type (West et al., 1975; Tueller et al., 1979). Depending on the site, the dominant species of pines and junipers will vary, but include some combination of *Pinus edulis, P. monophylla,* and *Juniperus osteosperma* or *J. scopulorum* for most Utah localities. Generally, junipers decrease and pines increase as elevation rises. Many pygmy conifer stands, especially at lower elevations, are quite open and have a sparse understory despite the fact that many species are known to occur with these conifers.

Mountain Mahogany-Oak Scrub.—Along the lower slopes of the Wasatch Range, one sees large stands of Gambel oak (*Quercus gambelii*) mixed with *Acer, Amelanchier, Cercocarpus* (especially *C. ledifolius*), and *Symphoricarpos*. Whereas this vegetation type is conspicuous because of its fall coloration, it is little studied (Harper et al., 1985; Hayward, 1948) and no consensus exists as to its subdivisions. At upper elevations, Gambel oak is replaced by conifers, especially pines and firs.

MONTANE CONIFER FORESTS

At elevations above the pygmy conifer forests and below the spruce-fir forest, several prominent combinations of conifers occur. These vary depending on elevation, soil acidity, and site dryness. The four types that have been delimited for Utah usually contain Douglas fir (*Pseudotsuga menziesii*), ponderosa pine (*Pinus ponderosa*), or a combination of the two as dominants.

Arizona Pine Forest.—These are typical ponderosa pine stands, often on dry, acidic soils. Lower elevation stands are quite open and are often underlain with dense grass stands (*Festuca, Muhlenbergia, Poa*) that carry fires and prevent establishment of young pines, except during rare episodes of good seedbeds, appropriate weather, and an absence of fire. In many Utah sites, open ponderosa stands have manzanita (*Arctostaphylos*) as an understory.

Pine-Douglas Fir Forest.—This combination of ponderosa pine and Douglas fir occurs as a discrete community mainly as a southeastern Utah outlier of a vegetation type more characteristic of Arizona, New Mexico, and southern Colorado. Such mixed stands with an open aspect and shrubby ground layer are unusual in Utah.

Douglas Fir Forest.—At higher elevations in some of our mountains, one finds ponderosa pine stands mixed with Douglas fir that appear to belong to the preceeding vegetation type. These are usually successional sites that will give way to Douglas fir climax forest. Often lodgepole pine (*Pinus contorta*) is a component of such areas. White fir (*Abies concolor*) and blue spruce (*Picea pungens*) occur spottily in this vegetation type, usually in canyon bottoms. White fir grows at elevations as low as 1,515 m, whereas blue spruce is seldom found below 1,970 m. Most sites have fairly good understories of *Berberis, Symphoricarpos, Physocarpus,* and some grasses.

Spruce-Fir-Douglas Fir.—This vegetation type is characterized by an increased abundance of white fir and blue spruce, in association with Douglas fir. Such sites occur in the Uinta Mountains and are increasingly common in mountains in the southern half of the state where mixed conifer stands may easily contain five species. A deciduous layer of small trees and shrubs gives this southern forest a different look than that of forests in northern Utah where the same three species occur.

SUBALPINE FORESTS AND WOODLANDS

Spruce-fir forests in Utah occur primarily in the subalpine zones of mountain ranges. The predominant tree species are subalpine fir (*Abies lasiocarpa*) and Engelmann spruce (*Picea engelmannii*), although they do not always occur together. Anywhere one looks in the Rocky Mountains, spruce-fir forests appear quite similar. In well-developed stands, few understory herbs occur, although woody, low-growing *Vaccinium* sp. may be abundant. More open stands have more diverse understories. Middle successional stages are dominated by the ubiquitous aspen (*Populus tremuloides*).

Southwestern Spruce-Fir Forest.—Forests designated by Küchler (1964) as this type occur only in the LaSal and Abajo Mountains. Their affinities are with the spruce-fir forests of southern Colorado and extreme northern New Mexico. This type is differentiated mainly by the presence of corkbark fir (*Abies lasiocarpa* var. *arizonica*). Although this is not a sufficient reason, in my view, to distinguish these forests; they do seem to have fewer broad-leafed shrubs and herbs in their lower layers.

Western Spruce-Fir Forest.—These are the typical subalpine forests scattered widely along the length of the Wasatch Range, in the Uintas, and in other isolated Utah ranges at higher elevations (MacMahon and Andersen, 1982). In addition to Engelmann spruce and subalpine fir stands, lodgepole pine can be locally common after fires, or may even be a climax species in isolated parts of the Uinta Mountains (Mauk and Henderson, 1984).

The common understory species of the spruce-fir forests vary from place to place depending on local microclimates and soils, but common plants include *Vaccinium scoparium, Arnica cordifolia, Pedicularis racemosa, Calamagrostis canadensis, Acer glabrum, Sorbus scopulina, Berberis repens,* or *Paxistima myrsinites.*

On adverse sites including dry, exposed ridge tops, limber pine (*Pinus flexilis*) may be the dominant tree, although it also occurs in less extreme habitats. Bristlecone pine (*Pinus longaeva*) is also found on some dry, exposed ridge tops and cliff edges, mainly in the western and southwestern parts of the state.

At timberline, dwarfed forms may include odd mixtures of pines, spruces, and firs, depending on local conditions and the biogeographic history of the particular mountain range.

ALPINE VEGETATION

Truly alpine vegetation in Utah occurs well above 2,750 m. Species composition varies greatly from one site to another, making generalizations difficult. Additionally, few detailed alpine vegetation studies are available for the state (Billings, 1978; Briggs and MacMahon, 1982, 1983; Hayward, 1952; McMillan, 1948).

Alpine Meadows.—Although Küchler (1964) maps this particular vegetation type, several variants are subsumed under this title. These differ principally in the degree to which they are covered by snow in winter, the rockiness of the soil, and the amount of soil "wetness". *Geum rossii* is common on exposed rocky sites whereas *Deschampsia caespitosa* is more often a plant of snow-covered areas or wet meadows. Many sites that have extreme exposures and shallow rocky soils are characterized by cushion plants such as *Silene acaulis* and *Paronychia pulvinata.* A number of species of sedge (*Carex*) dominate both wet and dry sites. On many sites, species of *Potentilla, Danthonia, Polygonum, Kobresia, Arenaria,* and *Draba* may be codominants.

AZONAL VEGETATION TYPES

Most of the vegetation described above is correlated, in broad terms, with regional climatic zones. Several of the vegetation types, however, are related to local conditions that occur within a variety of zones rather than within any one climatic zone.

Tule Marshes.—Wet areas that are dominated by bulrushes (*Scirpus*) and cattail (*Typha*) are common throughout the valleys of Utah. Sedges (*Carex*) are also frequently present and may dominate in shallow waters.

Riparian and Canyon Woodlands.—In upland areas these include willows (*Salix*), mountain alder (*Alnus incana*), narrowleaf cottonwood (*Populus angustifolia*), water birch (*Betula occidentalis*), and box elder (*Acer negundo*). These woodlands present a marked contrast to riparian woodlands of lower areas where one of the following often dominate: sandbar willow (*Salix exigua*), Fremont cottonwood (*Populus fremontii*), Russian olive (*Eleagnus angustifolia*), or tamarisk (*Tamarix*) .

"Desert" Areas Without Vegetation.—When sites are extreme because of salinity, soil crusting, or soil instability (e.g., very active sand dunes), no appreciable vegetation occurs. The vast salt flats around the Great Salt Lake fit this category, one that Küchler (1964) erects, but never discusses. Such areas are not always confined to zones that we would classify as deserts; for example, the Coral Pink Sand Dunes of Kane County, sit among pines and junipers.

Figure 4 indicates, as did Küchler (1964), that a small area just north of Kanab has as its potential natural vegetation a wheatgrass-bluegrass community that generally occurs in the Pacific Northwest. Whereas some of Küchler's indicator species do occur in this area of Utah, I do not accept that they represent an outlier of this particular vegetation type and have thus ignored it in this introduction.

LITERATURE CITED

Billings, W. D. 1978. Alpine phytogeography across the Great Basin. In: Intermountain Biogeography: A symposium. Great Basin Nat. Mem. 2: 105-117.

Bowns, J. E.; N. E. West. 1976. Blackbrush (*Coleogyne ramosissima* Torr.) on southwestern Utah rangelands. Utah Agric. Exper. Sta. Res. Rep. 27. Utah State University, Logan. 27 pp.

Briggs, G. M.; J. A. MacMahon. 1982. Structure of alpine plant communities near King's Peak, Uinta Mountains, Utah. Great Basin Nat. 42: 50-59.

_____ . 1983. Alpine and subalpine wetland plant communities of the Uinta Mountains, Utah. Great Basin Nat. 43: 523-530.

Harper, K. T.; F. J. Wagstaff; L. M. Kunzler. 1985. Biology and management of the Gambel oak vegetative type: A literature review. U.S. Forest Service, Gen. Tech. Rep. INT-179. Intermtn. Forest and Range Exper. Sta., Ogden, Utah. 31 pp.

Hayward, C. L. 1948. Biotic communities of the Wasatch chaparral, Utah. Ecol. Monog. 18: 473-506.

_____ . 1952. Alpine biotic communities of the Uinta Mountains, Utah. Ecol. Monogr. 22: 93-120.

Holdridge, L. R. 1967. Life zone ecology, rev. ed. Tropical Science Center, San Jose, Costa Rica.

Holmgren, N. H. 1972. Plant geography of the Intermountain Region. In: Intermountain flora, vol. 1, A. Cronquist, A. H. Holmgren, N. H. Holmgren, and J. L. Reveal, pp. 77-161. Hafner Publishing Co., New York.

Kleiner, E. F.; K. T. Harper. 1972. Environment and community organization in grasslands of Canyonlands National Park. Ecology 53: 299-309.

_____ . 1977. Occurrence of four major perennial grasses in relation to edaphic factors in a pristine community. J. Range Managem. 30: 286-289.

Küchler, A. W. 1964. Manual to accompany the map: Potential natural vegetation of the conterminous United States. American Geographical Society, Special Publ. 36. New York. 116 pp.

MacMahon, J. A.; D. C. Andersen. 1982. Subalpine forests: A world perspective with emphasis on western North America. Progress in Physical Geography 6: 368-425.

MacMahon, J. A.; F. H. Wagner. 1985. The Mohave, Sonoran and Chihuahuan deserts of North America. In: Hot deserts and arid shrublands A., M. Evenari et al., eds., pp. 105-202. Elsevier Science Publishers B. V., Amsterdam, The Netherlands.

MacMahon, J. A.; T. F. Wieboldt. 1978. Applying biogeographic principles to resource management: A case study evaluating Holdridge's life zone model. In: Intermountain biogeography: A symposium. Great Basin Nat. Mem. 2: 245-257.

Mauk, R. L.; J. A. Henderson. 1984. Coniferous forest habitat types of northern Utah. U.S. Forest Service, Gen. Tech. Rep. INT-170. Intermtn. Forest and Range Exper. Sta., Ogden, Utah. 89 pp.

McMillan, C. 1948. "A taxonomic and ecological study of the flora of the Deep Creek Mountains of central western Utah." University of Utah, Salt Lake City. Thesis.

Murphy, D. R. 1981. Vegetation zones. In: Atlas of Utah, D. C. Greer, K. D. Gurgel, W. L. Wahlquist, H. A. Christy, and G. B. Peterson, pp. 30-32. Brigham Young University Press, Provo, Utah.

Shultz, L. M. 1986. Taxonomic and geographic limits of *Artemisia* subgenus *Tridentatae* (Beetle) McArthur. In: The biology of *Artemisia* and *Chrysothamnus*, E. D. McArthur; B. L. Welch, eds., pp. 20-28. U.S. Forest Service, Intermtn. Research Sta., Ogden, Utah.

Tisdale, E. W.; M. Hironaka. 1981. The sagebrush-grass region: A review of the ecological literature. Forest, Wildlife and Range Exper. Sta. Bull. 33. University of Idaho, Moscow. 31 pp.

Tueller, P.T.; C. D. Beeson; R. J. Tausch; N. E. West; K. H. Rea. 1979. Pinyon-juniper woodlands of the Great Basin: Distribution, flora, vegetal cover. USDA Research Paper INT-229. Intermtn. Forest and Range Exper. Sta., Ogden, Utah. 22 pp.

West, N. E. 1983. Colorado Plateau-Mohavian blackbrush semi-desert. In: Temperate deserts and semi-deserts, N. E. West, ed., pp. 399-421. Elsevier Scientific Publishing Co., Amsterdam, The Netherlands.

_____ . 1988. Intermountain deserts, shrub steppes, and woodlands. In: North American terrestrial vegetation, M. G. Barbour and W. D. Billings, eds., pp. 209-230. Cambridge University Press, Cambridge.

West, N. E.; K. H. Rea; R. J. Tausch. 1975. Basic synecological relationships in juniper-pinyon woodlands. In: The pinyon-juniper ecosystem: A symposium, pp. 41-54. College of Natural Resources and Utah Agric. Exper. Sta., Logan.

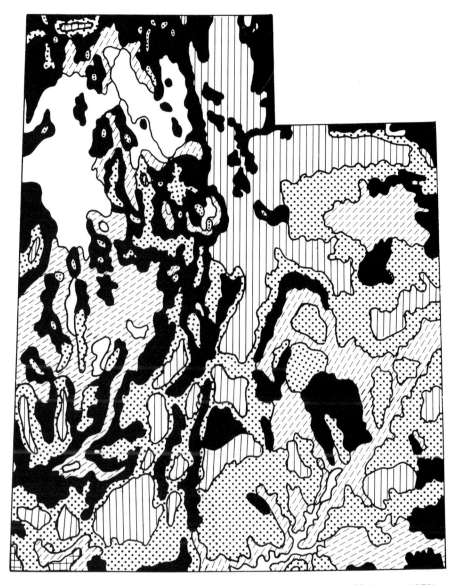

Fig. 1. Depiction of the Vegetation Zones of Utah (redrawn from Holmgren, 1972).

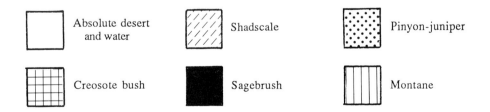

Absolute desert and water

Shadscale

Pinyon-juniper

Creosote bush

Sagebrush

Montane

Fig. 2. Depiction of the Vegetation Zones of Utah (redrawn from Murphy, 1981, but based on Holmgren, 1972).

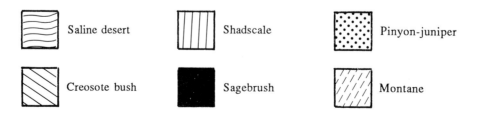

Saline desert   Shadscale   Pinyon-juniper

Creosote bush   Sagebrush   Montane

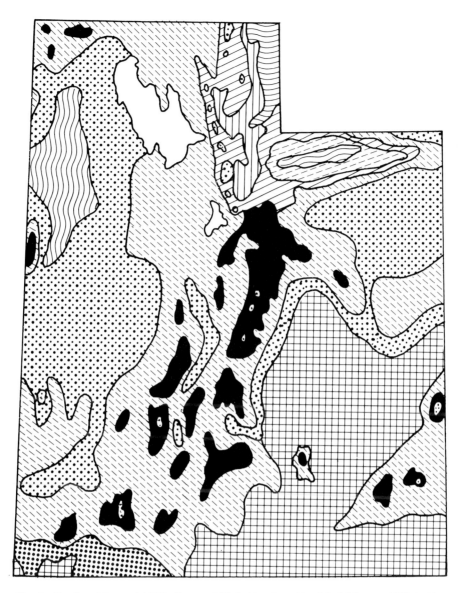

Fig. 3. Predicted Potential Life Zones of Utah (developed by MacMahon and Wieboldt, 1978, through application of a concept of life zones based on abiotic variables developed by Holdridge, 1967).

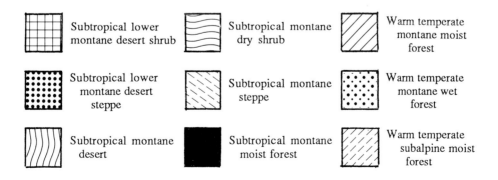

Subtropical lower
montane desert shrub

Subtropical montane
dry shrub

Warm temperate
montane moist
forest

Subtropical lower
montane desert
steppe

Subtropical montane
steppe

Warm temperate
montane wet
forest

Subtropical montane
desert

Subtropical montane
moist forest

Warm temperate
subalpine moist
forest

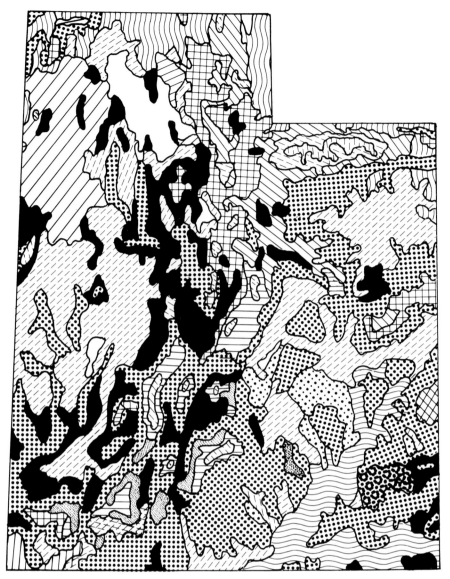

Fig. 4. Vegetation Types of Utah (based on a floristic classification developed and mapped by Küchler, 1964).

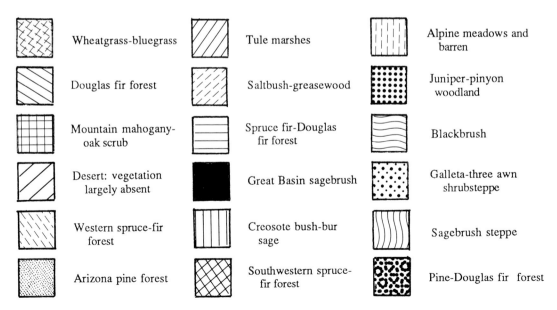

Wheatgrass-bluegrass

Douglas fir forest

Mountain mahogany-oak scrub

Desert: vegetation largely absent

Western spruce-fir forest

Arizona pine forest

Tule marshes

Saltbush-greasewood

Spruce fir-Douglas fir forest

Great Basin sagebrush

Creosote bush-bur sage

Southwestern spruce-fir forest

Alpine meadows and barren

Juniper-pinyon woodland

Blackbrush

Galleta-three awn shrubsteppe

Sagebrush steppe

Pine-Douglas fir forest

MAPS DEPICTING SPECIES DISTRIBUTION

1. ACERACEAE

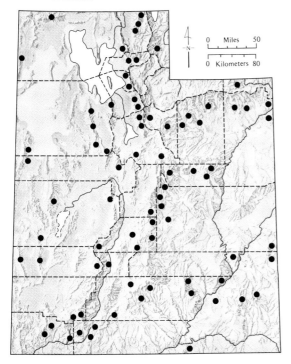

1. *Acer glabrum* Torr. Rocky Mountain maple. Apr.-Sept. Native tree or shrub, important component of mountain brush communities; streambanks, mesic slopes, 1450-3030 m.

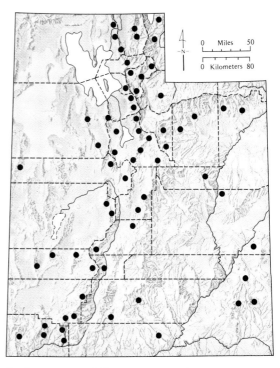

2. *Acer grandidentatum* Nutt. Bigtooth maple. May-Oct. Native tree, often codominant with *Quercus gambelii*; mountain brush communities, streambanks, mesic slopes, 1360-2790 m.

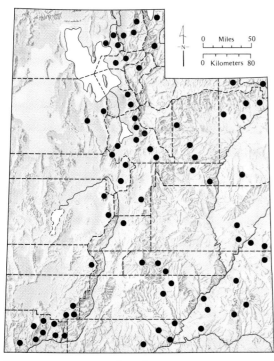

3. *Acer negundo* L. Boxelder. Apr.-Aug. Native tree; along waterways, cultivated, escaping and persistent in moist to mesic sites, 1210-2430 m.

2. AGAVACEAE

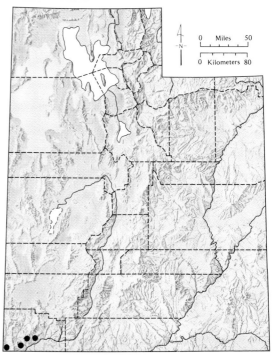

1. *Agave utahensis* Engelm. Utah century plant. Mar.-June. Native perennial; rock crevices in creosote bush communities, 970-1520 m.

1

2. AGAVACEAE

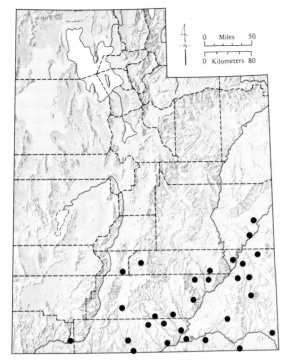

2. *Yucca angustissima* Trel. Narrowleaf yucca. Apr.-July. Native perennial; desert shrub communities, 1060-2430 m.

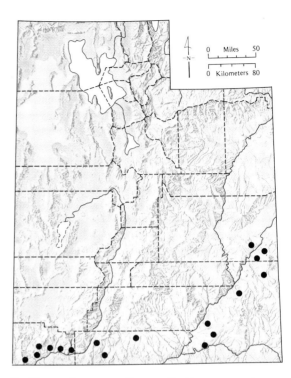

3. *Yucca baccata* Torr. Datil yucca. Apr.-June. Native perennial; creosote bush, desert shrub communities, 850-2120 m.

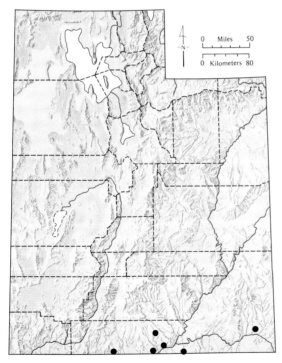

4. *Yucca baileyi* Woot. & Standl. Bailey yucca. Apr.-June. Native perennial; desert shrub communities, 1090-2000 m.

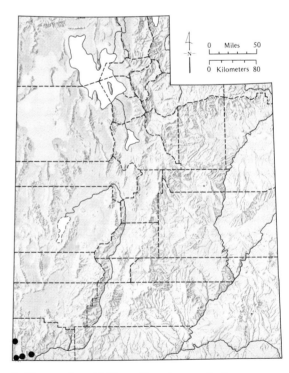

5. *Yucca brevifolia* Engelm. Joshua tree. Apr.-May. Native treelike perennial, codominant with *Larrea tridentata* ; 810-1210 m.

2. AGAVACEAE

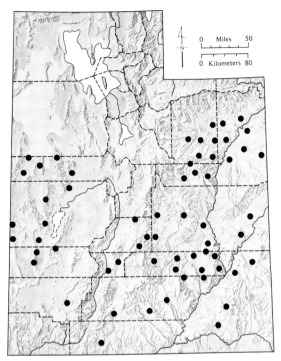

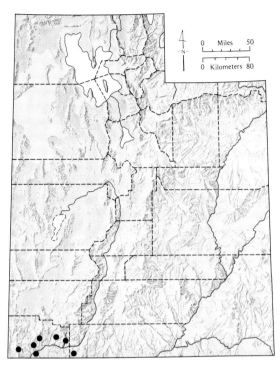

6. *Yucca harrimaniae* Trel. Harriman yucca. May-June. Native perennial; desert shrub to pinyon-juniper communities, 1300-2090 m.

7. *Yucca utahensis* McKelvey Soaptree or Utah yucca. Apr.-June. Native perennial; creosote bush, desert shrub communities, 850-1880 m.

3. AIZOACEAE

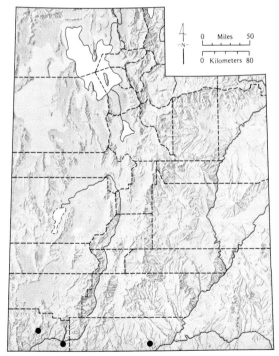

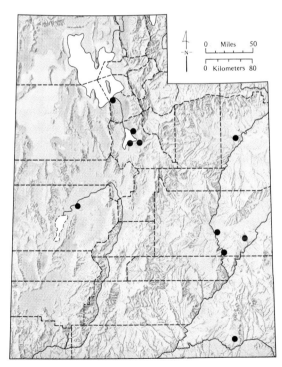

1. *Mollugo cerviana* (L.) Ser. Carpetweed. Sept.-Nov. Introduced annual; desert shrub communities, 970-1580 m.

2. *Sesuvium verrucosum* Raf. Sea purslane. June-Sept. Native perennial herb; greasewood communities, 1270-1370 m.

3

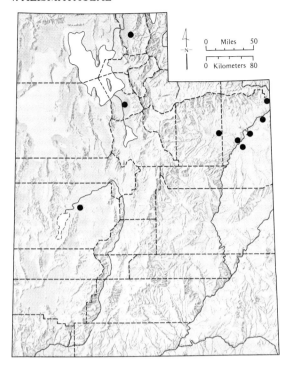

1. *Alisma gramineum* Lej. June-Aug. Native perennial herb; shallow water or stranded in mud, 1300-1670 m.

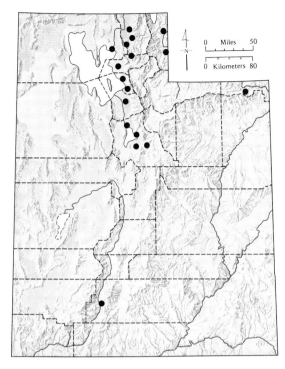

2. *Alisma plantago-aquatica* L. June-Sept. Circumboreal perennial herb; submerged in or emergent from shallow water, 1270-2120 m.

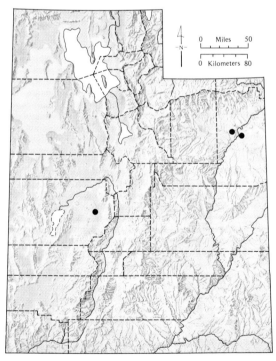

3. *Echinodorus rostratus* (Nutt.) Gray Burhead. July-Aug. Native annual; submerged in or emergent from fresh to saline water, 1360-1430 m.

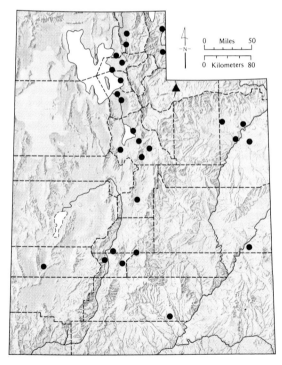

4. *Sagittaria cuneata* Sheld. Arrowhead. June-Aug. Native perennial herb; emergent from shallow water, 1270-2730 m.

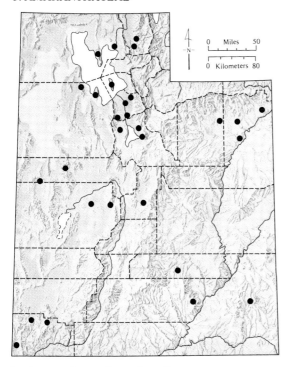

1. *Amaranthus albus* L. Tumbling pigweed. June-Oct. Native annual; waste places, 780-2430 m.

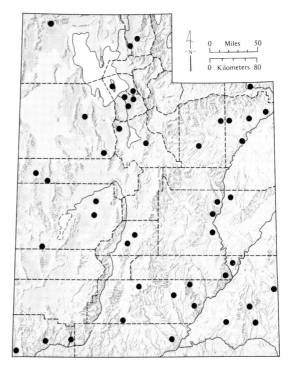

2. *Amaranthus blitoides* Wats. Prostrate pigweed. June-Oct. Native annual; waste places, 1270-2730 m.

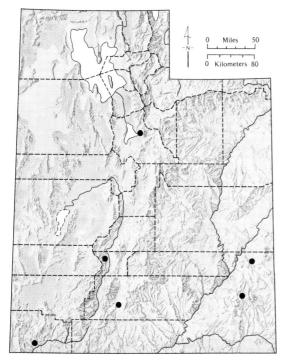

3. *Amaranthus powellii* Wats. Powell pigweed. July-Aug. Native annual; desert shrub communities, 1690-2300 m.

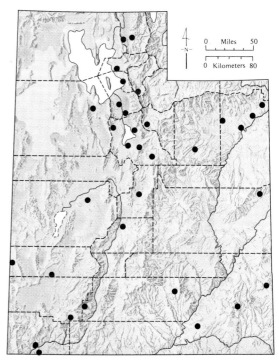

4. *Amaranthus retroflexus* L. Redroot pigweed. June-Sept. Native perennial herb; waste places, 1300-2280 m.

5. AMARANTHACEAE

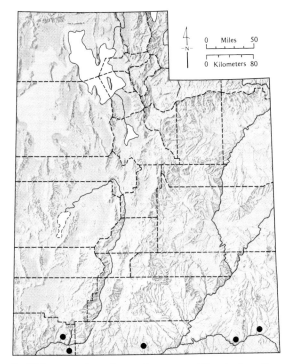

5. *Tidestromia lanuginosa* (Nutt.) Standl.
Woolly tidestromia. July-Sept. Native annual;
desert shrub communities, 1300-1370 m.

6. *Tidestromia oblongifolia* (Wats.) Standl.
Honey-sweet tidestromia. June-Sept. Native
perennial herb; creosote bush, desert shrub
communities, 840-1370 m.

6. ANACARDIACEAE

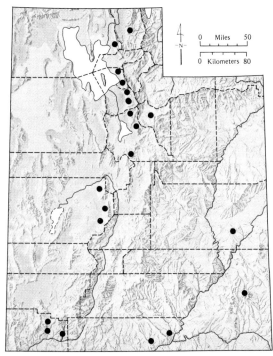

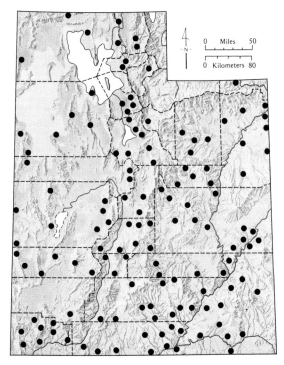

1. *Rhus glabra* L. Smooth sumac. June-July.
Native shrub or small tree; dry open slopes, 990-
1820 m.

2. *Rhus trilobata* Nutt. Squawbush;
skunkbush. Apr.-June. Native shrub; dry to mesic
slopes, streamside, 910-2120 m.

6. ANACARDIACEAE

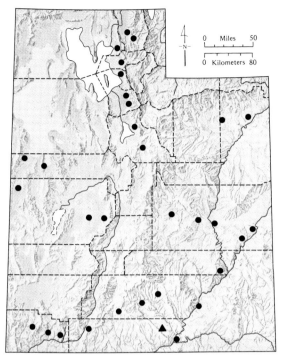

3. *Toxicodendron rydbergii* (Small) Greene
Poison ivy. Apr.-July. Native subshrub or shrub;
streamside, woods, waste places, 910-2730 m.

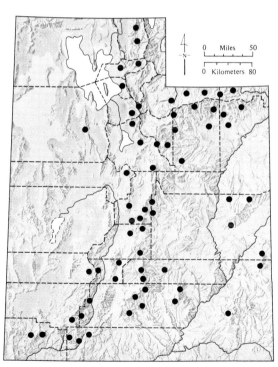

2. *Angelica pinnata* Wats. Small-leaf
angelica. June-Sept. Native perennial herb;
streamside, meadows, under aspen, openings in
conifer forests, 1520-3330 m.

7. APIACEAE

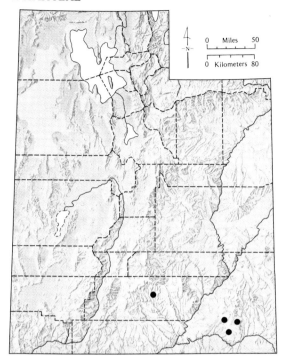

1. *Aletes macdougalii* Coult. & Rose May-
June. Native perennial herb; rock crevices,
pinyon-juniper, limber pine, bristlecone pine
communities, 1270-2740 m.

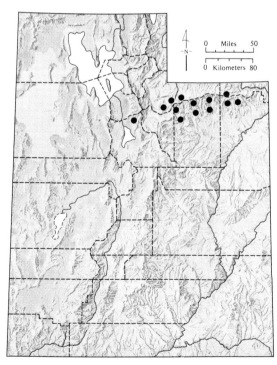

3. *Angelica roseana* Henderson Rock
angelica. July-Sept. Native perennial herb; open
rocky sites, 2120-3570 m.

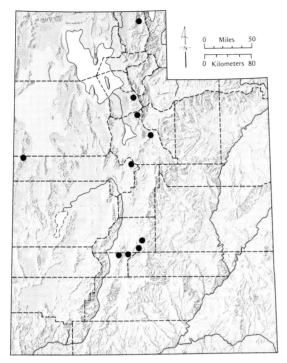

4. *Angelica wheeleri* Wats. Wheeler or Utah angelica. July-Sept. Native perennial herb; streamside, other wet sites, 1420-3050 m.

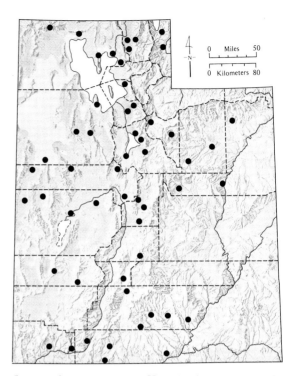

5. *Berula erecta* (Huds.) Cov. Cutleaf waterparsnip. June-Sept. Native perennial herb; shallow, often brackish water, wet mud, 850-2130 m.

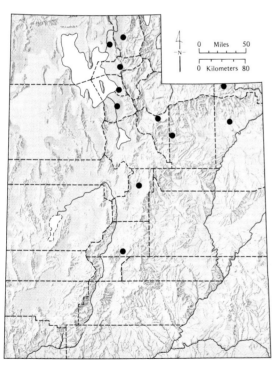

6. *Carum carvi* L. Caraway. May-July. Introduced biennial; cultivated, escaping and persistent, 1300-2120 m.

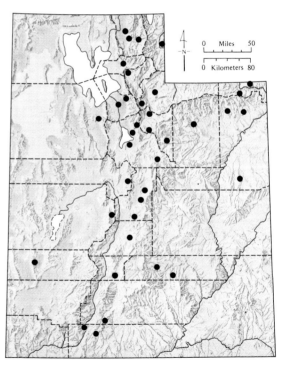

7. *Cicuta maculata* L. Water hemlock. June-Sept. Native perennial herb; along waterways, in marshes, 1300-2320 m.

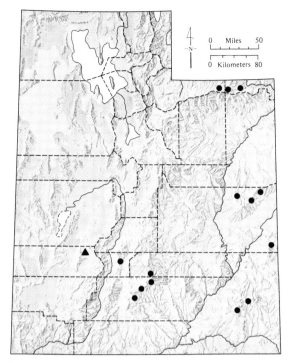

8. *Conioselinum scopulorum* (Gray) Coult. & Rose   June-Aug.   Native perennial herb; streamside, 2600-3200 m.

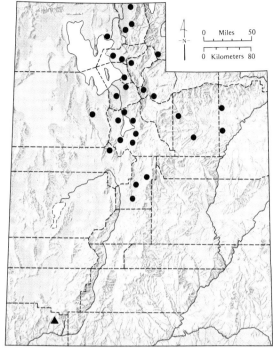

9. *Conium maculatum* L.   Poison hemlock. May-Aug.   Introduced biennial; moist sites, waste places, 1400-2990 m.

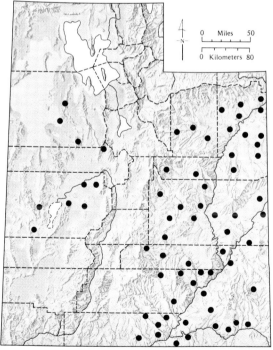

10. *Cymopterus acaulis* (Pursh) Raf. Stemless springparsley.   Apr.-May.   Native perennial herb; salt desert shrub, desert shrub, pinyon-juniper communities, 1300-1970 m.

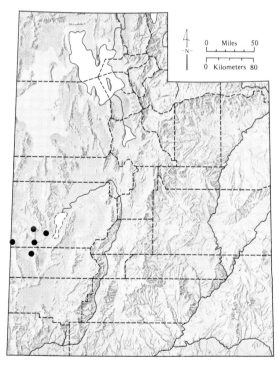

11. *Cymopterus basalticus* Jones   Basalt springparsley.   May-June.   Native perennial herb; shadscale, desert shrub communities, 1510-1990 m.

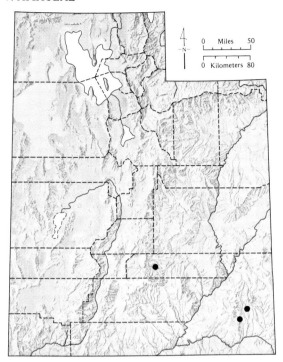

12. *Cymopterus beckii* Welsh & Goodrich
Pinnate springparsley. Apr.-June. Native
perennial herb; pinyon-juniper, mountain brush
communities, 1700-2150 m.

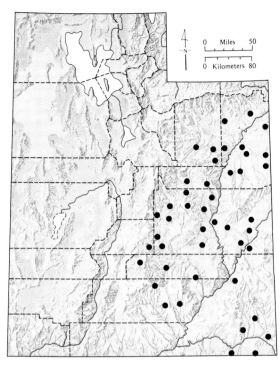

13. *Cymopterus bulbosus* A. Nels. Onion
spring-parsley. Apr.-May. Native perennial herb;
desert shrub, juniper communities, 1220-2010 m.

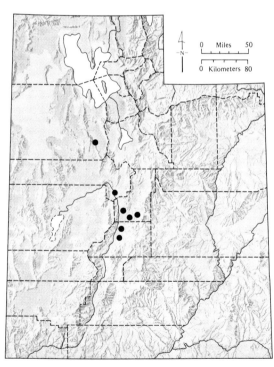

14. *Cymopterus coulteri* (Jones) Math.
Coulter springparsley. Apr.-June. Native
perennial herb; shadscale, sagebrush, desert shrub,
juniper communities, 1510-1700 m.

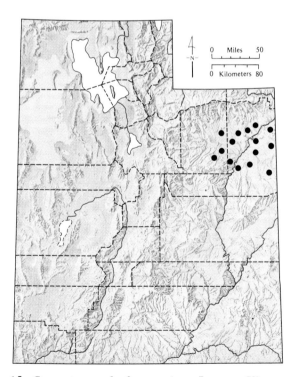

15. *Cymopterus duchesnensis* Jones Uinta
Basin springparsley. Apr.-June. Native perennial
herb; sagebrush, desert shrub to pinyon-juniper
communities, 1420-1850 m.

7. APIACEAE

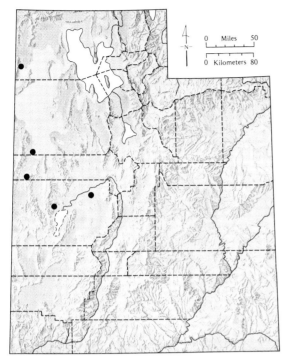

16. *Cymopterus globosus* (Wats.) Wats. Globe springparsley. Apr.-May. Native perennial herb; desert shrub communities, 1400-1530 m.

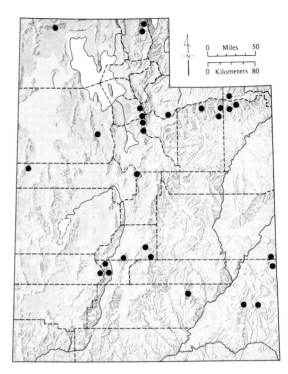

17. *Cymopterus hendersonii* (Coult. & Rose) Cronq. Mountain rockparsley. June-Aug. Native perennial herb; rocky sites, spruce-fir, alpine communities, 2740-3660 m.

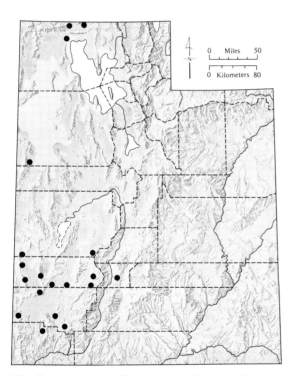

18. *Cymopterus ibapensis* Jones Ibapah springparsley. Apr.-June. Native perennial herb; greasewood, sagebrush, pinyon-juniper communities, 1520-2730 m.

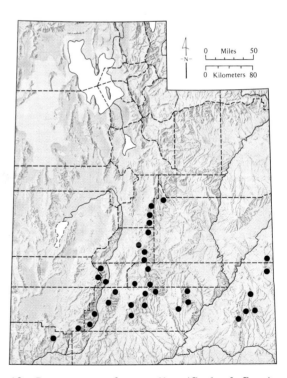

19. *Cymopterus lemmonii* (Coult. & Rose) Dorn June-Aug. Native perennial herb; grass-forb, aspen, spruce-fir, alpine communities, 2370-3600 m.

11

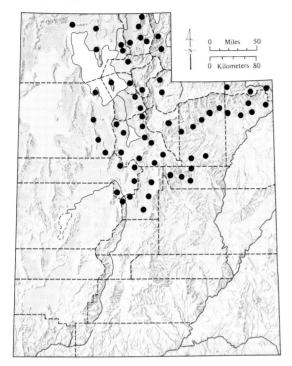

20. *Cymopterus longipes* Wats. Longfoot springparsley. Mar.-May. Native perennial herb; sagebrush, mountain brush, pinyon-juniper communities, 1300-3160 m.

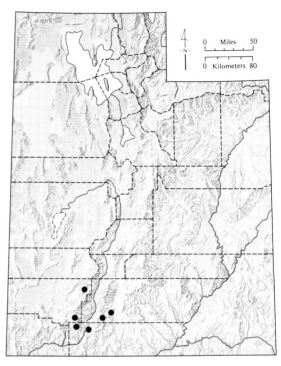

21. *Cymopterus minimus* (Math.) Math. Least springparsley. May-July. Native perennial herb; talus, bristlecone pine, ponderosa pine, spruce-fir communities, 2190-3030 m.

22. *Cymopterus multinervatus* (Coult. & Rose) Tides. Mar.-June. Native perennial herb; desert shrub, sagebrush communities, 1220-1520 m.

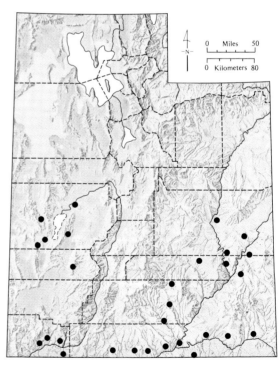

23. *Cymopterus newberryi* (Wats.) Jones Sweetroot springparsley. Apr.-May. Native perennial herb; shadscale, desert shrub, sagebrush, juniper communities, 850-1830 m.

7. APIACEAE

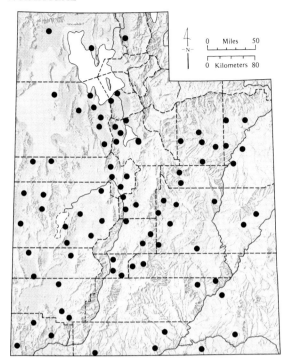

24. *Cymopterus purpurascens* (Gray) Jones Wide-wing springparsley. Mar.-June. Native perennial herb; salt desert shrub, desert shrub to ponderosa pine communities, 1060-2750 m.

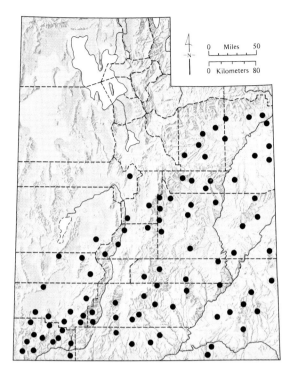

25. *Cymopterus purpureus* Wats. Apr.-July. Native perennial herb; sagebrush, desert shrub to limber pine communities, 1100-2880 m.

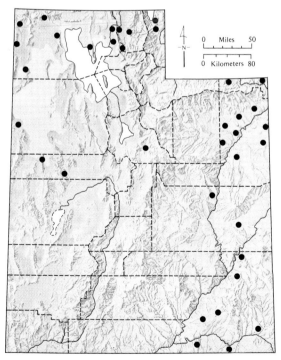

26. *Cymopterus terebinthinus* (Hook.) T. & G. May-June. Native perennial herb; desert shrub to mountain brush communities, rocky outcrops, 1360-2560 m.

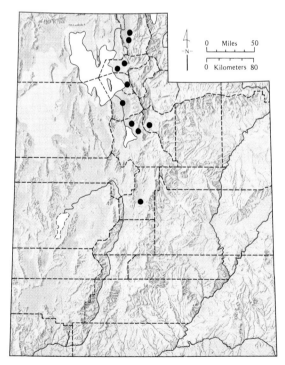

27. *Daucus carota* L. Carrot. July-Oct. Introduced biennial; cultivated, escaping and persistent, 1270-1700 m.

13

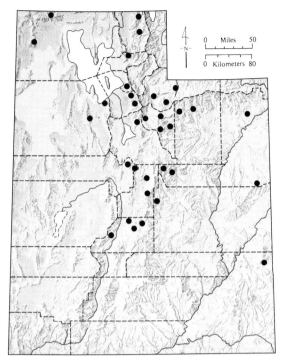

28. *Heracleum lanatum* Michx. Cow parsnip.
May-Aug. Native perennial herb; streamside, wet
meadows, other moist sites, 1430-2930 m.

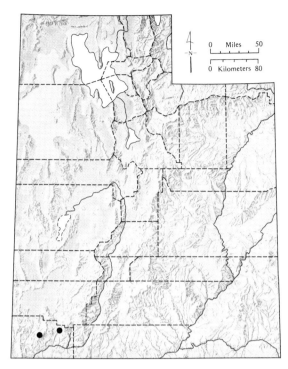

29. *Hydrocotyle verticillata* Thunb. Water
pennywort. Apr.-Oct. Native perennial herb; in
water or wet soil, 850-1820 m.

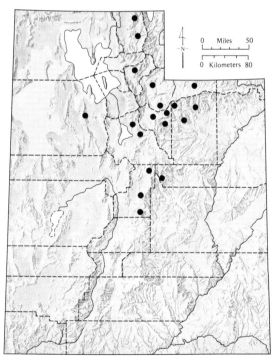

30. *Ligusticum filicinum* Wats. Fernleaf
ligusticum. June-Aug. Native perennial herb;
sagebrush, aspen, spruce-fir communities, 1910-
3400 m.

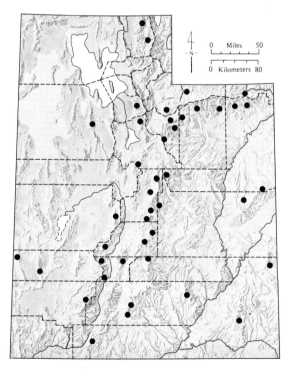

31. *Ligusticum porteri* Coult. & Rose
Southern ligusticum. June-Aug. Native perennial
herb; sagebrush, aspen, spruce-fir communities,
2250-3170 m.

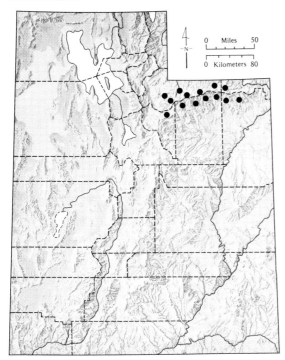

32. *Ligusticum tenuifolium* W a t s .
Slenderleaf ligusticum. July-Sept. Native
perennial herb; moist meadows, streamside, 2420-
3420 m.

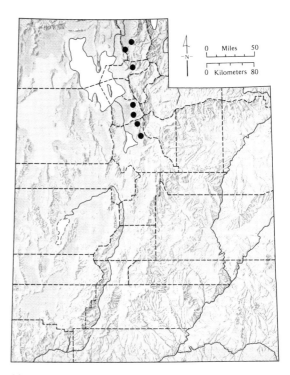

33. *Lomatium ambiguum* (Nutt.) Coult. &
Rose Wyeth biscuitroot. May-July. Native
perennial herb; sagebrush, mountain brush
communities, 1510-1980 m.

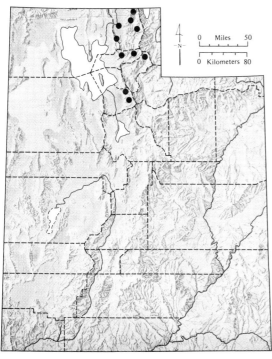

34. *Lomatium bicolor* (Wats.) Coult. & Rose
Wasatch biscuitroot. May-July. Native perennial
herb; sagebrush, mountain brush, aspen, meadow
communities, 1510-2440 m.

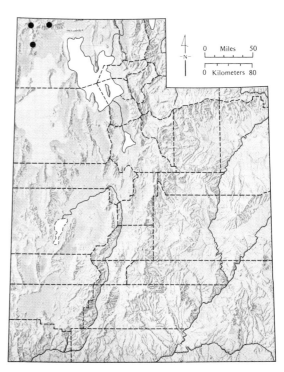

35. *Lomatium cous* (Wats.) Coult. & Rose
Cous biscuitroot. Apr.-June. Native perennial
herb; sagebrush-grass communities, 2420-2560 m.

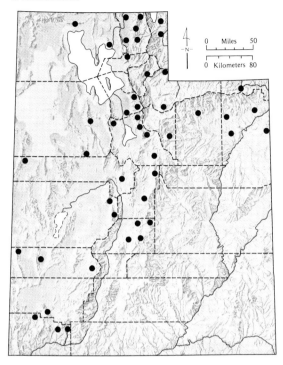

36. ***Lomatium dissectum*** (Nutt.) Math. & Const. Fernleaf or giant biscuitroot. Apr.-June. Native perennial herb; oak-maple, aspen, aspen-fir communities, 1280-3170 m.

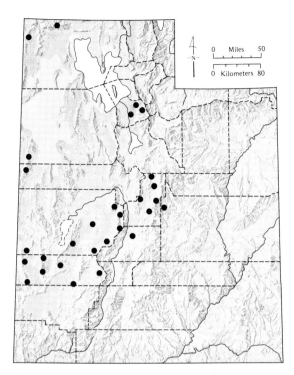

37. ***Lomatium foeniculaceum*** (Nutt.) Coult. & Rose Desert parsley. Apr.-July. Native perennial herb; shadscale, sagebrush, pinyon-juniper, mountain brush communities, 1250-2730 m.

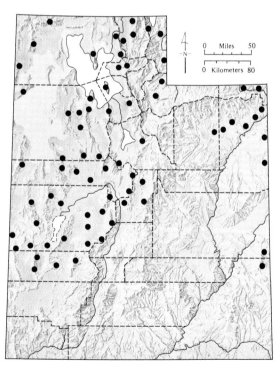

38. ***Lomatium grayi*** (Coult. & Rose) Coult. & Rose Milfoil biscuitroot. Mar.-July. Native perennial herb; desert shrub to ponderosa pine, Douglas fir communities, 1300-2840 m.

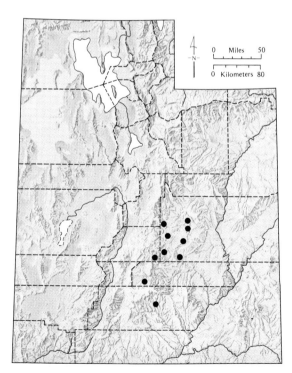

39. ***Lomatium junceum*** Barneby & N. Holmgren Rush lomatium. May-June. Native perennial herb; shadscale, desert shrub to ponderosa pine and Douglas fir communities, 1600-2490 m.

16

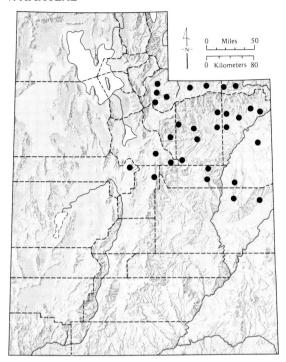

40. *Lomatium juniperinum* (Jones) Coult. & Rose   Juniper biscuitroot. May-July. Native perennial herb; sagebrush, mountain brush, pinyon-juniper, aspen-fir, alpine communities, 1820-3220 m.

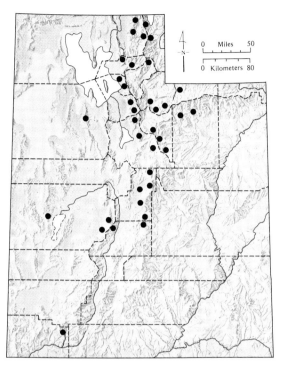

41. *Lomatium graveolens* (Wats) Dorn & Hartman   Stinking lomatium. May-Aug. Native perennial herb; sagebrush, mountain brush, spruce-fir communities, 1810-3250 m.

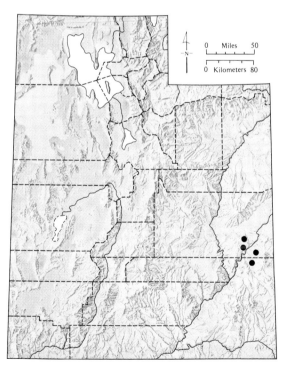

42. *Lomatium latilobum* (Rydb.) Math. Broadlobe or Canyonlands biscuitroot. Apr.-June. Native perennial herb; desert shrub, pinyon-juniper communities, 1510-2090 m.

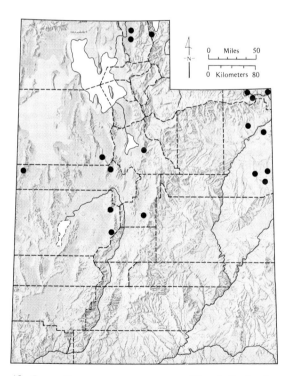

43. *Lomatium macrocarpum* (Nutt.) Coult. & Rose   Bigseed biscuitroot. Apr.-June. Native perennial herb; desert shrub, sagebrush, pinyon-juniper communities, 1480-2550 m.

7. APIACEAE

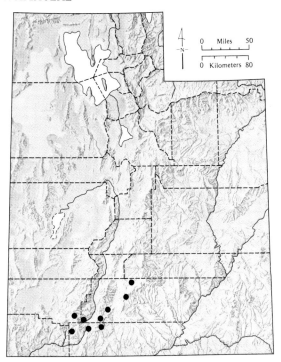

44. *Lomatium minimum* (Math.) Math. Least lomatium. June-July. Native perennial herb; forb-grass, ponderosa pine communities, rocky ridges, 1970-3180 m.

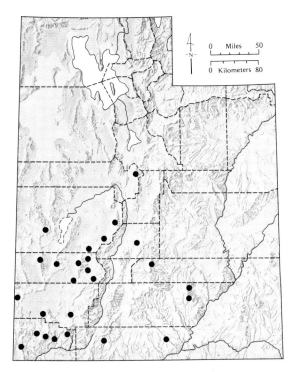

45. *Lomatium nevadense* (Wats.) Coult. & Rose Nevada biscuitroot. Apr.-June. Native perennial herb; desert shrub to ponderosa pine communities, 1510-2280 m.

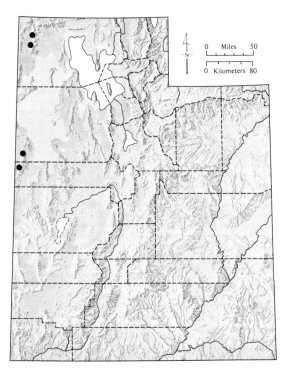

46. *Lomatium nudicaule* (Pursh) Coult. & Rose Barestem biscuitroot. Apr.-June. Native perennial herb; sagebrush, pinyon-juniper communities, 1570-2530 m.

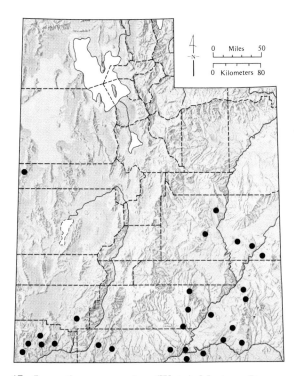

47. *Lomatium parryi* (Wats.) Macbr. Parry biscuitroot. May-June. Native perennial herb; creosote bush, desert shrub, pinyon-juniper, mountain brush communities, 970-2430 m.

18

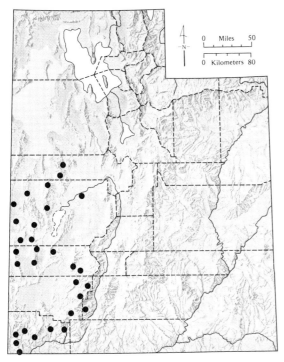

48. Lomatium scabrum (Coult. & Rose) Math.
Rough biscuitroot. Apr.-June. Native perennial
herb; creosote bush, desert shrub, pinyon-juniper,
mountain brush communities, 970-2670 m.

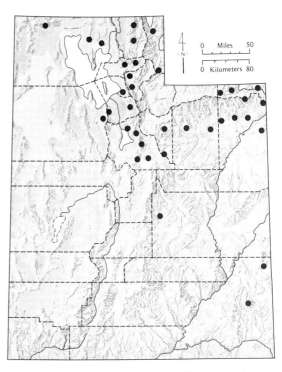

49. Lomatium triternatum (Pursh) Coult. &
Rose Ternate lomatium. Apr.-July. Native
perennial herb; sagebrush to aspen communities,
dry meadows, 1300-2890 m.

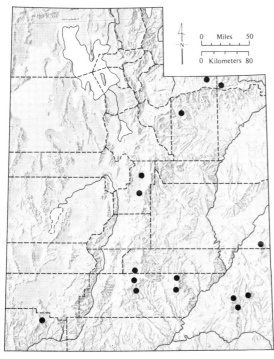

50. Oreoxis alpina (Gray) Coult. & Rose
Alpine oreoxis. June-Aug. Native perennial herb;
forb-grass, limber pine, spruce, alpine
communities, 2440-3640 m.

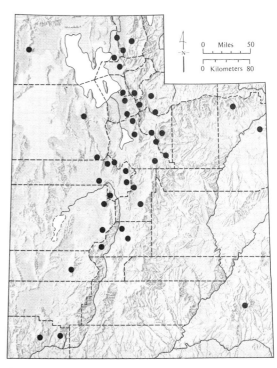

51. Orogenia linearifolia Wats. Indian
potato. Mar.-June. Native perennial herb; moist
slopes, often in snowmelt, mountain brush to
aspen-conifer communities, 1360-2850 m.

7. APIACEAE

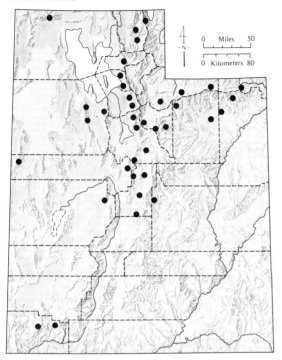

52. **Osmorhiza chilensis** H. & A. Spreading sweetroot. May-Aug. Native perennial herb; shaded sites in oak-maple, aspen-fir, streamside communities, 1520-3030 m.

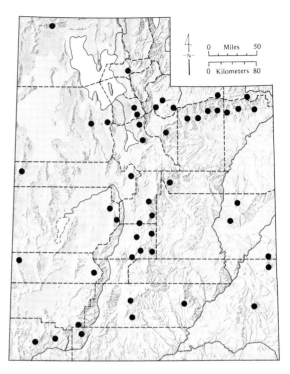

53. **Osmorhiza depauperata** Phil. Bluntseed sweetroot. May-Aug. Native perennial herb; shaded sites in oak-maple to spruce-fir communities, 1450-3200 m.

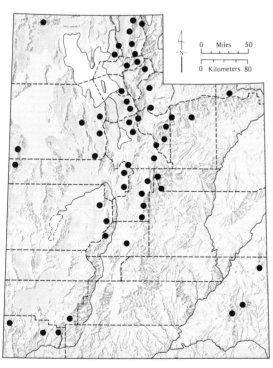

54. **Osmorhiza occidentalis** (Nutt.) Torr. Sweet Cicely. May-Aug. Native perennial herb; oak-maple, spruce-fir, streamside communities, 1750-3170 m.

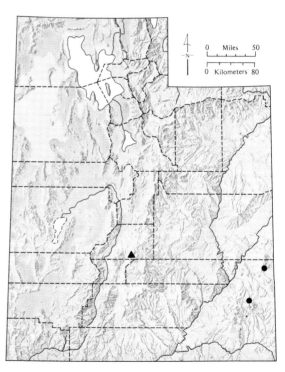

55. **Oxypolis fendleri** (Gray) Heller Fendler cowbane. July-Aug. Native perennial herb; streamside, 2720-2970 m.

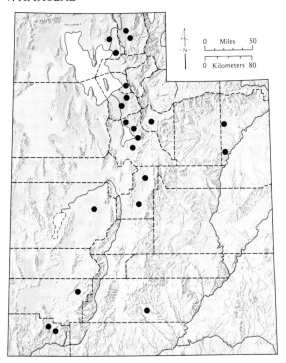

56. *Pastinaca sativa* L. Parsnip. May-Sept. Introduced biennial; roadsides, along waterways, other disturbed sites, 1300-2370 m.

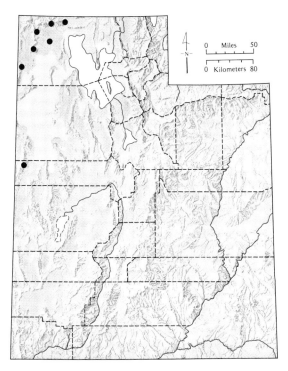

57. *Perideridia bolanderi* (Gray) Nels. & Macbr. Bolander yampah. May-July. Native perennial herb; sagebrush, juniper, mountain brush communities, 1520-2430 m.

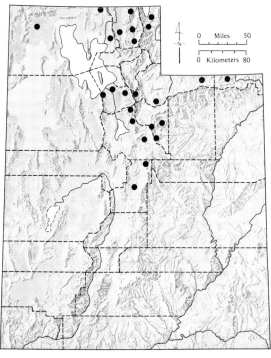

58. *Perideridia gairdneri* (H. & A.) Math. Common yampah; false yarrow. July-Sept. Native perennial herb; sagebrush, oak-maple, aspen, streamside communities, 1420-2670 m.

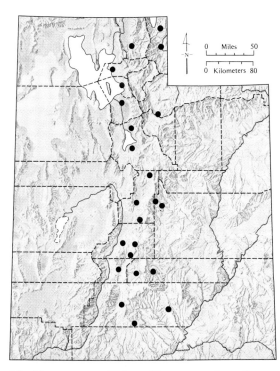

59. *Sium suave* Walt. Water parsnip. June-Aug. Native perennial herb; moist sites, shallow water, 1300-2970 m.

7. APIACEAE

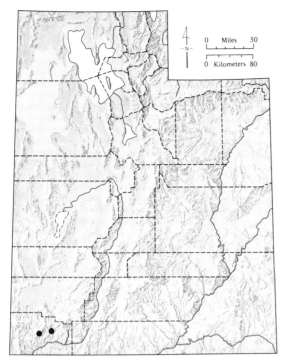

60. *Yabea microcarpa* (H. & A.) Kozo-Polj. Hedge parsley. Apr.-May. Native annual; turbinella live oak communities, 910-1120 m.

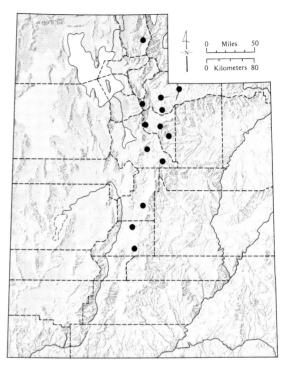

61. *Zizia aptera* (Gray) Fern. Zizia. June-Aug. Native perennial herb; streamside, meadow communities, 1720-2520 m.

8. APOCYNACEAE

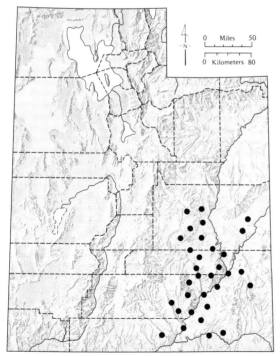

1. *Amsonia eastwoodiana* Rydb. Eastwood bluestar. Apr.-May. Native perennial herb; desert shrub communities, 1060-1820 m.

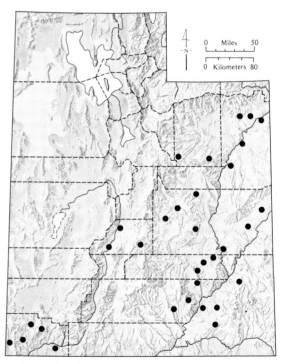

2. *Amsonia jonesii* Woodson Jones bluestar. Apr.-May. Native perennial herb; desert shrub, pinyon-juniper communities, 1270-1700 m.

8. APOCYNACEAE

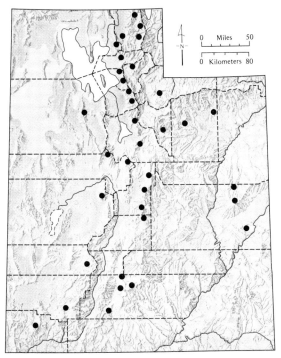

3. *Apocynum androsaemifolium* L. Spreading dogbane. July-Aug. Native perennial herb; open sites in oak-maple to spruce-fir communities, 1510-2580 m.

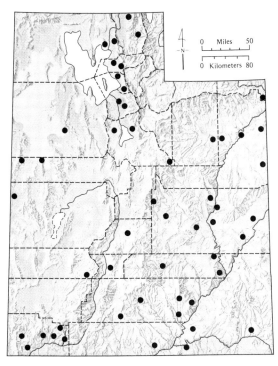

4. *Apocynum cannabinum* L. Common dogbane; Indian hemp. June-Aug. Native perennial herb; along waterways, margins of springs, waste places, 780-1700 m.

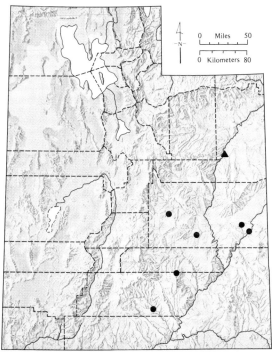

5. *Cycladenia humilis* Benth. Low cycladenia. May-June. Native perennial herb; desert shrub communities, 1510-1700 m.

9. ASCLEPIADACEAE

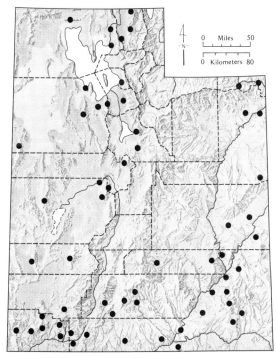

1. *Asclepias asperula* (Dcne.) Woodson Spider milkweed; antelope horns. May-July. Native perennial herb; desert shrub, mountain brush, pinyon-juniper communities, 1360-2580 m.

23

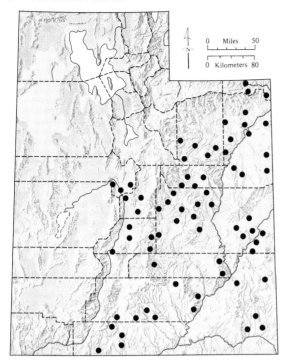

2. *Asclepias cryptoceras* Wats. Pallid milkweed; cow cabbage. May-June. Native perennial herb; shadscale to pinyon-juniper communities, 1240-2030 m.

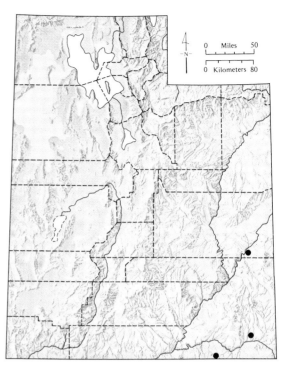

3. *Asclepias cutleri* Woodson Cutler milkweed. Apr.-May. Native perennial herb; sand dunes, 1300-1430 m.

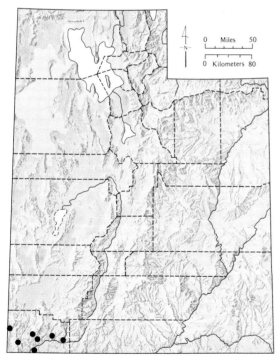

4. *Asclepias erosa* Torr. Desert milkweed. May-Aug. Native perennial herb; creosote bush, desert shrub communities, 860-1090 m.

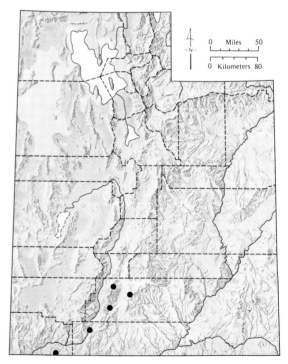

5. *Asclepias hallii* Gray Hall milkweed. July-Aug. Native perennial herb; sagebrush to limber pine communities, 2090-3030 m.

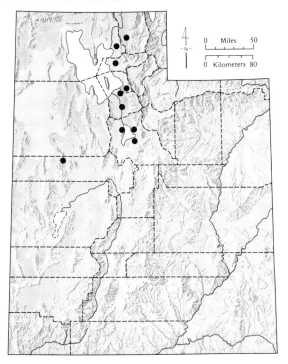

6. *Asclepias incarnata* L. Swamp milkweed. July-Aug. Native perennial herb; along waterways, other moist sites, 1270-1370 m.

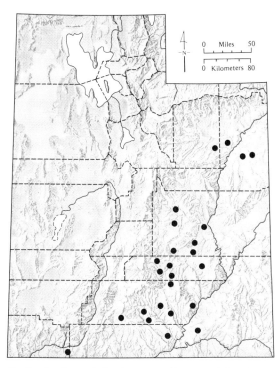

7. *Asclepias labriformis* Jones May-July. Native perennial herb; sand dunes, juniper communities, 1360-1700 m.

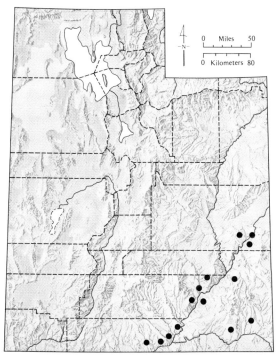

8. *Asclepias latifolia* (Torr.) Raf. Broadleaf milkweed. June-Sept. Native perennial herb; hanging garden, desert shrub communities, 1090-2120 m.

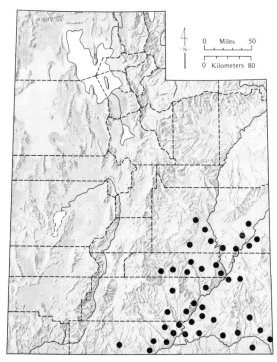

9. *Asclepias macrosperma* Eastw. Bigseed milkweed. May-June. Native perennial herb; sand dunes, desert shrub, pinyon-juniper communities, 1240-1700 m.

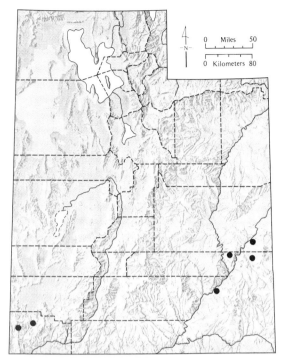

10. *Asclepias rusbyi* (Vail) Woodson Rusby milkweed. June-July. Native perennial herb; desert shrub, pinyon-juniper communities, 1510-2090 m.

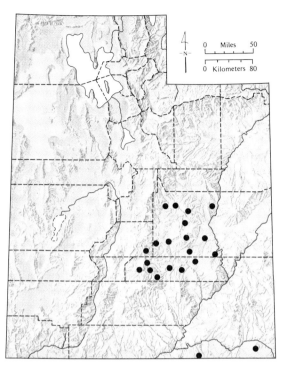

11. *Asclepias ruthiae* Maguire Ruth milkweed. May-June. Native perennial herb; shadscale, desert shrub communities, 1240-1550 m.

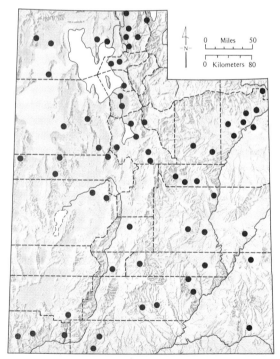

12. *Asclepias speciosa* Torr. Showy or common milkweed. June-July. Native perennial herb; mesic to moist, often disturbed sites, 780-2430 m.

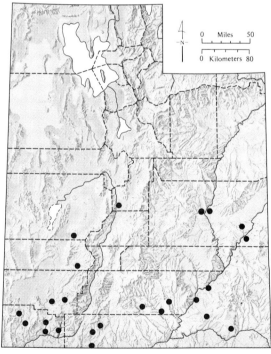

13. *Asclepias subverticillata* (Gray) Vail Whorled or poison milkweed. June-Aug. Native perennial herb; waste places, 910-1640 m.

9. ASCLEPIADACEAE

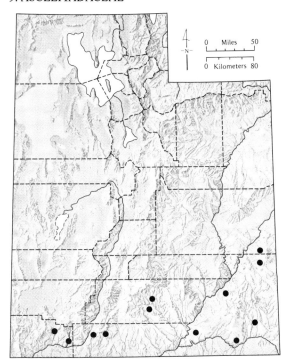

14. *Asclepias tuberosa* L.   Butterflyweed; orange milkweed. May-July. Native perennial herb; desert shrub communities, rocky slopes, 1360-1760 m.

15. *Sarcostemma cynanchoides* Dcne. Climbing milkweed. July-Aug. Native perennial herb; along waterways, rock ledges, 910-1310 m.

10. ASTERACEAE

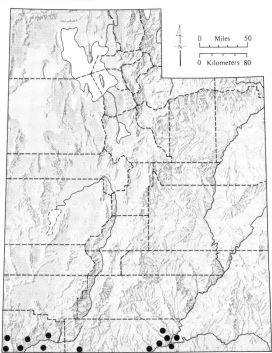

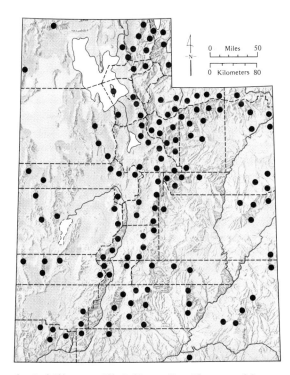

1. *Acamptopappus sphaerocephalus* (H. & G.) Gray Rayless goldenhead. Mar.-Sept. Native shrub; creosote bush, desert shrub communities, 730-1550 m.

2. *Achillea millefolium* L. Yarrow. May-Sept. Circumboreal perennial herb; sagebrush, pinyon-juniper, ponderosa pine, mountain brush communities to above timberline, 1270-3550 m.

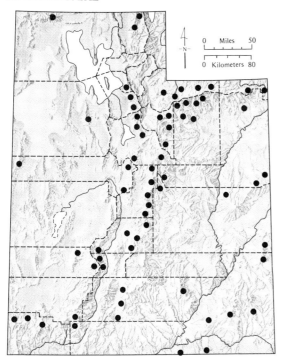

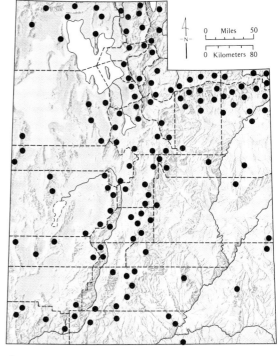

3. *Agoseris aurantiaca* (Hook.) Greene
Orange agoseris. July-Sept. Native perennial herb;
mountain brush to alpine meadow communities,
1360-3430 m.

4. *Agoseris glauca* (Pursh) Raf. Mountain
dandelion. May-Sept. Native perennial herb;
sagebrush communities to above timberline, 1270-
3600 m.

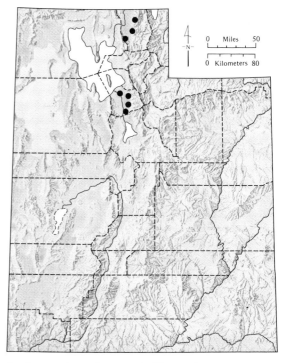

5. *Agoseris grandiflora* (Nutt.) Greene
Bigflower agoseris. May-July. Native perennial
herb; sagebrush communities, 1510-1670 m.

6. *Agoseris heterophylla* (Nutt.) Greene
Annual agoseris. May-June. Native annual; dry
meadows, sagebrush communities, 1270-1520 m.

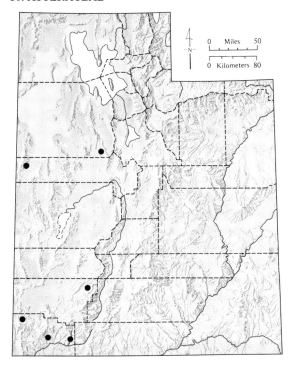

7. *Agoseris retrorsa* (Benth.) Greene
Spearleaf agoseris. June-Sept. Native perennial
herb; desert shrub, pinyon-juniper communities,
1360-2430 m.

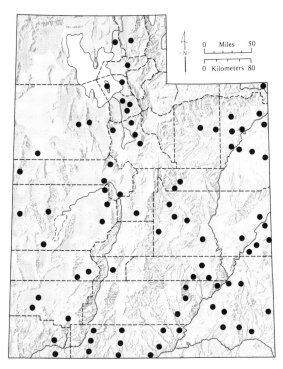

8. *Ambrosia acanthicarpa* Hook. Bur
ragweed; annual bursage. July-Oct. Native annual;
creosote bush to sagebrush and pinyon-juniper
communities, often in disturbed sites, 1060-2430
m.

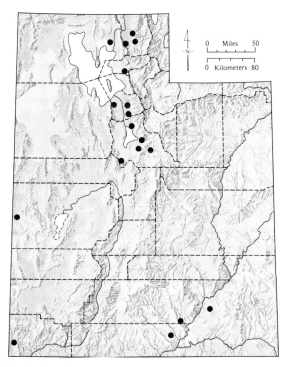

9. *Ambrosia artemisiifolia* L. Common
ragweed. Aug.-Oct. Native annual; fallow fields,
roadsides, ditchbanks and other disturbed sites, salt
tolerant, 820-1970 m.

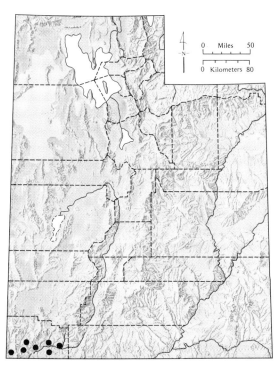

10. *Ambrosia dumosa* (Gray) Payne
Thornbush or white bursage. Mar.-Oct. Native
shrub; Joshua tree, creosote bush communities,
790-1220 m.

10. ASTERACEAE

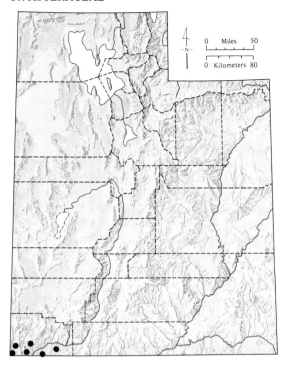

11. **Ambrosia eriocentra** (Gray) Payne Woolly bursage. Apr.-June. Native shrub; dry washes in Joshua tree, creosote bush communities, 790-910 m.

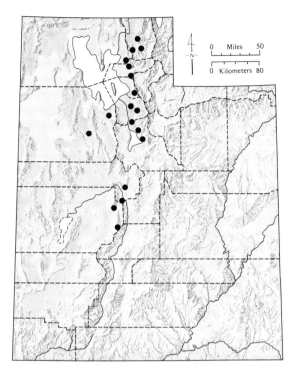

12. **Ambrosia psilostachya** DC. Western ragweed. July-Oct. Native perennial herb; salt desert shrub to mountain brush communities, often in the wake of disturbance, 1300-1820 m.

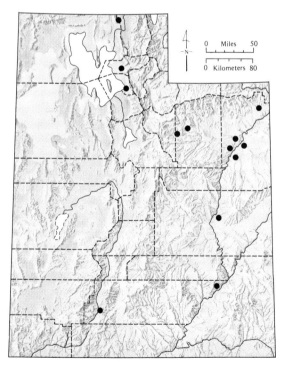

13. **Ambrosia tomentosa** Nutt. Low ragweed or skeletonleaf bursage. June-Sept. Native perennial herb; moist to dry, disturbed sites, greasewood to aspen communities, 1360-2730 m.

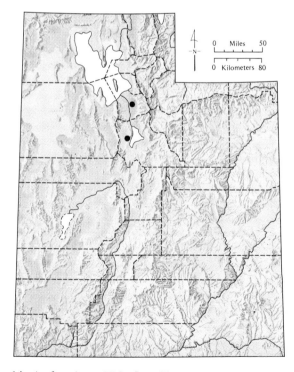

14. **Ambrosia trifida** L. Giant ragweed. June-Aug. Introduced annual; disturbed, usually irrigated sites, 1360-1430 m.

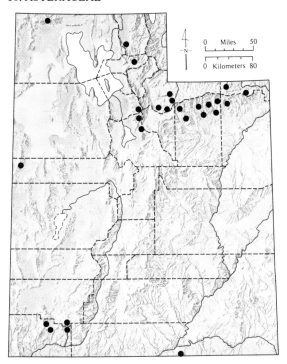

15. *Anaphalis margaritacea* (L.) Benth. & Hook. Pearly everlasting. July-Sept. Native perennial herb; open to shaded sites, oak-maple to aspen-conifer communities, 1300-3340 m.

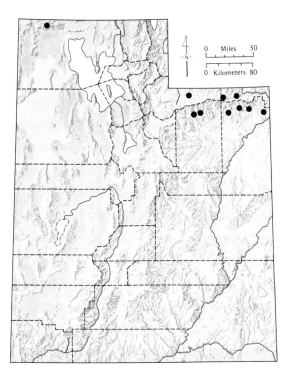

16. *Antennaria anaphaloides* Rydb. Pearly pussytoes. June-Aug. Native perennial herb; sagebrush, mountain brush, aspen-conifer communities, 2120-3180 m.

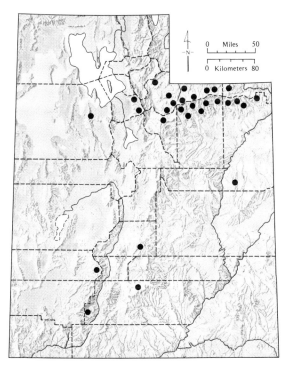

17. *Antennaria corymbosa* E. Nels. Flattop; plains pussytoes. June-Sept. Native perennial herb; moist to dry meadows, streamside in conifer communities to above timberline, 2120-3940 m.

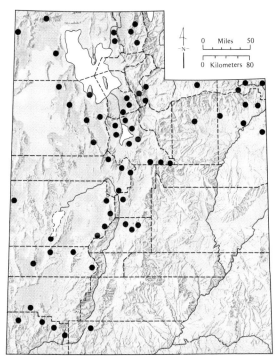

18. *Antennaria dimorpha* (Nutt.) T. & G. Low pussytoes. Apr.-July. Native perennial herb; sagebrush, pinyon-juniper, mountain brush to ponderosa pine, lodgepole pine communities, 1270-2580 m.

31

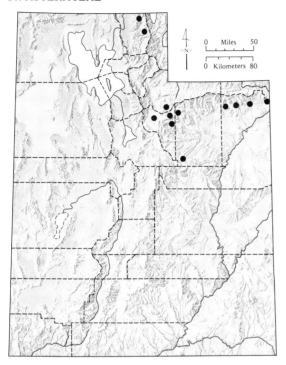

19. *Antennaria luzuloides* T. & G. Rush pussytoes. July-Aug. Native perennial herb; aspen-conifer communities, 1970-3090 m.

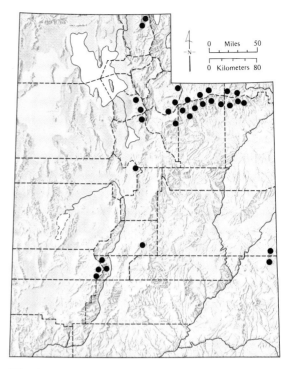

20. *Antennaria media* Greene Alpine pussytoes. June-Sept. Native perennial herb; aspen-conifer communities to above timberline, 2730-3490 m.

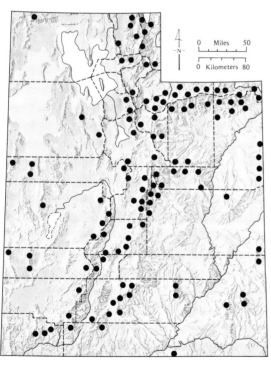

21. *Antennaria microphylla* Rydb. Rosy pussytoes. June-Aug. Native perennial herb; sagebrush, juniper, aspen-conifer, alpine meadow communities, 1510-3640 m.

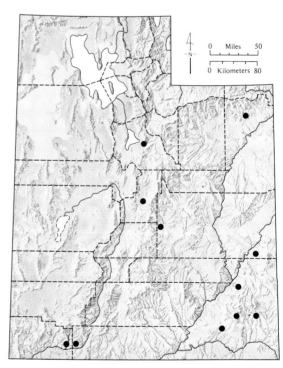

22. *Antennaria neglecta* Greene Field pussytoes. July-Aug. Native perennial herb; pinyon-juniper, ponderosa pine communities, 1510-2640 m.

10. ASTERACEAE

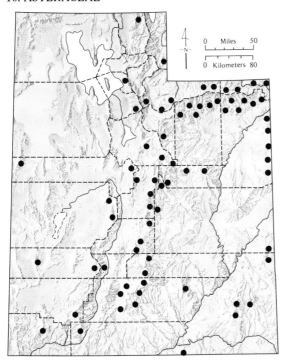

23. *Antennaria parvifolia* Nutt. Small-leaf pussytoes. May-Aug. Native perennial herb; sagebrush, pinyon-juniper, mountain brush to conifer communities, 1970-3030 m.

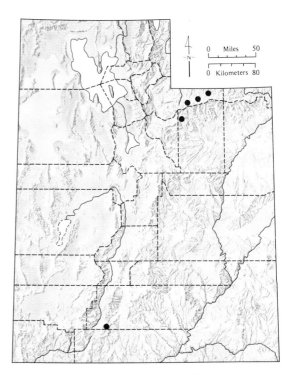

24. *Antennaria pulcherrima* (Hook.) Greene Showy pussytoes. July-Aug. Native perennial herb; moist meadows, marshes, streamside, 2570-2880 m.

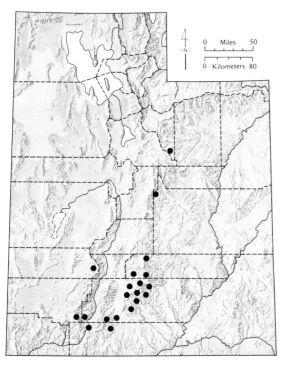

25. *Antennaria rosulata* Rydb. Woolly pussytoes. June-Aug. Native perennial herb; ponderosa pine, aspen, spruce-fir, alpine meadow communities, 2120-3340 m.

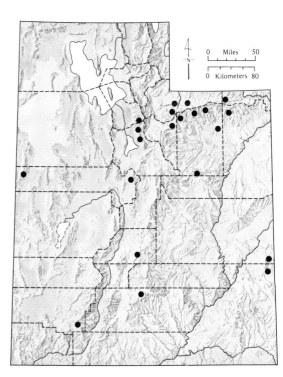

26. *Antennaria umbrinella* Rydb. Umber pussytoes. July-Aug. Native perennial herb; subalpine meadows to above timberline, 2730-3640 m.

33

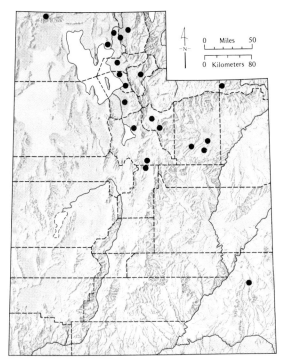

27. *Anthemis cotula* L. Mayweed chamomile or dogfennel. June-Sept. Introduced annual; roadsides, fallow fields, other disturbed sites, 1270-2430 m.

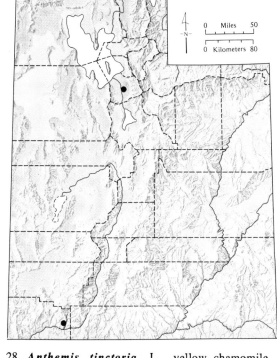

28. *Anthemis tinctoria* L. yellow chamomile. July-Sept. Introduced perennial herb; cultivated, escaping and persistent, 1670-2280 m.

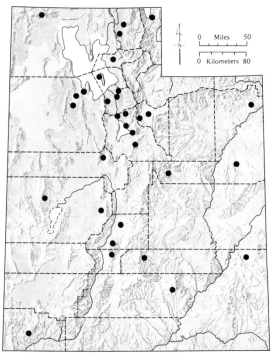

29. *Arctium minus* (Hill) Bernh. Burdock. July-Oct. Introduced biennial; disturbed sites, 910-1970 m.

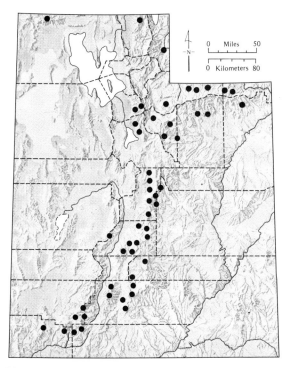

30. *Arnica chamissonis* Less. Chamisso arnica. July-Sept. Native perennial herb; along streams and lake shores in mountain brush, aspen-conifer communities, 1570-3330 m.

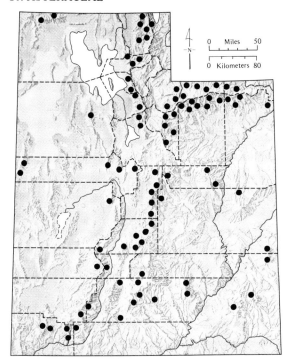

31. *Arnica cordifolia* Hook. Heartleaf arnica.
May-Aug. Native perennial herb; shady sites,
mountain brush to conifer communities, open rocky
places at higher elevations, 1570-3490 m.

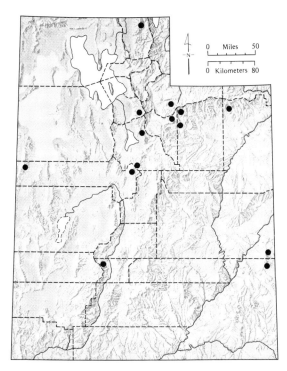

32. *Arnica diversifolia* Greene July-Aug.
Native perennial herb; streamside, meadows, talus
in spruce-fir communities to above timberline,
2570-3340 m.

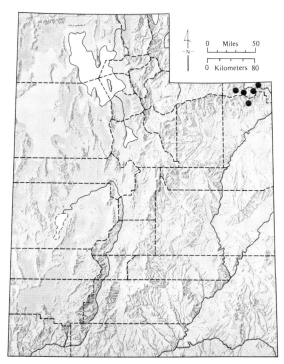

33. *Arnica fulgens* Pursh Orange arnica.
June-Aug. Native perennial herb; sagebrush
communities, 1970-2830 m.

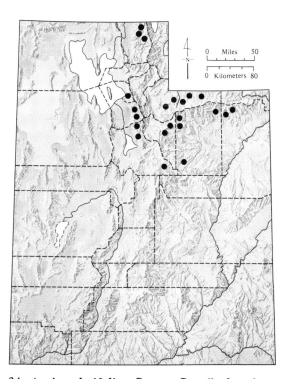

34. *Arnica latifolia* Bong. Broadleaf arnica.
July-Aug. Native perennial herb; rocky or shady
sites, spruce-fir, lodgepole pine communities,
2570-3340 m.

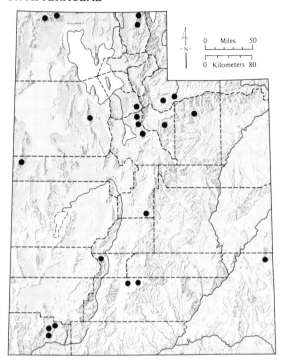

35. *Arnica longifolia* D. C. Eat. Longleaf arnica. July-Sept. Native perennial herb; streamside, talus in aspen-conifer communities, 2120-3340 m.

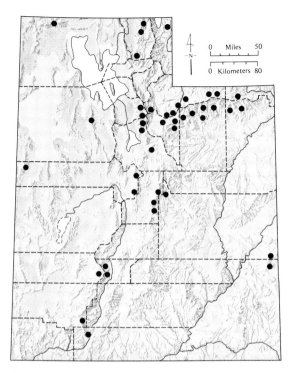

36. *Arnica mollis* Hook. Hairy arnica. July-Sept. Native perennial herb; streamside, moist meadows, talus in aspen-conifer communities, 2420-3550 m.

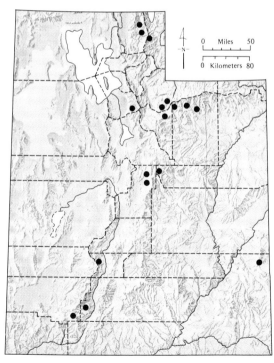

37. *Arnica parryi* Gray Parry arnica. July-Sept. Native perennial herb; aspen, spruce-fir communities, 2480-3180 m.

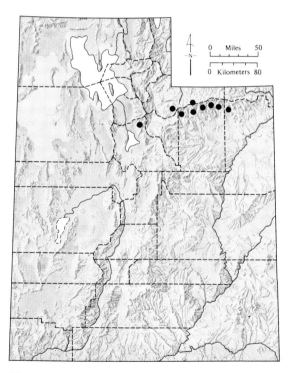

38. *Arnica rydbergii* Greene Rydberg arnica. July-Aug. Native perennial herb; spruce-fir, lodgepole pine communities, 3030-3340 m.

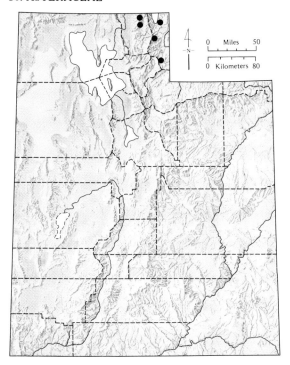

39. *Arnica sororia* Greene   Sister arnica. June-July.   Native perennial herb; sagebrush, aspen communities, 2120-2430 m.

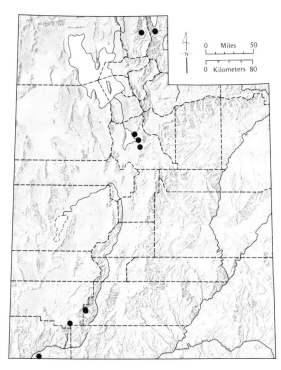

40. *Artemisia absinthium* L. Wormwood; absinthe. July-Sept. Introduced perennial herb; along waterways, roadsides, in fallow fields, other disturbed sites,1270-1670 m.

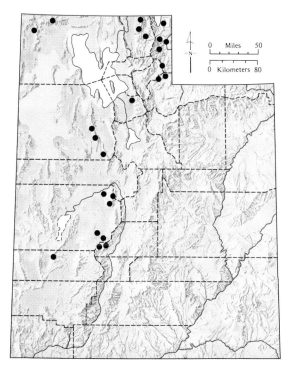

41. *Artemisia arbuscula* Nutt. Low sagebrush. June-Oct. Native shrub, shallow soil, sagebrush, pinyon-juniper, mountain brush, spruce-fir communities, 1400-3200 m.

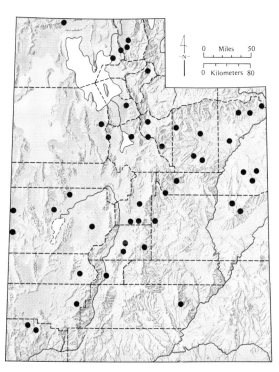

42. *Artemisia biennis* Willd.   Biennial sagewort. July-Sept. Native annual or biennial; along waterways, roadsides, other disturbed sites from salt desert shrub to aspen-fir communities, 1300-2880 m.

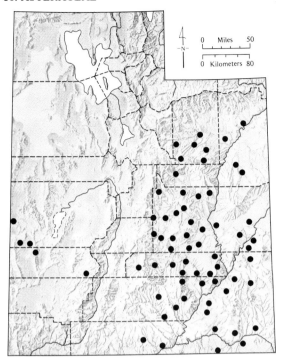

43. *Artemisia bigelovii* Gray Bigelow sagebrush. June-Oct. Native shrub or subshrub; desert shrub to pinyon-juniper communities, 1060-2460 m.

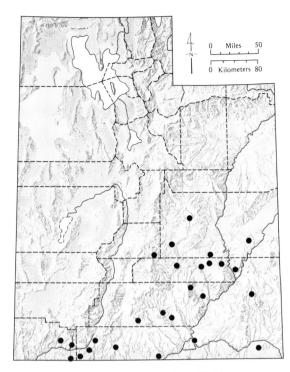

44. *Artemisia campestris* L. Field sagewort. July-Sept. Circumboreal perennial herb; shadscale, desert shrub, pinyon-juniper, mountain brush communities, typically in sandy sites, 1060-2730 m.

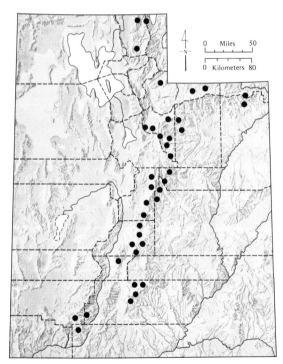

45. *Artemisia cana* Pursh Silver sagebrush. Aug.-Oct. Native shrub; grassy slopes, streambanks, wet meadows, 1810-3180 m.

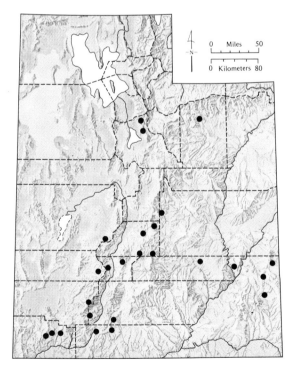

46. *Artemisia carruthii* Carruth Carruth sagewort. Aug.-Oct. Native perennial herb; desert shrub, pinyon-juniper, mountain brush, ponderosa pine, aspen, spruce-fir communities, 1820-3030 m.

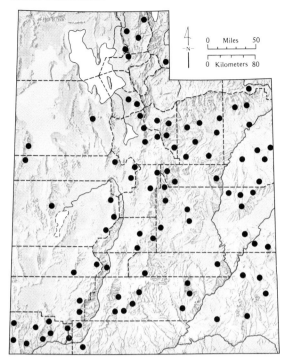

47. *Artemisia dracunculus* L. Tarragon. July-Oct. Native perennial herb; creosote bush to conifer communities, 840-3340 m.

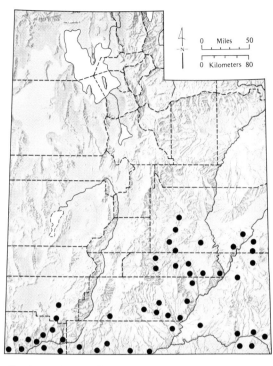

48. *Artemisia filifolia* Torr. Sand sagebrush. Aug.-Oct. Native shrub or subshrub; dunes or sandy sites in creosote bush, desert shrub communities, 840-1820 m.

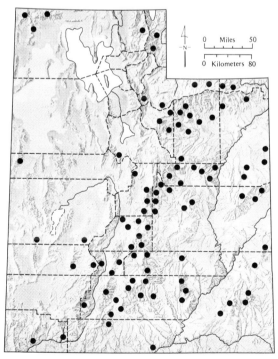

49. *Artemisia frigida* Willd. Fringed sagebrush. June-Sept. Native perennial herb or subshrub; creosote bush to alpine communities, 970-3400 m.

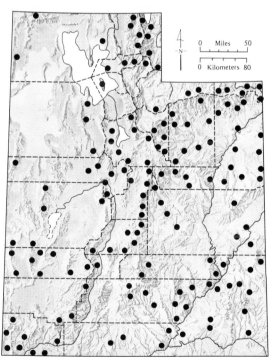

50. *Artemisia ludoviciana* Nutt. Foothill sage. July-Oct. Native perennial herb; creosote bush to alpine communities, 820-3490 m.

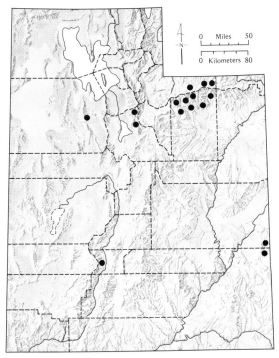

51. *Artemisia michauxiana* Bess. Michaux sagewort. July-Sept. Native perennial herb ; aspen, spruce-fir communities to above timberline, often in rocky places, 2570-3640 m.

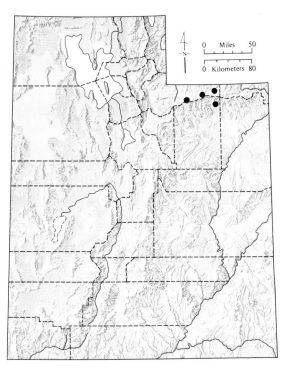

52. *Artemisia norvegica* Fries Norway sagewort. July-Sept. Native perennial herb; meadow, spruce-fir, lodgepole pine communities, talus, above timberline, 3030-3500 m.

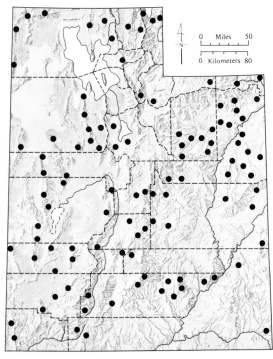

53. *Artemisia nova* A. Nels. Black sagebrush. July-Oct. Native shrub; salt desert shrub, desert shrub, pinyon-juniper to mountain brush communities, 1210-2880 m.

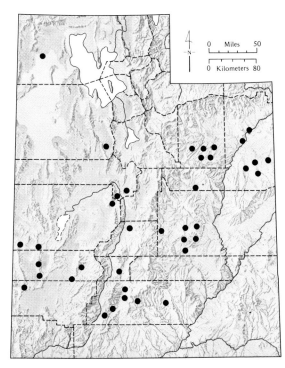

54. *Artemisia pygmaea* Gray Pigmy sagebrush. July-Sept. Native shrub; shadscale, desert shrub to pinyon-juniper communities, 1510-2270 m.

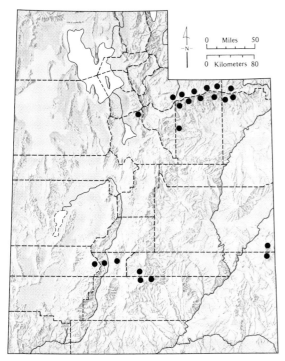

55. *Artemisia scopulorum* Gray Dwarf sagewort. July-Sept. Native perennial herb; meadows, talus, and open rocky places in lodgepole pine and spruce-fir communities to above timberline, 3030-3940 m.

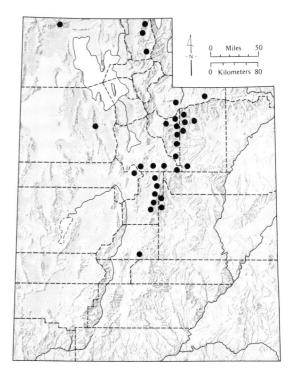

56. *Artemisia spiciformis* Osterh. Osterhout sagebrush. Aug.-Oct. Native shrub; mountain brush to spruce-fir communities, 2120-3030 m.

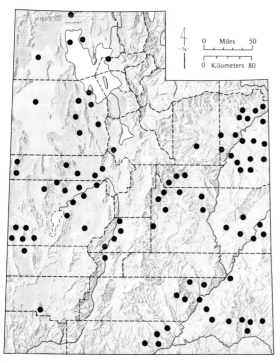

57. *Artemisia spinescens* D. C. Eat. Bud sagebrush; budsage. Apr.-June. Native shrub; shadscale, desert shrub communities, 1210-1970 m.

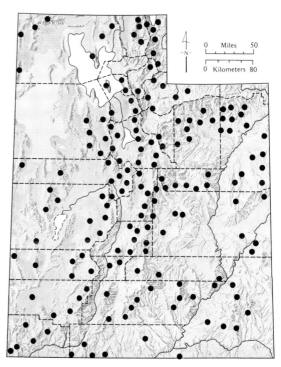

58. *Artemisia tridentata* Nutt. Sagebrush. Aug.-Oct. Native shrub; desert shrub communities to timberline, dominant over large areas, 1210-3030 m.

41

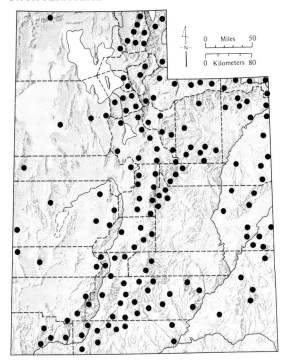

59. *Aster ascendens* Lindl. Pacific aster. July-Oct. Native perennial herb; creosote bush to conifer communities, 760-3180 m.

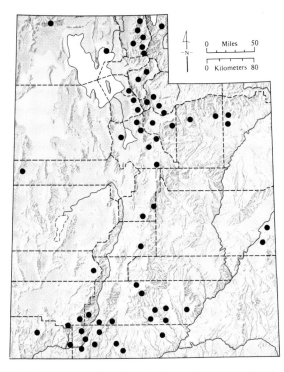

60. *Aster eatonii* (Gray) Howell Aug.-Sept. Native perennial herb; along waterways, wet meadows and other moist sites in mountain brush to conifer communities, 1270-3030 m.

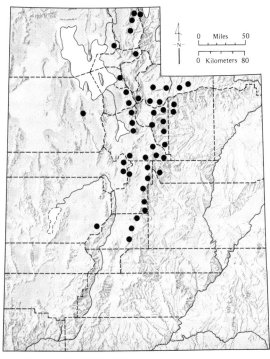

61. *Aster engelmannii* (D. C. Eat.) Gray Engelmann aster. July-Sept. Native perennial herb; mountain brush to conifer communities, 1970-3030 m.

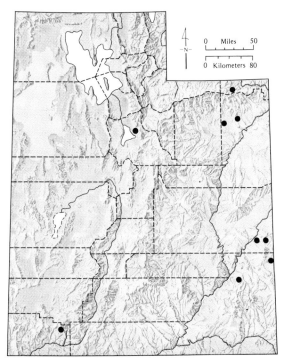

62. *Aster ericoides* L. July-Sept. Native perennial herb; along drainages and seep margins, meadows, hanging gardens, 1060-1820 m.

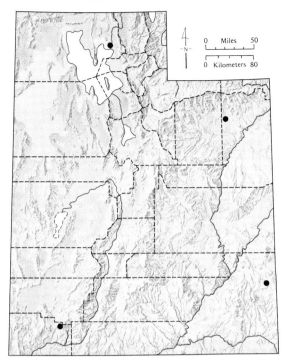

63. *Aster falcatus* Lindl. Sickle aster. July-
Sept. Native perennial herb; sagebrush, mountain
brush, ponderosa pine communities, 1300-1820 m.

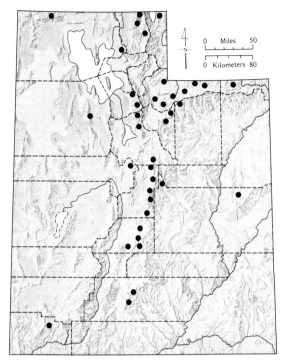

64. *Aster foliaceus* Lindl. Leafybract aster.
July-Sept. Native perennial herb; meadows,
openings in mountain brush, aspen, spruce-fir,
lodgepole pine communities, 1970-3240 m.

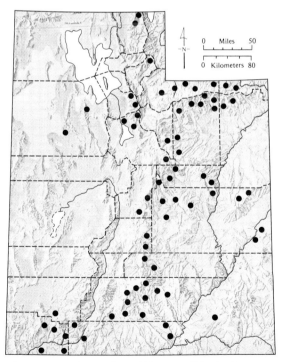

65. *Aster glaucodes* Blake Blueleaf aster.
July-Oct. Native perennial herb; moist to dry sites,
creosote bush to conifer communities, 820-3640 m.

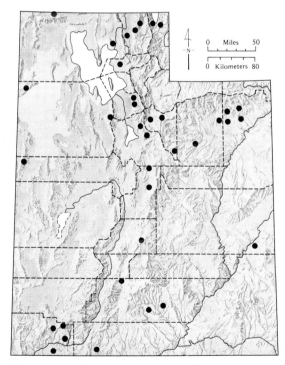

66. *Aster hesperius* Gray Siskiyou aster.
July-Sept. Native perennial herb; wet meadows,
along waterways, 850-2670 m.

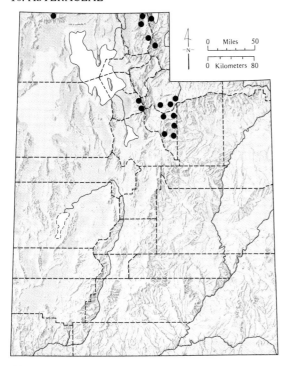

67. *Aster integrifolius* Nutt. Thickstem aster. July-Sept. Native perennial herb; meadows, mountain brush to conifer communities, 1970-3120 m.

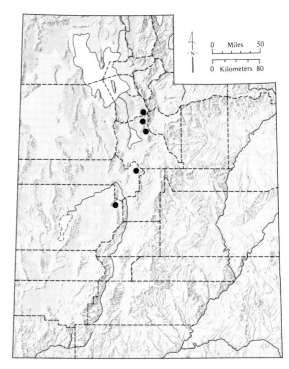

68. *Aster kingii* D. C. Eat. King aster. July-Aug. Native perennial herb; talus, rocky ridges, 1720-3030 m.

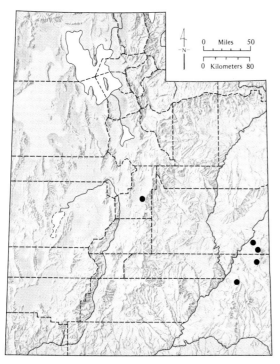

69. *Aster laevis* L. Smooth aster. July-Sept. Native perennial herb; along waterways, often in disturbed sites, 1060-2330 m.

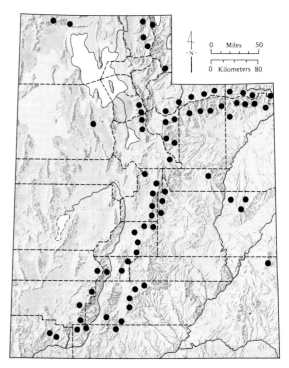

70. *Aster occidentalis* (Nutt.) T. & G. Western aster. July-Sept. Native perennial herb; meadows and streamside in aspen, spruce-fir, lodgepole pine communities, 1660-3270 m.

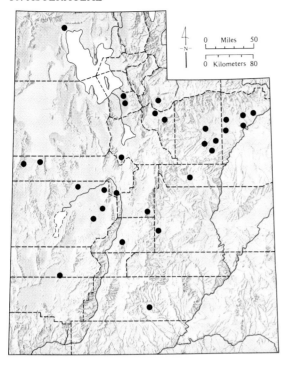

71. *Aster pauciflorus* Nutt. Alkali aster. July-Sept. Native perennial herb; moist, often alkaline or saline sites, 1360-2120 m.

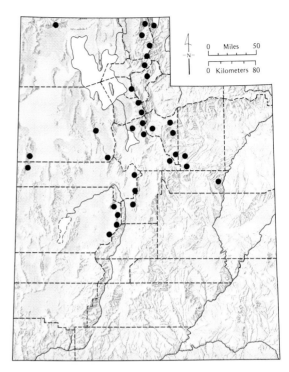

72. *Aster perelegans* Nels. & Macbr. Nuttall aster. July-Sept. Native perennial herb; sagebrush to aspen, spruce-fir communities, 1970-2880 m.

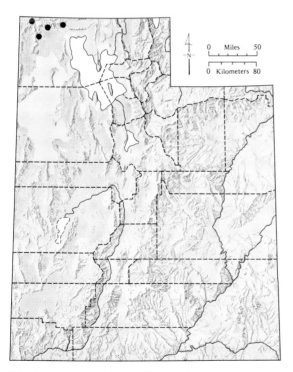

73. *Aster scopulorum* Gray Crag aster. June-Sept. Native perennial herb; sagebrush communities, 1820-2730 m.

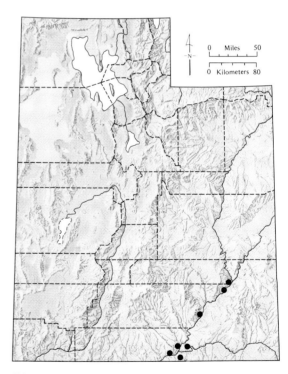

74. *Aster spinosus* Benth. Mexican devilweed. June-Oct. Native perennial herb; along waterways, 1120-1180 m.

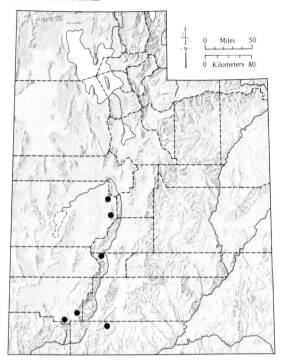

75. *Aster wasatchensis* (Jones) Blake Wasatch aster. July-Sept. Native perennial herb; pinyon-juniper to aspen, spruce-fir communities, 1820-2880 m.

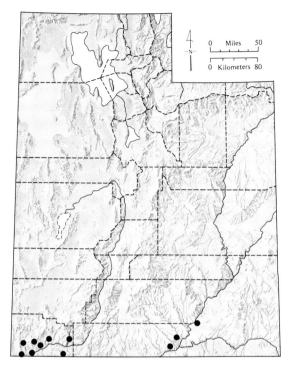

76. *Baccharis emoryi* Gray Emory baccharis. July-Oct. Native shrub; along waterways and washes in creosote bush, desert shrub communities, 760-1150 m.

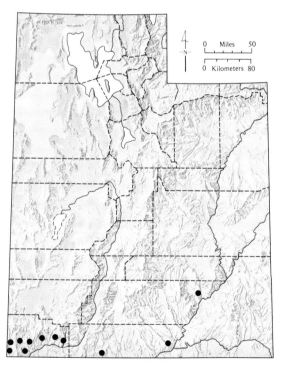

77. *Baccharis glutinosa* Pers. Seepwillow baccharis. Apr.-Oct. Native shrub; along waterways and washes, near seeps in creosote bush communities, 790-1340 m.

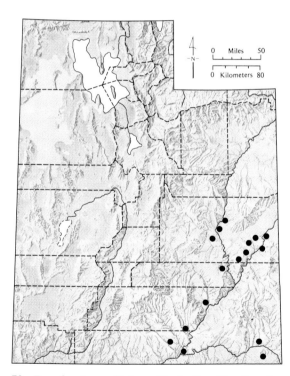

78. *Baccharis salicina* T. & G. Rio Grande baccharis. Apr.-Oct. Native shrub; along waterways and moist washes in desert shrub communities, 1150-1460 m.

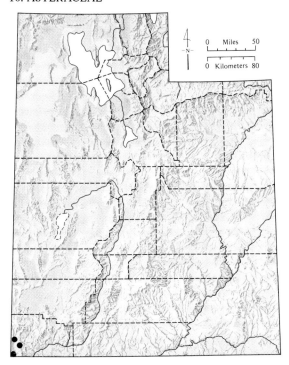

79. *Baccharis sergiloides* Gray Squaw waterweed. Apr.-Oct. Native shrub; along waterways and moist washes in creosote bush communities, 790-1090 m.

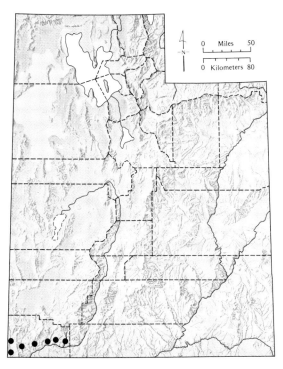

80. *Baccharis viminea* DC. Mulefat. Apr.-June. Native shrub; along waterways and moist washes in creosote bush communities, 760-1150 m.

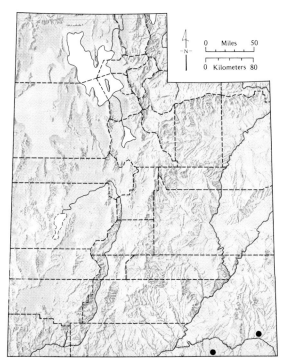

81. *Baccharis wrightii* Gray May-June. Native shrub; moist to dry washes in desert shrub communities, 1330-1520 m.

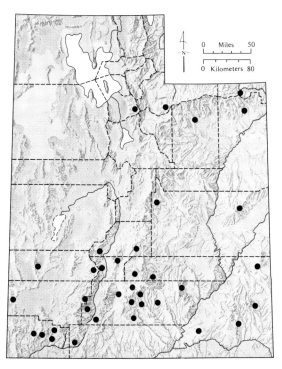

82. *Bahia dissecta* (Gray) Britt. Ragleaf bahia. July-Sept. Native perennial herb; sagebrush, pinyon-juniper, mountain brush to conifer communities, 1600-2790 m.

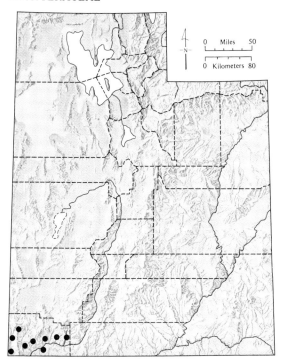

83. *Baileya multiradiata* Harv. & Gray Desert marigold. Mar.-Nov. Native biennial or perennial; creosote bush, desert shrub communities, 665-1370 m.

84. *Baileya pleniradiata* Harv. & Gray Apr.-Oct. Native annual or perennial; creosote bush communities, 730-1060 m.

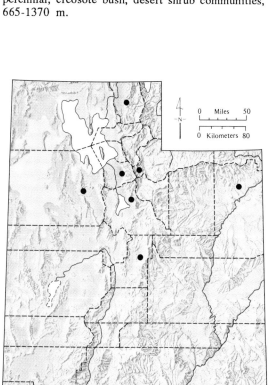

85. *Balsamita major* Desf. Costmary. July-Oct. Introduced perennial herb; cultivated, escaping and persistent, 1360-2120 m.

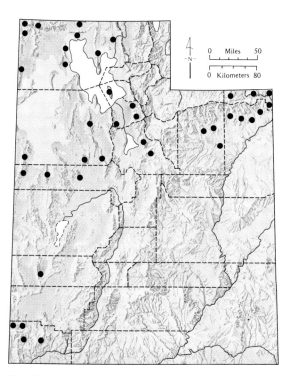

86. *Balsamorhiza hispidula* Sharp May-June. Native perennial herb; sagebrush, mountain brush and pinyon-juniper communities, 1210-3170 m.

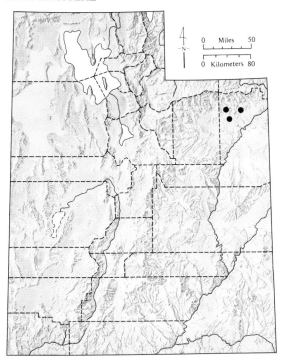

87. **Balsamorhiza hookeri** Nutt. Hooker balsamroot. Apr.-July. Native perennial herb; shadscale, desert shrub to ponderosa pine communities, 1360-2880 m.

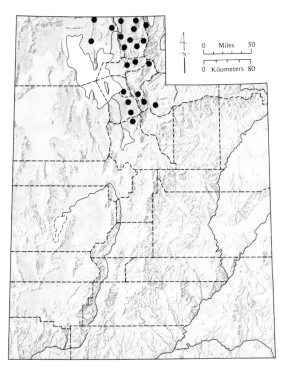

88. **Balsamorhiza macrophylla** Nutt. Cutleaf balsamroot. Apr.-June. Native perennial herb; mesic slopes in sagebrush, mountain brush communities, 1360-2490 m.

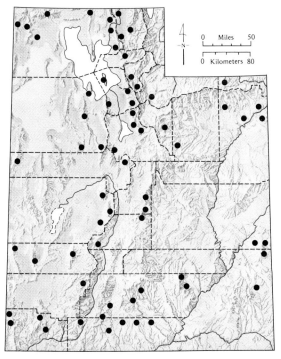

89. **Balsamorhiza sagittata** (Pursh) Nutt. Arrowleaf balsamroot. Apr.-June. Native perennial herb; sagebrush, pinyon-juniper, mountain brush to conifer communities, 1210-2730 m.

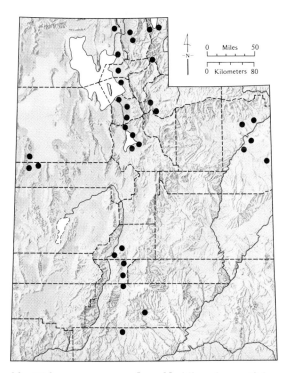

90. **Bidens cernua** L. Nodding beggartick. June-Sept. Native annual; moist, often disturbed sites in meadows, along waterways, 1360-2270 m.

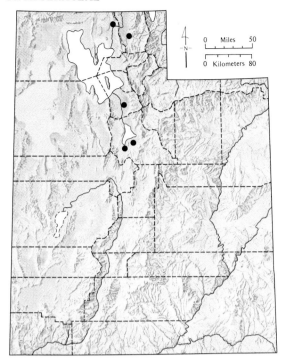

91. **Bidens comosa** (Gray) Wieg. July-Sept. Cosmopolitan annual; wet waste places, 1360-1520 m.

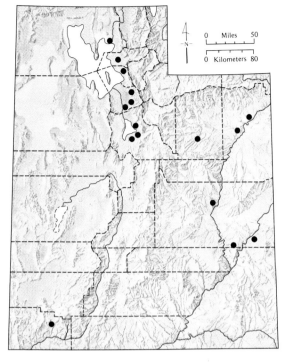

92. **Bidens frondosa** L. Devil's beggarticks. June-Aug. Native annual; wet, often disturbed sites along waterways, in meadows, 1060-1520 m.

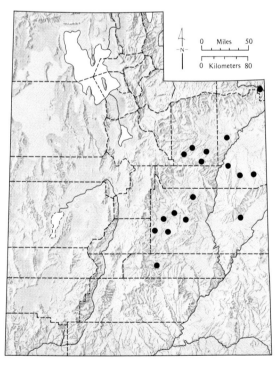

93. **Bolophyta ligulata** (Jones) W. A. Weber Liguled parthenium. May-June. Native perennial herb; rocky sites in shadscale, desert shrub, pinyon-juniper communities, 1510-2120 m.

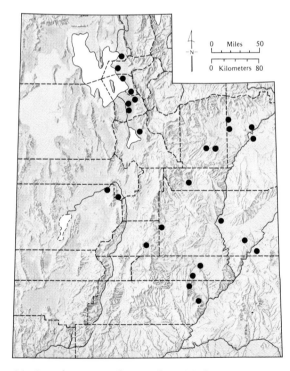

94. **Brachyactis ciliata** (Ledeb.) Ledeb. Aug.-Oct. Native annual; wet, often saline sites in marshes, along waterways and pond margins, 1210-1700 m.

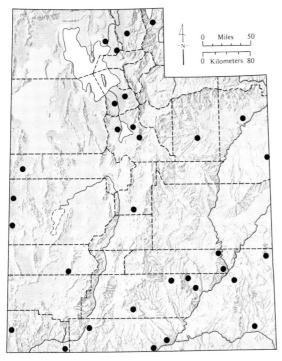

95. *Brachyactis frondosa* (Nutt.) Gray Aug.-Sept. Native annual; along waterways, in salt grass meadows, greasewood communities, 850-2120 m.

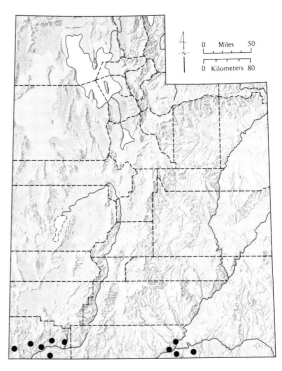

96. *Brickellia atractyloides* Gray Spiny brickellbush. Apr.-June. Native shrub; rocky sites in creosote bush communities, 760-1060 m.

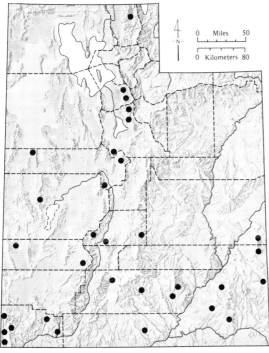

97. *Brickellia californica* (T. & G.) Gray California brickellbush. July-Oct. Native subshrub; rocky sites in creosote bush, mountain brush and pinyon-juniper communities, 760-2310 m.

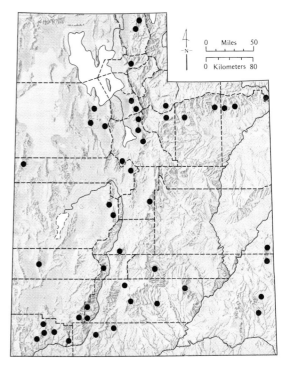

98. *Brickellia grandiflora* (Hook.) Nutt. Tasselflower brickellbush. July-Oct. Native perennial herb; moist to dry, often rocky slopes in mountain brush, pinyon-juniper, ponderosa pine, bristlecone pine and other conifer communities, 1210-3030 m.

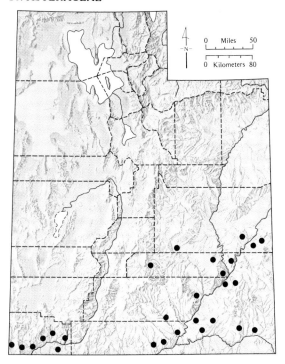

99. *Brickellia longifolia* Wats. Longleaf brickellbush. July-Oct. Native shrub; margins of seeps, hanging gardens, streamside, in creosote bush, desert shrub communities, 760-1820 m.

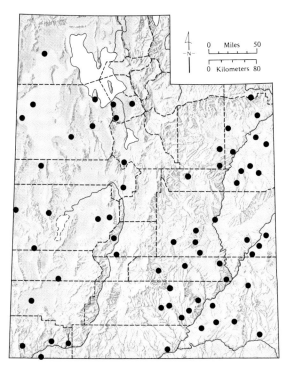

100. *Brickellia microphylla* (Nutt.) Gray Littleleaf brickellbush. Aug.-Oct. Native shrub or subshrub; dry rocky slopes in creosote bush, shadscale, desert shrub, pinyon-juniper communities, 880-2280 m.

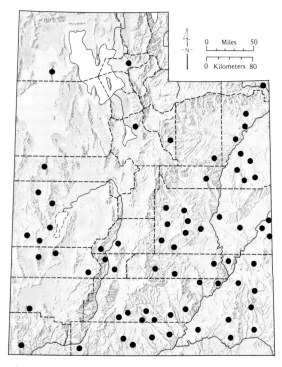

101. *Brickellia oblongifolia* Nutt. Mojave brickellbush. May-Aug. Native perennial herb or subshrub; shadscale, desert shrub, pinyon-juniper, ponderosa pine communities, 1210-2430 m.

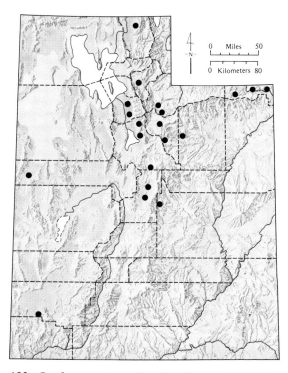

102. *Carduus nutans* L. Nodding musk thistle. May-Sept. Introduced annual or biennial; roadsides, fields, disturbed slopes, 1420-2580 m.

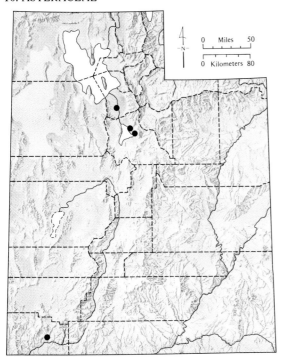

103. *Centaurea calcitrapa* L. Starthistle; lime knapweed. July-Sept. Introduced biennial; roadsides and other disturbed sites, 1300-1670 m.

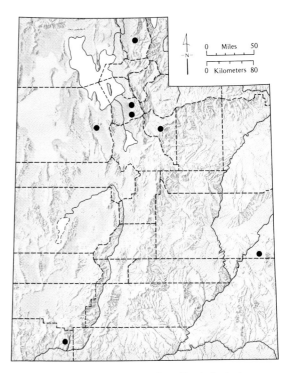

104. *Centaurea cyanus* L. Bachelor's button. May-Aug. Introduced annual; cultivated, escaping and persistent, 1060-2430 m.

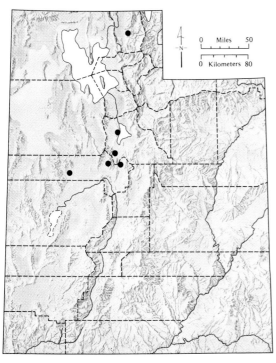

105. *Centaurea diffusa* Lam. Diffuse knapweed. May-July. Introduced annual or biennial; roadsides, 1360-1970 m.

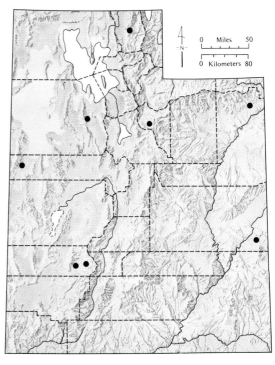

106. *Centaurea maculosa* Lam. Spotted knapweed. July-Aug. Introduced biennial or perennial; disturbed sites, 1510-2120 m.

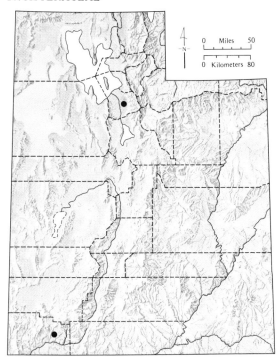

107. *Centaurea melitensis* L. Black knapweed. Introduced annual; disturbed sites, 910-1370 m.

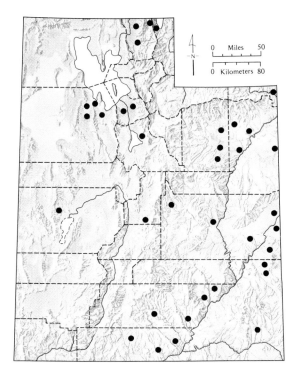

108. *Centaurea repens* L. Russian knapweed. June-Sept. Introduced perennial herb; disturbed sites, 1430-2280 m.

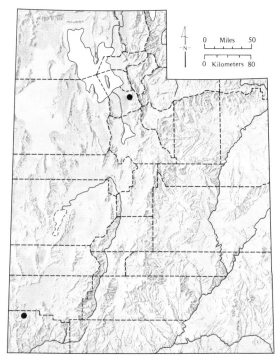

109. *Centaurea scabiosa* L. Gritty knapweed. July-Sept. Introduced perennial herb; cultivated, escaping and persistent, 1660-1850 m.

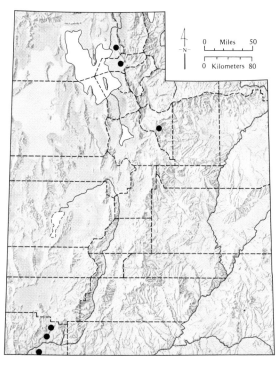

110. *Centaurea solstitialis* L. Yellow starthistle. June-Sept. Introduced annual or biennial; disturbed sites, 820-1970 m.

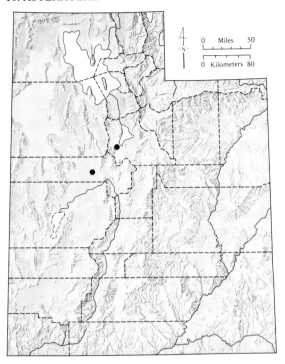

111. *Centaurea squarrosa* Willd. Square-twig knapweed. May-July. Introduced perennial herb; roadsides, 1360-1970 m.

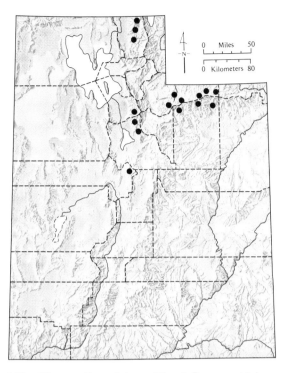

112. *Chaenactis alpina* (Gray) Jones Alpine dusty maiden. July-Sept. Native perennial herb; open rocky sites in aspen, spruce-fir communities to above timberline, 2880-3790 m.

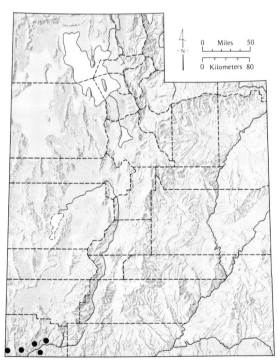

113. *Chaenactis carphoclinia* Gray Strawbed dustymaiden. Mar.-May. Native annual; creosote bush communities, 850-1060 m.

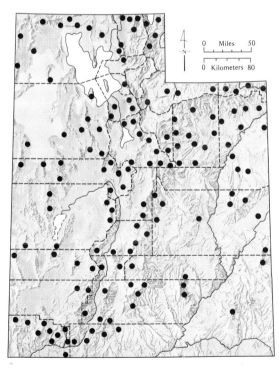

114. *Chaenactis douglasii* (Hook.) H. & A. Douglas dustymaiden. May-Sept. Native perennial herb; shadscale, desert shrub, pinyon-juniper to aspen-conifer communities, 1210-2880 m.

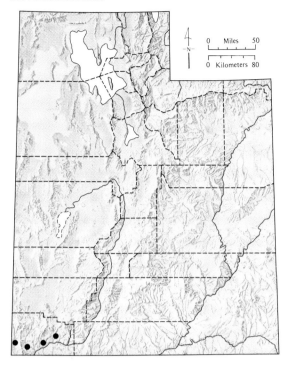

115. *Chaenactis fremontii* Gray Fremont dustymaiden. Mar.-May. Native annual; creosote bush communities, 790-970 m.

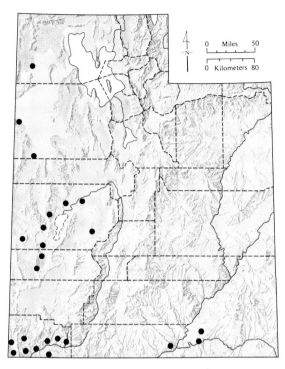

116. *Chaenactis macrantha* D. C. Eat. Bighead dustymaiden. Apr.-June. Native annual; creosote bush, shadscale, desert shrub to pinyon-juniper communities, 850-2060 m.

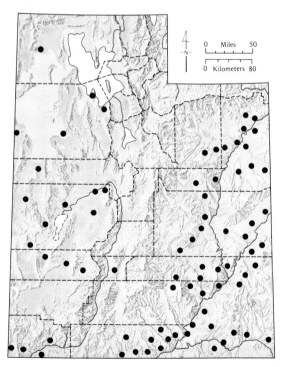

117. *Chaenactis stevioides* H. & A. Steve's dustymaiden. Apr.-June. Native annual; creosote bush, shadscale, desert shrub communities, 850-1820 m.

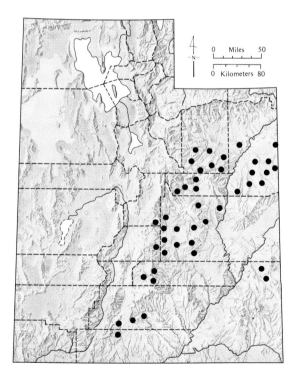

118. *Chamaechaenactis scaposa* (Eastw.) Rydb. Apr.-July. Native perennial herb; shadscale, desert shrub, pinyon-juniper, ponderosa pine communities, 1670-2550 m.

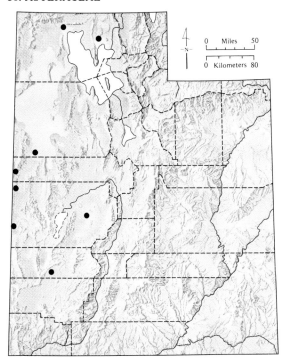

119. *Chrysothamnus albidus* (Jones) Greene Alkali rabbitbrush. Aug.-Sept. Native shrub; salt desert shrub communities, 1390-1550 m.

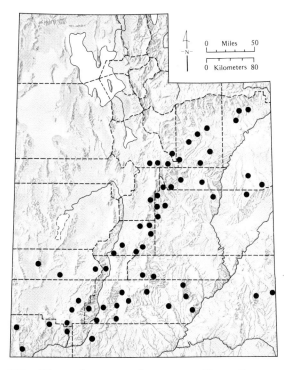

120. *Chrysothamnus depressus* Nutt. Dwarf rabbitbrush. July-Sept. Native shrub; sagebrush, pinyon-juniper, mountain brush to conifer communities, 1880-2880 m.

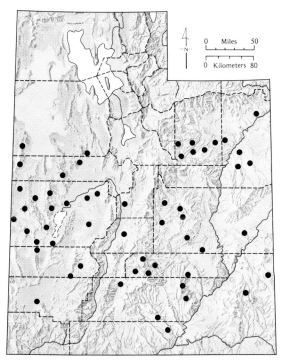

121. *Chrysothamnus greenei* (Gray) Greene Greene rabbitbrush. July-Sept. Native shrub; shadscale, desert shrub communities, 1360-1970 m.

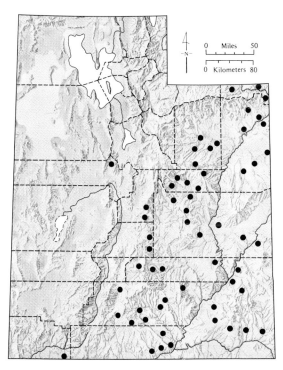

122. *Chrysothamnus linifolius* Greene Spreading rabbitbrush. July-Oct. Native shrub; margins of seeps and springs, streamside, 1060-2280 m.

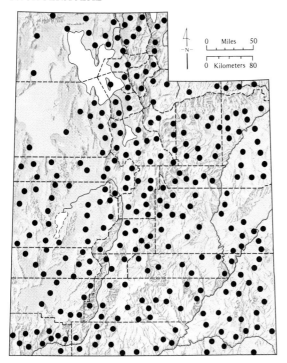

123. *Chrysothamnus nauseosus* (Pall.) Britt. Rubber rabbitbrush. Aug.-Oct. Native shrub, an important component of the sagebrush community; creosote bush to conifer communities, 850-3030 m.

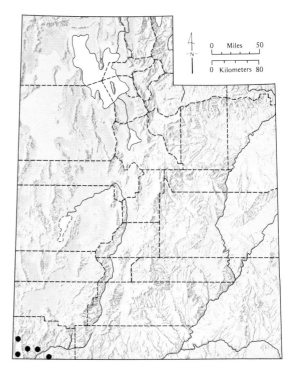

124. *Chrysothamnus paniculatus* (Gray) Hall Desert rabbitbrush. Aug.-Oct. Native shrub; creosote bush communities, 665-1120 m.

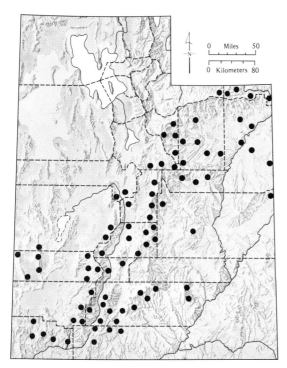

125. *Chrysothamnus parryi* (Gray) Greene Parry rabbitbrush. Aug.-Oct. Native shrub; sagebrush, pinyon-juniper to aspen communities, 1360-2700 m.

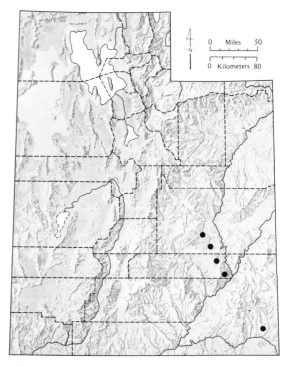

126. *Chrysothamnus pulchellus* (Gray) Greene Southwest rabbitbrush. Aug.-Oct. Native shrub; shadscale, desert shrub, pinyon-juniper communities, 1970-2120 m.

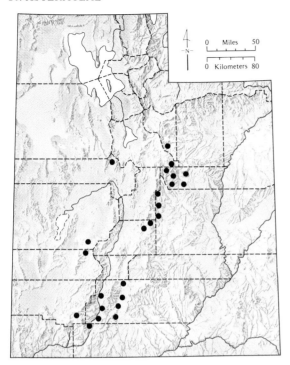

127. *Chrysothamnus vaseyi* (Gray) Greene Vasey rabbitbrush. July-Oct. Native shrub; mountain brush to ponderosa pine communities, 1820-2730 m.

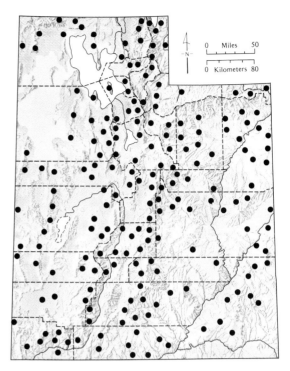

128. *Chrysothamnus viscidiflorus* (Hook.) Nutt. Mountain rabbitbrush. July-Oct. Native shrub; shadscale, desert shrub to conifer communities, 1030-3090 m.

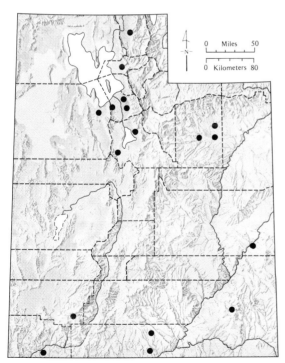

129. *Cichorium intybus* L. Chickory. Aug.-Oct. Introduced perennial herb; roadsides, other disturbed sites, 910-1970 m.

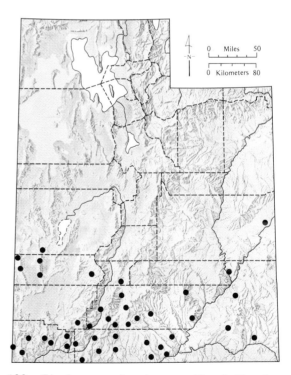

130. *Cirsium arizonicum* (Gray) Petrak Arizona thistle. June-Sept. Native biennial or perennial; shadscale, desert shrub to spruce-fir communities, 1150-3180 m.

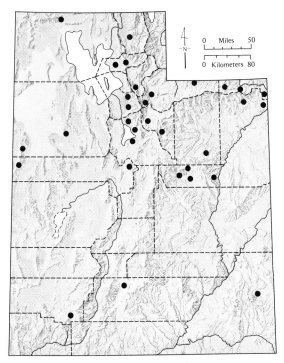

131. *Cirsium arvense* (L.) Scop. Canada thistle. Apr.-Sept. Introduced perennial herb; moist waste places, 1090-2370 m.

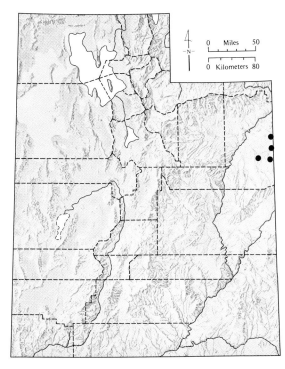

132. *Cirsium barnebyi* Welsh & Neese Barneby thistle. May-Aug. Native perennial herb; sagebrush, juniper communities, 1520-2260 m.

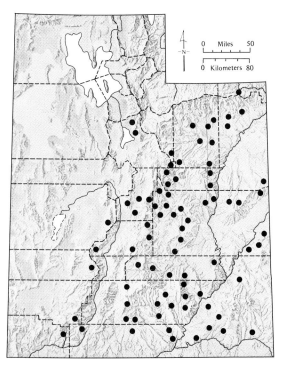

133. *Cirsium calcareum* (Jones) Woot. & Standl. Limestone thistle. May-Sept. Native perennial herb; moist to dry meadows, desert shrub to aspen-fir communities, 1060-2880 m.

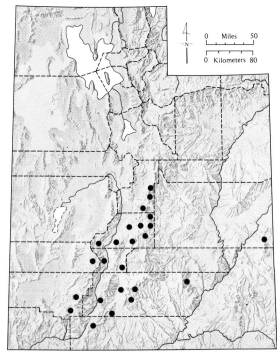

134. *Cirsium clavatum* (Jones) Petrak Club thistle. July-Sept. Native perennial herb; meadows, sagebrush to aspen, spruce-fir communities, 2420-3150 m.

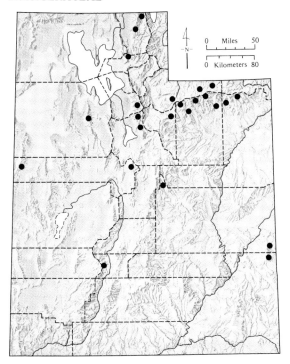

135. *Cirsium eatonii* (Gray) Robins. Eaton
thistle. July-Oct. Native perennial herb; lodgepole
pine, aspen, spruce-fir communities to above
timberline, 2270-3650 m.

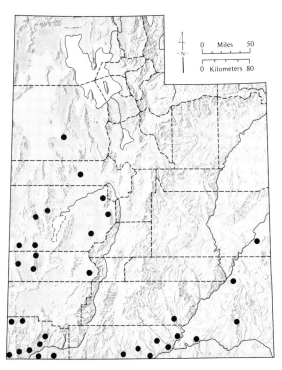

136. *Cirsium neomexicanum* Gray New
Mexico thistle. Mar.-July. Native biennial; rocky
sites in creosote bush, shadscale, desert shrub,
pinyon-juniper communities, 790-2030 m.

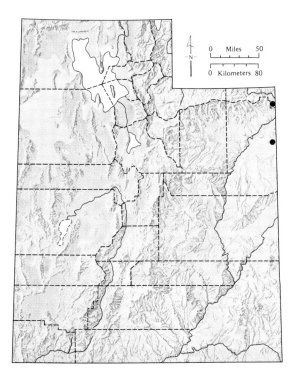

137. *Cirsium ownbeyi* Welsh Ownbey thistle.
July-Aug. Native perennial herb; streamside in
sagebrush-juniper communities, 1970-2430 m.

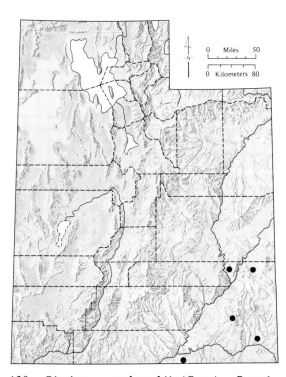

138. *Cirsium rothrockii* (Gray) Petrak
Rothrock thistle. July-Sept. Native perennial
herb; desert shrub to ponderosa pine communities,
1820-2550 m.

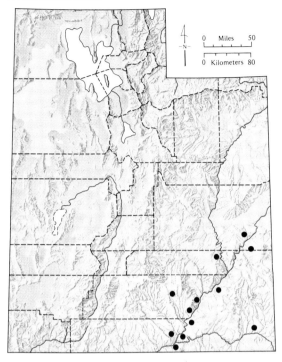

139. *Cirsium rydbergii* Petrak Rydberg thistle. July-Sept. Native perennial herb; margins of seeps, hanging gardens, 1150-1370 m.

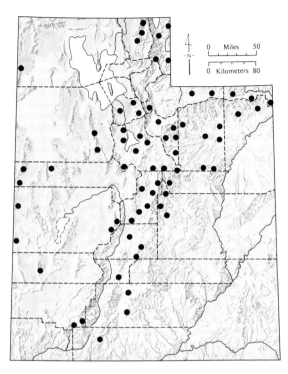

140. *Cirsium scariosum* Nutt. Meadow thistle. June-Sept. Native perennial herb; wet, often saline meadows, near springs, streamside, 1360-3150 m.

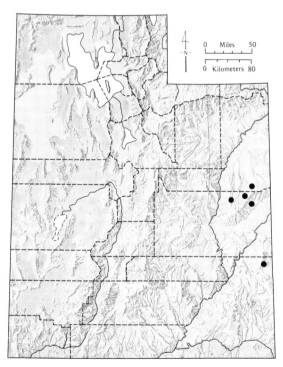

141. *Cirsium scopulorum* (Greene) Ckll. Mountain thistle. July-Sept. Native perennial herb; sagebrush, aspen, spruce-fir communities, 1820-2730 m.

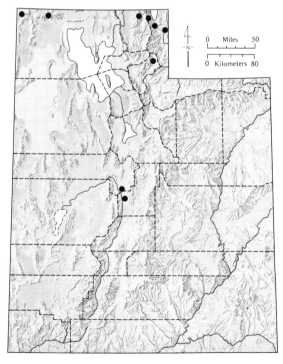

142. *Cirsium subniveum* Rydb. Snow thistle. July-Sept. Native perennial herb; pinyon-juniper communities, 2270-2730 m.

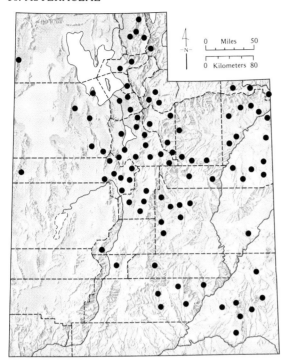

143. *Cirsium undulatum* (Nutt.) Spreng. Wavyleaf thistle. May-Sept. Native perennial herb; desert shrub to aspen-fir communities, 1360-2730 m.

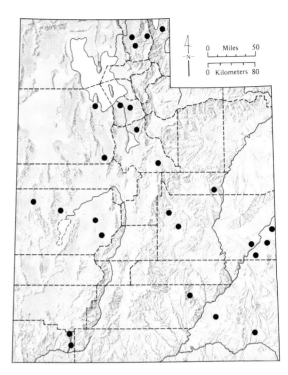

144. *Cirsium utahense* Petrak Utah thistle. July-Sept. Native perennial herb; creosote bush to aspen communities, 850-2580 m.

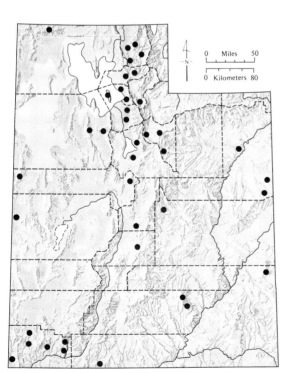

145. *Cirsium vulgare* (Savi) Ten. Bull thistle. July-Oct. Introduced perennial herb; disturbed sites, 1060-2580 m.

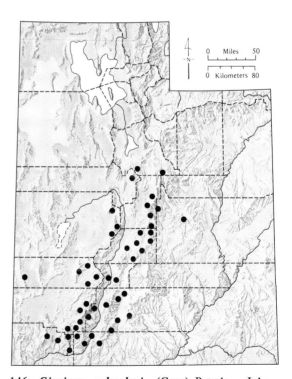

146. *Cirsium wheeleri* (Gray) Petrak July-Sept. Native perennial herb; pinyon-juniper, mountain brush to spruce-fir communities, 1970-2880 m.

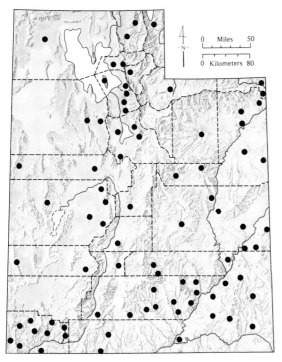

147. *Conyza canadensis* (L.) Cronq. Canada horseweed. July-Oct. Native annual; moist, mostly disturbed sites, 790-2580 m.

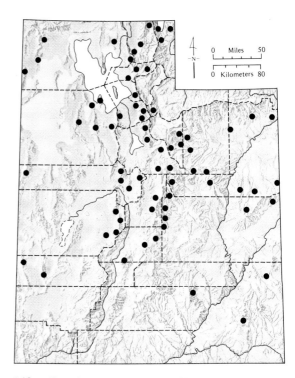

148. *Crepis acuminata* Nutt. Tapertip hawksbeard. May-Aug. Native perennial herb; dry open slopes in sagebrush, mountain brush to aspen, spruce-fir communities, 1420-2880 m.

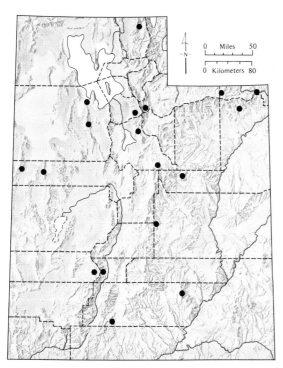

149. *Crepis atrabarba* Heller Black hawksbeard. June-Aug. Native perennial herb; open slopes in sagebrush, mountain brush, ponderosa pine, aspen, spruce-fir communities, 1630-3030 m.

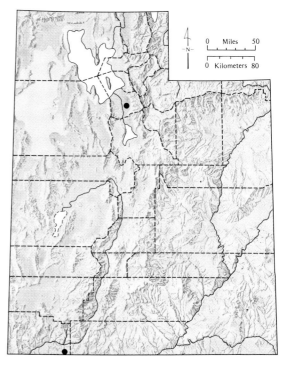

150. *Crepis capillaris* (L.) Wallr. Thread hawksbeard. Aug.-Oct. Introduced annual; disturbed sites, 1360-1880 m.

10. ASTERACEAE

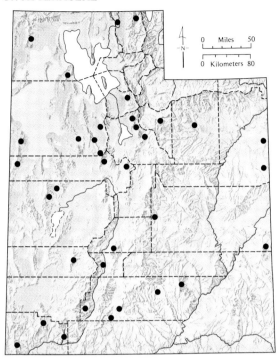

151. *Crepis intermedia* Gray Gray hawksbeard. May-July. Native perennial herb; open slopes in sagebrush, mountain brush, pinyon-juniper communities, 1360-2430 m.

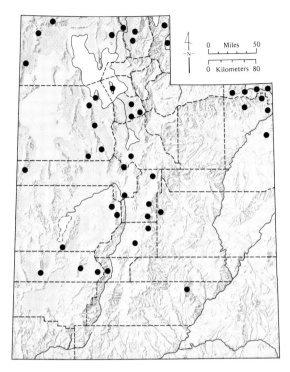

152. *Crepis modocensis* Greene Low hawksbeard. May-July. Native perennial herb; open rocky slopes in sagebrush, mountain brush, pinyon-juniper, aspen, spruce-fir communities, 1300-3150 m.

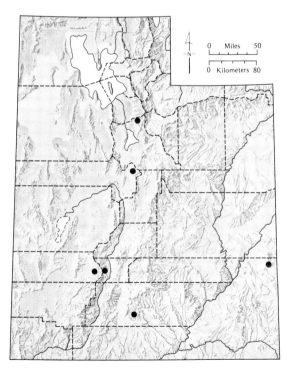

153. *Crepis nana* Richards. Tiny hawksbeard. July-Aug. Native perennial herb; subalpine to alpine communities, chiefly in talus, 2790-3490 m.

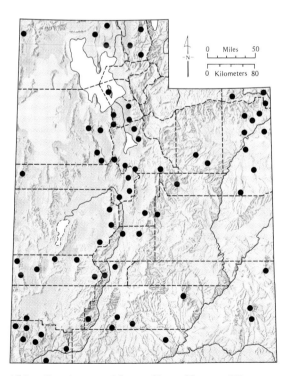

154. *Crepis occidentalis* Nutt. Western hawksbeard. May-July. Native perennial herb; shadscale, sagebrush, pinyon-juniper, ponderosa pine, aspen communities, 1210-2730 m.

65

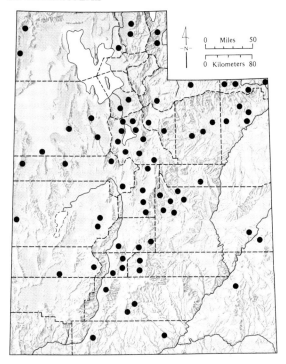

155. *Crepis runcinata* (James) T. & G.
Meadow hawksbeard. May-Sept. Native perennial
herb; moist, often saline meadows, along
lakeshores, near springs, 1270-2880 m.

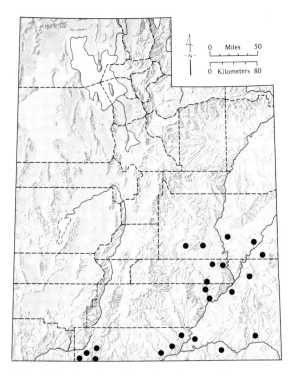

156. *Dicoria brandegei* Gray Brandegee
dicoria. Aug.-Oct. Native annual; sand dunes in
desert shrub communities, 1120-1670 m.

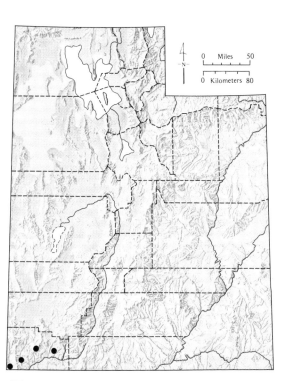

157. *Dicoria canescens* Gray Gray dicoria.
Sept.-Oct. Native annual; sand dunes in creosote
bush communities, 790-1150 m.

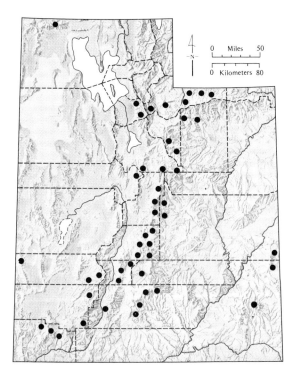

158. *Dugaldia hoopesii* (Gray) Rydb. Orange
sneezeweed. May-Aug. Native perennial herb;
meadows and streamside in sagebrush, mountain
brush, aspen, spruce-fir communities, 1820-
3550 m.

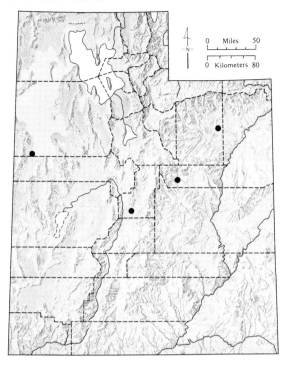

159. *Dyssodia papposa* (Vent.) Hitchc. Pappas dogweed. Aug.-Sept. Native annual; desert shrub communities, often roadside, 1450-1820 m.

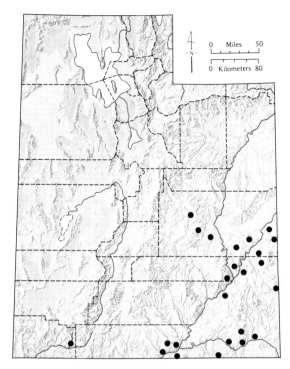

160. *Encelia frutescens* Gray Bush encelia. Apr.-Oct. Native shrub; rocky sites in shadscale, desert shrub communities, 1390-1610 m.

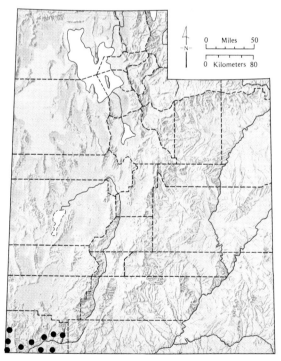

161. *Encelia virginensis* A. Nels. White-bush encelia. Apr.-Oct. Native shrub; creosote bush, Joshua tree communities, 790-1060 m.

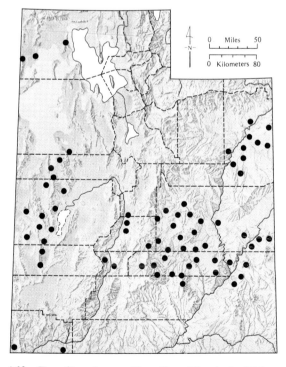

162. *Enceliopsis nudicaulis* (Gray) A. Nels. False sunflower. May-July. Native perennial herb; shadscale, desert shrub, pinyon-juniper communities, 1090-1880 m.

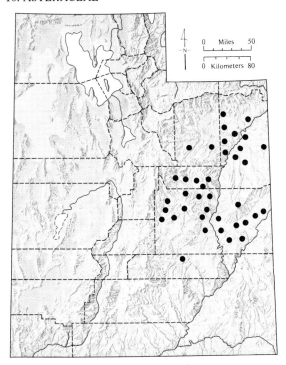

163. *Enceliopsis nutans* (Eastw.) A. Nels. Nodding enceliopsis. May-June. Native perennial herb; shadscale, mat saltbush, desert shrub communities, 1390-1820 m.

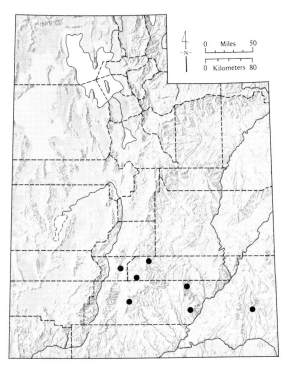

164. *Erigeron abajoensis* Cronq. Abajo fleabane. July-Sept. Native perennial herb; pinyon-juniper, ponderosa pine, spruce-fir communities, 2270-3400 m.

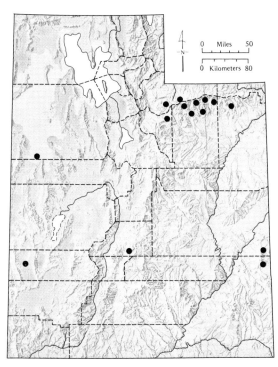

165. *Erigeron acris* L. Bitter fleabane. July-Aug. Circumboreal perennial herb; desert shrub, pinyon-juniper to lodgepole pine, aspen, spruce-fir communities, 1300-3460 m.

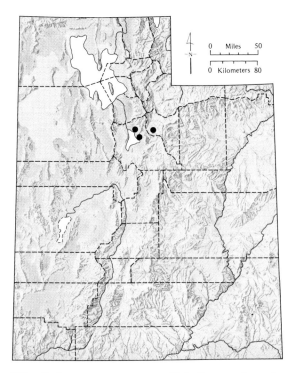

166. *Erigeron annuus* (L.) Pers. Annual fleabane. June-Aug. Introduced annual; disturbed sites, 1360-2180 m.

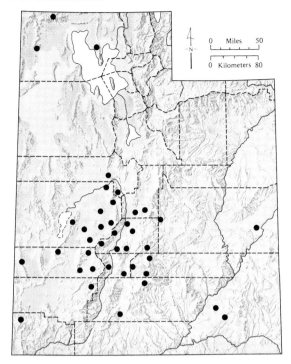

167. *Erigeron aphanactis* (Gray) Greene
Hairy fleabane. May-June. Native perennial herb;
shadscale, desert shrub to aspen communities,
1300-2730 m.

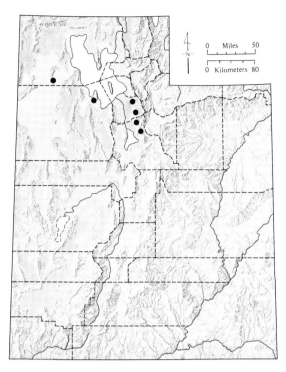

168. *Erigeron arenarioides* (D. C. Eat.)Gray
Wasatch fleabane. July-Sept. Native perennial
herb; rock crevices, 2120-3030 m.

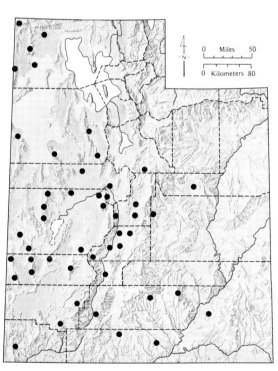

169. *Erigeron argentatus* Gray Silver
fleabane. May-June. Native perennial herb;
greasewood, shadscale, desert shrub, pinyon-
juniper, mountain brush communities, 1330-
2420 m.

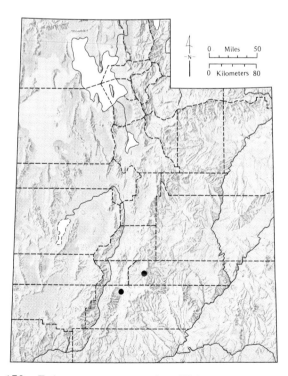

170. *Erigeron awapensis* Welsh Awapa
fleabane. June-July. Native perennial herb;
sagebrush, pinyon-juniper communities, 1810-
1970 m.

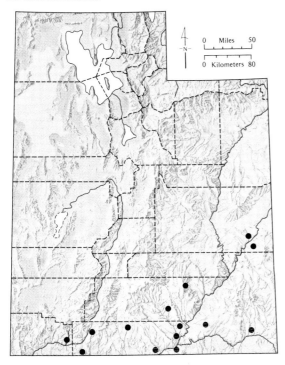

171. *Erigeron bellidiastrum* Nutt. Little daisy fleabane. May-June. Native annual or biennial; desert shrub, pinyon-juniper communities, 1060-1670 m.

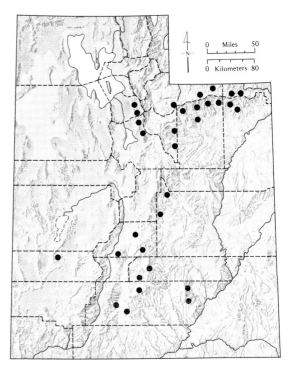

172. *Erigeron caespitosus* Nutt. Tufted fleabane. May-July. Native perennial herb; sagebrush communities to above timberline, 2270-3490 m.

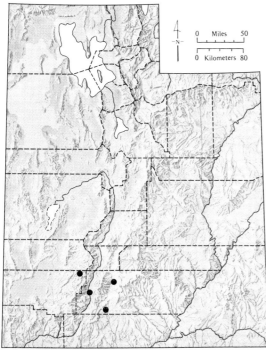

173. *Erigeron canus* Gray Hoary fleabane. July-Aug. Native perennial herb; talus in pinyon-juniper, ponderosa pine communities, 2150-2460 m.

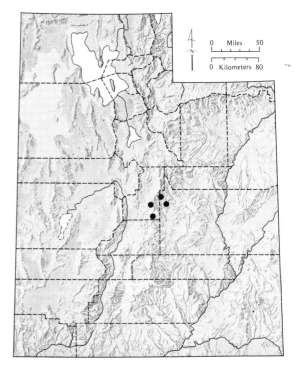

174. *Erigeron carringtonae* Welsh Carrington fleabane. July-Aug. Native perennial herb; meadows, escarpment margins, often on Flagstaff Limestone, 2970-3400 m.

10. ASTERACEAE

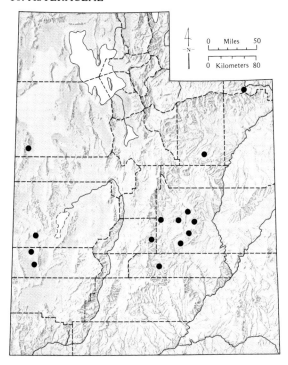

175. *Erigeron compactus* Blake Compact fleabane. June-July. Native perennial herb; shadscale, desert shrub, pinyon-juniper communities, 1820-2240 m.

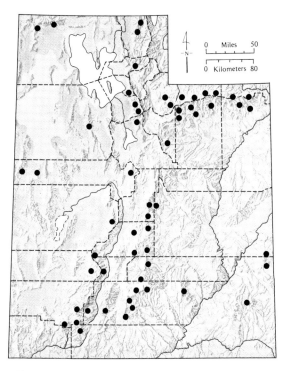

176. *Erigeron compositus* Pursh Fernleaf fleabane. June-Aug. Native perennial herb; aspen-conifer communities to above timberline, 2120-3940 m.

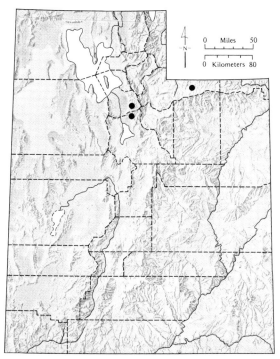

177. *Erigeron coulteri* Porter Coulter fleabane. July-Aug. Native perennial herb; moist sites in aspen, spruce-fir communities, 2270-3030 m.

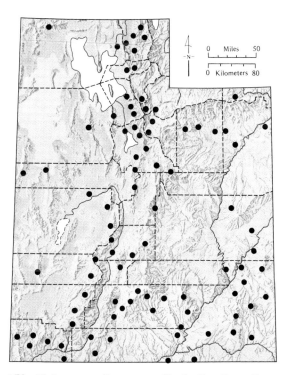

178. *Erigeron divergens* T. & G. Spreading fleabane. June-Aug. Native perennial herb; sagebrush, pinyon-juniper to aspen-fir communities, 1360-2730 m.

71

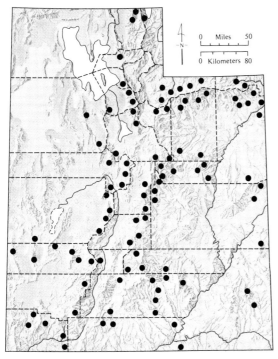

179. ***Erigeron eatonii*** Gray   Eaton fleabane.
May-Aug.   Native perennial herb; sagebrush,
pinyon-juniper, aspen-conifer communities to
above timberline, 1880-3610 m.

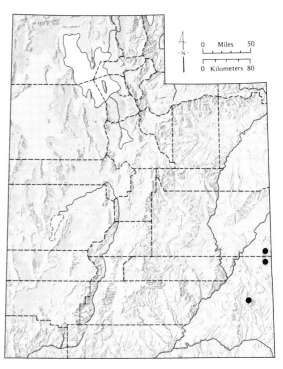

180. ***Erigeron elatior*** (Gray) Greene   Tall
fleabane.   July-Aug.   Native perennial herb;
meadows in aspen, spruce-fir communities, 2870-
3180 m.

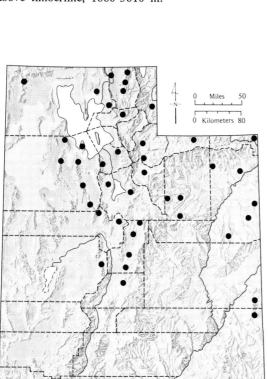

181. ***Erigeron   engelmannii***   A. Nels.
Engelmann fleabane. May-July. Native perennial
herb;   shadscale,   sagebrush,   pinyon-juniper
communities,   open   slopes   in   aspen-fir
communities, 1360-2850 m.

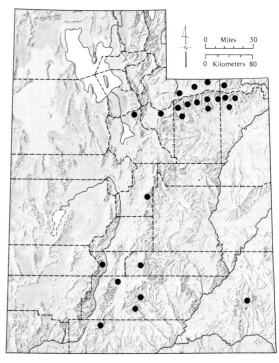

182. ***Erigeron eximius*** Greene   July-Aug.
Native perennial herb; shaded sites in aspen,
spruce-fir communities, 2330-3180 m.

72

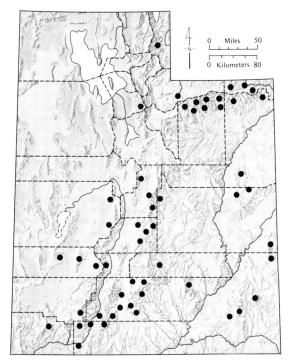

183. *Erigeron flagellaris* Gray Trailing fleabane. June-Aug. Native perennial herb; sagebrush, ponderosa pine, aspen, spruce-fir communities, 1820-3030 m.

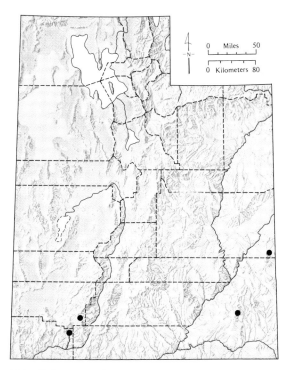

184. *Erigeron formosissimus* Greene Pretty fleabane. July-Sept. Native perennial herb; meadows in mountain brush, aspen communities, 1970-2580 m.

185. *Erigeron garrettii* A. Nels. Garrett fleabane. Aug.-Sept. Native perennial herb; moist rock crevices, cliffs, 2730-3780 m.

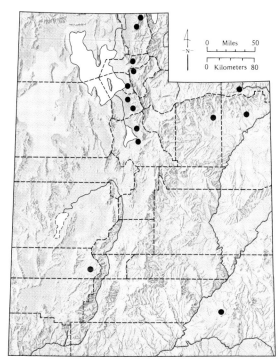

186. *Erigeron glabellus* Nutt. Smooth fleabane. June-July. Native biennial; moist meadows, streamsides, 1330-1820 m.

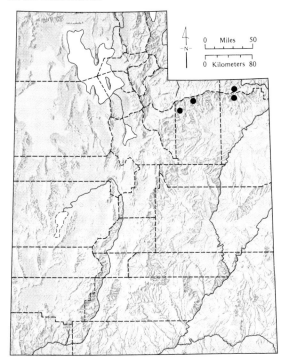

187. *Erigeron goodrichii* Welsh Goodrich fleabane. July-Aug. Native perennial herb; meadows and talus in spruce communities to above timberline, 3030-3400 m.

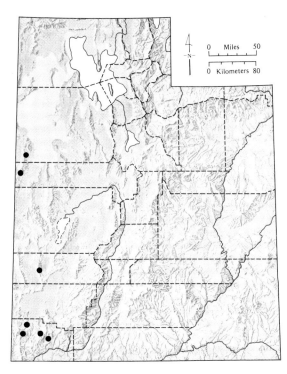

188. *Erigeron jonesii* Cronq. Jones fleabane. June-July. Native perennial herb; sagebrush, mountain brush, pinyon-juniper, ponderosa pine communities, 1510-2730 m.

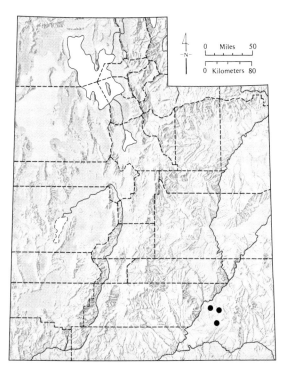

189. *Erigeron kachinensis* Welsh & Moore Kachina fleabane. Apr.-June. Native perennial herb; margins of seeps, hanging gardens, 1630-1730 m.

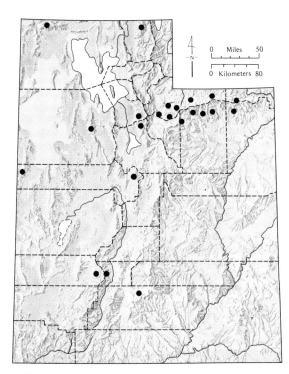

190. *Erigeron leiomerus* Gray Yellow fleabane. July-Aug. Native perennial herb; meadows and talus in lodgepole pine, spruce communities to above timberline, 2540-3620 m.

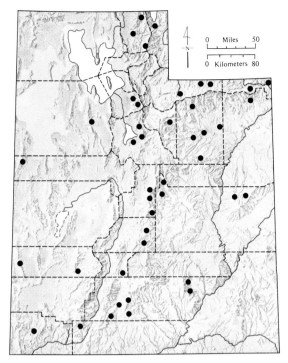

191. *Erigeron lonchophyllus* Hook. Spearleaf fleabane. June-Aug. Native perennial herb; wet meadows, marshes, streamside, near springs, 1300-2880 m.

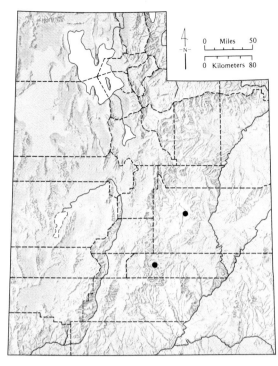

192. *Erigeron maguirei* Cronq. Maguire fleabane. May-June. Native perennial herb; rocky sites in desert shrub communities, 1660-1760 m.

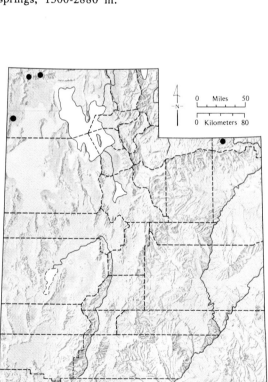

193. *Erigeron nanus* Nutt. Dwarf fleabane. June-July. Native perennial herb; sagebrush-grass communities, rocky ridges, 2120-3030 m.

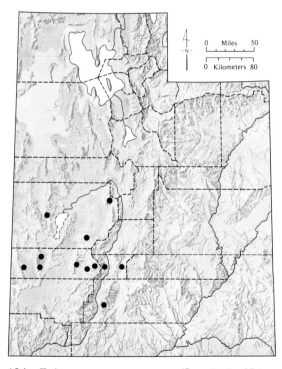

194. *Erigeron nauseosus* (Jones) A. Nels. Marysvale fleabane. June-July. Native perennial herb; rock crevices and talus in pinyon-juniper, mountain brush, fir communities, 1970-2730 m.

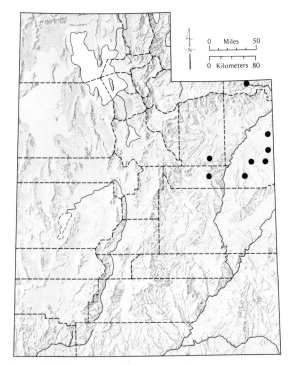

195. *Erigeron nematophyllus* Rydb. Needleleaf fleabane. May-Aug. Native perennial herb; sagebrush, pinyon-juniper communities, 1940-2880 m.

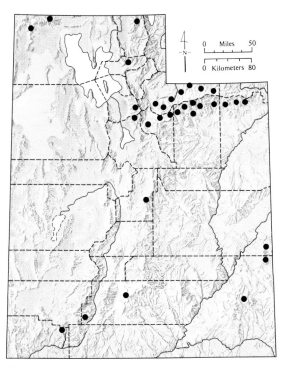

196. *Erigeron peregrinus* (Pursh) Greene Exotic fleabane. July-Sept. Native perennial herb; aspen, spruce-fir, lodgepole pine communities, 2420-3550 m.

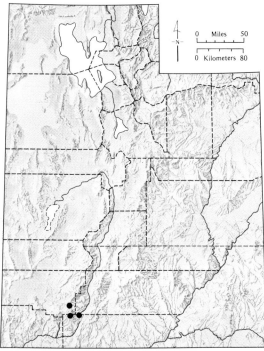

197. *Erigeron proselyticus* Nesom Professor fleabane. June-July. Native perennial herb; rocky sites in bristlecone pine, aspen, spruce-fir communities, 2290-2730 m.

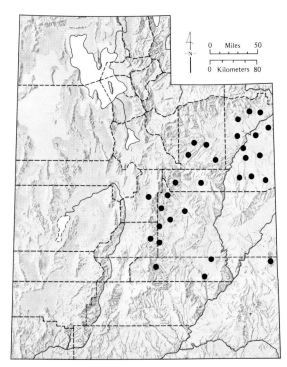

198. *Erigeron pulcherrimus* Heller Basin fleabane. May-June. Native perennial herb; greasewood, shadscale, mat saltbush, pinyon-juniper communities, 1300-1970 m.

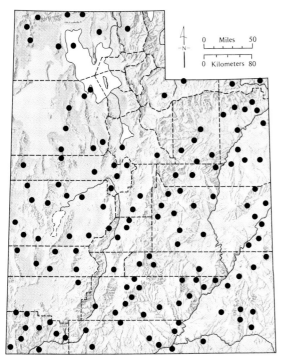

199. *Erigeron pumilus* Nutt. Low fleabane.
May-Aug. Native perennial herb; shadscale, desert
shrub, pinyon-juniper communities, 1060-2490 m.

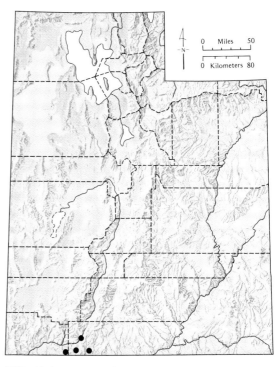

200. *Erigeron religiosus* Cronq. Religious
fleabane. May-June. Native biennial or perennial;
pinyon-juniper, ponderosa pine-oak communities,
1360-2120 m.

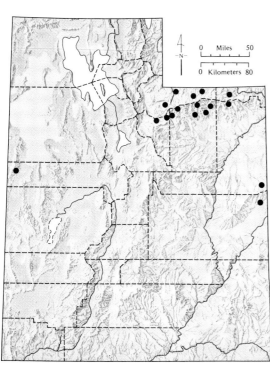

201. *Erigeron simplex* Greene Greene
fleabane. July-Aug. Native perennial herb;
lodgepole pine, spruce-fir communities to above
timberline, 3030-3730 m.

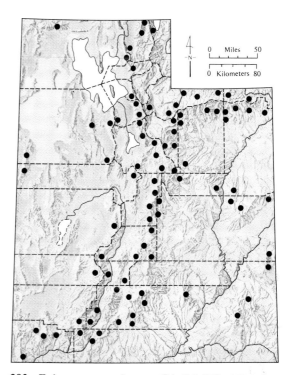

202. *Erigeron speciosus* (Lindl.) DC. Oregon
fleabane. July-Aug. Native perennial herb; shaded
sites in mountain brush, ponderosa pine, lodgepole
pine, aspen, spruce-fir communities, 1970-3340 m.

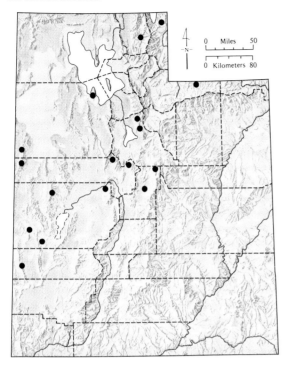

203. *Erigeron tener* Gray Soft fleabane. July-Aug. Native perennial herb; rocky sites in sagebrush, mountain brush, pinyon-juniper, fir communities, 1970-3340 m.

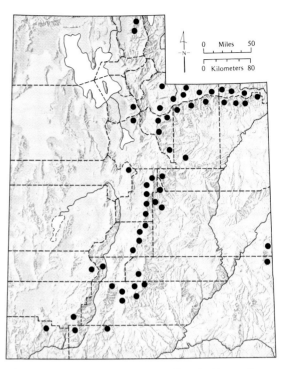

204. *Erigeron ursinus* D. C. Eat. Bear fleabane. July-Aug. Native perennial herb; moist to dry meadows, openings in lodgepole pine, aspen, spruce-fir communities, 2420-3640 m.

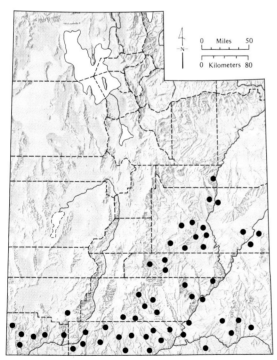

205. *Erigeron utahensis* Gray Utah fleabane. May-June. Native perennial herb; creosote bush, desert shrub, pinyon-juniper communities, 1360-2880 m.

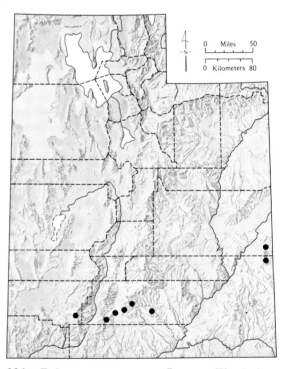

206. *Erigeron vagus* Pays. Wandering fleabane. July-Aug. Native perennial herb; rock crevices and talus in ponderosa, bristlecone pine communities, 2420-3180 m.

10. ASTERACEAE

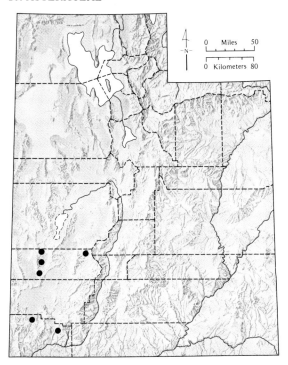

207. *Erigeron wahwahensis* Welsh Wah Wah fleabane. June-Aug. Native perennial herb; sagebrush, mountain brush, pinyon-juniper communities, 1450-2290 m.

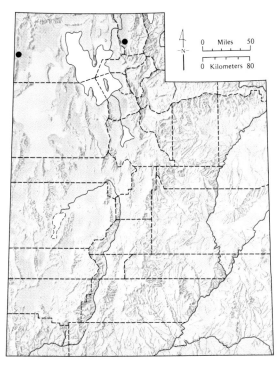

208. *Eriophyllum lanatum* (Pursh) Forbes Woolly eriophyllum. Apr.-June. Native perennial herb; sagebrush, curlleaf mountain mahogany, pinyon-juniper communities, 1630-2300 m.

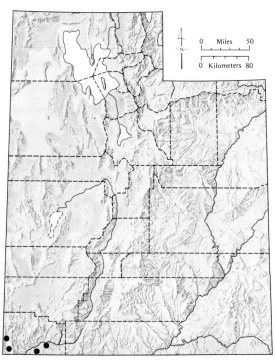

209. *Eriophyllum lanosum* (Gray) Gray Annual eriophyllum. Apr.-July. Native annual; creosote bush communities, 760-910 m.

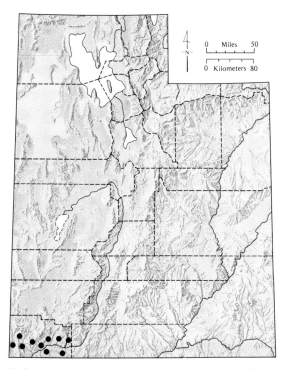

210. *Eriophyllum wallacei* (Gray) Gray Wallace eriophyllum. Feb.-May. Native annual; creosote bush, blackbrush communities, 820-1240 m.

79

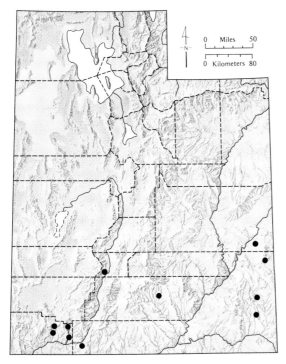

211. *Eupatorium herbaceum* (Gray) Greene Sept.-Oct. Native perennial herb; pinyon-juniper, oak, ponderosa pine communities, 1510-2290 m.

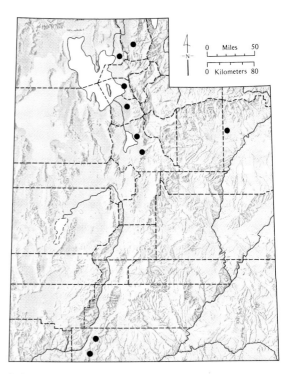

212. *Eupatorium maculatum* L. Spotted Joe-pye weed. July-Oct. Native perennial herb; wet meadows, marshes, streamsides, 1290-1670 m.

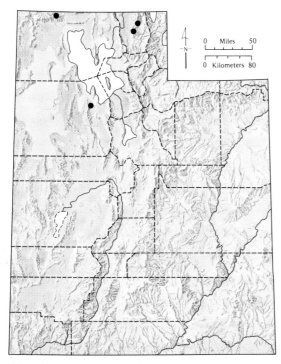

213. *Eupatorium occidentale* Hook. Western Joe-pye weed. July-Sept. Native perennial herb; rock crevices, talus, 1510-2730 m.

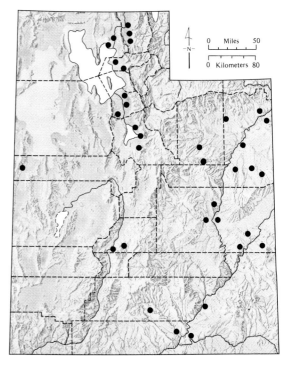

214. *Euthamia occidentalis* Nutt. Western goldenrod. July-Sept. Native perennial herb; wet meadows, marshes, streamside, 1060-1820 m.

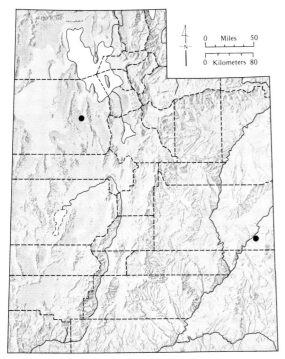

215. *Flaveria campestris* J. R. Johnst. Marshweed. Aug.-Sept. Native annual; near springs, streamsides, 1210-1460 m.

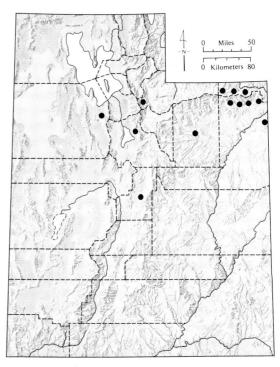

216. *Gaillardia aristata* Pursh Blanketflower. July-Aug. Native perennial herb; pinyon-juniper, ponderosa pine, aspen, spruce-fir communities, 1510-2850 m.

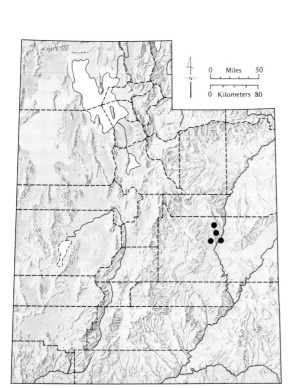

217. *Gaillardia flava* Rydb. Yellow blanketflower. May-July. Native perennial herb; moist meadows, streamside, 1090-1580 m.

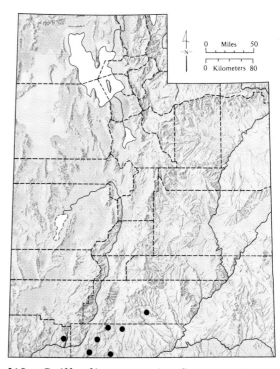

218. *Gaillardia parryi* Greene Parry blanketflower. May-Sept. Native perennial herb; pinyon-juniper, ponderosa pine communities, 1360-1970 m.

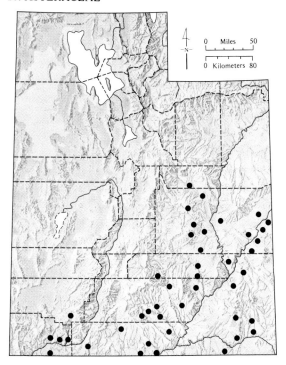

219. *Gaillardia pinnatifida* Torr. Apr.-July. Native perennial herb; shadscale, desert shrub to pinyon-juniper communities, 790-2090 m.

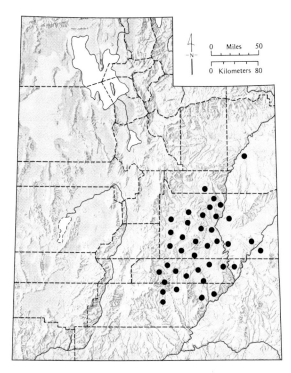

220. *Gaillardia spathulata* Gray Sword blanketflower. May-Aug. Native perennial herb; shadscale, mat saltbush, desert shrub communities, often roadside, 1090-2310 m.

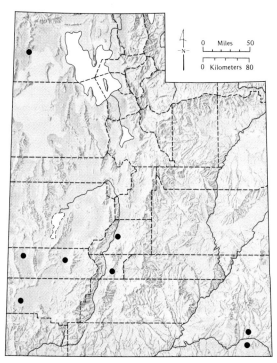

221. *Glyptopleura marginata* D. C. Eat. Border glyptopleura. May-July. Native annual; desert shrub communities, 1150-1520 m.

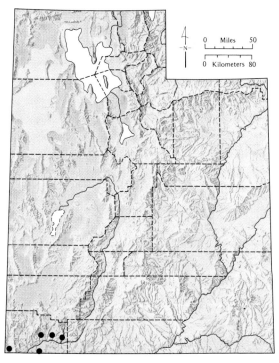

222. *Glyptopleura setulosa* Gray Bristle glyptopleura. Mar.-June. Native annual; creosote bush, Joshua tree communities, 690-910 m.

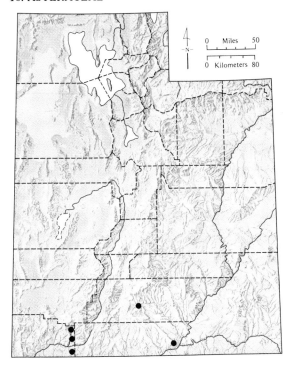

223. *Gnaphalium canescens* DC. Hoary cudweed. June-Sept. Native perennial herb; pinyon-juniper, ponderosa pine communities, 1210-2430 m.

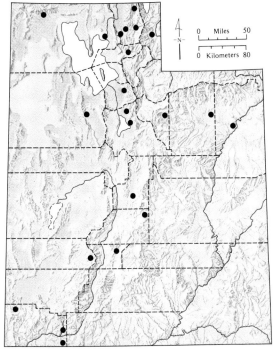

224. *Gnaphalium palustre* Nutt. Lowland cudweed. June-Sept. Native annual; wet to drying mud of lakes and ponds, 1360-2580 m.

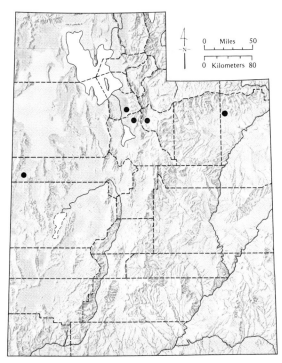

225. *Gnaphalium stramineum* H. B. K. Straw cudweed. June-Aug. Native annual or biennial; disturbed sites along waterways, 1360-2120 m.

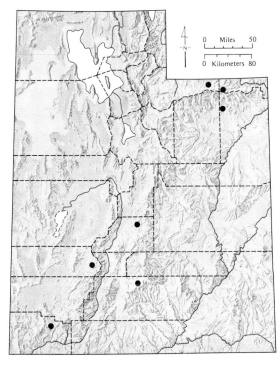

226. *Gnaphalium uliginosum* L. Marsh cudweed. Aug.-Sept. Introduced annual; wet to drying mud of lakes and ponds, 2270-2880 m.

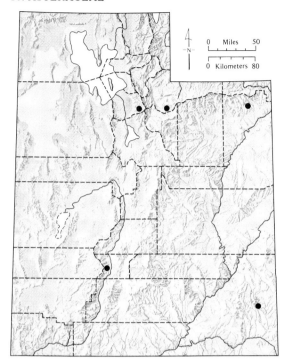

227. *Gnaphalium viscosum* H. B. K. Sticky cudweed. July-Sept. Native annual or biennial; mountain brush, ponderosa pine, aspen-fir communities, 1660-2930 m.

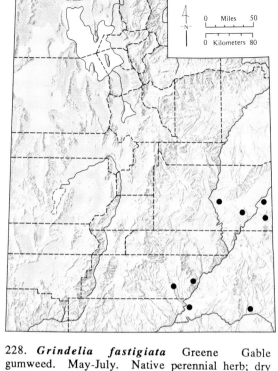

228. *Grindelia fastigiata* Greene Gable gumweed. May-July. Native perennial herb; dry washes in desert shrub communities, 1030-1820 m.

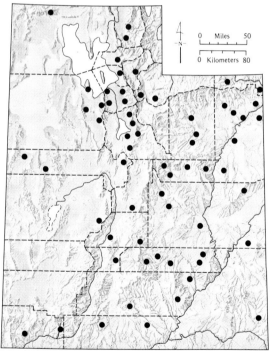

229. *Grindelia squarrosa* (Pursh) Dunal Curlycup gumweed. July-Oct. Native perennial herb; disturbed sites in salt desert shrub, sagebrush, mountain brush communities, 1180-2880 m.

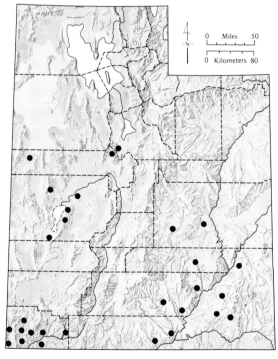

230. *Gutierrezia microcephala* (DC.) Gray Threadleaf snakeweed. July-Oct. Native shrub or subshrub; creosote bush, desert shrub, pinyon-juniper communities, 820-1520 m.

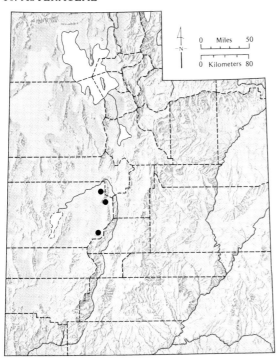

231. *Gutierrezia petradoria* (Welsh & Goodrich) Welsh Golden snakeweed. July-Sept. Native perennial herb; sagebrush, oakbrush, mountain mahogany, white fir communities, 1790-2640 m.

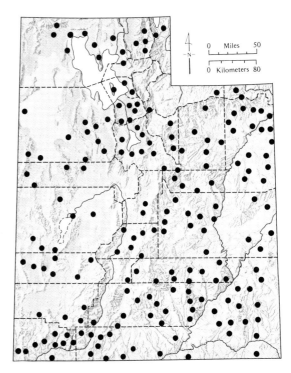

232. *Gutierrezia sarothrae* (Pursh) B. & R. Broom snakeweed. July-Oct. Native shrub or subshrub; creosote bush, sagebrush, rabbitbrush, pinyon-juniper communities, often in the wake of disturbance, 810-2880 m.

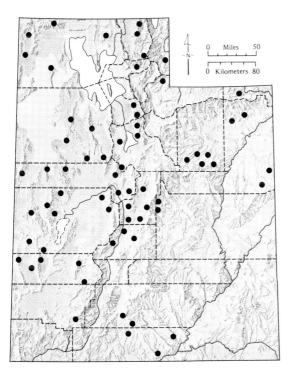

233. *Haplopappus acaulis* (Nutt.) Gray Goldenweed. May-July. Native perennial herb; barren rocky sites in sagebrush, mountain brush to bristlecone pine and spruce-fir communities, 1360-3180 m.

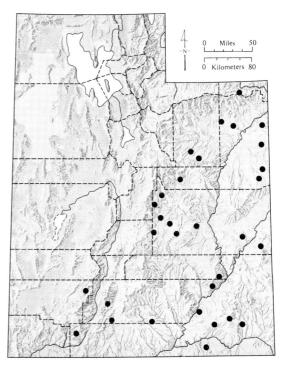

234. *Haplopappus armerioides* (Nutt.) Gray Thrifty goldenweed. May-July. Native perennial herb; barren rocky sites in desert shrub to ponderosa pine communities, 1210-2430 m.

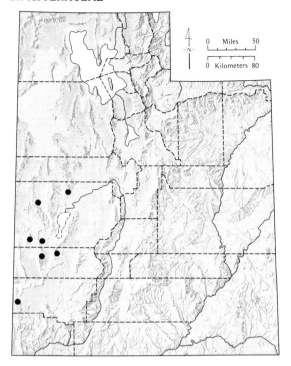

235. *Haplopappus cervinus* Wats. Deer goldenweed. Sept.-Oct. Native shrub; shadscale, sagebrush, pinyon-juniper communities, 1570-2310 m.

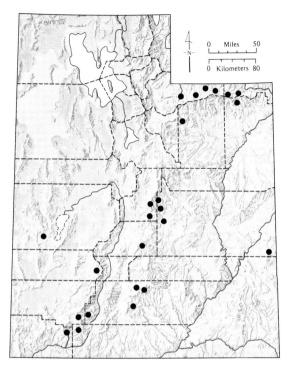

236. *Haplopappus clementis* (Rydb.) Blake Tranquil goldenweed. June-Aug. Native perennial herb; meadows in sagebrush to spruce-fir communities, 1970-3490 m.

237. *Haplopappus crispus* L. C. Anderson Pine Valley goldenweed. Sept.-Oct. Native shrub; aspen, ponderosa pine, fir communities, 1820-2580 m.

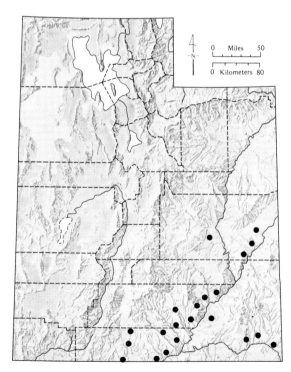

238. *Haplopappus drummondii* (T. & G.) Blake Drummond goldenweed. Aug.-Oct. Native subshrub; moist sites in salt grass meadows, greasewood, tamarix communities, 910-1220 m.

10. ASTERACEAE

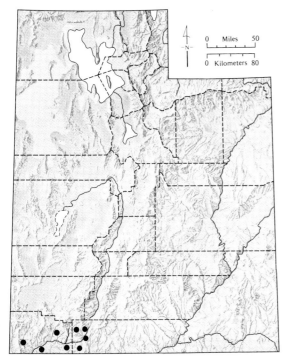

239. *Haplopappus gracilis* (Nutt.) Gray
Slender goldenweed. Apr.-Oct. Native annual;
creosote bush, desert shrub communities, 820-
1700 m.

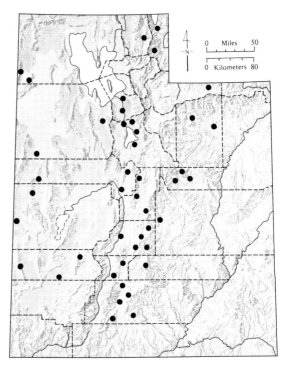

240. *Haplopappus lanceolatus* (Hook.) T.&G.
Lanceleaf goldenweed. Aug.-Oct. Native perennial
herb; wet saline meadows, 1300-2120 m.

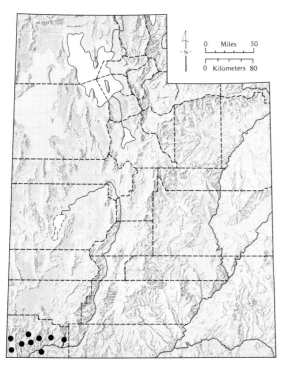

241. *Haplopappus linearifolius* DC.
Threadleaf goldenweed. Apr.-June. Native shrub;
creosote bush, Joshua tree, desert shrub
communities, 690-1370 m.

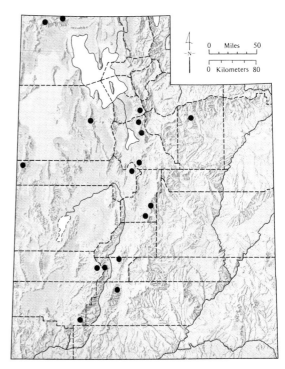

242. *Haplopappus macronema* Gray
Whitestem goldenweed. July-Sept. Native shrub;
aspen, spruce-fir communities to above timberline,
2120-3400 m.

87

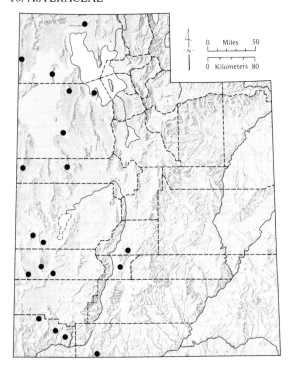

243. *Haplopappus nanus* (Nutt.) D. C. Eat. Dwarf goldenweed. July-Sept. Native shrub; rock crevices in desert shrub to pinyon-juniper communities, 1240-1910 m.

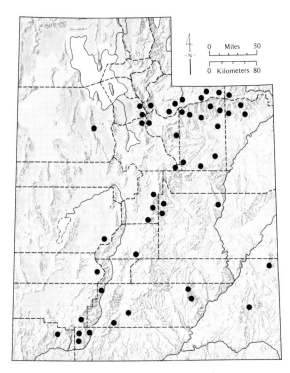

244. *Haplopappus parryi* Gray Parry goldenweed. July-Sept. Native perennial herb; lodgepole pine, aspen, spruce-fir communities to above timberline, 1720-3490 m.

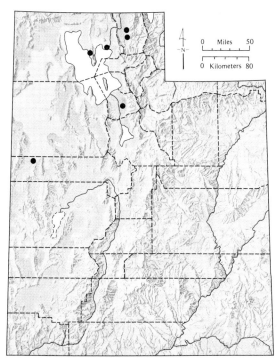

245. *Haplopappus racemosus* (Nutt.) Torr. Cluster goldenweed. July-Aug. Native perennial herb; saline meadows, 1290-1580 m.

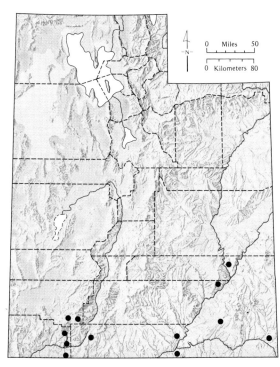

246. *Haplopappus scopulorum* (Jones) Blake Rocky Mountain goldenweed. Aug.-Oct. Native shrub; desert shrub, pinyon-juniper communities, 1360-1600 m.

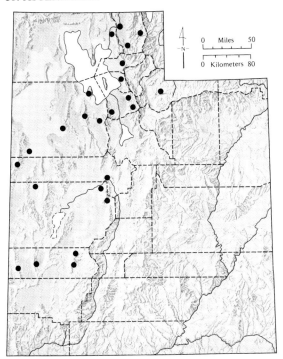

247 *Haplopappus watsonii* Gray Watson goldenweed. July-Sept. Native shrub; rock crevices in desert shrub, pinyon-juniper, mountain brush, ponderosa pine communities, 1330-2640 m.

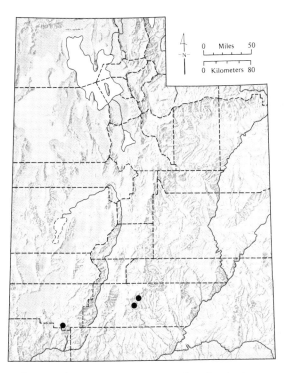

248. *Haplopappus zionis* L. C. Anderson Cedar Breaks goldenweed. July-Sept. Native shrub; ponderosa pine, spruce-fir communities, 2440-3050 m.

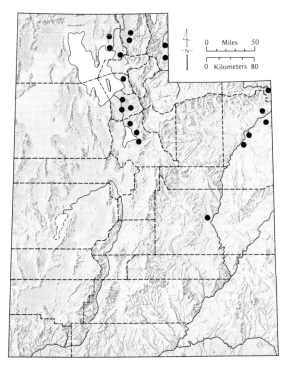

249. *Helenium autumnale* L. Autumn sneezeweed. July-Sept. Native perennial herb; meadows, marshes, streamside, often in disturbed sites, 1270-1820 m.

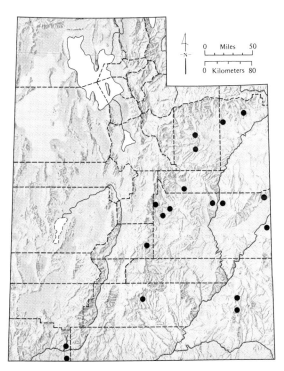

250. *Helianthella microcephala* (Gray) Gray Purpledisk sunflower. June-Sept. Native perennial herb; rocky sites in desert shrub, pinyon-juniper, ponderosa pine, aspen, spruce-fir communities, 1720-2790 m.

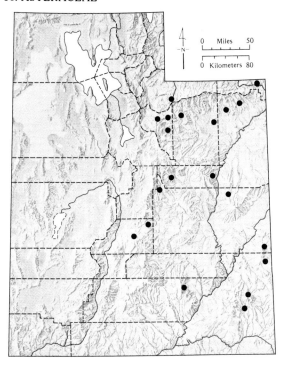

251. *Helianthella quinquenervis* (Hook.)
Gray Fivenerve sunflower. July-Aug. Native
perennial herb; openings in mountain brush, aspen,
spruce-fir communities, 2300-3180 m.

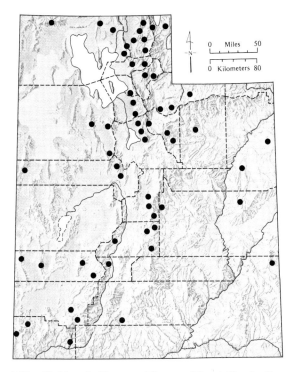

252. *Helianthella uniflora* (Nutt.) T. & G.
Little sunflower. May-Aug. Native perennial herb;
open, rocky sites in sagebrush to aspen, spruce-fir
communities, 1360-3150 m.

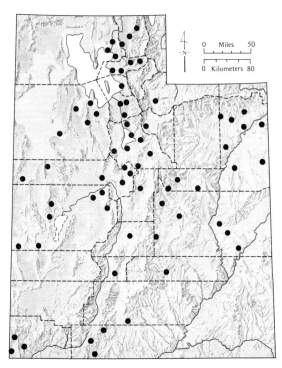

253. *Helianthus annuus* L. Common
sunflower. June-Oct. Native annual; desert shrub to
pinyon-juniper communities, chiefly in disturbed
sites, 1060-2280 m.

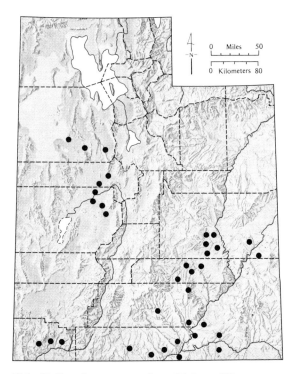

254. *Helianthus anomalus* Blake Western or
sand sunflower. May-Sept. Native annual; desert
shrub to pinyon-juniper communities, commonly in
dunes or other sandy sites, 1060-1940 m.

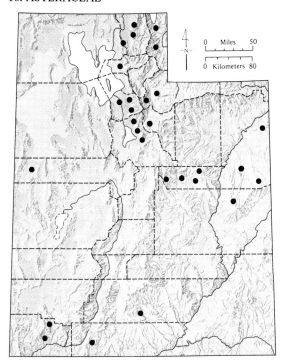

255. *Helianthus nuttallii* T. & G. Nuttall sunflower. July-Sept. Native perennial herb; wet meadows, along waterways, margins of seeps and springs, 1300-2670 m.

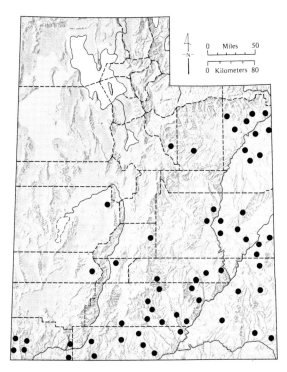

256. *Helianthus petiolaris* Nutt. Prairie sunflower. May-Sept. Native annual; shadscale, desert shrub to pinyon-juniper communities, 970-1670 m.

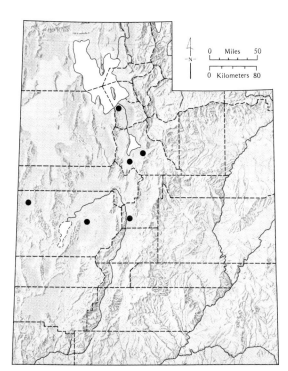

257. *Heliomeris hispida* (Gray) Ckll. Hairy goldeneye. July-Sept. Native annual; saline meadows and marshes, 1180-1400 m.

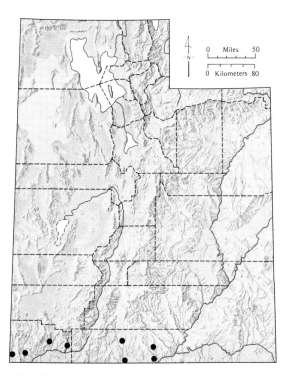

258. *Heliomeris longifolia* (Robins. & Greenm.) Ckll. Longleaf goldeneye. July-Oct. Native annual; shadscale, mat saltbush, desert shrub communities, 1060-1400 m.

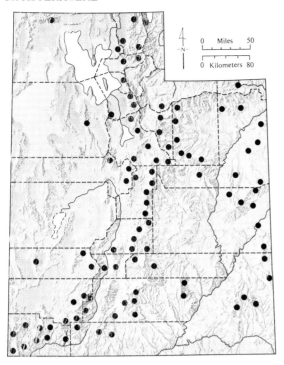

259. *Heliomeris multiflora* Nutt. Showy goldeneye. June-Sept. Native perennial herb; shadscale, desert shrub to aspen, spruce-fir communities, 1360-3090 m.

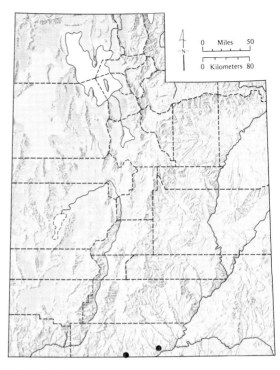

260. *Heliomeris soliceps* (Barneby) Yates Tropic goldeneye. May-Sept. Native annual; mat saltbush communities, 1000-1400 m.

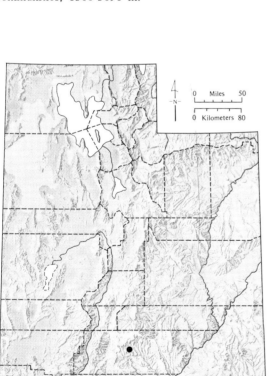

261. *Heterotheca jonesii* (Blake) Welsh & Atwood Jones golden aster. June-Aug. Native perennial herb; rocky sites in pinyon-juniper, ponderosa pine communities, 1420-2880 m.

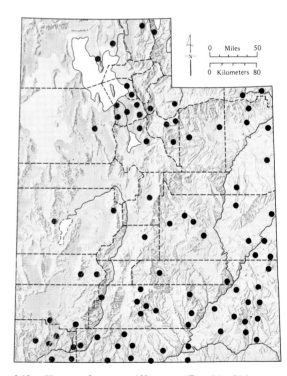

262. *Heterotheca villosa* (Pursh) Shinners Hairy goldenaster. May-Oct. Native perennial herb; creosote bush to aspen, ponderosa pine communities, 970-3090 m.

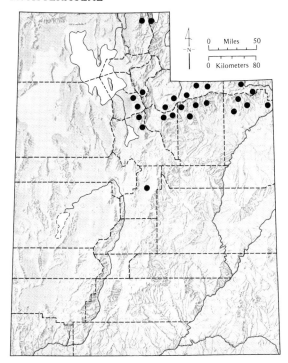

263. *Hieracium albiflorum* Hook. White hawkweed. July-Sept. Native perennial herb; shady sites in aspen, spruce-fir communities, 1880-3400 m.

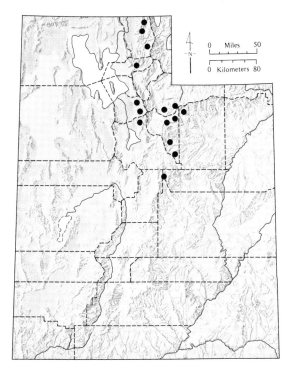

264. *Hieracium cynoglossoides* Arv.-Touv. Houndstongue hawkweed. July-Sept. Native perennial herb; grass-forb to aspen, spruce-fir communities, 2000-2970 m.

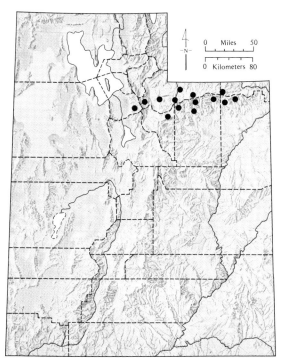

265. *Hieracium gracile* Hook. Slender hawkweed. July-Sept. Native perennial herb; aspen, spruce-fir communities, 2910-3400 m.

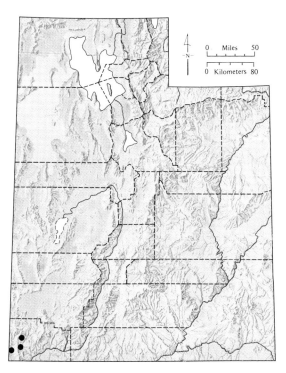

266. *Hulsea heterochroma* Gray May-June. Native perennial herb; pinyon-juniper communities, 1360-1580 m.

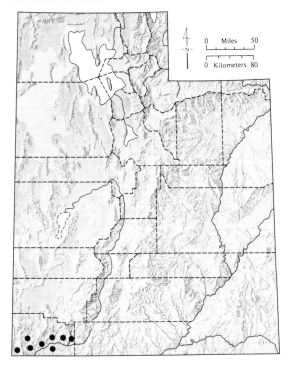

267. *Hymenoclea salsola* T. & G. Burrobrush. Apr.-June. Native perennial herb; creosote bush communities, 665-1090 m.

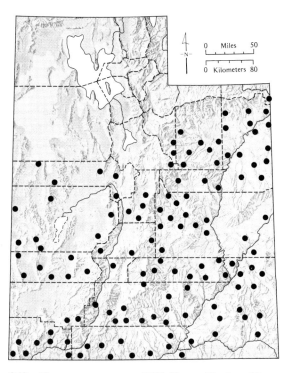

268. *Hymenopappus filifolius* Hook. May-Aug. Native perennial herb; creosote bush, shadscale, desert shrub communities to above timberline, 970-3430 m.

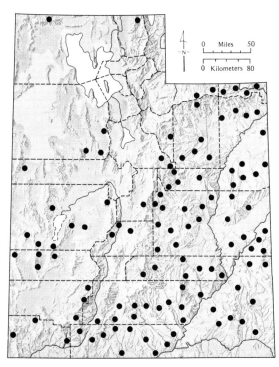

269. *Hymenoxys acaulis* (Pursh) Parker Stemless woollybase. May-July. Native perennial herb; barren rocky sites in shadscale, desert shrub communities to above timberline, 1360-3580 m.

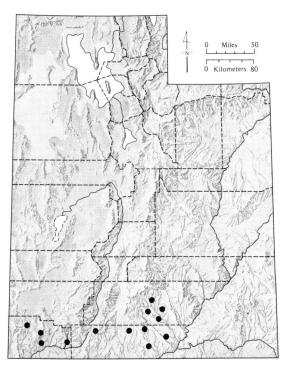

270. *Hymenoxys cooperi* (Gray) Ckll. Ragged rustlers. May-June. Native biennial or perennial herb; sagebrush, pinyon-juniper communities, 940-2370 m.

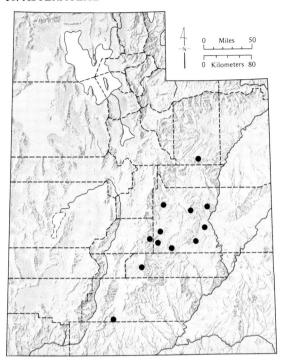

271. *Hymenoxys depressa* (T. & G.) Welsh & Reveal Cushion hymenoxys. May-June. Native perennial herb; sagebrush, pinyon-juniper communities, 2120-2580 m.

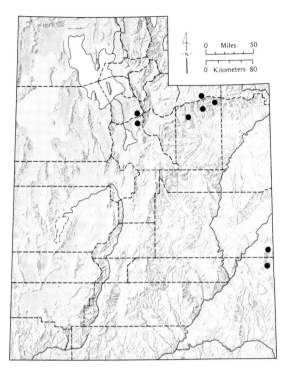

272. *Hymenoxys grandiflora* (T. & G.) Parker Graylocks or alpine hymenoxys. July-Sept. Native perennial herb; krummholz, alpine meadows to rocky sites above timberline, 3030-3820 m.

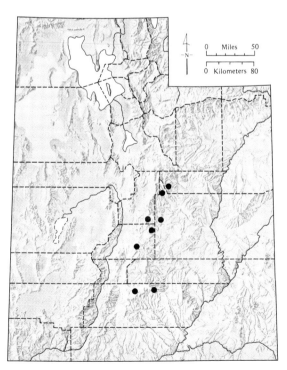

273. *Hymenoxys helenioides* (Rydb.) Ckll. June-Aug. Native perennial herb; meadow, sagebrush to aspen communities, 2720-3030 m.

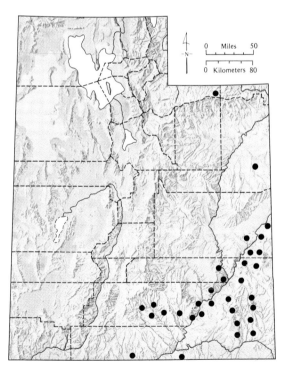

274. *Hymenoxys ivesiana* (Greene) Parker May-June. Native perennial herb; barren rocky sites in desert shrub, pinyon-juniper communities, 1820-2270 m.

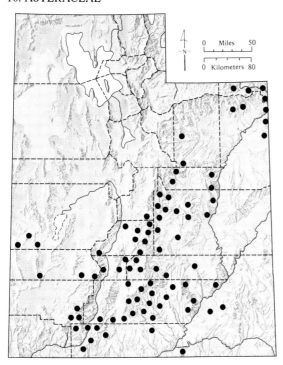

275. *Hymenoxys richardsonii* (Hook.) Ckll.
Pingue; Colorado rubberplant. June-Aug. Native
perennial herb; shadscale, sagebrush to ponderosa
pine, bristlecone pine communities, 1510-3060 m.

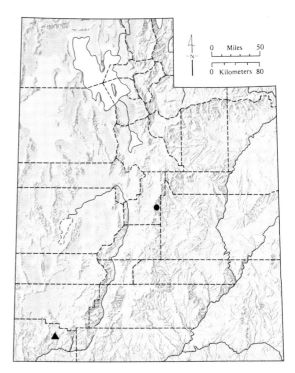

276. *Hymenoxys subintegra* Ckll. June-July.
Native biennial or perennial; ponderosa pine,
aspen, spruce-fir communities, 1970-2270 m.

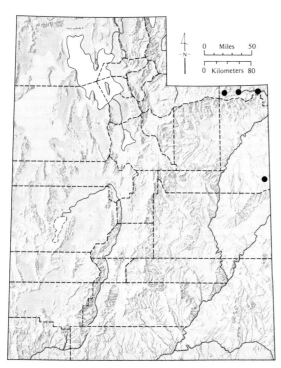

277. *Hymenoxys torreyana* (Nutt.) Parker
June-July. Native perennial herb; sagebrush,
pinyon-juniper, mountain brush communities,
1820-2120 m.

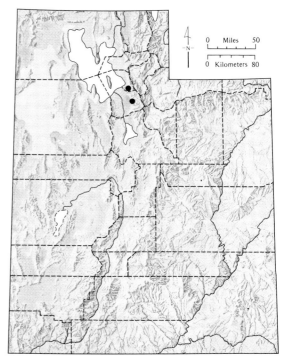

278. *Hypochaeris radicata* L. Cat's ears.
Aug.-Sept. Introduced perennial herb; disturbed
sites, 1420-1490 m.

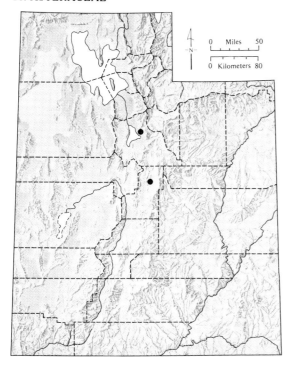

279. *Inula helenium* L. Elecampane. June-July. Introduced perennial herb; wet meadows, along waterways, usually in the wake of disturbance, 1240-1820 m.

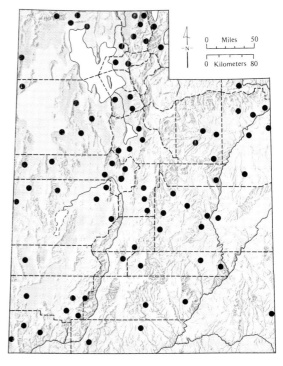

280. *Iva axillaris* Pursh Poverty sumpweed. June-Sept. Native perennial herb; salt desert shrub to aspen communities, 1300-2430 m.

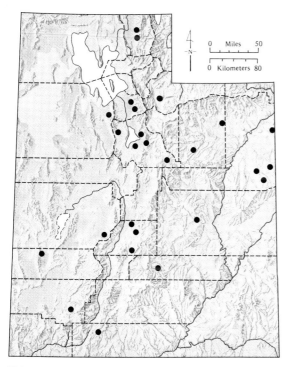

281. *Iva xanthifolia* Nutt. Rag sumpweed; marsh elder. July-Sept. Native perennial herb; disturbed sites in open to wooded areas, 1300-2120 m.

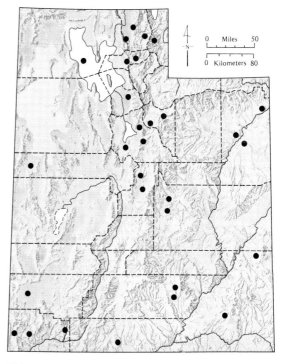

282. *Lactuca serriola* L. Wild or prickly lettuce. July-Sept. Native annual or biennial; dry to moist, disturbed sites, 730-2270 m.

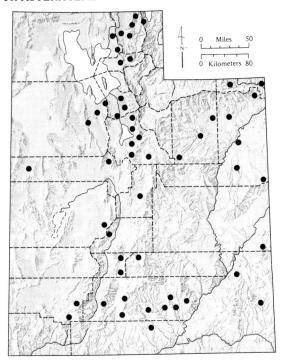

283. *Lactuca tatarica* (L.) C. A. Mey. Blue lettuce. June-Sept. Native perennial herb; moist meadows, along waterways and roadsides, 1270-2730 m.

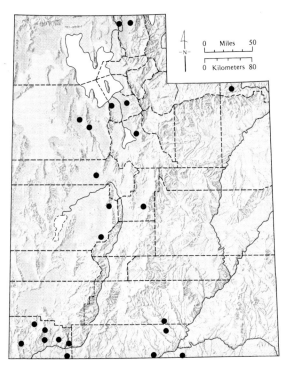

284. *Layia glandulosa* (Hook.) H. & A. Tidytips. Apr.-July. Native annual; desert shrub, sagebrush, pinyon-juniper communities, 1210-1820 m.

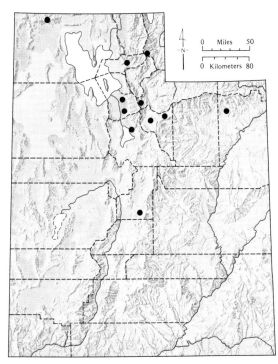

285. *Leucanthemum vulgare* Lam. Ox-eye daisy. June-Sept. Introduced perennial herb; disturbed sites, 1300-3120 m.

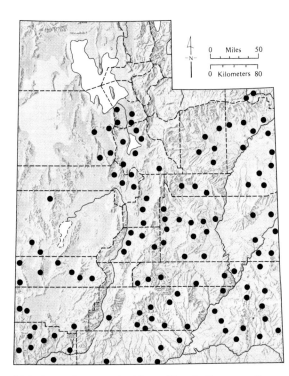

286. *Leucelene ericoides* (Torr.) Greene Rose heath. Apr.-Aug. Native perennial herb; shadscale, desert shrub to pinyon-juniper, ponderosa pine communities, 1000-2520 m.

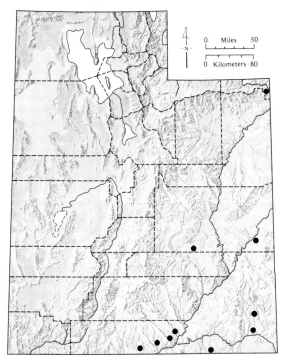

287. *Lygodesmia arizonica* Tomb Arizonica skeletonweed. May-Aug. Native perennial herb; desert shrub communities, 1300-1550 m.

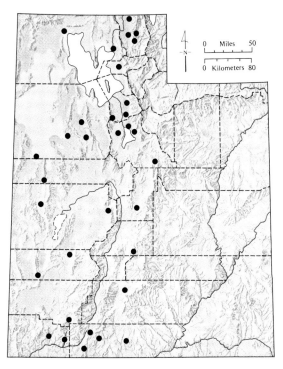

288. *Lygodesmia dianthopsis* (D. C. Eat.) Tomb Smoothseed skeletonweed. May-July. Native perennial herb; salt desert shrub, desert shrub to pinyon-juniper communities, 1330-1760 m.

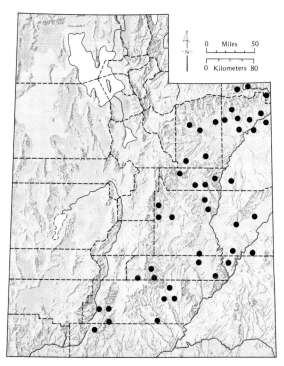

289. *Lygodesmia grandiflora* (Nutt.) T. & G. Largeflower skeletonweed. May-Aug. Native perennial herb; desert shrub to pinyon-juniper communities, 1360-2730 m.

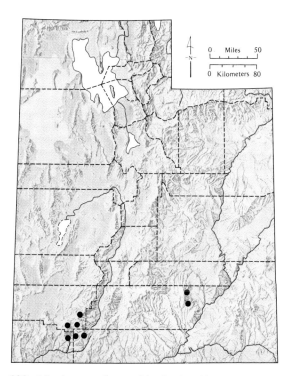

290. *Machaeranthera bigelovii* (Gray) Greene Bigelow tansyaster. July-Aug. Native perennial herb; pinyon-juniper, ponderosa pine, aspen-fir communities, 2120-3030 m.

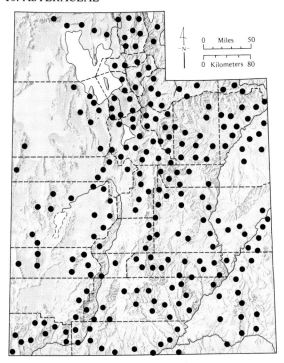

291. *Machaeranthera canescens* (Pursh) Gray
Hoary tansyaster. June-Oct. Native biennial or
perennial; salt desert shrub to lodgepole pine,
spruce-fir communities, 1060-3030 m.

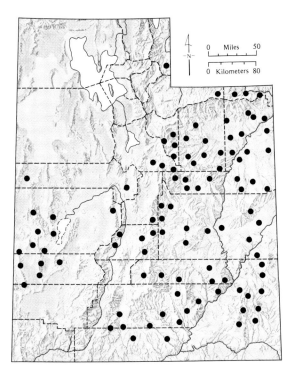

292. *Machaeranthera grindelioides* (Nutt.)
Shinners Gumweed tansyaster. May-July. Native
perennial herb; shadscale, desert shrub, sagebrush,
pinyon-juniper communities, 1360-2400 m.

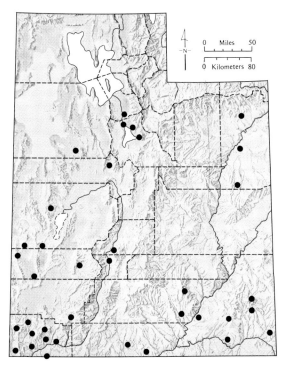

293. *Machaeranthera leucanthemifolia*
(Greene) Greene White tansyaster. June-Oct.
Native biennial or perennial; creosote bush, desert
shrub communities, 850-1670 m.

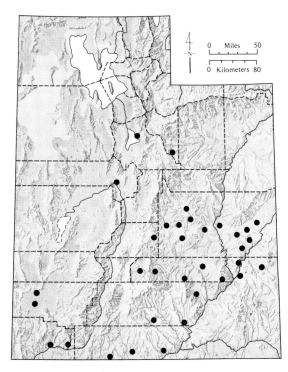

294. *Machaeranthera tanacetifolia* (H. B.
K.) Nees Tansyleaf tansyaster. May-June. Native
annual; desert shrub communities, 1090-1700 m.

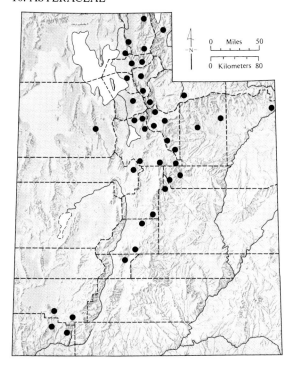

295. *Madia glomerata* Hook. Mountain or
cluster tarweed. July-Sept. Native annual; open
slopes in sagebrush, aspen, spruce-fir communities,
1820-2880 m.

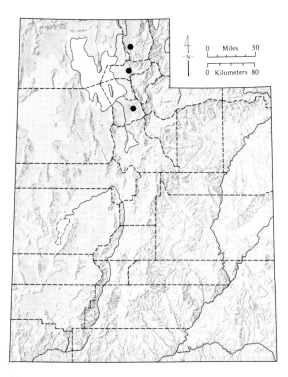

296. *Madia gracilis* (Smith) Keck Slender
tarweed. June-Sept. Native annual; open slopes in
sagebrush, mountain brush communities, 1510-
2120 m.

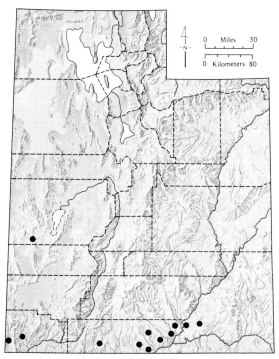

297. *Malacothrix californica* DC. California
desert dandelion. Apr.-Aug. Native annual;
creosote bush, desert shrub communities, 730-
1520 m.

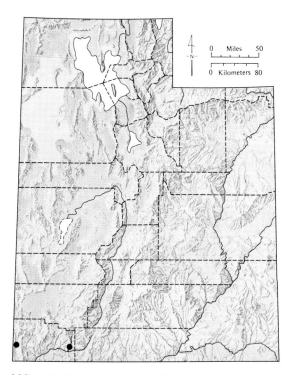

298. *Malacothrix clevelandii* Gray
Cleveland desert dandelion. May-June. Native
annual; pinyon-juniper, turbinella live oak
communities, 1210-1610 m.

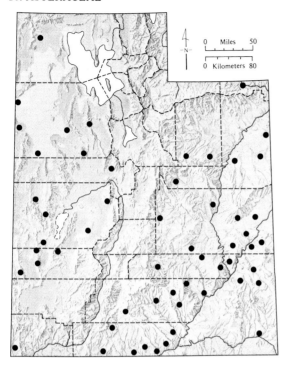

299. *Malacothrix sonchoides* (Nutt.) T.&G. Sowthistle desert dandelion. Apr.-June. Native annual; creosote bush, desert shrub to pinyon-juniper communities, 820-1970 m.

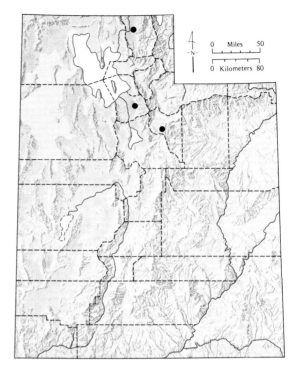

300. *Matricaria chamomilla* L. Chamomile mayweed. June-Oct. Introduced annual; disturbed sites, 1390-2430 m.

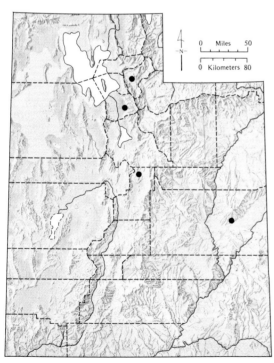

301. *Matricaria maritima* L. Dog chamomile; seashore mayweed. June-Sept. Introduced biennial or perennial; disturbed sites, 1300-2730 m.

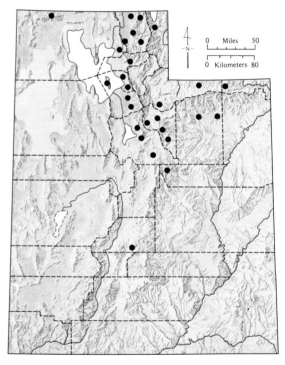

302. *Matricaria matricarioides* (Less.) Porter Pineapple weed. Mar.-Sept. Introduced annual; disturbed sites, 1300-2730 m.

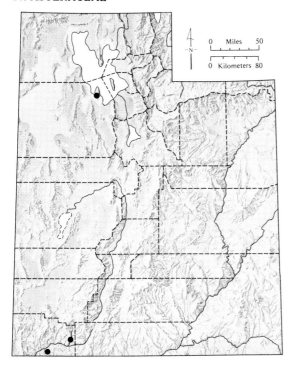

303. *Microseris lindleyi* (DC.) Gray Lindley microseris. Apr.-June. Native annual; creosote bush, desert shrub communities, 820-1370 m.

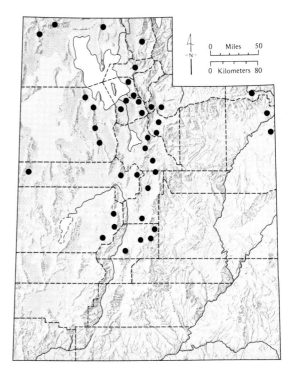

304. *Microseris nutans* (Geyer) Schultz-Bip. Nodding microseris. Apr.-June. Native annual; sagebrush to aspen-fir communities, 1450-2520 m.

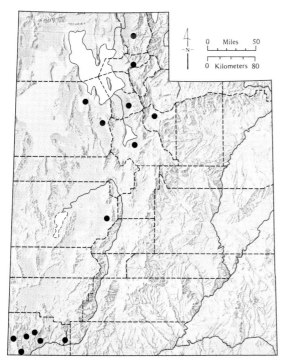

305. *Onopordum acanthium* L. Scotch cotton-thistle. June-July. Introduced biennial; waste places, 1030-2270 m.

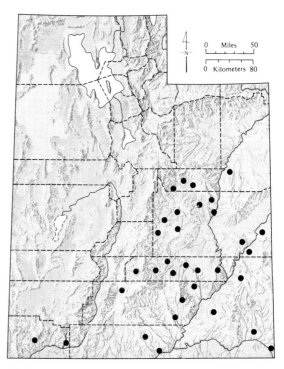

306. *Oxytenia acerosa* Nutt. Copperweed. July-Sept. Native perennial herb; wet, often saline sites, seep and spring margins, along waterways, 1360-2120 m.

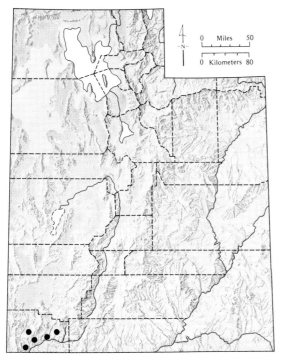

307. *Palafoxia arida* Turner & Morris
Spanish needle. June-Oct. Native annual; creosote
bush communities, 665-970 m.

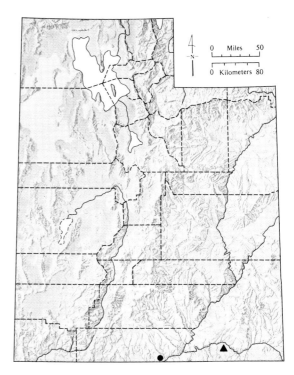

308. *Pectis angustifolia* Torr. July-Sept.
Native annual; desert shrub communities, 1210-
1370 m.

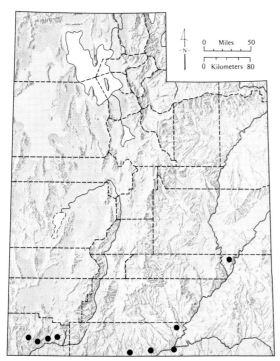

309. *Pectis papposa* H. & G. Chinchweed.
Aug.-Oct. Native annual; creosote bush, desert
shrub communities, 730-1460 m.

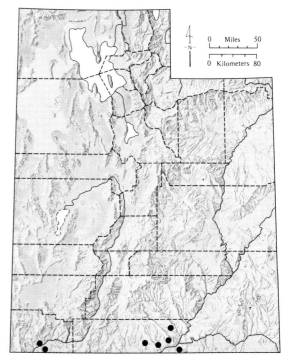

310. *Perezia wrightii* Gray Brownfoot. May-
June. Native perennial herb; creosote bush, desert
shrub, juniper communities, 820-1390 m.

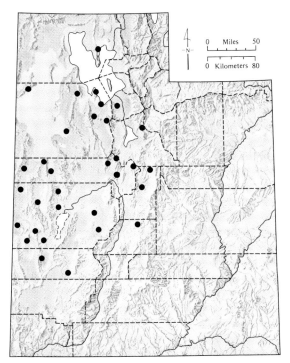

311. *Perityle stansburii* (Gray) J. F. Macbr. Stansbury rockdaisy. May-Sept. Native perennial herb; rock crevices in desert shrub to pinyon-juniper communities, 1210-1820 m.

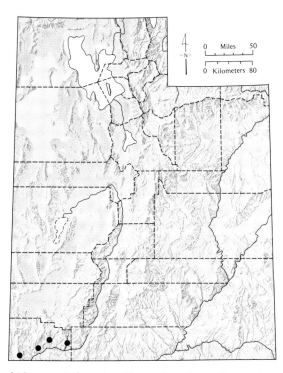

312. *Perityle tenella* (Jones) J. F. Macbr. Jones rockdaisy. May-June. Native perennial herb; rock crevices in desert shrub to pinyon-juniper communities, 820-1970 m.

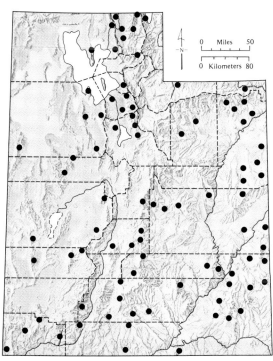

313. *Petradoria pumila* (Nutt.) Greene Rock goldenrod. June-Aug. Native perennial herb; desert shrub to ponderosa pine communities, 1270-2880 m.

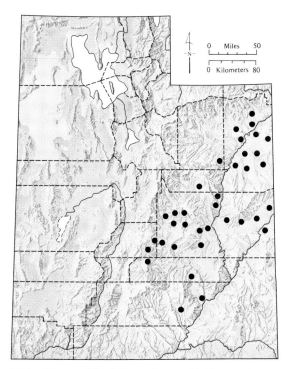

314. *Platyschkuhria integrifolia* (Gray) Rydb. May-July. Native perennial herb; shadscale, mat saltbush, desert shrub, pinyon-juniper communities, 1090-2360 m.

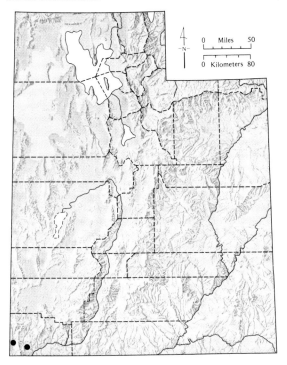

315. *Pluchea camphorata* (L.) DC. May-June.
Native perennial herb; along waterways in creosote
communities, 970-1090 m.

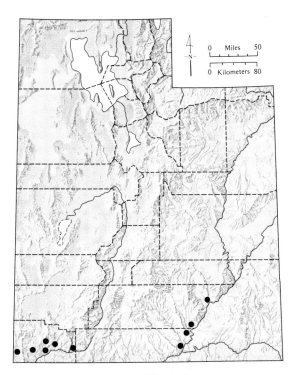

316. *Pluchea sericea* (Nutt.) Cov. Arrowweed.
May-July. Native shrub; along waterways in
creosote bush communities, 665-1090 m.

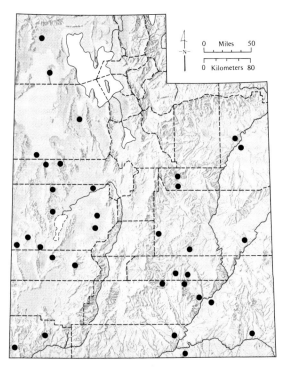

317. *Prenanthella exigua* (Gray) Rydb. May-
July. Native annual; creosote bush, shadscale,
desert shrub, pinyon-juniper communities, 760-
1820 m.

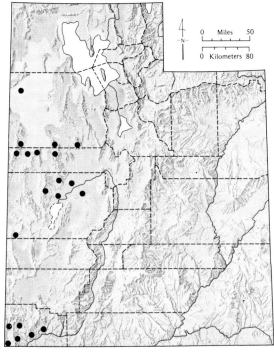

318. *Psathyrotes annua* (Nutt.) Gray May-
Sept. Native annual; creosote bush, salt desert
shrub, pinyon-juniper communities, 760-1430 m.

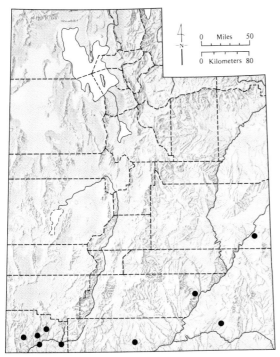

319. ***Psathyrotes pilifera*** Gray Aug.-Sept. Native annual; creosote bush, desert shrub communities, 850-2060 m.

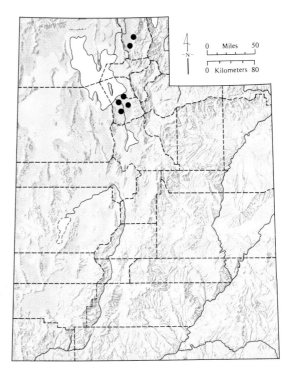

320. ***Psilocarphus brevissimus*** Nutt. June-Sept. Native annual; drying mud, usually of saline sites, 1300-1700 m.

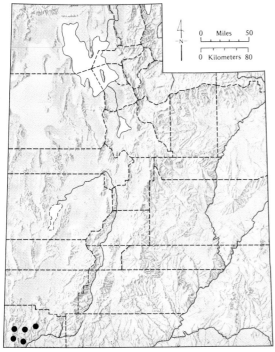

321. ***Psilostrophe cooperi*** (Gray) Greene Whitestem paperflower. Apr.-Sept. Native shrub; creosote bush communities, 820-970 m.

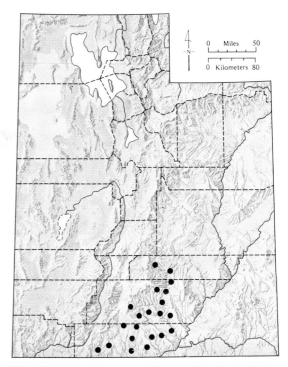

322. ***Psilostrophe sparsiflora*** (Gray) A. Nels. Greenstem paperflower. Apr.-Sept. Native perennial herb; shadscale, desert shrub, pinyon-juniper communities, 1390-2000 m.

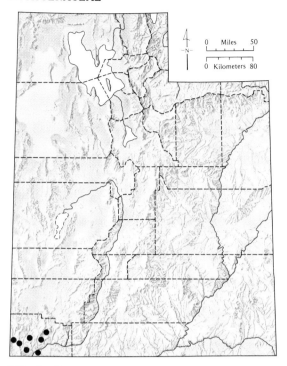

323. *Rafinesquia neomexicana* Gray Desert chicory. Mar.-June. Native annual; creosote bush communities, 790-970 m.

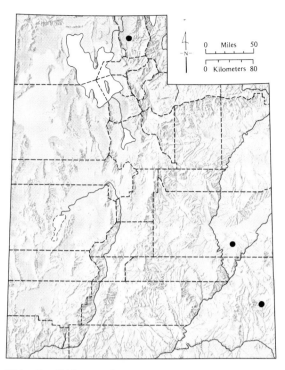

324. *Ratibida columnifera* (Nutt.) Woot. & Standl. Prairie coneflower. June-Aug. Native perennial herb; sagebrush communities, often in disturbed sites, 1360-2300 m.

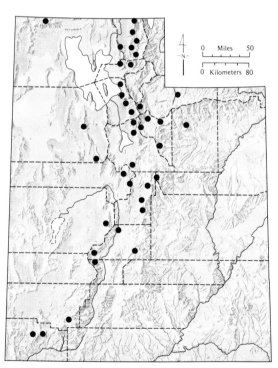

325. *Rudbeckia occidentalis* Nutt. Western coneflower. June-Aug. Native perennial herb; mountain brush to aspen, spruce-fir communities, 1880-3030 m.

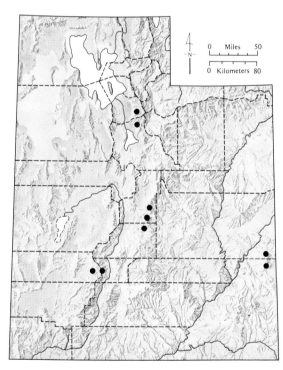

326. *Senecio amplectens* Gray Alpine groundsel. July-Sept. Native perennial herb; spruce-fir communities to above timberline, 2730-3940 m.

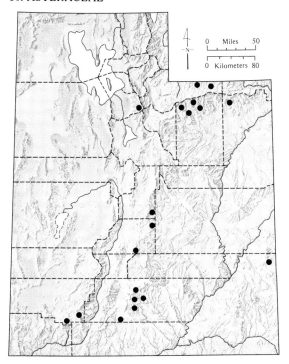

327. *Senecio atratus* Greene   Black groundsel.
July-Sept. Native perennial herb; aspen, spruce-fir
communities, often on rocky sites, 2770-3240 m.

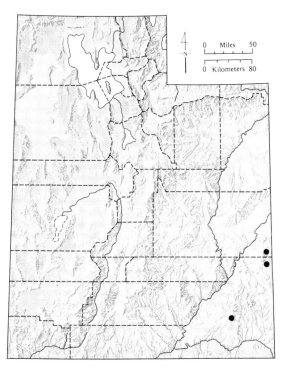

328. *Senecio bigelovii* Gray   Bigelow
groundsel. July-Aug. Native perennial herb;
ponderosa pine, aspen, spruce-fir communities,
2510-3640 m.

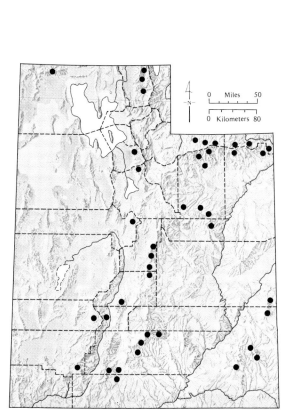

329. *Senecio canus* Hook. Woolly groundsel.
July-Aug. Native perennial herb; rocky sites in
pinyon-juniper communities to above timberline,
2120-3640 m.

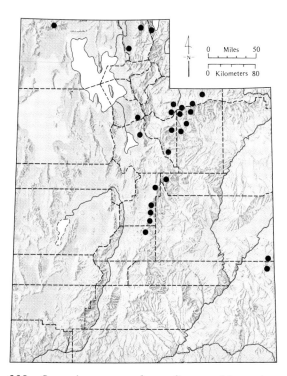

330. *Senecio crassulus* Gray   Mountain
meadow or thickleaf groundsel. July-Aug. Native
perennial herb; rocky sites in aspen, spruce-fir
communities, 1820-3400 m.

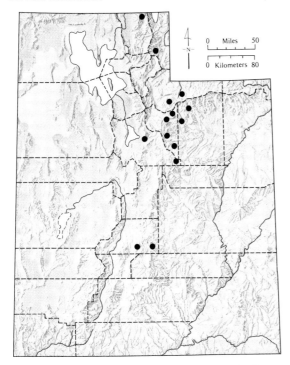

331. *Senecio crocatus* Rydb. Saffron groundsel. July-Aug. Native perennial herb; streamside and other moist sites in mountain brush to aspen, spruce-fir communities, 1820-2880 m.

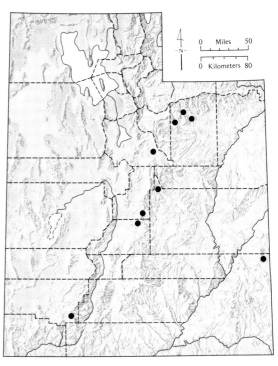

332. *Senecio dimorphophyllus* Greene Splitleaf groundsel. July-Aug. Native perennial herb; wet meadows, mountain brush, aspen, spruce-fir communities, 1820-3140 m.

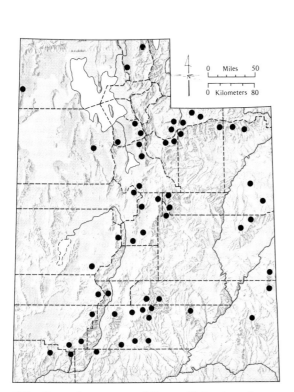

333. *Senecio eremophilus* Richards. June-Sept. Native perennial herb; mountain brush to lodgepole pine, spruce-fir communities, 1600-3430 m.

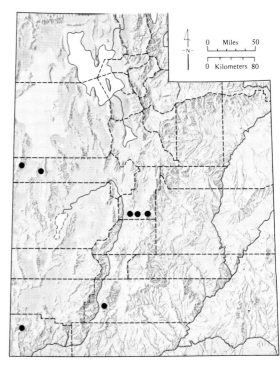

334. *Senecio fendleri* Gray Fendler groundsel. July-Aug. Native perennial herb; rocky sites, 1600-3000 m.

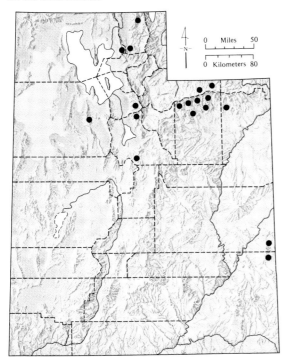

335. *Senecio fremontii* T. & G. Fremont groundsel. July-Aug. Native perennial herb; rocky sites in aspen, spruce-fir communities to above timberline, 2570-3640 m.

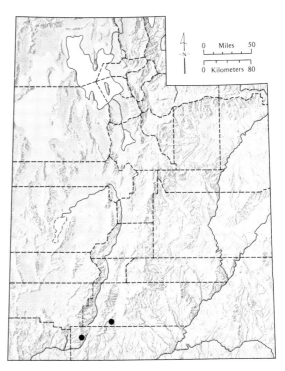

336. *Senecio hartianus* Heller June-Aug. Native perennial herb; pinyon-juniper, ponderosa pine communities, 1880-2240 m.

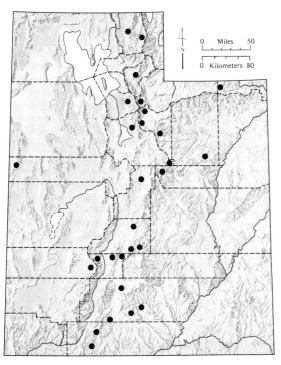

337. *Senecio hydrophilus* Nutt. Water groundsel. July-Sept. Native perennial herb; wet, sometimes saline meadows, along waterways, pond margins, 1300-2730 m.

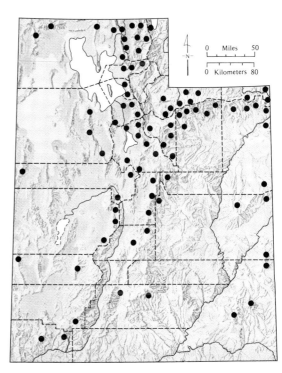

338. *Senecio integerrimus* Nutt. Lambstongue or Columbia groundsel. Apr.-Aug. Native perennial herb; open slopes in sagebrush to aspen, spruce-fir communities, 1360-3340 m.

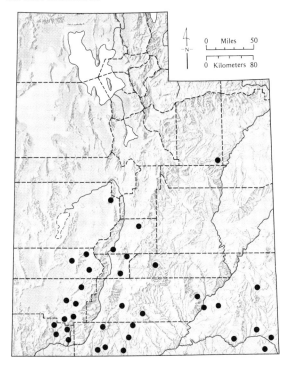

339. *Senecio longilobus* Benth. May-Sept. Native perennial herb; creosote bush, desert shrub to pinyon-juniper communities, 910-2180 m.

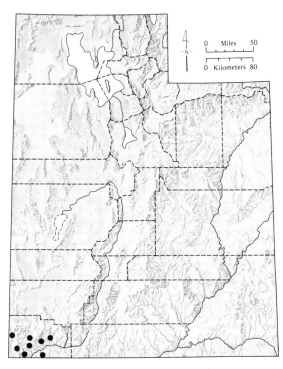

340. *Senecio monoensis* Greene May-Oct. Native subshrub; creosote bush, desert shrub communities, 670-1370 m.

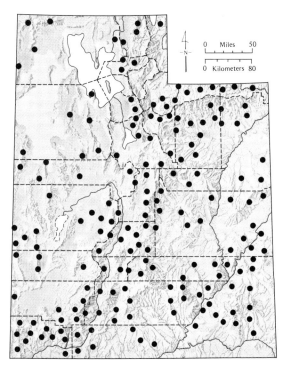

341. *Senecio multilobatus* T. & G. Lobeleaf groundsel. Apr.-Aug. Native perennial herb; creosote bush to aspen, spruce-fir communities, 820-3180 m.

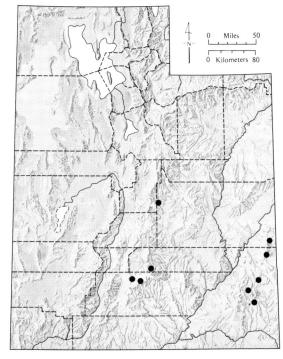

342. *Senecio neomexicanus* Gray New Mexico groundsel. May-July. Native perennial herb; mountain brush to ponderosa pine, aspen communities, 2180-3250 m.

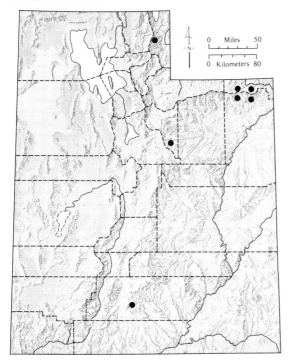

343. *Senecio pauperculus* Michx. Balsam groundsel. July-Aug. Native perennial herb; moist sites in lodgepole, aspen, spruce-fir communities, 2270-2730 m.

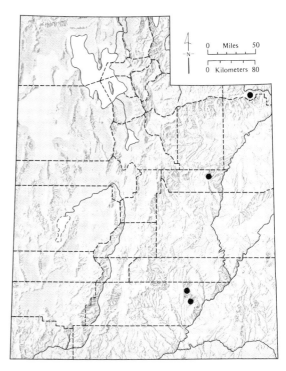

344. *Senecio pudicus* Greene Shy groundsel. June-Aug. Native perennial herb; open meadows and rocky ridges in aspen, spruce-fir communities, 2120-3180 m.

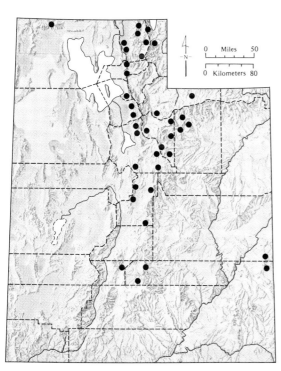

345. *Senecio serra* Hook. Butterweed. July-Aug. Native perennial herb; mountain brush, aspen, spruce-fir communities, 1820-3360 m.

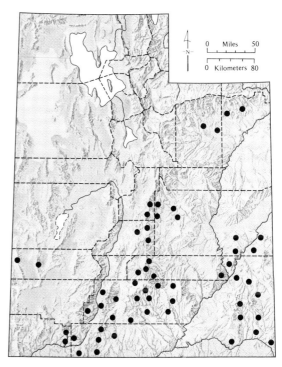

346. *Senecio spartioides* T. & G. Broom groundsel. July-Oct. Native perennial herb; open slopes in oak, pinyon-juniper, mountain brush, aspen communities, 1060-2730 m.

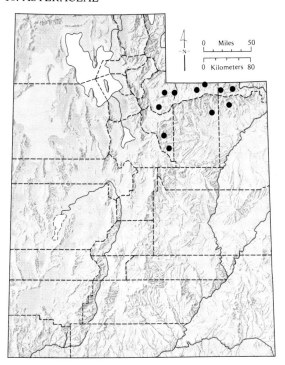

347. *Senecio sphaerocephalus* Greene Ballhead groundsel. July-Aug. Native perennial herb; lodgepole pine, spruce-fir communities, 2270-3030 m.

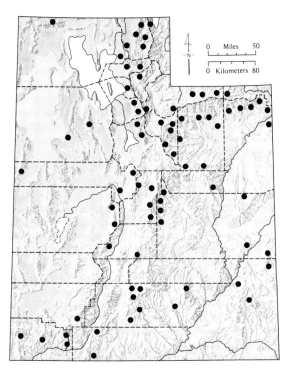

348. *Senecio streptanthifolius* Greene May-Aug. Native perennial herb; sagebrush, mountain brush communities to above timberline, 1360-3520 m.

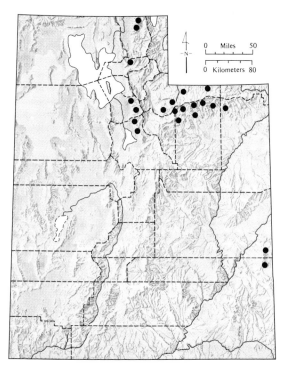

349. *Senecio triangularis* Hook. Arrowleaf groundsel. July-Aug. Native perennial herb; mountain brush to lodgepole pine, spruce-fir communities, 1820-3430 m.

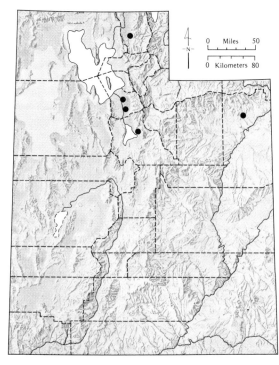

350. *Senecio vulgaris* L. Common groundsel. Apr.-Oct. Introduced annual; disturbed sites, 1300-1520 m.

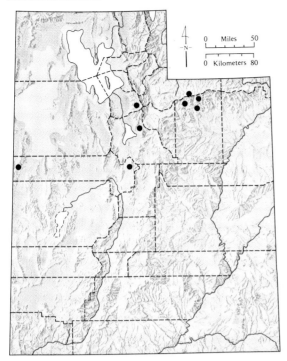

351. *Senecio werneriaefolius* (Gray) Gray
Hoary groundsel. July-Aug. Native perennial herb;
spruce-fir communities to above timberline, 3030-
3640 m.

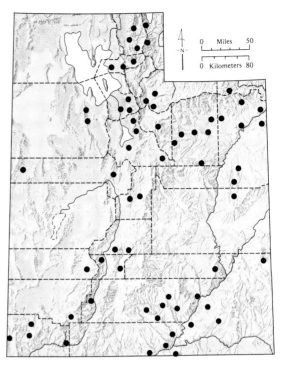

352. *Solidago canadensis* L. Goldenrod.
Aug.-Oct. Native perennial herb; along waterways
and in other mesic sites in creosote bush to
mountain brush communities, 910-2120 m.

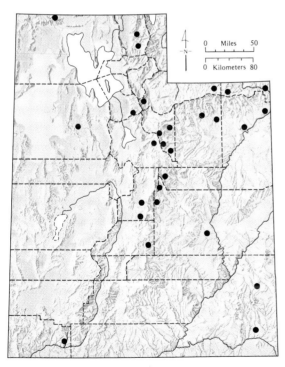

353. *Solidago missouriensis* Nutt. Missouri
goldenrod. July-Sept. Native perennial herb;
streamside, other moist sites in sagebrush to fir
communities, 1510-2880 m.

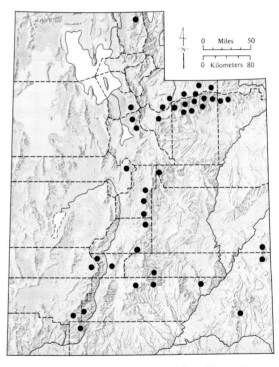

354. *Solidago multiradiata* Ait. Mountain or
low goldenrod. June-Sept. Native perennial herb;
lodgepole, aspen, spruce-fir communities, 2270-
3640 m.

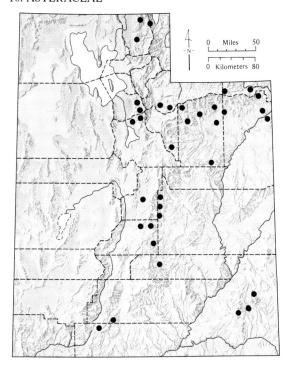

355. *Solidago nana* Nutt. Dwarf goldenrod. July-Sept. Native perennial herb; wet meadows, along waterways, or other moist sites in mountain brush, ponderosa pine, aspen, spruce-fir communities, 1970-3090 m.

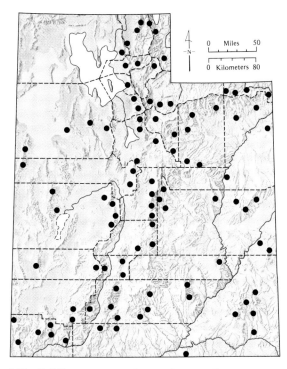

356. *Solidago sparsiflora* Gray Fewflowered goldenrod. July-Sept. Native perennial herb; pinyon-juniper, mountain brush, ponderosa pine, aspen, spruce-fir communities, 1780-3030 m.

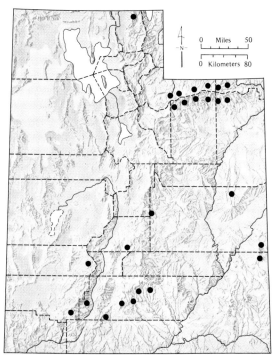

357. *Solidago spathulata* DC. Coast goldenrod. July-Oct. Native perennial herb; aspen, spruce-fir communities to above timberline, 2570-3490 m.

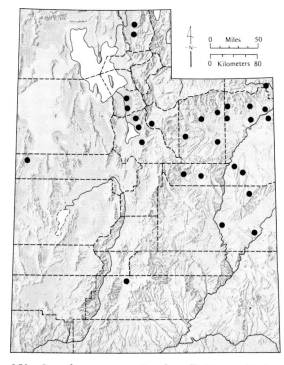

358. *Sonchus arvensis* L. Field sowthistle. July-Sept. Introduced perennial herb; disturbed sites, 1360-1970 m.

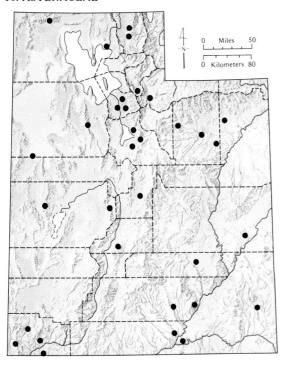

359. *Sonchus asper* (L.) Hill Spiny sowthistle. June-Sept. Introduced annual; disturbed sites, 760-2430 m.

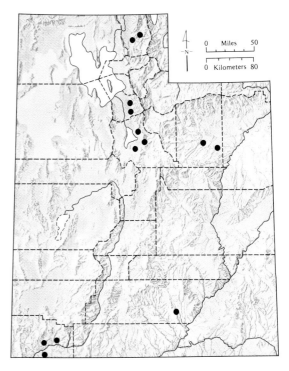

360. *Sonchus oleraceus* L. Common sowthistle. Apr.-Aug. Introduced annual; disturbed sites, 760-1880 m.

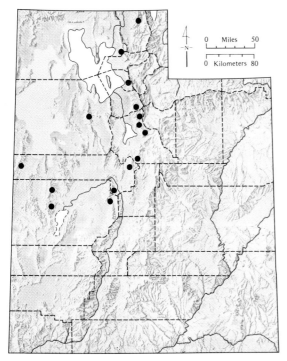

361. *Sphaeromeria diversifolia* (D. C. Eat.) Rydb. July-Sept. Native subshrub; mountain brush to aspen, spruce-fir communities, 1510-3180 m.

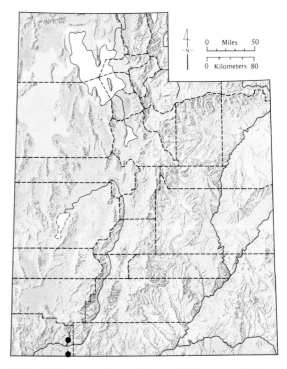

362. *Sphaeromeria ruthiae* Holmgren, Shultz, & Lowrey Aug.-Oct. Native perennial herb; rock crevices in cliffs, sandy sites in ponderosa pine communities, 1450-1970 m.

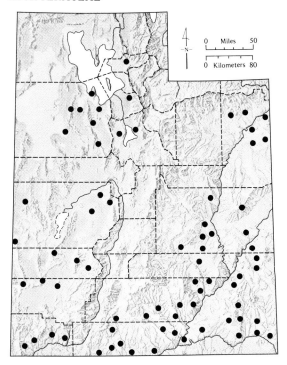

363. *Stephanomeria exigua* Nutt. Small wirelettuce. June-Sept. Native annual or biennial; creosote bush, desert shrub to pinyon-juniper communities, 730-1970 m.

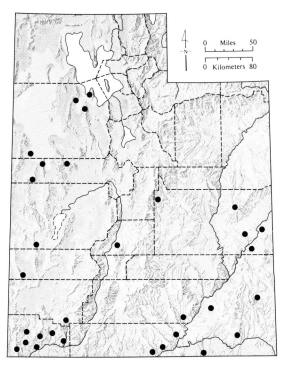

364. *Stephanomeria pauciflora* (Torr.) A. Nels. Slimflower wirelettuce. July-Sept. Native perennial herb; creosote bush, desert shrub, ponderosa pine communities, 665-2430 m.

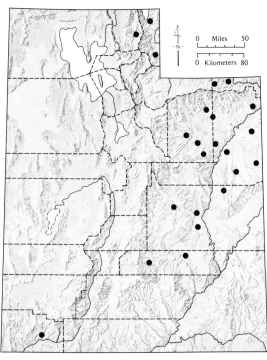

365. *Stephanomeria runcinata* Nutt. Desert wirelettuce. June-Sept. Native perennial herb; salt desert shrub to pinyon-juniper communities, 1150-2270 m.

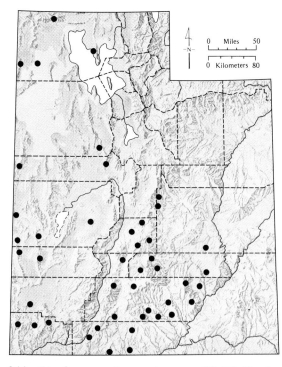

366. *Stephanomeria spinosa* (Nutt.) Tomb Thorn wirelettuce. July-Sept. Native perennial herb; desert shrub, pinyon-juniper to ponderosa pine, aspen-fir communities, 1510-2730 m.

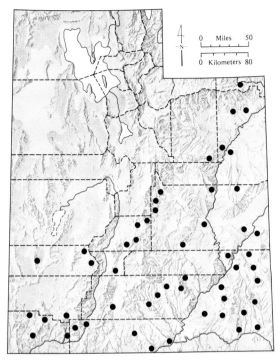

367. *Stephanomeria tenuifolia* (Torr.) Hall Slender wirelettuce. May-Oct. Native perennial herb; desert shrub, sagebrush, pinyon-juniper, ponderosa pine, Douglas fir communities, 1060-2730 m.

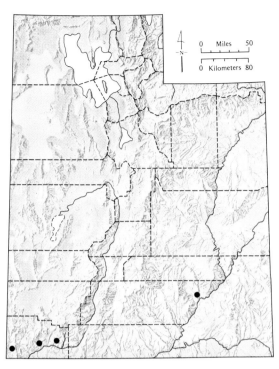

368. *Stylocline micropoides* Gray Desert neststraw. Mar.-May. Native annual; creosote bush, desert shrub communities, 820-1060 m.

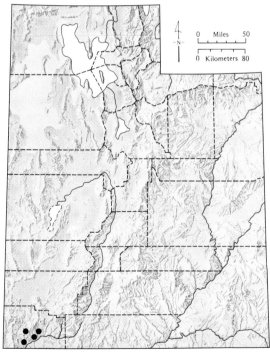

369. *Syntrichopappus fremontii* Gray Apr.-May. Native annual; creosote bush, desert shrub, juniper communities, 665-1370 m.

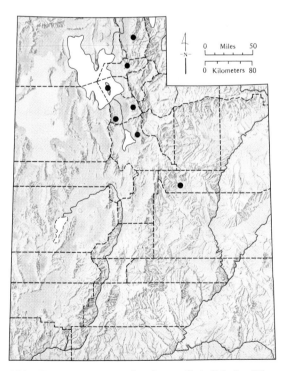

370. *Tanacetum parthenium* (L.) Schultz-Bip. Feverfew. June-Sept. Introduced perennial herb; cultivated, occasionally escaping and persisting, 1360-1520 m.

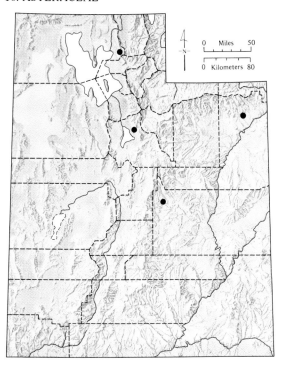

371. **Tanacetum vulgare** L. Common tansy.
Aug.-Sept. Introduced perennial herb; disturbed
sites, 1360-1820 m.

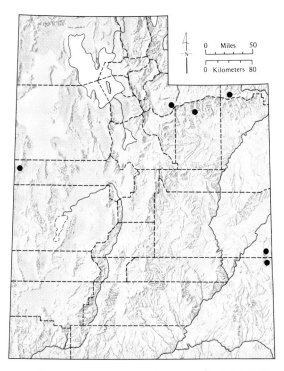

372. **Taraxacum ceratophorum** (Ledeb.) DC.
Rough dandelion. July-Sept. Circumboreal
perennial herb; meadows in spruce-fir, krummholz
communities, 2870-3640 m.

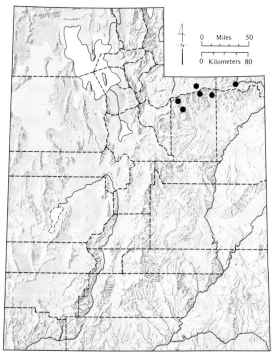

373. **Taraxacum lyratum** (Ledeb.) DC. Alpine
dandelion. July-Sept. Native perennial herb;
meadows in spruce-fir communities to above
timberline, 2970-3640 m.

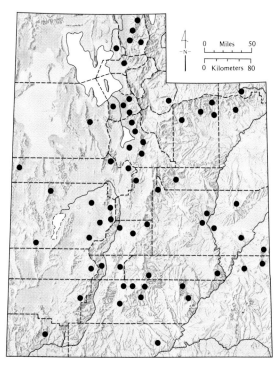

374. **Taraxacum officinale** Weber Common
dandelion. Mar.-Sept. Introduced perennial herb;
disturbed sites in creosote bush to aspen, spruce-fir
communities, 760-3640 m.

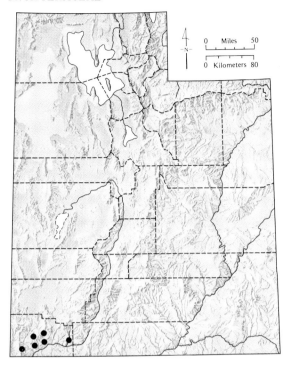

375. *Tetradymia axillaris* A. Nels. Longspine horsebrush. Apr.-June. Native shrub; creosote bush, desert shrub communities, 760-1520 m.

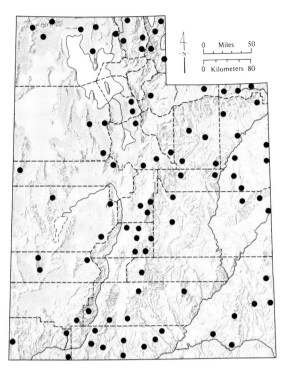

376. *Tetradymia canescens* DC. Gray horsebrush. June-Oct. Native shrub; sagebrush, mountain brush to aspen-conifer communities, 1360-2890 m.

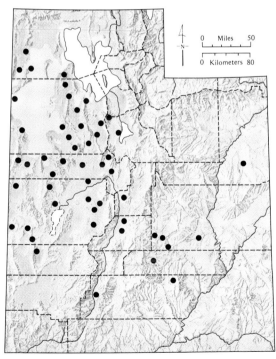

377. *Tetradymia glabrata* Gray Littleleaf horsebrush. Apr.-Aug. Native shrub; greasewood, shadscale, sagebrush, juniper communities, 1360-2270 m.

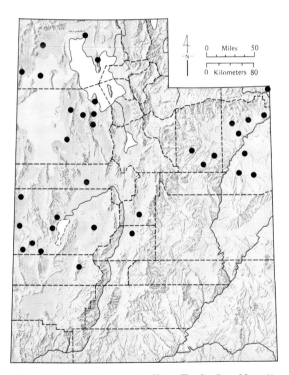

378. *Tetradymia nuttallii* T. & G. Nuttall horsebrush. May-July. Native shrub; shadscale, greasewood, sagebrush, pinyon-juniper communities, 1510-1970 m.

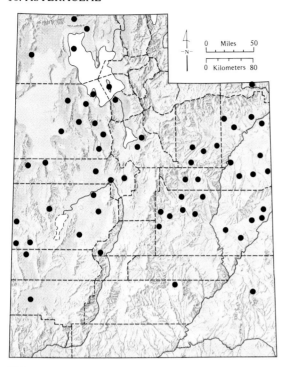

379. *Tetradymia spinosa* H. & A. Spiny horsebrush. May-June. Native shrub; shadscale, greasewood, sagebrush, pinyon-juniper communities, 1210-1820 m.

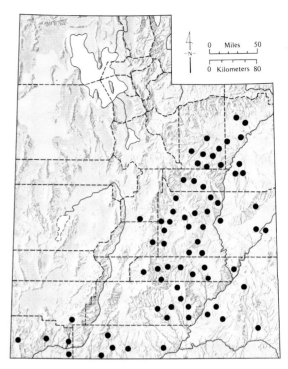

380. *Thelesperma subnudum* Gray Barestem greenthread. May-July. Native perennial herb; desert shrub, shadscale, pinyon-juniper communities, 970-2430 m.

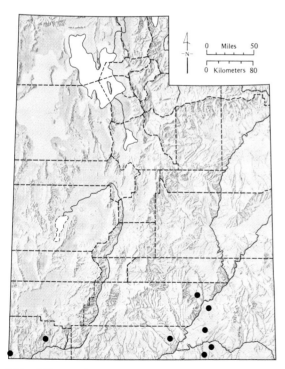

381. *Thymophylla acerosa* (DC.) Strother Prickleleaf dogweed. Apr.-Nov. Native perennial herb; sand dunes in creosote bush communities, 970-1180 m.

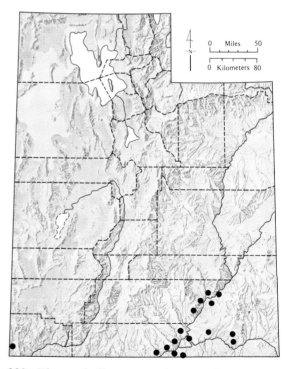

382. *Thymophylla pentachaeta* (DC.) Small Firehair dogweed. Apr.-Sept. Native perennial herb; creosote bush, Joshua tree, desert shrub communities, 1000-1580 m.

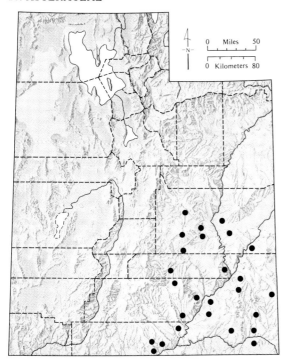

383. *Townsendia annua* Beaman Annual townsendia. Apr.-June. Native annual; desert shrub communities, 1060-1640 m.

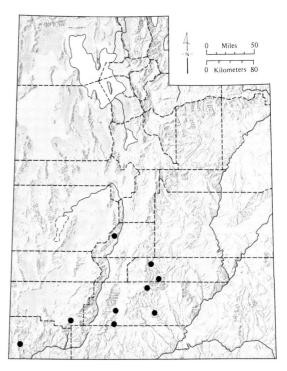

384. *Townsendia exscapa* (Richards.) Porter Stemless townsendia. May-July. Native perennial herb; sagebrush, ponderosa pine, aspen-fir communities, 1970-2640 m.

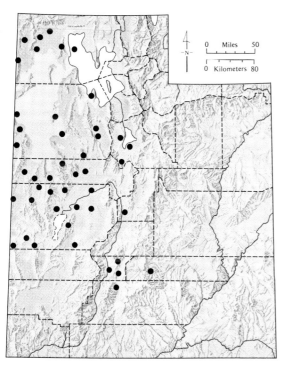

385. *Townsendia florifer* (Hook.) Gray Showy townsendia. May-June. Native perennial herb; salt desert shrub, desert shrub communities, 1390-1820 m.

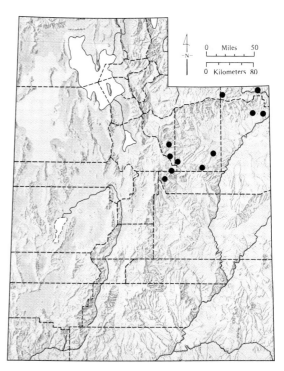

386. *Townsendia hookeri* Beaman Hooker townsendia. May-July. Native perennial herb; sagebrush, aspen-fir communities, 1910-2730 m.

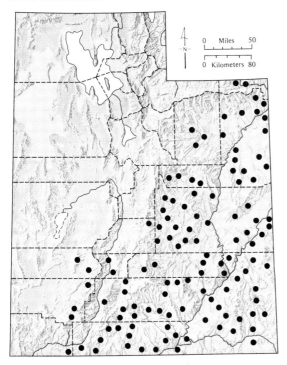

387. *Townsendia incana* Nutt. Hoary townsendia. Apr.-June. Native perennial herb; shadscale, mat saltbush, desert shrub to pinyon-juniper communities, windswept ridges, 1210-2790 m.

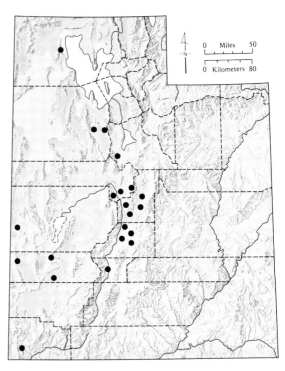

388. *Townsendia jonesii* (Beaman) Reveal Jones townsendia. May-June. Native perennial herb; shadscale, desert shrub, sagebrush, pinyon-juniper communities, 1360-1820 m.

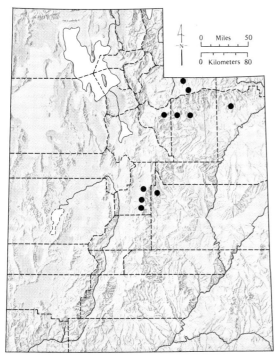

389. *Townsendia leptotes* (Gray) Osterh. Common townsendia. June-July. Native perennial herb; grass-forb-sagebrush communities, 2720-3090 m.

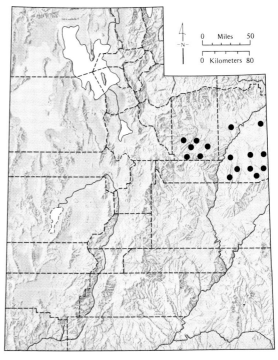

390. *Townsendia mensana* Jones Table townsendia. Apr.-June. Native perennial herb; shadscale, sagebrush, pinyon-juniper communities, 1820-2880 m.

124

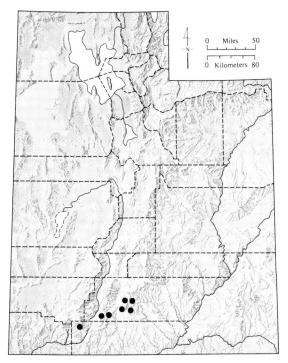

391. *Townsendia minima* Eastw. Least townsendia. Apr.-July. Native perennial herb; rocky sites in bristlecone pine, ponderosa pine, fir communities, 2420-2580 m.

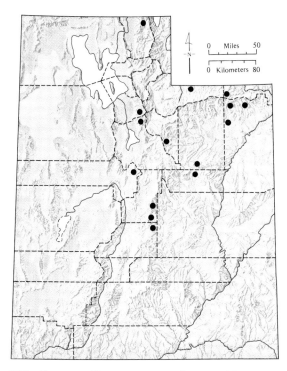

392. *Townsendia montana* Jones Mountain townsendia. July-Aug. Native perennial herb; lodgepole pine, aspen, spruce-fir communities, 2570-3330 m.

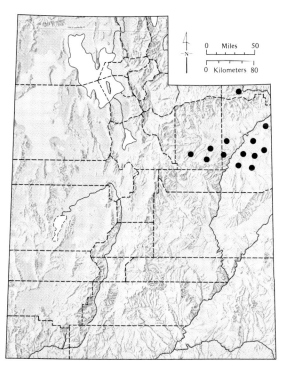

393. *Townsendia strigosa* Nutt. Hairy townsendia. June-Aug. Native biennial; shadscale, desert shrub, pinyon-juniper communities, 1450-1820 m.

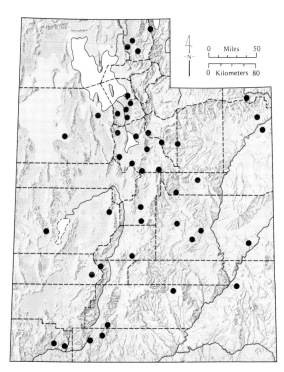

394. *Tragopogon dubius* Scop. Yellow salsify; goatsbeard. May-July. Introduced annual or biennial; disturbed sites, 1360-2880 m.

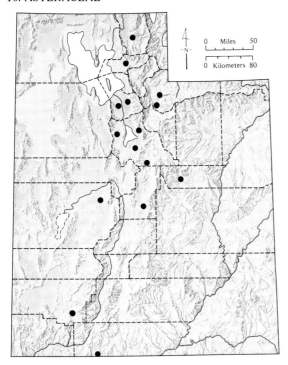

395. *Tragopogon porrifolius* L. Purple
salsify; oyster plant. May-July. Introduced
biennial; disturbed sites, 1450-2270 m.

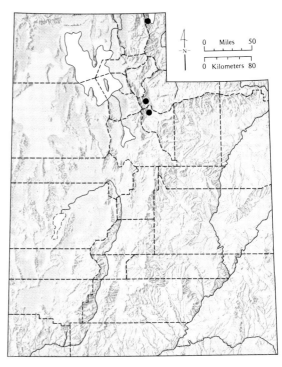

396. *Tragopogon pratensis* L. Meadow
salsify. May-June. Introduced biennial; disturbed
sites, 1360-1670 m.

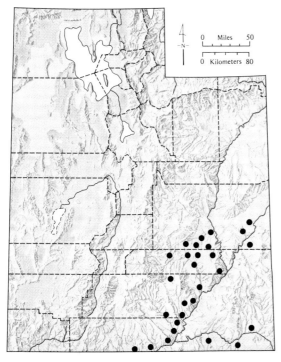

397. *Vanclevea stylosa* (Eastw.) Greene Pillar
vanclevea. July-Oct. Native annual or biennial;
desert shrub communities, 1060-1660 m.

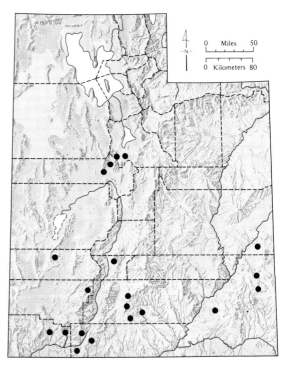

398. *Verbesina encelioides* (Cav.) Benth. &
Hook. Golden crownbeard. June-Sept. Native
perennial herb; desert shrub to ponderosa pine
communities, often roadside, 1150-2120 m.

10. ASTERACEAE

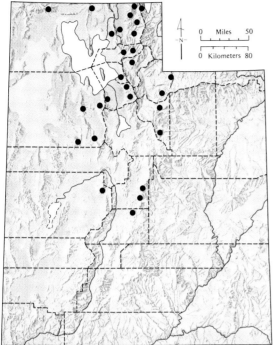

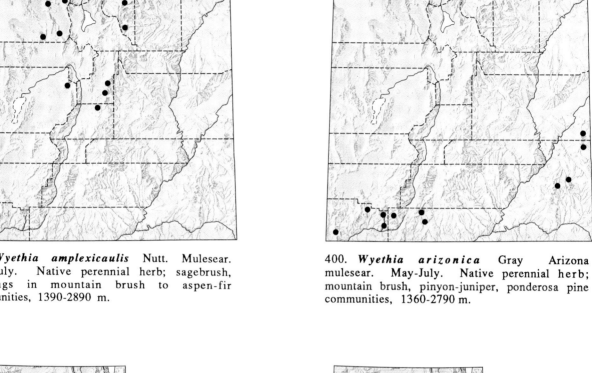

399. *Wyethia amplexicaulis* Nutt. Mulesear. May-July. Native perennial herb; sagebrush, openings in mountain brush to aspen-fir communities, 1390-2890 m.

400. *Wyethia arizonica* Gray Arizona mulesear. May-July. Native perennial herb; mountain brush, pinyon-juniper, ponderosa pine communities, 1360-2790 m.

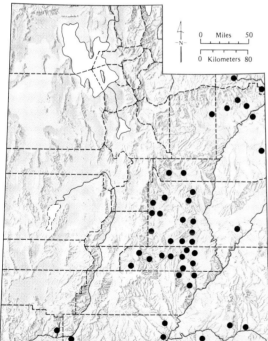

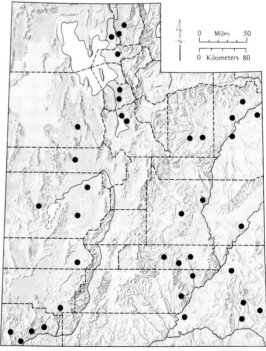

401. *Wyethia scabra* Hook. Badlands mulesear. May-July. Native perennial herb; desert shrub, pinyon-juniper, ponderosa pine communities, often on sand dunes, 1090-2270 m.

402. *Xanthium strumarium* L. Cocklebur. Aug.-Oct. Introduced annual; disturbed sites, 760-1970 m.

127

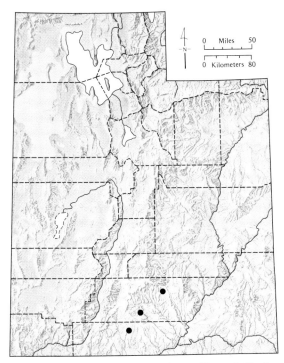

403. *Xylorhiza confertifolia* (Cronq.) T. J. Watson   Henrieville woodyaster.   May-June. Native perennial herb; shadscale to pinyon-juniper communities, 1450-2240 m.

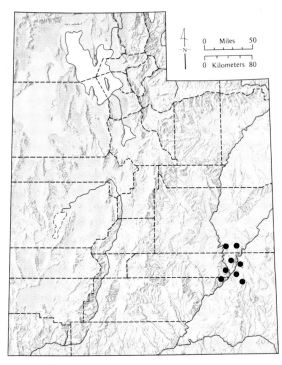

404. *Xylorhiza glabriuscula* Nutt.   Smooth woodyaster.   May-July.   Native perennial herb; shadscale, desert shrub communities, 1450-1940 m.

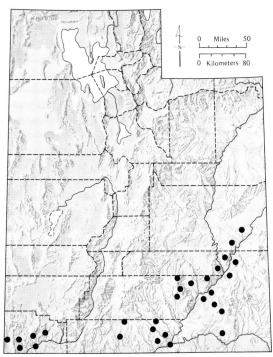

405. *Xylorhiza tortifolia* (T. & G.) Greene Mar.-June.   Native perennial herb or subshrub; creosote bush, shadscale, mat saltbush, desert shrub, pinyon-juniper communities, 790-1970 m.

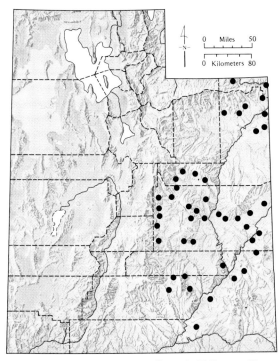

406. *Xylorhiza venusta* (Jones) Heller   Cisco woodyaster.   Apr.-June.   Native perennial herb; shadscale, mat saltbush, desert shrub communities, 1150-2060 m.

11. BERBERIDACEAE

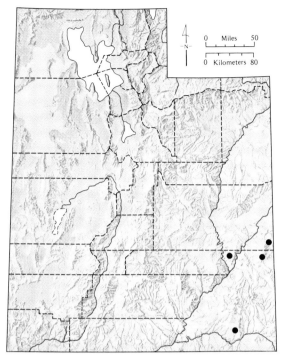

1. ***Berberis fendleri*** Gray   May-June.   Fendler barberry.   Native shrub; pinyon-juniper, Douglas fir, hanging garden communities, 1750-2060 m.

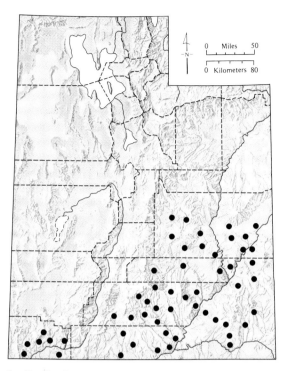

2. ***Berberis fremontii*** Torr.   Fremont barberry.   Apr.-May.   Native shrub; open hillsides, creosote bush to pinyon-juniper communities, 810-2430 m.

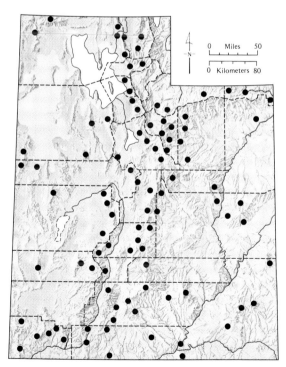

3. ***Berberis repens*** Lindl.   Oregon grape. Apr.-June.   Native shrub; shaded sites in oak-maple, aspen-fir, spruce-fir communities, 1210-3340 m.

12. BETULACEAE

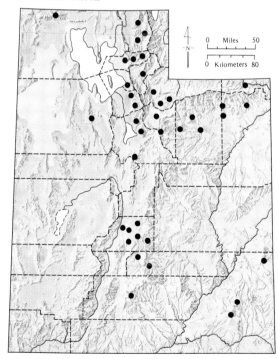

1. ***Alnus incana*** (L.) Moench   White or mountain alder.   Mar.-June.   Native tree or shrub; streamside, 1240-2730 m.

12. BETULACEAE

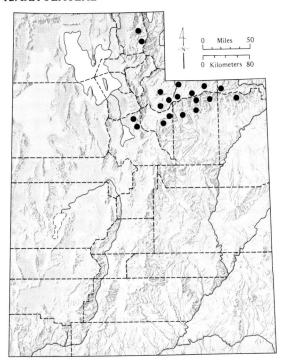

2. ***Betula glandulosa*** Michx. Bog birch.
July-Aug. Native shrub; streamside, wet meadows,
2120-3340 m.

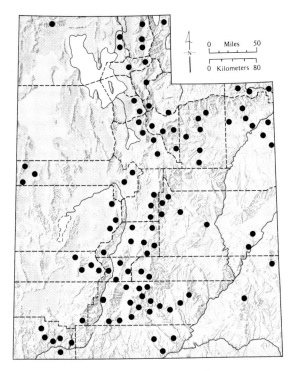

3. ***Betula occidentalis*** Hook. Western water
birch. Apr.-June. Native tree or shrub; streamside,
1210-2730 m.

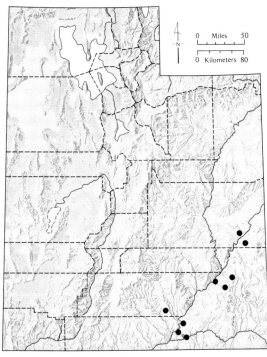

4. ***Ostrya knowltonii*** Cov. Western
hophornbeam. Apr.-May. Native tree; streamside,
hanging gardens, 1210-1730 m.

13. BIGNONIACEAE

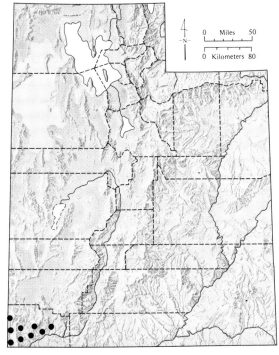

1. ***Chilopsis linearis*** (Cav.) Sweet Desert
willow. July-Aug. Native shrub or small tree;
along waterways and washes, 810-1060 m.

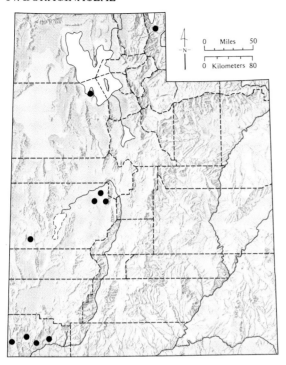

1. *Amsinckia intermedia* Fisch. & Mey. Fireweed fiddleneck. Mar.-May. Native annual; dry waste places, 840-2120 m.

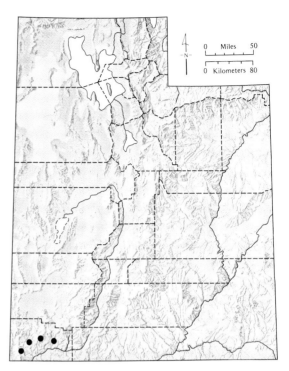

2. *Amsinckia menziesii* (Lehm.) Nels. & Macbr. Menzies fiddleneck. Mar.-Apr. Native annual; dry sites, rock crevices, 840-910 m.

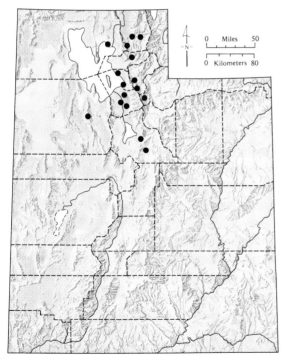

3. *Amsinckia retrorsa* Suksd. Rough fiddleneck. Apr.-Aug. Native annual; dry to moist, often disturbed sites, 1270-2280 m.

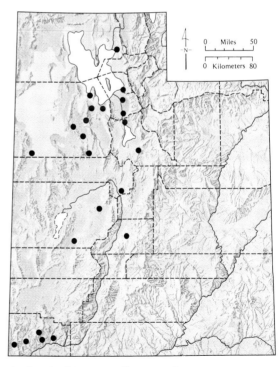

4. *Amsinckia tessellata* Gray Western fiddleneck; devil's lettuce. Apr.-July. Native annual; creosote bush to juniper communities, often in disturbed sites, 840-1820 m.

14. BORAGINACEAE

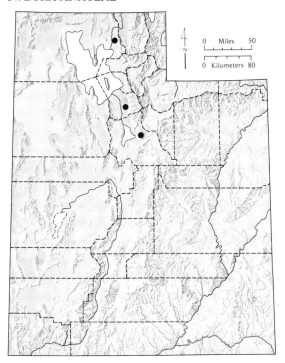

5. *Anchusa azurea* Mill. Blue alkanet. May-June. Introduced perennial herb; cultivated, escaping and persistent, 13600-1460 m.

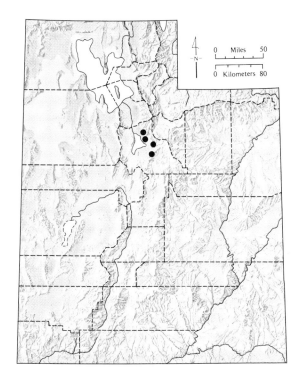

6. *Anchusa officinalis* L. Bugloss alkanet. May-July. Introduced perennial herb; cultivated, escaping and persistent, 1630-2280 m.

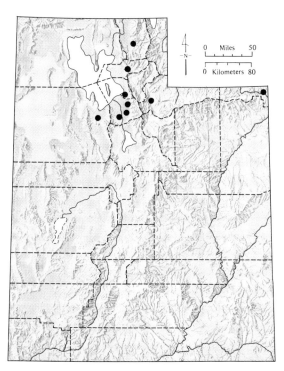

7. *Asperugo procumbens* L. Catchweed. Apr.-June. Introduced annual; mesic to dry, disturbed sites, 1270-2210 m.

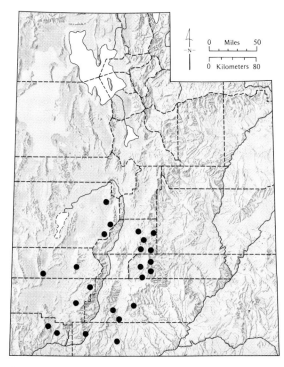

8. *Cryptantha abata* Johnst. Low cryptanth. Apr.-May. Native perennial herb; sagebrush, pinyon-juniper, ponderosa pine communities, 1510-2550 m.

132

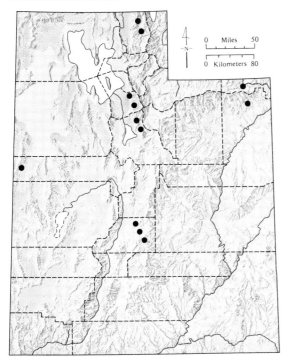

9. *Cryptantha affinis* (Gray) Greene   May-July.   Native annual; shaded sites in oak-maple, aspen, ponderosa pine communities, 1480-2610 m.

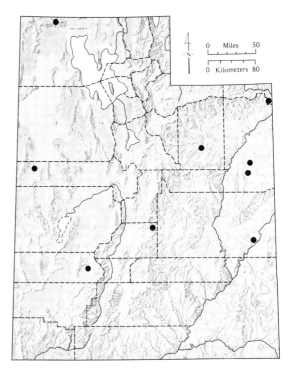

10. *Cryptantha ambigua* (Gray) Greene Wilkes cryptanth. June-July. Native annual; open slopes, sagebrush, mountain brush, pinyon-juniper, aspen communities, 1510-2910 m.

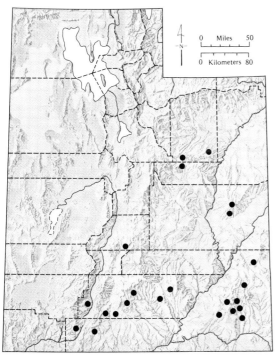

11. *Cryptantha bakeri* (Greene) Pays. Baker cryptanth. Apr.-June. Native perennial herb; pinyon-juniper to ponderosa pine communities, 1510-2580 m.

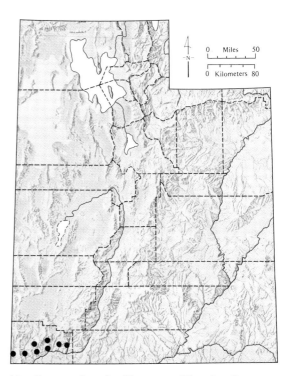

12. *Cryptantha barbigera* (Gray) Greene Bearded cryptanth. Apr.-May. Native annual; creosote bush, sagebrush, juniper communities, 810-1520 m.

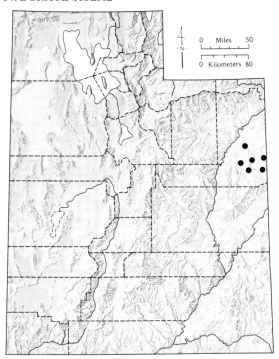

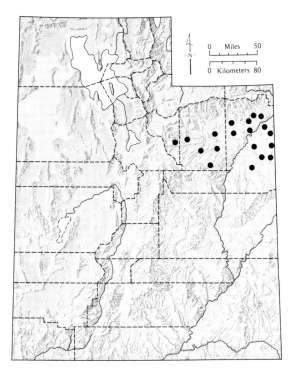

13. *Cryptantha barnebyi* Johnst. Barneby cryptanth. May-June. Native perennial herb; barren shale knolls of the Green River Formation in shadscale, sagebrush, pinyon-juniper communities, 1810-1970 m.

14. *Cryptantha breviflora* (Osterh.) Pays. Smallflower or Uinta Basin cryptanth. Apr.-June. Native perennial herb; desert shrub, sagebrush, pinyon-juniper communities, 1670-2120 m.

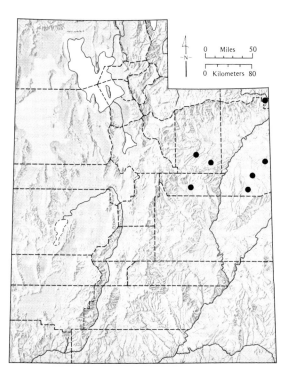

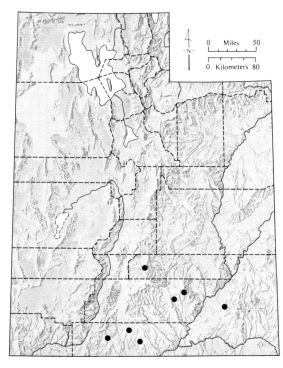

15. *Cryptantha caespitosa* (A. Nels.) Pays. Tufted or spreading cryptanth. May-June. Native perennial herb; sagebrush, pinyon-juniper communities, 1510-2180 m.

16. *Cryptantha capitata* (Eastw.) Johnst. Head cryptanth. May-July. Native perennial herb; ponderosa pine, pinyon-juniper communities, 2090-2430 m.

14. BORAGINACEAE

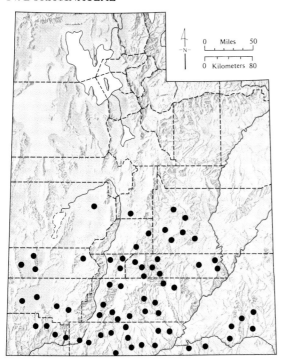

17. *Cryptantha cinerea* (Greene) Cronq. Gray cryptanth. May-Aug. Native perennial herb;. shadscale, sagebrush, pinyon-juniper, ponderosa pine communities, 1300-3030 m.

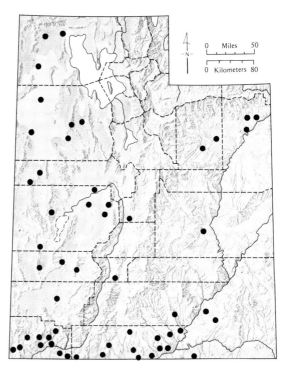

18. *Cryptantha circumscissa* (H. & A.) Johnst. Matted or cushion cryptanth. Apr.-June. Native annual; creosote bush to juniper communities, 840-1820 m.

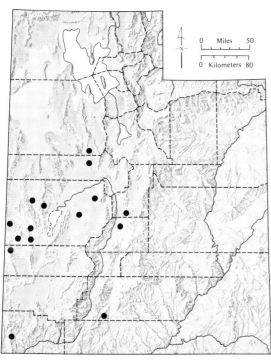

19. *Cryptantha compacta* Higgins Mound or compact cryptanth. May-June. Native perennial herb; salt desert shrub, desert shrub communities, 1510-2820 m.

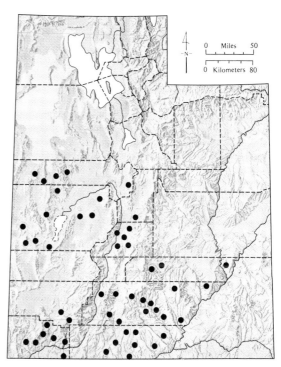

20. *Cryptantha confertiflora* (Greene) Pays. Golden cryptanth. Apr.-June. Native perennial herb; greasewood, desert shrub to ponderosa pine communities, 1060-2210 m.

135

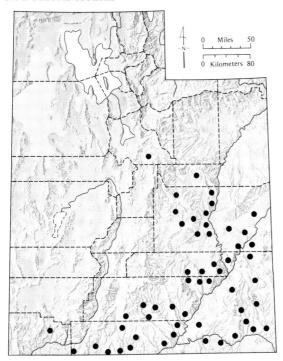

21. *Cryptantha crassisepala* (T. & G.) Greene Plains cryptanth. May-June. Native annual; sand dunes, greasewood, pinyon-juniper communities, 1060-1790 m.

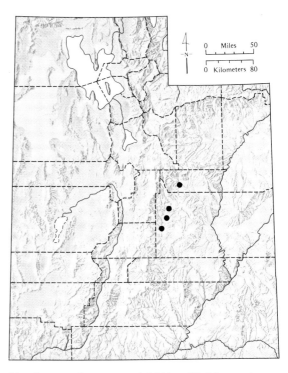

22. *Cryptantha creutzfeldtii* Welsh Apr.-May. Native perennial herb; Mancos Shale in shadscale and mat saltbush communities, 1660-1970 m.

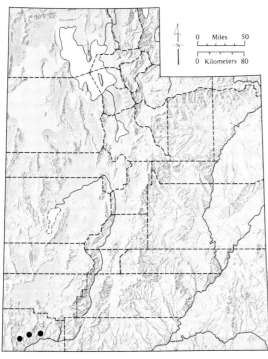

23. *Cryptantha decipiens* (Jones) Heller Beguiling cryptanth. Apr.-May. Native annual; rocky ledges, creosote bush communities, 910-1060 m.

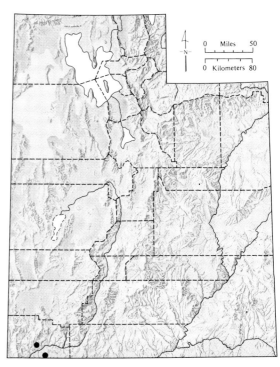

24. *Cryptantha dumetorum* (Greene) Greene Bramble or scrambling cryptanth. Mar.-May. Native annual; creosote bush, desert shrub communities, 810-970 m.

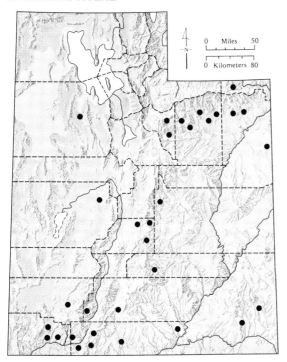

25. *Cryptantha fendleri* (Gray) Greene   June-Aug. Native annual; sagebrush, juniper, ponderosa pine communities, 1510-2610 m.

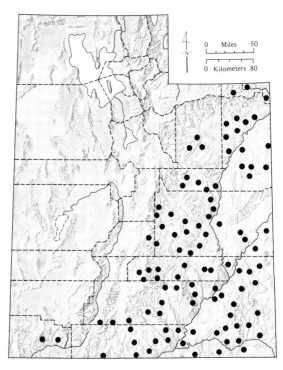

26. *Cryptantha flava* (A. Nels.) Pays.   Yellow cryptanth.   Apr.-July.   Native perennial herb; shadscale to pinyon-juniper communities, 1150-2430 m.

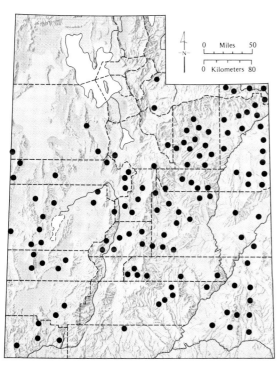

27. *Cryptantha flavoculata* (A. Nels.) Pays. Yelloweye cryptanth. May-June. Native perennial herb; sagebrush to pinyon-juniper communities, 970-2730 m.

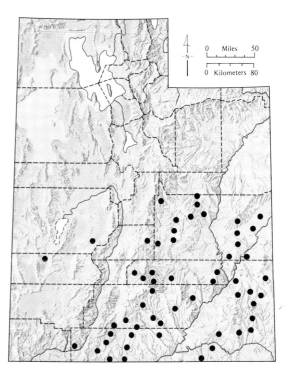

28. *Cryptantha fulvocanescens* (Wats.) Pays. Tawny or plateau cryptanth. May-June. Native perennial herb; dry sandy sites, pinyon-juniper communities, 1450-2520 m.

137

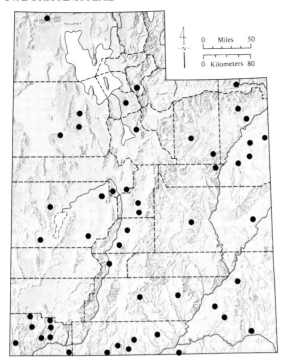

29. *Cryptantha gracilis* Osterh. Slender cryptanth. Apr.-June. Native annual; grass-sagebrush, oak, pinyon-juniper communities, 1210-1970 m.

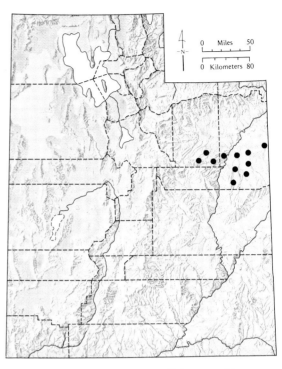

30. *Cryptantha grahamii* Johnst. Fragrant cryptanth. May-June. Native perennial herb; Green River Formation in desert shrub communities, 1510-2060 m.

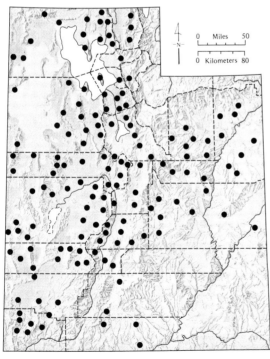

31. *Cryptantha humilis* (Greene) Pays. Cat's eye. Apr.-June. Native perennial herb; dry open slopes, shadscale to pinyon-juniper communities, 1060-2120 m.

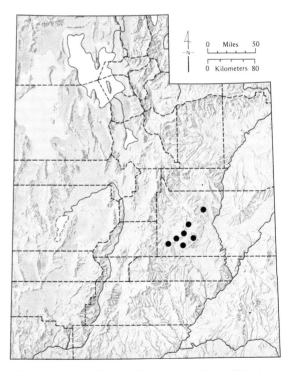

32. *Cryptantha johnstonii* Higgins Johnston cryptanth. May-June. Native perennial herb; pinyon-juniper communities, 1390-2120 m.

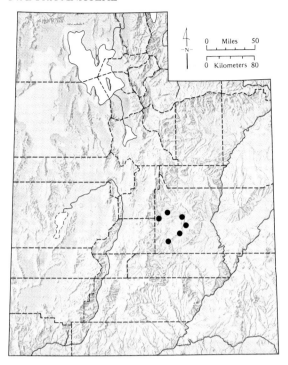

33. *Cryptantha jonesiana* (Pays.) Pays. Jones or San Rafael cryptanth. May-June. Native perennial herb; shadscale, desert shrub, pinyon-juniper communities, 1390-1970 m.

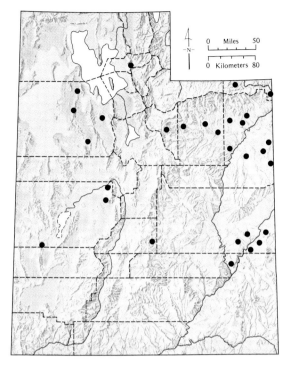

34. *Cryptantha kelseyana* Greene Kelsey cryptanth. June-July. Native annual; sagebrush, pinyon-juniper communities, 1390-2490 m.

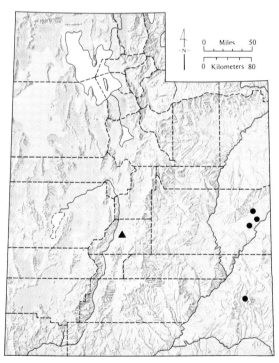

35. *Cryptantha longiflora* (A. Nels.) Pays. May-June. Native perennial herb; desert shrub, pinyon-juniper communities, 1270-1670 m.

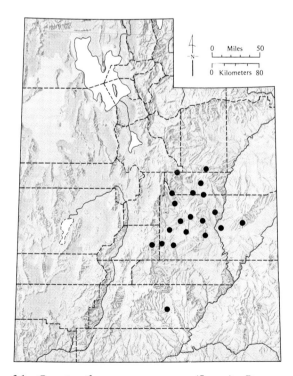

36. *Cryptantha mensana* (Jones) Pays. Carbon cryptanth. May-June. Native perennial herb; shadscale, desert shrub communities, 1270-2280 m.

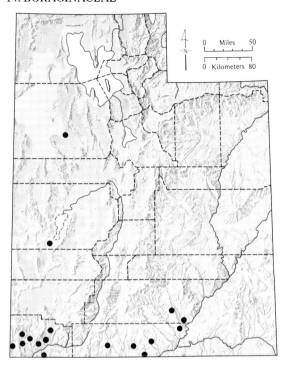

37. *Cryptantha micrantha* (Torr.) Johnst. Redroot cryptanth. Mar.-June. Native annual; sand dunes, desert shrub, sagebrush communities, waste places, 910-1460 m.

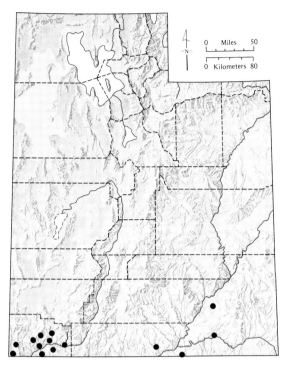

38. *Cryptantha nevadensis* Nels. & Kenn. Nevada cryptanth. Apr.-May. Native annual; creosote bush, desert shrub, turbinella live oak communities, 910-1310 m.

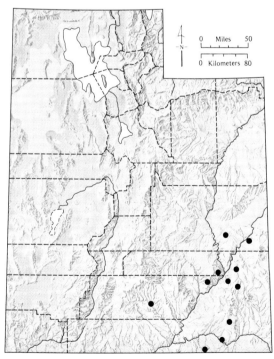

39. *Cryptantha osterhoutii* (Pays.) Pays. Osterhout cryptanth. May-June. Native perennial herb; desert shrub, oak, pinyon-juniper communities, 1360-1880 m.

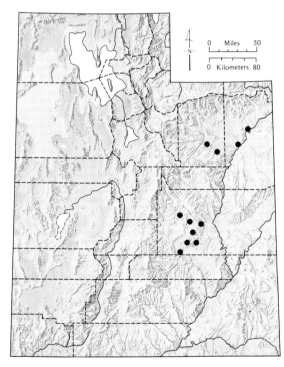

40. *Cryptantha paradoxa* (A. Nels.) Pays. May-June. Native perennial herb; barren clay, rocky sites in shadscale, desert shrub, pinyon-juniper communities, 1510-2060 m.

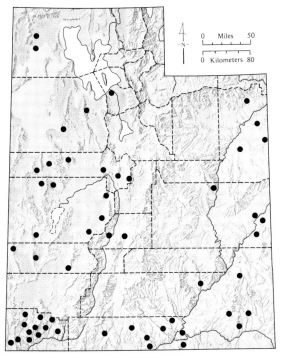

41. *Cryptantha pterocarya* (Torr.) Greene Winged-nut cryptanth. Apr.-June. Native annual; creosote bush, desert shrub, pinyon-juniper communities, 840-1880 m.

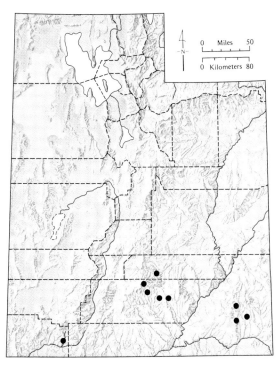

42. *Cryptantha pustulosa* (Rydb.) Pays. San Juan cryptanth. Apr.-May. Native perennial herb; sagebrush, mountain brush communities, 1510-2000 m.

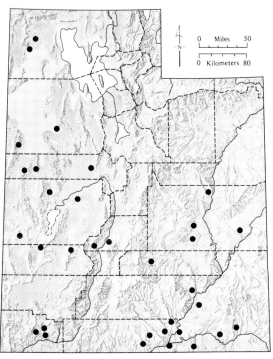

43. *Cryptantha recurvata* Cov. Bent-nut cryptanth. Apr.-June. Native annual; desert shrub, juniper communities, 910-1580 m.

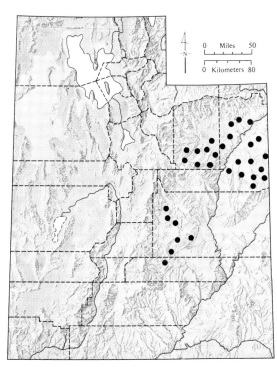

44. *Cryptantha rollinsii* Johnst. Rollins cryptanth. May-July. Native perennial herb; desert shrub, pinyon-juniper communities, 1510-2280 m.

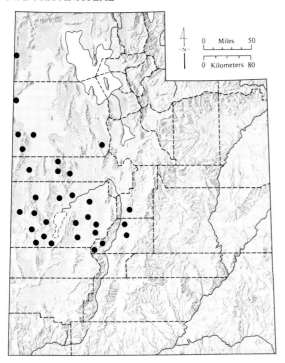

45. ***Cryptantha rugulosa*** (Pays.) Pays. May-July. Native perennial herb; salt desert shrub, desert shrub, sagebrush communities, 1210-1900 m.

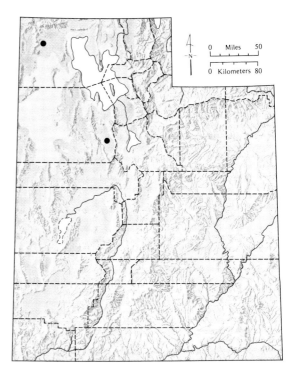

46. ***Cryptantha scoparia*** A. Nels. Broom cryptanth. June-July. Native annual; desert shrub communities, 1510-1650 m.

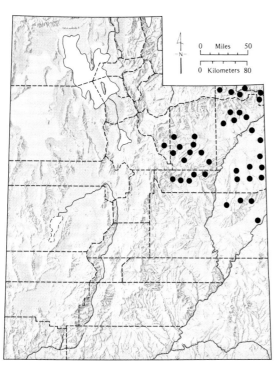

47. ***Cryptantha sericea*** (Gray) Pays. Silky cryptanth. May-Aug. Native perennial herb; sagebrush, pinyon-juniper, aspen-fir communities, 1660-2580 m.

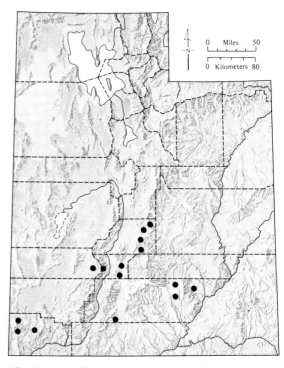

48. ***Cryptantha setosissima*** (Gray) Pays. Bristly cryptanth. June-Aug. Native perennial herb; sagebrush, mountain brush, pinyon-juniper communities, 1570-2730 m.

142

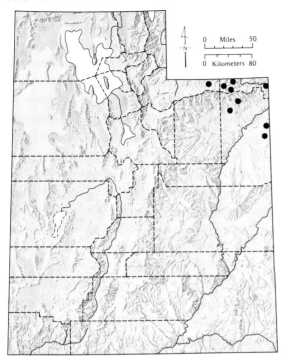

49. *Cryptantha stricta* (Osterh.) Pays. Erect cryptanth. May-Aug. Native perennial herb; sagebrush, pinyon-juniper, mountain brush communities, 1810-2580 m.

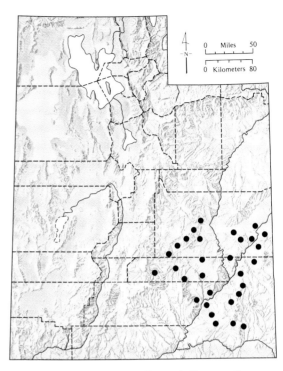

50. *Cryptantha tenuis* (Eastw.) Pays. Canyon cryptanth. May-June. Native perennial herb; desert shrub communities, 1300-1820 m.

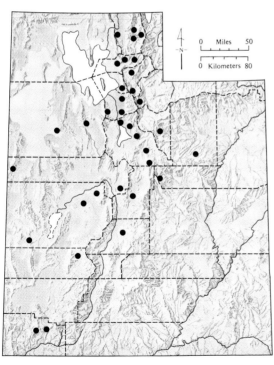

51. *Cryptantha torreyana* (Gray) Greene Torrey cryptanth. June-Aug. Native annual; dry slopes, sagebrush, oak-maple, aspen-fir communities, 1300-2880 m.

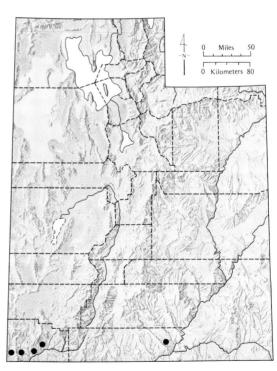

52. *Cryptantha utahensis* (Gray) Greene Utah cryptanth. Apr.-May. Native annual; creosote bush, desert shrub communities, 810-1370 m.

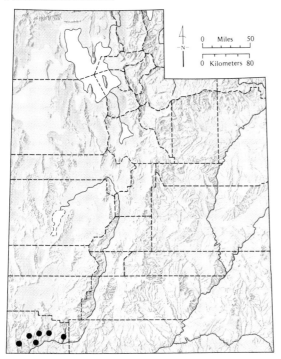

53. *Cryptantha virginensis* (Jones) Pays. Virgin River cryptanth. Apr.-May. Native perennial herb; creosote bush to pinyon-juniper communities, 910-1210 m.

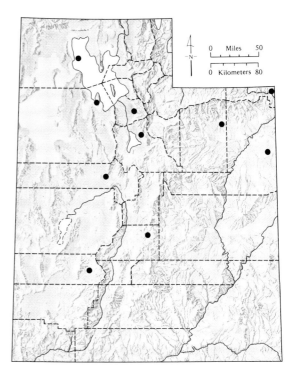

54. *Cryptantha watsonii* (Gray) Greene Watson cryptanth. May-July. Native annual; sagebrush to ponderosa pine communities, 1270-2490 m.

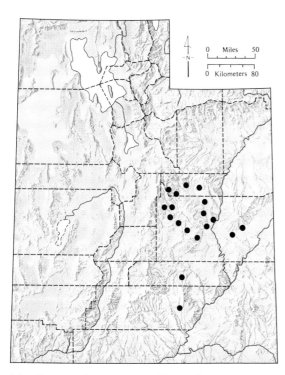

55. *Cryptantha wetherillii* (Eastw.) Pays. Apr.-June. Native perennial herb; greasewood, mat saltbush to pinyon-juniper communities, 1270-1670 m.

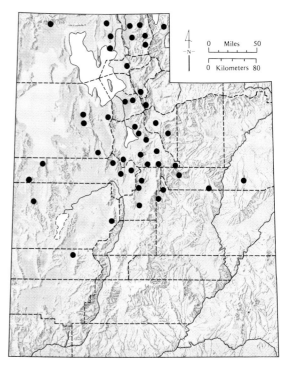

56. *Cynoglossum officinale* L. Hounds-tongue. June-Aug. Introduced biennial; disturbed mesic sites in oak to aspen communities, 1360-2790 m.

14. BORAGINACEAE

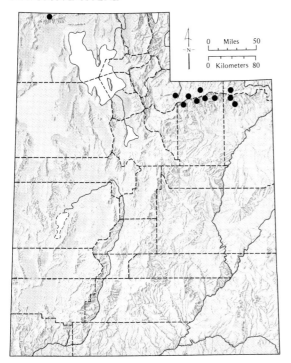

57. *Eritrichium nanum* (Vill.) Schrad. Blue-eyes. June-Aug. Native perennial herb; rocky summits, meadows, 3030-3940 m.

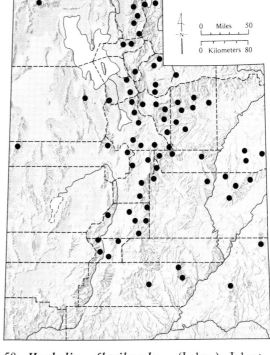

58. *Hackelia floribunda* (Lehm.) Johnst. Showy stickseed. June-Aug. Native biennial to perennial; sagebrush to aspen-fir communities, 1510-3030 m.

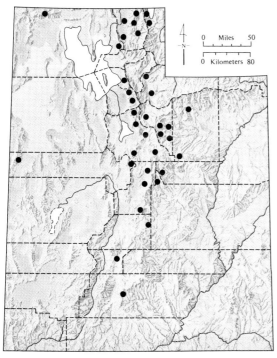

59. *Hackelia micrantha* (Eastw.) Gentry Smallflower stickseed or tickweed. July-Aug. Native perennial herb; sagebrush to aspen-spruce-fir communities, 2120-3030 m.

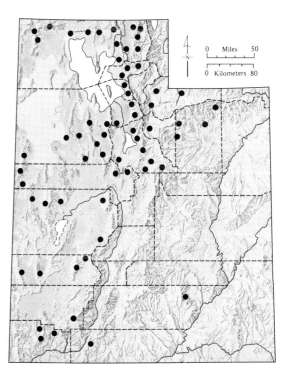

60. *Hackelia patens* (Nutt.) Johnst. Spotted stickseed. May-July. Native perennial herb; sagebrush, mountain brush, pinyon-juniper to spruce-fir communities, 1360-2880 m.

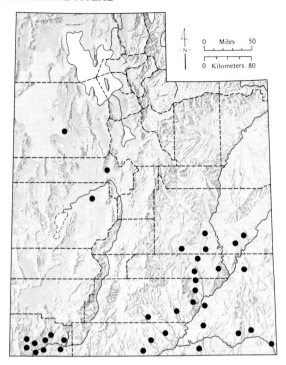

61. *Heliotropium convolvulaceum* (Nutt.) Gray Bindweed heliotrope. June-Sept. Native annual; sand dunes, shadscale, desert shrub communities, 880-1550 m.

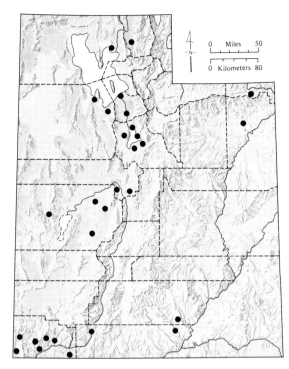

62. *Heliotropium curassavicum* L. Salt heliotrope. May-Aug. Native perennial herb; moist sites in creosote bush, salt desert shrub to juniper communities, 810-1520 m.

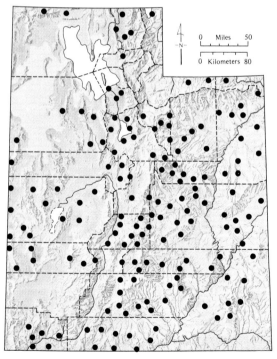

63. *Lappula redowskii* (Hornem.) Greene Western stickseed. May-Aug. Native annual; disturbed sites, greasewood to aspen communities, 910-2940 m.

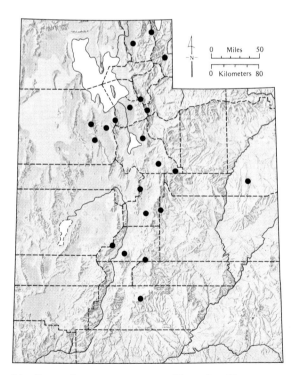

64. *Lappula squarrosa* (Retz.) Dumort. European stickseed. May-Aug. Introduced annual; disturbed sites in sagebrush-grass communities, 1240-2240 m.

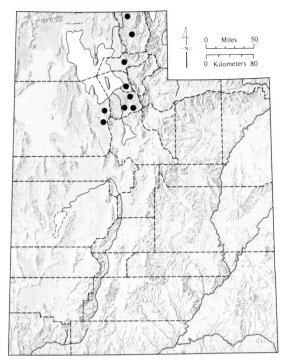

65. Lithospermum arvense L. Gromwell.
Apr.-June. Introduced annual; waste places, grassy
slopes, oak-maple communities, 1300-1940 m.

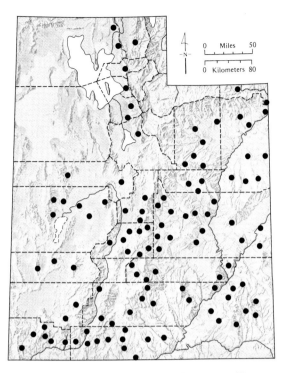

66. Lithospermum incisum Lehm. Showy
stoneseed. May-June. Native perennial herb;
desert shrub, sagebrush to ponderosa pine
communities, 1360-2730 m.

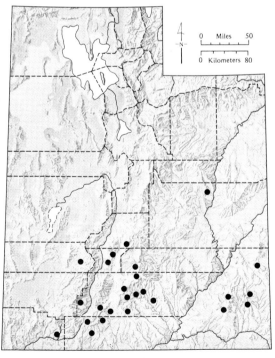

67. Lithospermum multiflorum Torr. Southwestern stoneseed. June-Aug. Native perennial
herb; sagebrush to aspen, spruce-fir communities,
2120-3030 m.

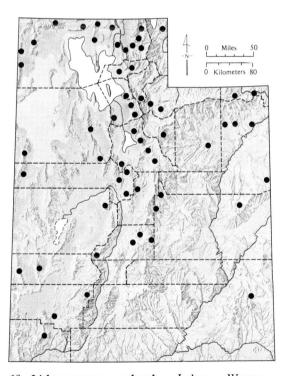

68. Lithospermum ruderale Lehm. Western
stoneseed. Apr.-Aug. Native perennial herb;
grassy slopes, sagebrush, oak, juniper, aspen
communities, 1330-2670 m.

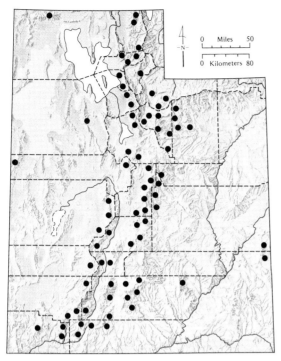

69. **Mertensia arizonica** Greene Aspen bluebell. May-Aug. Native perennial herb; oak-maple, aspen-fir, meadow communities, 1810-3340 m.

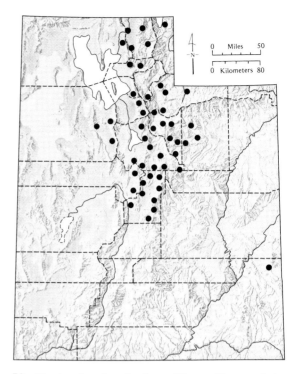

70. **Mertensia brevistyla** Wats. Short-styled bluebell. Apr.-July. Native perennial herb; sagebrush, oak-maple, mountain brush communities, 1450-2790 m.

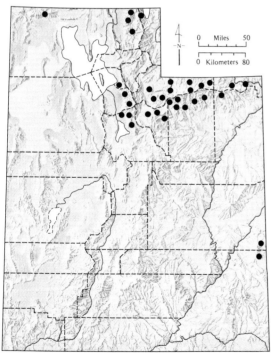

71. **Mertensia ciliata** (Torr.) G. Don Mountain bluebell. June-Aug. Native perennial herb; streamside, wet meadow, spruce-fir communities, 1970-3790 m.

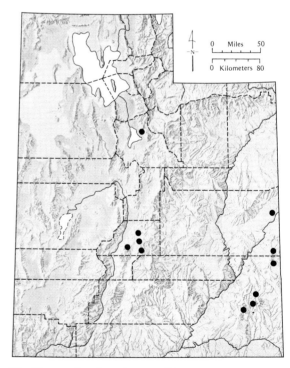

72. **Mertensia franciscana** Heller Franciscan bluebell. May-Aug. Native perennial herb; streamside, aspen, spruce-fir communities, 2120-3030 m.

14. BORAGINACEAE

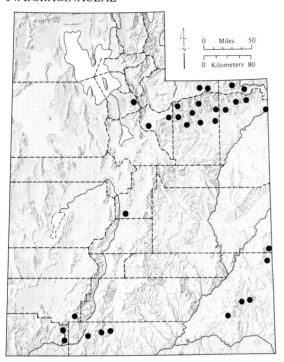

73. *Mertensia fusiformis* Greene Spindle-rooted bluebell. June-Aug. Native perennial herb; sagebrush to ponderosa pine communities, 1810-3030 m.

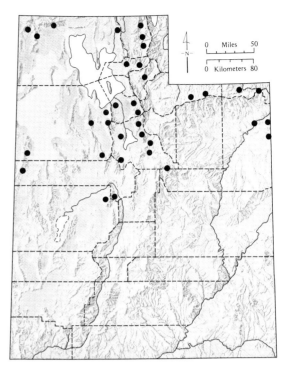

74. *Mertensia oblongifolia* (Nutt.) G. Don Western or sagebrush bluebell. May-July. Native perennial herb; open slopes to shade in sagebrush to conifer communities, 1420-3030 m.

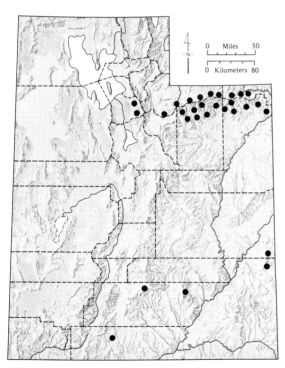

75. *Mertensia viridis* A. Nels. Greenleaf bluebell. May-Aug. Native perennial herb; rocky sites in oakbrush, spruce-fir, alpine communities, 1660-3940 m.

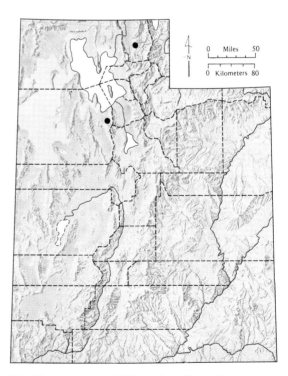

76. *Myosotis scorpioides* L. True forget-me-not. June-Sept. Introduced perennial herb; cultivated, escaping and persistent along waterways, 1390-1520 m.

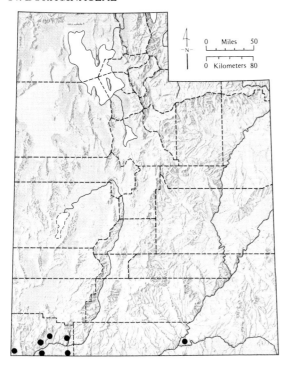

77. *Pectocarya heterocarpa* (Johnst.) Johnst. Mixed-nut combseed. Mar.-Apr. Native annual; open slopes in creosote bush, desert shrub communities, 810-970 m.

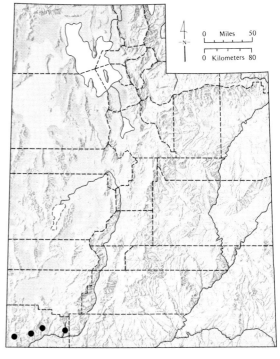

78. *Pectocarya setosa* Gray Saucer or bristly combseed. Apr.-May. Native annual; sagebrush, pinyon-juniper communities, 810-1060 m.

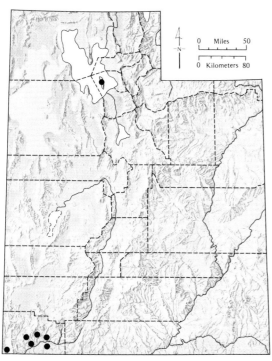

79. *Plagiobothrys arizonicus* (Gray) Greene Arizona popcornflower. Mar.-May. Native annual; Joshua tree, desert shrub communities, 810-1120 m.

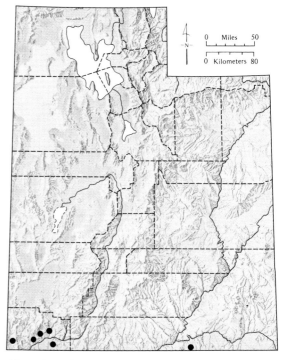

80. *Plagiobothrys jonesii* Gray Jones or Mojave popcornflower. Apr.-May. Native annual; creosote bush, desert shrub communities, 810-1060 m.

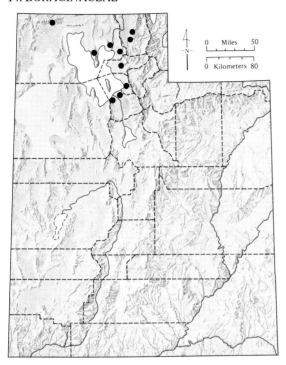

81. *Plagiobothrys leptocladus* (Greene) Johnst. Alkali popcornflower. Apr.-June. Native annual; salt desert shrub communities, 1270-1370 m.

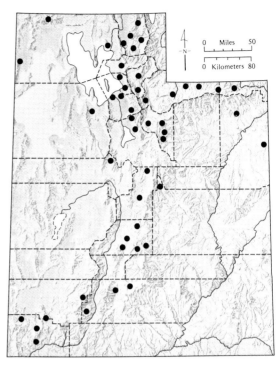

82. *Plagiobothrys scouleri* (H. & A.) Johnst. Scouler or meadow popcornflower. June-Aug. Native annual; moist sites, salt desert shrub to aspen-fir communities, 880-2880 m.

83. *Plagiobothrys tenellus* (Nutt.) Gray Slender popcornflower. Apr.-June. Native annual; sagebrush, pinyon-juniper communities, 1270-1430 m.

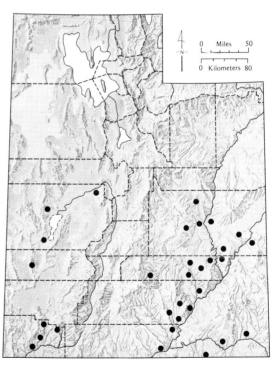

84. *Tiquilia latior* (Johnst.) A. Richardson Matted tiquilia. May-Aug. Native perennial herb; desert shrub communities, 810-1670 m.

14. BORAGINACEAE

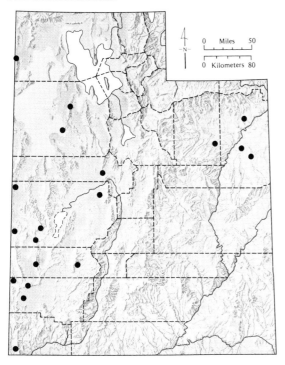

85. *Tiquilia nuttallii* (Hook.) A. Richardson
Nuttall or rosette tiquilia. May-Sept. Native
annual; sand dunes, 810-1820 m.

15. BRASSICACEAE

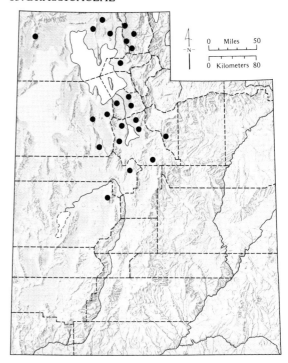

1. *Alyssum alyssoides* (L.) L. Alyssum.
Apr.-July. Introduced annual; disturbed sites in
grass-forb, sagebrush, oak communities, 1300-
2150 m.

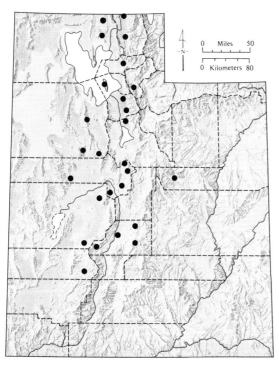

2. *Alyssum desertorum* Stapf Desert
alyssum. Apr.-May. Introduced annual; disturbed
sites in grass-forb, sagebrush, pinyon-juniper
communities, 1330-2150 m.

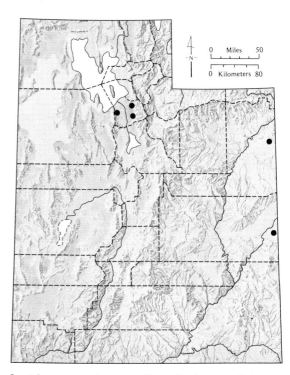

3. *Alyssum minus* (L.) Rothm. Lesser
alyssum. May-June. Introduced annual; disturbed
sites in grass-forb, sagebrush, pinyon-juniper
communities, 1300-1880 m.

152

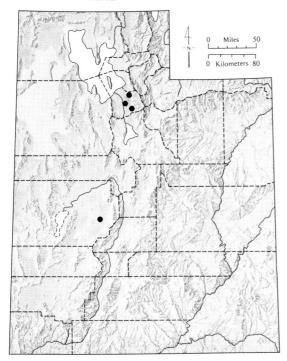

4. ***Alyssum szowitsianum*** Fisch. & Mey. Szowits alyssum. Apr.-June. Introduced annual; disturbed sites in grass-forb, sagebrush, pinyon-juniper communities, 1330-1910 m.

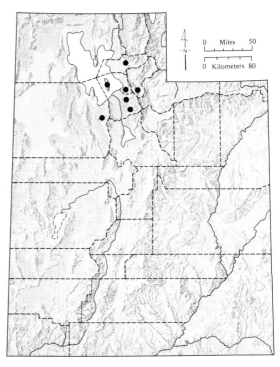

5. ***Arabidopsis thaliana*** (L.) Heynh. Mouse-ear cress. Mar.-June. Introduced annual; disturbed sites in grass-forb, oak communities, 1300-2120 m.

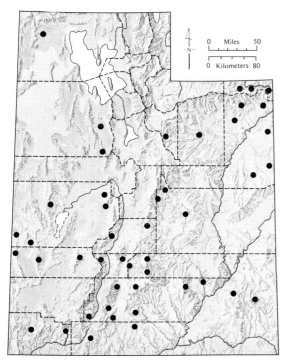

6. ***Arabis demissa*** Greene   May-June. Native perennial herb; open slopes, sagebrush, pinyon-juniper communities, 1660-3030 m.

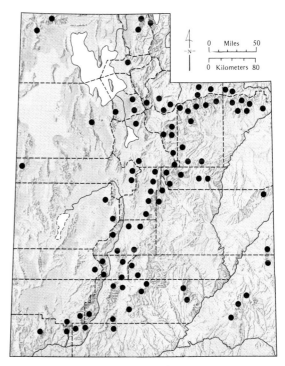

7. ***Arabis drummondii*** Gray   Drummond rockcress. June-Sept. Native perennial herb; oak to aspen-fir, meadow, ponderosa pine communities, rocky slopes, 1940-3790 m.

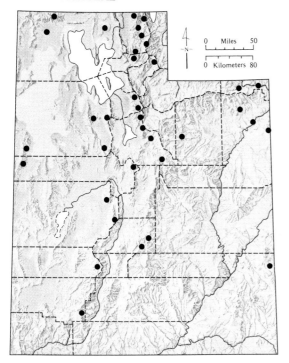

8. *Arabis glabra* (L.) Bernh. Tower rockcress.
May-Aug. Native perennial herb; sagebrush to
aspen-fir, streamside communities, 1630-3180 m.

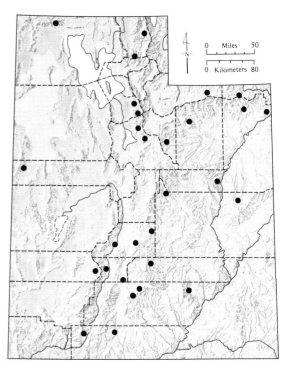

9. *Arabis hirsuta* (L.) Scop. Hairy rockcress.
May-Aug. Native perennial herb; sagebrush to
aspen-fir, streamside communities, 1510-3030 m.

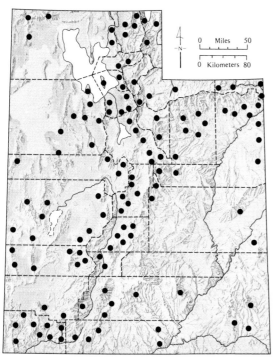

10. *Arabis holboellii* Hornem. Holboell
rockcress. Apr.-July. Native perennial herb; desert
shrub to conifer communities, 1270-3210 m.

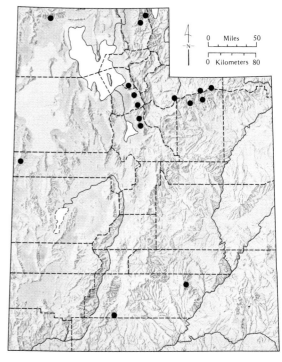

11. *Arabis lemmonii* Wats. May-Aug.
Lemmon rockcress. Native perennial herb; exposed
rocky slopes, alpine meadows, 2420-3940 m.

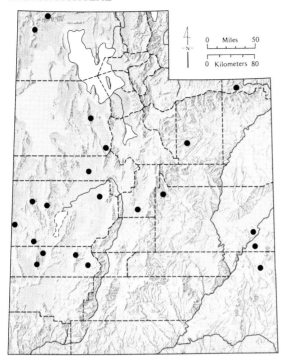

12. *Arabis lignifera* A. Nels. May-June.
Native perennial herb; shadscale, desert shrub to
pinyon-juniper communities, 1270-2000 m.

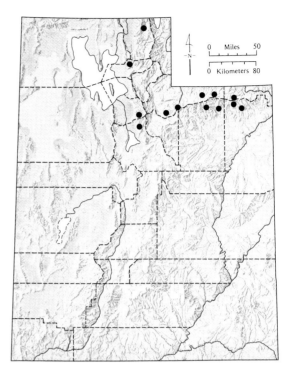

13. *Arabis lyallii* Wats. Lyall rockcress.
July-Aug. Native perennial herb; subalpine fir,
krummholz communities, exposed alpine ridges,
2570-3640 m.

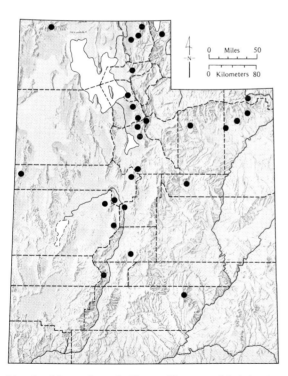

14. *Arabis microphylla* Nutt. Littleleaf
rockcress. Apr.-June. Native perennial herb; oak-
sagebrush to conifer communities, rocky slopes,
1450-3030 m.

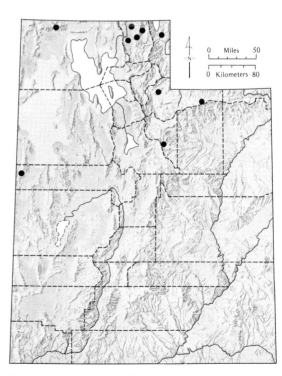

15. *Arabis nuttallii* Robins. Nuttall
rockcress. May-July. Native perennial herb;
sagebrush, mountain brush, meadow communities,
1360-2940 m.

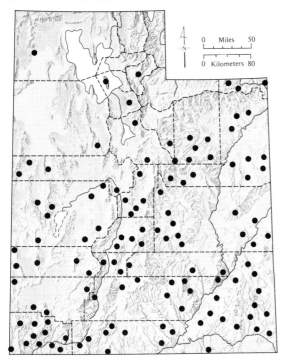

16. *Arabis perennans* Wats. Common rockcress. Apr.-June. Native perennial herb; creosote bush, desert shrub to ponderosa pine communities, 810-3030 m.

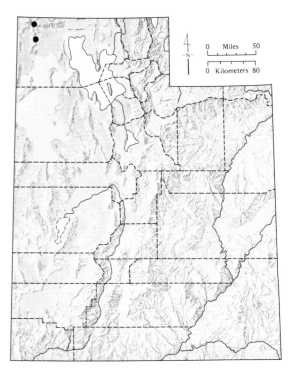

17. *Arabis puberula* Nutt. Hoary rockcress. May-June. Native perennial herb; dry rocky slopes, sagebrush communities, 810-2120 m.

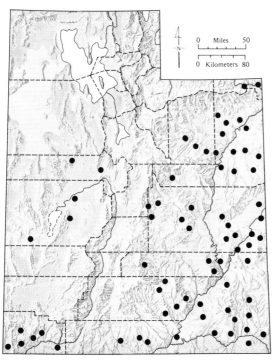

18. *Arabis pulchra* Jones Pretty rockcress. Apr.-June. Native perennial herb; Joshua tree to pinyon-juniper communities, 810-2060 m.

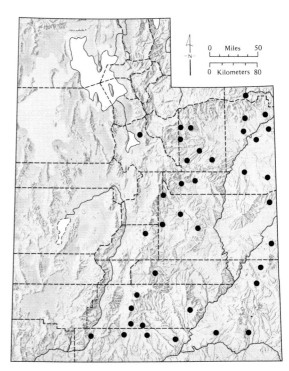

19. *Arabis selbyi* Rydb. Selby rockcress. Apr.-June. Native perennial herb; sagebrush to ponderosa pine communities, 1510-2610 m.

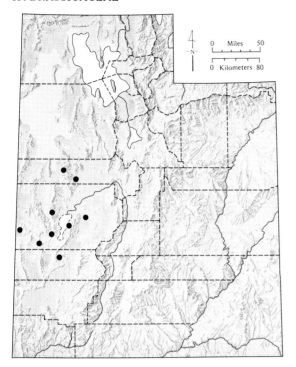

20. *Arabis shockleyi* Munz Munz rockcress.
May-June. Native perennial herb; shadscale, desert
shrub, sagebrush communities, 1420-2180 m.

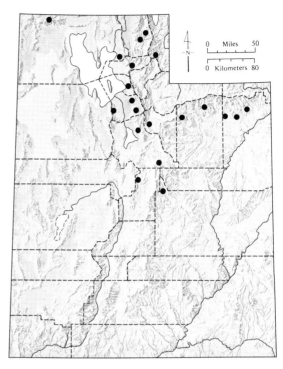

21. *Arabis sparsiflora* Nutt. Sicklepod
rockcress. Apr.-July. Native perennial herb;
grass-forb, pinyon-juniper, oak-maple
communities, 1330-2670 m.

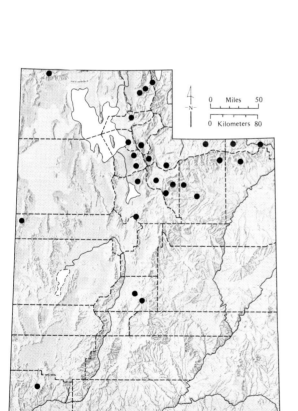

22. *Barbarea orthoceras* Ledeb. Erectpod
wintercress. May-July. Circumboreal perennial
herb; moist meadows, streamside, open woods,
1510-3210 m.

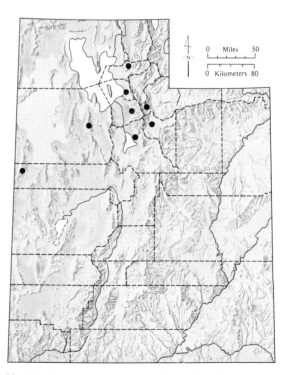

23. *Barbarea vulgaris* R. Br. Yellowrocket
wintercress. May-Oct. Introduced perennial herb;
waste places, oak-maple, meadow communities,
1300-2280 m.

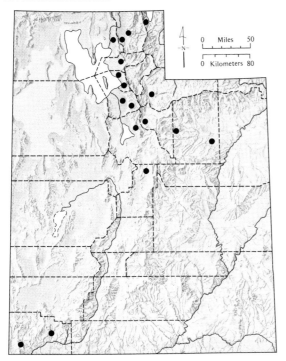

24. *Brassica campestris* L. Bird-rape mustard. Apr.-July. Introduced annual; waste places, 810-3000 m.

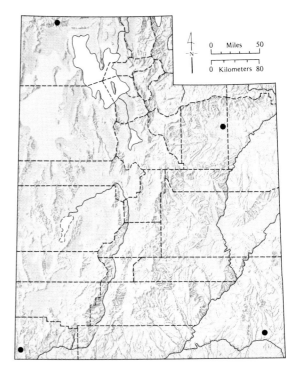

25. *Brassica juncea* (L.) Czern. Indian mustard. Apr.-July. Introduced annual; waste places, sagebrush to aspen communities, 810-2430 m.

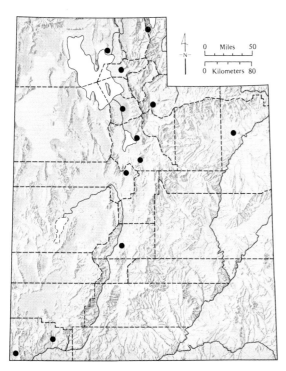

26. *Brassica kaber* (DC.) Wheel. Charlock mustard. Mar.-July. Introduced annual; roadsides, fields, along waterways, 810-1970 m.

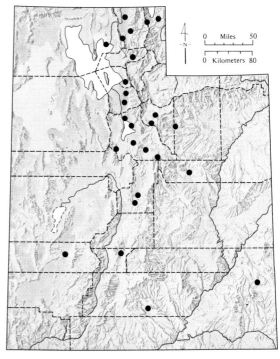

27. *Brassica nigra* (L.) Koch Black mustard. May-Sept. Introduced annual; cultivated fields, roadsides, clearings in oak-maple communities, 1270-2250 m.

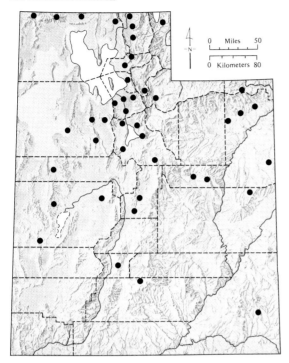

28. *Camelina microcarpa*   DC.   Falseflax.
Apr.-July. Introduced annual; waste places, fields,
open slopes, 1270-2730 m.

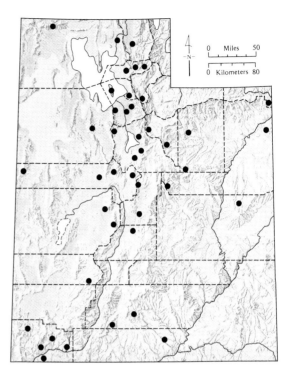

29. *Capsella bursa-pastoris* (L.) Medic.
Shepherd's purse. Mar.-Sept. Introduced annual;
waste places, open slopes, 840-2910 m.

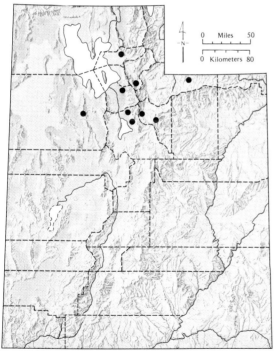

30. *Cardamine breweri* Wats.   Brewer
bittercress.   Apr.-May.   Native perennial herb;
streamside, seep margins, 1660-2430 m.

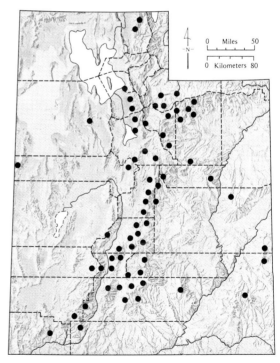

31. *Cardamine cordifolia* Gray Heartleaf
bittercress. May-Aug. Native perennial herb;
streamside, seep margins, 1660-3580 m.

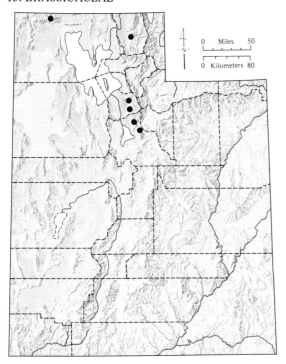

32. *Cardamine hirsuta* L. Hairy bittercress. Apr.-June. Introduced annual; disturbed moist sites, 1360-1820 m.

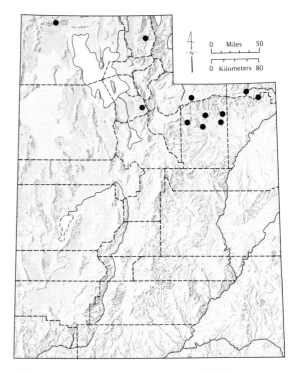

33. *Cardamine pensylvanica* Willd. June-Aug. Native perennial herb; streamside, other moist sites, 1540-2460 m.

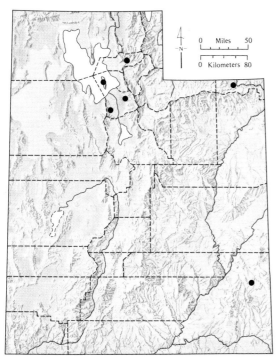

34. *Cardaria chalepensis* (L.) Hand.-Mazz. Cabin whitetop. May-July. Introduced perennial herb; disturbed moist sites, 1600-1820 m.

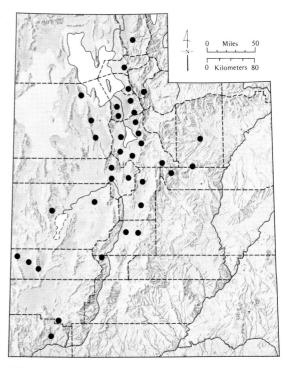

35. *Cardaria draba* (L.) Desv. Whitetop. May-July. Introduced perennial herb; disturbed sites, greasewood to mountain brush communities, 1330-2670 m.

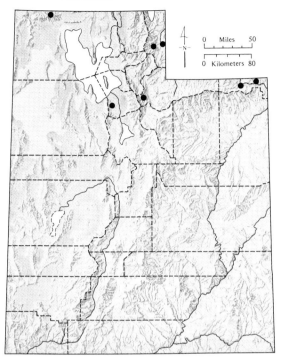

36. *Cardaria pubescens* (Mey.) Jarm. Hairy whitetop. June-July. Native perennial herb; waste places, cultivated fields, 1510-2240 m.

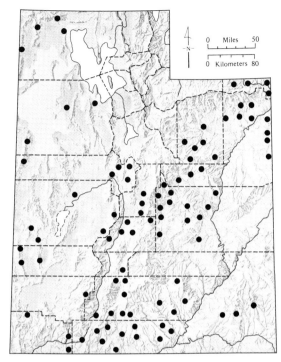

37. *Caulanthus crassicaulis* (Torr.) Wats. Thickstem wildcabbage. May-Aug. Native perennial herb; desert shrub, sagebrush, pinyon-juniper, ponderosa pine communities, 1570-3180 m.

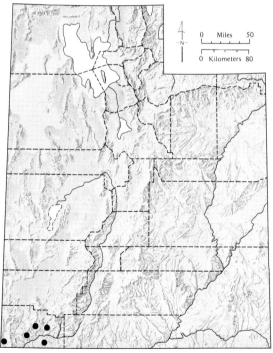

38. *Caulanthus lasiophyllus* (H. & A.) Pays. Apr.-May. Native annual; creosote bush communities, 810-1030 m.

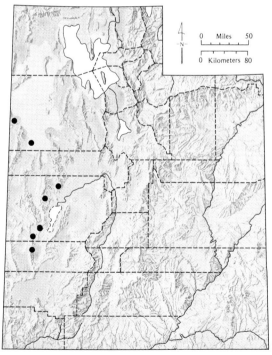

39. *Caulanthus pilosus* Wats. Hairy wild-cabbage. Apr.-May. Native annual or biennial; shadscale, desert shrub communities, 1360-1820 m.

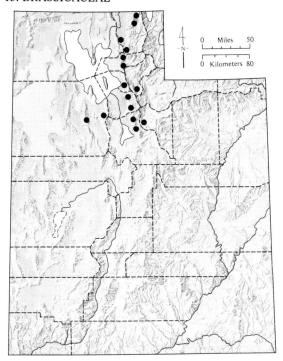

40. *Chlorocrambe hastata* (Wats.) Rydb. Mountain mustard. June-Aug. Native perennial herb; streamside, mountain brush, aspen communities, 1810-3030 m.

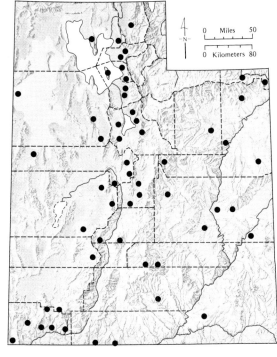

41. *Chorispora tenella* (Pall.) DC. Musk mustard. Apr.-July. Introduced annual; disturbed sites, 800-2280 m.

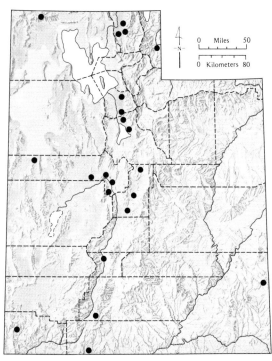

42. *Conringia orientalis* (L.) Dumort. Hare's ear mustard. May-June. Introduced annual; disturbed sites, open slopes, 1360-2120 m.

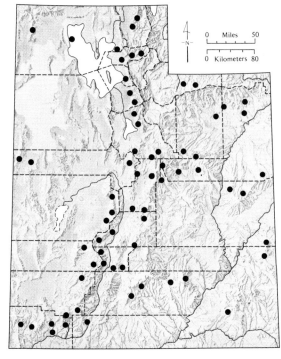

43. *Descurainia californica* (Gray) Schulz California tansymustard. Apr.-Aug. Native annual or biennial; streamside, mountain brush, aspen communities, 1630-3460 m.

162

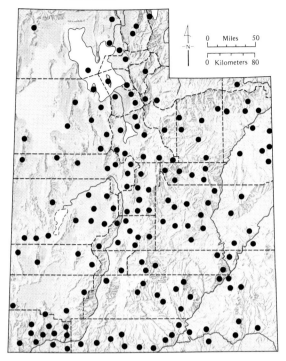

44. *Descurainia pinnata* (Walt.) Britton
Pinnate tansymustard. Mar.-Sept. Native annual;
greasewood to pinyon-juniper, mountain brush,
ponderosa pine communities, 840-2910 m.

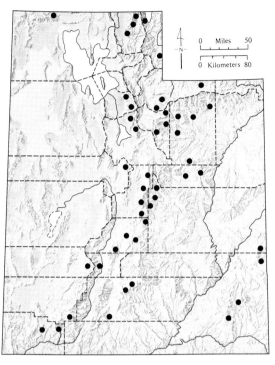

45. *Descurainia richardsonii* (Sweet) Schulz
Richardson tansymustard. July-Aug. Native annual
or biennial; sagebrush to spruce-fir, mountain
meadow communities, 1390-3340 m.

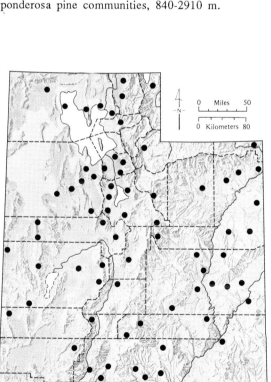

46. *Descurainia sophia* (L.) Prantl   Flixweed.
Mar.-July. Introduced annual; disturbed sites,
greasewood to open grassy slopes, 840-2580 m.

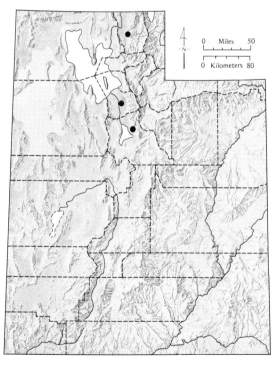

47. *Diplotaxis muralis* (L.) DC.   May-June.
Introduced annual or biennial; waste places, 1300-
1520 m.

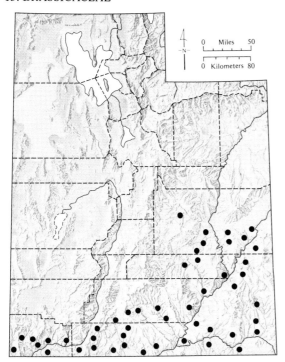

48. **Dithyrea wislizenii** Engelm. Spectacle pod. Apr.-June. Native annual; sandy sites, creosote bush, desert shrub communities, 810-2300 m.

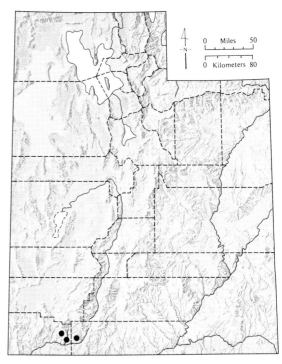

49. **Draba asprella** Greene Rough draba. Apr.-May. Native perennial herb; rocky slopes, oak, ponderosa pine communities, 1720-2120 m.

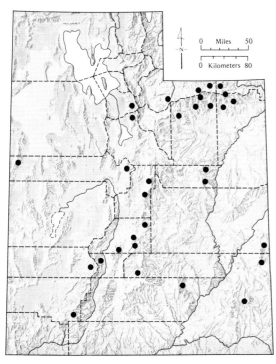

50. **Draba aurea** Vahl Golden draba. June-Aug. Native perennial herb; streamside, aspen, spruce-fir communities, alpine meadows, exposed ridges, 2700-3940 m.

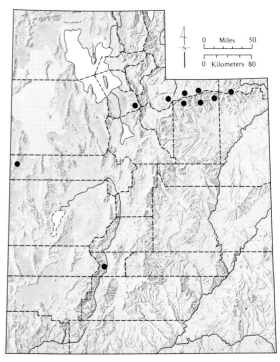

51. **Draba cana** Rydb. June-Aug. Native perennial herb; spruce-fir communities, meadows, talus, krummholz, 3180-3640 m.

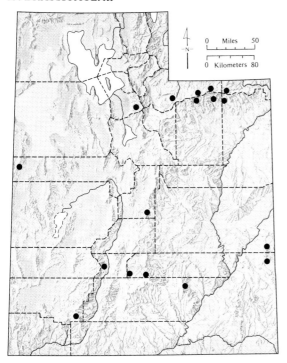

52. *Draba crassifolia* R. Grah. Rocky Mountain draba. July-Sept. Native perennial herb; conifer communities, talus, meadows, rocky ridges, 2880-3490 m.

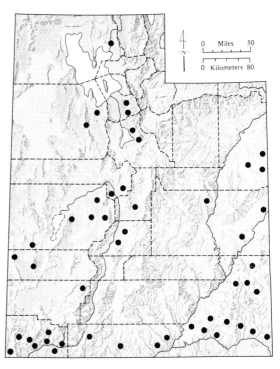

53. *Draba cuneifolia* T. & G. Wedgeleaf draba. Mar.-June. Native annual; creosote bush, pinyon-juniper, mountain brush, ponderosa pine communities, 810-2520 m.

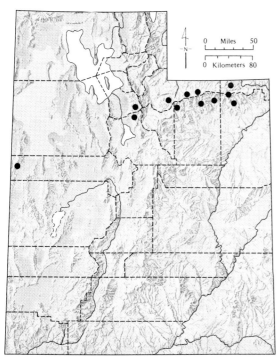

54. *Draba densifolia* T. & G. Rockcress draba. June-Aug. Native perennial herb; wet alpine meadows, exposed rocky ridges, 3030-3490 m.

55. *Draba incerta* Pays. June-July. Native perennial herb; exposed rocky ridges, talus, 2780-2970 m.

165

15. BRASSICACEAE

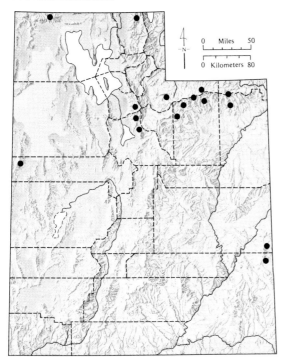

56. **Draba lonchocarpa** Rydb. Spearfruit draba. June-Aug. Native perennial herb; open rocky slopes, alpine meadows, 2360-3640 m.

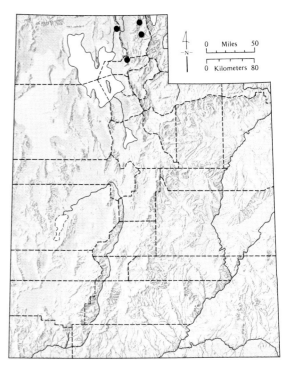

57. **Draba maguirei** C. L. Hitchc. Maguire draba. June-July. Native perennial herb; conifer communities, talus, rocky ridges, 1810-2730 m.

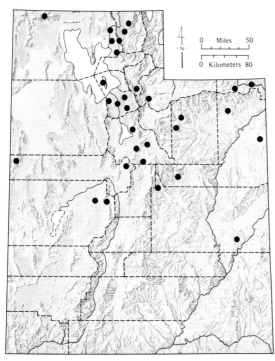

58. **Draba nemorosa** L. Woods draba. Apr.-June. Native annual; grass-forb, sagebrush, oak, ponderosa pine communities, 1280-2520 m.

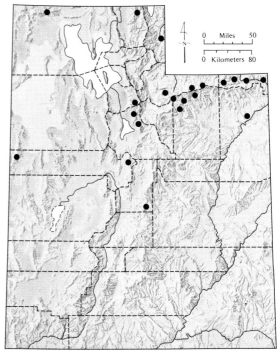

59. **Draba oligosperma** Hook. Doublecomb draba. June-Aug. Native perennial herb; pinyon-juniper, ponderosa pine, spruce-fir communities, exposed alpine ridges, 2120-3790 m.

166

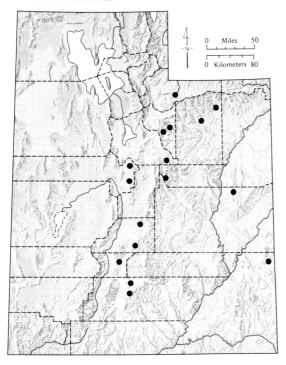

60. ***Draba rectifructa*** C. L. Hitchc. Mountain draba. May-June. Native annual; meadows, grassy slopes, aspen, spruce-fir communities, 2120-3030 m.

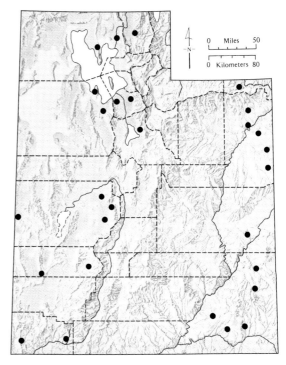

61. ***Draba reptans*** (Lam.) Fern. Dwarf draba. Apr.-June. Native annual; desert shrub, grass-forb, juniper, oak communities, 1280-2120 m.

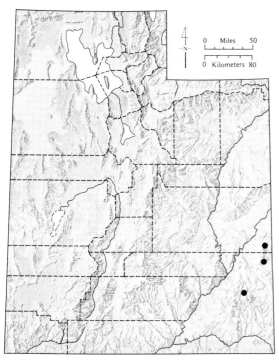

62. ***Draba spectabilis*** Greene Splendid draba. June-July. Native perennial herb; oak, conifer communities, alpine ridges, 2480-3640 m.

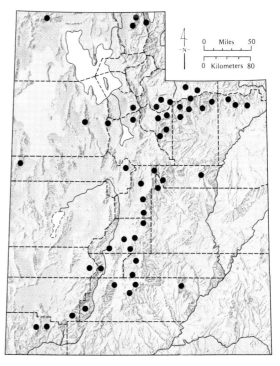

63. ***Draba stenoloba*** Ledeb. Alaska draba. May-Aug. Native annual to perennial herb; sagebrush to spruce-fir communities, meadows, alpine ridges, 1810-3490 m.

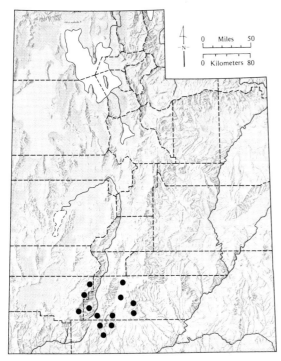

64. *Draba subalpina* Goodm. & Hitchc. Breaks draba. May-July. Native perennial herb; pinyon-juniper, bristlecone pine, spruce-fir communities, alpine slopes, 2210-3430 m.

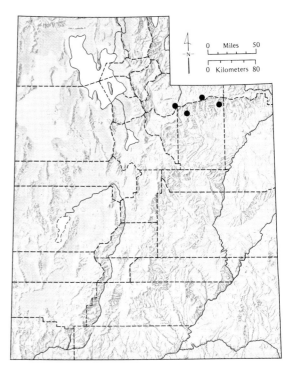

65. *Draba ventosa* Gray Wind draba. July-Aug. Native perennial herb; talus, exposed rocky slopes, 3300-3640 m.

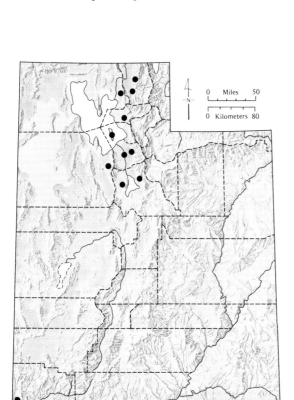

66. *Draba verna* L. Mar.-May. Spring draba. Introduced annual; waste places, greasewood to oak-sagebrush communities, 1300-1640 m.

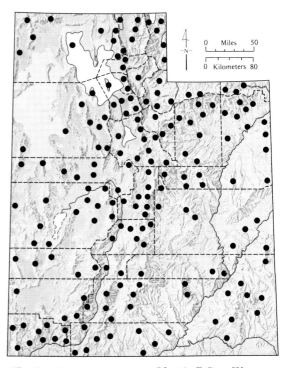

67. *Erysimum asperum* (Nutt.) DC. Western wallflower. Apr.-Aug. Native biennial or perennial herb; desert shrub communities to above timberline, 810-3640 m.

168

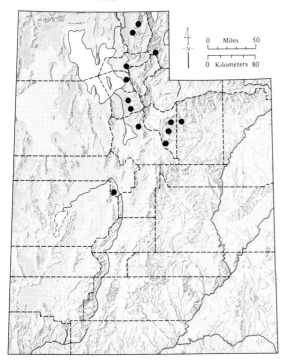

68. **Erysimum cheiranthoides** L. Treacle wallflower. May-July. Native annual or biennial; moist sites, meadows and roadsides, 1420-2430 m.

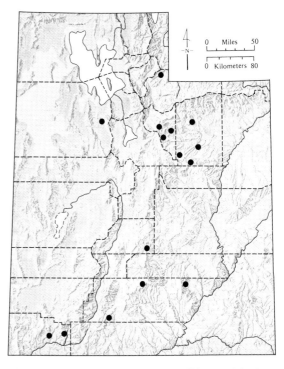

69. **Erysimum inconspicuum** (Wats.) MacM. Small wallflower. May-July. Native biennial or perennial herb; sagebrush to aspen, spruce-fir communities, 1360-2730 m.

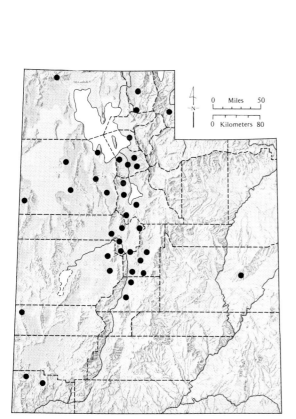

70. **Erysimum repandum** L. Spreading wallflower. Apr.-June. Introduced annual; disturbed sites, 1270-2060 m.

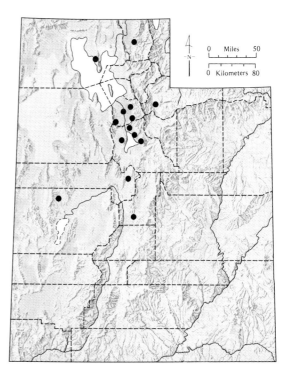

71. **Euclidium syriacum** (L.) R. Br. Syrian mustard. May-June. Introduced annual; waste places, dry foothills, 1300-1640 m.

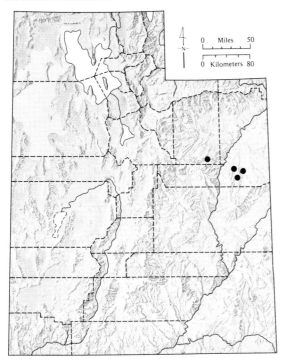

72.*Glaucocarpum suffrutescens (Roll.)
Roll. Toadflax cress. Apr.-May. Native perennial
herb; Green River Formation shales in desert shrub,
pinyon-juniper communities, 1940-1970 m.

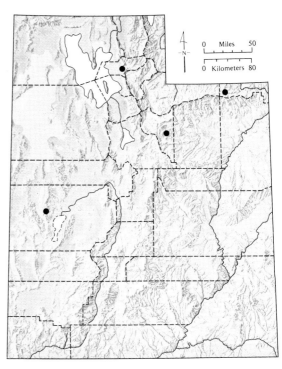

73. Halimolobos virgata (Nutt.) Schulz
Strictweed. July-Aug. Introduced annual or
biennial; meadows, mountain brush communities,
1420-2730 m.

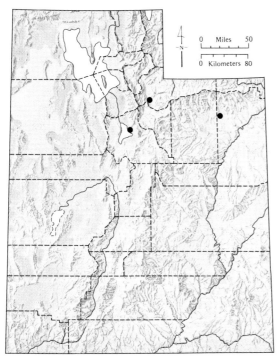

74. Hesperis matronalis L. Dame's rocket.
May-July. Introduced perennial herb; cultivated,
escaping and persistent, 1360-1880 m.

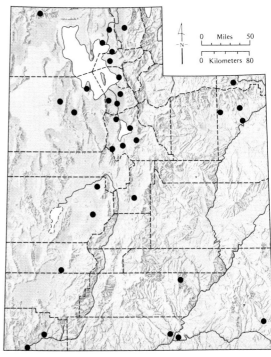

75. Hutchinsia procumbens (L.) Desv.
Hutchins mustard. Apr.-May. Native annual; salt
desert shrub, salt grass meadows, margins of hot
springs, hanging gardens, 840-2120 m.

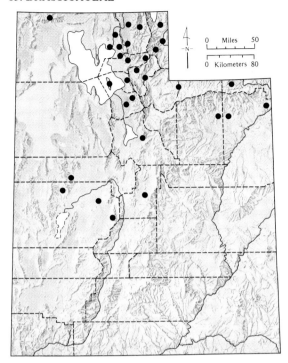

76. *Isatis tinctoria* L. Dyer's woad. May-June.
Introduced biennial or perennial herb; roadsides,
fallow fields, dry foothills, 1300-2580 m.

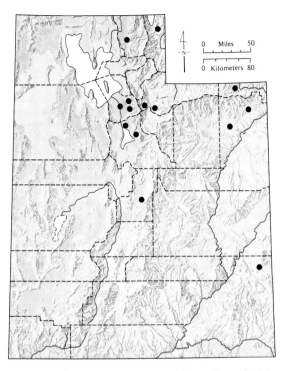

77. *Lepidium campestre* (L.) R. Br. Field
pepperweed. May-July. Introduced annual;
disturbed sites, greasewood to dry foothill
communities, 1300-2400 m.

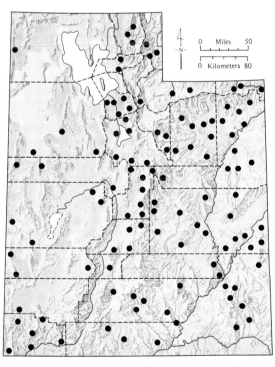

78. *Lepidium densiflorum* Schrad. Prairie
pepperweed. Apr.-Sept. Native annual; greasewood
communities to open woods, often in disturbed
sites, 840-3030 m.

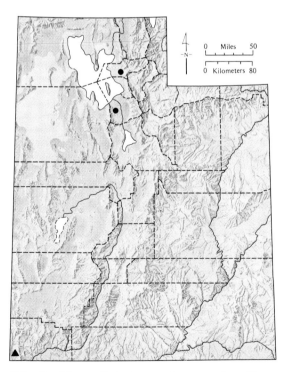

79. *Lepidium dictyotum* Gray Apr.-May.
Native annual; salt grass meadow, salt desert shrub
communities, 1270-1310 m.

15. BRASSICACEAE

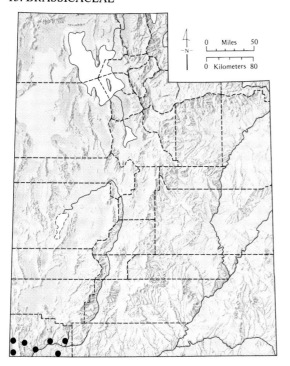

80. **Lepidium fremontii** Wats. Desert pepperweed. Apr.-May. Native perennial herb or subshrub; creosote bush, desert shrub communities, 810-1100 m.

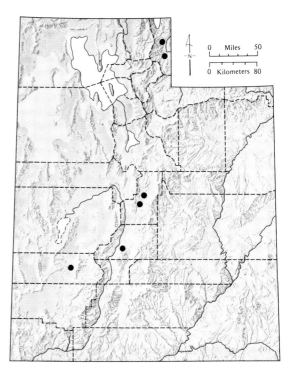

81. **Lepidium integrifolium** Nutt. May-July. Native perennial herb; salt grass meadows, 1510-1910 m.

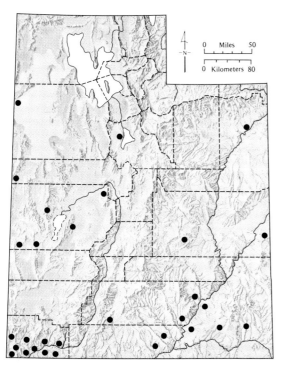

82. **Lepidium lasiocarpum** Nutt. Shaggyfruit pepperweed. Feb.-May. Native annual; creosote bush, desert shrub communities, 810-2120 m.

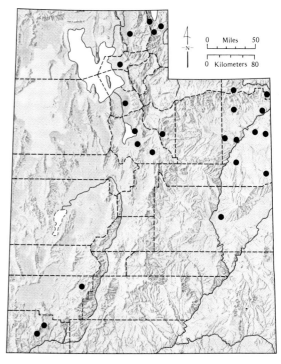

83. **Lepidium latifolium** L. Perennial pepperweed. July-Aug. Introduced perennial herb; disturbed mesic to moist sites, 1280-2150 m.

172

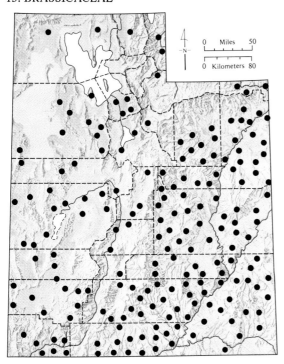

84. *Lepidium montanum* Nutt. Mountain pepperweed. Apr.-Aug. Native perennial herb; desert shrub communities to alpine slopes, 810-3030 m.

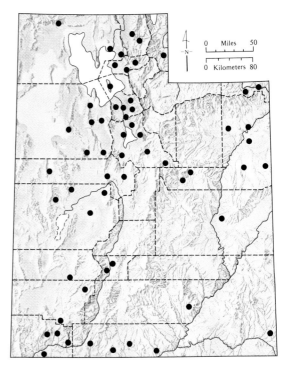

85. *Lepidium perfoliatum* L. Clasping-leaf pepperweed. Apr.-July. Introduced annual; disturbed sites, greasewood communities to open slopes, 810-2430 m.

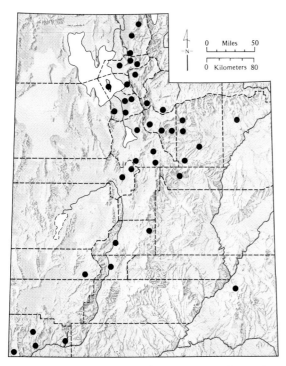

86. *Lepidium virginicum* L. Virginia pepperweed. Apr.-July. Native annual; disturbed sites, grass-sagebrush communities, streamside, 1060-2730 m.

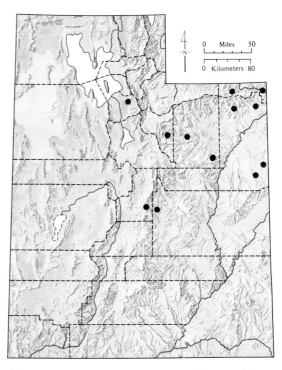

87. *Lesquerella alpina* (Nutt.) Wats. June-July. Native perennial herb; pinyon-juniper communities to dry open slopes, 1840-2370 m.

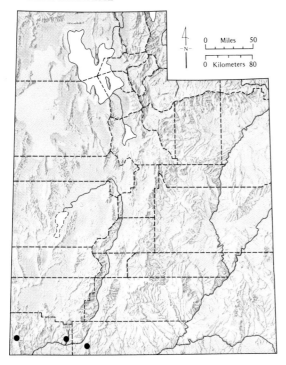

88. *Lesquerella arizonica* Wats. Arizona bladderpod. May-June. Native perennial herb; sagebrush, oak-mountain brush, pinyon-juniper communities, 1510-2150 m.

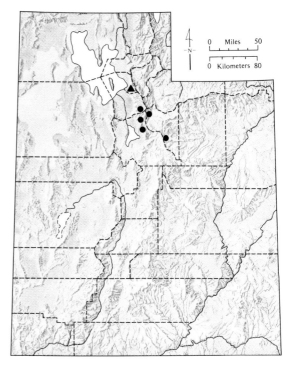

89. *Lesquerella garrettii* Pays. Garrett bladderpod. June-Aug. Native perennial herb; open woods, exposed rocky ridges, 3030-3640 m.

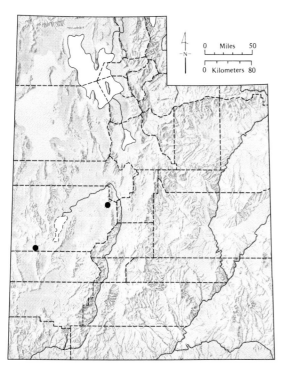

90. *Lesquerella goodrichii* Roll. Goodrich bladderpod. May-June. Native perennial herb; pinyon-juniper, aspen-fir communities, 2180-2430 m.

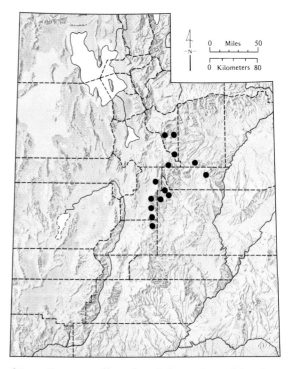

91. *Lesquerella hemiphysaria* Maguire Skyline bladderpod. May-Aug. Native perennial herb; spruce-fir, meadows, rocky ridgetops, 2120-3030 m.

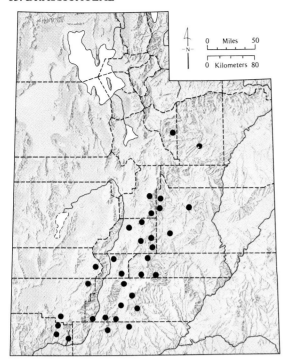

92. *Lesquerella intermedia* (Wats.) Heller Watson bladderpod. May-Aug. Native perennial herb; sagebrush, pinyon-juniper, ponderosa pine communities, 1360-2910 m.

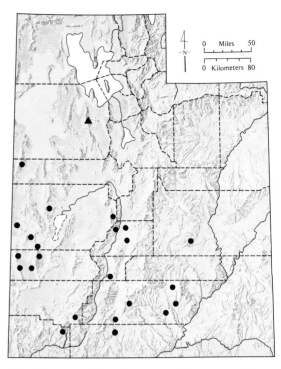

93. *Lesquerella kingii* Wats. King bladderpod. May-July. Native perennial herb; sagebrush, pinyon-juniper, ponderosa pine communities, 1360-3340 m.

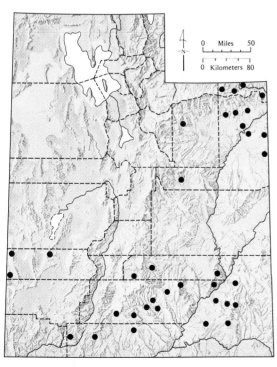

94. *Lesquerella ludoviciana* (Nutt.) Wats. Silver bladderpod. May-July. Native perennial herb; sagebrush, pinyon-juniper, ponderosa pine, spruce-fir communities, 1510-2730 m.

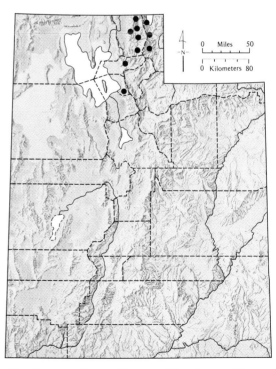

95. *Lesquerella multiceps* Maguire Many-headed bladderpod. May-Aug. Native perennial herb; oak, aspen communities, rocky slopes, 1810-2940 m.

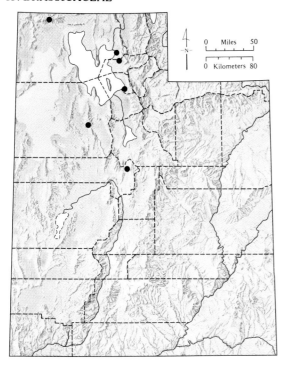

96. *Lesquerella occidentalis* Wats. Western bladderpod. May-Aug. Native perennial herb; sagebrush-grass, pinyon-juniper, aspen, spruce-fir communities, talus, 1970-3340 m.

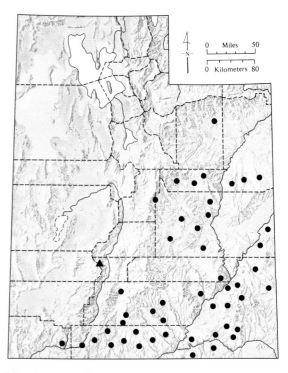

97. *Lesquerella rectipes* Woot. & Standl. Colorado bladderpod. June-Aug. Native perennial herb; desert shrub, sagebrush, pinyon-juniper, ponderosa pine communities, 1180-2550 m.

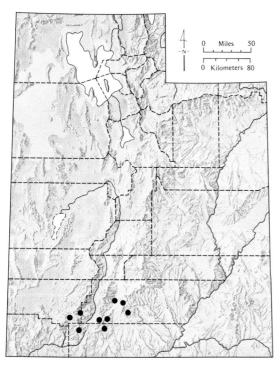

98. *Lesquerella rubicundula* Roll. Breaks bladderpod. May-July. Native perennial herb; juniper, spruce-fir, bristlecone pine, ponderosa pine communities, 2120-3340 m.

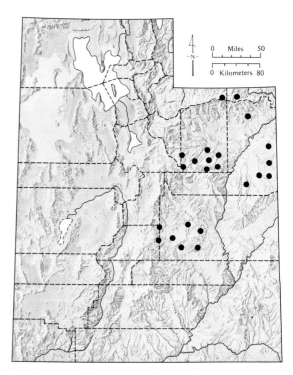

99. *Lesquerella subumbellata* Roll. Rollins bladderpod. May-July. Native perennial herb; sagebrush, pinyon-juniper, Douglas fir communities, 1720-2430 m.

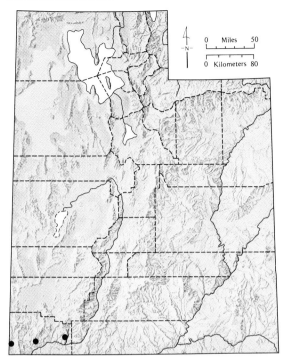

100. *Lesquerella tenella* A. Nels. Slender bladderpod. Mar.-Apr. Native annual; Joshua tree, creosote bush, desert shrub, juniper communities, 840-1120 m.

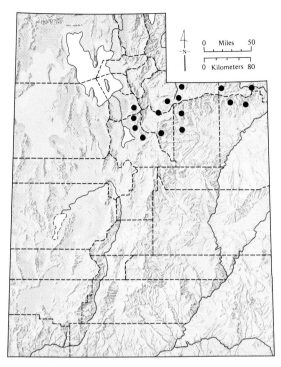

101. *Lesquerella utahensis* Rydb. Utah bladderpod. June-Aug. Native perennial herb; openings in spruce-fir, krummholz communities, 2720-3340 m.

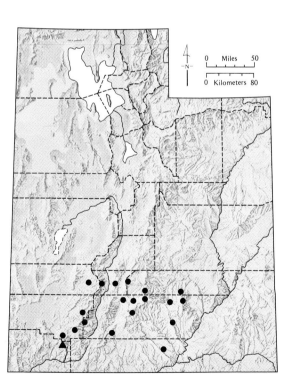

102. *Lesquerella wardii* Wats. Ward bladderpod. June-July. Native perennial herb; sagebrush, oak, ponderosa pine, meadow, aspen, spruce-fir, alpine communities, 1810-3340 m.

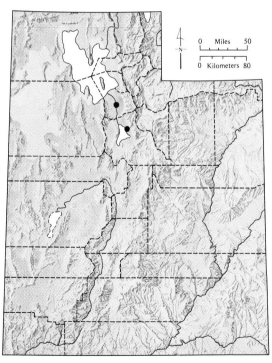

103. *Lobularia maritima* (L.) Desv. Sweet alyssum. June-Aug. Introduced annual; cultivated, escaping and persistent, 1270-1520 m.

15. BRASSICACEAE

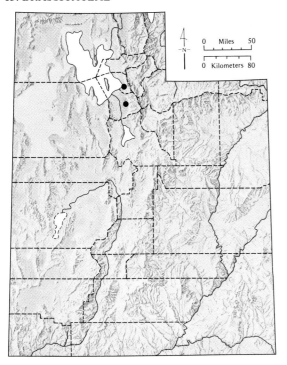

104. *Lunaria annua* L. Honesty. May-July. Introduced annual; cultivated, escaping and persistent, 1360-1460 m.

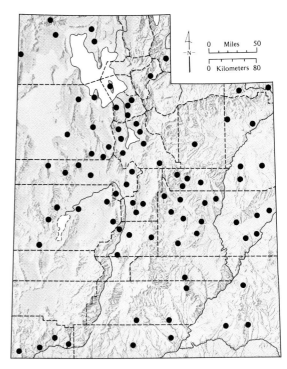

105. *Malcolmia africana* R. Br. African mustard. Apr.-July. Introduced annual; roadsides and other disturbed sites, 840-2670 m.

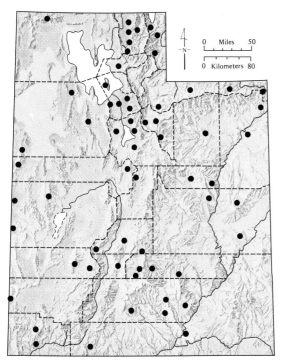

106. *Nasturtium officinale* R. Br. Watercress. May-Aug. Introduced perennial herb; slow-moving streams, shallow water of marshes, meadows, 910-2730 m.

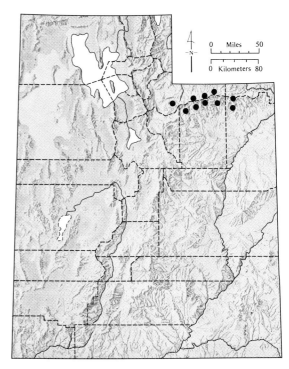

107. *Parrya rydbergii* Botsch. Uinta parrya. July-Aug. Circumboreal perennial herb; talus, alpine slopes, 3180-3940 m.

178

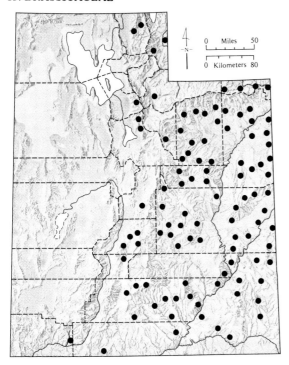

108. *Physaria acutifolia* Rydb. Rydberg twinpod. Apr.-June. Native perennial herb; desert shrub, sagebrush, pinyon-juniper, other pine communities, talus, 1270-3430 m.

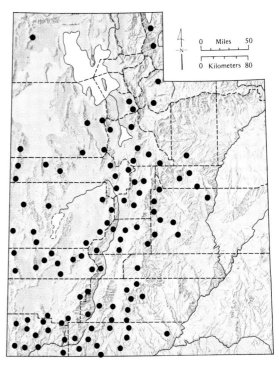

109. *Physaria chambersii* Roll. Chamber twinpod. Apr.-June. Native perennial herb; desert shrub to ponderosa pine and spruce-fir communities, meadows, talus, 940-3400 m.

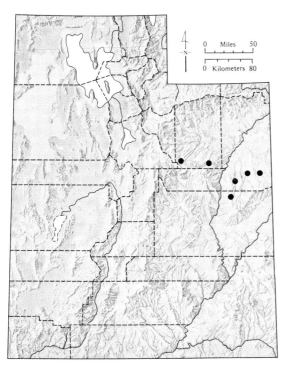

110. *Physaria floribunda* Rydb. May-June. Native perennial herb; soils developed on clay and shale in pinyon-juniper communities, 1720-2180 m.

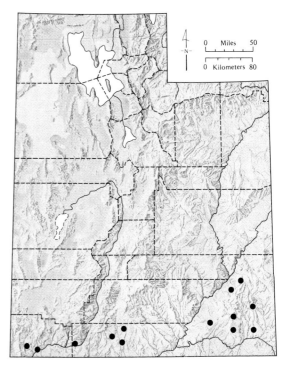

111. *Physaria newberryi* Gray Newberry twinpod. Apr.-June. Native perennial herb; creosote bush to pinyon-juniper communities, 880-1880 m.

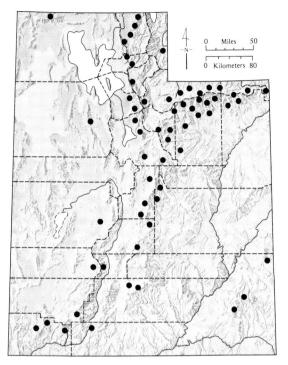

112. *Rorippa curvipes* Greene May-Aug.
Native annual to perennial herb; streamside, margins
of ponds, seeps and springs, 1300-3430 m.

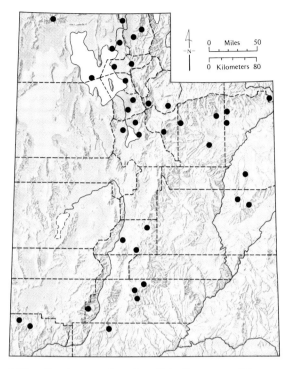

113. *Rorippa palustris* (L.) Besser Marsh
yellowcress. May-Aug. Circumboreal annual or
biennial; streamside, margins of ponds, seeps and
springs, 1300-2800 m.

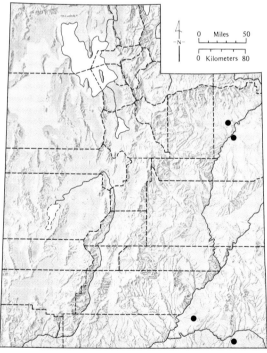

114. *Rorippa sinuata* (Nutt.) Hitchc. Apr.-
Sept. Native perennial herb; streamside, margins
of ponds, seeps and springs, 1130-1430 m.

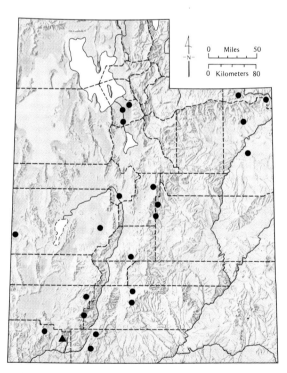

115. *Rorippa tenerrima* Greene July-Aug.
Native annual; streamside, margins of ponds, seeps
and springs, 1300-2910 m.

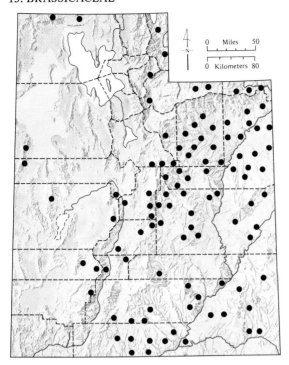

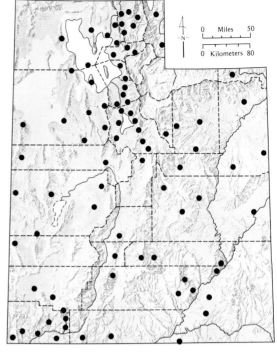

116. *Schoenocrambe linifolia* (Nutt.) Greene May-July. Native perennial herb; shadscale, desert shrub, sagebrush, pinyon-juniper to aspen communities, 1210-2670 m.

117. *Sisymbrium altissimum* L. Jim Hill mustard. May-July. Introduced annual; dry, disturbed sites, 1300-2400 m.

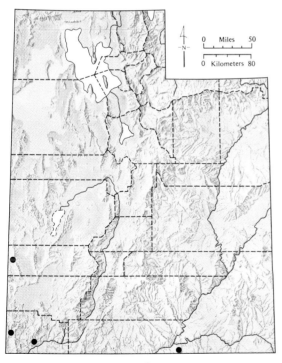

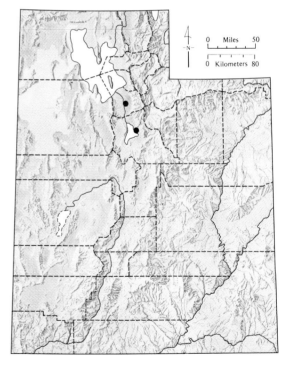

118. *Sisymbrium irio* L. London rocket. Mar.-Apr. Introduced annual; dry waste places, 840-1670 m.

119. *Sisymbrium officinale* (L.) Scop. Hedge mustard. May-Sept. Introduced annual; disturbed sites, 1300-1370 m.

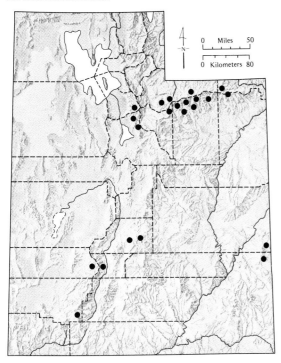

120. *Smelowskia calycina* C. A. Mey. June-Aug. Native perennial herb; open, usually rocky slopes, 2720-3940 m.

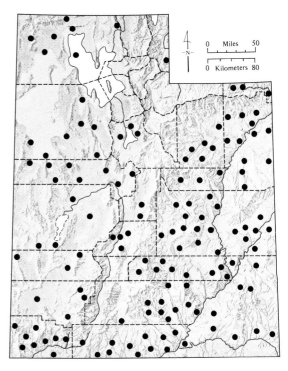

121. *Stanleya pinnata* (Pursh) Britton Prince's plume. May-Aug. Native perennial herb; greasewood, shadscale, desert shrub to ponderosa pine communities, 910-2780 m.

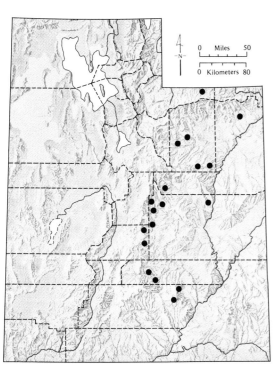

122. *Stanleya viridiflora* Nutt. Green prince's plume. July-Aug. Native perennial herb; sagebrush, pinyon-juniper, ponderosa pine communities, 1510-2730 m.

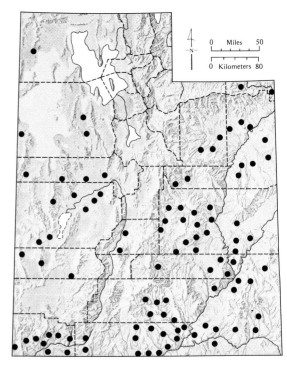

123. *Streptanthella longirostris* (Wats.) Rydb. Mar.-June. Native annual; creosote bush, desert shrub, pinyon-juniper communities, grassy slopes, 840-2340 m.

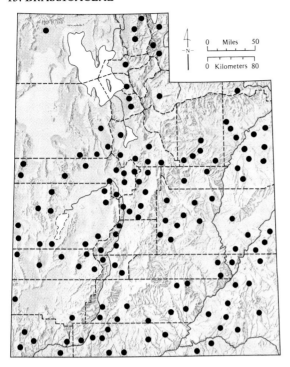

124. *Streptanthus cordatus* Nutt. Twistflower. June-Aug. Native perennial herb; desert shrub, sagebrush, oak, pinyon-juniper, fir communities, 1060-2940 m.

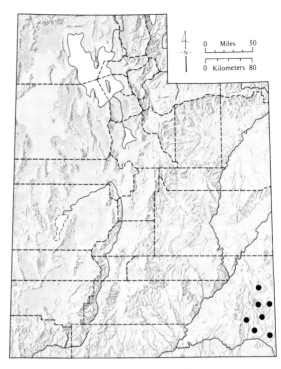

125. *Thelypodiopsis aurea* (Eastw.) Rydb. Apr.-May. Native biennial or perennial herb; desert shrub, sagebrush, pinyon-juniper communities, 1300-2120 m.

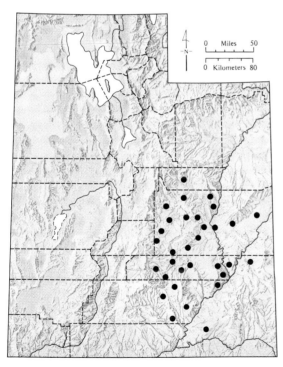

126. *Thelypodiopsis divaricata* (Roll.) Welsh & Reveal Mar.-May. Native annual or biennial; shadscale, desert shrub, pinyon-juniper communities, 1210-2060 m.

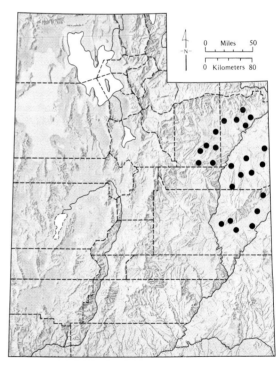

127. *Thelypodiopsis elegans* (Jones) Rydb. May-July. Native annual or biennial; shadscale, desert shrub, sagebrush, pinyon-juniper communities, 1450-2000 m.

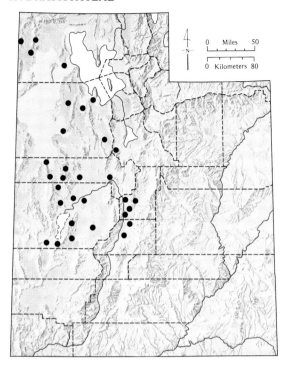

128. *Thelypodiopsis vermicularis* (Welsh & Reveal) Roll. May-June. Native annual or biennial; salt desert shrub, desert shrub communities, 1330-1670 m.

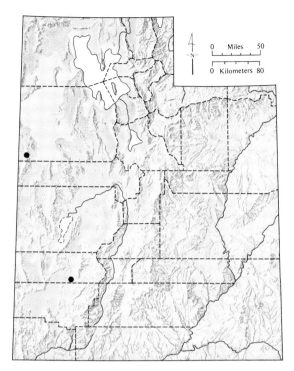

129. *Thelypodium flexuosum* Robins. May-June. Native biennial or perennial herb; greasewood communities, 1510-1670 m.

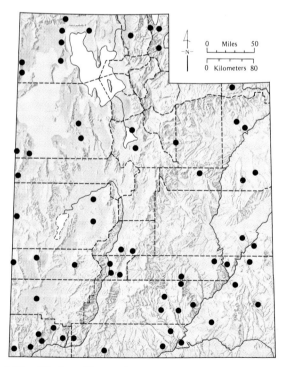

130. *Thelypodium integrifolium* (Nutt.) Endl. July-Aug. Native biennial; moist sites, salt grass meadow, greasewood to pinyon-juniper communities, 840-2430 m.

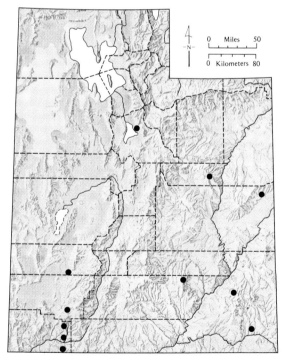

131. *Thelypodium laxiflorum* Al-Shehbaz Looseflower thelypody. June-Aug. Native biennial; mountain brush, pinyon-juniper, bristlecone pine, ponderosa pine, aspen-fir communities,1210-3030 m.

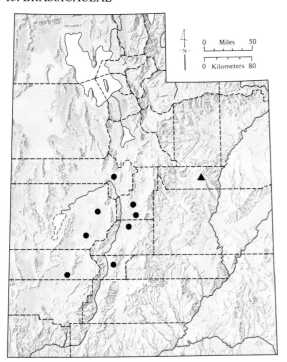

132. ***Thelypodium rollinsii*** Al-Shehbaz
June-Oct. Native biennial; moist sites in salt grass
meadow, greasewood, streamside communities,
1420-1580 m.

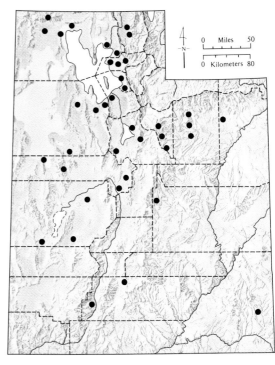

133. ***Thelypodium sagittatum*** (Nutt.) Endl.
Arrowleaf thelypody. Apr.-June. Native biennial
or perennial herb; salt desert shrub, sagebrush-
grass communities, 1300-3120 m.

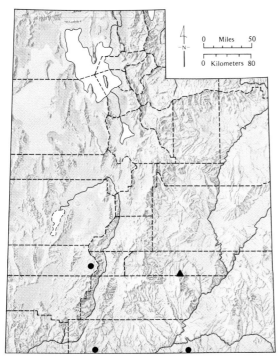

134. ***Thelypodium wrightii*** Gray July-Aug.
Native biennial; desert shrub, pinyon-juniper,
ponderosa pine communities, 1840-2640 m.

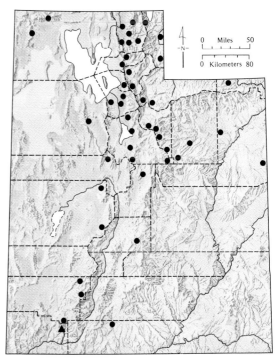

135. ***Thlaspi arvense*** L. Field pennycress.
Apr.-Aug. Introduced annual; disturbed sites, 1300-
1700 m.

15. BRASSICACEAE

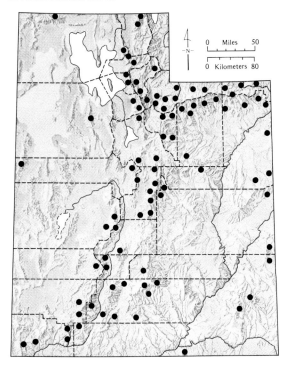

136. *Thlaspi montanum* L. May-Aug.
Circumboreal perennial herb; mesic to moist sites, sagebrush, mountain brush to spruce-fir, alpine communities, 1060-3640 m.

137. *Thysanocarpus curvipes* Hook. Sand fringepod. Apr.-May. Native annual; creosote bush, desert shrub communities, 840-1520 m.

16. CACTACEAE

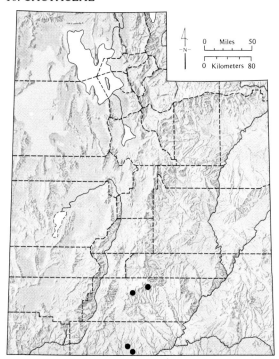

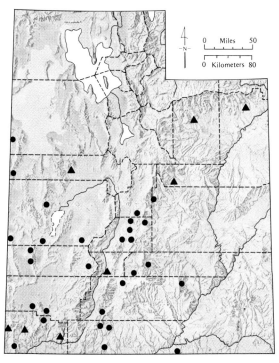

1. *Coryphantha missouriensis* (Sw.) Britt. & Rose Missouri coryphantha. May-June. Native perennial; open rocky slopes in desert shrub, juniper, ponderosa pine communities, 1450-2730 m.

2. *Coryphantha vivipara* (Nutt.) Britt. & Rose Viviparous coryphantha. May-July. Native perennial; open rocky slopes in desert shrub, sagebrush, pinyon-juniper communities, 910-2580 m.

16. CACTACEAE

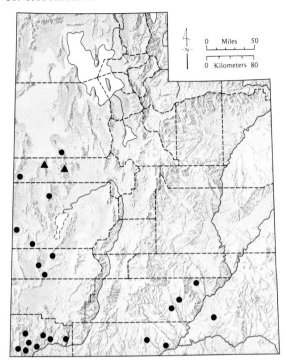

3. *Echinocereus engelmannii* (Parry) Lem. Engelmann hedgehog cactus. May-June. Native perennial; open rocky slopes in creosote bush, desert shrub, pinyon-juniper, mountain brush communities, 880-1880 m.

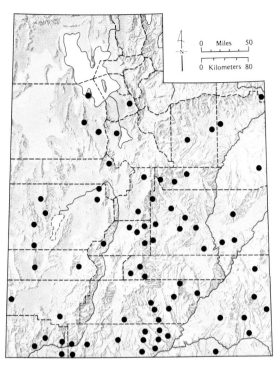

4. *Echinocereus triglochidiatus* Engelm. Claret cup. May-July. Native perennial; open rocky slopes in salt desert shrub, pinyon-juniper, sagebrush communities, 970-2730 m.

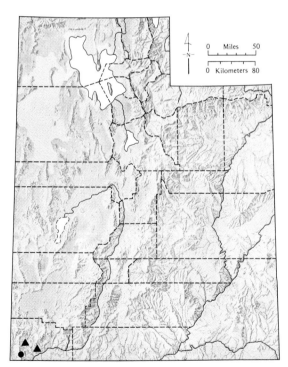

5. *Neolloydia johnsonii* (Parry) L. Benson Johnson neolloydia. Apr.-May. Native perennial; creosote bush, desert shrub communities, 810-1210 m.

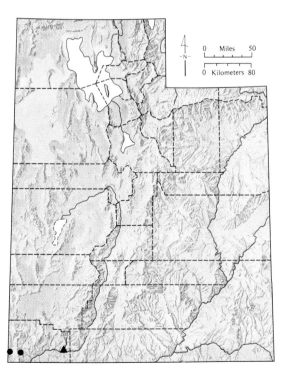

6. *Opuntia acanthocarpa* Engelm. & Bigel. Buckhorn cholla. Apr.-May. Native shrub; Joshua tree, creosote bush communities, 810-1060 m.

187

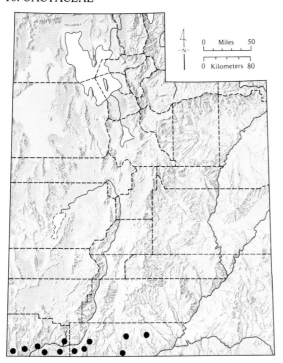

7. *Opuntia basilaris* Engelm. & Bigel. Beavertail pricklypear. Apr.-May. Native perennial; cliffs and rocky sites in creosote bush, desert shrub, pinyon-juniper communities, 810-2060 m.

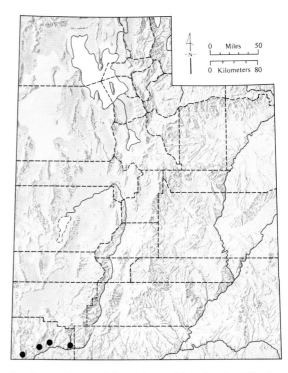

8. *Opuntia chlorotica* Engel. & Bigel. Pancake pricklypear. May-June. Native shrubby perennial; desert shrub communities, 970-1210 m.

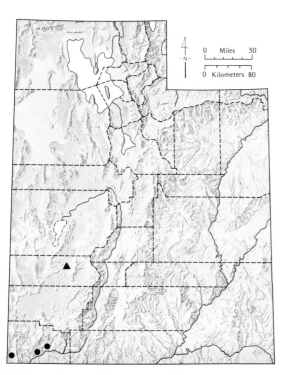

9. *Opuntia echinocarpa* Engel. & Bigel. Strawtop pricklypear; silver or golden cholla. Apr.-May. Native shrub; sandy sites in desert shrub, pinyon-juniper communities, 810-1210 m.

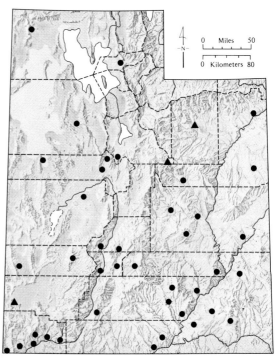

10. *Opuntia erinacea* Engelm. & Bigel. Grizzlybear pricklypear. May-July. Native perennial; creosote bush, desert shrub, shadscale, pinyon-juniper, ponderosa pine, aspen communities, 1270-2790 m.

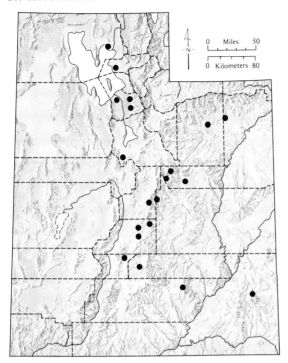

11. *Opuntia fragilis* (Nutt.) Haw. June-July. Little or brittle pricklypear. Native perennial; sagebrush, pinyon-juniper, mountain brush, aspen communities, 1270-2580 m.

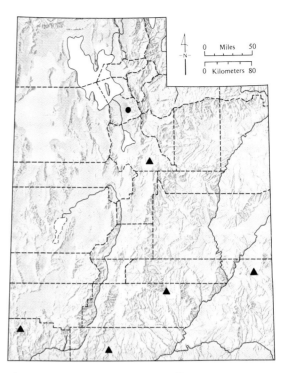

12. *Opuntia macrorhiza* Engelm. Plains pricklypear. May-June. Native perennial; pinyon-juniper, mountain brush communities, 1360-1730 m.

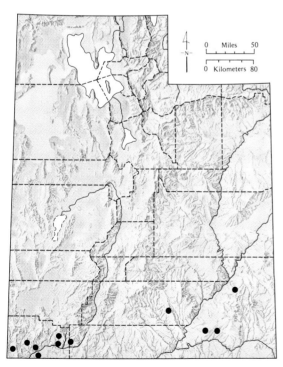

13. *Opuntia phaeacantha* Engelm. Berry pricklypear. May-June. Native perennial; creosote bush, desert shrub, sagebrush, pinyon-juniper, oak communities, 910-2000 m.

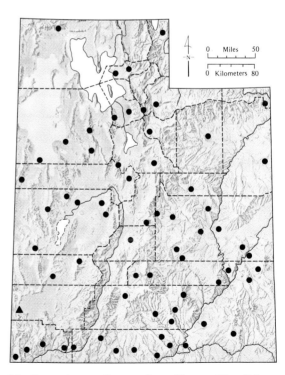

14. *Opuntia polyacantha* Haw. May-July. Native perennial; salt bush, desert shrub, sagebrush, pinyon-juniper, oak, aspen communities, 1060-2180 m.

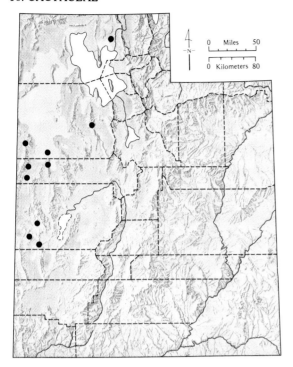

15. *Opuntia pulchella* Engelm. Sand cholla. May-June. Native perennial; sandy or rocky alluvial fans in desert shrub, shadscale communities, 1360-1520 m.

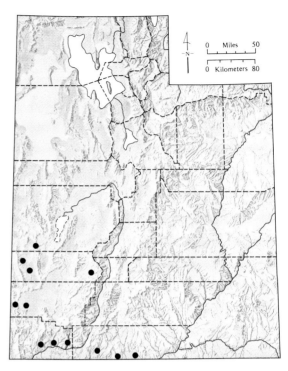

16. *Opuntia whipplei* Engelm. & Bigel. Whipple cholla. May-June. Native shrubby or mat-forming perennial; creosote bush, desert shrub, pinyon-juniper communities, 970-1970 m.

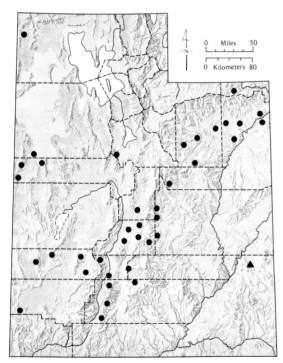

17. *Pediocactus simpsonii* (Engelm.) Britt. & Rose Simpson pediocactus. May-June. Native perennial; shadscale, desert shrub, sagebrush, pinyon-juniper, conifer communities, 1450-2730 m.

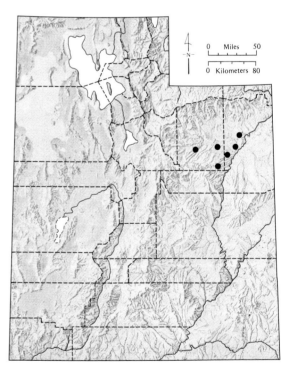

18.**Sclerocactus glaucus* (K. Schum) L. Benson May-June. Native perennial; shadscale, desert shrub communities, 1360-1520 m.

16. CACTACEAE

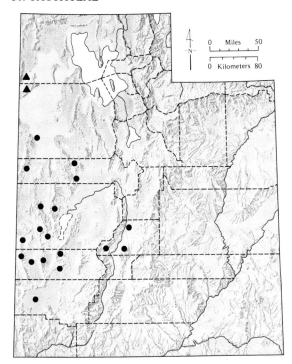

19. *Sclerocactus pubispinus* (Engelm.) L. Benson May-June. Native perennial; salt desert shrub, desert shrub, sagebrush, pinyon-juniper communities, 1690-1940 m.

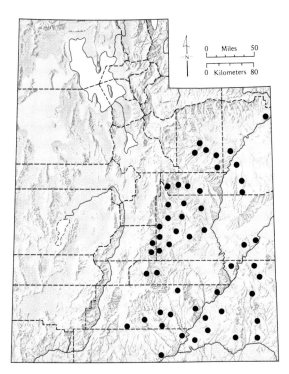

20. *Sclerocactus whipplei* (Engelm. & Bigel.) Britt. & Rose May-June. Native perennial; shadscale, desert shrub to ponderosa pine communities, 1570-2430 m.

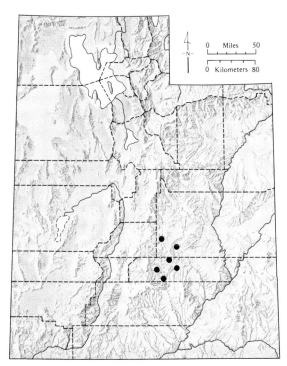

21. **Sclerocactus wrightiae* L. Benson Wright fishhook cactus. May-June. Native perennial; shadscale, desert shrub to juniper communities, 1360-1730 m.

17. CALLITRICHACEAE

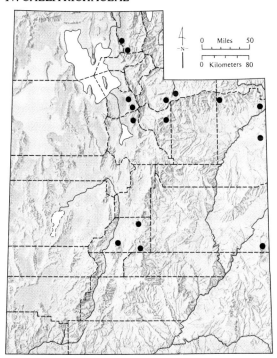

1. *Callitriche hermaphroditica* L. Secret waterstarwort. July-Aug. Native annual to perennial herb; sluggish streams, reservoirs, ponds, lakes, 1630-3180 m.

17. CALLITRICHACEAE

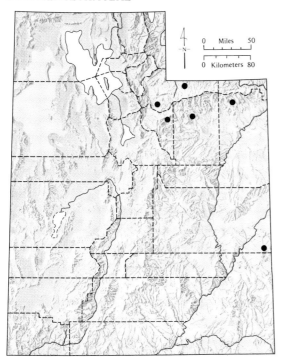

2. *Callitriche heterophylla* Pursh Larger waterstarwort. Aug.-Sept. Native annual to perennial herb; sluggish streams, ponds, lakes, 2120-3150 m.

3. *Callitriche palustris* L. Common waterstarwort. July-Oct. Circumboreal annual to perennial herb; sluggish streams, ponds, lakes, 1940-3340 m.

18. CAMPANULACEAE

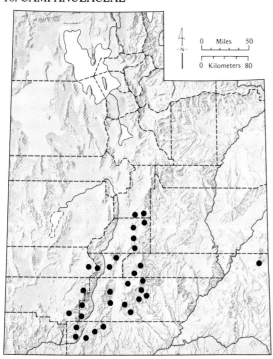

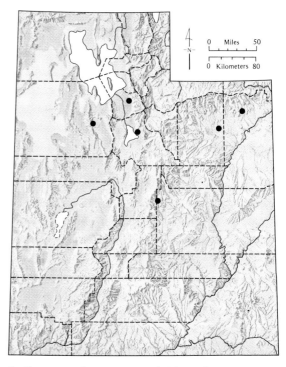

1. *Campanula parryi* Gray Parry bellflower. June-Aug. Native perennial herb; sagebrush, ponderosa pine, spruce-fir, meadow communities, 1970-3180 m.

2. *Campanula rapunculoides* L. Creeping bellflower. July-Oct. Introduced perennial herb; roadsides, gardens, other disturbed sites, 1300-2490 m.

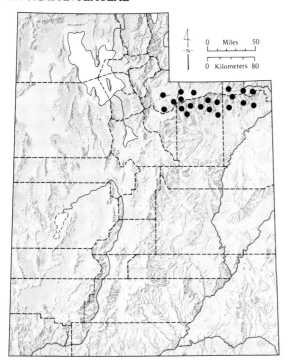

3. *Campanula rotundifolia* L. American
bellflower. July-Sept. Circumboreal perennial
herb; rocky sites, streamside, meadows, lodgepole
pine, aspen, spruce-fir communities, talus, 1510-
3640 m.

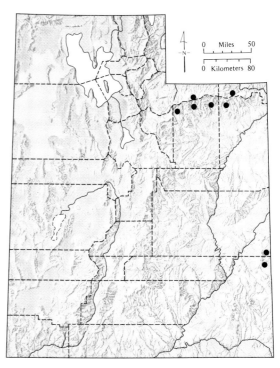

4. *Campanula uniflora* L. Singleflower
bellflower. July-Aug. Circumboreal perennial
herb; sedge meadow, spruce-fir, alpine
communities, 3630-3940 m.

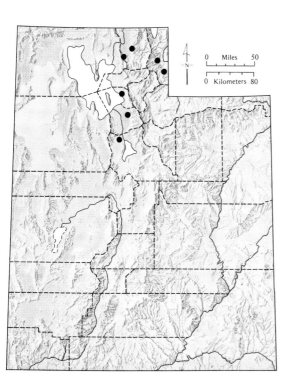

5. *Downingia laeta* (Greene) Greene July-
Sept. Native annual; shallow water, drying mud
flats, 1330-1640 m.

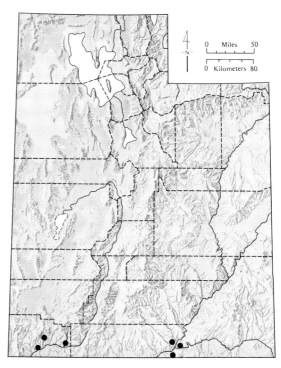

6. *Lobelia cardinalis* L. Scarlet lobelia.
May-Sept. Native perennial herb; shaded canyons,
seep margins, stream banks, other moist places,
1000-1610 m.

18. CAMPANULACEAE

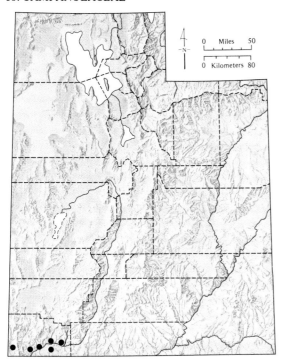

7. Nemacladus glanduliferus Jeps. Threadplant. Apr.-May. Native annual; creosote bush, bursage communities, 910-1060 m.

8. Porterella carnosula (H. & A.) Torr. Fleshy porterella. June-Aug. Native annual; shallow water, wet meadows, 2880-3030 m.

19. CANNABACEAE

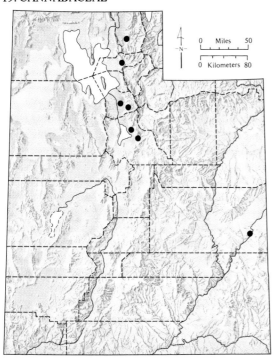

1. Cannabis sativa L. Marijuana; hemp. July-Sept. Introduced annual; cultivated and escaping, 1300-1520 m.

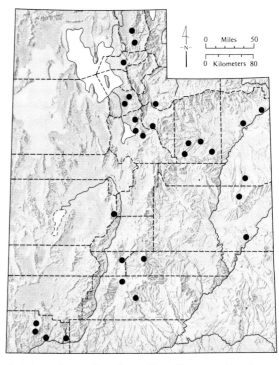

2. Humulus lupulus L. Hops. July-Aug. Native perennial vine; irrigated fields, streamside, wet meadows, 1300-2430 m.

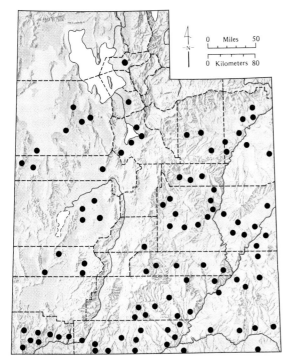

1. *Cleome lutea* Hook. Yellow beeplant. Apr.-Aug. Native annual; shadscale, desert shrub to pinyon-juniper communities, often in the wake of disturbance, 840-1970 m.

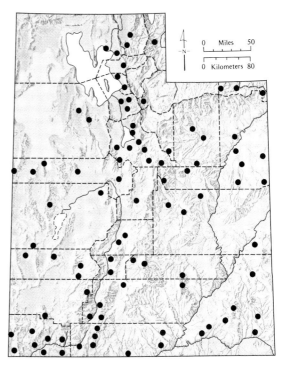

2. *Cleome serrulata* Pursh   Rocky Mountain beeplant. June-Sept. Native annual; shadscale, desert shrub, sagebrush, meadow communities, often in the wake of disturbance, 910-2430 m.

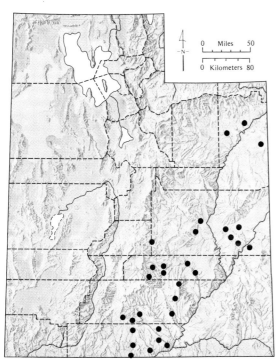

3. *Cleomella palmerana* Jones   Palmer cleomella. May-July. Native annual; mat saltbush, shadscale, desert shrub communities, 1210-1940 m.

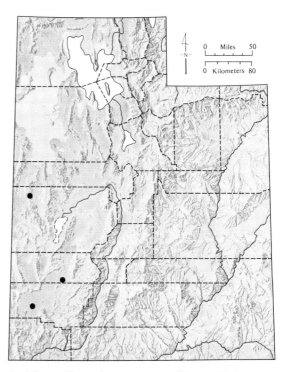

4. *Cleomella plocasperma* Wats. Twistseed cleomella. June-Aug. Native annual; salt grass, salt desert shrub communities, 1060-1820 m.

195

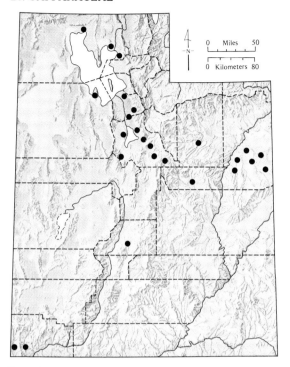

5. *Polanisia dodecandra* (L.) DC. Clammy weed. July-Aug. Native annual; greasewood, sagebrush, oak communities, often in the wake of disturbance, 810-1580 m.

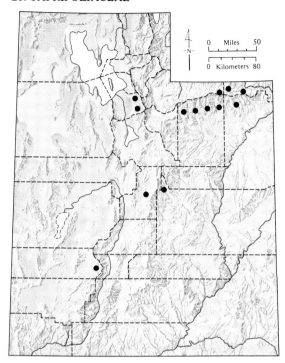

1. *Linnaea borealis* L. Linnaeus twinflower. June-Sept. Circumboreal subshrub; streamside, meadow, lodgepole pine, aspen, spruce-fir communities, 1810-2880 m.

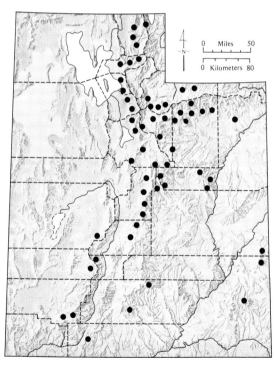

2. *Lonicera involucrata* (Rich.) Spreng. Bearberry honeysuckle. June-Aug. Native shrub; streamside, meadows, shaded sites in lodgepole pine, aspen, spruce-fir communities, 1510-3340 m.

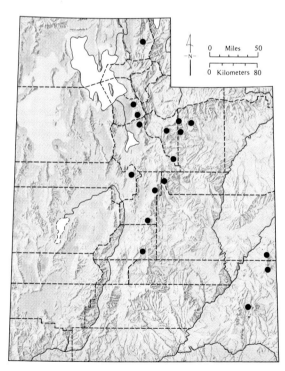

3. *Lonicera utahensis* Wats. Utah honeysuckle. Apr.-July. Native shrub; maple, aspen, spruce-fir communities, 1970-2670 m.

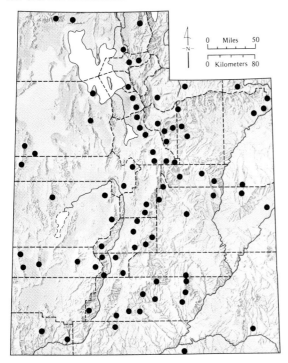

4. *Sambucus cerulea* Raf. Blue elderberry.
June-Aug. Native shrub, an important component
of the mountain brush community; sagebrush,
juniper, oak-maple, ponderosa pine, aspen, spruce-
fir communities, moist slopes, 1510-2730 m.

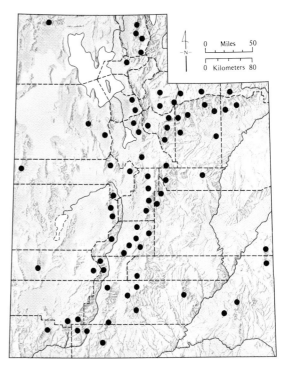

5. *Sambucus racemosa* L. Red elderberry.
June-Aug. Circumboreal shrub; mountain brush,
aspen, spruce-fir, meadow, streamside communities,
1810-3340 m.

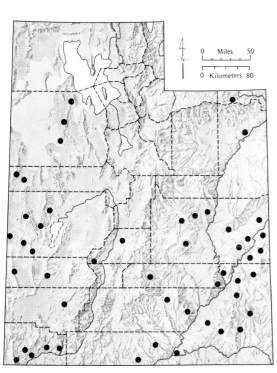

6. *Symphoricarpos longiflorus* Gray
Longflower snowberry. Apr.-June. Native shrub;
shadscale, desert shrub, pinyon-juniper, sagebrush
communities, 910-2280 m.

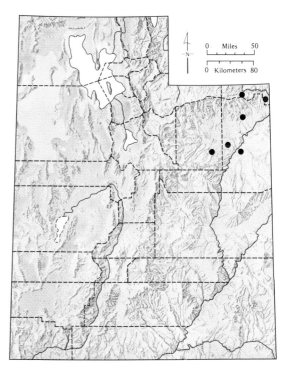

7. *Symphoricarpos occidentalis* Hook.
Western snowberry. June-Aug. Native shrub;
streamside, wet meadows, 1510-1820 m.

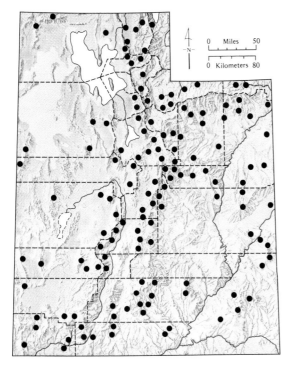

8. *Symphoricarpos oreophilus* Gray Mountain snowberry. May-Aug. Native shrub, an important component of the mountain brush community; sagebrush, pinyon-juniper, mountain brush, ponderosa pine, aspen, spruce-fir communities, 1630-3280 m.

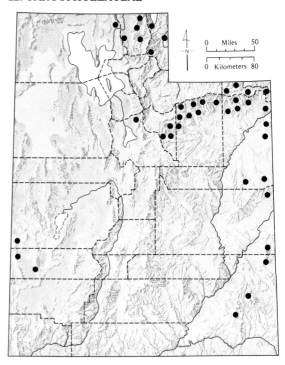

1. *Arenaria congesta* Nutt. Ballhead sandwort. June-Aug. Native perennial herb; pinyon-juniper, sagebrush, mountain brush, ponderosa pine, lodgepole pine, aspen, spruce-fir, alpine communities, 1510-3490 m.

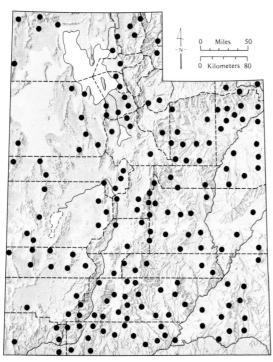

2. *Arenaria fendleri* Gray Fendler sandwort. May-Aug. Native perennial herb; shadscale, sagebrush, pinyon-juniper, ponderosa pine, bristlecone pine, mountain brush, spruce-fir, alpine communities, 1420-3790 m.

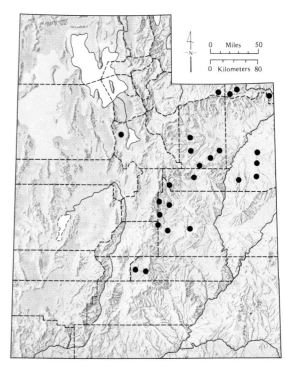

3. *Arenaria hookeri* Nutt. Hooker sandwort. June-July. Native perennial herb; barren rocky ridges in sagebrush, pinyon-juniper communities, 1720-2910 m.

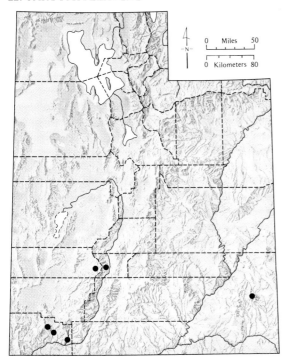

4. *Arenaria lanuginosa* (Michx.) Rohrb. Woolly sandwort. June-Sept. Native perennial herb; Douglas fir-white fir communities, 1240-2180 m.

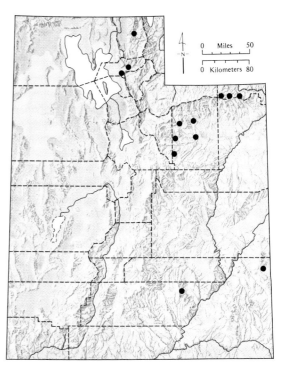

5. *Arenaria lateriflora* L. May-Aug. Circumboreal perennial herb; wet meadow, lodgepole pine, aspen, spruce-fir communities, 1540-2730 m.

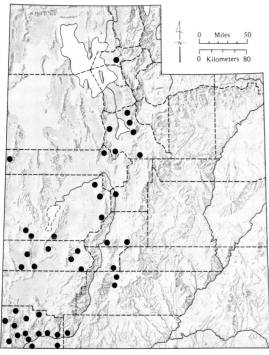

6. *Arenaria macradenia* Wats. Big sandwort. Apr.-July. Native subshrub; Joshua tree, pinyon-juniper, mountain brush, ponderosa pine, aspen, spruce-fir, alpine meadow communities, 810-2970 m.

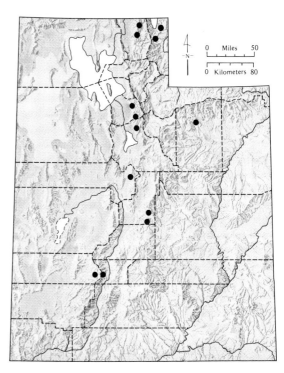

7. *Arenaria nuttallii* Pax Nuttall sandwort. June-Aug. Native perennial herb; chiefly in talus, 2060-3640 m.

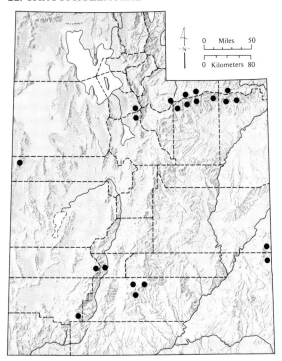

8. *Arenaria obtusiloba* (Rydb.) Fern. Arctic sandwort. July-Aug. Native perennial herb; lodgepole pine, spruce-fir, alpine communities, 2880-3990 m.

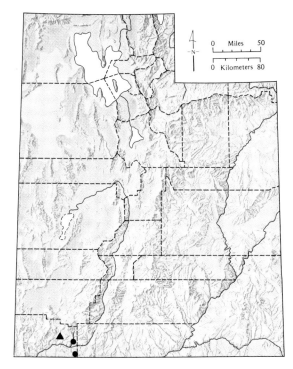

9. *Arenaria pusilla* Wats. Pretty sandwort. Apr.-May. Native annual; ponderosa pine, mountain brush communities, 1510-1640 m.

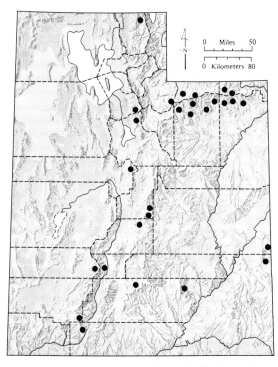

10. *Arenaria rubella* (Wahl.) J. E. Sm. Red sandwort. June-Aug. Native biennial or perennial herb; lodgepole pine, spruce-fir, meadow, alpine communities, 2300-3790 m.

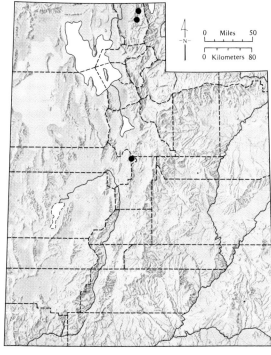

11. *Arenaria serpyllifolia* L. July-Sept. Introduced annual; mountain brush, spruce-fir communities, 2180-2550 m.

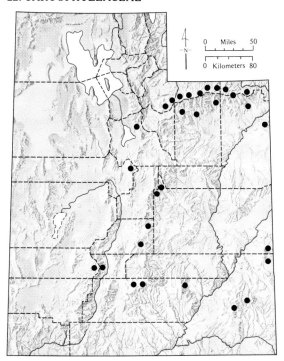

12. *Cerastium arvense* L. Field chickweed. June-Aug. Circumboreal perennial herb; sagebrush, pinyon-juniper, ponderosa pine, lodgepole pine, aspen, alpine meadow communities, 1360-3910 m.

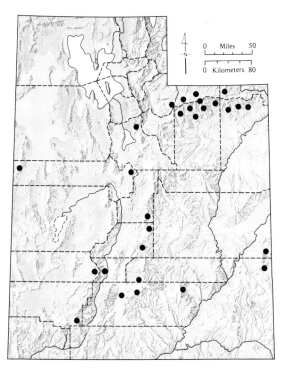

13. *Cerastium beeringianum* Cham. & Schlecht. Beering chickweed. June-Aug. Native perennial herb; silver sagebrush, lodgepole pine, aspen, spruce-fir, alpine communities, 2120-3880 m.

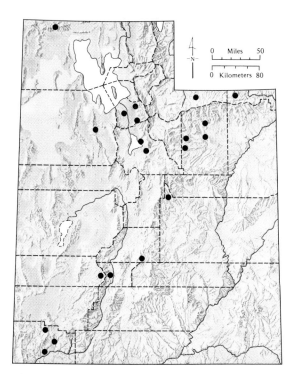

14. *Cerastium fontanum* Baumg. Mouse-ear chickweed. May-Sept. Introduced biennial or perennial herb; lawns, other disturbed sites, riparian communities, 840-2730 m.

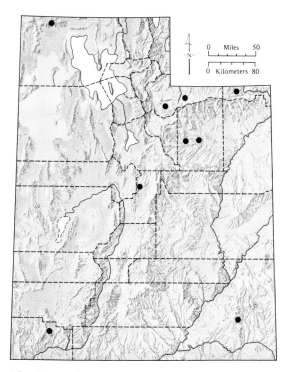

15. *Cerastium nutans* Raf. Nodding chickweed. May-Aug. Native annual; sagebrush, meadow communities, 2120-2910 m.

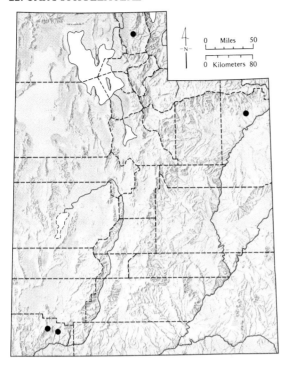

16. *Gypsophila paniculata* L. Baby's breath. June-Aug. Introduced perennial herb; cultivated, escaping and persistent, 2060-2120 m.

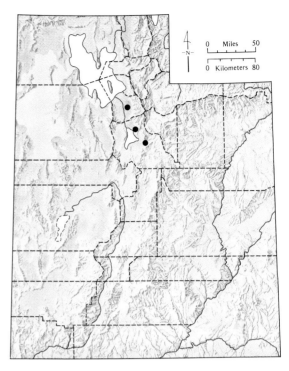

17. *Gypsophila scorzonerifolia* Ser. Aug.-Sept. Introduced perennial herb; moist roadsides, pastures, 1300-1370 m.

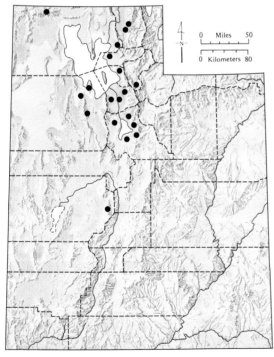

18. *Holosteum umbellatum* L. Umbrella holosteum. Apr.-May. Introduced annual; greasewood to mountain brush communities, 1280-1970 m.

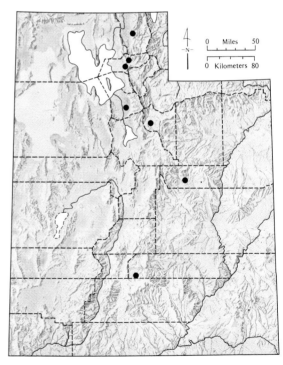

19. *Lychnis alba* Mill. Whitecockle. June-July. Introduced perennial herb; disturbed sites, 1330-2910 m.

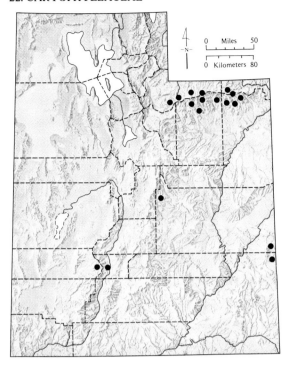

20. *Lychnis apetala* L. Mountain campion. July-Aug. Circumboreal perennial herb; spruce-fir, sedge meadows, alpine communities, 3330-3710 m.

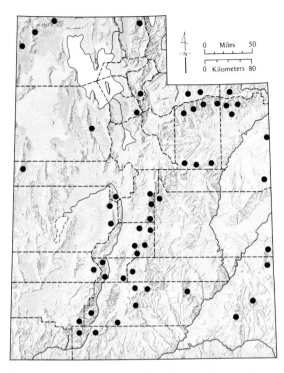

21. *Lychnis drummondii* (Hook.) Wats. July-Sept. Native perennial herb; pinyon-juniper, ponderosa pine, lodgepole pine, aspen, spruce-fir, alpine communities, 2120-3550 m.

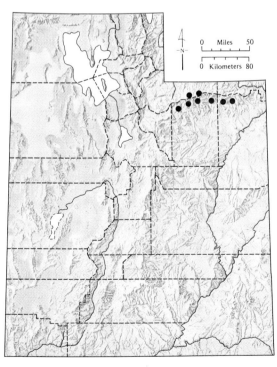

22. *Paronychia pulvinata* Gray Rocky Mountain nailwort. July-Aug. Native perennial herb; meadows and rocky ridges in spruce-fir, alpine communities, 3330-3790 m.

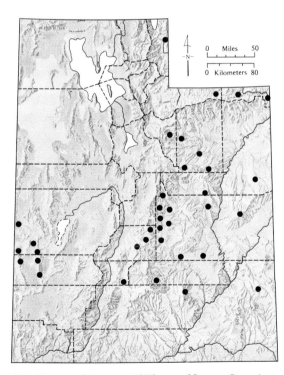

23. *Paronychia sessiliflora* Nutt. Creeping nailwort. June-Aug. Native perennial herb; barren rocky ridges in shadscale, sagebrush, pinyon-juniper communities, 1510-2730 m.

203

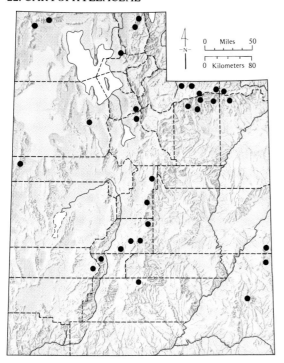

24. *Sagina saginoides* (L.) Karst. Arctic pearlwort. June-Aug. Circumboreal biennial or perennial herb; streamside, lake margins, conifer communities, open, often rocky slopes, 1810-3490 m.

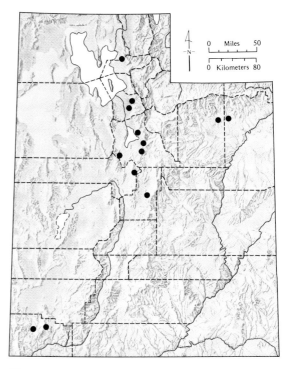

25. *Saponaria officinalis* L. Bouncing bet. July-Sept. Introduced perennial herb; cultivated, escaping and persistent, 1300-2280 m.

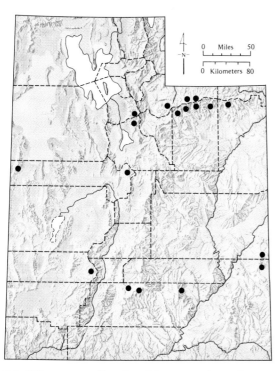

26. *Silene acaulis* L. Moss campion. June-July. Circumboreal perennial herb; spruce-fir, alpine communities, 2660-3940 m.

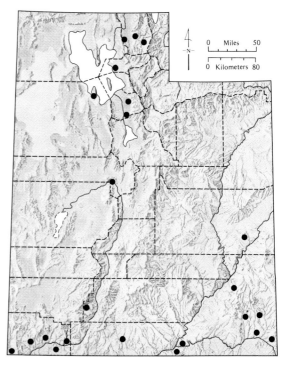

27. *Silene antirrhina* L. Sleepy catchfly. Apr.-July. Native annual; creosote bush, desert shrub, pinyon-juniper, mountain brush communities, 970-2120 m.

204

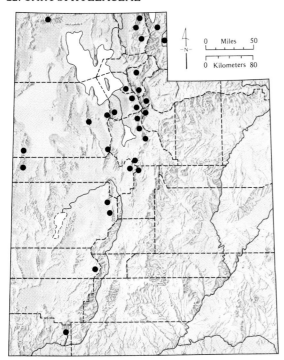

28. *Silene douglasii* Hook. Drummond campion. June-Aug. Native perennial herb; sagebrush, mountain brush, grass-forb, conifer communities, 1510-3340 m.

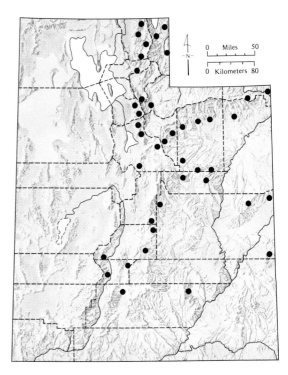

29. *Silene menziesii* Hook. Menzies campion. June-Aug. Native perennial herb; mountain brush, aspen, conifer communities, 1660-3150 m.

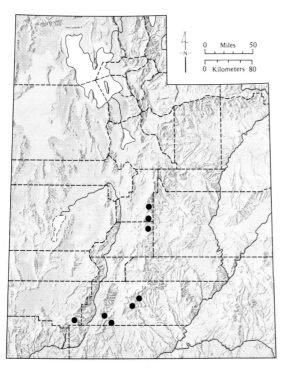

30. *Silene petersonii* Maguire Peterson campion. June-Aug. Native perennial herb; barren rocky slopes in ponderosa pine, bristlecone pine, spruce-fir communities, 2120-3400 m.

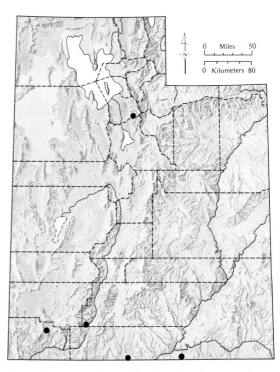

31. *Silene scouleri* Hook. Scouler campion. Aug.-Sept. Native perennial herb; pinyon-juniper, ponderosa pine communities, 2120-2880 m.

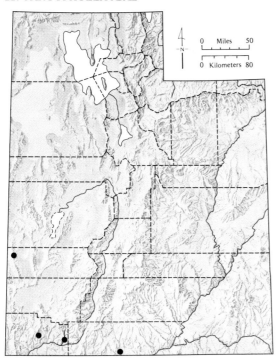

32. *Silene verecunda* Wats.   Spring campion.
June-Aug.   Native perennial herb; pinyon-juniper,
mountain brush communities, 1060-2730 m.

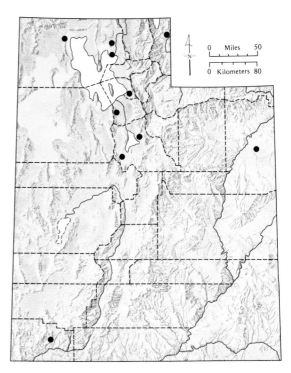

33. *Spergularia marina* (L.) Griseb.   Salt
marsh sandspurry. June-Aug. Introduced annual or
biennial; salt desert shrub, streamside, pond and
lake margins, 1060-1820 m.

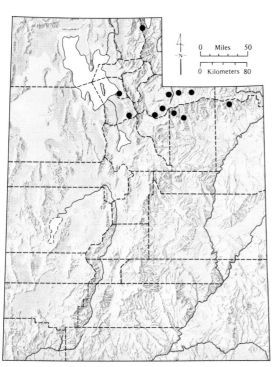

34. *Spergularia rubra* (L.) J. & C. Presl   Red
sandspurry. July-Aug. Introduced annual; mountain
brush to subalpine meadow communities, often on
disturbed sites, 2270-3030 m.

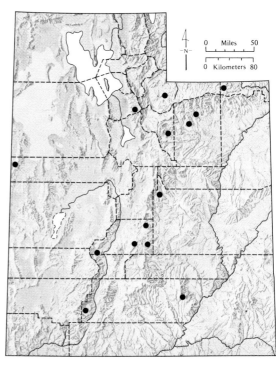

35. *Stellaria calycantha* (Ledeb.) Bong.
Calyxeye starwort. June-Aug. Circumboreal
perennial herb; aspen, ponderosa pine, lodgepole
pine, spruce-fir communities, 2210-3150 m.

206

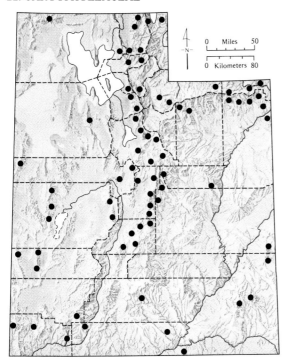

36. *Stellaria jamesiana* Torr. James chickweed. May-Aug. Native perennial herb; sagebrush, mountain brush, ponderosa pine, bristlecone pine, aspen, spruce-fir communities, 1510-3210 m.

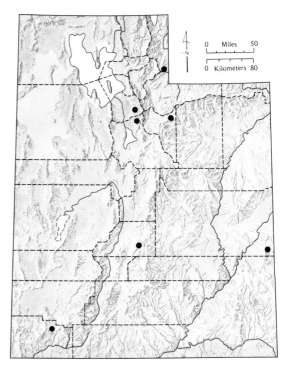

37. *Stellaria longifolia* Willd. Longleaf starwort. July-Aug. Native perennial herb; streamside, meadows, 2030-2880 m.

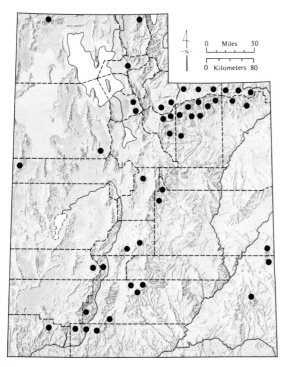

38. *Stellaria longipes* Goldie Longstalk starwort. May-Aug. Native perennial herb; streamside, wet meadows, alpine communities, 1690-3640 m.

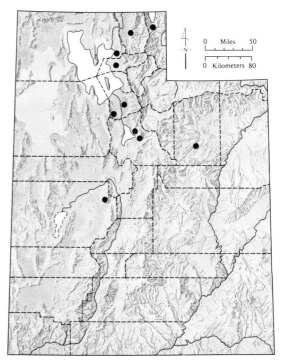

39. *Stellaria media* (L.) Vill. Common chickweed. Apr.-Nov. Introduced annual; disturbed, mostly irrigated sites, 1330-1820 m.

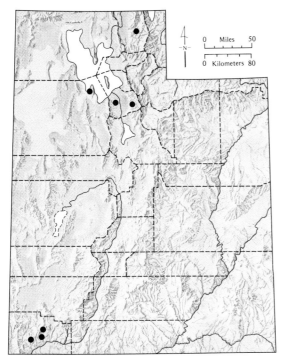

40. *Stellaria nitens* Nutt. Apr.-May.
Handsome starwort. Native annual; meadows, open
grassy slopes, 910-2940 m.

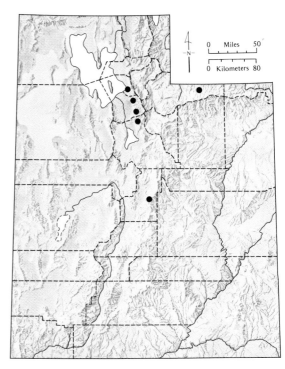

41. *Stellaria obtusa* Engelm. Blunt starwort.
July-Sept. Native perennial herb; moist sites in
sagebrush, aspen, spruce-fir, meadow, alpine
communities, 1910-3340 m.

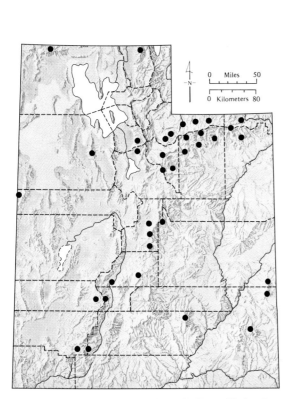

42. *Stellaria umbellata* Kar. & Kir. Umbrella
starwort. June-Aug. Native perennial herb; moist
sites in aspen, lodgepole pine, spruce-fir, alpine
communities, 2300-3490 m.

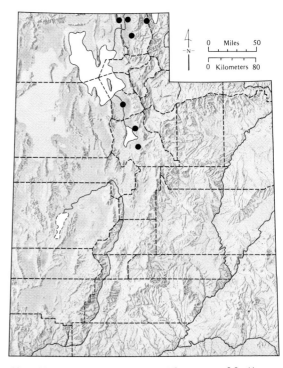

43. *Vaccaria pyramidata* Medicus
Cowcockle. May-Aug. Introduced annual; open
sites in sagebrush, mountain brush communities,
1300-2550 m.

23. CELASTRACEAE

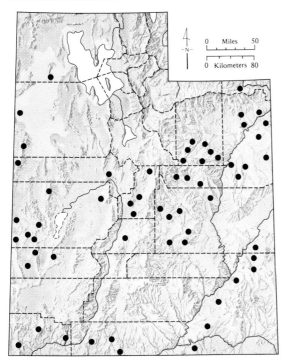

1. ***Forsellesia spinescens*** (Gray) Greene Greasebush. May-June. Native shrub; desert shrub to pinyon-juniper communities, 1360-2310 m.

24. CERATOPHYLLACEAE

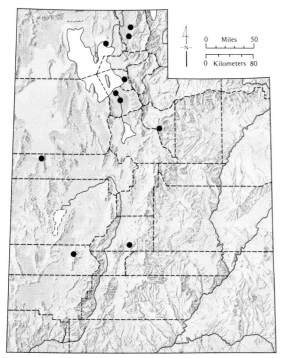

1. ***Ceratophyllum demersum*** L. Hornwort. June-Sept. Cosmopolitan perennial herb; fresh or brackish, slow-moving or standing water, 1270-1370 m.

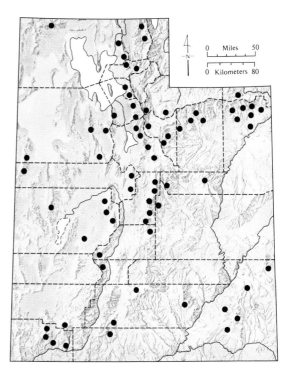

2. ***Paxistima myrsinites*** (Pursh) Raf. Mountain lover. May-Aug. Native shrub; shaded sites in oak, maple, aspen, spruce-fir communities, occasionally on open rocky slopes, 1450-3340 m.

25. CHENOPODIACEAE

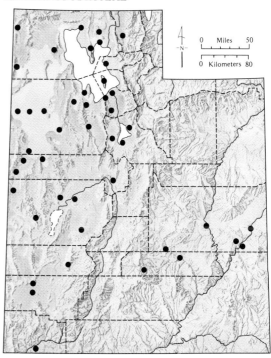

1. ***Allenrolfea occidentalis*** (Wats.) Kuntze Pickleweed; iodine bush. May-July. Native subshrub or shrub, an important component of the salt desert shrub community; moderately moist saline sites, 750-1610 m.

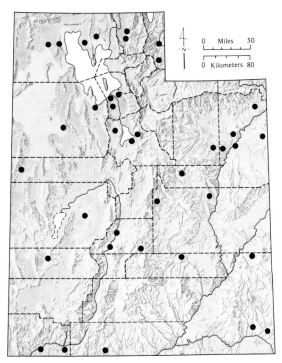

2. *Atriplex argentea* Nutt. Silver orach. June-
Aug. Native annual; salt desert shrub, commonly
shadscale and greasewood communities, 840-
1820 m.

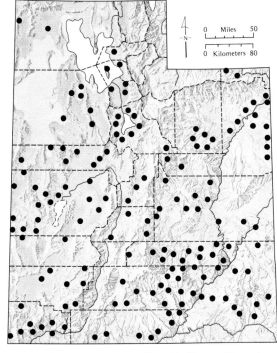

3. *Atriplex canescens* (Pursh) Nutt. Fourwing
saltbush. May-Aug. Native shrub; creosote bush,
greasewood, desert shrub, sagebrush, mountain
brush, pinyon-juniper communities, 840-2430 m.

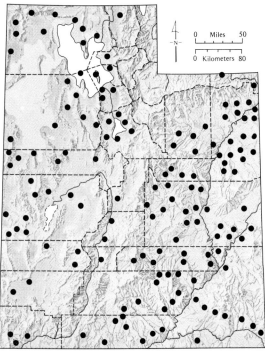

4. *Atriplex confertifolia* (Torr. & Frem.)
Wats. Shadscale. May-Aug. Native shrub;
greasewood, mat saltbush, salt desert shrub,
sagebrush, pinyon-juniper communities, dominant
over large areas, 840-2280 m.

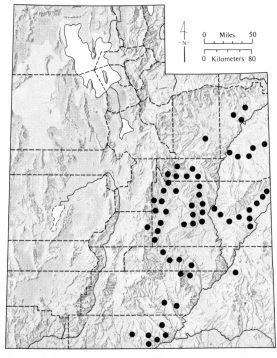

5. *Atriplex corrugata* Wats. Mat saltbush.
Apr.-July. Native shrub; salt desert shrub
communities, often codominant with *Atriplex
gardneri*, 1210-2120 m.

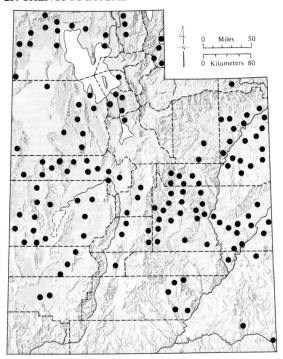

6. *Atriplex gardneri* (Moq.) D. Dietr. Gardner saltbush. June-July. Native shrub or subshrub; saltgrass, salt desert shrub, sagebrush communities, 1210-2150 m.

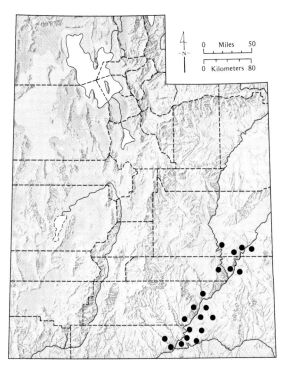

7. *Atriplex garrettii* Rydb. Garrett saltbush. July-Aug. Native shrub or subshrub; shadscale, desert shrub communities, talus, 1030-1880 m.

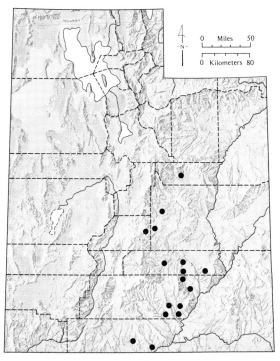

8. *Atriplex graciliflora* Jones Blue Valley orach. Apr.-May. Native annual; salt desert shrub communities, 1120-1880 m.

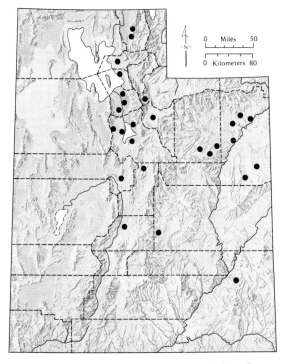

9. *Atriplex heterosperma* Bunge May-Sept. Introduced annual; salt desert shrub communities, fallow fields, along waterways, 1270-1970 m.

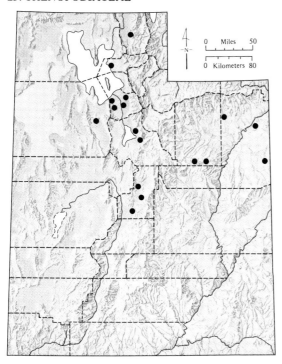

10. *Atriplex hortensis* L. Garden orach. June-Aug. Introduced annual; disturbed saline sites, 1300-2120 m.

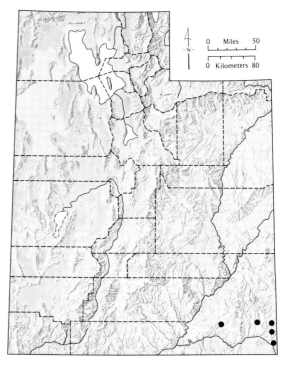

11. *Atriplex obovata* Moq. Mound or New Mexico saltbush. Apr.-June. Native shrub; salt desert shrub communities, 1120-1310 m.

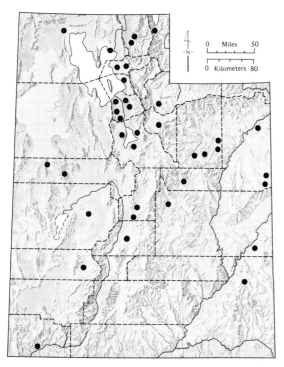

12. *Atriplex patula* L. Fat-hen or spear orach. July-Oct. Circumboreal annual; salt grass, greasewood, and other halophytic communities, often in disturbed sites, 840-2000 m.

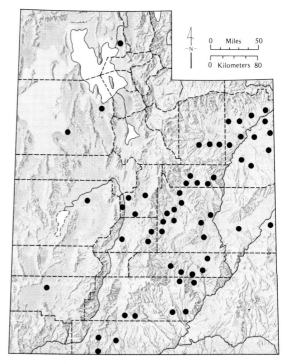

13. *Atriplex powellii* Wats. Powell orach. June-Oct. Native annual; salt desert shrub, desert shrub, pinyon-juniper communities, 1300-2180 m.

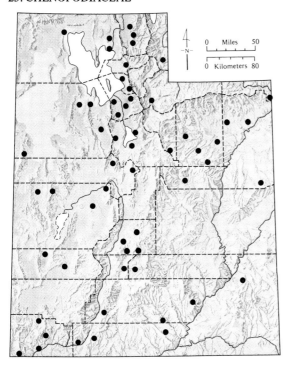

14. *Atriplex rosea* L. Tumbling orach. Aug.-Oct. Introduced annual; disturbed, often saline sites, 810-2250 m.

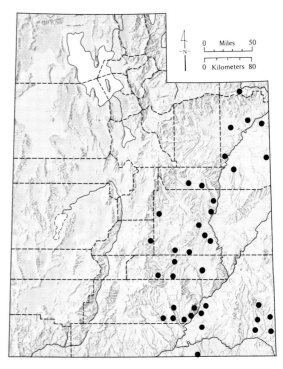

15. *Atriplex saccaria* Wats. Stalked orach. May-Aug. Native annual; salt desert shrub, desert shrub, pinyon-juniper communities, 1120-1970 m.

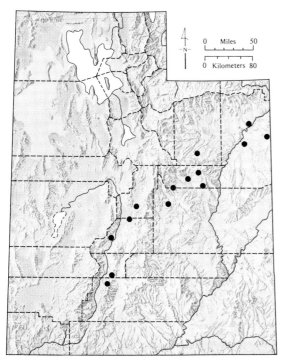

16. *Atriplex wolfii* Wats. Wolf orach. Aug.-Sept. Native annual; salt desert shrub communities, 1360-2120 m.

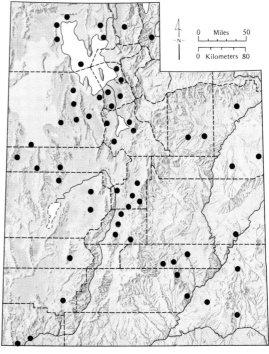

17. *Bassia hyssopifolia* (Pall.) Kuntze Smotherweed. July-Sept. Introduced annual; disturbed, usually saline sites, 810-2370 m.

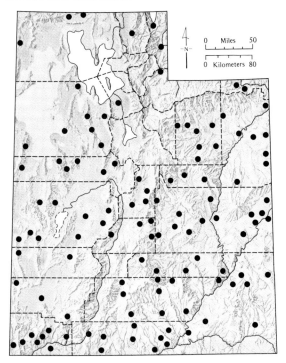

18. *Ceratoides   lanata* (Pursh) Howell
Winterfat; white sage. May-Aug. Native shrub;
creosote bush, shadscale, desert shrub, sagebrush,
pinyon-juniper communities, 800-2820 m.

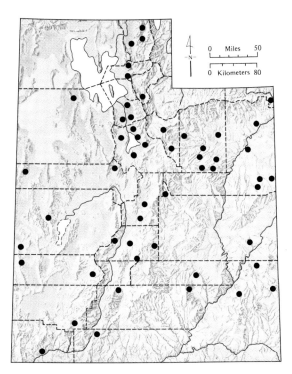

19. *Chenopodium   album* L. Lambsquarter.
July-Sept. Introduced annual; gardens, fields, other
disturbed sites, 840-3030 m.

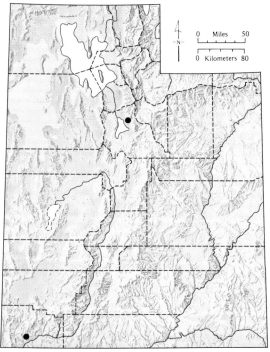

20. *Chenopodium   ambrosioides* L.
Wormseed; Mexican tea. July-Sept. Introduced
annual; disturbed sites, 840-1370 m.

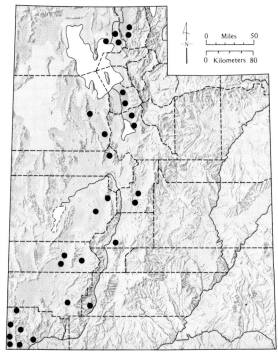

21. *Chenopodium   botrys* L. Jerusalem oak.
June-Oct. Introduced annual; disturbed sites, 800-
1970 m.

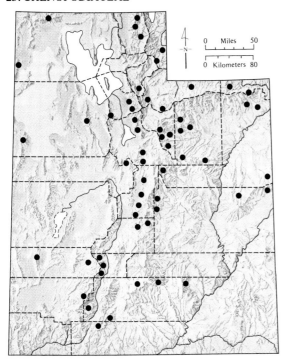

22. Chenopodium capitatum (L.) A s c h .
Strawberry blite. June-Aug. Circumboreal annual;
mountain brush, ponderosa pine, lodgepole pine,
aspen, spruce-fir communities, 1300-3600 m.

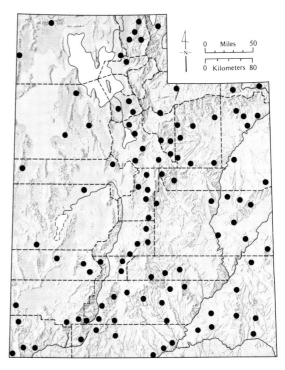

23. Chenopodium fremontii Wats. Fremont
goosefoot. July-Sept. Native annual; creosote
bush, shadscale, desert shrub, pinyon-juniper to
aspen, spruce-fir communities, 840-3180 m.

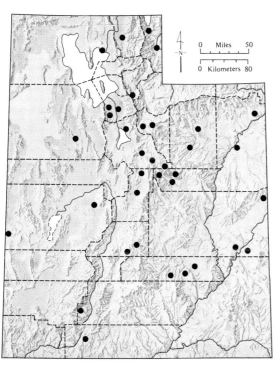

24. Chenopodium glaucum L. Oakleaf
goosefoot. July-Sept. Circumboreal annual;
disturbed, often saline sites along waterways, in
pastures and meadows, pinyon-juniper to spruce-fir
communities, 1210-2730 m.

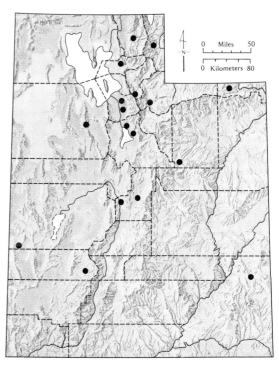

25. Chenopodium hybridum L. M a p l e l e a f
goosefoot. July-Aug. Circumboreal annual;
sagebrush, mountain brush, pinyon-juniper to aspen
communities, 1840-2430 m.

215

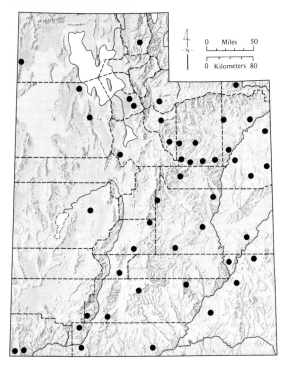

26. *Chenopodium leptophyllum* (Moq.) Wats. Narrowleaf goosefoot. July-Sept. Native annual; creosote bush, salt desert shrub, desert shrub, mountain brush, aspen communities, 840-2880 m.

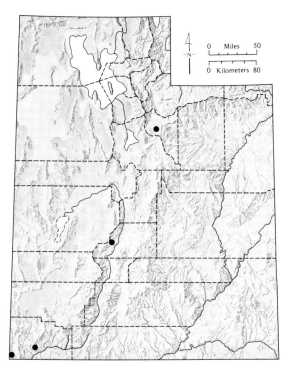

27. *Chenopodium murale* L. Nettleleaf goosefoot. May-Oct. Introduced annual; disturbed sites, 840-2120 m.

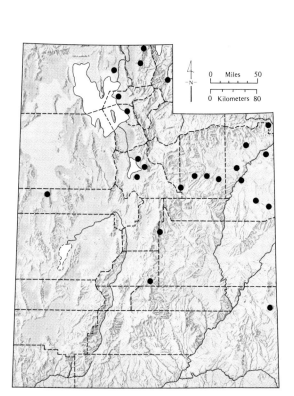

28. *Chenopodium rubrum* L. Red goosefoot. June-Sept. Native annual; disturbed, moist, chiefly saline sites, 1330-2430 m.

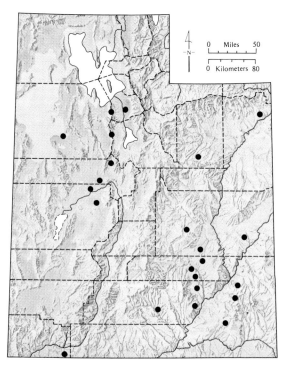

29. *Corispermum villosum* Rydb. Bugseed. June-Sept. Native annual; dunes and other sandy sites in desert shrub to pinyon-juniper communities, 1060-2430 m.

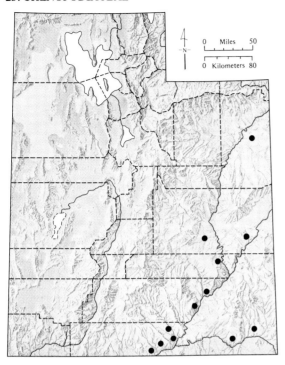

30. *Cycloloma atriplicifolium* (Spreng.) Coult. Winged pigweed. June-Sept. Native annual; sandy sites in desert shrub communities, 1090-1460 m.

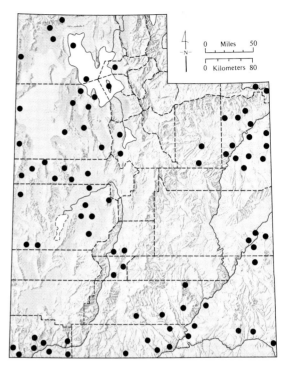

31. *Grayia spinosa* (Hook.) Moq. Spiny hopsage. Apr.-July. Native shrub; creosote bush, shadscale, sagebrush to pinyon-juniper communities, 800-1820 m.

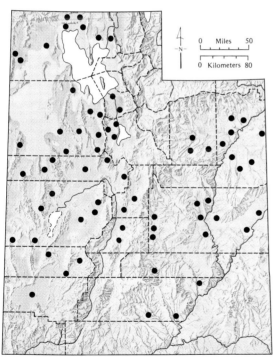

32. *Halogeton glomeratus* (Bieb.) C. A. Mey. Halogeton. June-Sept. Introduced annual; disturbed, often saline sites, 1210-2000 m.

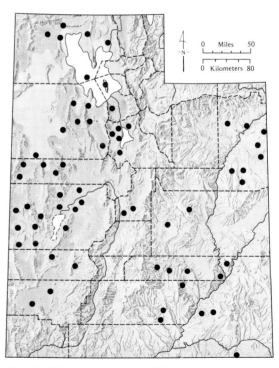

33. *Kochia americana* Wats. Gray or green Molly. June-Sept. Native perennial herb or subshrub; salt desert shrub, sagebrush communities, 1260-1970 m.

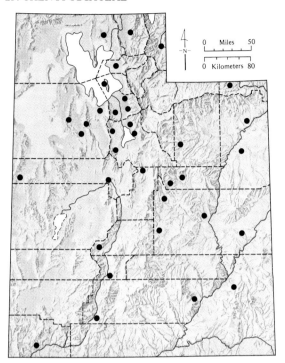

34. Kochia scoparia (L.) Schrad. Summer cypress. July-Oct. Introduced annual; waste places, 930-1940 m.

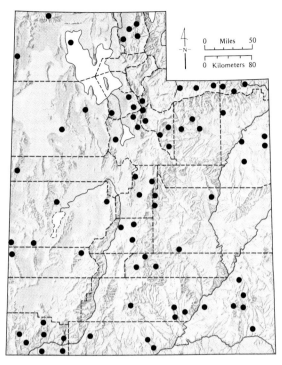

35. Monolepis nuttalliana (Schult.) Greene Poverty weed. June-Sept. Native annual; creosote bush, salt desert shrub, desert shrub to aspen-conifer communities, often in the wake of disturbance, 900-3280 m.

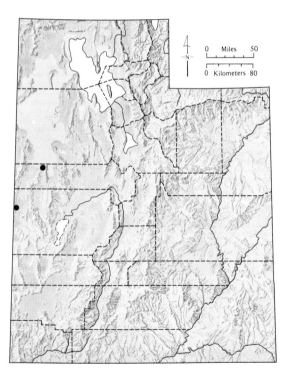

36. Nitrophila occidentalis (Moq.) Wats. Western miterwort. Aug.-Sept. Native perennial herb; saline sites, 1360-1460 m.

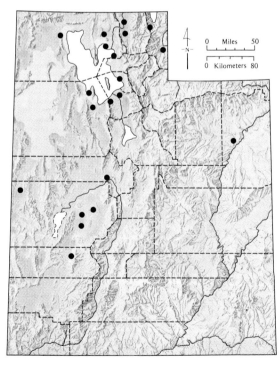

37. Salicornia europaea L. Annual samphire. July-Sept. Cosmopolitan annual; moist saline sites, 1270-1460 m.

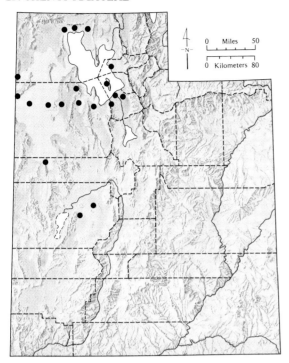

38. *Salicornia utahensis* Tides. Utah samphire. June-Sept. Native perennial herb; moist saline sites in annual samphire, iodine bush communities, 1270-1430 m.

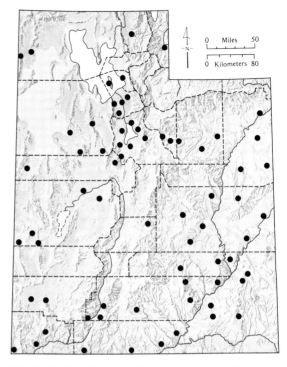

39. *Salsola iberica* Sennen & Pau Russian thistle; tumbleweed. June-Sept. Introduced annual; disturbed sites, 810-2430 m.

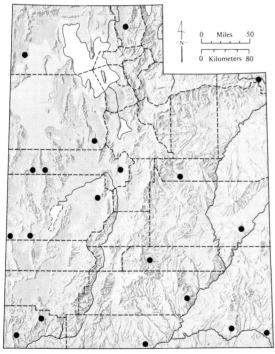

40. *Salsola paulsenii* Litv. Barbwire Russian thistle. June-Sept. Introduced annual; disturbed sites, 910-1820 m.

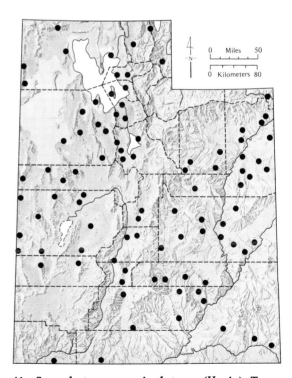

41. *Sarcobatus vermiculatus* (Hook.) Torr. Greasewood. July-Sept. Native shrub; a major component of the salt desert shrub community, 840-2120 m.

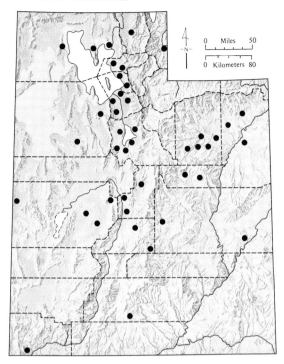

42. *Suaeda calceoliformis* (Hook.) Moq.
Broom seepweed. July-Sept. Native perennial
herb; salt desert shrub communities, 840-2520 m.

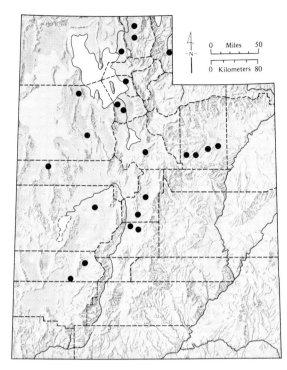

43. *Suaeda occidentalis* (Wats.) Wats. July-
Sept. Native annual; salt desert shrub communities,
1280-1520 m.

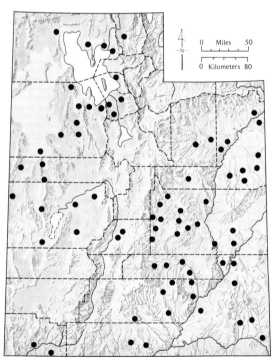

44. *Suaeda torreyana* Wats. Bush seepweed.
July-Sept. Native subshrub or shrub; salt desert
shrub communities, 840-1520 m.

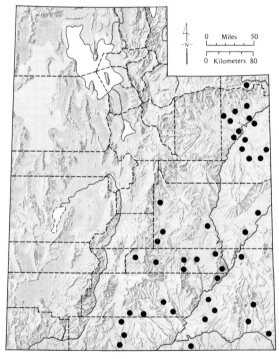

45. *Zuckia brandegei* (Gray) Welsh & Stutz
Spineless hopsage. June-Sept. Native shrub;
shadscale, mat saltbush, desert shrub communities,
1360-2180 m.

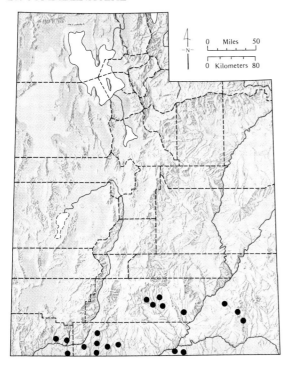

1. *Tradescantia occidentalis* (Britt.) Smyth
Prairie spiderwort. May-Aug. Native perennial
herb; sandy sites in desert shrub, pinyon-juniper,
ponderosa pine communities, 1240-1970 m.

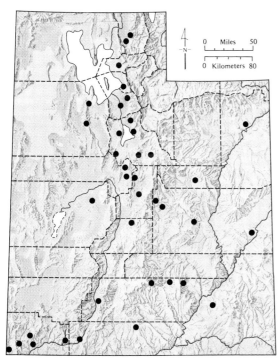

2. *Convolvulus arvensis* L. Field bindweed or
creeping Jenny. May-Sept. Introduced perennial
herb; cultivated and waste places, 840-2060 m.

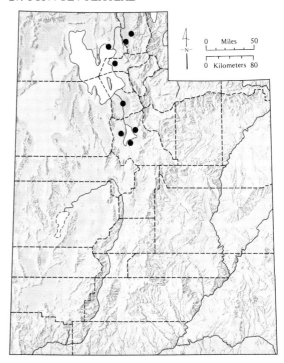

1. *Calystegia sepium* (L.) R. Br. Hedge
bindweed. June-Aug. Native vinelike perennial
herb; disturbed sites, often along waterways, 1270-
1310 m.

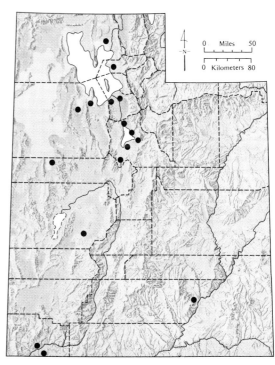

3. *Cressa truxillensis* H. B. K. Alkali weed.
June-Sept. Native perennial herb; salt desert shrub
communities, 1210-1520 m.

27. CONVOLVULACEAE

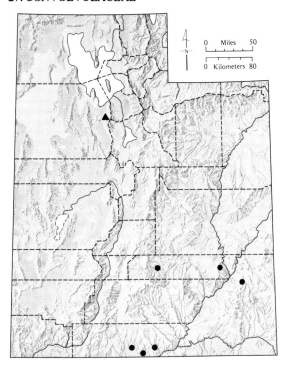

4. *Evolvulus nuttallianus* Roem. & Schult. Wild morning glory. May-June. Native vinelike perennial herb; sandy sites in desert shrub communities, 1270-1700 m.

28. CORNACEAE

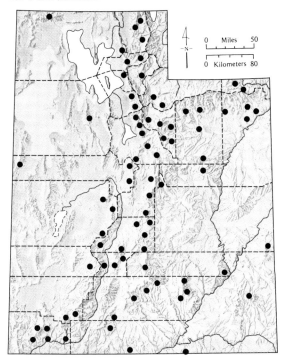

1. *Cornus sericea* L. Red-osier dogwood. Apr.-Sept. Native shrub; streamside, marshes, 970-2730 m.

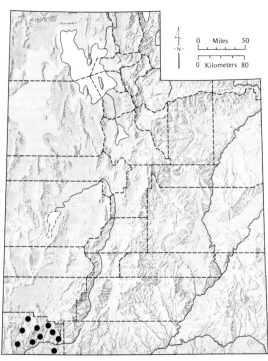

2. *Garrya flavescens* Wats. Yellowleaf silktassel. Apr.-June. Native shrub; desert shrub, pinyon-juniper, ponderosa pine communities, 970-2420 m.

29. CRASSULACEAE

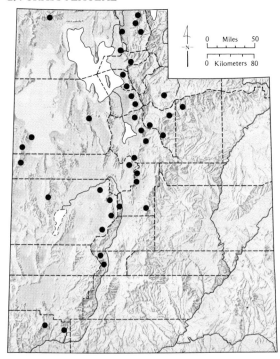

1. *Sedum debile* Wats. Orpine stonecrop. June-Aug. Native perennial herb; rock crevices, meadows, streamside in mountain brush to spruce-fir communities, 1450-3030 m.

29. CRASSULACEAE

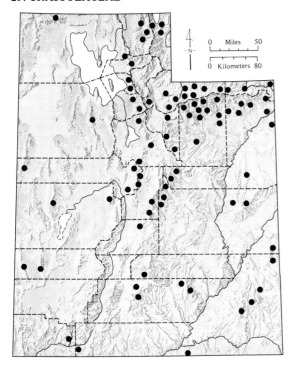

2. *Sedum lanceolatum* Torr. Lanceleaf stonecrop. June-Aug. Native perennial herb; rocky sites in sagebrush, pinyon-juniper, lodgepole pine, ponderosa pine, aspen communities, 1510-3640 m.

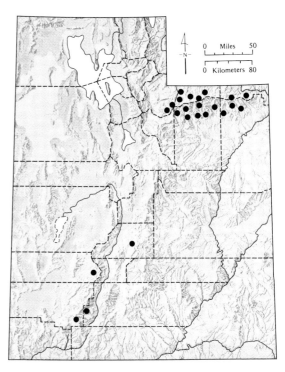

3. *Sedum rhodanthum* Gray Redpod stonecrop. July-Aug. Native perennial herb; wet meadows, streamside, lake margins, 2660-3640 m.

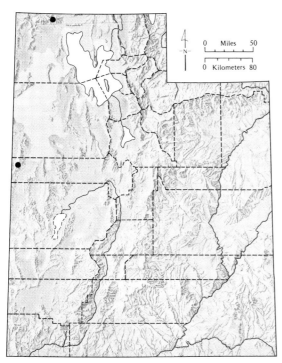

4. *Sedum rosea* (L.) Scop. Roseroot stonecrop. July-Aug. Native perennial herb; rocky sites, meadows, 2720-3340 m.

30. CUCURBITACEAE

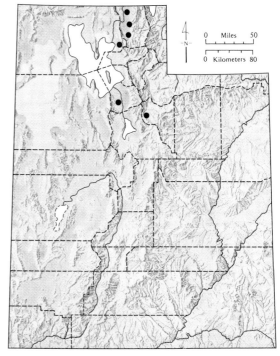

1. *Bryonia alba* L. White bryony. June-Sept. Introduced perennial vine; along fences, 1360-1640 m.

223

30. CUCURBITACEAE

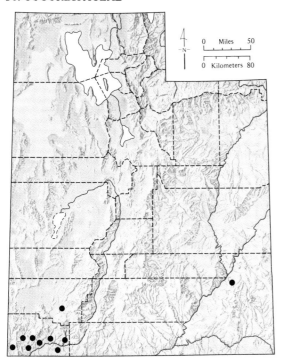

2. Cucurbita foetidissima H. B. K. Buffalo gourd. Apr.-July. Native perennial herb; creosote bush communities, 840-1060 m.

3. Echinocystis lobata (Michx.) T. & G. Wild mock cucumber. Aug.-Sept. Introduced annual vine; cultivated, escaping and persistent, 1330-1400 m.

31. CUPRESSACEAE

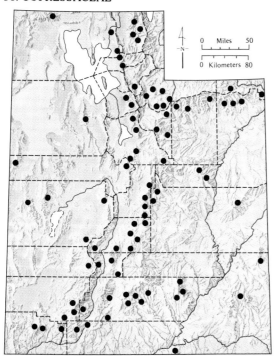

1. Juniperus communis L. Common juniper. Circumboreal shrub; shaded sites in aspen, conifer communities, exposed rocky slopes at higher elevations, 2120-3490 m.

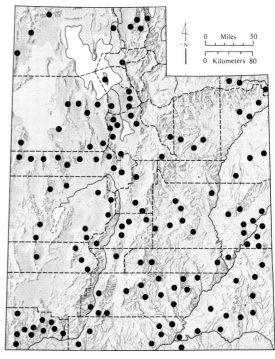

2. Juniperus osteosperma (Torr.) Little Utah juniper. Native tree; dominant over large areas, often in association with *Pinus monophylla* or *P. edulis*, 1210-2280 m.

31. CUPRESSACEAE

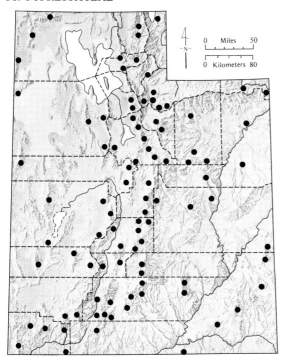

3. *Juniperus scopulorum* Sarg. Rocky Mountain juniper. Native tree; mountain brush, ponderosa pine, aspen communities, often streamside, 1210-2430 m.

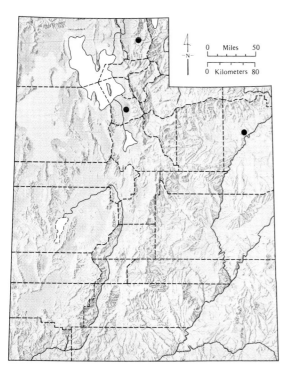

2. *Cuscuta cephalanthii* Engelm. Butterbrush dodder. Sept.-Oct. Native annual; parasitic on a wide range of hosts, 1300-1430 m.

32. CUSCUTACEAE

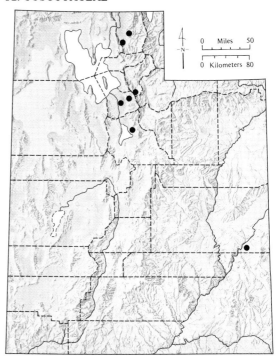

1. *Cuscuta approximata* Bab. Alfalfa dodder. June-Sept. Introduced annual; parasitic on a wide range of hosts, especially alfalfa, 1330-2280 m.

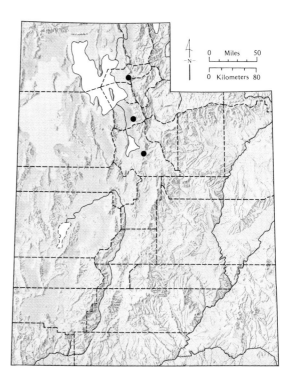

3. *Cuscuta cuspidata* Engelm. Aug.-Oct. Native annual; parasitic on a number of hosts with an apparent preference for species of Asteraceae, 1300-1370 m.

225

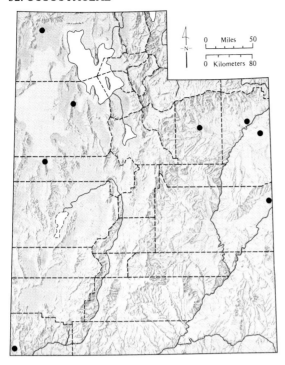

4. Cuscuta denticulata Engelm. Desert dodder.
June-Aug. Native annual; parasitic chiefly on desert
shrubs, 1300-1430 m.

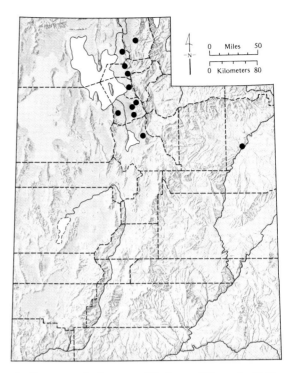

5. Cuscuta indecora Choisy   Bigseed alfalfa
dodder. Aug.-Oct. Native annual; parasitic on
many hosts, often on alfalfa and species of
Asteraceae, 1300-1550 m.

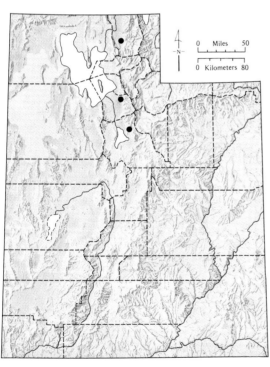

6. Cuscuta megalocarpa Rydb. July-Aug.
Native annual; parasitic on a number of hosts,
among them various species of *Salix* , 2210-
2280 m.

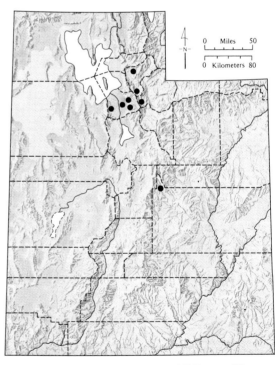

7. Cuscuta occidentalis Millsp. Western
dodder. July-Aug. Native annual; parasitic on
numerous hosts, among them various weeds and
grasses, 1300-2370 m.

226

32. CUSCUTACEAE

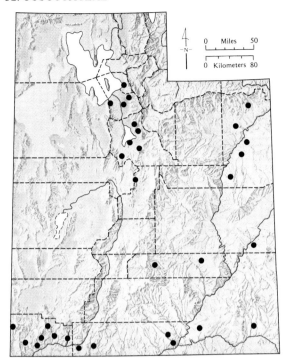

8. *Cuscuta pentagona* Engelm. Western field dodder. June-Aug. Native annual; parasitic on a wide variety of hosts including species of Convolvulaceae and Asteraceae, 1270-2280 m.

9. *Cuscuta salina* Engelm. Saltmarsh dodder. Aug.-Sept. Native annual; parasitic on halophytic herbs and shrubs, 880-1290 m.

33. CYPERACEAE

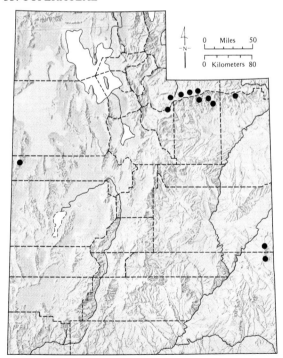

1. *Carex albonigra* Mack. Black and white sedge. July-Aug. Native perennial; talus, meadows, 3430-3810 m.

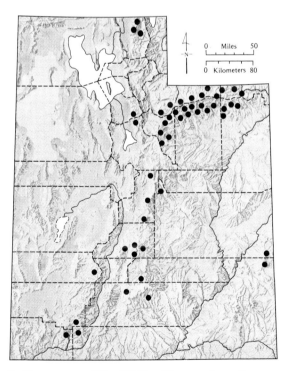

2. *Carex aquatilis* Wahl. Water sedge. June-Aug. Circumboreal perennial; marshes, streamside, lake shores, wet meadows, 2190-3480 m.

227

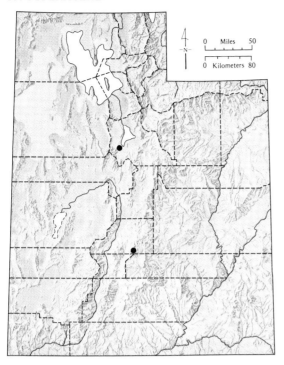

3. *Carex atherodes* Spreng. Slough sedge.
June-Aug. Circumboreal perennial; pond margins,
streamside, 1370-2700 m.

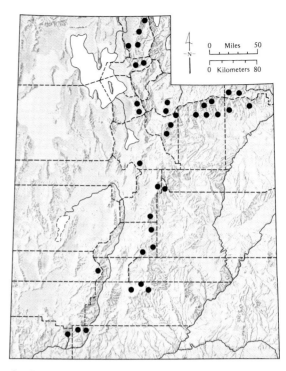

4. *Carex athrostachya* Olney Slenderbeak
sedge. May-Aug. Native perennial; wet meadows,
margins of ponds and lakes, 1820-3480 m.

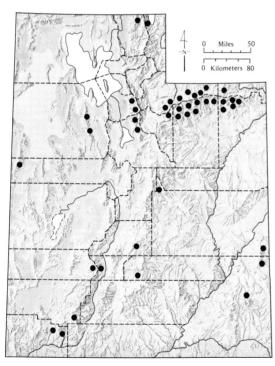

5. *Carex atrata* L. Blackrobed sedge. July-Aug.
Circumboreal perennial; moist sites in oak-
ponderosa pine to alpine communities, talus, 2280-
3850 m.

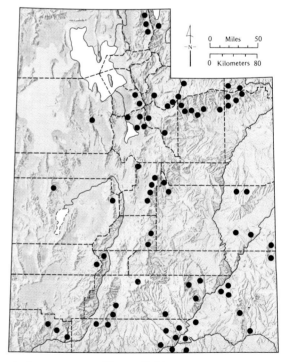

6. *Carex aurea* Nutt. Golden sedge. Apr.-Aug.
Native perennial; hanging gardens, streamside, near
seeps and springs, wet meadows, 1140-3350 m.

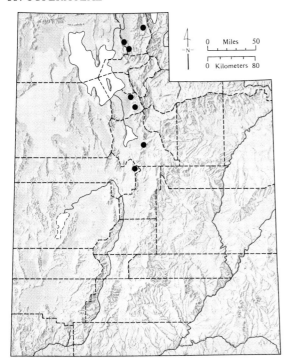

7. *Carex backii* F. Boott Rocky Mountain sedge. May-July. Native perennial; oak-maple communities, 1720-1980 m.

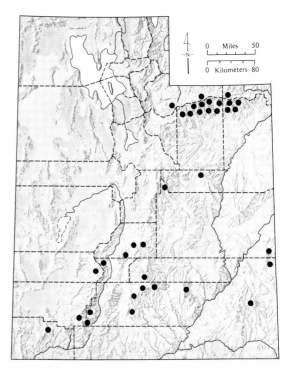

8. *Carex bella* Bailey Showy sedge. July-Sept. Native perennial; ponderosa pine, lodgepole pine, spruce-fir, alpine communities, 2630-3320 m.

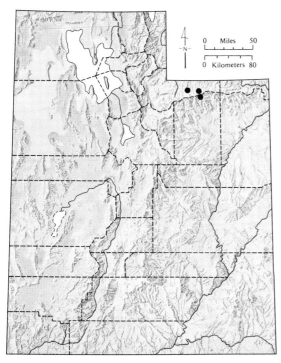

9. *Carex bipartita* All. July-Aug. Circumboreal perennial; wet alpine meadows, 3330-3640 m.

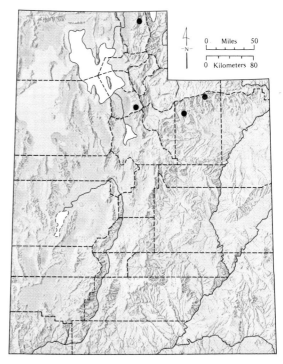

10. *Carex breweri* F. Boott Brewer sedge. July-Aug. Native perennial; wet to dry, sometimes rocky sites, 2780-3030 m.

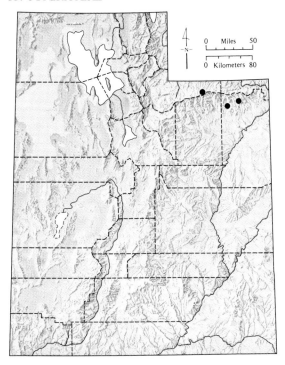

11. *Carex brunnescens* (Pers.) Poir. Brown sedge. May-Aug. Circumboreal perennial; wet meadows, 2250-2960 m.

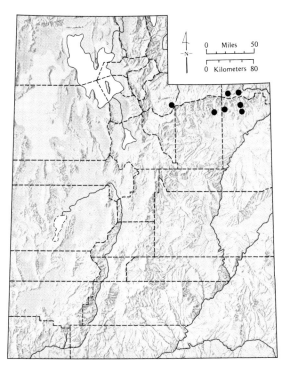

12. *Carex buxbaumii* Wahl. Buxbaum sedge. June-Aug. Circumboreal perennial; wet meadows, 2250-2940 m.

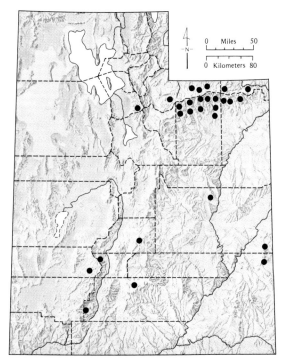

13. *Carex canescens* L. Pale sedge. June-Aug. Circumboreal perennial; streamside, pond and lake margins, wet meadows, 1920-3480 m.

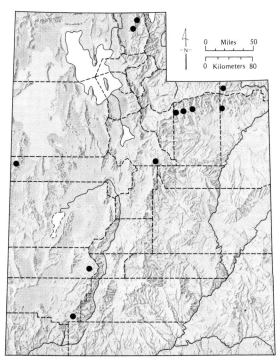

14. *Carex capillaris* L. Hairlike sedge. June-Aug. Circumboreal perennial; streamside, wet meadows, 2440-2840 m.

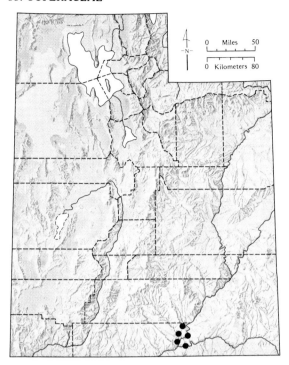

15. *Carex curatorum* Stacey Canyonlands sedge. July-Aug. Native perennial; hanging gardens, riparian communities, 1150-1340 m.

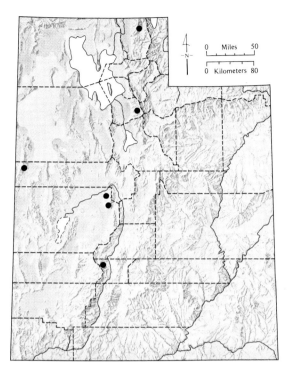

16. *Carex deweyana* Schwein. Dewey sedge. May-July. Native perennial; oak, aspen, fir communities, 2190-2950 m.

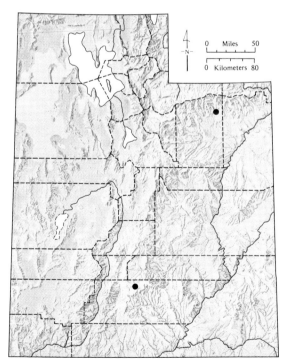

17. *Carex diandra* Schrank June-July. Circumboreal perennial; wet meadows, 2210-2270 m.

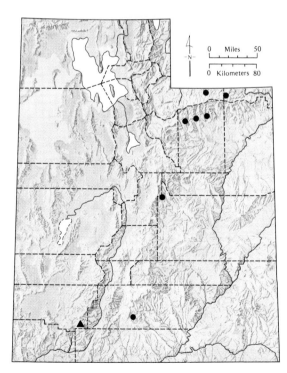

18. *Carex dioica* L. Yellow bog sedge. June-July. Circumboreal perennial; wet meadows, 2740-3130 m.

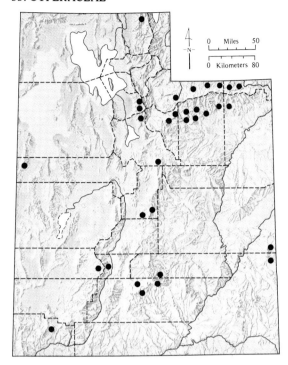

19. *Carex disperma* Dewey   Softleaf sedge.
June-Aug. Circumboreal perennial; streamside, wet
meadows, 2280-3050 m.

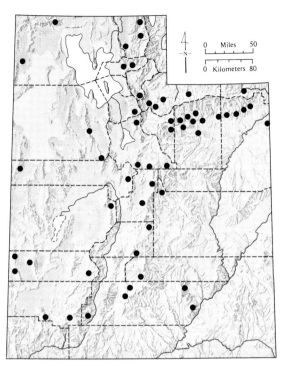

20. *Carex douglasii* F. Boott   Douglas
sedge. Apr.-Aug. Native perennial; chiefly dry
sites in pinyon-juniper, sagebrush to conifer
communities, 1510-3090 m.

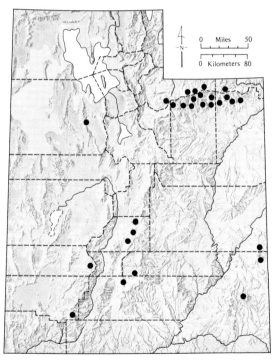

21. *Carex ebenea* Rydb. Ebony sedge. July-
Aug. Native perennial; openings in lodgepole
pine, spruce, alpine communities, 2870-3550 m.

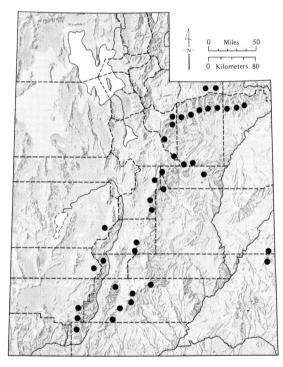

22. *Carex egglestonii* Mack.   Eggleston
sedge. July-Aug. Native perennial; openings in
aspen, spruce-fir, alpine communities, 2420-
3430 m.

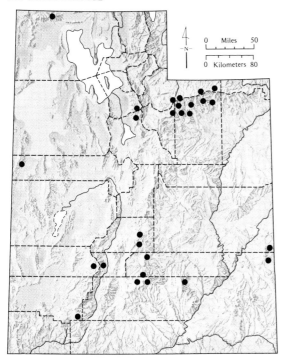

23. *Carex elynoides* Holm   Kobresia or blackroot sedge.   June-Aug.   Native perennial; krummholz, alpine communities, 2860-3900 m.

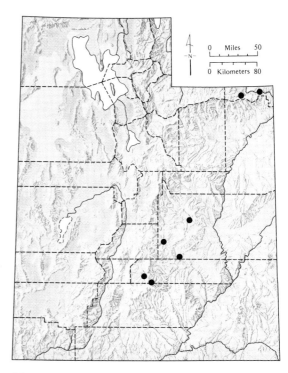

24. *Carex filifolia* Nutt.   Threadleaf sedge. Apr.-July.   Native perennial; desert shrub to pinyon-juniper communities, 1670-2230 m.

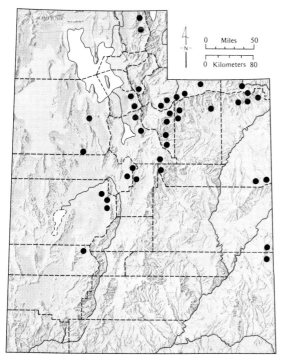

25. *Carex geyeri* F. Boott   Elk sedge.   Apr.-July.   Native perennial; mountain brush to aspen, spruce-fir communities, 1830-3300 m.

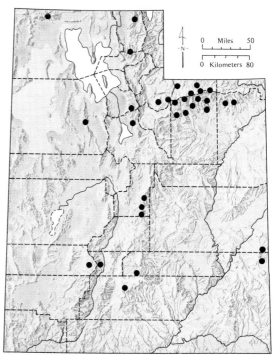

26. *Carex haydeniana* Olney   Cloud sedge. June-Aug.   Native perennial; spruce-fir, krummholz, alpine communities, 2630-3940 m.

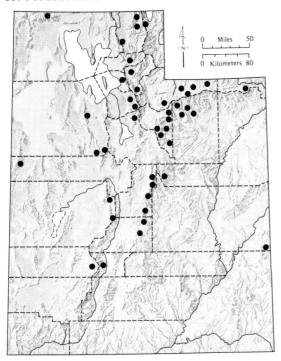

27. *Carex hoodii* F. Boott Hood sedge. May-July. Native perennial; sagebrush, mountain brush to spruce-fir communities, 2090-3030 m.

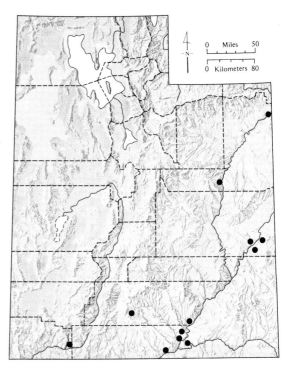

28. *Carex hystricina* Willd. Bottlebrush sedge. May-June. Native perennial; streamside, wet meadows, 1370-1920 m.

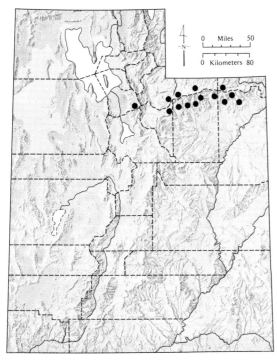

29. *Carex illota* Bailey Sheep sedge. June-Aug. Native perennial; pond and lake margins, streamside, wet meadows, 2270-3490 m.

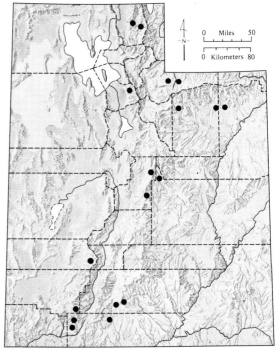

30. *Carex interior* Bailey Inland sedge. May-July. Native perennial; wet meadows, 1890-3170 m.

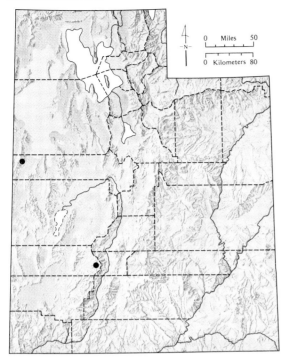

31. ***Carex jonesii*** Bailey   Jones sedge. June-
Sept. Native perennial; streamside, wet meadows,
2590-2840 m.

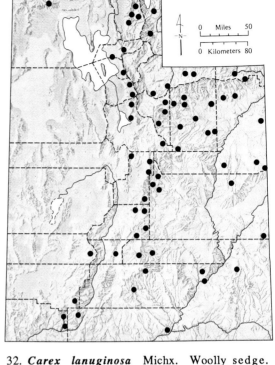

32. ***Carex lanuginosa*** Michx. Woolly sedge.
May-Sept. Native perennial; margins of ponds and
lakes, streamside, wet meadows, 1240-2790 m.

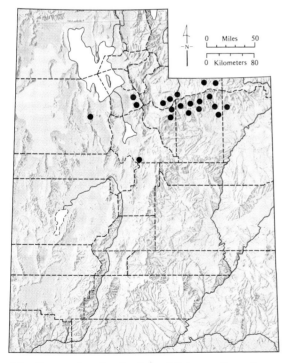

33. ***Carex lenticularis*** Michx.   June-Aug.
Native perennial; sites adjoining springs, ponds,
and lakes, streamside, wet meadows, 1860-3260 m.

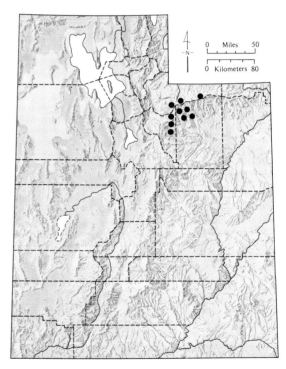

34. ***Carex leporinella*** Mack.   Sierra hare
sedge. July-Aug. Native perennial; margins of
ponds and lakes, wet to dry meadows, 2830-
3200 m.

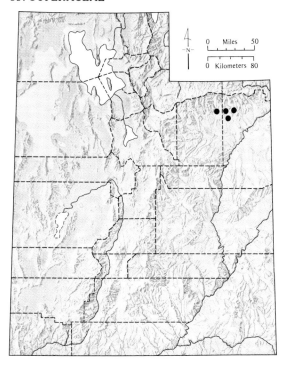

35. *Carex leptalea* Wahl. Flaccid sedge. May-Aug. Native perennial; shady wet sites, 2200-2350 m.

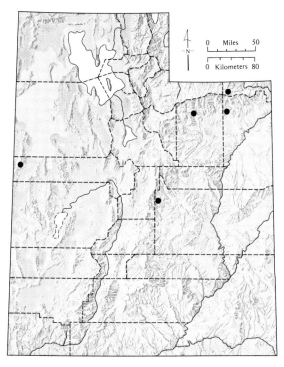

36. *Carex limnophila* Herm. Pond sedge June-July. Native perennial; wet meadows, 2160-2750 m.

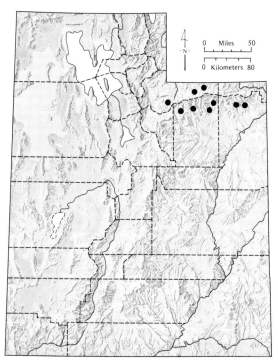

37. *Carex limosa* L. Mud sedge. June-Aug. Circumboreal perennial; wet meadows, 2950-3200 m.

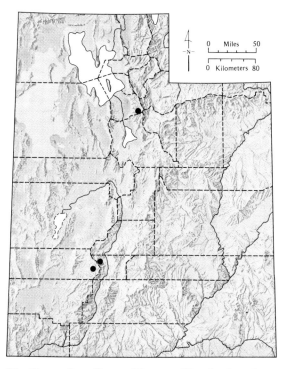

38. *Carex luzulina* Olney Woodrush sedge. June-Aug. Native perennial; streamside, wet meadows, openings in spruce-fir communities, 2950-3350 m.

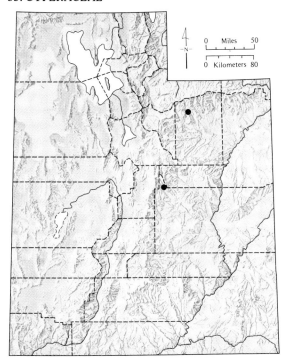

39. *Carex microglochin* Wahl. July-Aug.
Native perennial; wet meadows, 2800-2830 m.

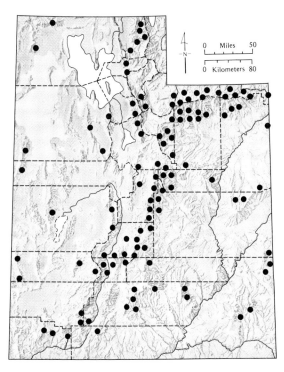

40. *Carex microptera* Mack. Smallwing sedge.
June-Aug. Native perennial; margins of ponds and
lakes, streamside, wet meadows, 1520-3420 m.

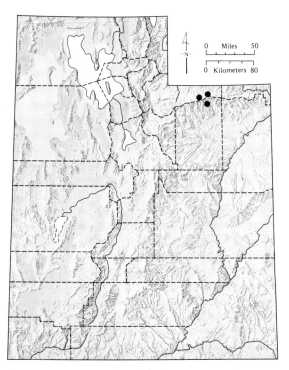

41. *Carex misandra* R. Br. Shortleaf sedge.
July-Aug. Circumboreal perennial; open slopes,
alpine meadows, 3600-3690 m.

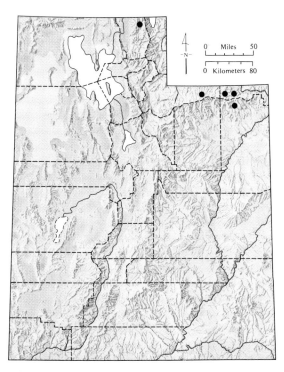

42. *Carex multicostata* Mack. Many-ribbed
sedge. June-Aug. Native perennial; streamside,
wet meadows, 2620-2840 m.

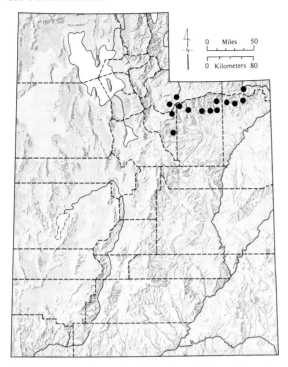

43. *Carex muricata* L. May-Aug. Circumboreal perennial; wet meadows, 2250-3780 m.

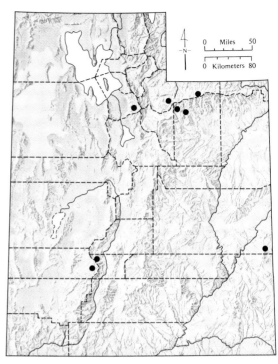

44. *Carex nardina* Fries   Spikenard sedge. June-Aug.   Circumboreal perennial; moist to dry open slopes, talus, cliff crevices, 3050-3510 m.

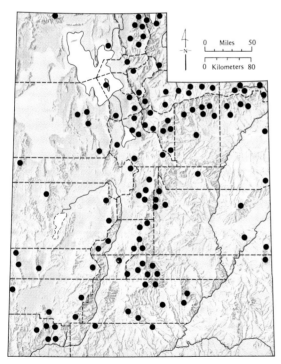

45. *Carex nebrascensis* Dewey   Nebraska sedge.   May-July.   Native perennial; marshes, along waterways, near springs and ponds, wet meadows, 1360-3070 m.

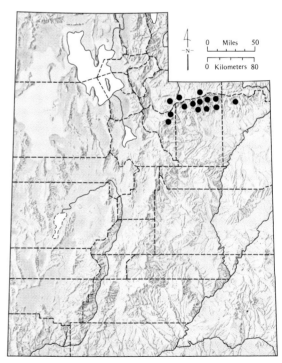

46. *Carex nelsonii* Mack. Nelson sedge. July-Aug.   Native perennial; streamside, moist to dry meadows, alpine slopes, 2830-3870 m.

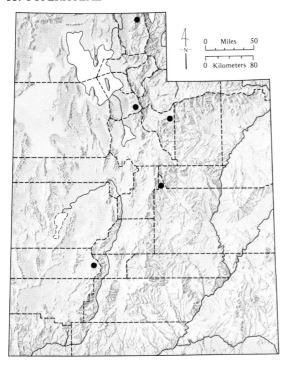

47. *Carex neurophora* Mack. Nerved alpine sedge. July-Aug. Native perennial; streamside, wet meadows, 2500-2960 m.

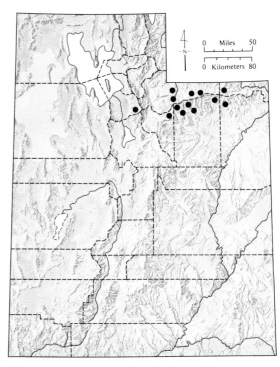

48. *Carex nigricans* C. A. Mey. Black alpine sedge. June-Aug. Native perennial; moist woods, streamside, wet to dry meadows, 2430-3380 m.

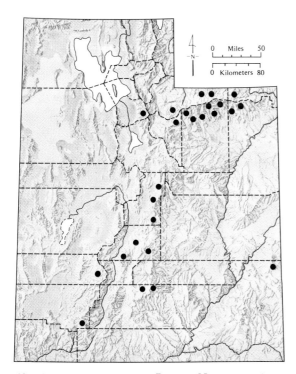

49. *Carex norvegica* Retz. Norway sedge. June-Aug. Circumboreal perennial; streamside, openings in aspen-conifer communities, wet meadows, 2250-3370 m.

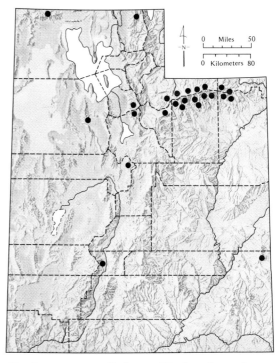

50. *Carex nova* Bailey Black sedge. June-Aug. Native perennial; openings in lodgepole pine and spruce forests, alpine meadows, 2790-3690 m.

239

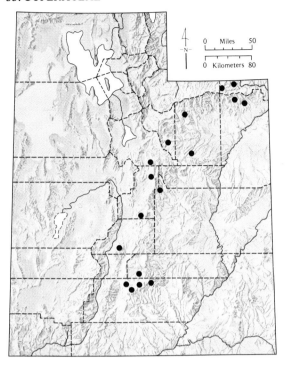

51. *Carex obtusata* Lilj. Blunt sedge. May-July. Native perennial; dry meadows, mountain brush to aspen, spruce-fir communities, 1980-3050 m.

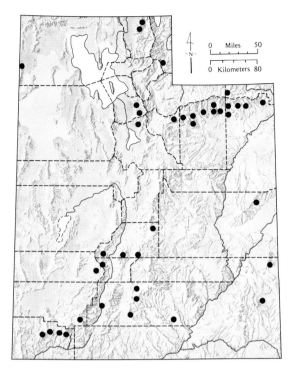

52. *Carex occidentalis* Bailey Western sedge. June-Aug. Native perennial; oak-maple, mountain brush, ponderosa pine, aspen, spruce-fir communities, 1830-3230 m.

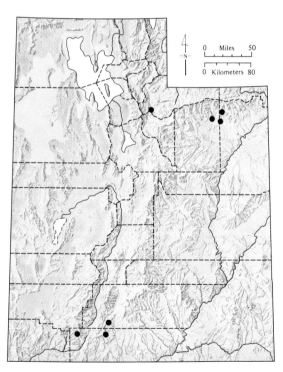

53. *Carex oederi* Retz. Green sedge. June-Aug. Circumboreal perennial; along waterways, wet meadow communities, 1760-2750 m.

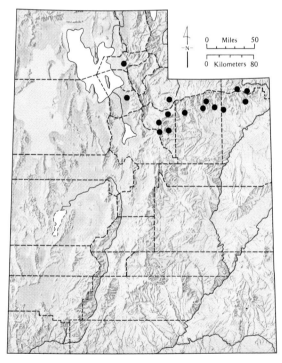

54. *Carex pachystachya* Steud. Chamisso sedge. May-Aug. Native perennial; near springs, streamside, wet meadows, 1430-2470 m.

33. CYPERACEAE

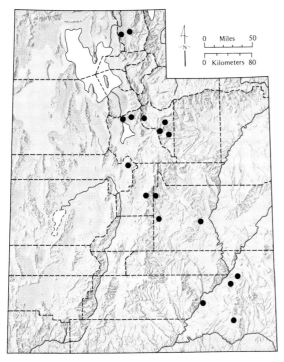

55. *Carex parryana* Dewey Parry sedge. May-July. Native perennial; wet meadows, near seeps and springs, 1220-3110 m.

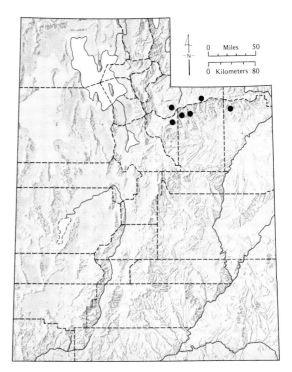

56. *Carex paupercula* Michx. Poor sedge. June-Aug. Circumboreal perennial; wet meadows, 2870-3110 m.

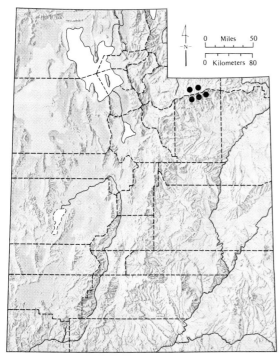

57. *Carex paysonis* Clokey Payson sedge. July-Aug. Native perennial; meadows, alpine slopes, 3290-3660 m.

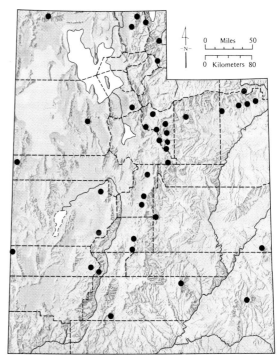

58. *Carex petasata* Dewey Liddon sedge. May-July. Native perennial; sagebrush, grass-forb, mountain brush, aspen communities, 2070-3050 m.

241

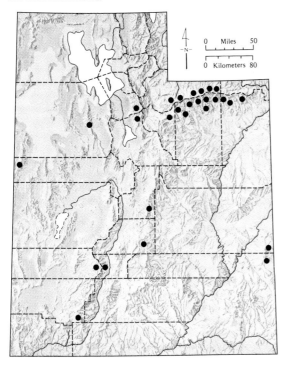

59. *Carex phaeocephala* Piper Dunhead sedge. June-Aug. Native perennial; lodgepole pine, spruce-fir, krummholz communities, rocky alpine slopes, 2830-3500 m.

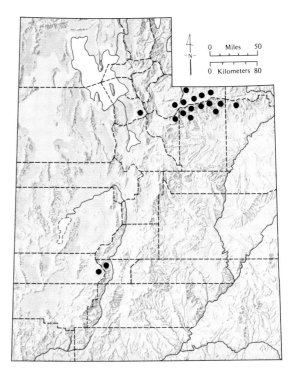

60. *Carex praeceptorum* Mack. July-Aug. Native perennial; margins of ponds and lakes, wet meadows, near seeps and springs, 3030-3400 m.

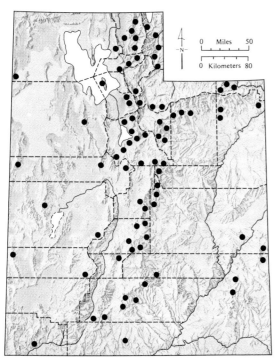

61. *Carex praegracilis* W. Boott Blackcreeper sedge. May-Aug. Native perennial; along waterways, margins of ponds and lakes, wet meadows, near seeps and springs, 850-2970 m.

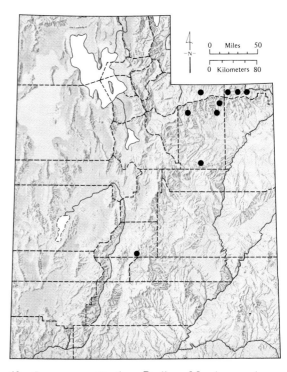

62. *Carex praticola* Rydb. Meadow sedge. June-Aug. Native perennial; openings in lodgepole pine, aspen, spruce-fir communities, 2740-3140 m.

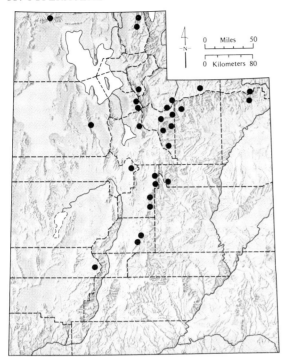

63. *Carex raynoldsii* Dewey   Raynolds sedge.
June-Aug. Native perennial; moist to dry meadows,
openings in aspen, spruce-fir communities, 2190-
3170 m.

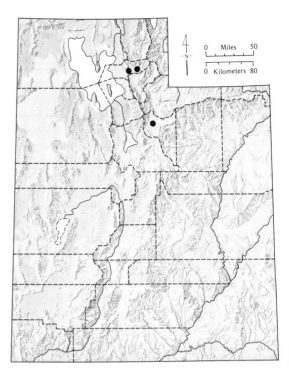

64. *Carex retrorsa* Schwein. Knotsheath sedge.
May-Sept.   Native perennial; streamside, wet
meadows, 1400-1830 m.

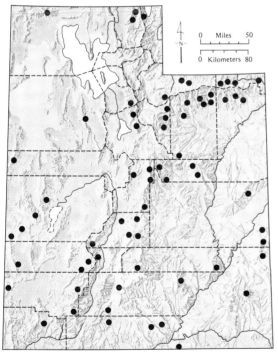

65. *Carex rossii* F. Boott   Ross sedge. May-
Aug. Native perennial; sagebrush, pinyon-juniper
to aspen, spruce-fir, alpine communities, 1340-
3450 m.

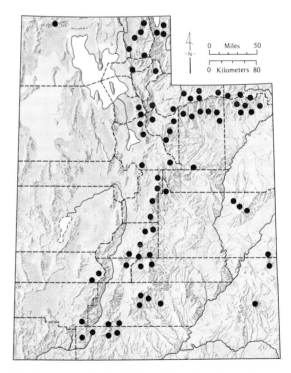

66. *Carex rostrata* Stokes Beaked sedge. June-
Aug. Circumboreal perennial; wet meadows, 1830-
3200 m.

243

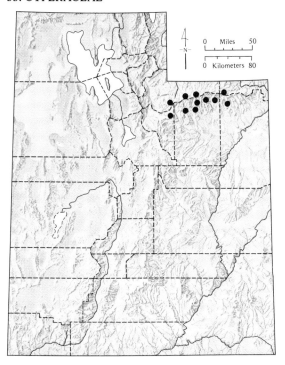

67. *Carex rupestris* All. Curly sedge. July-Aug. Circumboreal perennial; alpine meadows, krummholz communities, 3200-3660 m.

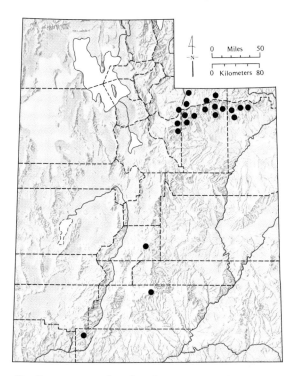

68. *Carex saxatilis* L. Rock sedge. June-Aug. Circumboreal perennial; margins of ponds and lakes, wet meadows, 2740-3810 m.

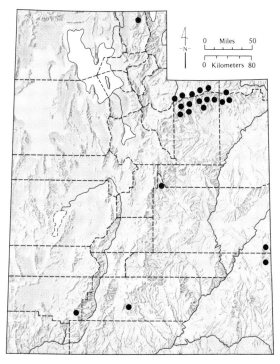

69. *Carex scirpoidea* Michx. False bulrush sedge. June-Aug. Native perennial; dry meadows, openings in spruce, lodgepole pine forests, krummholz, alpine communities, 2890-4100 m.

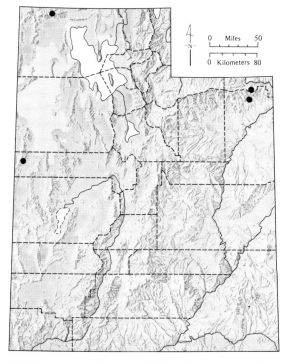

70. *Carex scopulorum* Holm Mountain sedge. June-Aug. Native perennial; streamsides, wet meadows, 2370-2790 m.

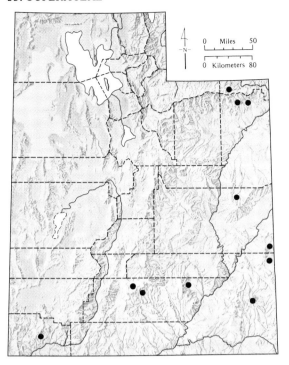

71. *Carex siccata* Dewey Silvertop sedge. June-Aug. Native perennial; sagebrush, oakbrush, ponderosa pine, aspen, spruce-fir communities, 910-3170 m.

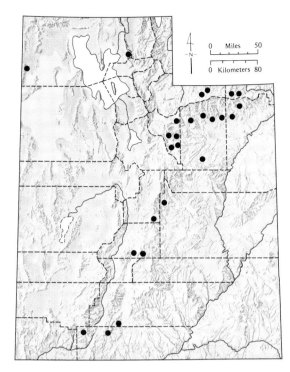

72. *Carex simulata* Mack. June-Aug. Native perennial; streamside, wet meadows, 2280-2870 m.

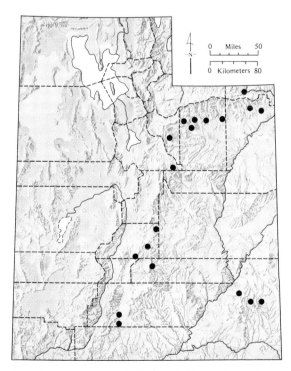

73. *Carex stenophylla* Wahl. Narrowleaf sedge. June-July. Native perennial; sagebrush-grass, pinyon-juniper communities, windswept slopes, 1920-3270 m.

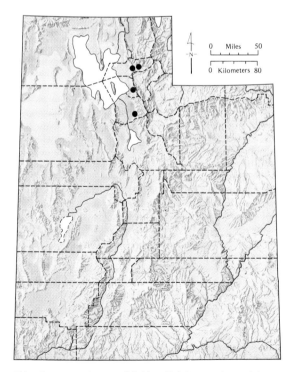

74. *Carex stipata* Muhl. Prickly sedge. May-Aug. Native perennial; wet sandy meadows, 1520-1830 m.

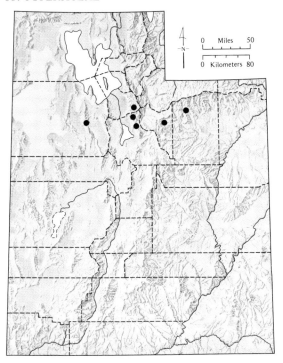

75. *Carex straminiformis* Bailey   Shasta
sedge.   July-Aug.   Native perennial; grass-forb,
spruce communities, exposed rocky ridges, 2740-
3140 m.

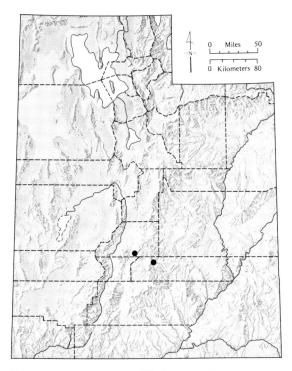

76. *Carex subfusca* W. Boott   Rusty sedge.
June-Aug.   Native perennial; dry meadows, 2120-
2880 m.

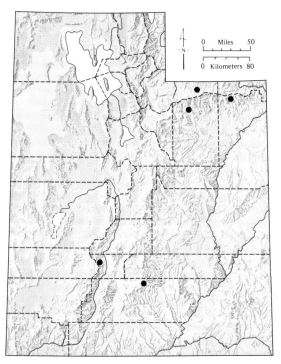

77. *Carex subnigricans* Stacey   Dark alpine
sedge.   July-Aug.   Native perennial; wet meadows,
2960-3360 m.

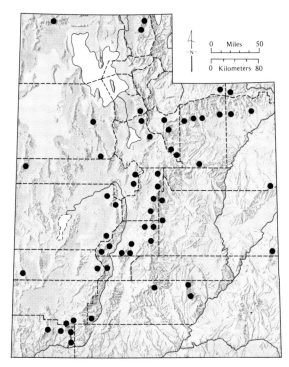

78. *Carex vallicola* Dewey   Valley sedge.
May-July.   Native perennial; sagebrush-grass,
mountain brush, ponderosa pine, aspen, spruce-fir
communities, 1670-3010 m.

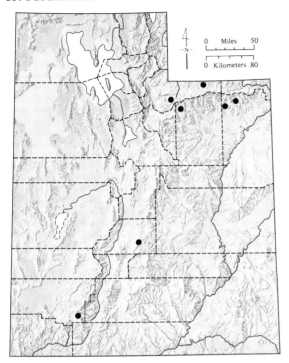

79. *Carex vesicaria* L. Blister sedge. June-
Aug. Circumboreal perennial; boggy meadows,
lake shores, often in shallow water, 3000-3050 m.

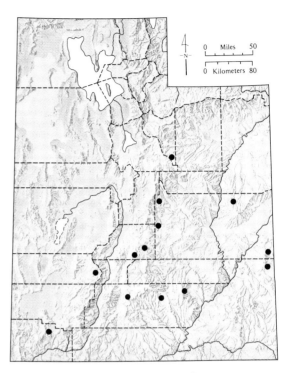

80. *Carex xerantica* Bailey Dryland sedge.
July-Aug. Native perennial; grass-forb
communities, open woods, 2620-3510 m.

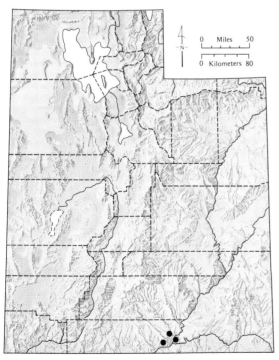

81. *Cladium californicum* (Wats.) O'Neill
California sawgrass. May-June. Native perennial;
hanging gardens, 1120-1150 m.

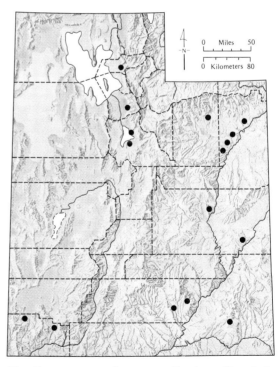

82. *Cyperus aristatus* Rottb. Bearded
flatsedge. June-Aug. Cosmopolitan annual; along
waterways, near seeps and springs, disturbed sites
in meadows, 1220-2010 m.

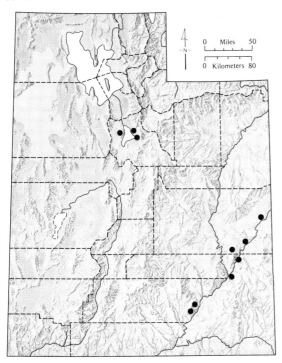

83. *Cyperus erythrorhizos* Muhl. Redroot flatsedge. June-Sept. Native annual; pond and lake margins, river bars, 1500-1820 m.

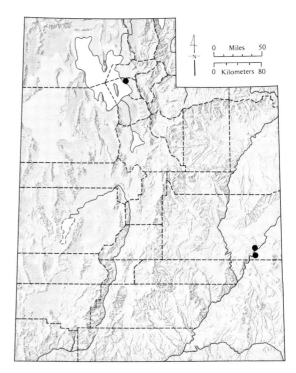

84. *Cyperus esculentus* L. Yellow or chufa flatsedge. May-Sept. Introduced perennial; along waterways, invading irrigated sites, 840-1750 m.

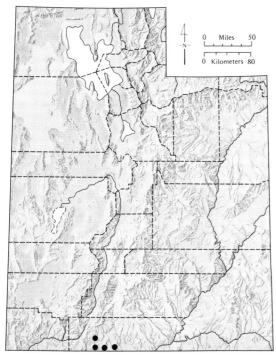

85. *Cyperus schweinitzii* Torr. Schweinitz flatsedge. June-Aug. Native perennial; dunes, sandy sites in desert shrub, juniper communities, 1730-1980 m.

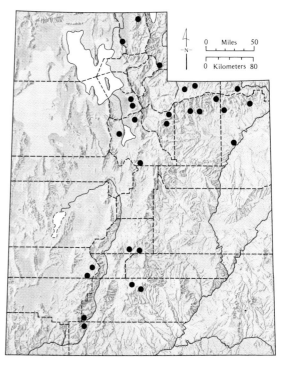

86. *Eleocharis acicularis* (L.) R. & S. Needle spikerush. June-Sept. Circumboreal perennial; along waterways, pond and lake margins, boggy meadows, often in shallow water, 1310-3250 m.

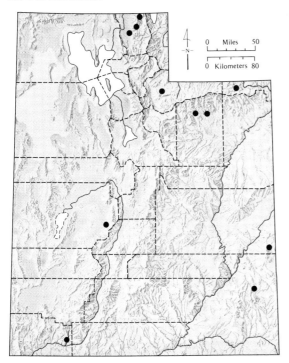

87. *Eleocharis bolanderi* Gray Bolander
spikerush. May-July. Native perennial; wet
meadows, 1450-2590 m.

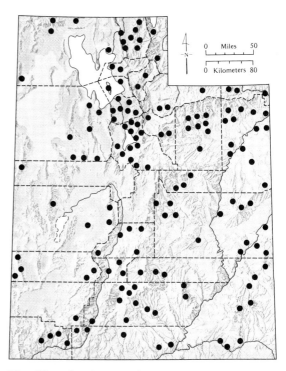

88. *Eleocharis palustris* (L.) R. & S.
Common spikerush. May-Aug. Circumboreal
perennial; streamside, pond and lake margins, wet
meadows, 1130-3200 m.

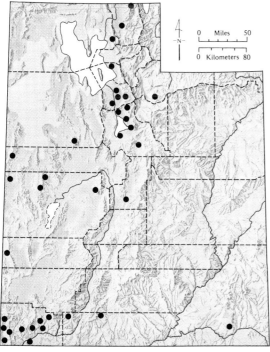

89. *Eleocharis parishii* Britt. Parish
spikerush. Apr.-Sept. Native perennial; near seeps
and springs, pond and lake margins, wet meadows,
770-2700 m.

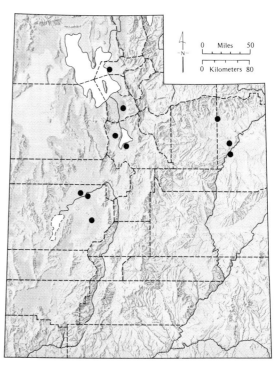

90. *Eleocharis parvula* (R. & S.) Bluff. &
Fingerh. Dwarf spikerush. June-Sept. Native
perennial; flood plains, drying margins of lakes
and ponds, 1250-1770 m.

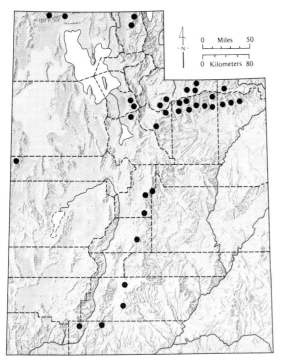

91. *Eleocharis pauciflora* (Lightf.) Link June-Aug. Circumboreal perennial; streamside, wet meadows, 2080-3370 m.

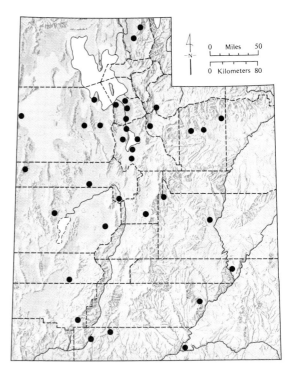

92. *Eleocharis rostellata* (Torr.) Torr. Beaked spikerush. June-Aug. Native perennial; along waterways, marshes, near seeps and springs, alkali tolerant, 1280-2250 m.

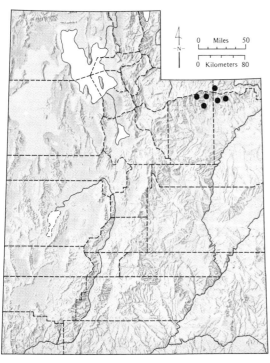

93. *Eriophorum polystachion* L. Many-spike cottonsedge. July-Aug. Circumboreal perennial; wet meadows, 2740-3390 m.

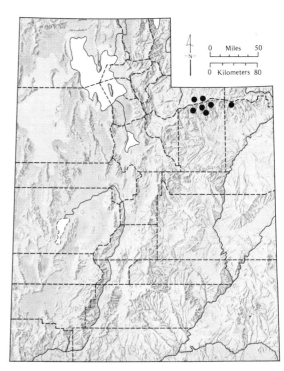

94. *Eriophorum scheuchzeri* Hoppe Scheuchzeri cottonsedge. July-Aug. Circumboreal perennial; wet meadows, lakeshores, 3350-3810 m.

250

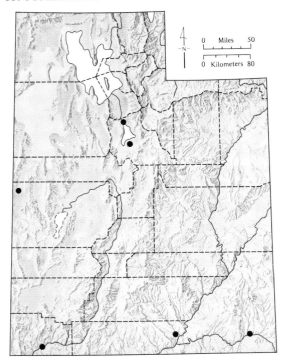

95. *Fimbristylis spadicea* (L.) Vahl July-Aug. Native perennial; hanging gardens, streamside, pond and lake margins, wet meadows, alkali tolerant, 1120-1380 m.

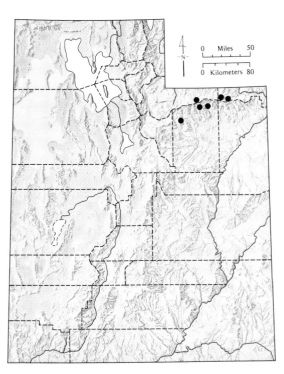

96. *Kobresia bellardii* (All.) Degland July-Aug. Circumboreal perennial; talus, other rocky sites above timberline, 3200-3630 m.

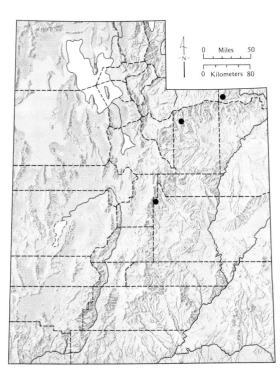

97. *Kobresia simpliciuscula* (Wahl.) Mack. June-Aug. Circumboreal perennial; wet meadows, 2580-2790 m.

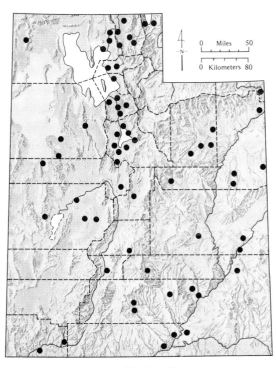

98. *Scirpus acutus* Bigel. Hardstem bulrush; tule. June-Aug. Native perennial; flood plains, marshes, pond and lake margins, near seeps and springs, 1090-2200 m.

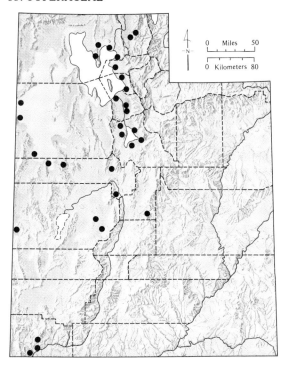

99. *Scirpus americanus* Pers. American threesquare bulrush. June-Sept. Native perennial; marshes, pond and lake margins, near seeps and springs, salt tolerant, 730-1510 m.

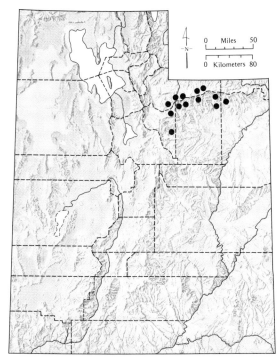

100. *Scirpus cespitosus* L. Deerhair bulrush. July-Aug. Circumboreal perennial; wet meadows, 2890-3420 m.

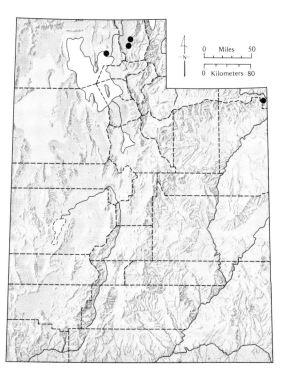

101. *Scirpus fluviatilis* (Torr.) Gray River bulrush. June-Aug. Native perennial; marshes, along waterways, 1380-1650 m.

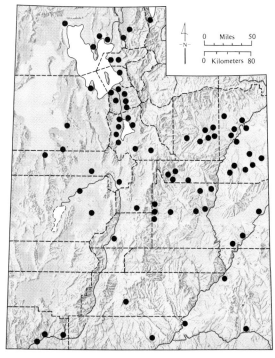

102. *Scirpus maritimus* L. Alkali bulrush. June-Sept. Circumboreal perennial; marshes, along waterways, pond and lake margins, wet meadows, alkali and salt tolerant, 830-2080 m.

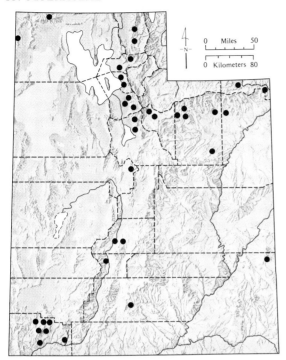

103. *Scirpus microcarpus* Presl Panicled bulrush. June-Aug. Native perennial; along waterways, wet meadows, 1370-2890 m.

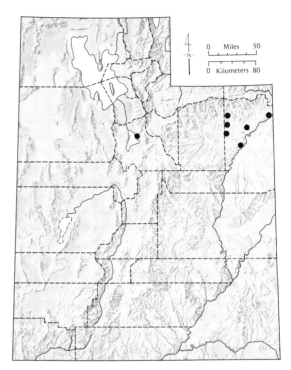

104. *Scirpus pallidus* (Britt.) Fern. Pale bulrush. June-Aug. Native perennial; along waterways, 1370-1710 m.

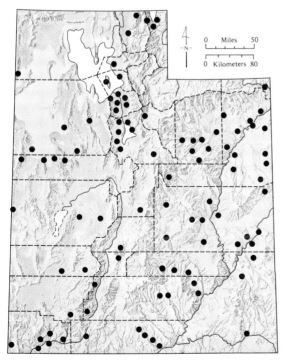

105. *Scirpus pungens* Vahl Common threesquare bulrush. May-Aug. Cosmopolitan perennial; marshes, along waterways, pond and lake margins, near seeps and springs, salt tolerant, 850-2290 m.

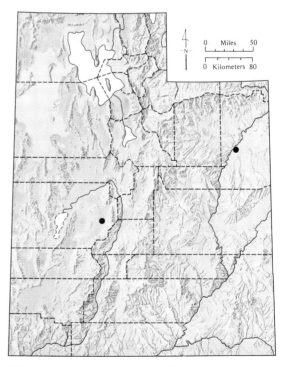

106. *Scirpus supinus* L. Sharpscale bulrush. May-Sept. Cosmopolitan annual; flood plains, drying mud flats along pond and lake margins, 1380-1420 m.

33. CYPERACEAE

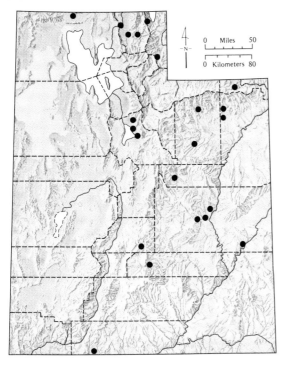

107. **Scirpus validus** Vahl Softstem bulrush.
June-Aug. Native perennial; along waterways,
pond and lake margins, 1220-1880 m.

34. DIPSACACEAE

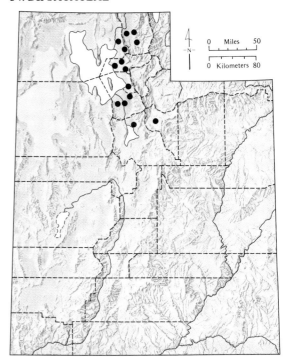

1. **Dipsacus sylvestris** Huds. Wild teasel.
May-Sept. Introduced biennial; moist waste places,
1300-1520 m.

35. ELAEAGNACEAE

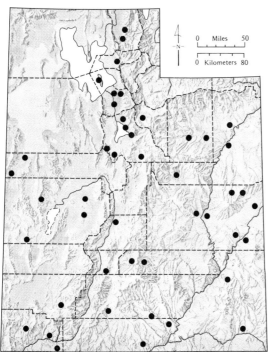

1. **Elaeagnus angustifolia** L. Russian olive.
May-July. Introduced tree or shrub; cultivated,
escaping and well established in moist sites, 810-
2090 m.

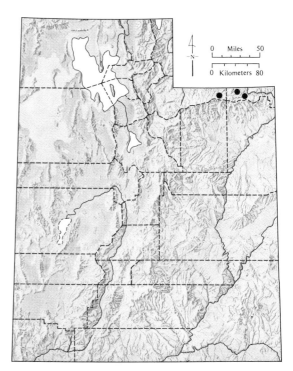

2. **Elaeagnus commutata** Bernh. Silverberry.
June-July. Native shrub or small tree; moist sites,
commonly streamside, 1970-2430 m.

35. ELAEAGNACEAE

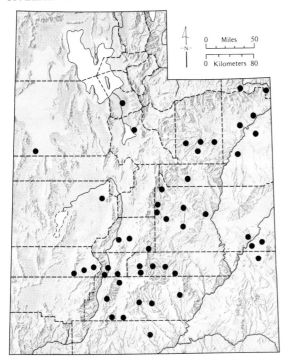

3. *Shepherdia argentea* (Pursh) Nutt. Silver buffaloberry. Apr.-May. Native shrub or small tree; streamside and moist meadows in pinyon-juniper, oak, ponderosa pine communities, 1330-2280 m.

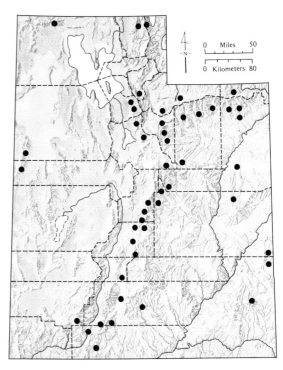

4. *Shepherdia canadensis* (L.) Nutt. Russet buffaloberry. May-July. Native shrub; shaded sites in aspen, spruce-fir communities, 2040-3340 m.

36. ELATINACEAE

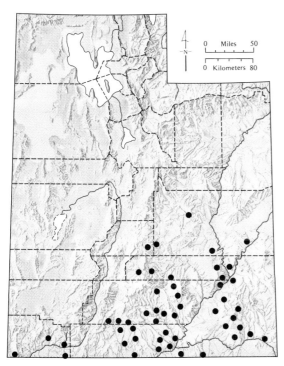

5. *Shepherdia rotundifolia* Parry Roundleaf buffaloberry. Mar.-May. Native shrub; creosote bush to pinyon-juniper communities, frequently cliff-dwelling, 970-2670 m.

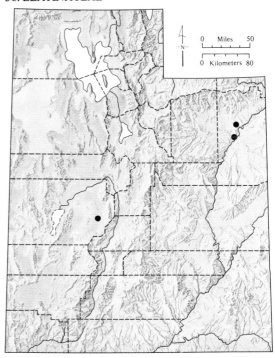

1. *Bergia texana* (Hook.) Seub. June-Aug. Native annual; moist meadows, streamside, salt tolerant, 1360-1680 m.

36. ELATINACEAE

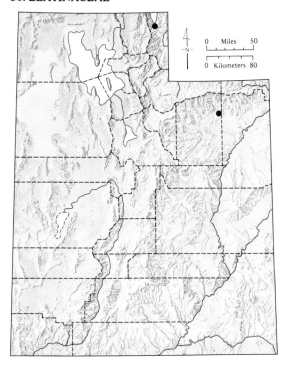

2. ***Elatine brachysperma*** Gray Shortseed waterwort. July-Aug. Native annual; drying mud flats, 1810-2280 m.

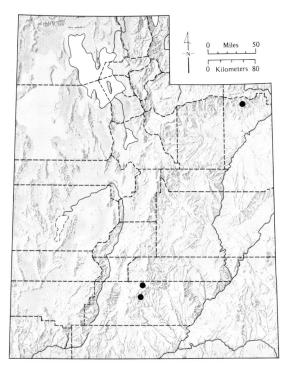

3. ***Elatine rubella*** Rydb. Aug.-Sept. Native annual; drying mud flats, 2720-2880 m.

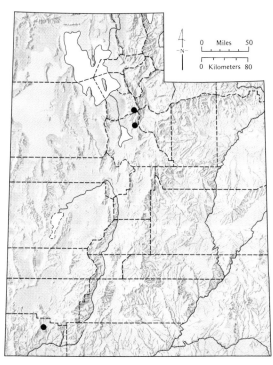

4. ***Elatine triandra*** Schk. Three-lobed waterwort. Aug.-Sept. Native annual; drying mud flats, 2640-2730 m.

37. EPHEDRACEAE

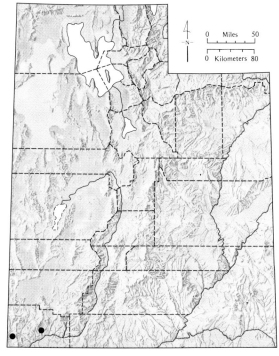

1. ***Ephedra fasciculata*** A. Nels. Nevada jointfur. Native shrub; rocky sites in creosote bush communities, 750-910 m.

37. EPHEDRACEAE

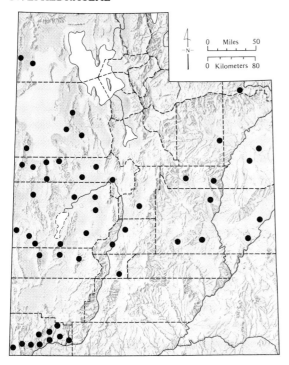

2. *Ephedra nevadensis* Wats. Nevada Mormon tea. Native shrub; creosote bush, shadscale, desert shrub, juniper communities, 910-2280 m.

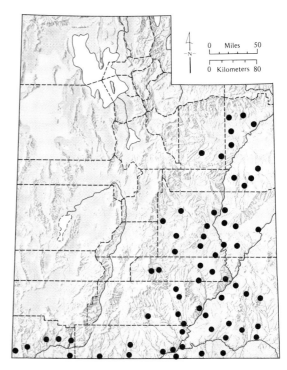

3. *Ephedra torreyana* Wats. Native shrub; creosote bush, desert shrub to pinyon-juniper communities, 810-1730 m.

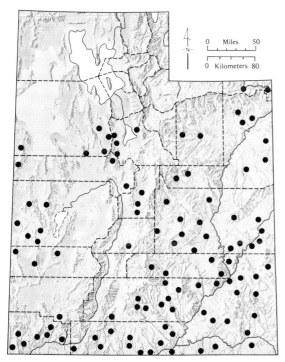

4. *Ephedra viridis* Cov. Mormon tea. Native shrub; rocky slopes, often as soil binder, creosote bush to pinyon-juniper communities, 840-2730 m.

38. EQUISETACEAE

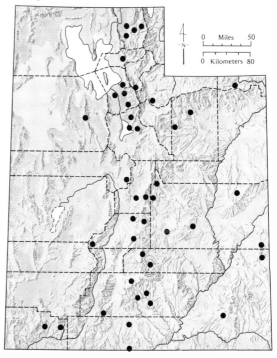

1. *Equisetum arvense* L. Field horsetail. Apr.-July. Cosmopolitan; aerial stems annual; marshes, streambanks, wet meadows, 1300-3030 m.

257

38. EQUISETACEAE

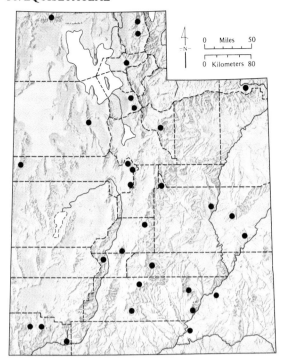

2. *Equisetum hyemale* L. Western scouring rush. May-Oct. Circumboreal; aerial stems perennial; streambanks, 910-2430 m.

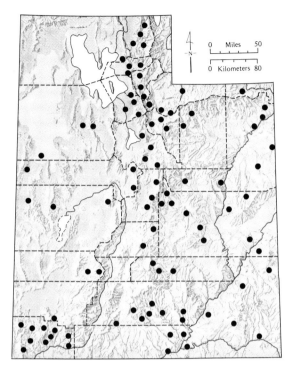

3. *Equisetum laevigatum* A. Br. Smooth horsetail. May-Oct. Native; aerial stems biennial; streamside, moist to dry, often disturbed sites in meadows, 940-2850 m.

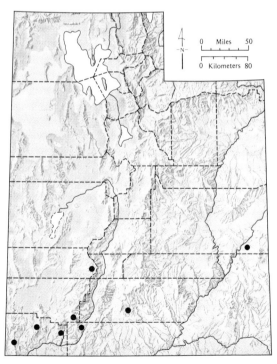

4. *Equisetum variegatum* Schleich. Variegated horsetail. July-Sept. Circumboreal; aerial stems perennial; streamside, wet meadows, 2660-3150 m.

39. ERICACEAE

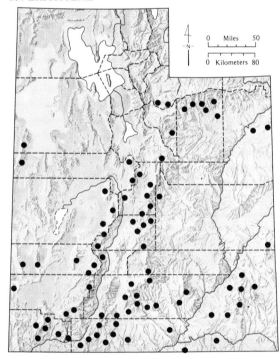

1. *Arctostaphylos patula* Greene Greenleaf manzanita. Apr.-July. Native shrub; mountain brush, pinyon pine, ponderosa pine, lodgepole pine communities, 1360-2730 m.

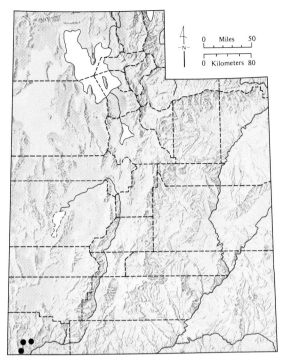

2. *Arctostaphylos pringlei* Parry Pink-bracted manzanita. Apr.-June. Native shrub; oak, pinyon-juniper communities, 1510-2120 m.

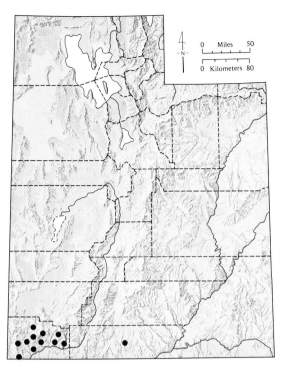

3. *Arctostaphylos pungens* H. B. K. Mexican manzanita. Apr.-June. Native shrub; desert shrub, juniper communities, open rocky ridges, 1060-1880 m.

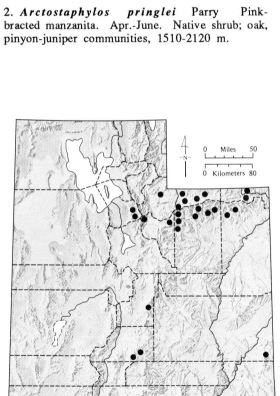

4. *Arctostaphylos uva-ursi* (L.) Spreng. Bearberry. June-July. Circumboreal shrub; conifer communities, open rocky ridges, 2140-3500 m.

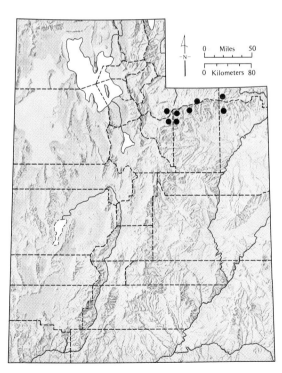

5. *Gaultheria humifusa* (Grah.) Rydb. Western wintergreen. July-Aug. Native subshrub; moist openings in conifer communities, 2880-3350 m.

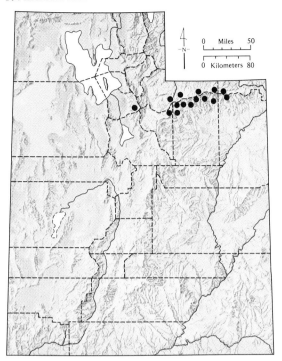

6. *Kalmia polifolia* Wang. Bog or swamp laurel. July-Aug. Native shrub; moist meadows, lakeshores, shaded sites in spruce-fir forests, 2940-3490 m.

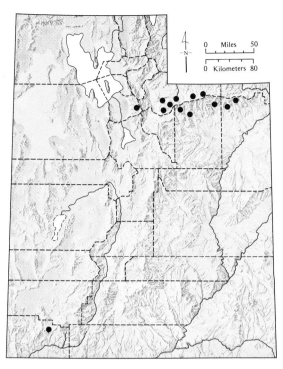

7. *Ledum glandulosum* Nutt. Labrador tea. June-Aug. Native shrub; streamside, moist meadows, rock crevices, 2450-3280 m.

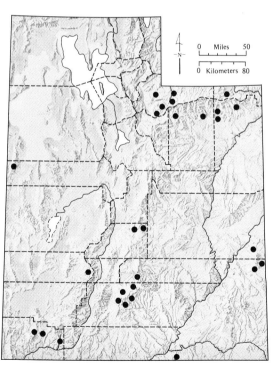

8. *Pterospora andromedea* Nutt. Pinedrops. July-Aug. Native perennial herb; shaded sites in aspen, spruce-fir, ponderosa pine, lodgepole pine communities, 2420-3250 m.

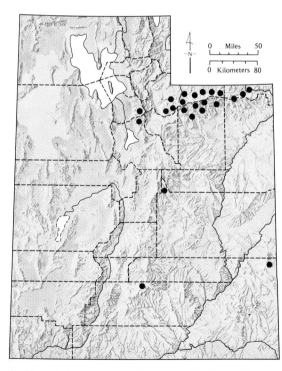

9. *Vaccinium caespitosum* Michx. Dwarf blueberry. June-Aug. Native subshrub; streamside, meadows, rocky sites, 2420-3340 m.

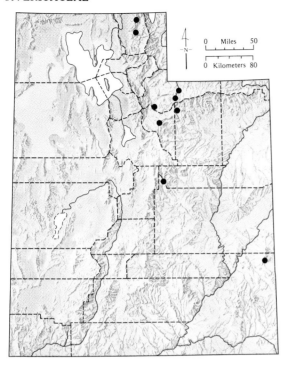

10. *Vaccinium membranaceum* Dougl. Big blueberry. June-July. Native shrub; shaded sites in spruce-fir, lodgepole pine forests, 2480-3120 m.

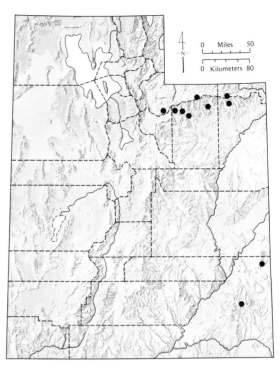

11. *Vaccinium myrtillus* L. Myrtle whortleberry; bilberry. June-Aug. Native subshrub; shaded sites in conifer forests, 2300-3340 m.

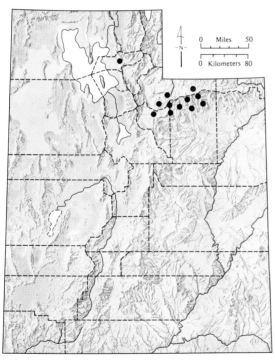

12. *Vaccinium occidentale* Gray Western bog blueberry. June-Aug. Native shrub; meadows, shaded sites in conifer forests, 3030-3490 m.

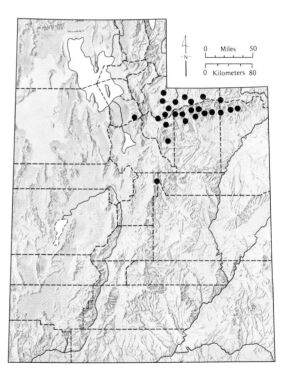

13. *Vaccinium scoparium* Leiberg Grouse whortleberry. June-Aug. Native subshrub; shaded sites in conifer forests, 2720-3410 m.

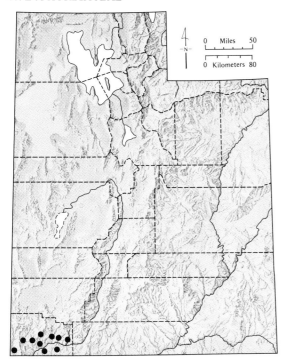

1. *Croton californicus* Muell.-Arg. June-Oct. Native perennial herb; sandy sites in creosote bush communities, 840-1210 m.

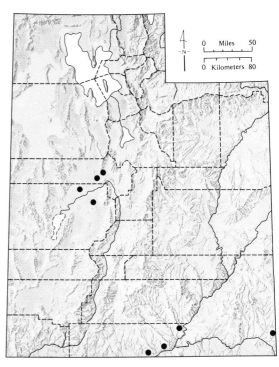

2. *Croton texensis* (Klotzsch) Muell.-Arg. June-Aug. Native annual; dunes, other sandy sites in desert shrub communities, 1120-1670 m.

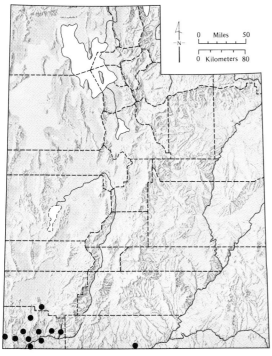

3. *Euphorbia albomarginata* T. & G. Whitemargin spurge. Apr.-June. Native perennial herb; creosote bush to desert shrub, pinyon-juniper communities, 800-1820 m.

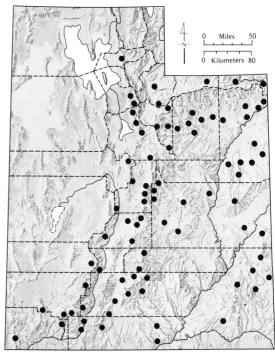

4. *Euphorbia brachycera* Engelm. Shorthorn spurge. June-Aug. Native perennial herb; shadscale, desert shrub to pinyon-juniper, aspen-conifer communities, 1420-3180 m.

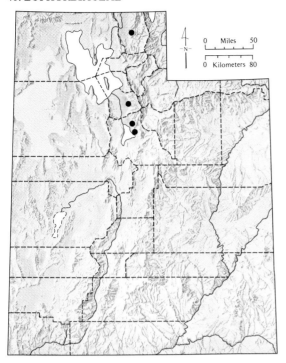

5. *Euphorbia cyparissias* L. Cypress spurge. May-July. Introduced perennial herb; cultivated, escaping and persistent, 1300-1370 m.

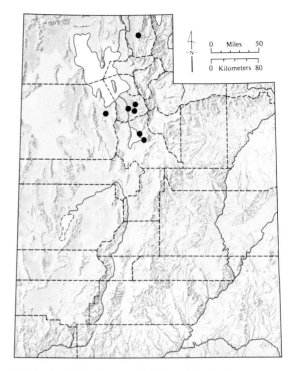

6. *Euphorbia dentata* Michx. Toothed spurge. July-Aug. Introduced annual; invading cultivated areas, roadsides and other disturbed sites, 1300-1400 m.

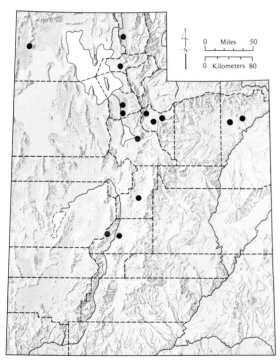

7. *Euphorbia esula* L. Leafy spurge. May-July. Introduced perennial herb; roadsides, fallow fields, other disturbed sites, 1300-2880 m.

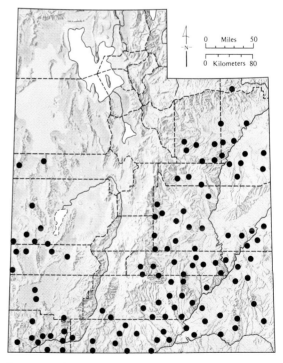

8. *Euphorbia fendleri* T. & G. Fendler spurge. May-Aug. Native perennial herb; creosote bush to pinyon-juniper communities, 900-2280 m.

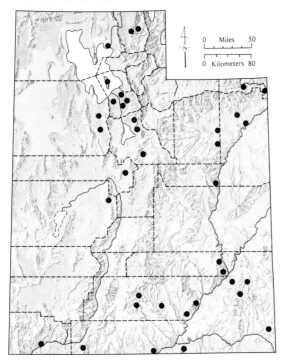

9. **Euphorbia glyptosperma** Engelm. Ridgeseed spurge. July-Aug. Native annual; invading gardens, roadsides, and disturbed sites in salt desert shrub to mountain brush communities, 840-2090 m.

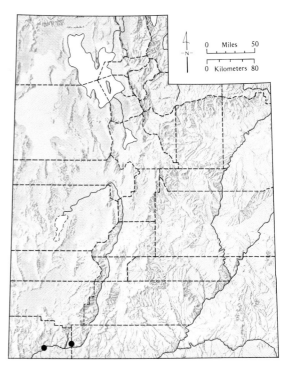

10. **Euphorbia hyssopifolia** L. Hyssop spurge. Mar.-May. Native annual; disturbed sites in creosote bush communities, 840-1210 m.

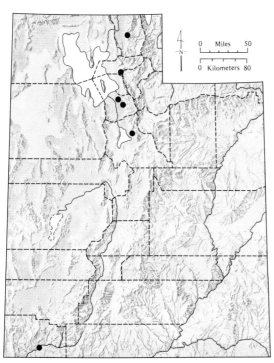

11. **Euphorbia maculata** L. Spotted spurge. July-Oct. Introduced annual; invading lawns, other cultivated areas and disturbed sites, 1020-1370 m.

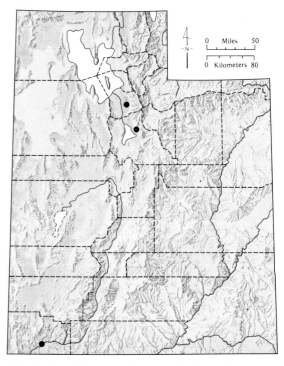

12. **Euphorbia marginata** Pursh Snow-on-the-mountain spurge. July-Sept. Introduced annual; cultivated, escaping and occasionally persistent, 1300-1400 m.

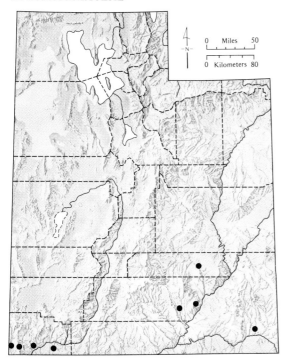

13. *Euphorbia micromera* Boiss. Littleleaf spurge. July-Sept. Native annual; creosote bush, desert shrub communities, 840-1610 m.

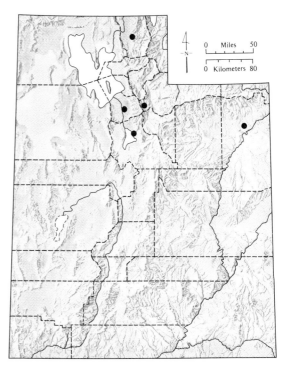

14. *Euphorbia myrsinites* L. Myrtle spurge. Apr.-July. Introduced perennial herb; cultivated, escaping and persistent, 1300-2060 m.

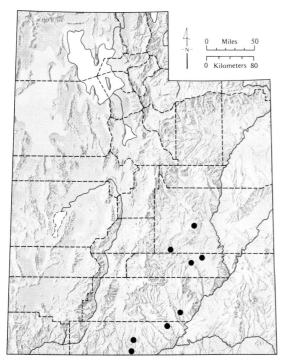

15. *Euphorbia nephradenia* Barneby Utah spurge. June-Aug. Native annual; desert shrub communities, 1150-1610 m.

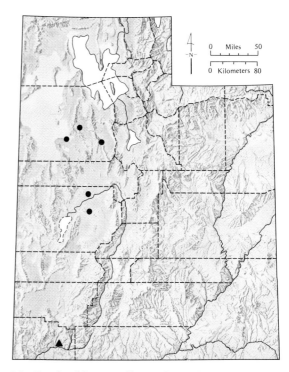

16. *Euphorbia ocellata* D. & H. Little-eye spurge. July-Sept. Native annual; dunes and other sandy, sometimes saline sites, 1390-1550 m.

40. EUPHORBIACEAE

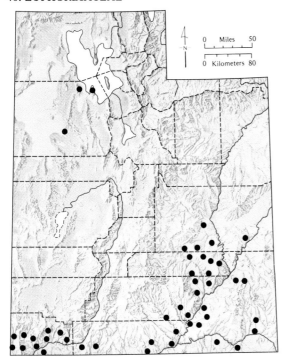

17. *Euphorbia parryi* Engelm. Dune spurge. June-Oct. Native annual; dunes, other sandy sites in creosote bush to desert shrub, pinyon-juniper communities, 840-1850 m.

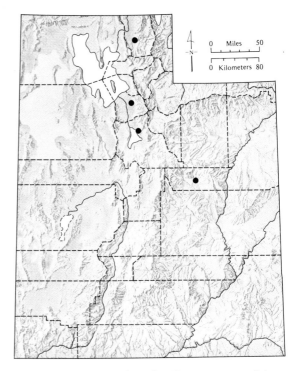

18. *Euphorbia peplus* L. Petty spurge. July-Sept. Introduced annual; invading cultivated sites, 1360-1430 m.

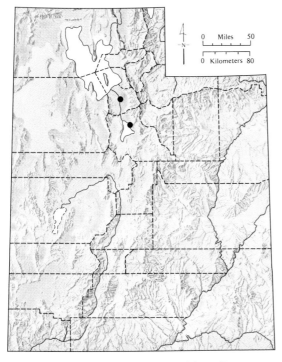

19. *Euphorbia prostrata* Ait. Prostrate spurge. July-Sept. Introduced annual; invading gardens and lawns, 1300-1370 m.

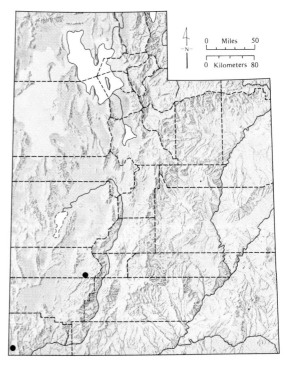

20. *Euphorbia revoluta* Engelm. July-Aug. Native annual; creosote bush to pinyon-juniper communities, 850-2000 m.

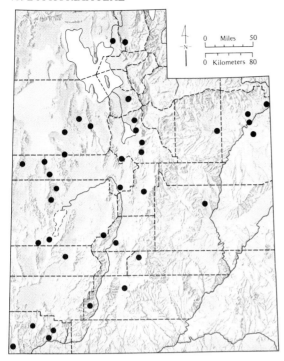

21. *Euphorbia serpyllifolia* Pers. Thymeleaf spurge. July-Oct. Native annual; creosote bush, salt desert shrub, desert shrub to aspen, ponderosa pine communities, occasionally weedy, 840-2730 m.

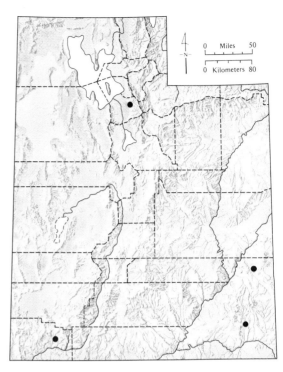

22. *Euphorbia spathulata* Lam. Prairie or beaver spurge. May-June. Native annual; desert shrub, sagebrush, pinyon-juniper communities, 1300-1400 m.

23. *Reverchonia arenaria* Gray Aug.-Sept. Native annual; dunes, other sandy sites in desert shrub communities, 910-1820 m.

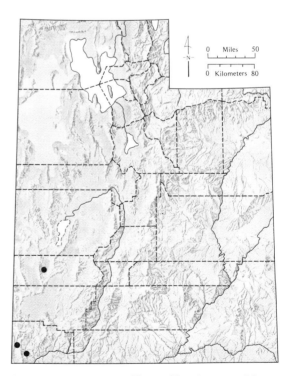

24. *Tragia ramosa* Torr. Noseburn. May-Sept. Native perennial herb; rock crevices, dry cliffs, creosote bush to desert shrub communities, 910-1970 m.

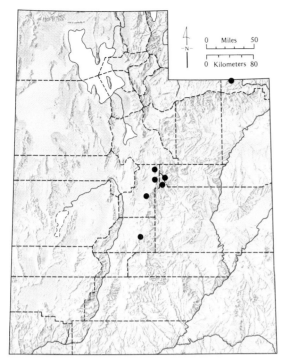

1. *Astragalus adsurgens* Pall. Standing milkvetch. May-Aug. Native perennial herb; open sites in sagebrush to aspen, ponderosa pine communities, 1970-3150 m.

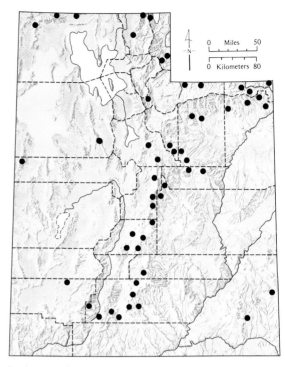

2. *Astragalus agrestis* G. Don Purple or field milkvetch. Apr.-July. Native perennial herb; open sites in sagebrush to aspen, conifer communities, moist meadows, 1360-3120 m.

3. *Astragalus alpinus* L. Alpine milkvetch. July-Aug. Circumboreal perennial herb; moist sites in aspen, conifer communities, 2420-2700 m.

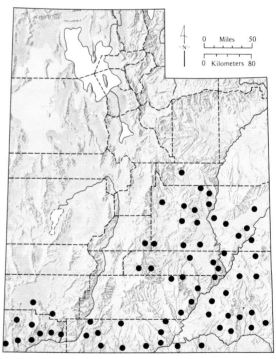

4. *Astragalus amphioxys* Gray Crescent milkvetch. Apr.-June. Native perennial herb; creosote bush, desert shrub to pinyon-juniper, mountain brush communities, 810-2490 m.

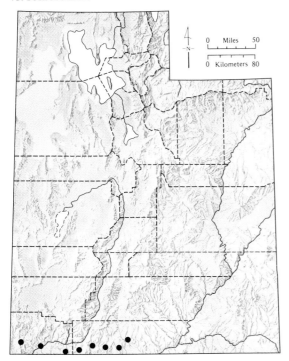

5. *Astragalus ampullarius* Wats. Gumbo milkvetch. May-June. Native perennial herb; creosote bush, shadscale, desert shrub communities, 950-1630 m.

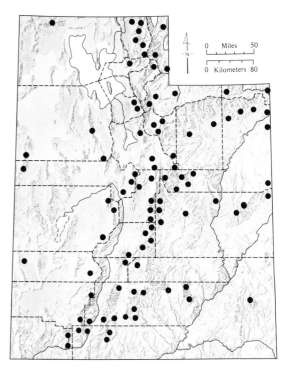

6. *Astragalus argophyllus* T. & G. Silverleaf milkvetch. Apr.-June. Native perennial herb; sagebrush to aspen, conifer communities, 1420-3030 m.

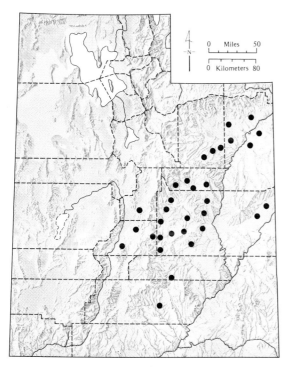

7. *Astragalus asclepiadoides* Jones Milkweed milkvetch. May-June. Native perennial herb; mat saltbush, shadscale communities, 1420-2300 m.

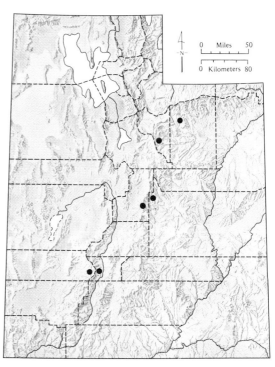

8. *Astragalus australis* (L.) Lam. Subarctic or Indian milkvetch. June-Aug. Circumboreal perennial herb; alpine rocky ridges, talus, 2840-3610 m.

41. FABACEAE

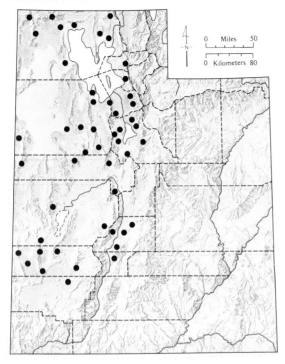

9. *Astragalus beckwithii* T. & G. Beckwith milkvetch. Apr.-June. Native perennial herb; shadscale, sagebrush-grass, pinyon-juniper, mountain brush communities, 1300-2450 m.

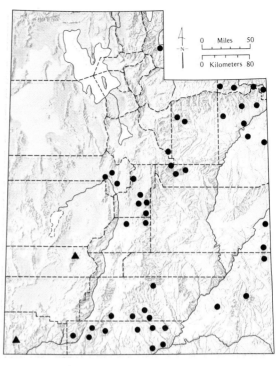

10. *Astragalus bisulcatus* (Hook.) Gray Two-grooved milkvetch. May-July. Native perennial herb; salt desert shrub, sagebrush, pinyon-juniper, mountain brush communities, 1460-2580 m.

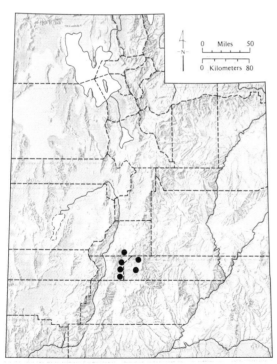

11. *Astragalus bodinii* Sheld. Bodin milkvetch. July-Aug. Native perennial herb; moist meadows, 2120-2270 m.

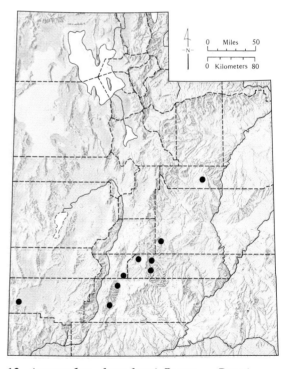

12. *Astragalus brandegei* Porter Brandegee milkvetch. May-Sept. Native perennial herb; sandy to rocky sites in oakbrush, pinyon-juniper communities, 1810-2300 m.

270

41. FABACEAE

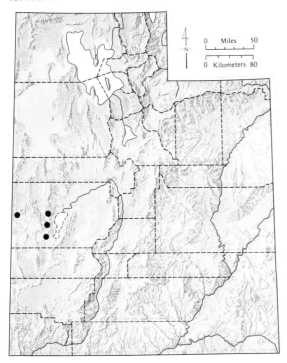

13. *Astragalus callithrix* Barneby Callaway milkvetch. Apr.-June. Native perennial herb; dunes and other sandy sites in sagebrush, juniper communities, 1540-1700 m.

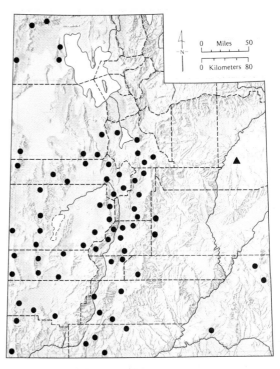

14. *Astragalus calycosus* Wats. Torrey milkvetch. Apr.-July. Native perennial herb; barren sites with shadscale, desert shrub, pinyon-juniper communities to exposed alpine ridges, 1570-3340 m.

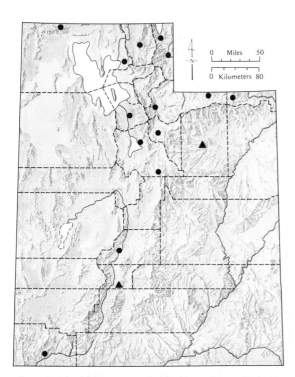

15. *Astragalus canadensis* L. Canada milkvetch. Apr.-July. Native perennial herb; streamside, pond and lake margins, moist meadows, 910-2330 m.

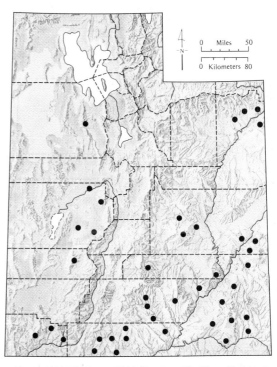

16. *Astragalus ceramicus* Sheld. Painted milkvetch. May-July. Native perennial herb; dunes, other sandy to rocky sites in desert shrub to pinyon-juniper communities, 1210-2430 m.

271

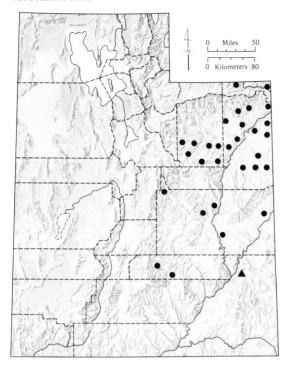

17. *Astragalus chamaeleuce* Gray Cicada milkvetch; popper. Apr.-June. Native perennial herb; barren slopes in shadscale, desert shrub, pinyon-juniper communities, 1420-2400 m.

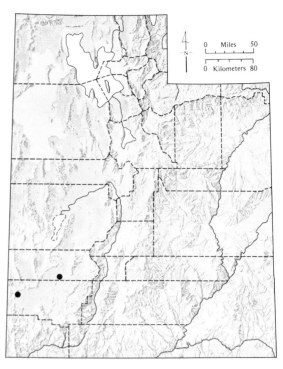

18. *Astragalus chamaemeniscus* Barneby Dwarf crescent milkvetch. Apr.-May. Native perennial herb; sagebrush, pinyon-juniper communities, 1510-1610 m.

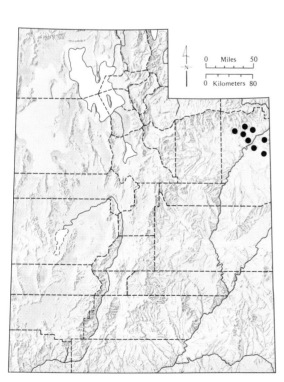

19. *Astragalus chloodes* Barneby Grass milkvetch. May-June. Native perennial herb; rocky sites in desert shrub, mountain brush, pinyon-juniper communities, 1450-1820 m.

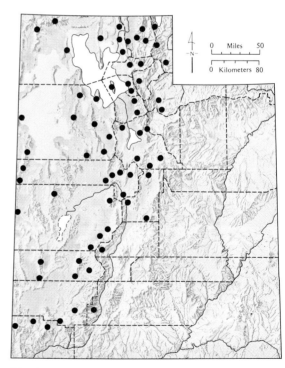

20. *Astragalus cibarius* Sheld. Silky loco milkvetch. Apr.-July. Native perennial herb; shadscale, sagebrush-grass, pinyon-juniper communities, 1270-2880 m.

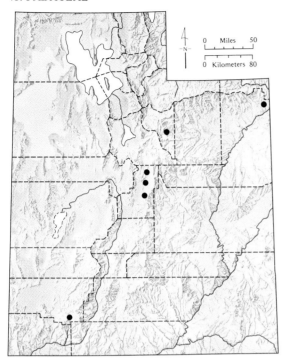

21. *Astragalus cicer* L. Chickpea milkvetch.
May-Aug. Introduced perennial herb; cultivated,
escaping and persistent, 2150-2910 m.

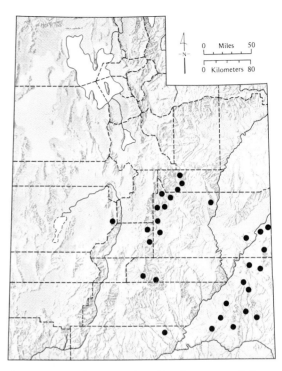

22. *Astragalus coltonii* Jones Colton
milkvetch. Apr.-June. Native perennial herb;
rocky sites in desert shrub, sagebrush-grass,
mountain brush, pinyon-juniper communities,
1540-2880 m.

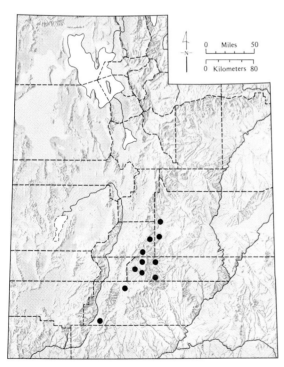

23. *Astragalus consobrinus* (Barneby) Welsh
Solemn or Bicknell milkvetch. Apr.-June. Native
perennial herb; desert shrub-grass, pinyon-juniper
communities, 1570-2580 m.

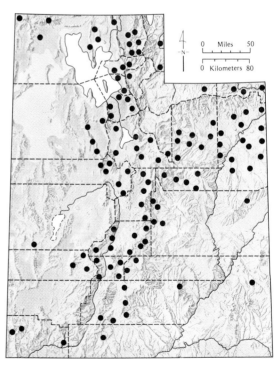

24. *Astragalus convallarius* Greene Timber
milkvetch. May-July. Native perennial herb;
desert shrub, pinyon-juniper, ponderosa pine, oak-
aspen communities, 1270-2770 m.

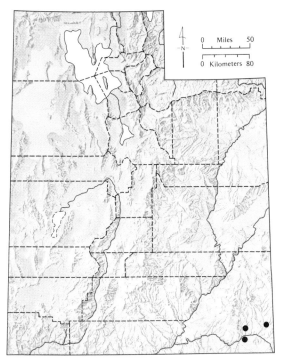

25. *Astragalus cronquistii* Barneby
Cronquist milkvetch. Apr.-May. Native perennial
herb; desert shrub communities, 1330-1490 m.

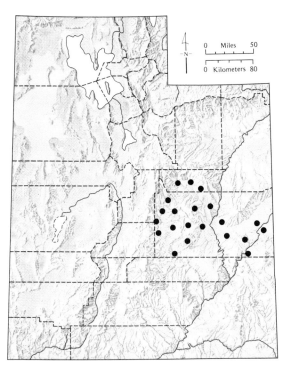

26. *Astragalus cymboides* Jones Canoe
milkvetch. May-June. Native perennial herb; mat
saltbush, shadscale, desert shrub, pinyon-juniper
communities, 1570-2280 m.

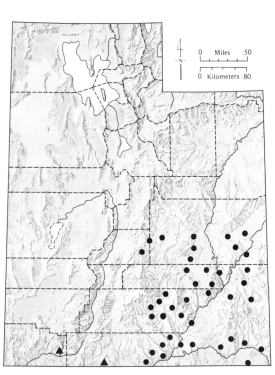

27. *Astragalus desperatus* Jones Rimrock
milkvetch. Apr.-June. Native perennial herb;
rocky sites in desert shrub, pinyon-juniper
communities, 1300-1210 m.

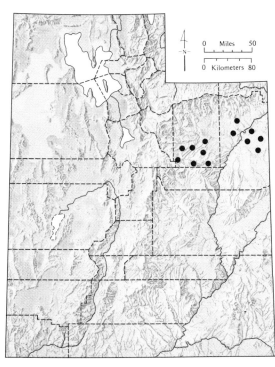

28. *Astragalus detritalis* Jones Debris
milkvetch. May-June. Native perennial herb;
shadscale, desert shrub, pinyon-juniper
communities, 1630-2430 m.

274

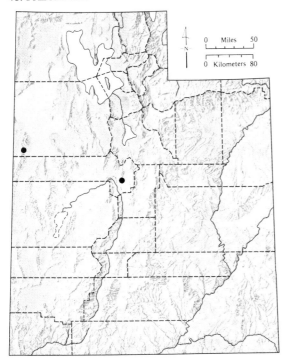

29. *Astragalus diversifolius* Gray Meadow milkvetch. May-June. Native perennial herb; moist saline meadows, 1420-1670 m.

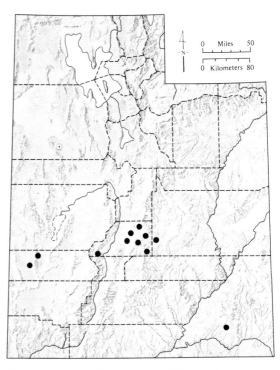

30. *Astragalus drummondii* Hook. Drummond milkvetch. May-July. Native perennial herb; mountain brush, pinyon-juniper, ponderosa pine communities, 1970-2790 m.

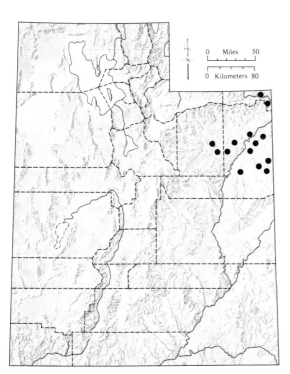

31. *Astragalus duchesnensis* Jones Duchesne milkvetch. Apr.-June. Native perennial herb; shadscale, desert shrub, pinyon-juniper communities, 1450-1790 m.

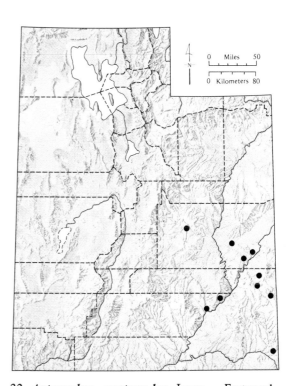

32. *Astragalus eastwoodae* Jones Eastwood milkvetch. Apr.-May. Native perennial herb; shadscale, desert shrub, pinyon-juniper communities, 1450-1670 m.

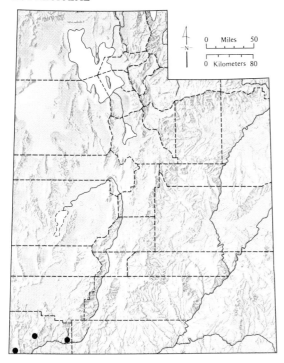

33. *Astragalus ensiformis* Jones Pagumpa milkvetch. Apr.-May. Native perennial herb; creosote bush to pinyon-juniper communities, 1210-1460 m.

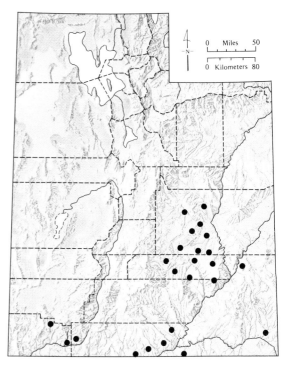

34. *Astragalus episcopus* Wats. Bishop milkvetch. May-June. Native perennial herb; shadscale, desert shrub, pinyon-juniper communities, 1270-1970 m.

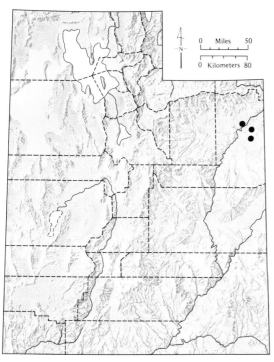

35. *Astragalus equisolensis* Neese & Welsh Horseshoe milkvetch. May-June. Native perennial herb; desert shrub communities, 1480-1550 m.

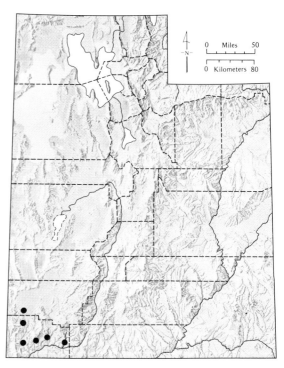

36. *Astragalus eremiticus* Sheld. Hermit milkvetch. Apr.-May. Native perennial herb; desert shrub, pinyon-juniper communities, 1130-1970 m.

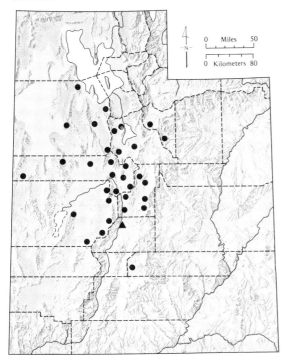

37. *Astragalus eurekensis* Jones Eureka milkvetch. Apr.-June. Native perennial herb; sagebrush, pinyon-juniper, mountain brush communities, 1330-2880 m.

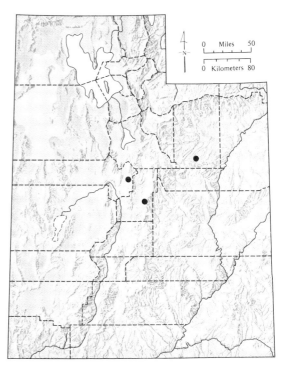

38. *Astragalus falcatus* Lam. Russian sickle milkvetch. June-Aug. Introduced perennial herb; cultivated as a soil stabilizer, escaping and persistent, 1660-2150 m.

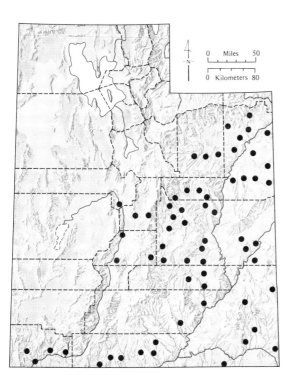

39. *Astragalus flavus* Nutt. Yellow milkvetch. Apr.-June. Native perennial herb; creosote bush, mat saltbush, shadscale, pinyon-juniper communities, 840-1970 m.

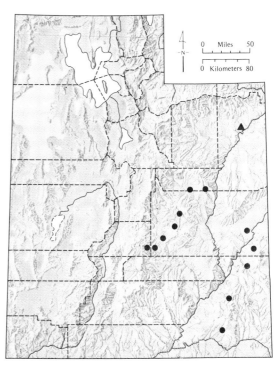

40. *Astragalus flexuosus* (Hook.) G. Don Pliant milkvetch. May-July. Native perennial herb; shadscale, desert shrub, oak, pinyon-juniper communities, 1420-2120 m.

41. FABACEAE

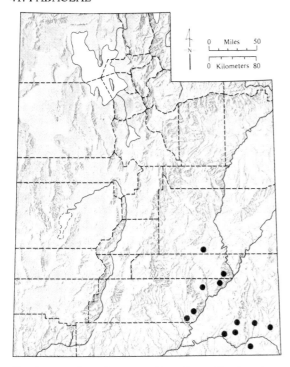

41. *Astragalus fucatus* Barneby   Hopi milk-vetch.   Apr.-June.   Native perennial herb; desert shrub communities, 1380-1940 m.

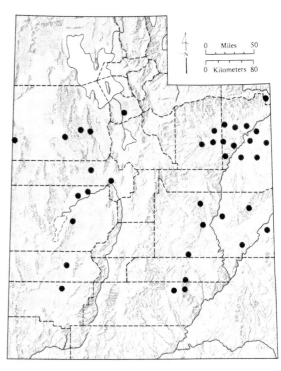

42. *Astragalus geyeri* Gray   Geyer milkvetch. Apr.-May.   Native annual; dunes and other sandy sites in desert shrub communities, 1300-1820 m.

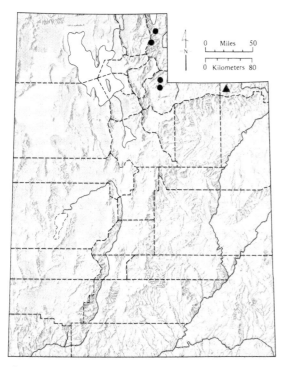

43. *Astragalus gilviflorus* Sheld.   Threeleaf or plains milkvetch.   Apr.-May.   Native perennial herb; barren sites in sagebrush communities, 1940-2090 m.

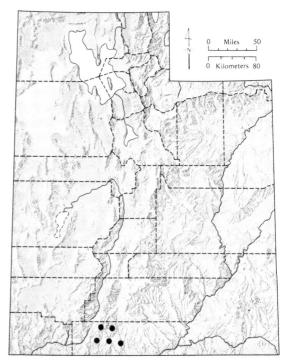

44. *Astragalus hallii* Gray   Hall milkvetch. May-June.   Native perennial herb; oakbrush, pinyon-juniper communities, 1750-2300 m.

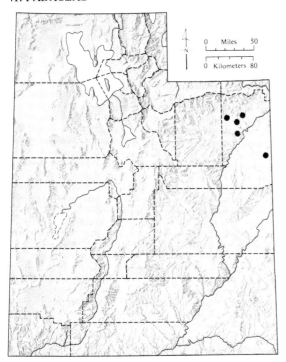

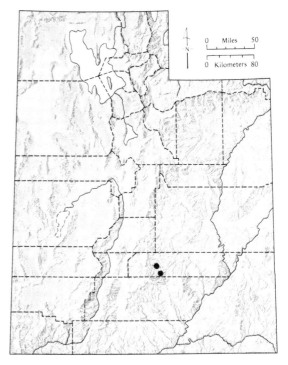

45. *Astragalus hamiltonii* Porter Hamilton milkvetch. May-June. Native perennial herb; desert shrub, pinyon-juniper communities, 1570-1820 m.

46. *Astragalus harrisonii* Barneby Harrison milkvetch. Apr.-May. Native perennial herb; pinyon-juniper communities, 1600-2940 m.

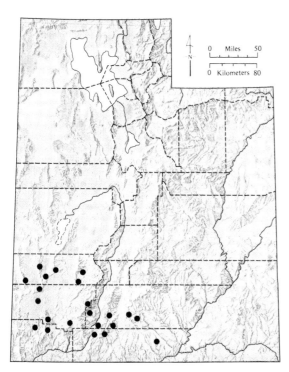

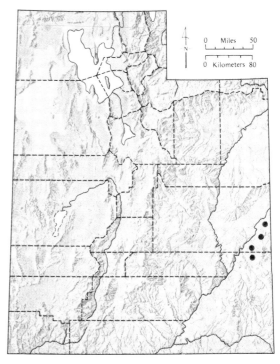

47. *Astragalus humistratus* Gray Groundcover milkvetch. May-Aug. Native perennial herb; desert shrub, pinyon-juniper, ponderosa pine communities, 1510-2580 m.

48. *Astragalus iselyi* Welsh Isely milkvetch. Apr.-May. Native perennial herb; shadscale, pinyon-juniper communities, 1450-1730 m.

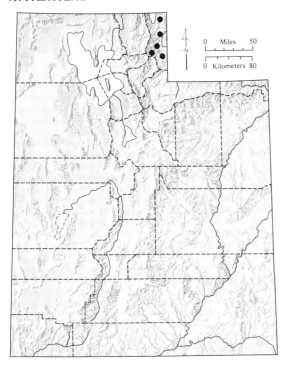

49. *Astragalus jejunus* Wats. Starveling milkvetch. May-July. Native perennial herb; barren sites in sagebrush-juniper communities, 1930-2120 m.

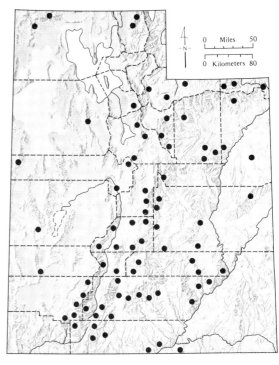

50. *Astragalus kentrophyta* Gray May-Aug. Native perennial herb; desert shrub, pinyon-juniper, ponderosa pine, spruce-fir communities, 1510-3520 m.

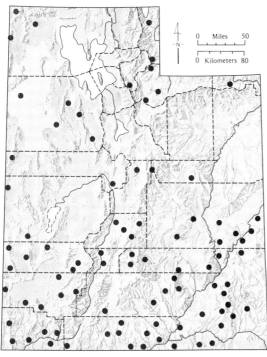

51. *Astragalus lentiginosus* Hook. Specklepod or freckled milkvetch. Apr.-June. Native perennial herb; creosote bush, desert shrub, pinyon-juniper communities, 840-2430 m.

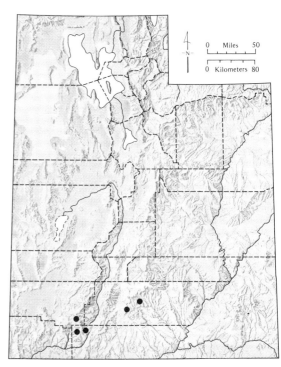

52. *Astragalus limnocharis* Barneby Navajo Lake milkvetch. June-Aug. Native perennial herb; lakeshores and rocky sites on the Wasatch Formation, 2420-3340 m.

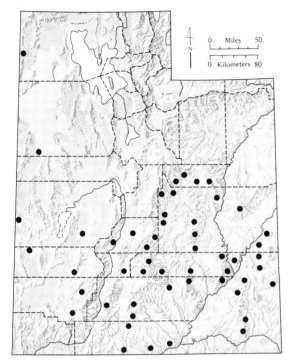

53. *Astragalus lonchocarpus* Torr. Great rushy milkvetch. May-June. Native perennial herb; mat saltbush, desert shrub, pinyon-juniper communities, 1510-2220 m.

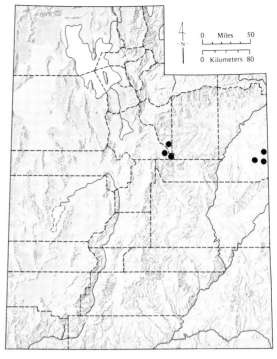

54. *Astragalus lutosus* Jones Dragon milkvetch. May-June. Native perennial herb; barren sites in shadscale, desert shrub to pinyon-juniper, conifer communities, 1570-1700 m.

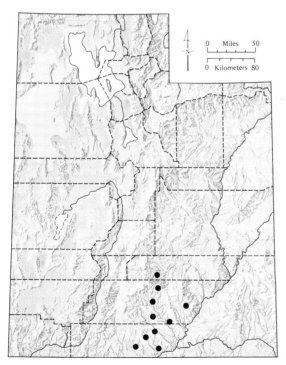

55. *Astragalus malacoides* Barneby Kaiparowits milkvetch. Apr.-May. Native perennial herb; shadscale, desert shrub, pinyon-juniper communities, 1450-2300 m.

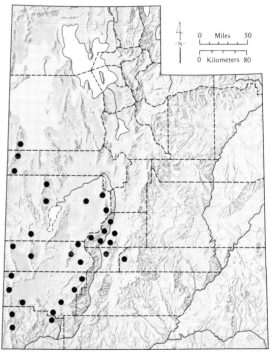

56. *Astragalus marianus* (Rydb.) Barneby Sevier milkvetch. May-June. Native perennial herb; sagebrush, pinyon-juniper, oak, aspen-fir communities, 1700-2730 m.

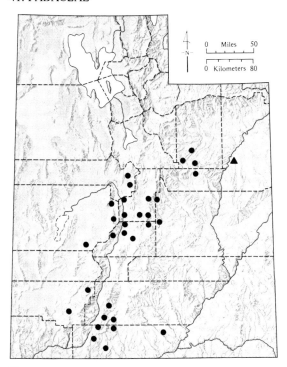

57. *Astragalus megacarpus* (Nutt.) Gray
Great bladdery milkvetch. Apr.-June. Native
perennial herb; open sites in shadscale-sagebrush,
pinyon-juniper, oak, ponderosa pine, aspen
communities, 1630-3030 m.

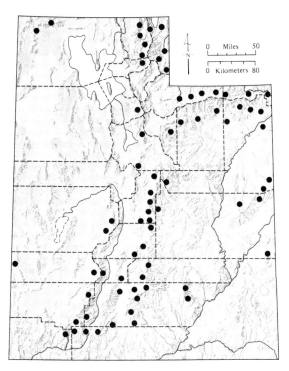

58. *Astragalus miser* Hook. Weedy milkvetch.
May-Aug. Native perennial herb; mountain brush,
aspen-conifer, rocky alpine meadow communities,
1810-3430 m.

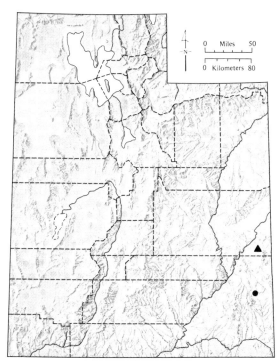

59. *Astragalus missouriensis* Nutt. May-
July. Native perennial herb; sagebrush, pinyon-
juniper communities, 1740-2500 m.

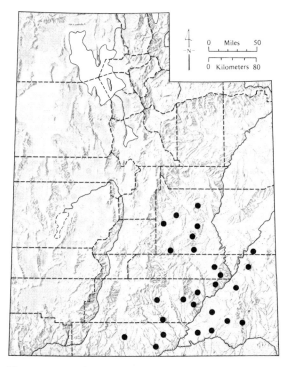

60. *Astragalus moencoppensis* Jones
Moenkopi milkvetch. May-June. Native perennial
herb; shadscale, desert shrub, pinyon-juniper
communities, 1330-2150 m.

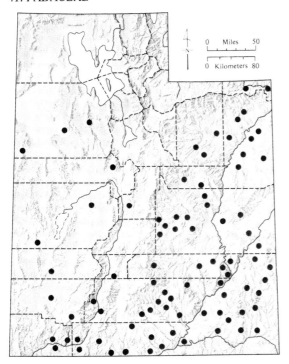

61. *Astragalus mollissimus* Torr. Woolly locoweed. Mar.-June. Native perennial herb; salt desert shrub, desert shrub, pinyon-juniper communities, 1330-2180 m.

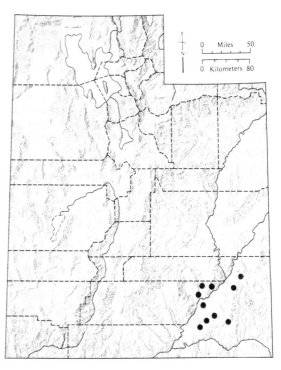

62. *Astragalus monumentalis* Barneby Monument milkvetch. Apr.-Aug. Native perennial herb; desert shrub, pinyon-juniper communities, 1150-1900 m.

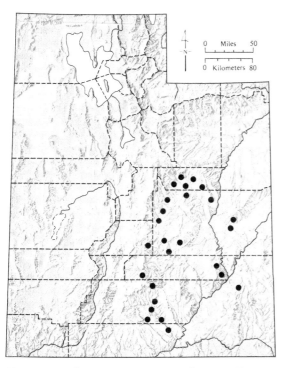

63. *Astragalus musiniensis* Jones Ferron milkvetch. May-June. Native perennial herb; shadscale, mat saltbush, desert shrub, pinyon-juniper communities, 1540-2090 m.

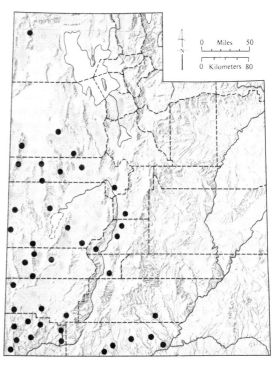

64. *Astragalus newberryi* Gray Newberry milkvetch. Mar.-June. Native perennial herb; salt desert shrub, desert shrub, mountain brush, pinyon-juniper communities, 1150-2120 m.

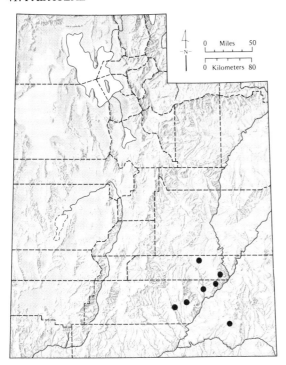

65. *Astragalus nidularius* Barneby Birdnest
milkvetch. Apr.-May. Native perennial herb;
desert shrub, pinyon-juniper communities, 1270-
1970 m.

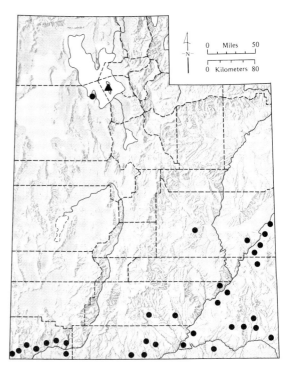

66. *Astragalus nuttallianus* A. DC. Small-
flowered milkvetch. Mar.-May. Native annual;
creosote bush, desert shrub, pinyon-juniper
communities, 840-1820 m.

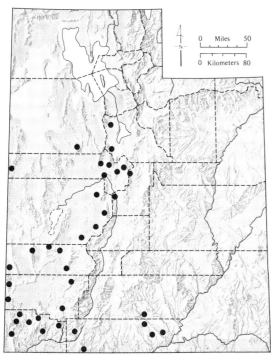

67. *Astragalus oophorus* Wats. Spindle or
egg milkvetch. Apr.-July. Native perennial herb;
shadscale, sagebrush, desert shrub communities,
1360-2180 m.

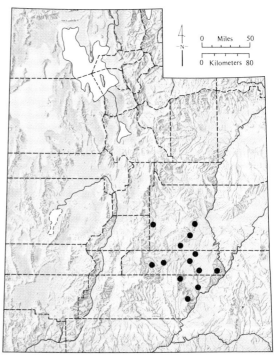

68. *Astragalus pardalinus* (Rydb.) Barneby
Panther milkvetch. May-June. Native perennial
herb; desert shrub, pinyon-juniper communities,
1390-1760 m.

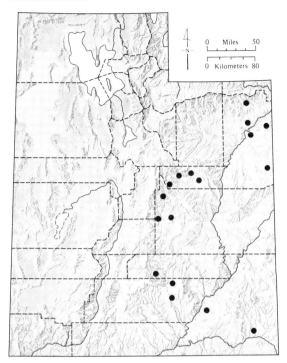

69. *Astragalus pattersonii* Brand. Patterson milkvetch. May-June. Native perennial herb; shadscale, desert shrub, pinyon-juniper communities, 1470-2400 m.

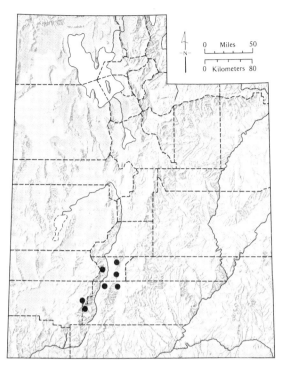

70.*Astragalus perianus* Barneby Rydberg milkvetch. June-Aug. Native perennial herb; barren rocky sites in aspen-fir, alpine communities, 2250-3200 m.

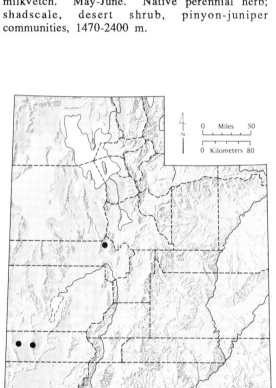

71. *Astragalus pinonis* Jones Pinyon milkvetch. May-July. Native perennial herb; sagebrush, pinyon-juniper communities, 1650-1820 m.

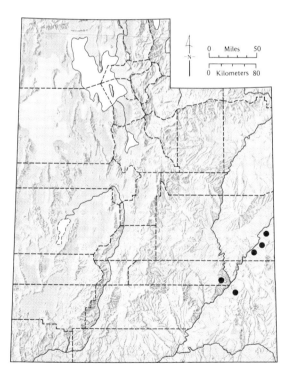

72. *Astragalus piscator* Barneby & Welsh Mar.-June. Native perennial herb; desert shrub communities, 1550-1750 m.

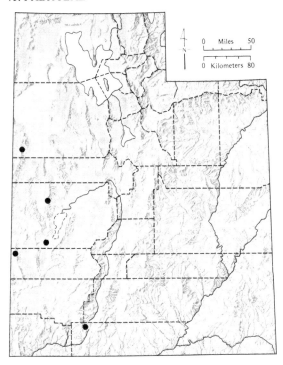

73. *Astragalus platytropis* Gray Broadkeeled milkvetch. July-Aug. Native perennial herb; talus, rocky ridges, 2400-2880 m.

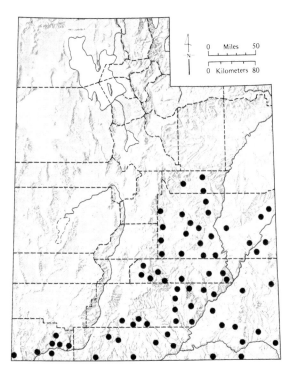

74. *Astragalus praelongus* Sheld. Stinking milkvetch. Apr.-July. Native perennial herb; creosote bush, salt desert shrub, desert shrub, pinyon-juniper communities, 840-2150 m.

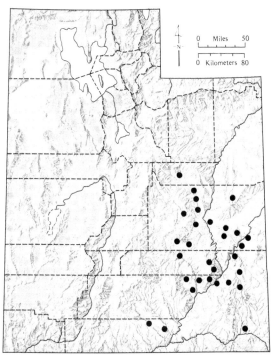

75. *Astragalus preussii* Gray Preuss milkvetch. Apr.-May. Native perennial herb; shadscale, mat saltbush, desert shrub communities, 1100-1950 m.

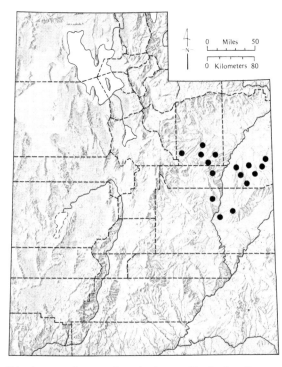

76. *Astragalus pubentissimus* T. & G. Green River milkvetch. May-July. Native perennial herb; shadscale, desert shrub, pinyon-juniper communities, 1350-2180 m.

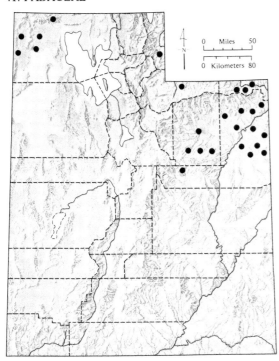

77. *Astragalus purshii* Hook. Woollypod or Pursh milkvetch. May-June. Native perennial herb; sagebrush, desert shrub, pinyon-juniper communities, 1570-2550 m.

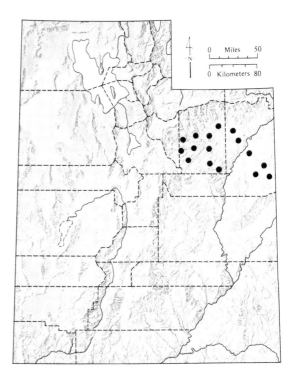

78. *Astragalus racemosus* Pursh Alkali milkvetch. May-June. Native perennial herb; shadscale, desert shrub, pinyon-juniper communities, 1570-1970 m.

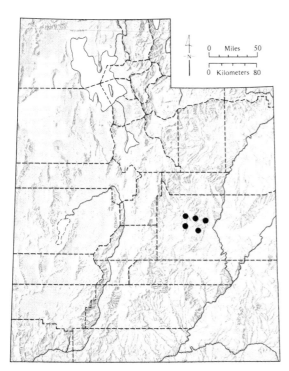

79. *Astragalus rafaelensis* Jones San Rafael milkvetch. Apr.-May. Native perennial herb; shadscale, desert shrub communities, 1370-1670 m.

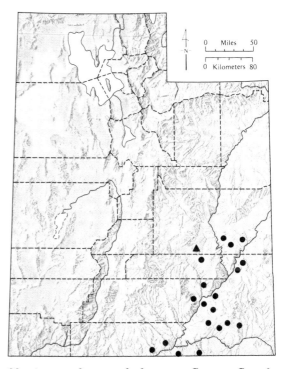

80. *Astragalus sabulonum* Gray Gravel milkvetch. Apr.-June. Native annual or biennial; shadscale, desert shrub, pinyon-juniper communities, 1130-2130 m.

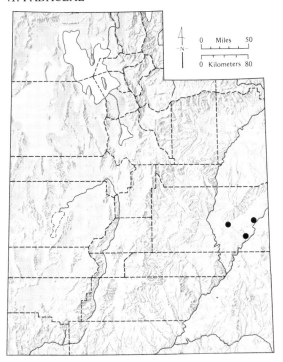

81. *Astragalus sabulosus* Jones Cisco milkvetch. Apr.-May. Native perennial herb; shadscale, mat saltbush, desert shrub communities, 1250-1550 m.

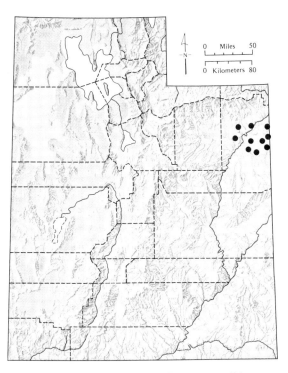

82. *Astragalus saurinus* Barneby Dinosaur milkvetch. May-June. Native perennial herb; shadscale, desert shrub, pinyon-juniper communities, 1450-2000 m.

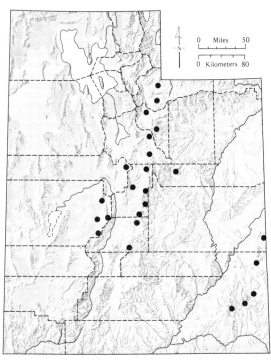

83. *Astragalus scopulorum* Porter Rocky Mountain milkvetch. May-July. Native perennial herb; sagebrush, mountain brush, pinyon-juniper, ponderosa pine, aspen-fir communities, 1870-2870 m.

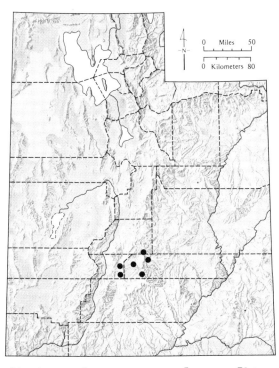

84. *Astragalus serpens* Jones Plateau milkvetch. May-Aug. Native perennial herb; sagebrush, pinyon-juniper, aspen-fir communities, 2070-2760 m.

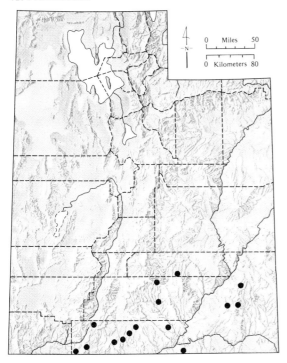

85. *Astragalus sesquiflorus* Wats. Sandstone milkvetch. May-July. Native perennial herb; rock crevices and talus in desert shrub to ponderosa pine, aspen communities, 1510-3000 m.

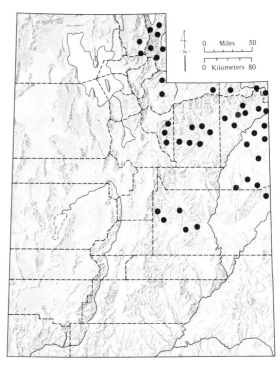

86. *Astragalus spatulatus* Sheld. Tufted or draba milkvetch. May-Aug. Native perennial herb; barren sites in sagebrush, mountain brush, pinyon-juniper communities, 1540-2430 m.

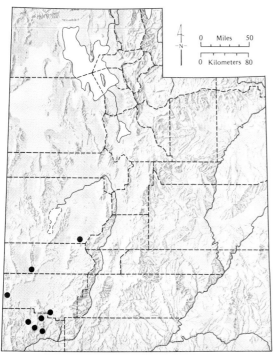

87. *Astragalus straturensis* Jones Silver Reef milkvetch. May-June. Native perennial herb; sagebrush, oakbrush, pinyon-juniper communities, 1570-2130 m.

88. *Astragalus striatiflorus* Jones Escarpment milkvetch. Apr.-May. Native perennial herb; sandy sites in desert shrub communities, 1360-1910 m.

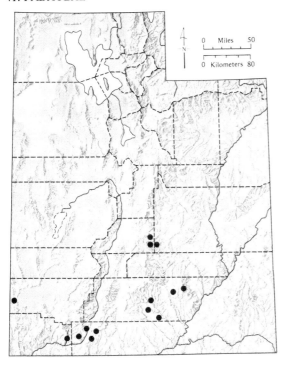

89. *Astragalus subcinereus* Gray Siler milkvetch. May-Aug. Native perennial herb; sagebrush, pinyon-juniper, ponderosa pine communities, 1660-2430 m.

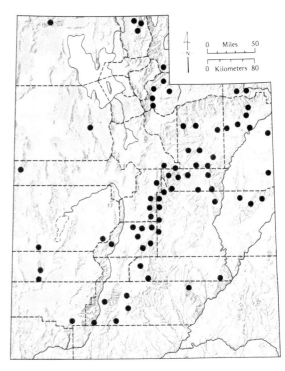

90. *Astragalus tenellus* Pursh Pulse milkvetch. June-Aug. Native perennial herb; sagebrush, mountain brush to spruce-fir communities, 1850-3030 m.

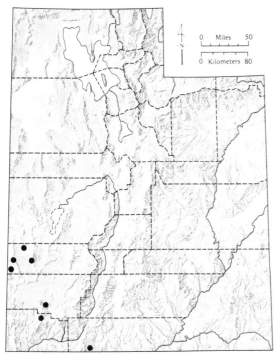

91. *Astragalus tetrapterus* Gray Fourwing milkvetch. May-June. Native perennial herb; sagebrush to pinyon-juniper communities, 1350-2270 m.

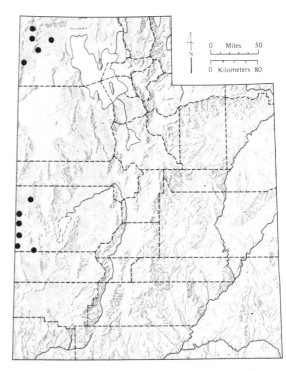

92. *Astragalus toanus* Jones Mar.-June. Native perennial herb; salt desert shrub, pinyon-juniper communities, 1270-1820 m.

41. FABACEAE

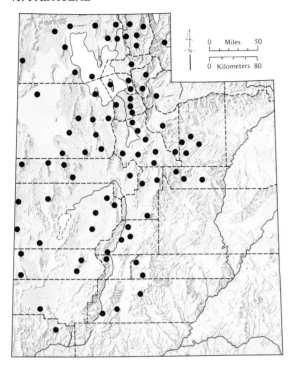

93. *Astragalus utahensis* (Torr.) T. & G. Utah milkvetch. Apr.-May. Native perennial herb; grass-sagebrush, pinyon-juniper, oakbrush communities, 1210-2300 m.

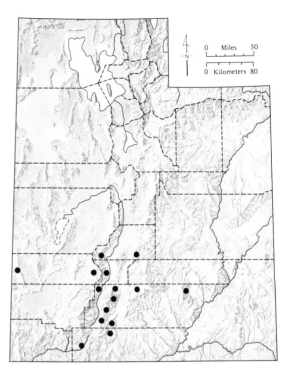

94. *Astragalus wardii* Gray Ward milkvetch. May-Sept. Native perennial herb; greasewood, sagebrush, pinyon-juniper, ponderosa pine, aspen-fir communities, 1510-2980 m.

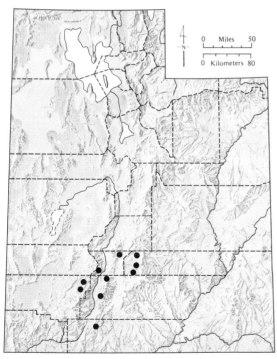

95. *Astragalus welshii* Barneby Welsh milkvetch. May-June. Native perennial herb; sagebrush, pinyon-juniper, aspen communities, 2135-2810 m.

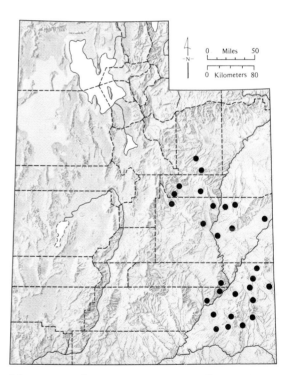

96. *Astragalus wingatanus* Wats. Fort Wingate milkvetch. Apr.-June. Native perennial herb; shadscale, desert shrub, pinyon-juniper communities, 1390-2310 m.

41. FABACEAE

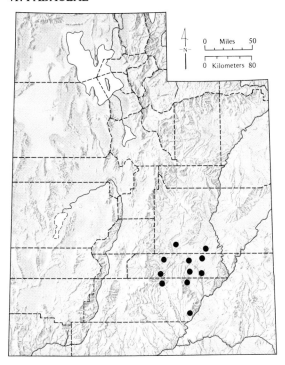

97. *Astragalus woodruffii* Jones Woodruff milkvetch. May-June. Native perennial herb; dunes, other sandy sites in desert shrub communities, 1300-1650 m.

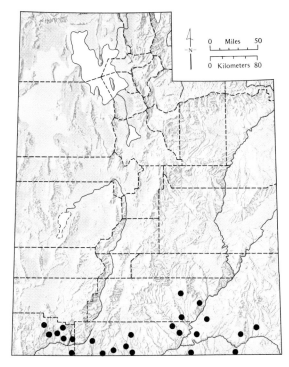

98. *Astragalus zionis* Jones Zion milkvetch. Apr.-May. Native perennial herb; desert shrub, pinyon-juniper communities, 970-2200 m.

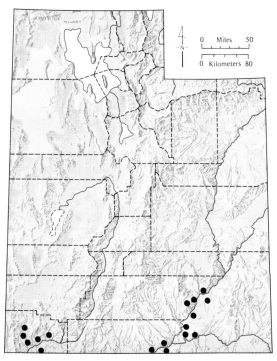

99. *Cercis occidentalis* Gray Western redbud. Mar.-May. Native tree or shrub; sandstone canyons in desert shrub communities, 810-1210 m.

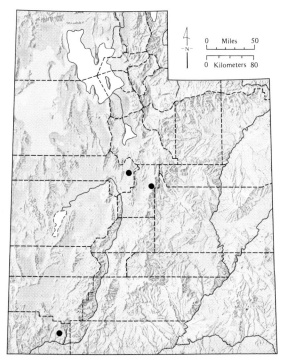

100. *Colutea arborescens* L. Bladder senna. June-July. Introduced shrub; cultivated, escaping and persistent, 1660-2100 m.

292

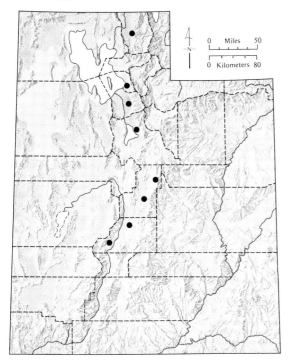

101. *Coronilla varia* L. Crownvetch. June-July. Introduced perennial herb; cultivated, escaping and persistent, 1510-1790 m.

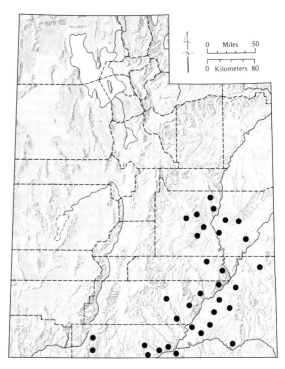

102. *Dalea flavescens* (Wats.) Welsh Kanab prairie clover. May-July. Native perennial herb; sandy sites in desert shrub, pinyon-juniper communities, 1300-1730 m.

103. *Dalea lanata* Spreng. Woolly dalea. July-Sept. Native perennial herb; sandy sites in creosote bush, desert shrub communities, 970-1330 m.

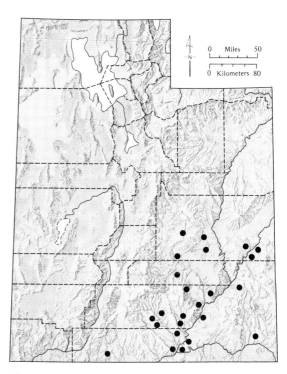

104. *Dalea oligophylla* (Torr.) Shinners Western prairie clover. June-Sept. Native perennial herb; hanging gardens, desert shrub, pinyon-juniper communities, 970-2000 m.

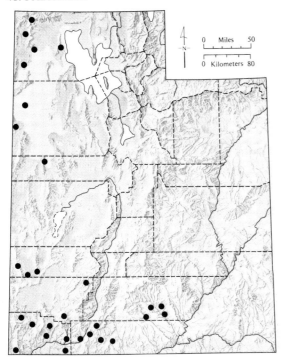

105. *Dalea searlsiae* (Gray) Barneby Searls dalea. May-July. Native perennial herb; creosote bush, desert shrub, pinyon-juniper, oakbrush communities, 850-2300 m.

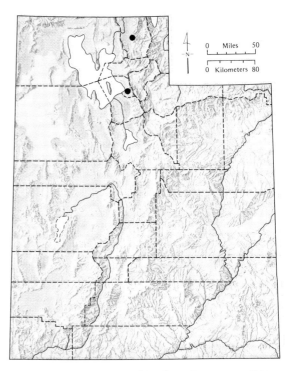

106. *Galega officinalis* L. Goatsrue. July-Aug. Introduced perennial herb; waste places, 1500-1600 m.

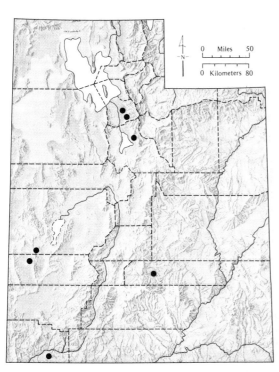

107. *Gleditsia triacanthos* L. Honey locust. Apr.-May. Introduced tree; cultivated, escaping and persistent, 1030-1670 m.

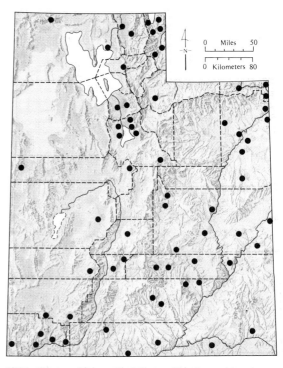

108. *Glycyrrhiza lepidota* Pursh American licorice. May-Aug. Native perennial herb; moist sites in greasewood, desert shrub, pinyon-juniper communities, 800-2420 m.

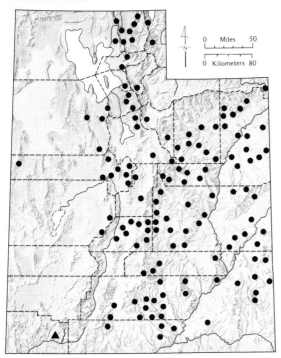

109. *Hedysarum boreale* Nutt. Northern
sweetvetch. Apr.-July. Native perennial herb;
grass-sagebrush, desert shrub to aspen-ponderosa
pine communities, 1240-2760 m.

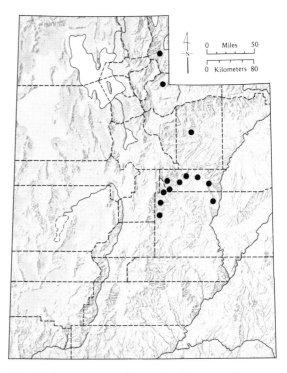

110. *Hedysarum occidentale* Greene Western
sweetvetch. June-July. Native perennial herb;
sagebrush, mountain brush, aspen, spruce-fir
communities, 1900-2500 m.

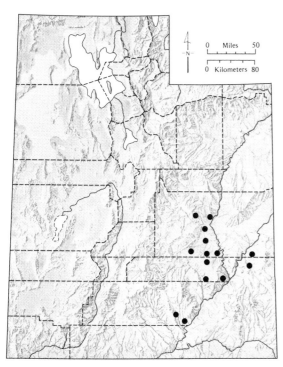

111. *Hoffmanseggia repens* (Eastw.) Ckll.
Creeping rushpea. May-June. Native perennial
herb; sandy sites in desert shrub communities,
1210-1660 m.

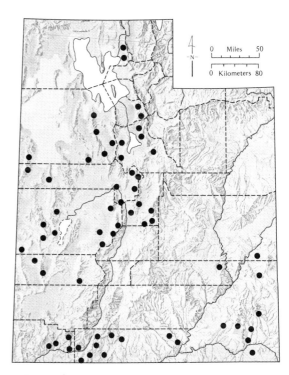

112. *Lathyrus brachycalyx* Rydb. Purple
peavine. Apr.-June. Native perennial herb; desert
shrub, pinyon-juniper, mountain brush
communities, 1210-2300 m.

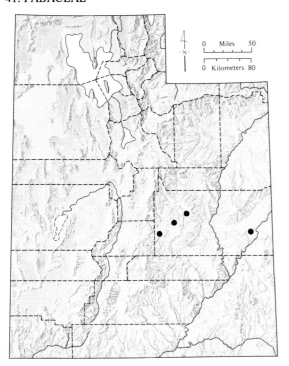

113. *Lathyrus eucosmus* Butters & St. John May-June. Native perennial herb; shadscale, desert shrub communities, 1510-1850 m.

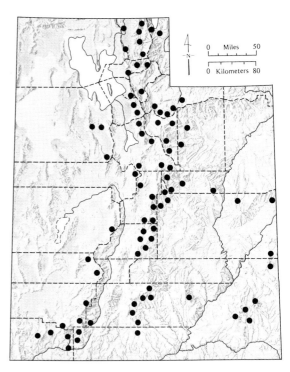

114. *Lathyrus lanszwertii* Kell. Thickleaf sweetpea. May-Aug. Native perennial herb; mountain brush, aspen, spruce-fir communities, 1690-3460 m.

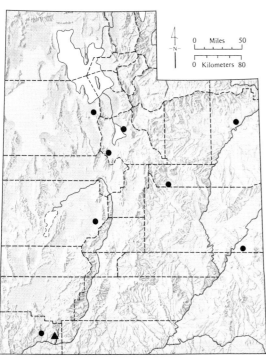

115. *Lathyrus latifolius* L. Perennial sweetpea. June-July. Introduced perennial herb; cultivated, escaping and persistent, 1360-1690 m.

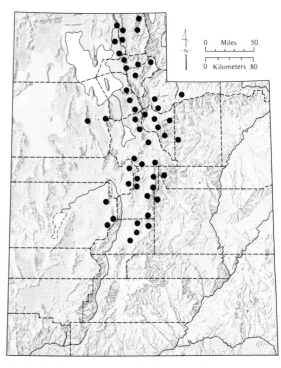

116. *Lathyrus pauciflorus* Fern. Wild sweetpea. Apr.-Aug. Native perennial herb; sagebrush-oak to aspen-conifer communities, 1360-3030 m.

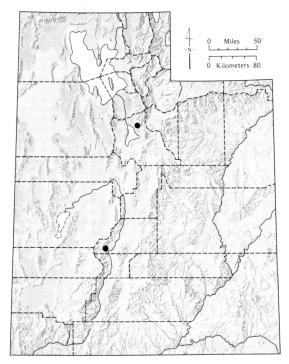

117. *Lathyrus sylvestris* L. Scots sweetpea.
June-July. Introduced perennial herb; cultivated,
escaping and persistent, 1450-2120 m.

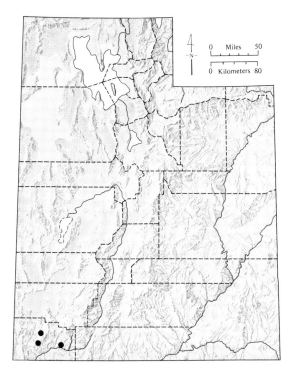

118. *Lotus denticulatus* (Drew) Greene
Mojave trefoil. May-June. Native annual; creosote
bush to mountain brush communities, 880-2120 m.

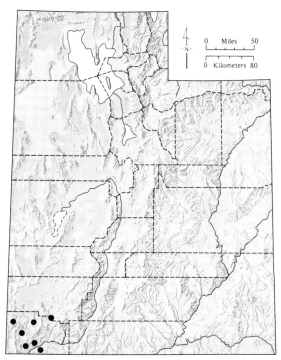

119. *Lotus humistratus* Greene   Foothill
trefoil. Apr.-May. Native annual; creosote bush
communities, 820-970 m.

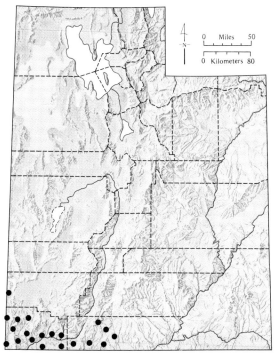

120. *Lotus plebeius* (Brandeg.) Barneby
Common trefoil. Apr.-Oct. Native perennial herb;
creosote bush to pinyon-juniper communities, 850-
1970 m.

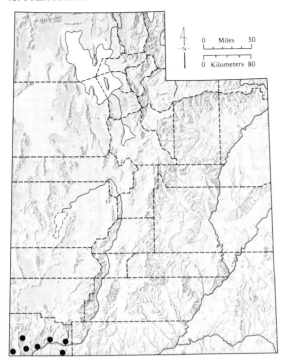

121. **Lotus rigidus** (Benth.) Greene Bush trefoil. Mar.-Apr. Native suffrutescent perennial herb; creosote bush, desert shrub communities, 820-1270 m.

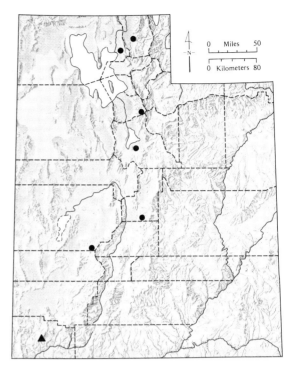

122. **Lotus tenuis** Willd. Slender trefoil. July-Aug. Introduced perennial herb; cultivated, escaping and persistent, 1390-2430 m.

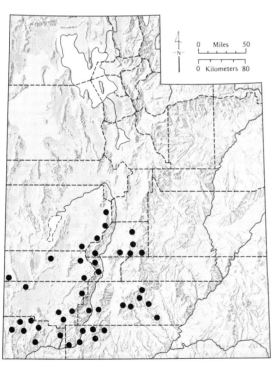

123. **Lotus utahensis** Ottley Utah trefoil. May-July. Native perennial herb; sagebrush, pinyon-juniper to aspen-conifer communities, 1640-2790 m.

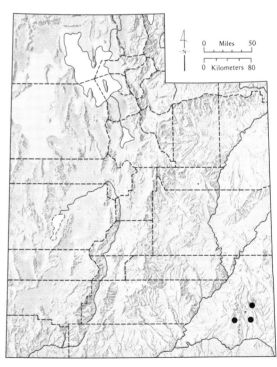

124. **Lotus wrightii** (Gray) Greene Wright trefoil. June-July. Native perennial herb; pinyon-juniper, ponderosa pine communities, 2000-2120 m.

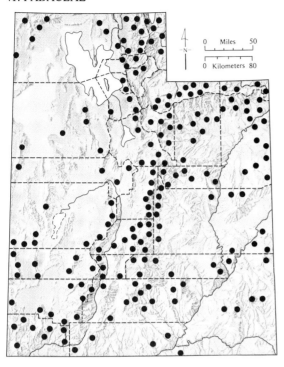

125. *Lupinus argenteus* Pursh   Silvery lupine.
Apr.-Sept.   Native perennial herb; grass-sagebrush
to aspen, spruce-fir communities, alpine ridges,
1510-3330 m.

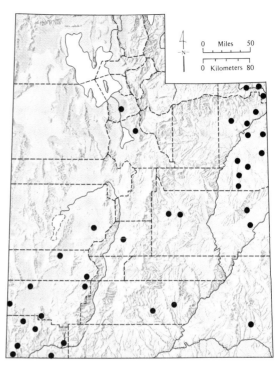

126. *Lupinus brevicaulis* Wats.   Shortstem
lupine.   Apr.-June.   Native annual; creosote bush,
shadscale, desert shrub, sagebrush, pinyon-juniper
communities, 900-2030 m.

127. *Lupinus concinnus* Agardh   Elegant
lupine.   Apr.-May.   Native annual; creosote bush
communities, 850-1000 m.

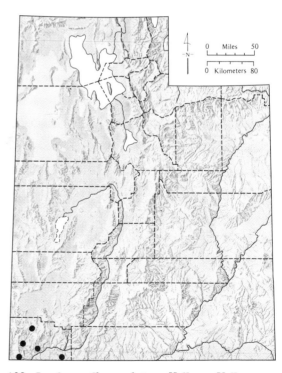

128. *Lupinus flavoculatus* Heller   Yelloweye
lupine.   May-June.   Native annual; creosote bush to
pinyon-juniper communities, 850-1970 m.

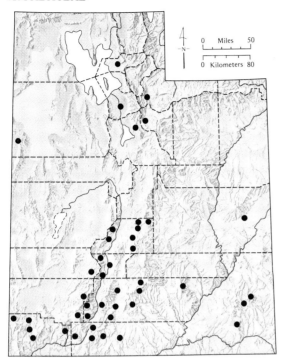

129. *Lupinus kingii* Wats. King lupine. June-Aug. Native annual; sagebrush, pinyon-juniper, ponderosa pine communities, 1420-3030 m.

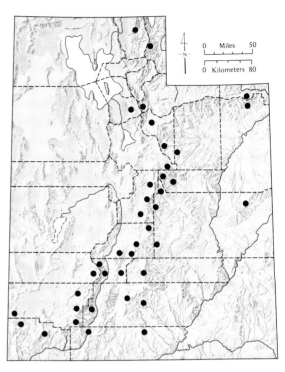

130. *Lupinus lepidus* Lindl. Neat lupine. July-Aug. Native perennial herb; open sites in sagebrush, aspen, spruce-fir communities, 1900-3400 m.

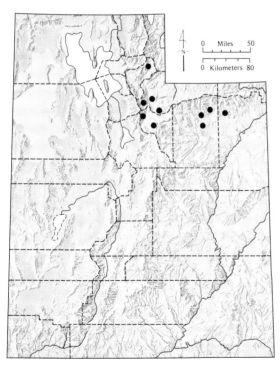

131. *Lupinus leucophyllus* Lindl. Velvet or whiteleaf lupine. June-Aug. Native perennial herb; grass-sagebrush, mountain brush, aspen-conifer communities, 1700-2430 m.

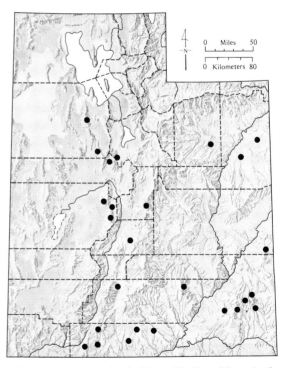

132. *Lupinus polyphyllus* Lindl. Many-leaf lupine. May-Aug. Native perennial herb; sagebrush, mountain brush, pinyon-juniper, aspen-conifer communities, 1790-2970 m.

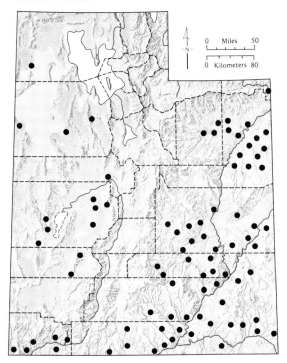

133. *Lupinus pusillus* Pursh   Dwarf lupine.
Apr.-June.   Native annual; sandy sites in creosote
bush, shadscale, desert shrub, pinyon-juniper
communities, 910-1820 m.

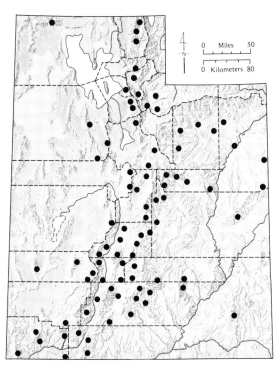

134. *Lupinus sericeus* Pursh   Silky lupine.
May-Sept.   Native perennial herb; sagebrush,
pinyon-juniper to ponderosa pine, aspen, spruce-fir
communities, 1360-3000 m.

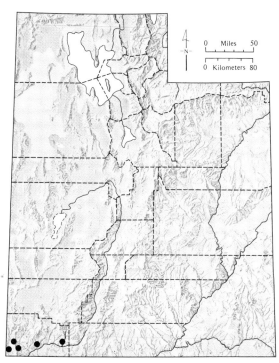

135. *Lupinus sparsiflorus* Benth.   Mojave
lupine.   Mar.-May.   Native annual; creosote bush
communities, 800-1000 m.

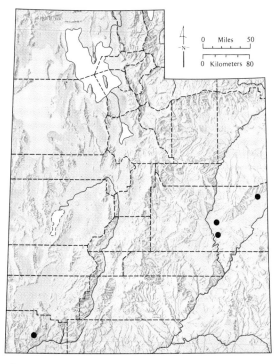

136. *Medicago falcata* L.   Yellow alfalfa.
June-July.   Introduced perennial herb; disturbed
sites, 1360-2120 m.

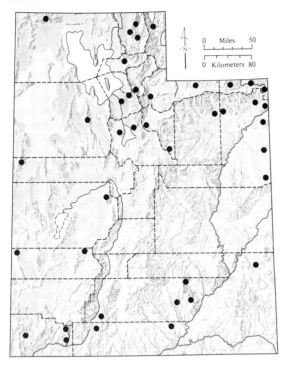

137. *Medicago lupulina* L. Black medick.
May-July. Introduced annual to perennial; waste
places, 940-2390 m.

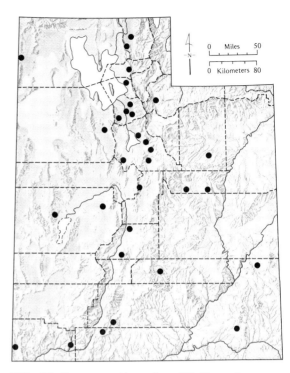

138. *Medicago sativa* L. Alfalfa or lucerne.
June-Sept. Introduced perennial herb; cultivated,
escaping and persistent in waste places, 820-
1940 m.

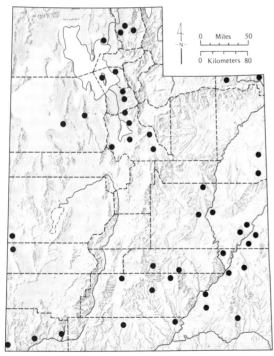

139. *Melilotus alba* Medic. White sweetclover.
June-Aug. Introduced annual or biennial; disturbed
sites, 800-1820 m.

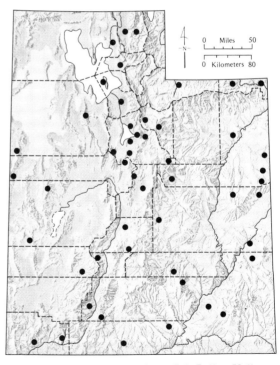

140. *Melilotus officinalis* (L.) Pall. Yellow
sweetclover. May-July. Introduced annual or
biennial; disturbed sites, 800-2120 m.

41. FABACEAE

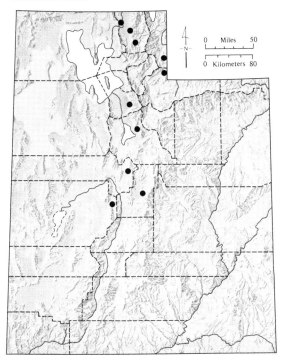

141. *Onobrychis viciifolia* Scop. Sainfoin; holy clover. June-July. Introduced perennial herb; cultivated, escaping and persistent, 1360-2060 m.

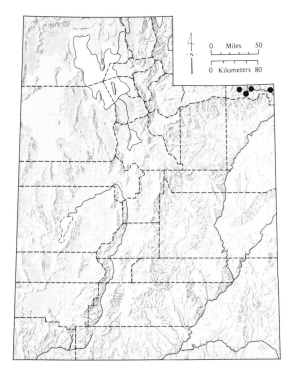

142. *Oxytropis besseyi* (Rydb.) Blank. Bessey locoweed. May-June. Native perennial herb; pinyon-juniper communities, 1730-1880 m.

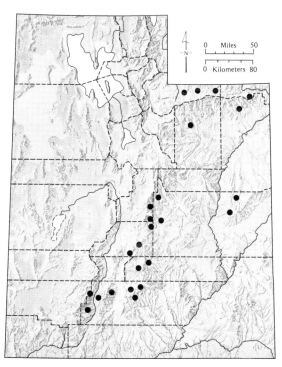

143. *Oxytropis deflexa* (Pall.) DC. Hangpod locoweed. June-Aug. Circumboreal perennial herb; meadows, openings in aspen-conifer communities, 2400-3330 m.

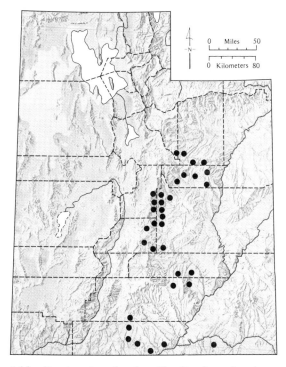

144. *Oxytropis lambertii* Pursh Lambert locoweed. June-July. Native perennial herb; desert shrub, grass-sagebrush, pinyon-juniper communities, 1390-3030 m.

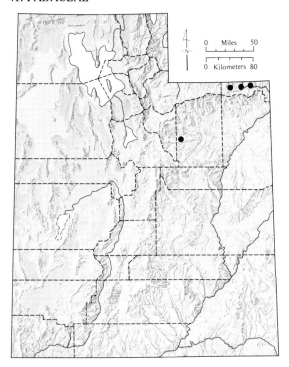

145. *Oxytropis multiceps* T. & G. Rocky Mountain locoweed. May-July. Native perennial herb; pinyon-juniper communities, 1800-2000 m.

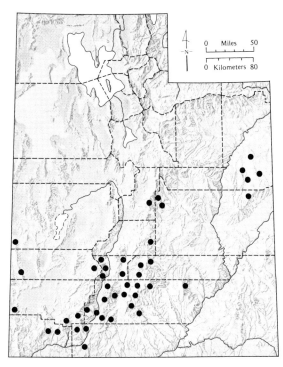

146. *Oxytropis oreophila* Gray Mountain locoweed. May-Sept. Native perennial herb; barren slopes in desert shrub, pinyon-juniper, ponderosa pine, bristlecone pine, spruce-fir, alpine communities, 1820-3450 m.

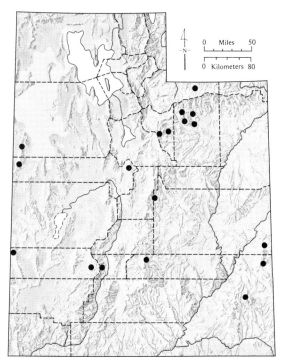

147. *Oxytropis parryi* Gray Parry locoweed. June-Aug. Native perennial herb; alpine meadows and exposed rocky slopes, 2640-3640 m.

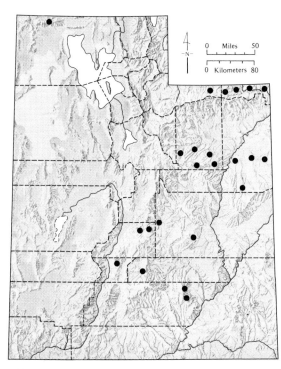

148. *Oxytropis sericea* Nutt. Silky or white locoweed. May-June. Native perennial herb; desert shrub, pinyon-juniper, sagebrush communities, 1670-3180 m.

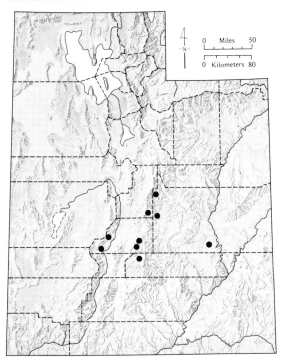

149. *Oxytropis viscida* Nutt. Sticky locoweed. June-July. Native perennial herb; open rocky slopes and ridges, 2390-3270 m.

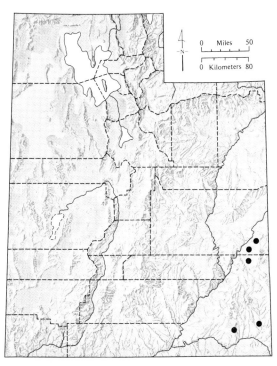

150. *Parryella filifolia* T. & G. Dunebroom. June-July. Native perennial herb; sand dunes, 1420-1580.

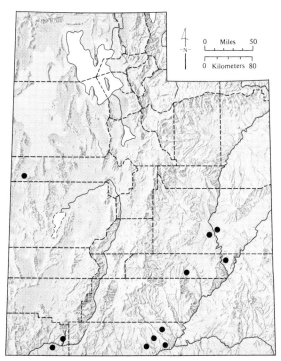

151. *Peteria thompsonae* Wats. Thompson peteria. May-June. Native perennial herb; desert shrub, pinyon-juniper communities, 1210-1520 m.

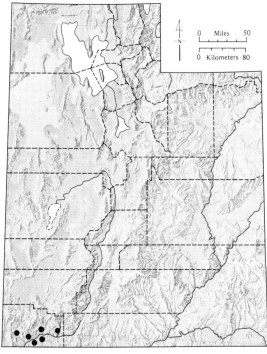

152. *Prosopis glandulosa* Torr. Mesquite. May-June. Native shrub or tree; creosote bush communities, 850-1060 m.

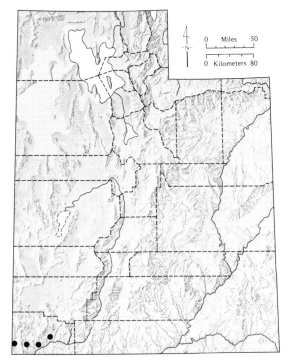

153. ***Prosopis pubescens*** Benth. Screwbean mesquite. May-June. Native perennial herb; creosote bush communities, 850-1120 m.

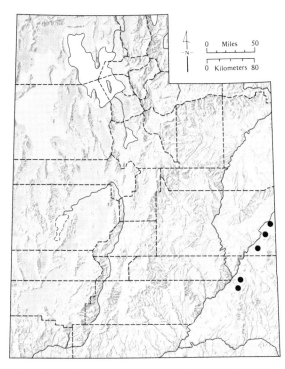

154. ***Psoralea aromatica*** Pays. Paradox breadroot. May-June. Native perennial herb; desert shrub, pinyon-juniper communities, 1450-1670 m.

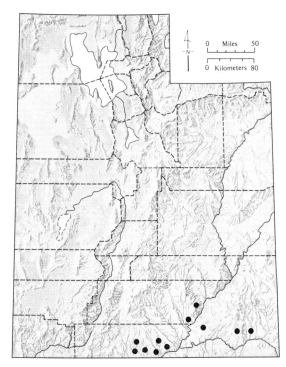

155. ***Psoralea juncea*** Eastw. Rush scurfpea. Apr.-June. Native perennial herb; dunes and other sandy sites in desert shrub communities, 1300-1670 m.

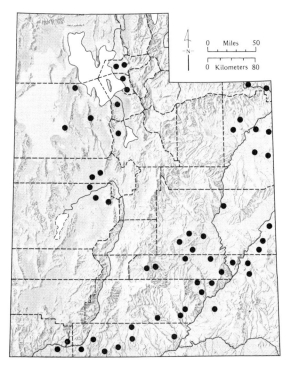

156. ***Psoralea lanceolata*** Pursh Dune or lemon scurfpea. May-Aug. Native perennial herb; dunes and other sandy sites in desert shrub communities, 1290-1850 m.

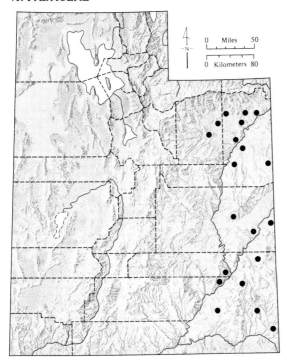

157. *Psoralea megalantha* Woot. & Standl. Large-flowered breadroot. May-July. Native perennial herb; shadscale, desert shrub, pinyon-juniper communities, 1240-1670 m.

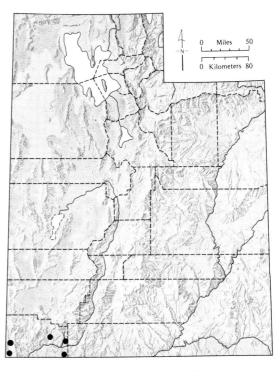

158. *Psoralea mephitica* Wats. Skunk breadroot. May-June. Native perennial herb; creosote bush, desert shrub, pinyon-juniper communities, 910-1360 m.

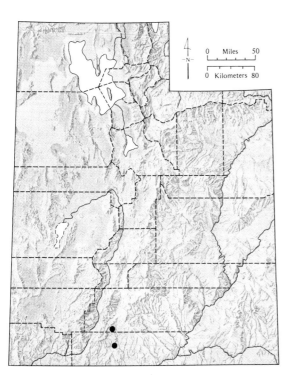

159. *Psoralea pariensis* Welsh & Atwood Paria breadroot. June-July. Native perennial herb; pinyon-juniper, ponderosa pine communities, 2300-2420 m.

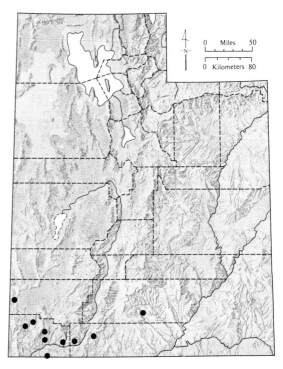

160. *Psoralea tenuiflora* Pursh Prairie scurfpea. June-Sept. Native perennial herb; sagebrush, oakbrush, pinyon-juniper communities, 1390-2120 m.

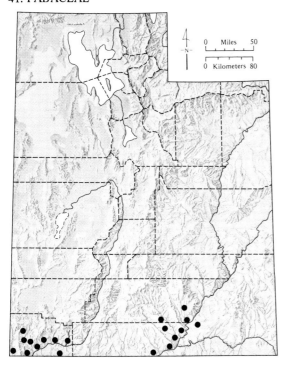

161. *Psorothamnus fremontii* (Torr.) Barneby
Fremont indigo bush. May-June. Native shrub;
creosote bush, desert shrub communities, 800-
1520 m.

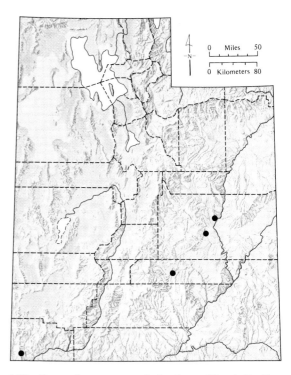

162. *Psorothamnus polydenius* (Torr.) Rydb.
Glandular indigo bush. May-June. Native shrub;
Joshua tree, creosote bush, shadscale, mat saltbush
communities, 820-1520 m.

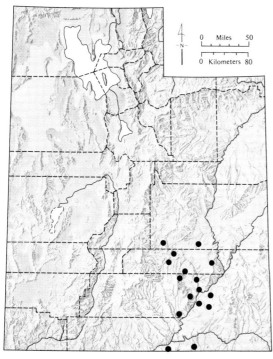

163. *Psorothamnus thompsonae* (Vail) Welsh
& Atwood Thompson indigo bush. May-Aug.
Native shrub; shadscale, desert shrub, pinyon-
juniper communities, 1060-2270 m.

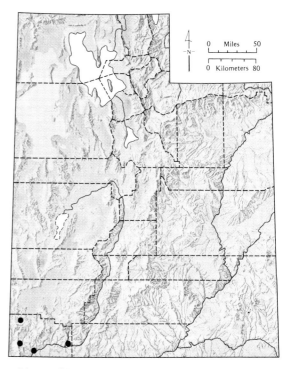

164. *Robinia neomexicana* Gray New
Mexico locust. Apr.-May. Native tree or shrub;
creosote bush, mountain brush communities, 850-
1520 m.

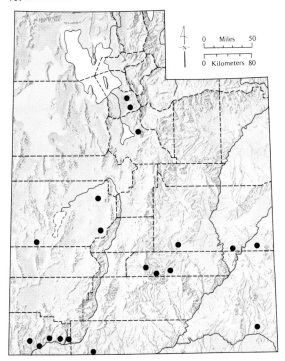

165. **Robinia pseudoacacia** L. Black locust.
Apr.-June. Introduced tree; cultivated, escaping and
persistent, 910-1550 m.

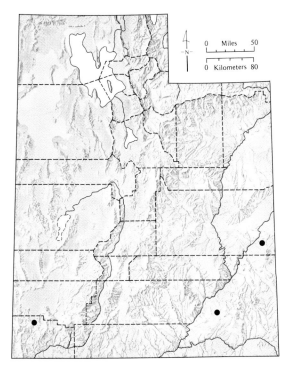

166. **Sophora nuttalliana** Turner Silky
sophora. May-June. Native perennial herb; sandy
sites in desert shrub communities, 1330-1670 m.

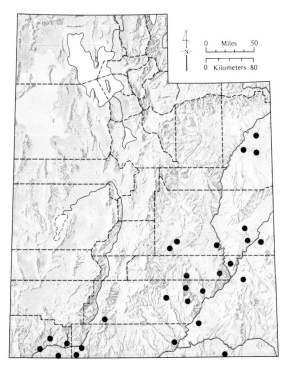

167. **Sophora stenophylla** Gray Silvery
sophora. Apr.-July. Native perennial herb; dunes
and other sandy sites in creosote bush, desert
shrub, pinyon-juniper communities, 850-1850 m.

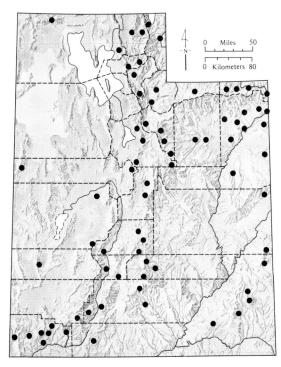

168. **Thermopsis rhombifolia** Richards.
Golden pea. May-July. Native perennial herb;
streamside, moist meadows, shady sites in aspen,
pine communities, 1330-3180 m.

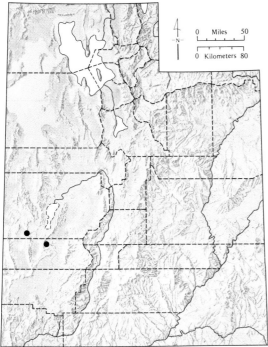

169. **Trifolium andersonii** Gray Anderson clover. May-June. Native perennial herb; barren sites in pinyon-juniper communities, 2220-2440 m.

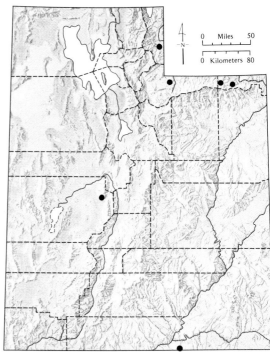

170. **Trifolium andinum** Nutt. Andean clover. May-June. Native perennial herb; barren sites in mountain brush, ponderosa pine, fir communities, 2000-2930 m.

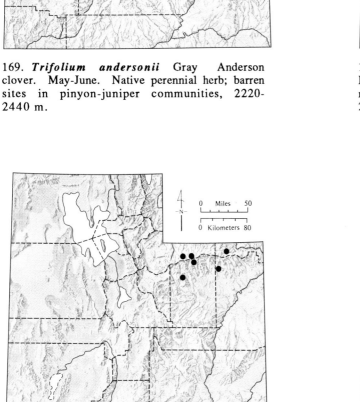

171. **Trifolium dasyphyllum** T. & G. Uinta clover. June-Aug. Native perennial herb; alpine meadows and exposed ridges, 3030-3900 m.

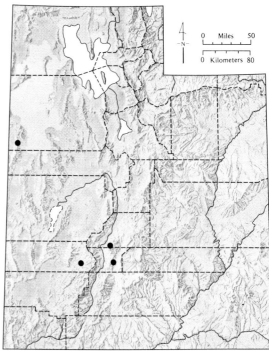

172. **Trifolium eriocephalum** Nutt. Woolly clover. June-Aug. Native perennial herb; moist meadows, 1510-2120 m.

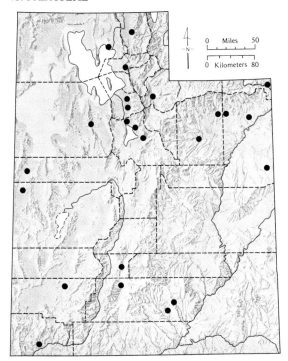

173. *Trifolium fragiferum* L. Strawberry clover. July-Sept. Introduced perennial herb; cultivated as a component of lawns, escaping and persistent, 1270-2060 m.

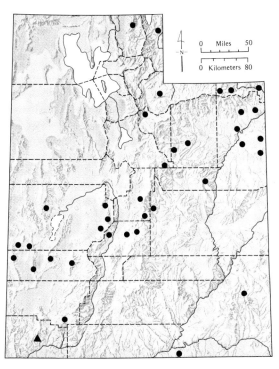

174. *Trifolium gymnocarpon* Nutt. Nuttall or hollyleaf clover. Apr.-July. Native perennial herb; desert shrub, pinyon-juniper to aspen, spruce-fir communities, 1730-3090 m.

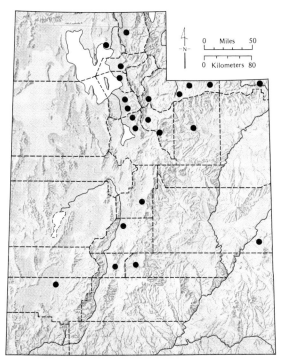

175. *Trifolium hybridum* L. Alsike clover. June-Sept. Introduced perennial herb; cultivated, escaping and persistent, 1390-2730 m.

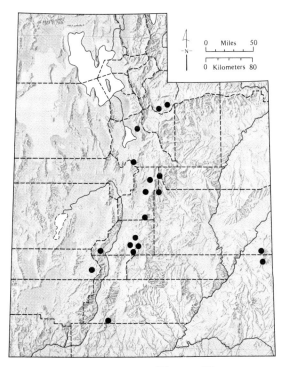

176. *Trifolium kingii* Wats. King clover. June-Aug. Native perennial herb; moist meadows, streamside in mountain brush to aspen, spruce-fir communities, 2270-3260 m.

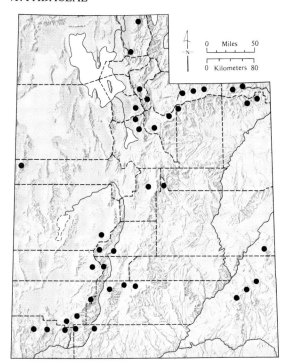

177. *Trifolium longipes* Nutt. Longstalk or Rydberg clover. May-Aug. Native perennial herb; meadows, streamside in mountain brush to aspen, spruce-fir communities, 1820-3300 m.

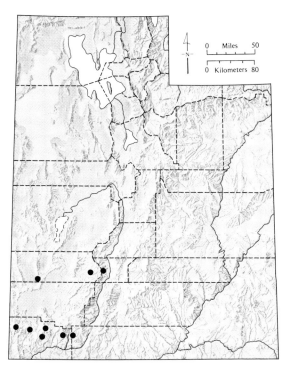

178. *Trifolium macilentum* Greene Lean clover. May-June. Native perennial herb; oak, ponderosa pine, aspen, spruce-fir, subalpine meadow communities, 1970-2910 m.

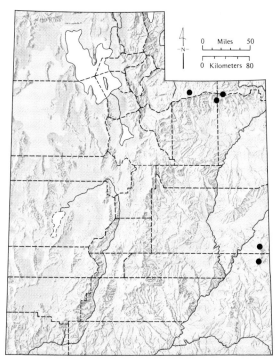

179. *Trifolium nanum* Torr. Dwarf clover. June-Aug. Native perennial herb; alpine meadows, rocky ridges, 3290-3940 m.

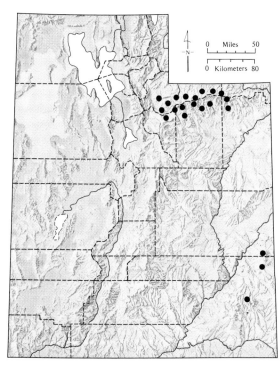

180. *Trifolium parryi* Gray Parry clover. June-Aug. Native perennial herb; meadows and talus in lodgepole pine, subalpine fir communities to above timberline, 2680-3790 m.

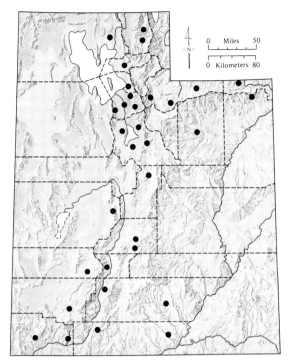

181. *Trifolium pratense* L. Red clover. May-Sept. Introduced perennial herb; cultivated, escaping and persistent, 1300-3180 m.

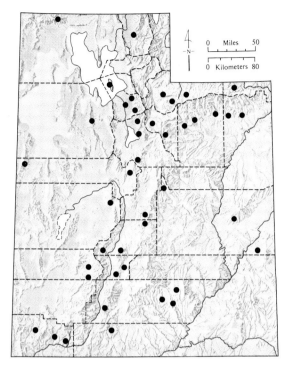

182. *Trifolium repens* L. White clover. May-July. Introduced perennial herb; cultivated, escaping and persistent, 1300-2580 m.

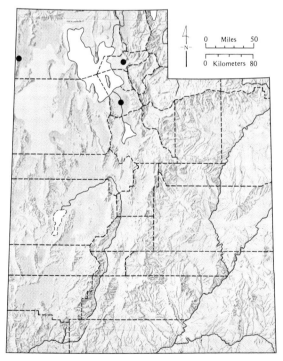

183. *Trifolium variegatum* Nutt. Whitetip or variegated clover. June-July. Native annual; moist to dry meadows, along waterways, 1270-1300 m.

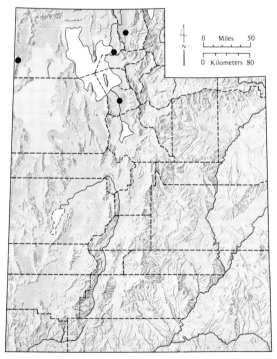

184. *Trifolium wormskjoldii* Lehm. Wormskjold clover. May-July. Native perennial herb; moist meadows, streamside, pond margins, 1280-1520 m.

41. FABACEAE

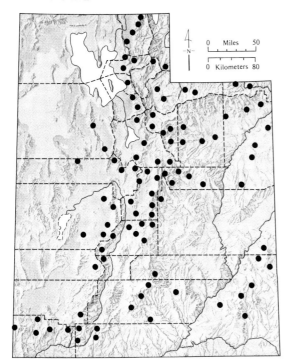

185. *Vicia americana* Willd. American vetch.
Apr.-Aug. Native perennial herb; sagebrush,
pinyon-juniper, mountain brush to aspen, spruce-fir
communities, 1360-3180 m.

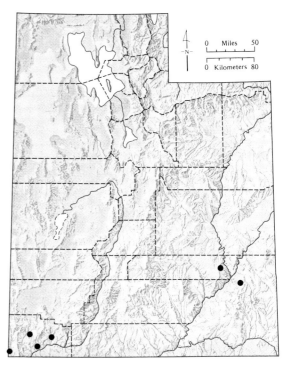

186. *Vicia ludoviciana* Nutt. Louisiana vetch.
Apr.-May. Native annual; creosote bush to pinyon-
juniper communities, 850-1820 m.

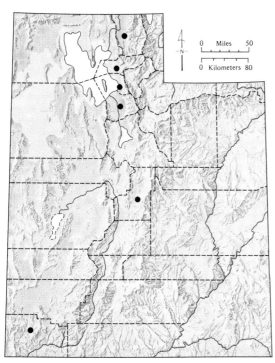

187. *Vicia villosa* Roth Hairy vetch. May-
Sept. Introduced annual; invading cultivated and
other disturbed sites, 1300-2430 m.

42. FAGACEAE

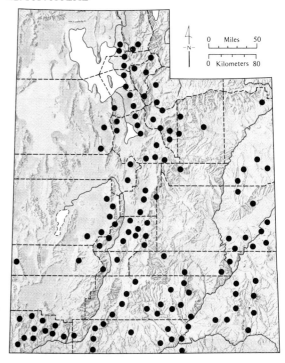

1. *Quercus gambelii* Nutt. Gambel oak. Apr.-
June. Native tree or shrub; dominant over large
areas, a major component of the mountain brush
community; sagebrush, to aspen, pinyon-juniper,
ponderosa pine communities, 1000-3030 m.

42. FAGACEAE

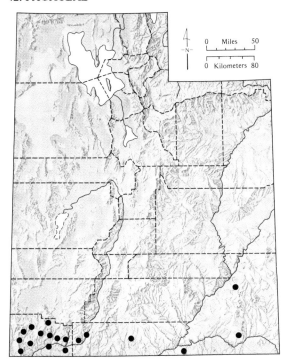

2. *Quercus turbinella* Greene   Turbinella live oak. Apr.-June.   Native shrub or small tree; creosote bush to desert shrub communities, 800-1970 m.

3. *Quercus undulata* Torr. Wavyleaf oak. Apr.-June.   Native shrub or small tree; desert shrub communities, a soil binder, 1000-1970 m.

43. FRANKENIACEAE

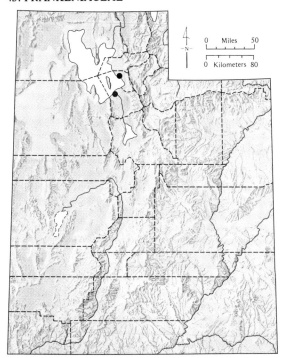

1. *Frankenia pulverulenta* L.   May-June. Introduced annual; moist sites in salt desert shrub, 1270-1290 m.

44. FUMARIACEAE

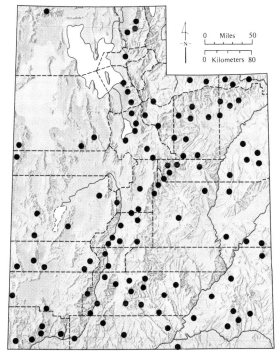

1. *Corydalis aurea* Willd.   Golden corydalis. Apr.-Sept.   Native annual or biennial; moist to dry, sometimes disturbed sites in creosote bush to aspen-conifer communities, 840-3330 m.

44. FUMARIACEAE

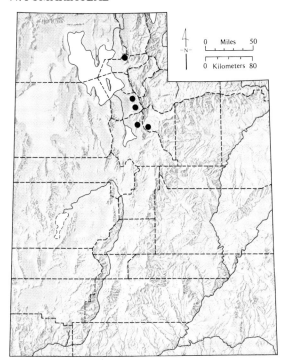

2. *Corydalis caseana* Gray   Fitweed corydalis.
June-July.   Native perennial herb; streamside,
sometimes in rushing water, lakeshores, spring
margins, 1880-2940 m.

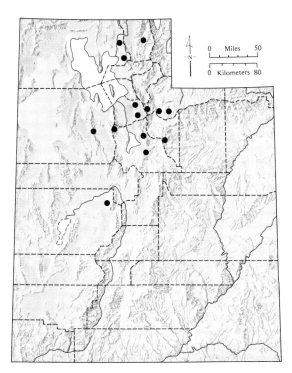

3. *Dicentra uniflora* Kell. Steershead.   Apr.-
May. Native perennial herb; open or shaded sites
in mountain brush to spruce-fir communities, often
in the wake of snowmelt, 1500-2970 m.

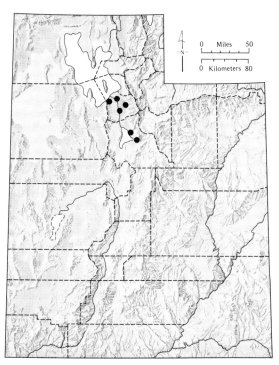

4. *Fumaria officinalis* L. Common fumitory.
Apr.-June. Introduced annual; waste places, 1270-
1730 m.

45. GENTIANACEAE

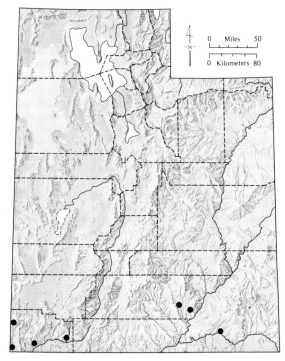

1. *Centaurium calycosum* (Buckl.) Fern.
Buckley centaury. June-July. Native annual; wet
meadows, streamside, near springs and seeps, 850-
2060 m.

316

45. GENTIANACEAE

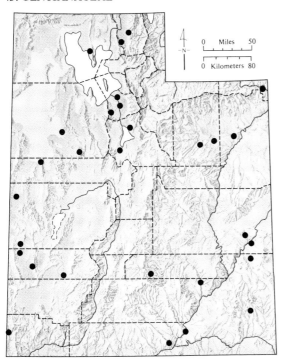

2. *Centaurium exaltatum* (Griseb.) Piper
Great Basin centaury. June-Sept. Native annual;
wet, often saline meadows, near springs and seeps,
1120-1940 m.

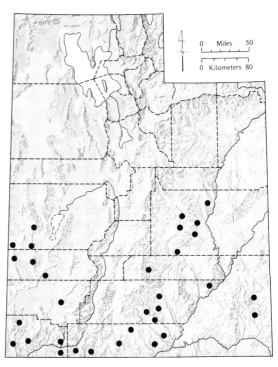

3. *Frasera albomarginata* Wats. White-
margined frasera. May-July. Native biennial;
shadscale, other desert shrub to pinyon-juniper
communities, 1210-2180 m.

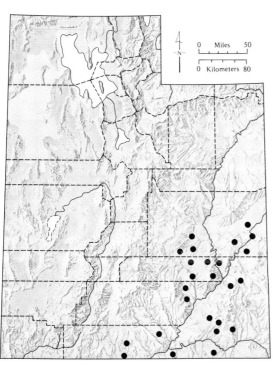

4. *Frasera paniculata* Torr. Utah frasera.
May-July. Native biennial; sandy sites in desert
shrub to pinyon-juniper communities, 1210-
1910 m.

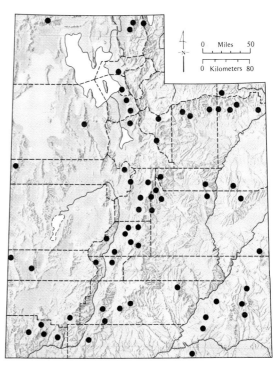

5. *Frasera speciosa* Griseb. Elkweed. June-
Aug. Native biennial; moist to mesic open slopes
in pinyon-juniper, oak, aspen, spruce-fir
communities, 1970-3430 m.

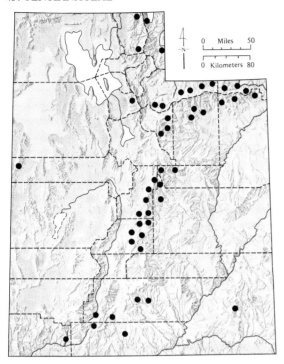

6. *Gentiana affinis* Griseb. Rocky Mountain gentian. Aug.-Sept. Native perennial herb; moist meadows, streamside in mountain brush to aspen-spruce-fir communities, 1790-2970 m.

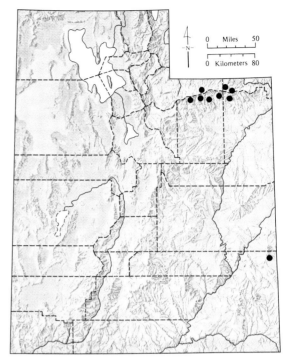

7. *Gentiana algida* Pall. Arctic gentian. Aug.-Sept. Native perennial herb; moist open sites in alpine communities, 3030-3940 m.

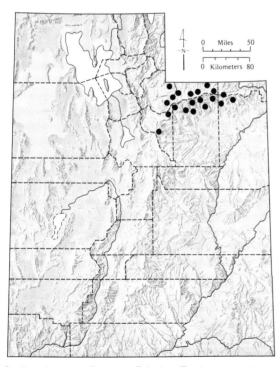

8. *Gentiana calycosa* Griseb. Explorer gentian. Aug.-Sept. Native perennial herb; streamside, moist sites in meadows, aspen-conifer, alpine communities, 2720-3540 m.

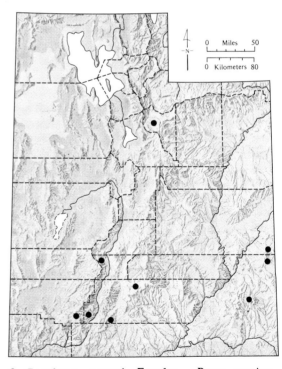

9. *Gentiana parryi* Engelm. Parry gentian. July-Sept. Native perennial herb; moist sites in mountain brush to aspen-conifer communities, 1970-3640 m.

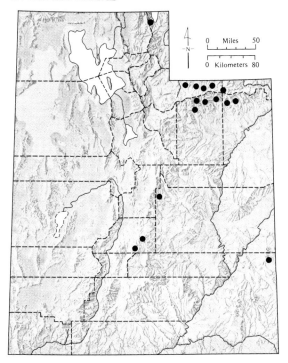

10. *Gentiana prostrata* Haenke Moss gentian. July-Aug. Native annual or biennial; streamside, wet meadows, 1850-3640 m.

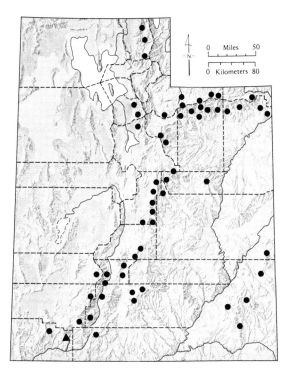

11. *Gentianella amarella* (L.) Börner Felwort. July-Aug. Native annual or biennial; wet to mesic sites in meadows and aspen-conifer communities, 2180-3790 m.

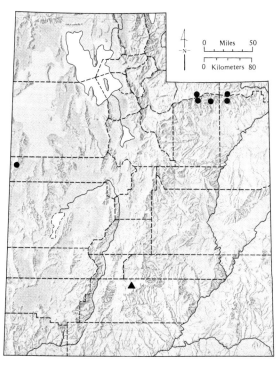

12. *Gentianella tenella* (Rottb.) Börner Lapland gentian. Aug.-Sept. Native annual; moist alpine meadows, 3180-3640 m.

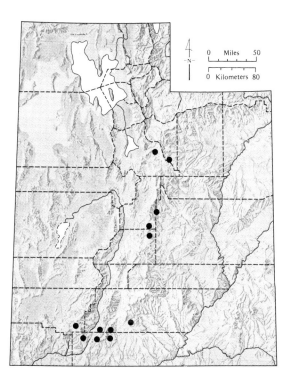

13. *Gentianella tortuosa* (Jones) J. Gillett Jones gentian. July-Aug. Native annual; calcareous ridges in bristlecone pine, spruce-fir communities, 2150-3250 m.

45. GENTIANACEAE

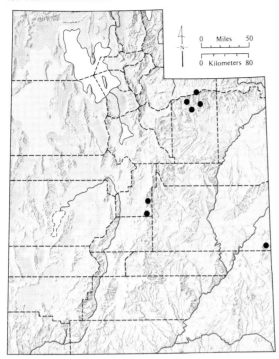

14. *Gentianopsis barbellata* (Engelm.) Iltis
Aug.-Sept. Native perennial herb; talus, rocky
slopes in conifer communities, 2940-3430 m.

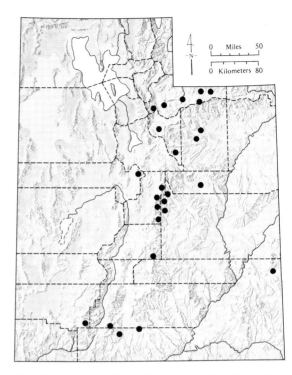

15. *Gentianopsis detonsa* (Rottb.) Ma
Meadow gentian. Aug.-Sept. Circumboreal annual;
streamside, wet meadows, 1660-3180 m.

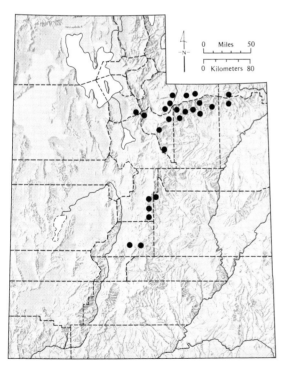

16. *Swertia perennis* L.   July-Aug.
Circumboreal perennial herb; marshes, streamside,
lakeshores, wet meadows, spruce-fir, lodgepole pine
communities, 2570-3550 m.

46. GERANIACEAE

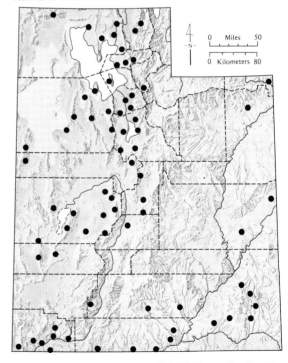

1. *Erodium cicutarium* (L.) L' Her. Storksbill.
Feb.-Nov. Introduced annual; disturbed sites in
numerous plant communities, 800-2460 m.

320

46. GERANIACEAE

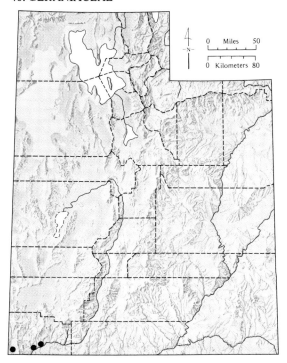

2. **_Erodium texanum_** Gray Tufted storksbill.
Apr.-May. Native annual; creosote bush
communities, 800-970 m.

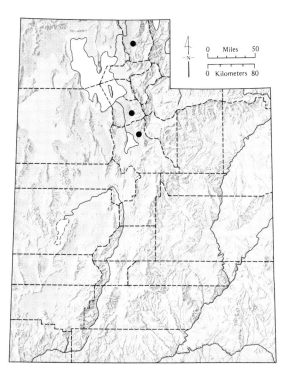

3. **_Geranium bicknellii_** Britt. Bicknell
cranesbill. June-Aug. Introduced annual or
biennial; disturbed sites, 1810-2430 m.

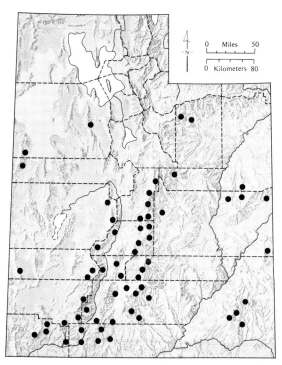

4. **_Geranium caespitosum_** James Small-leaf
geranium. June-Sept. Native perennial herb; moist
to dry, open sites from mountain brush to aspen-
conifer communities, 1300-3030 m.

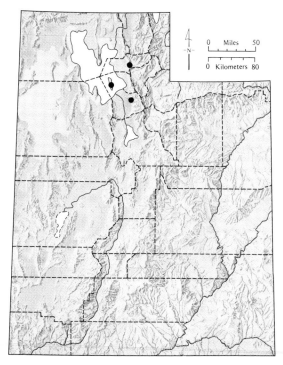

5. **_Geranium carolinianum_** L. Carolina
cranesbill. Apr.-July. Native annual or biennial;
disturbed sites, 1300-1360 m.

321

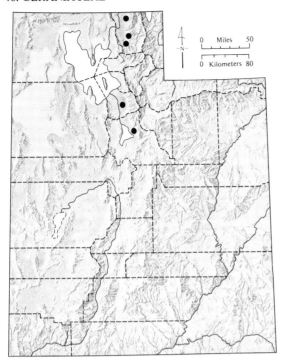

6. *Geranium pusillum* L. Slender cranesbill. May-Aug. Introduced annual or biennial; disturbed sites, 1360-1500 m.

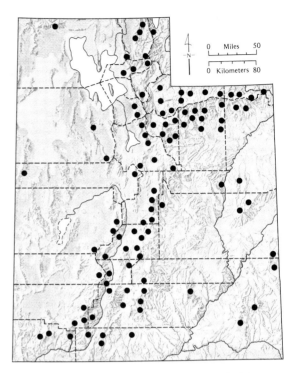

7. *Geranium richardsonii* Fisch. & Trautv. Richardson geranium. June-Sept. Native perennial herb; streamside, moist meadows, moist or shaded slopes in mountain brush to spruce-fir, pinyon-juniper, lodgepole pine, ponderosa pine communities, 1690-3340 m.

47. GROSSULARIACEAE

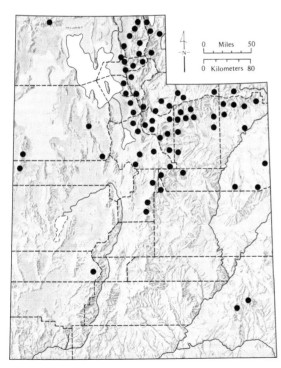

8. *Geranium viscosissimum* Fisch. & Mey. Sticky geranium. May-Sept. Native perennial herb; mesic to dry sites in mountain brush to aspen, spruce-fir communities, 1570-3200 m.

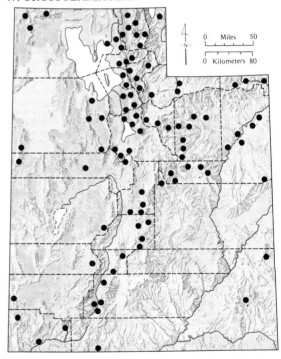

1. *Ribes aureum* Pursh Golden currant. Apr.-June. Native shrub; along waterways, other moist to mesic sites in creosote bush, greasewood-shadscale to conifer communities, 840-2580 m.

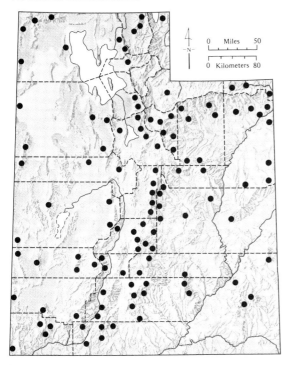

2. *Ribes cereum* Dougl. Wax or squaw currant. May-July. Native shrub; desert shrub to alpine communities, 1520-3640 m.

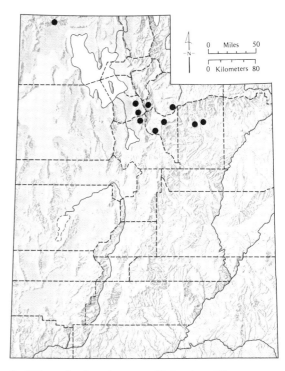

3. *Ribes hudsonianum* Richards. Western or wild black currant. May-July. Native shrub; streamside in mountain brush, aspen-conifer communities, 1450-2570 m.

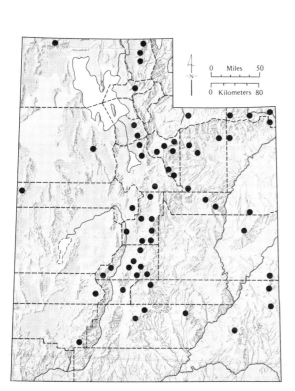

4. *Ribes inerme* Rydb. Whitestem gooseberry. May-July. Native shrub; streamside, moist sites in pinyon-juniper, mountain brush, aspen, spruce-fir communities, 1600-3150 m.

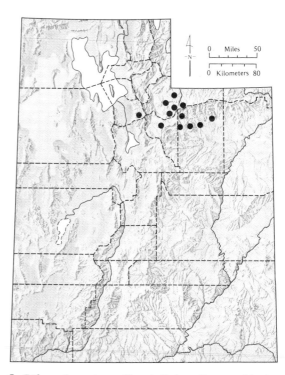

5. *Ribes lacustre* (Pers.) Poir. Swamp black gooseberry. July-Aug. Native shrub; streamside, rocky slopes in mountain brush, aspen, spruce-fir communities, 1970-3350 m.

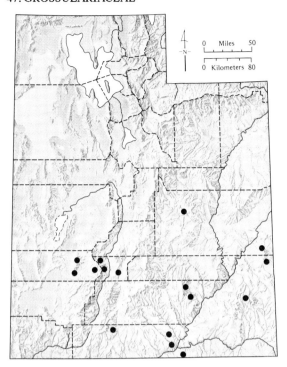

6. **Ribes leptanthum** Gray Trumpet gooseberry. May-June. Native shrub; pinyon-juniper, mountain brush to aspen, ponderosa pine communities, 1830-2590 m.

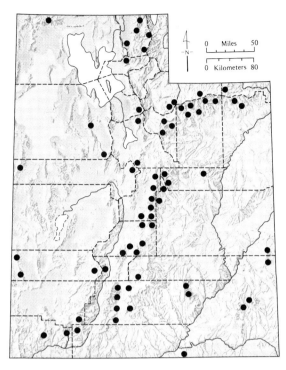

7. **Ribes montigenum** McClat. Alpine prickly currant. June-Aug. Native shrub; aspen-conifer, krummholz communities, talus, 2130-3780 m.

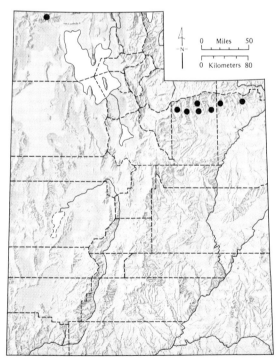

8. **Ribes setosum** Lindl. Missouri gooseberry. May-July. Native shrub; streamside, wet meadows, near seeps and springs, 2130-2800 m.

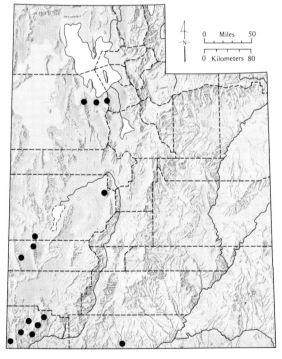

9. **Ribes velutinum** Greene Desert gooseberry. Mar.-July. Native shrub; creosote bush, sagebrush, desert shrub, pinyon-juniper, mountain brush communities, 1000-2320 m.

47. GROSSULARIACEAE

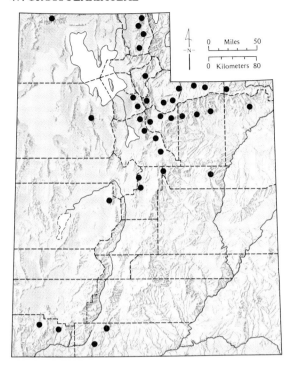

10. ***Ribes viscosissimum*** Pursh Sticky currant. May-July. Native shrub; streamside, meadows, shade of mountain brush to aspen-conifer communities, 1690-2930 m.

11. ***Ribes wolfii*** Roth. Rothrock or Wolf currant. June-Aug. Native shrub; streamside, mountain brush communities, often among rocks, shaded sites in conifer forests, 1640-3350 m.

48. HALORAGACEAE

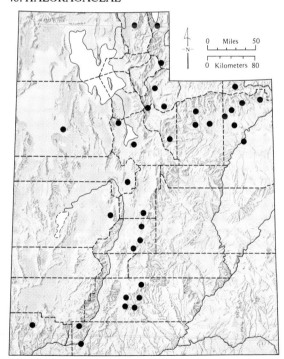

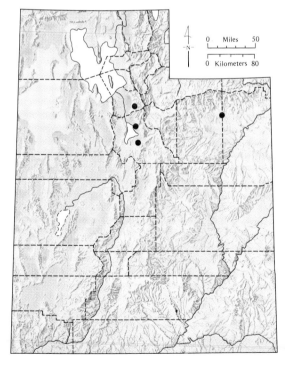

1. ***Myriophyllum exalbescens*** Fern. Apr.-June. Native perennial herb; ponds, slow-moving water, 1300-2730 m.

2. ***Myriophyllum verticillatum*** L. Apr.-June. Circumboreal perennial herb; ponds, slow-moving water, 1360-2420 m.

49. HIPPURIDACEAE

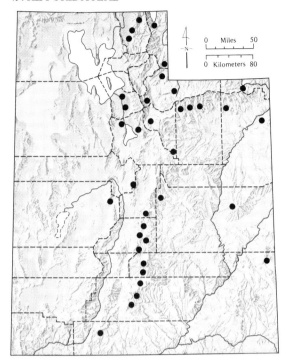

1. ***Hippuris vulgaris*** L. Common marestail. May-July. Circumboreal perennial herb; fresh or brackish shallow water of streams, ponds, marshes, drying mud flats, 1270-3120 m.

50. HYDROCHARITACEAE

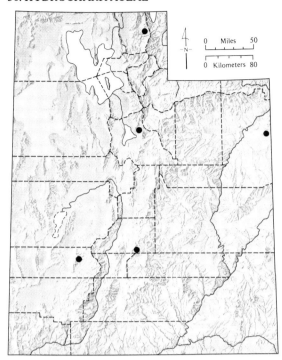

1. ***Elodea canadensis*** Michx. American waterweed. July-Sept. Native perennial herb; shallow water of streams and ponds, 1960-2730 m.

51. HYDROPHYLLACEAE

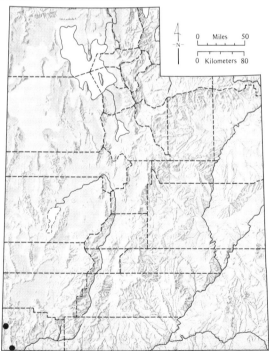

1. ***Emmenanthe penduliflora*** Benth. Whispering bells. Apr.-June. Native annual; desert shrub, juniper communities, 1150-1300 m.

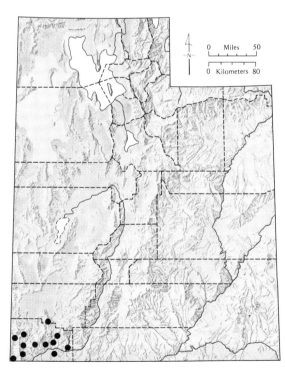

2. ***Eriodictyon angustifolium*** Nutt. Yerba santa. May-June. Native shrub; creosote bush to pinyon-juniper communities, 1000-2100 m.

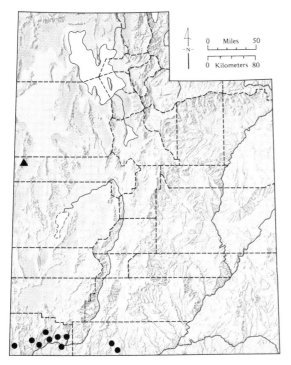

3. Eucrypta micrantha (Torr.) Heller Desert cucrypta. Mar.-Apr. Native annual; creosote bush to pinyon-juniper communities, 800-1580 m.

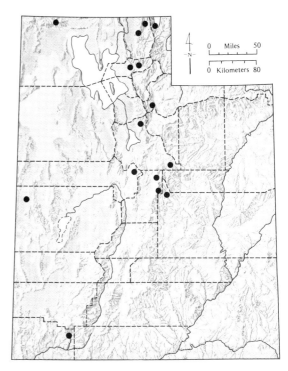

4. Hesperochiron pumilus (Griseb.) Porter Apr.-June. Native perennial herb; streamside, moist meadows, 1500-2580 m.

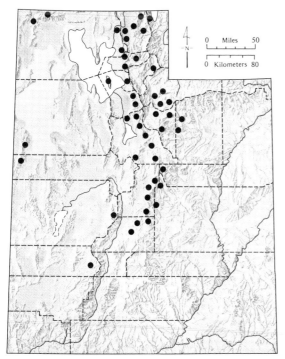

5. Hydrophyllum capitatum Benth. Ballhead waterleaf. Apr.-July. Native perennial herb; shaded sites in mountain brush to conifer communities, 1400-2730 m.

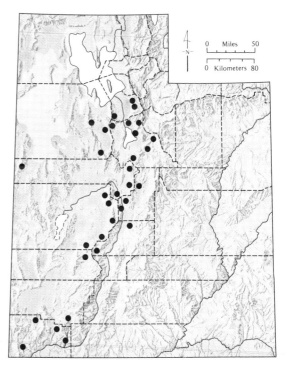

6. Hydrophyllum occidentale (Wats.) Gray Western waterleaf. Apr.-July. Native perennial herb; shaded sites in mountain brush to conifer communities, 1330-2730 m.

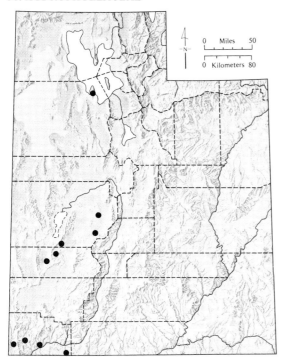

7. *Nama demissum* Gray Purplemat. Apr.-July. Native annual; creosote bush, greasewood, desert shrub communities, 800-1300 m.

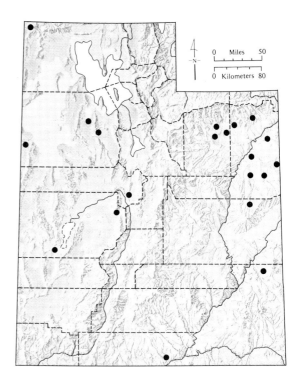

8. *Nama densum* Lemmon Compact or leafy nama. May-Sept. Native annual; shadscale, other desert shrub, juniper communities, 1090-1730 m.

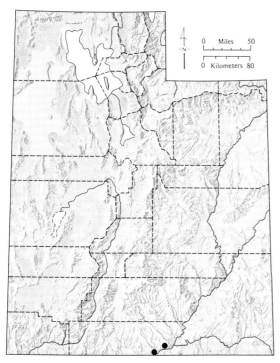

9. *Nama hispidum* Gray Hairy nama. Apr.-Sept. Native annual; desert shrub communities, 1270-1340 m.

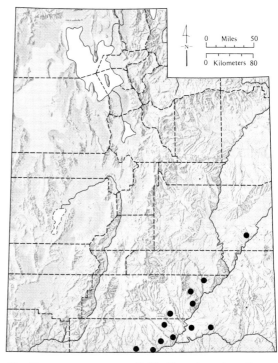

10. *Nama retrorsum* J. T. Howell Apr.-June. Native annual; desert shrub to pinyon-juniper communities, 1120-2120 m.

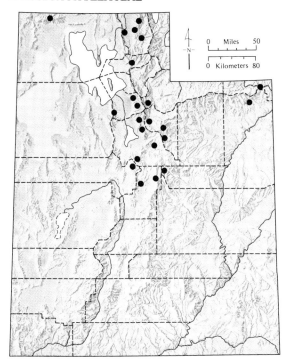

11. *Nemophila breviflora* Gray Woodlove;
Great Basin nemophila. May-July. Native annual;
shaded sites in mountain brush to aspen-fir
communities, 1450-2630 m.

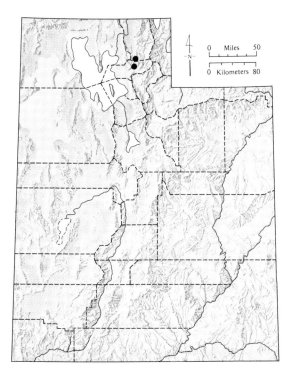

12. *Nemophila parviflora* Benth. Smallflower
nemophila. May-June. Native annual; shaded sites
under oakbrush, 1500-1660 m.

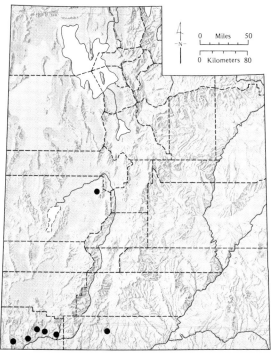

13. *Phacelia affinis* Gray Apr.-June. Native
annual; creosote bush to pinyon-juniper
communities, 910-1790 m.

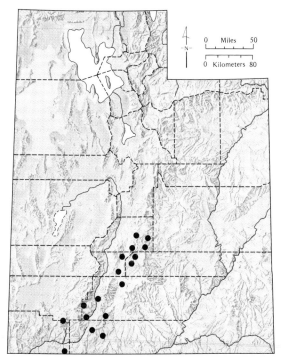

14. *Phacelia alba* Rydb. White phacelia. June-
Aug. Native annual; mountain brush to ponderosa
pine communities, 1360-2550 m.

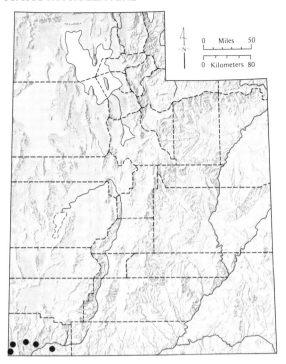

15. *Phacelia ambigua* Jones   Apr.-May.
Native annual; Joshua tree, creosote bush
communities, 810-910 m.

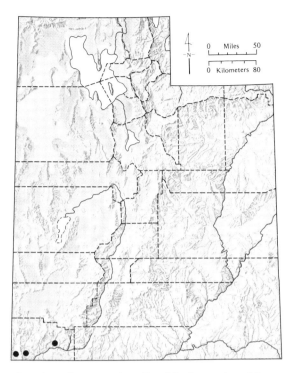

16. *Phacelia anelsonii* Macbr.   Apr.-May.
Native annual; Joshua tree, creosote bush
communities, 800-910 m.

17. *Phacelia cephalotes* Gray   Apr.-May.
Native annual; creosote bush, desert shrub
communities, 1060-1520 m.

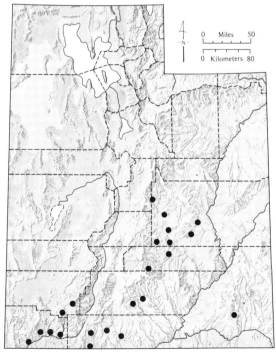

18. *Phacelia constancei* Atwood   May-Aug.
Native biennial; rocky sites in creosote bush to
ponderosa pine communities, 810-3030 m.

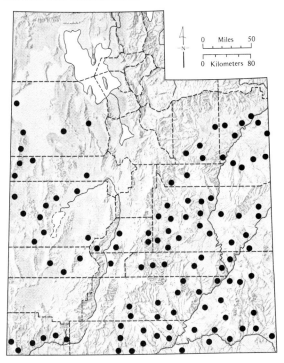

19. *Phacelia crenulata* Torr. Cutleaf helioptrope. Apr.-June. Native annual; creosote bush to ponderosa pine communities, 840-2580 m.

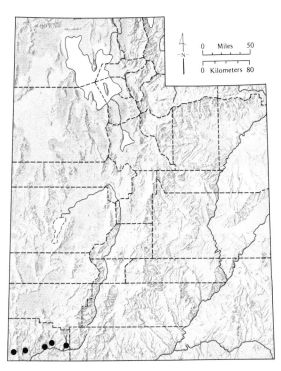

20. *Phacelia curvipes* Wats. Apr.-May. Native annual; creosote bush, pinyon-juniper communities, 840-2120 m.

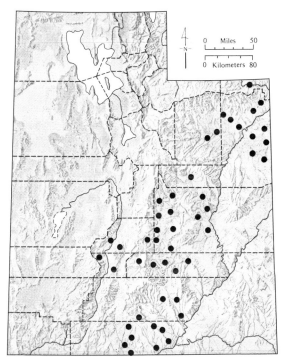

21. *Phacelia demissa* Gray Brittle phacelia. May-June. Native annual; greasewood, shadscale, mat saltbush communities, 1300-1970 m.

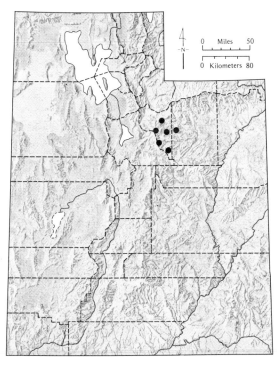

22. *Phacelia franklinii* (R. Br.) Gray July-Aug. Native annual or biennial; sagebrush-grass communities, 2300-2700 m.

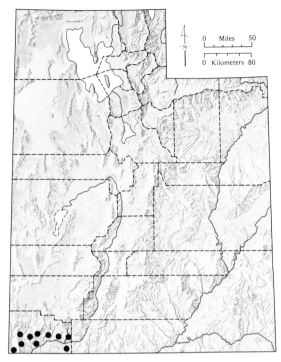

23. *Phacelia fremontii* Torr. Fremont phacelia. Apr.-May. Native annual; creosote bush, desert shrub communities, 800-1460 m.

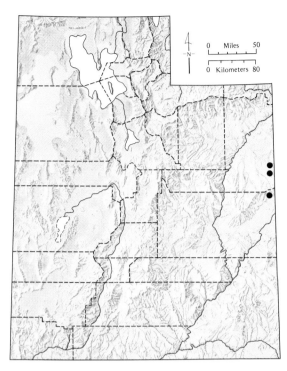

24. *Phacelia glandulosa* Nutt. May-Aug. Native annual or biennial; rocky sites in desert shrub, pinyon-juniper communities, 1510-2280 m.

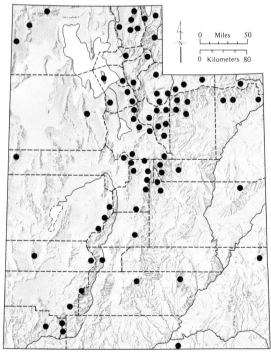

25. *Phacelia hastata* Lehm. June-Aug. Native perennial herb; mountain brush to conifer communities, talus, 1330-3490 m.

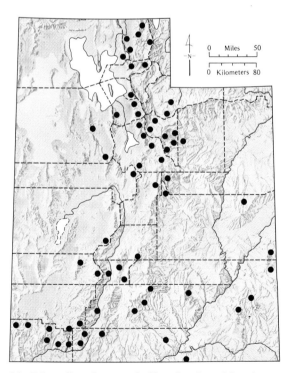

26. *Phacelia heterophylla* Pursh May-Aug. Native perennial herb; mountain brush to conifer communities, 1360-3340 m.

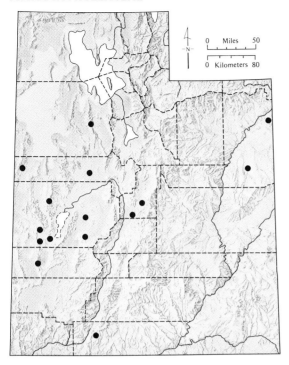

27. *Phacelia incana* Brand   Hoary phacelia. May-June. Native annual; desert shrub, pinyon-juniper communities, 1390-2370 m.

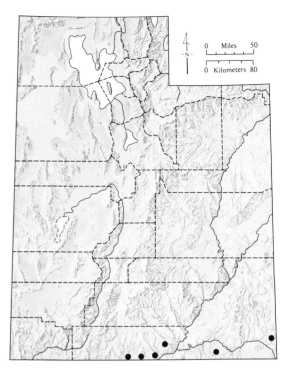

28. *Phacelia integrifolia* Torr.   Apr.-July. Native annual; shadscale, other desert shrub communities, 1270-1700 m.

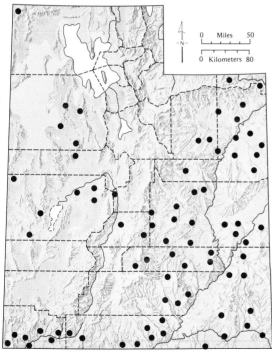

29. *Phacelia ivesiana* Torr.   Ives phacelia. May-June. Native annual; shadscale, other desert shrub, pinyon-juniper communities, 910-1940 m.

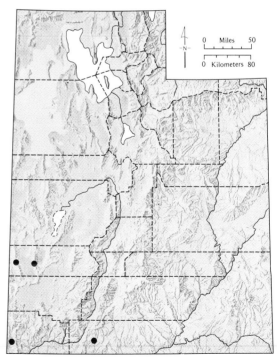

30. *Phacelia lemmonii* Gray   Mar.-July. Native annual; creosote bush, shadscale, pinyon-juniper communities, 860-2030 m.

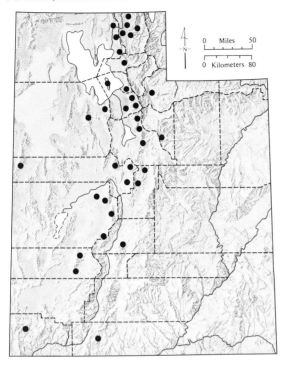

31. *Phacelia linearis* (Pursh) Holz. Threadleaf phacelia. May-June. Native annual; mountain brush to aspen-fir communities, 1360-2580 m.

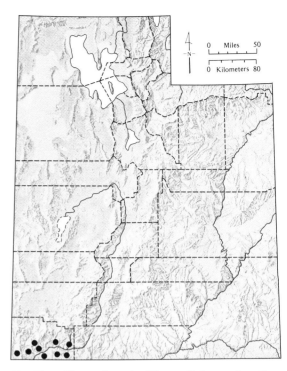

32. *Phacelia palmeri* Wats. Palmer phacelia. July-Aug. Native biennial; creosote bush, pinyon-juniper communities, 800-1820 m.

33. *Phacelia pulchella* Gray Apr.-Aug. Native annual; creosote bush, desert shrub communities, 910-1580 m.

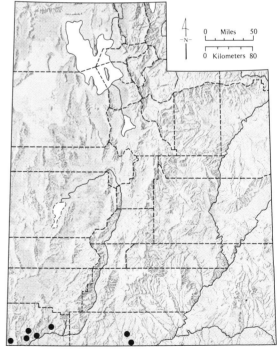

34. *Phacelia rotundifolia* Wats. Limestone phacelia. Mar.-Apr. Native annual; creosote bush communities, 800-1060 m.

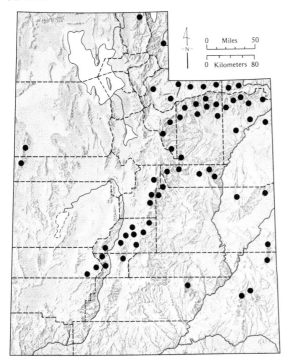

35. Phacelia sericea (Grah.) Gray June-Aug.
Native perennial herb; mountain brush to conifer
communities, 2120-3430 m.

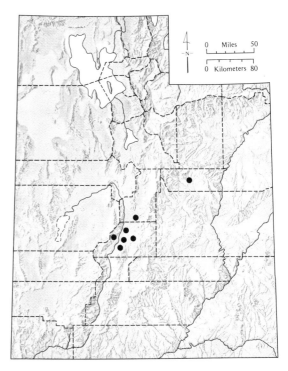

36. Phacelia utahensis Voss Utah phacelia.
June-July. Native biennial; shadscale, desert shrub,
pinyon-juniper communities, 1660-1730 m.

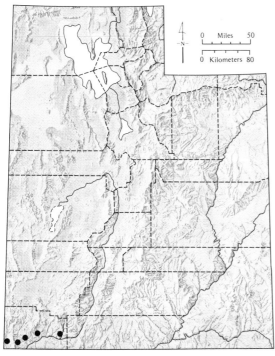

37. Phacelia vallis-mortae Voss Apr.-May.
Native annual; creosote bush communities, 840-
1220 m.

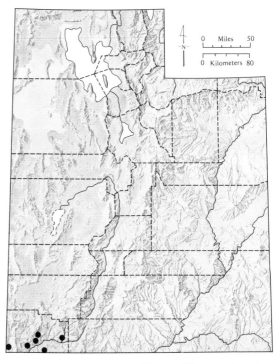

38. Tricardia watsonii Wats. Watson tricardia.
Mar.-Apr. Native perennial herb; creosote bush
communities, 800-1090 m.

52. HYPERICACEAE

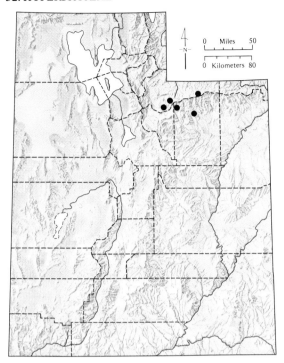

1. ***Hypericum anagalloides*** C. & S. Tinkers penny. Aug.-Sept. Native perennial herb; margins of ponds and lakes, 2720-3030 m.

2. ***Hypericum formosum*** H. B. K. Western St. Johnswort. July-Sept. Native perennial herb; marshes, streamside, moist meadows, 1300-3030 m.

53. IRIDACEAE

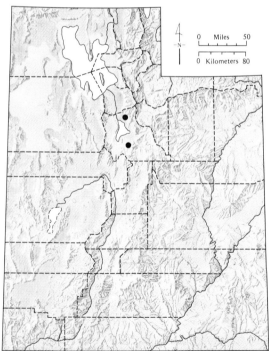

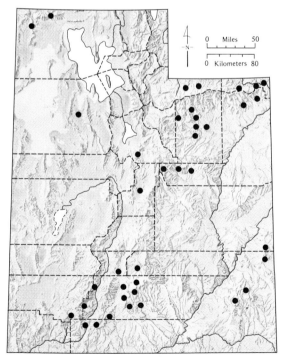

1. ***Iris germanica*** L. Fleur-de-lis. Apr.-May. Introduced perennial herb; cultivated, escaping and persistent, 1300-1370 m.

2. ***Iris missouriensis*** Nutt. Missouri iris. May-July. Native perennial herb; wet meadows, streamside, 1660-2880 m.

53. IRIDACEAE

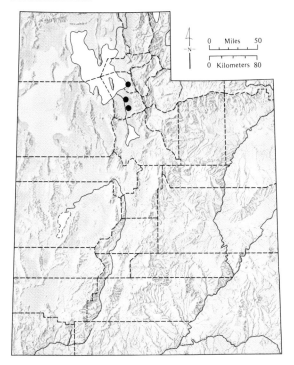

3. *Iris pseudacorus* L. Yellow flag or water iris. May-June. Introduced perennial herb; along waterways, in marshes, sometimes in shallow water, 1270-1300 m.

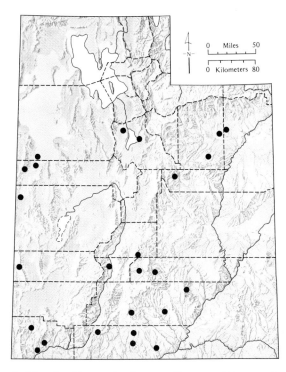

4. *Sisyrinchium demissum* Greene Blue-eyed grass. Apr.-Aug. Native perennial herb; margins of seeps and springs, marshes, wet meadows, 840-2370 m.

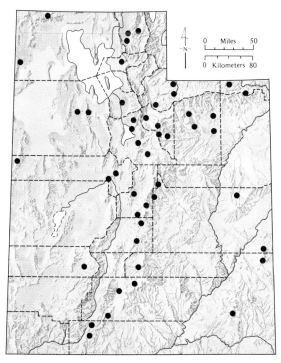

5. *Sisyrinchium idahoense* Bickn. May-July. Native perennial herb; near seeps and springs, in marshes, wet meadows, 1300-2670 m.

54. ISOETACEAE

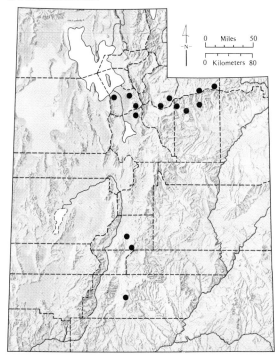

1. *Isoetes bolanderi* Engelm. Native perennial herb; shallow water of ponds and lakes, 1310-3230 m.

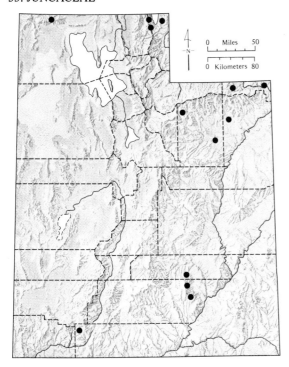

1. *Juncus alpinus* Vill. Northern rush. July-Sept. Circumboreal perennial; marshes, lake shores, streamside, 1520-2800 m.

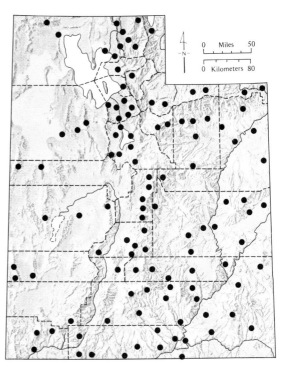

2. *Juncus arcticus* Willd. Wiregrass. May-Aug. Circumboreal perennial; marshes, streamside, pond margins, wet meadows, near seeps and springs, salt tolerant, 840-3050 m.

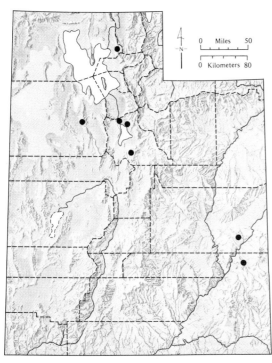

3. *Juncus articulatus* L. Jointed rush. June-July. Cosmopolitan perennial; lakeshores, streamside, wet meadows, 1220-2120 m.

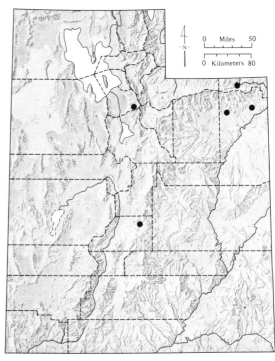

4. *Juncus bryoides* Herm. Minute rush. June-July. Native annual; shaded sites in mountain brush, ponderosa pine communities, 2400-2550 m.

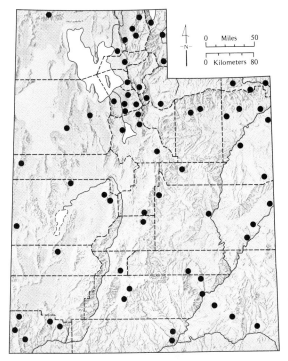

5. *Juncus bufonius* L. Toad rush. June-Aug.
Cosmopolitan annual; hanging gardens, near seeps
and springs, pond margins, wet meadows, 1130-
2850 m.

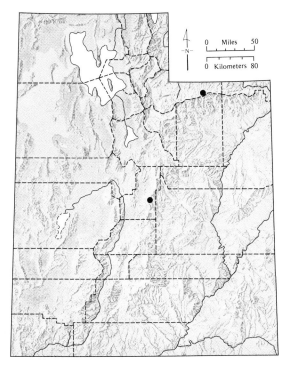

6. *Juncus castaneus* J. E. Sm. June-Aug.
Circumboreal perennial; wet meadows, 3180-
3400 m.

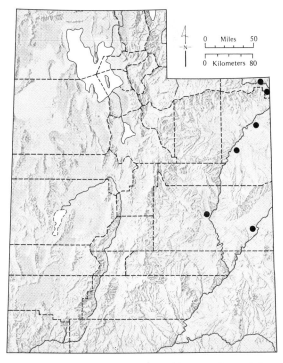

7. *Juncus compressus* Jacq. June-July.
Circumboreal perennial; marshes, streamside, 1220-
1680 m.

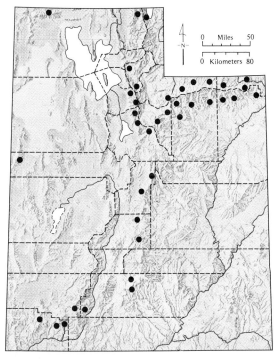

8. *Juncus confusus* Cov. June-Aug. Native
perennial; wet to dry sites in aspen, ponderosa
pine, lodgepole pine, spruce-fir communities,
1970-3180 m.

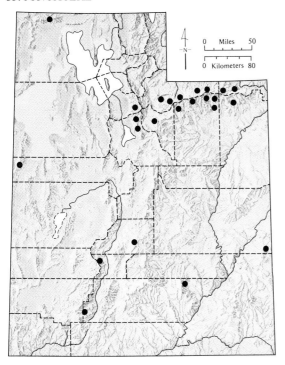

9. *Juncus drummondii* E. Mey. Drummond rush. June-Aug. Native perennial; wet to dry sites in lodgepole pine, spruce-fir, alpine meadow communities, 2420-3480 m.

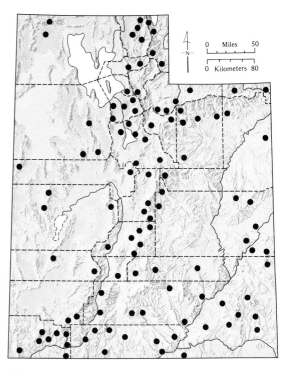

10. *Juncus ensifolius* Wikstr. Swordleaf rush. June-Aug. Native perennial; hanging gardens, pond margins, near seeps and springs, streamside, 850-3340 m.

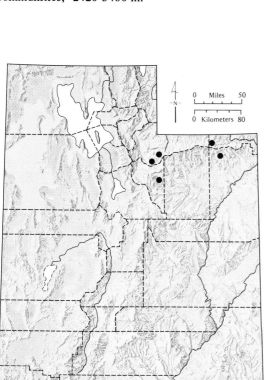

11. *Juncus filiformis* L. Thread rush. Aug.-Sept. Circumboreal perennial; streamside, wet alpine meadows, 2730-3340 m.

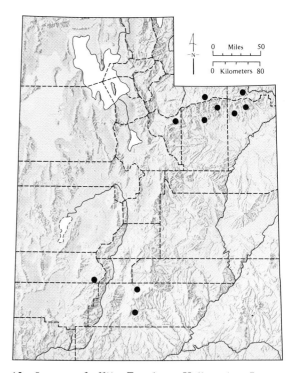

12. *Juncus hallii* Engelm. Hall rush. June-Aug. Native perennial; wet to dry meadows, pond margins, streamside, 2850-3280 m.

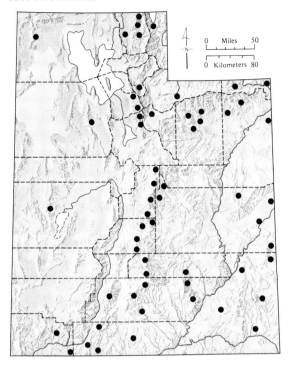

13. *Juncus longistylis* Torr. Longstyle rush.
June-Aug. Native perennial; wet meadows, near
seeps and springs, streamside, 1270-3350 m.

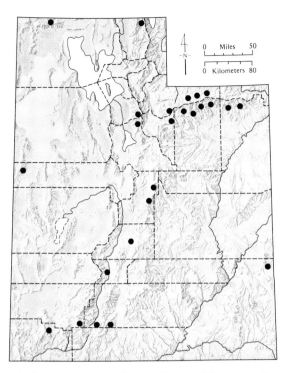

14. *Juncus mertensianus* Bong. Mertens rush.
July-Aug. Native perennial; pond margins, near
seeps and springs, streamside, wet meadows, 2430-
3420 m.

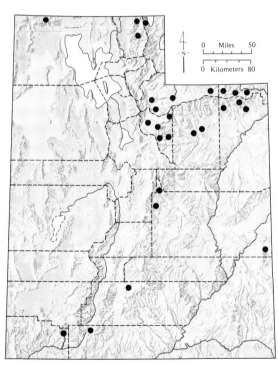

15. *Juncus nevadensis* Wats. Nevada rush.
July-Aug. Native perennial; wet to dry meadows,
1640-3050 m.

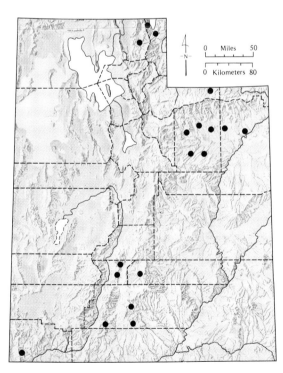

16. *Juncus nodosus* L. Knotted rush. June-
Sept. Native perennial; streamside, wet meadows,
1250-2430 m.

341

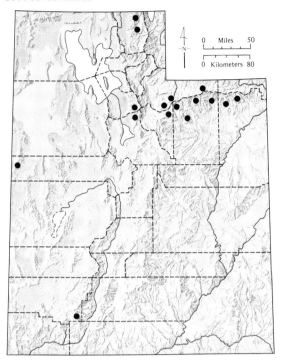

17. *Juncus parryi* Engelm. Parry rush. July-Aug. Native perennial; wet to dry, often rocky sites in lodgepole pine, spruce, alpine meadow communities, 2620-3490 m.

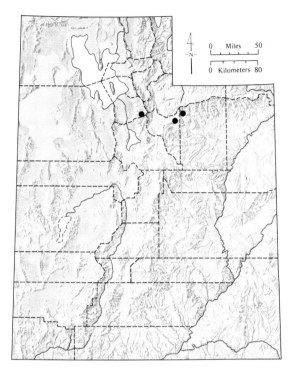

18. *Juncus regelii* Buch. Regel rush. Aug.-Sept. Native perennial; streamside, wet meadows, 2720-3060 m.

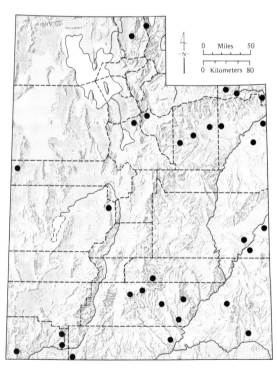

19. *Juncus tenuis* Willd. Poverty rush. June-Aug. Native perennial; hanging gardens, streamside, pond margins, wet meadows, 1130-2380 m.

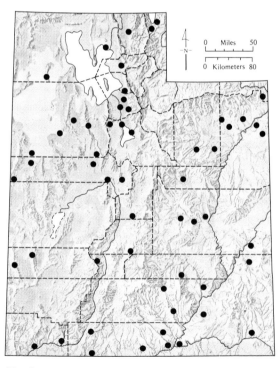

20. *Juncus torreyi* Cov. Torrey rush. June-Aug. Native perennial; along waterways, pond and lake margins, wet meadows, near seeps and springs, salt tolerant, 810-2010 m.

55. JUNCACEAE

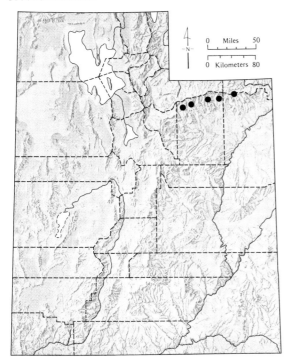

21. *Juncus triglumis* L.   Three-flowered rush.
July-Aug.   Circumboreal perennial; wet alpine
meadows, 2800-3810 m.

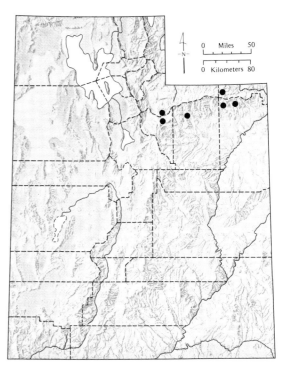

22. *Luzula campestris* (L.) DC.   Field or hairy
woodrush.   June-Aug.   Circumboreal perennial;
meadow, lodgepole pine, spruce communities,
2330-3110 m.

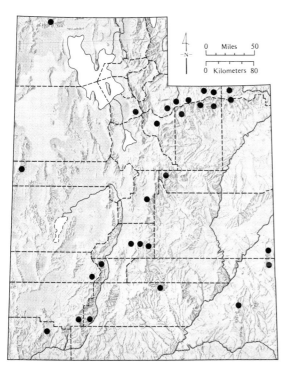

23. *Luzula parviflora* (Ehrh.) Desv.   Millett
woodrush.   June-Aug.   Circumboreal perennial;
streamside, wet meadows, shaded sites in ponderosa
pine, lodgepole pine, aspen, spruce-fir
communities, 2300-3490 m.

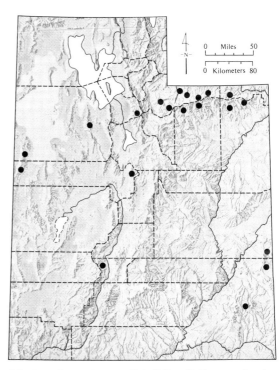

24. *Luzula spicata* (L.) DC.   Spike woodrush.
July-Sept.   Circumboreal perennial; dry to wet
meadows, streamside, shaded sites in lodgepole
pine, spruce-fir communities, exposed rocky slopes
above timberline, 2470-3810 m.

343

56. JUNCAGINACEAE

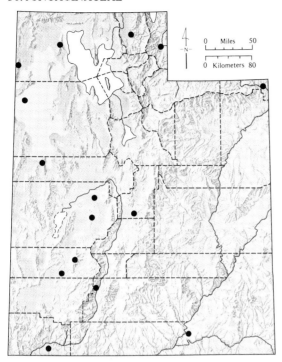

1. *Triglochin concinna* Davy Low arrowgrass. May-Aug. Native perennial herb; marshes, near seeps and springs, salt tolerant, 1280-1460 m.

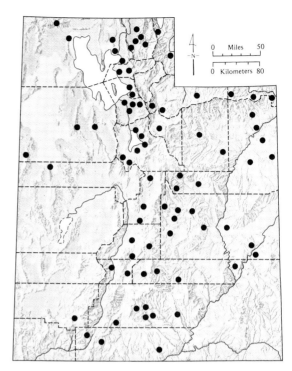

2. *Triglochin maritima* L. Maritime arrowgrass. May-Aug. Circumboreal perennial herb; marshes, wet meadows, salt tolerant, 1300-2670 m.

57. KRAMERIACEAE

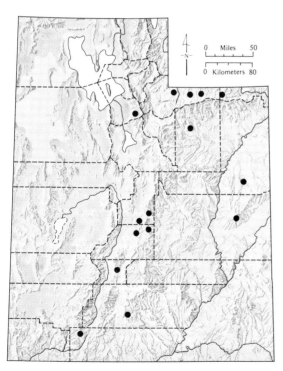

3. *Triglochin palustris* L. Marsh arrowgrass. June-Aug. Circumboreal perennial herb; wet meadows and other moist sites in ponderosa pine, lodgepole pine, aspen, spruce-fir communities, salt tolerant, 1510-2910 m.

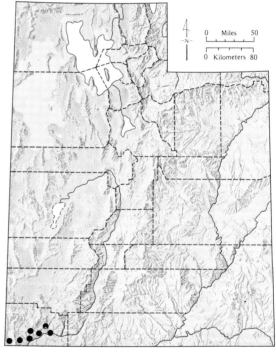

1. *Krameria parvifolia* Benth. Range ratany. Apr.-June. Native shrub; Joshua tree, creosote bush communities, 800-1000 m.

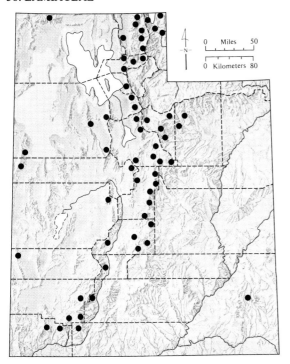

1. *Agastache urticifolia* (Benth.) Kuntze Horsemint. June-Aug. Native perennial herb; sagebrush to aspen-fir communities, 1660-2990 m.

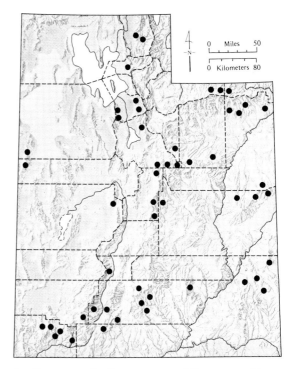

2. *Dracocephalum parviflorum* Nutt. American dragonhead. June-Aug. Native annual or perennial; sagebrush to aspen communities, 1630-2730 m.

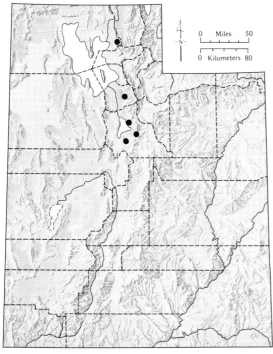

3. *Glecoma hederacea* L. Ground ivy. Apr.-July. Introduced perennial herb; disturbed sites, 1390-1580 m.

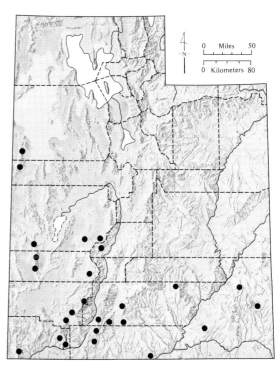

4. *Hedeoma drummondii* Benth. Mock pennyroyal. June-Aug. Native perennial herb; desert shrub to pinyon-juniper communities, 1120-2430 m.

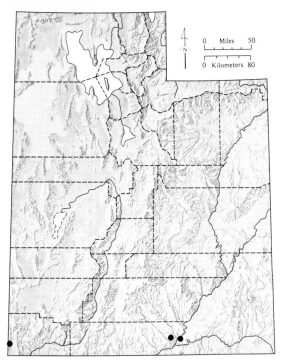

5. *Hedeoma nana* (Torr.) Briq. Dwarf pennyroyal. May-June. Native annual; hanging gardens, dry rocky slopes, pinyon-juniper communities, 1060-1150 m.

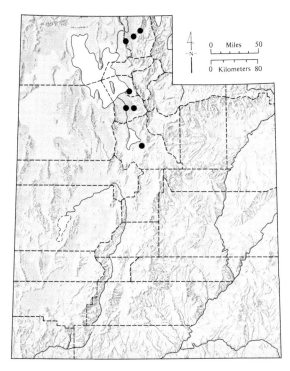

6. *Lamium amplexicaule* L. Deadnettle. Apr.-May. Introduced annual; roadsides, other disturbed sites, 1300-1580 m.

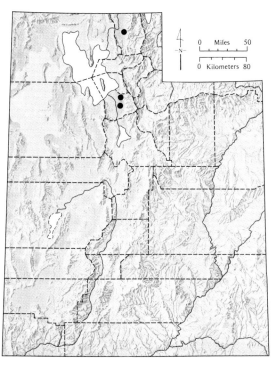

7. *Lamium purpureum* L. Purple deadnettle. May-June. Introduced annual; disturbed sites, 1360-1520 m.

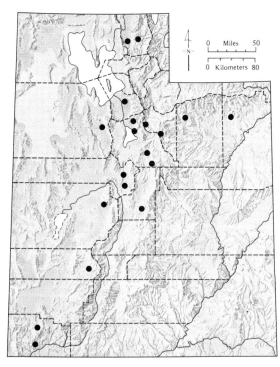

8. *Leonurus cardiaca* L. Motherwort. July-Aug. Introduced perennial herb; disturbed sites and established in mountain brush, aspen-conifer communities, 840-2280 m.

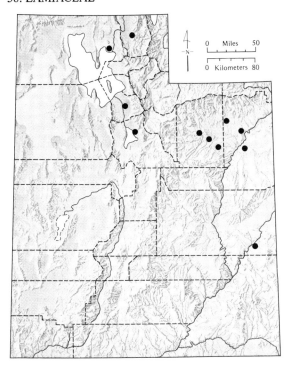

9. *Lycopus americanus* Barton American bugleweed. July-Aug. Native perennial herb; marshes, streamside, wet meadows, 1210-2310 m.

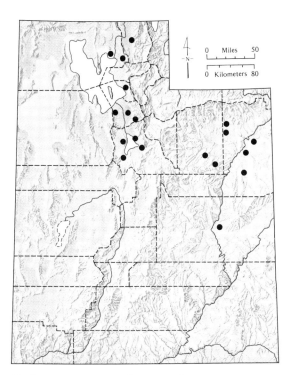

10. *Lycopus asper* Greene Rough bugleweed. July-Aug. Native perennial herb; along waterways, in marshes, wet meadows, 1280-1820 m.

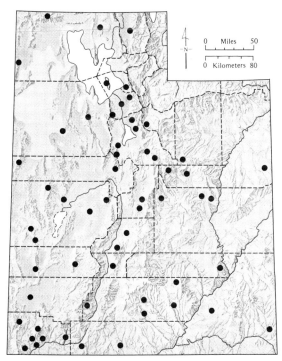

11. *Marrubium vulgare* L. Horehound. May-Aug. Introduced perennial herb; disturbed sites, especially along roadsides, 840-2430 m.

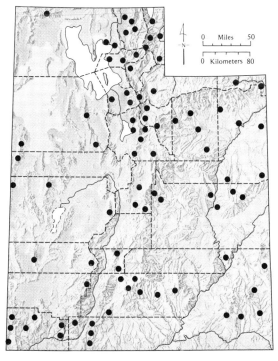

12. *Mentha arvensis* L. Field mint. July-Sept. Circumboreal perennial herb; along waterways, other moist places in creosote bush to conifer communities, 900-2850 m.

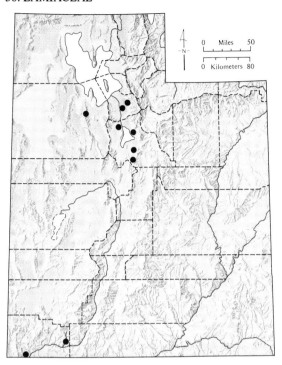

13. **Mentha piperita** L. Peppermint. July-Aug. Introduced perennial herb; cultivated, escaping and established in moist sites, especially along waterways, 1390-1580 m.

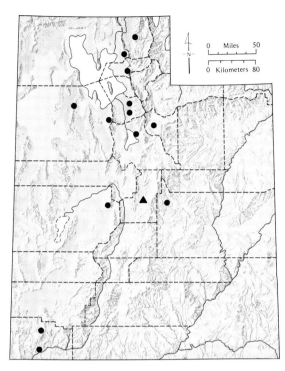

14. **Mentha spicata** L. Spearmint. July-Sept. Introduced perennial herb; along waterways, in wet meadows, 840-1880 m.

15. **Molucella laevis** L. Shellflower. May-June. Introduced annual; cultivated, escaping and persistent in disturbed sites in creosote bush to pinyon-juniper communities, 910-1520 m.

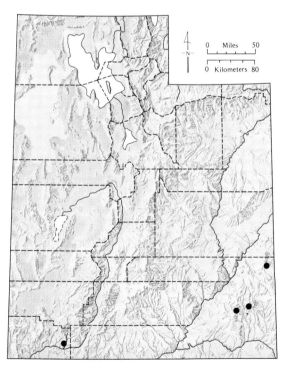

16. **Monarda fistulosa** L. Beebalm. July-Aug. Native perennial herb; moist, open sites in sagebrush, mountain brush communities, 1930-2090 m.

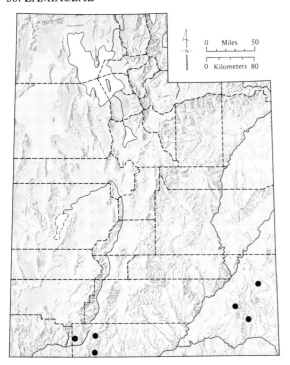

17. *Monarda pectinata* Nutt. Plains beebalm. June-July. Native annual; oak-sagebrush to pinyon-juniper communities, 1510-2060 m.

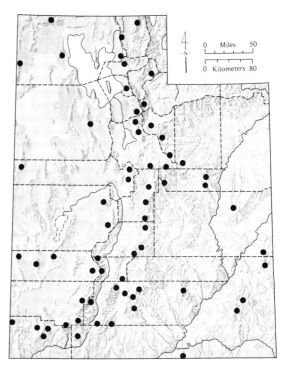

18. *Monardella odoratissima* Benth. Cloverhead horsemint. July-Aug. Native perennial herb; open rocky slopes, 1810-3340 m.

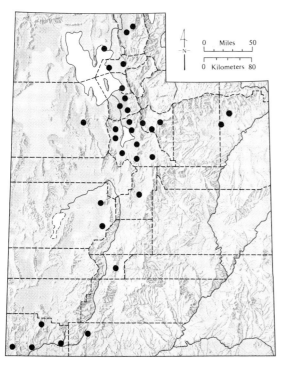

19. *Nepeta cataria* L. Catnip. July-Aug. Introduced perennial herb; along waterways, in moist to dry, often disturbed sites in sagebrush, mountain brush, aspen communities, 850-2090 m.

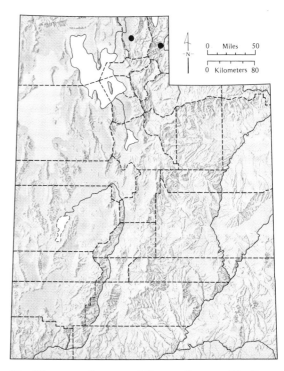

20. *Physostegia parviflora* Gray Obedient plant. July-Aug. Native perennial herb; along waterways, lakeshores, in marshes, 1390-1910 m.

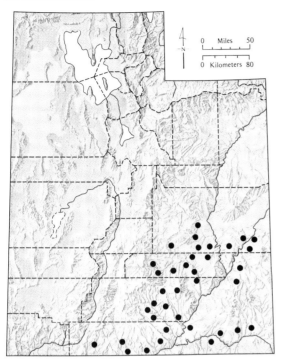

21. *Poliomintha incana* (Torr.) Gray Purple sage. May-June. Native shrub; dunes, other sandy sites in desert shrub communities, 1270-1820 m.

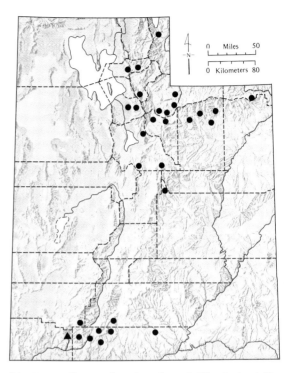

22. *Prunella vulgaris* L. Selfheal; healall. June-Aug. Cosmopolitan perennial herb; moist sites in sagebrush to conifer communities, 1510-3180 m.

23. *Salazaria mexicana* Torr. Bladder sage. Apr.-June. Native shrub; Joshua tree, creosote bush communities, 850-1220 m.

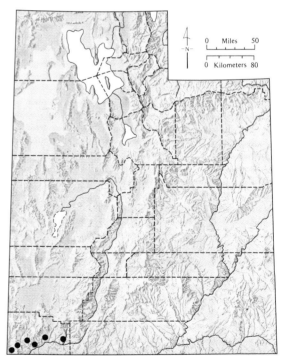

24. *Salvia columbariae* Benth. Chia. Apr.-May. Native annual; Joshua tree to pinyon-juniper communities, 840-1470 m.

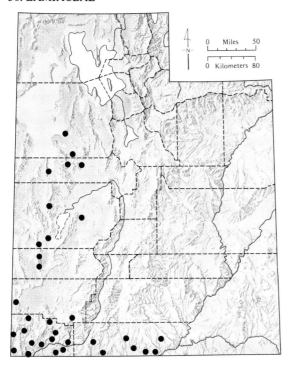

25. *Salvia dorrii* (Kell.) Abrams Dorr sage.
Apr.-Aug. Native shrub; dry, often rocky sites in
Joshua tree to pinyon-juniper communities,
occasionally near springs or in other moist sites,
840-1940 m.

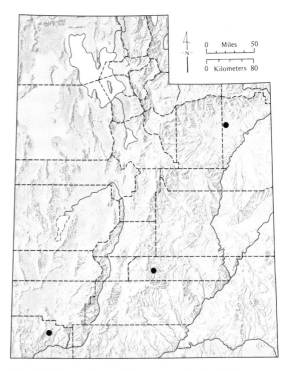

26. *Salvia reflexa* Hornem. Rocky Mountain
sage. Aug.-Sept. Native annual; dry, often
disturbed sites, 1360-1700 m.

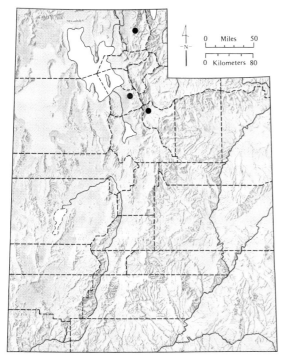

27. *Salvia sclarea* L. Clary. June-Aug.
Introduced biennial; adventive or escaped from
cultivation, persistent along roadsides, 1690-
1970 m.

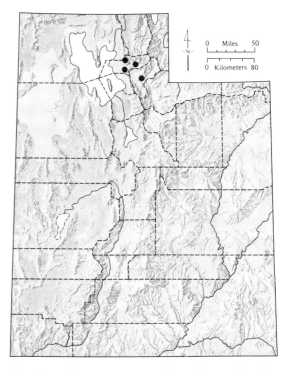

28. *Scutellaria antirrhinoides* Benth.
Skullcap. May-June. Native perennial herb; open
sites in mountain brush communities, 1360-
1520 m.

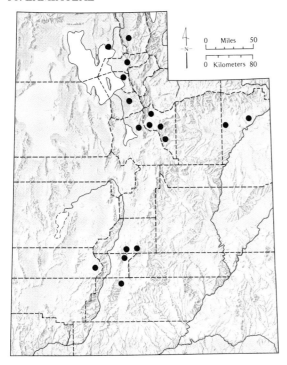

29. *Scutellaria galericulata* L. Littlecap skullcap. June-Aug. Circumboreal perennial herb; streamside, wet meadows, 1300-2700 m.

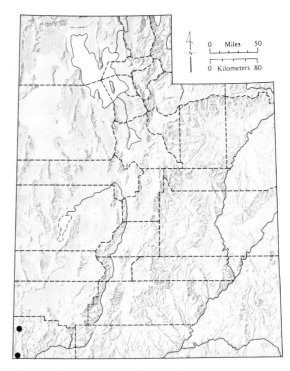

30. *Stachys albens* Gray White hedgenettle. June-July. Native perennial herb; marshes, streamside, 840-1220 m.

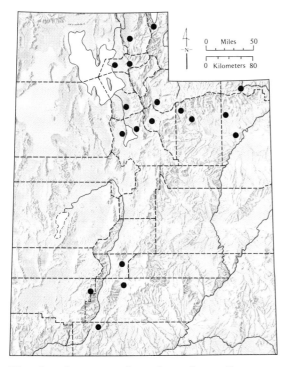

31. *Stachys palustris* L. Common hedgenettle; woundwort. June-Aug. Circumboreal perennial herb; streamside, lakeshores, meadows, 1330-2550 m.

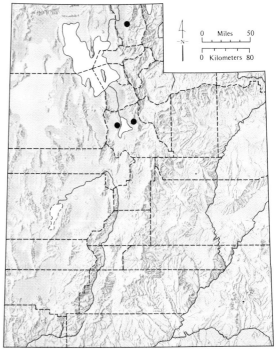

32. *Teucrium canadense* L. Canada germander. July-Aug. Native perennial herb; marshes, lakeshores, streamside, 1330-1820 m.

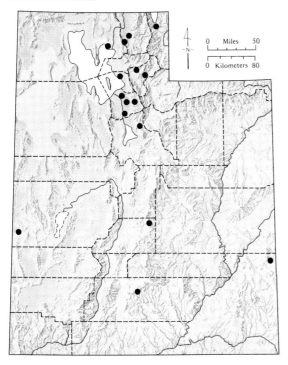

1. *Lemna minor* L. Lesser duckweed. June-Oct. Cosmopolitan perennial herb; standing or slow-moving water, 1270-2180 m.

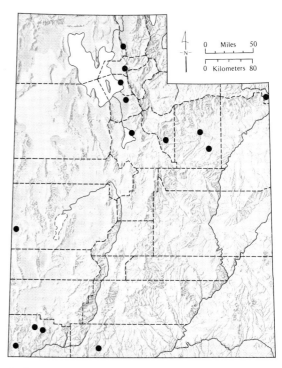

2. *Lemna minuta* Raf. June-Oct. Native perennial herb; standing or slow-moving water, 1300-1370 m.

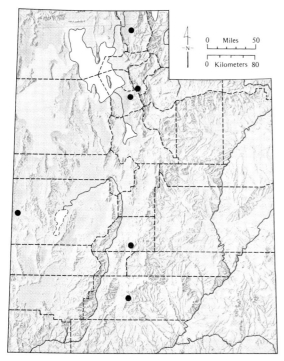

3. *Lemna trisulca* L. Ivy-leaf duckweed. June-Oct. Cosmopolitan perennial herb; standing or slow-moving water, 1300-2610 m.

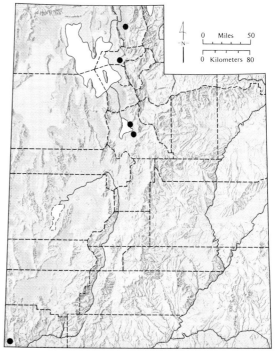

4. *Lemna valdiviana* Phil. June-Sept. Native perennial herb; standing or slow-moving water, 830-1370 m.

59. LEMNACEAE

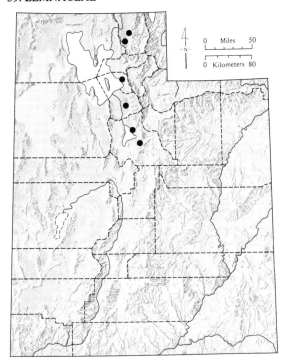

5. *Spirodela polyrhiza* (L.) Schleid. Giant duckmeat. June-Oct. Cosmopolitan perennial herb; standing or slow-moving water, 1270-1400 m.

6. *Wolffia punctata* Griseb. Watermeal. June-Oct. Native perennial herb; standing or slow-moving water, 1360-1460 m.

60. LENTIBULARIACEAE

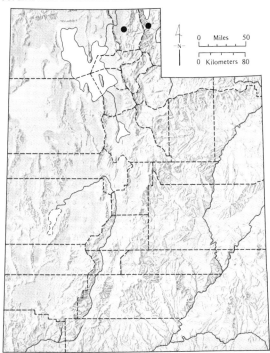

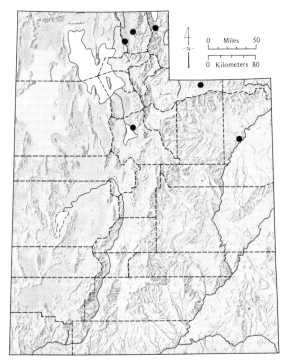

1. *Utricularia intermedia* Hayne Flatleaf bladderwort. July-Aug. Circumboreal perennial herb; standing or slow-moving water, 1360-1820 m.

2. *Utricularia minor* L. Lesser bladderwort. July-Aug. Circumboreal perennial herb; standing or slow-moving water, 1360-1820 m.

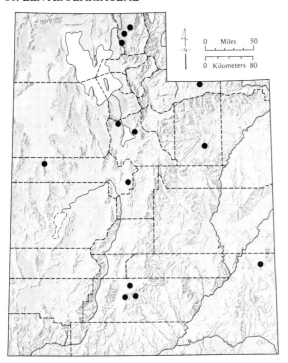

3. *Utricularia vulgaris* L. Common bladderwort. June-Sept. Circumboreal perennial herb; standing or slow-moving water, 1330-1820 m.

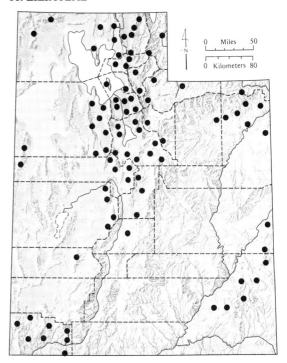

1. *Allium acuminatum* Hook. Tapertip onion. May-July. Native perennial herb; dry open sites in greasewood to aspen-fir communities, 1210-2490 m.

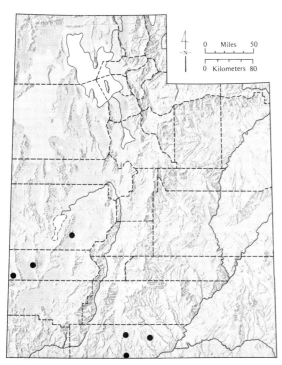

2. *Allium atrorubens* Wats. May-June. Native perennial herb; desert shrub communities, 1450-1930 m.

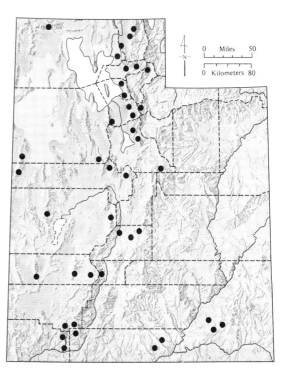

3. *Allium bisceptrum* Wats. Twincrest onion. Apr.-July. Native perennial herb; mountain brush to aspen communities, 1360-3120 m.

61. LILIACEAE

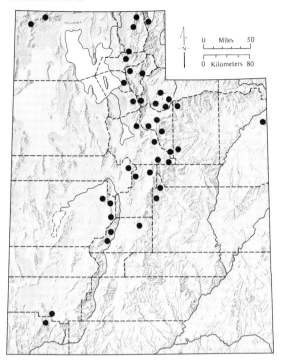

4. *Allium brandegei* Wats. Brandegee onion. May-July. Native perennial herb; sagebrush to conifer communities, 1730-3340 m.

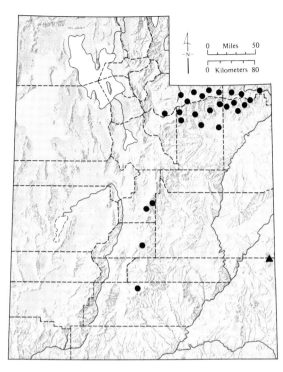

5. *Allium brevistylum* Wats. Shortstyle onion. July-Aug. Native perennial herb; moist sites in aspen, ponderosa pine communities, 2360-3210 m.

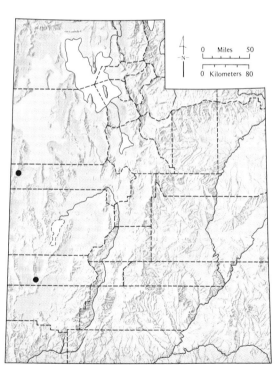

6. *Allium campanulatum* Wats. Dusky onion. June-July. Native perennial herb; shaded sites in mountain brush communities, 2120-2430 m.

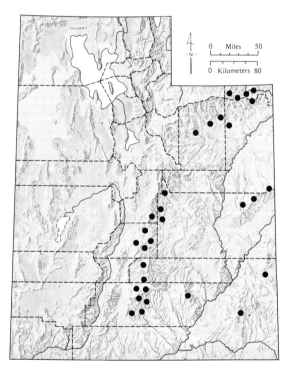

7. *Allium cernuum* Roth Nodding onion. July-Aug. Native perennial herb; open rocky sites in sagebrush to aspen communities, 1970-3500 m.

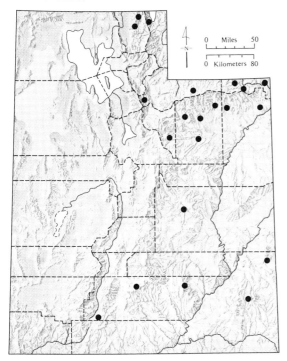

8. *Allium geyeri* Wats. Geyer onion. May-Sept. Native perennial herb; streamside, moist meadows, 2270-3520 m.

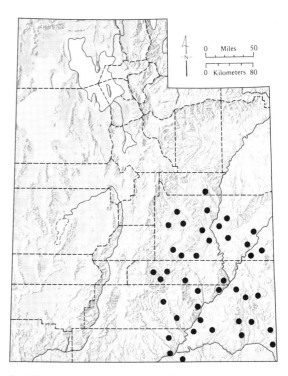

9. *Allium macropetalum* Rydb. Large-flowered onion. Apr.-May. Native perennial herb; desert shrub to pinyon-juniper communities, 1120-1930 m.

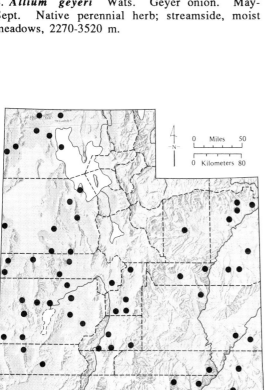

10. *Allium nevadense* Wats. Nevada onion. May-July. Native perennial herb; creosote bush to pinyon-juniper communities, 840-2440 m.

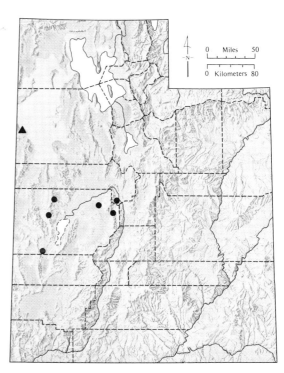

11. *Allium parvum* Kell. Small onion. May-June. Native perennial herb; desert shrub communities, 1660-2930 m.

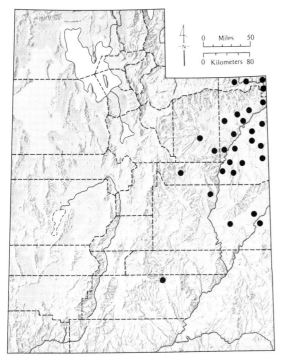

12. *Allium textile* Nels. & Macbr. Textile onion. May-June. Native perennial herb; shadscale to pinyon-juniper communities, 1420-2280 m.

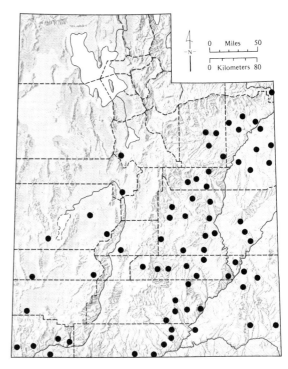

13. *Androstephium breviflorum* Wats. Funnel lily. Apr.-May. Native perennial herb; creosote bush, shadscale, mat saltbush, pinyon-juniper communities, 810-1970 m.

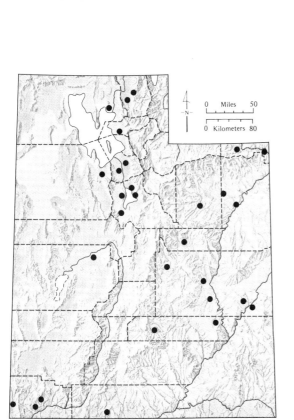

14. *Asparagus officinalis* L. Asparagus. June-July. Introduced perennial herb; cultivated, escaping and persistent, 800-1760 m.

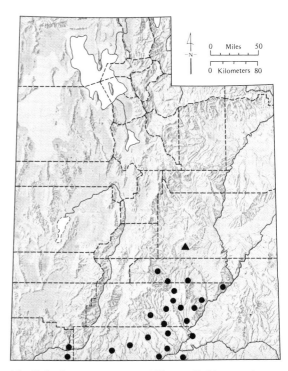

15. *Calochortus aureus* Wats. Golden mariposa lily. Apr.-June. Native perennial herb; desert shrub, pinyon-juniper communities, 1210-1700 m.

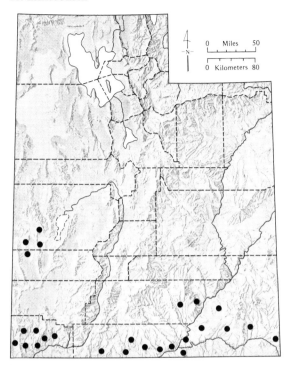

16. *Calochortus flexuosus* Wats. Weakstem mariposa lily. Apr.-June. Native perennial herb; desert shrub, pinyon-juniper communities, 840-1970 m.

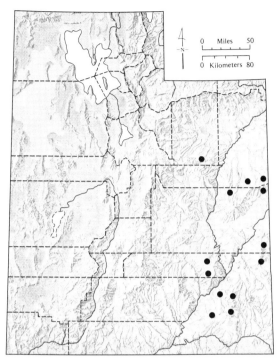

17. *Calochortus gunnisonii* Wats. Gunnison mariposa lily. June-July. Native perennial herb; mountain brush to conifer communities, 2120-3030 m.

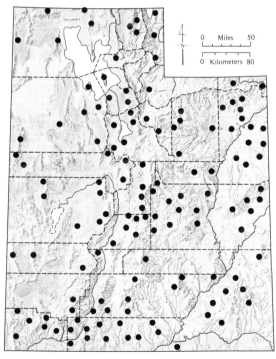

18. *Calochortus nuttallii* T. & G. Sego lily. May-Aug. Native perennial herb; open sites in shadscale, mat saltbush, desert shrub to ponderosa pine communities, 1150-2850 m.

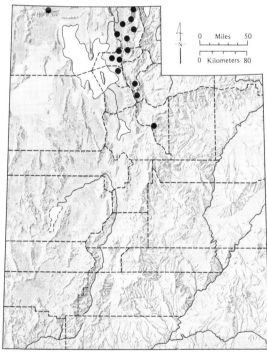

19. *Camassia quamash* (Pursh) Greene Camas. June-July. Native perennial herb; wet open sites in grass-sagebrush communities, 1630-2430 m.

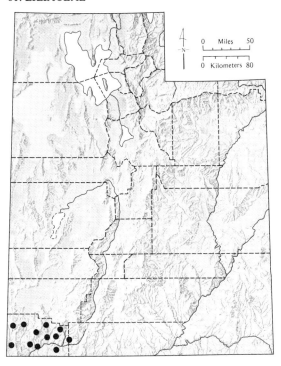

20. *Dichelostemma pulchellum* (Salisb.) Heller Bluedicks. Apr.-May. Native perennial herb; creosote bush, sagebrush, oakbrush communities, 850-1520 m.

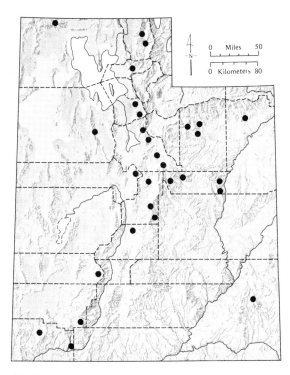

21. *Disporum trachycarpum* (Wats.) Benth. & Hook. Fairybells. Apr.-July. Native perennial herb; shaded sites in mountain brush to conifer communities, 1570-2430 m.

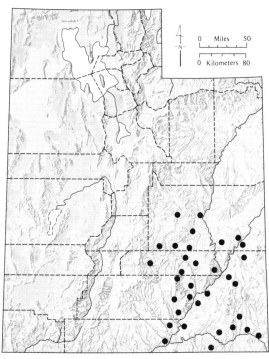

22. *Eremocrinum albomarginatum* (Jones) Jones Desert lily. Apr.-June. Native perennial herb; desert shrub to pinyon-juniper communities, 1150-1880 m.

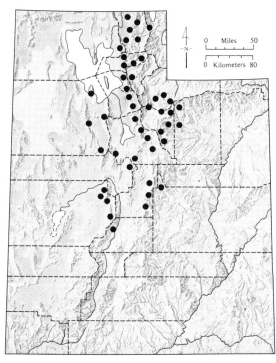

23. *Erythronium grandiflorum* Pursh Dogtooth violet. Apr.-July. Native perennial herb; mesic to moist sites, often in the wake of snowmelt, in mountain brush to conifer communities, 1390-3180 m.

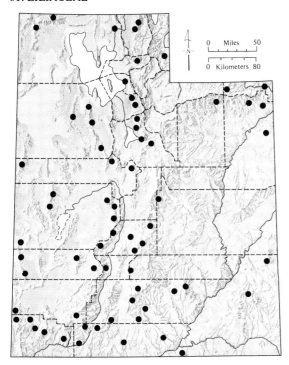

24. *Fritillaria atropurpurea* Nutt. Leopard lily. May-Aug. Native perennial herb; mountain brush, pinyon-juniper, aspen-fir communities, 1510-3180 m.

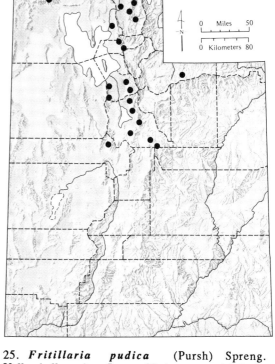

25. *Fritillaria pudica* (Pursh) Spreng. Yellowbells. Apr.-June. Native perennial herb; sagebrush to aspen communities, 1510-2550 m.

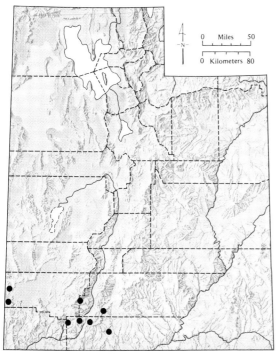

26. *Leucocrinum montanum* Gray Star lily. May-June. Native perennial herb; desert shrub, sagebrush, pinyon-juniper, ponderosa pine communities, 2000-2430 m.

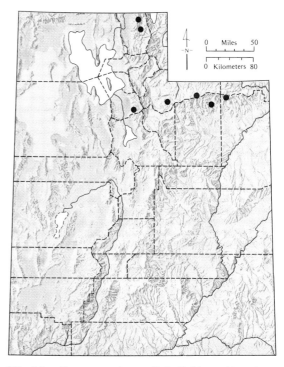

27. *Lloydia serotina* (L.) Rchb. Alp lily. June-July. Native perennial herb; wet meadows, rock crevices, exposed rocky slopes at and above timberline, 2270-3520 m.

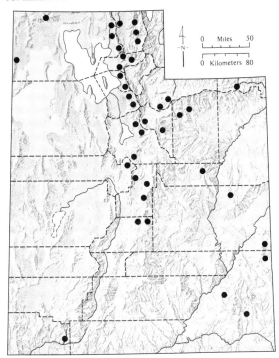

28. *Smilacina racemosa* (L.) Desf. False Solomon seal. May-July. Native perennial herb; shaded sites in mountain brush to conifer communities, 1210-3030 m.

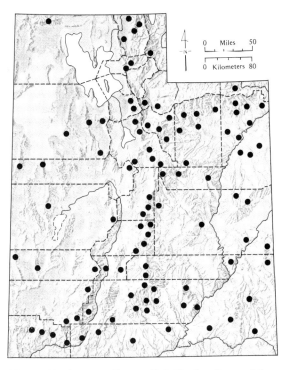

29. *Smilacina stellata* (L.) Desf. Starry false Solomon seal. Apr.-Aug. Native perennial herb; shaded sites in desert shrub to aspen-fir communities, 1210-3180 m.

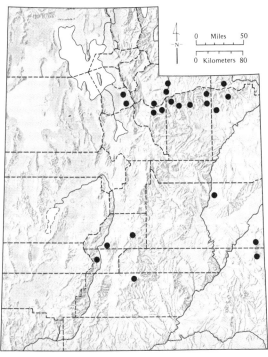

30. *Streptopus amplexifolius* (L.) DC. Twisted-stalk; cucumber root. June-July. Native perennial herb; shaded sites in aspen, spruce-fir communities, 1270-3030 m.

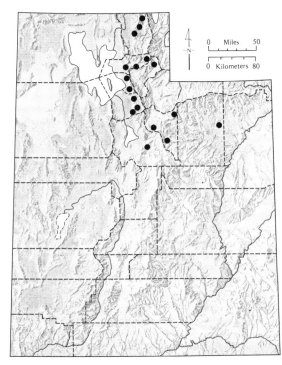

31. *Triteleia grandiflora* Lindl. Wild hyacinth. May-July. Native perennial herb; mountain brush to conifer communities, 1420-2430 m.

362

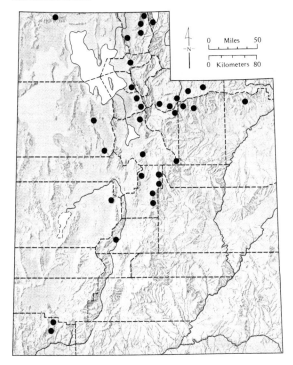

32. *Veratrum californicum* Durand False hellebore. May-Aug. Native perennial herb; moist meadows, open slopes, 1820-3090 m.

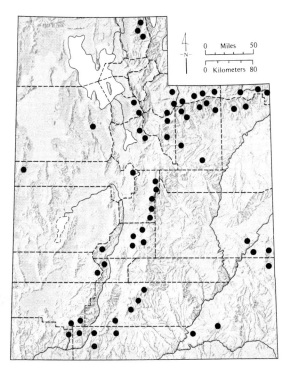

33. *Zigadenus elegans* Pursh Mountain death camas. June-Aug. Native perennial herb; moist, mostly protected sites in desert shrub to krummholz communities, 1120-3640 m.

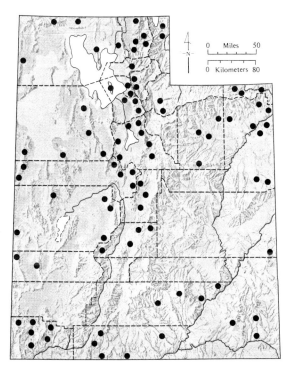

34. *Zigadenus paniculatus* (Nutt.) Wats. Foothill death camas. May-June. Native perennial herb; open sites in sagebrush-oak to ponderosa pine communities, 1210-2730 m.

62. LIMNANTHACEAE

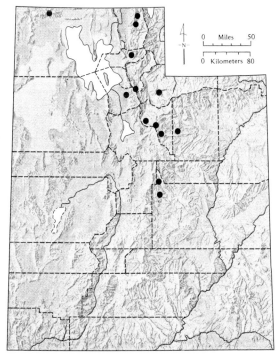

1. *Floerkea proserpinacoides* Willd. False mermaid. Apr.-July. Native annual; shaded sites in mountain brush to lodgepole pine communities, 1450-2600 m.

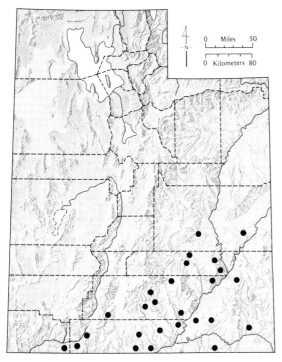

1. **Linum aristatum** Engelm. Broom flax.
May-Oct. Native annual; desert shrub to pinyon-
juniper communities, 1360-1970 m.

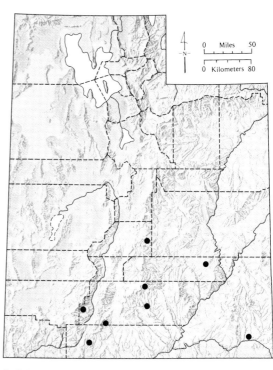

2. **Linum australe** Heller Small yellow flax.
June-Aug. Native annual; desert shrub to ponderosa
pine communities, 1210-2730.

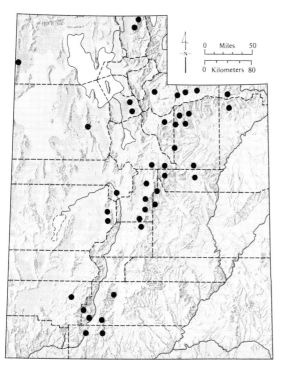

3. **Linum kingii** Wats. King flax. June-Aug.
Native perennial herb; open rocky sites in
mountain brush to conifer communities, 1390-
3280 m.

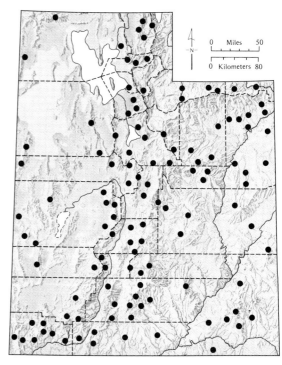

4. **Linum lewisii** Pursh Blue flax. May-July.
Native perennial herb; desert shrub, pinyon-juniper,
oak to aspen-fir communities, 1210-3150 m.

63. LINACEAE

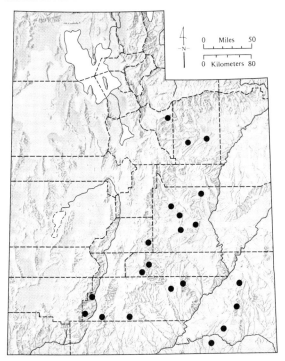

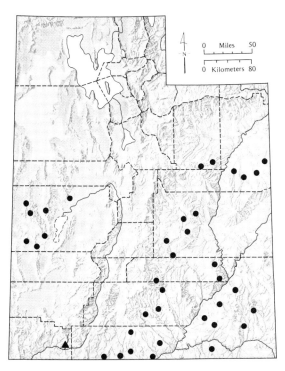

**5. *Linum puberulum* (Engelm.) Heller Downy flax. May-June. Native annual; desert shrub, pinyon-juniper communities, 1120-2610 m.

**6. *Linum subteres* (Trel.) Winkl. May-Oct. Native perennial herb; desert shrub, pinyon-juniper communities, 1360-2060 m.

64. LOASACEAE

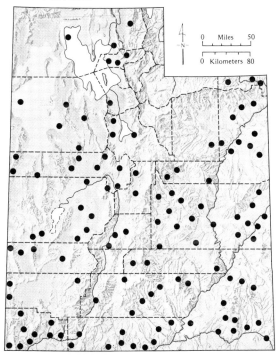

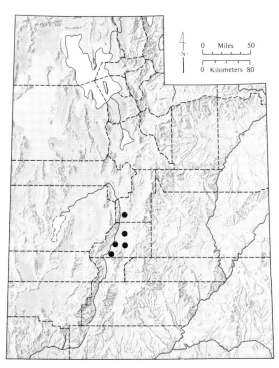

**1. *Mentzelia albicaulis* Hook. Whitestem blazing star. Mar.-June. Native annual; creosote bush to pinyon-juniper communities, 800-2420 m.

**2. *Mentzelia argillosa* J. Darl. Arapien stickleaf. May-Aug. Native perennial herb; open rocky sites in pinyon-juniper communities, 1700-1900 m.

365

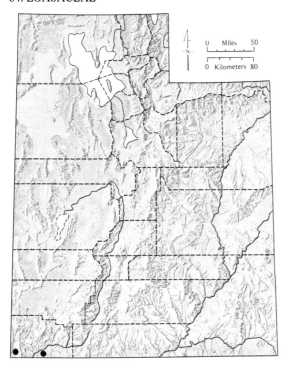

3. *Mentzelia californica* Thompson & Roberts California blazing star. Mar.-May. Native annual; Joshua tree, creosote bush communities, 810-850 m.

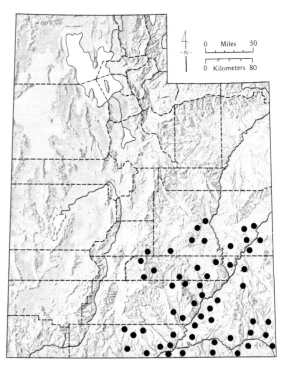

4. *Mentzelia cronquistii* Thompson & Prigge Cronquist stickleaf. May-Sept. Native perennial herb; desert shrub to pinyon-juniper communities, 970-2120 m.

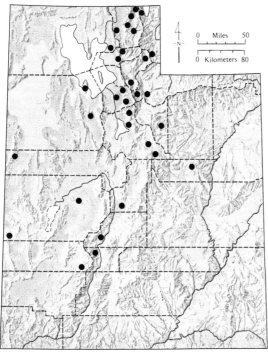

5. *Mentzelia dispersa* Wats. Bushy blazing star. May-July. Native annual; sagebrush to conifer communities, 1360-2870 m.

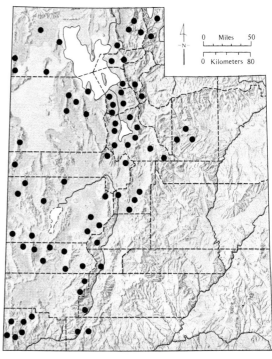

6. *Mentzelia laevicaulis* (Hook.) T. & G. Smoothstem blazing star. June-Oct. Native perennial herb; creosote bush to ponderosa pine communities, often in disturbed sites, 910-2440 m.

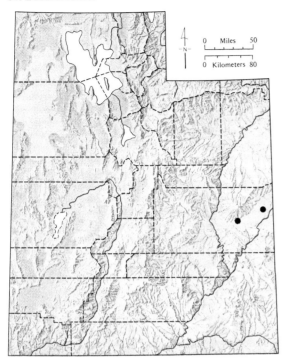

7. *Mentzelia marginata* (Osterh.) Thompson & Prigge May-July. Native biennial or perennial; shadscale, mat saltbush communities, 1510-1670 m.

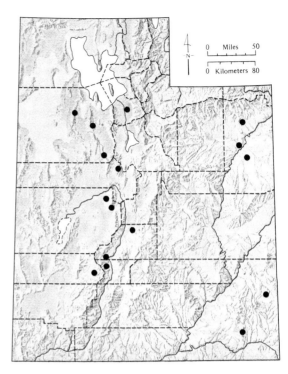

8. *Mentzelia montana* (A. Davids.) A. Davids. Mountain blazing star. May-July. Native annual; desert shrub communities, 1340-1730 m.

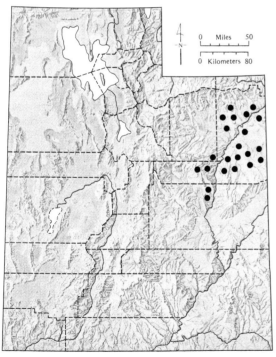

9. *Mentzelia multicaulis* (Osterh.) Goodm. Many-stem blazing star. May-Aug. Native perennial herb; shadscale, desert shrub, pinyon-juniper communities, 1510-2130 m.

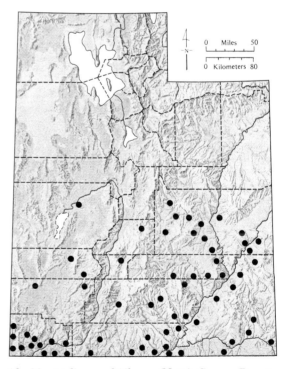

10. *Mentzelia multiflora* (Nutt.) Gray Desert blazing star. Apr.-Sept. Native perennial herb; creosote bush to pinyon-juniper, mountain brush communities, 800-2120 m.

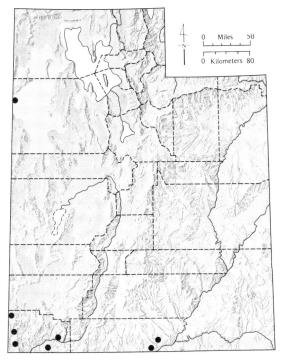

11. *Mentzelia obscura* Thompson & Roberts
May-June. Native annual; creosote bush, desert
shrub communities, 910-1750 m.

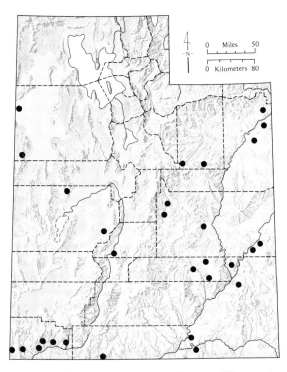

12. *Mentzelia pterosperma* Eastw. Wingseed
blazing star. Apr.-June. Native annual or
perennial; creosote bush, desert shrub communities,
810-1730 m.

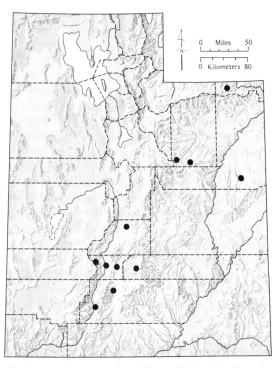

13. *Mentzelia pumila* (Nutt.) T. & G. Dwarf
blazing star. May-Aug. Native biennial or
perennial; desert shrub to ponderosa pine
communities, 1660-2730 m.

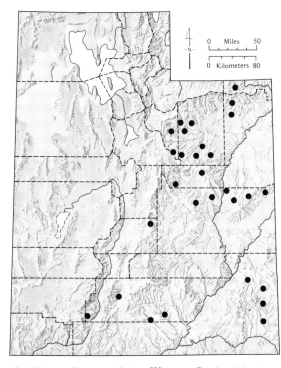

14. *Mentzelia rusbyi* Woot. Rusby blazing
star. June-Sept. Native biennial or perennial;
sagebrush, mountain brush to ponderosa pine
communities, 1830-2570 m.

64. LOASACEAE

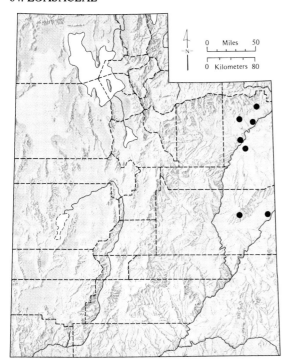

15. *Mentzelia thompsonii* Glad Thompson blazing star. May-June. Native annual; shadscale, desert shrub communities, 1450-1900 m.

16. *Petalonyx parryi* Gray Parry sandpaper plant. May-July. Native shrub or subshrub; creosote bush communities, 800-900 m.

65. LYTHRACEAE

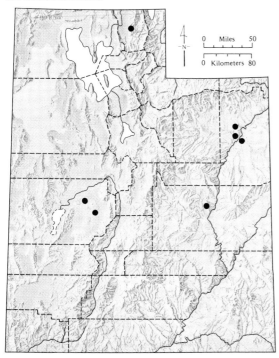

1. *Ammannia robusta* Heer & Regel Purple ammannia. July-Aug. Native annual; marshes, along waterways, drying mud flats, salt tolerant, 1210-1450 m.

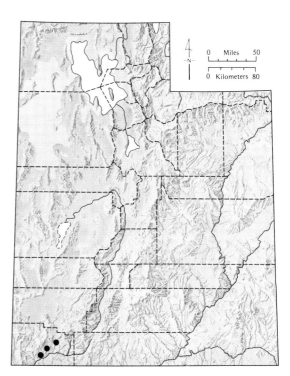

2. *Lythrum californicum* T. & G. California loosestrife. Apr.-Oct. Native perennial herb; marshes, along waterways, near springs and seeps, salt tolerant, 870-1340 m.

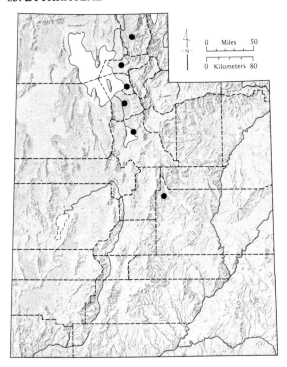

3. *Lythrum salicaria* L. Purple loosestrife. July-Aug. Introduced perennial herb; cultivated, escaping and established in moist, usually disturbed sites, 1270-1520 m.

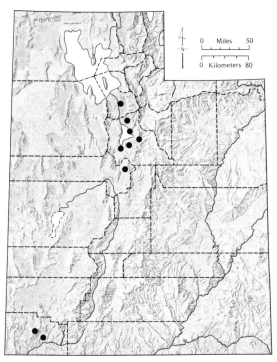

2. *Althaea rosea* (L.) Cav. Hollyhock. July-Sept. Introduced biennial or perennial; cultivated, escaping and persistent, 1300-1520 m.

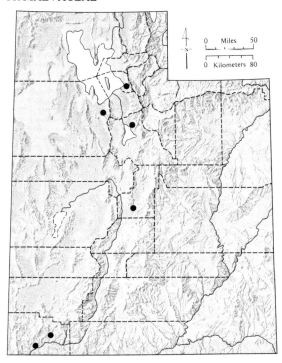

1. *Abutilon theophrasti* Medic. Velvetleaf. July-Sept. Introduced annual; irrigated sites and waste places, 910-1370 m.

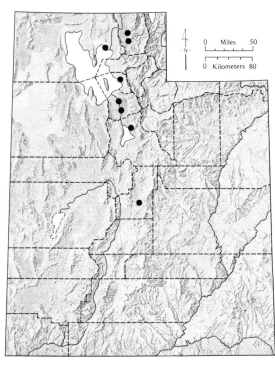

3. *Hibiscus trionum* L. Flower-of-an-hour. July-Aug. Introduced annual; weed of cultivated places, 1280-1460 m.

370

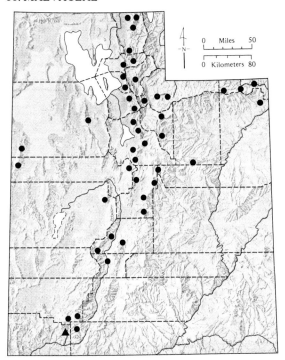

4. *Iliamna rivularis* (Dougl.) Greene   Wild hollyhock.   June-Sept.   Native perennial herb; streamside, mountain brush, 1660-2880 m.

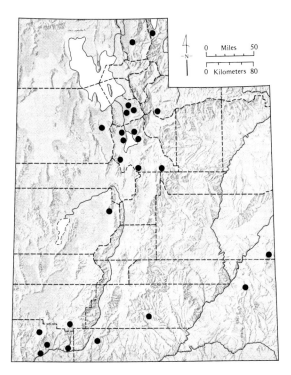

5. *Malva neglecta* Wallr.   Cheeses; cheeseweed. Apr.-Aug.   Introduced annual or biennial; irrigated sites and waste places, 910-2270 m.

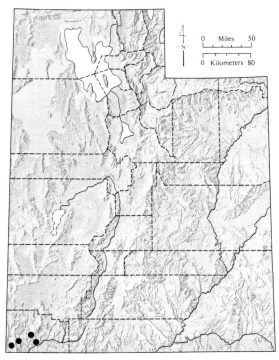

6. *Malvastrum exile* Gray   Mar.-May.   Native annual; creosote communities, 840-970 m.

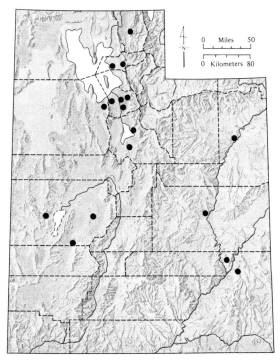

7. *Malvella leprosa* (Ort.) Krap.   Alkali mallow; dollar weed.   July-Oct.   Native perennial herb; saline meadows, 1410-1520 m.

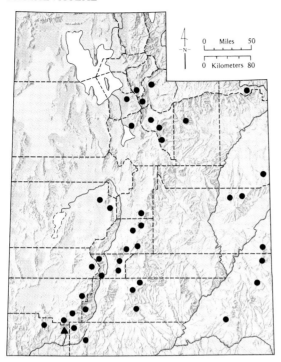

8. *Sidalcea candida* Gray White checkermallow. July-Aug. Native perennial herb; streamside, moist meadows, 1940-2880 m.

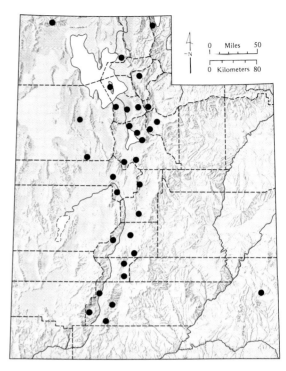

9. *Sidalcea neomexicana* Gray New Mexico checkermallow. June-Aug. Native perennial herb; moist, often saline meadows, 1300-2270 m.

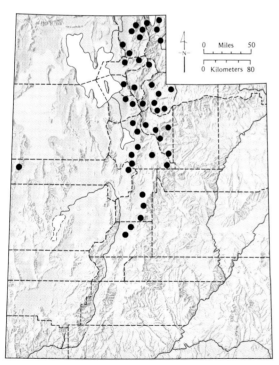

10. *Sidalcea oregana* (Nutt.) Gray Oregon checkermallow. June-Aug. Native perennial herb; moist meadows, streamside, mountain brush, aspen, lodgepole pine communities, 1510-2700 m.

11. *Sphaeralcea ambigua* Gray Desert globemallow. Mar.-Apr. Native perennial herb; creosote bush, desert shrub communities, 810-1060 m.

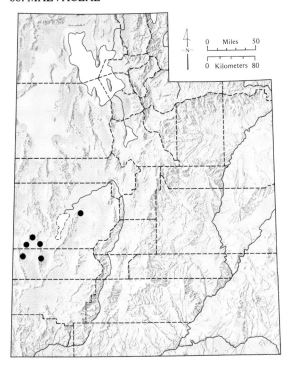

12. *Sphaeralcea caespitosa* Jones Tufted globemallow. May-July. Native perennial herb; dry rocky sites in shadscale, desert shrub communities, 1660-1820 m.

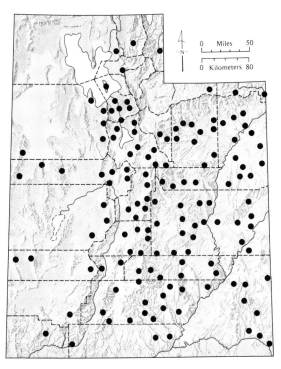

13. *Sphaeralcea coccinea* (Pursh) Rydb. Scarlet globemallow. Apr.-July. Native perennial herb; shadscale, desert shrub, sagebrush to ponderosa pine communities, 1330-2520 m.

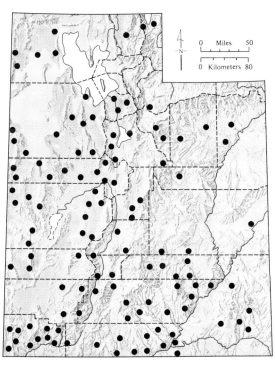

14. *Sphaeralcea grossulariifolia* (H. & A.) Rydb. Gooseberryleaf globemallow. Apr.-Sept. Native perennial herb; greasewood, shadscale, sagebrush, pinyon-juniper communities, 780-2120 m.

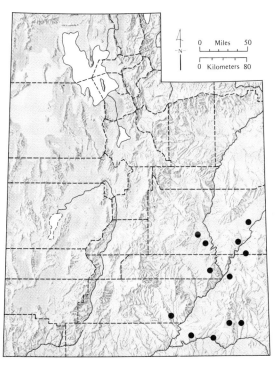

15. *Sphaeralcea leptophylla* (Gray) Rydb. Scaly globemallow. May-July. Native perennial herb; rock crevices, sandy sites in desert shrub communities, 1210-1520 m.

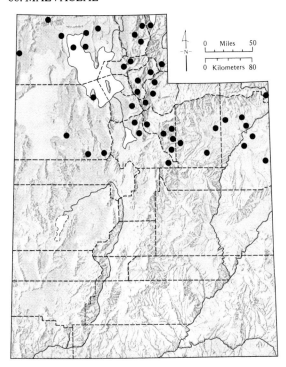

16. *Sphaeralcea munroana* (Dougl.) Spach. Munroe globemallow. May-July. Native perennial herb; shadscale, desert shrub, juniper, mountain brush communities, 1320-2030 m.

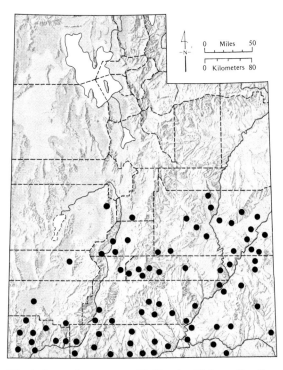

17. *Sphaeralcea parvifolia* A. Nels. Small-flowered globemallow. Apr.-July. Native perennial herb; creosote bush, shadscale, desert shrub to pinyon-juniper communities, 840-1970 m.

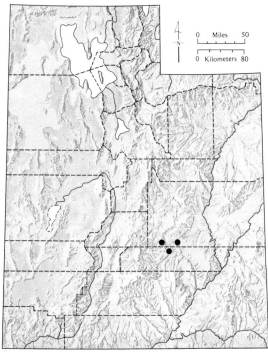

18. *Sphaeralcea psoraloides* Welsh Psoralea globemallow. June-July. Native perennial herb; desert shrub communities, 1390-1520 m.

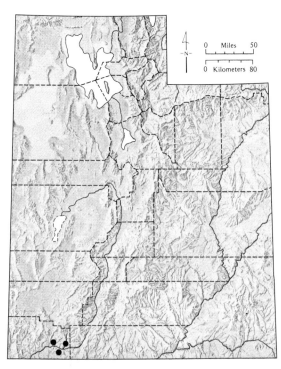

19. *Sphaeralcea rusbyi* Gray Rusby globemallow. May-July. Native perennial herb; creosote bush, desert shrub communities, 850-1210 m.

67. MARSILEACEAE

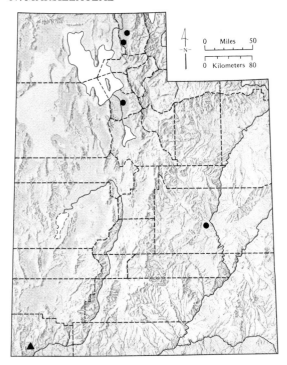

1. **Marsilea vestita** Hook. & Grev. Pepperwort or water clover. Native perennial herb; shallow water and mud of marshes, ponds, waterways, 1330-1820 m.

68. MARTYNIACEAE

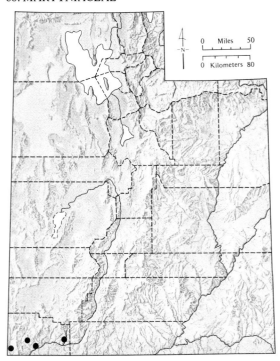

1. **Proboscidea parviflora** (Woot.) W. & S. Small-flowered unicorn plant. July-Oct. Native annual; creosote bush communities, 750-1060 m.

69. MENYANTHACEAE

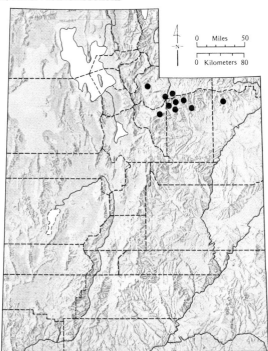

1. **Menyanthes trifoliata** L. Buckbean. Apr.-**Aug.** Circumboreal perennial herb; shallow water of ponds, meadows, lodgepole pine, spruce-fir communities, 3030-3340 m.

70. NAJADACEAE

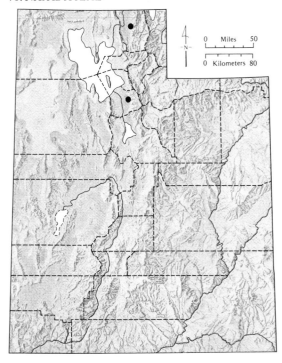

1. **Najas guadalupensis** (Spreng.) M o r o n g Southern waternymph. June-Aug. Native annual; shallow water of ponds, 1300-1370 m.

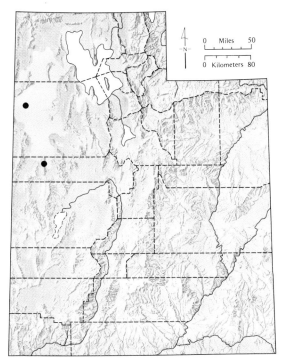

2. *Najas marina* L. Spiny waternymph. July-Sept. Introduced annual; warm brackish water of springs, 1330-1370 m.

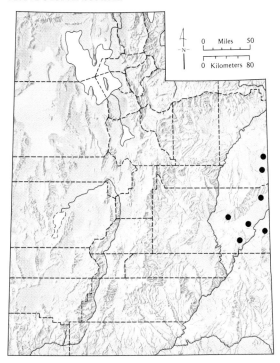

1. *Abronia argillosa* Welsh & Goodrich Clay verbena. May-June. Native perennial herb; shadscale, desert shrub communities, 1300-1820 m.

2. *Abronia fragrans* Hook. Fragrant sand verbena; snowball. Apr.-Sept. Native perennial herb; shadscale, desert shrub to ponderosa pine communities, 840-2460 m.

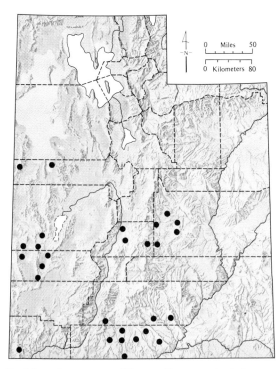

3. *Abronia nana* Wats. Low sand verbena. May-June. Native perennial herb; shadscale, desert shrub to pinyon-juniper communities, 1060-1970 m.

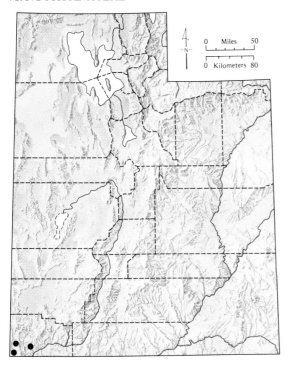

4. *Abronia villosa* Wats. Sticky sand verbena.
Mar.-Apr. Native annual; creosote bush
communities, 780-970 m.

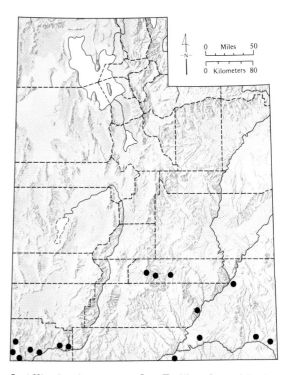

5. *Allionia incarnata* L. Trailing four o'clock.
June-Aug. Native annual to perennial; creosote
bush, shadscale, desert shrub communities, 780-
1820 m.

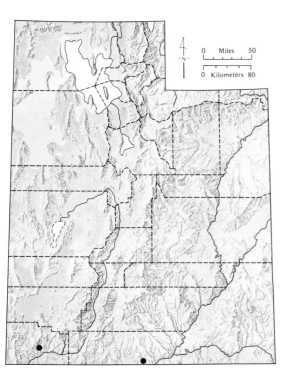

6. *Boerhaavia spicata* Choisy Spiderling.
Sept.-Oct. Native annual; creosote bush, desert
shrub communities, 970-1520 m.

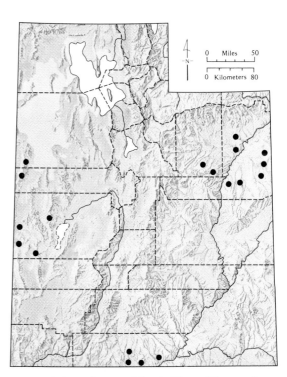

7. *Mirabilis alipes* (Wats.) Pilz Watson four
o'clock. Apr.-June. Native perennial herb;
greasewood, shadscale, desert shrub communities,
1240-1940 m.

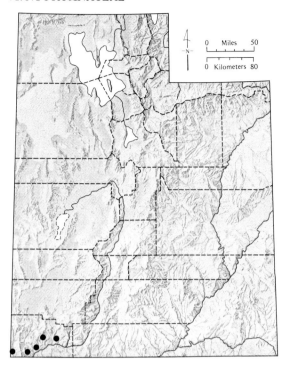

8. *Mirabilis bigelovii* Gray Bigelow four o'clock. Apr.-June. Native perennial herb; creosote bush communities, 810-970 m.

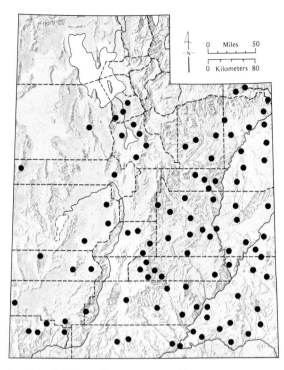

9. *Mirabilis linearis* (Pursh) Heimerl Narrowleaf or fringecup four o'clock. June-Oct. Native perennial herb; desert shrub to ponderosa pine communities, 1300-2580 m.

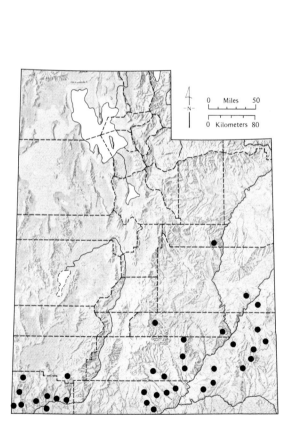

10. *Mirabilis multiflora* (Torr.) Gray Colorado four o'clock. Apr.-June. Native perennial herb; creosote bush to pinyon-juniper communities, 810-2280 m.

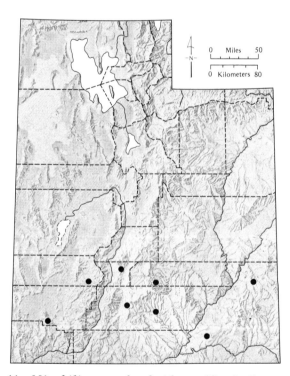

11. *Mirabilis oxybaphoides* (Gray) Gray Spreading four o'clock. Aug.-Sept. Native perennial herb; desert shrub to pinyon-juniper communities, 1660-2180 m.

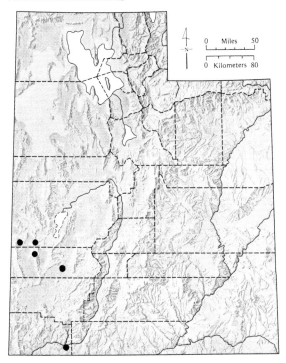

12. *Mirabilis pumila* (Standl.) Standl.
Standley four o'clock. July-Aug. Native perennial
herb; desert shrub communities, 1510-1760 m.

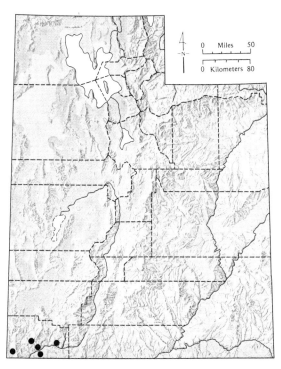

13. *Selinocarpus nevadensis* (Standl.) Fowler
& Turner Moonpod. May-June. Native perennial
herb; creosote communities, 780-1060 m.

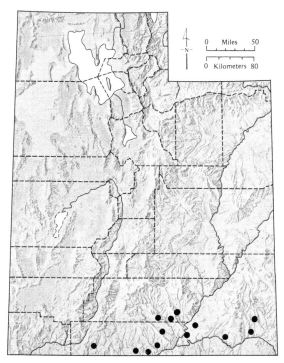

14. *Tripterocalyx carneus* (Greene) Galloway
Winged sand verbena. Apr.-July. Native annual;
desert shrub communities, 1060-1820 m.

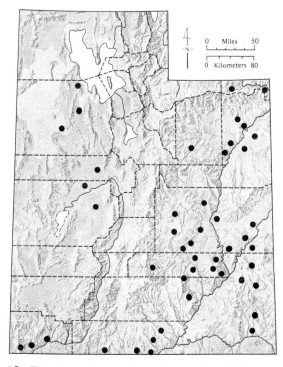

15. *Tripterocalyx micranthus* (Torr.) Hook.
Sandpuffs. May-July. Native annual; creosote
bush, shadscale, mat saltbush, desert shrub
communities, 1000-1820 m.

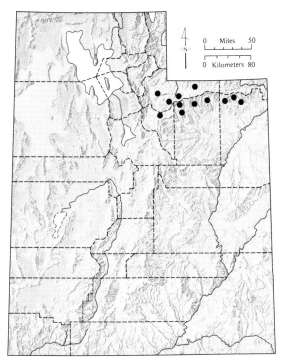

1. *Nuphar polysepalum* Engelm. Yellow pondlily. July-Aug. Native perennial herb; water of lakes and ponds, 2720-3300 m.

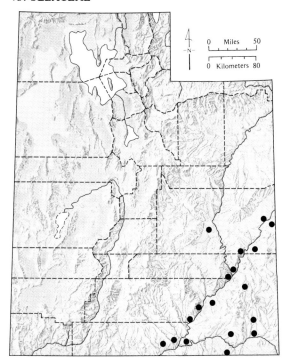

1. *Forestiera pubescens* Nutt. Desert olive. May-June. Native shrub; desert shrub, pinyon-juniper communities, 940-1790 m.

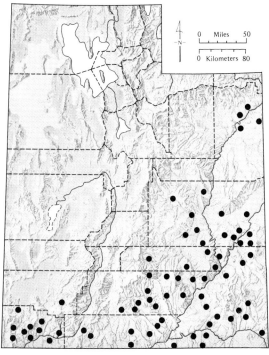

2. *Fraxinus anomala* Wats. Singleleaf ash. Apr.-July. Native shrub or small tree; creosote bush to pinyon-juniper communities, 910-2610 m.

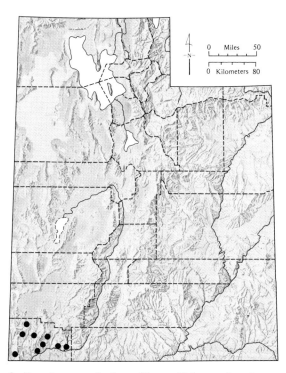

3. *Fraxinus velutina* Torr. Velvet ash. Apr.-June. Native tree; along creeks and washes in creosote communities, 780-1210 m.

380

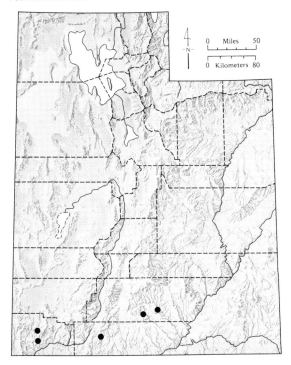

4. *Menodora scabra* Gray Rough menodora.
June-July. Native subshrub; pinyon-juniper
communities, 1510-1820 m.

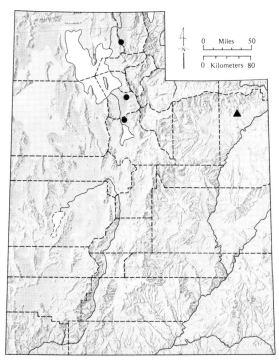

2. *Boisduvalia glabella* (Nutt.) Walp. Smooth
spike primrose. Aug.-Sept. Native annual; wet to
drying shores of ponds, lakes, reservoirs, 1510-
1820 m.

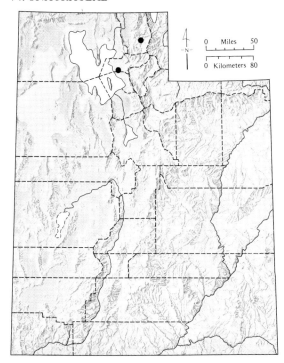

1. *Boisduvalia densiflora* (Lindl.) Wats.
Dense spike primrose. July-Sept. Native annual;
marshes, wet to drying shores of ponds, lakes,
1300-1430 m.

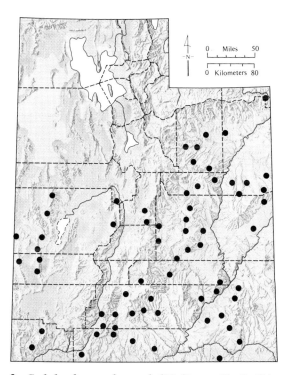

3. *Calylophus lavandulifolius* (T. & G.)
Raven Lavender evening primrose. May-Aug.
Native perennial herb; desert shrub to ponderosa
pine communities, 1360-2740 m.

381

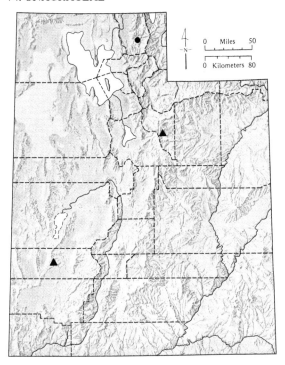

4. *Camissonia andina* (Nutt.) Raven May-July. Native annual; sagebrush, pinyon-juniper communities, 1360-1970 m.

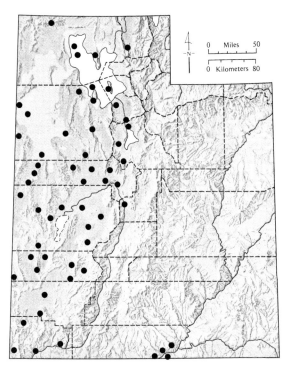

5. *Camissonia boothii* (Dougl.) Raven Apr.-Sept. Native annual; creosote bush, greasewood, shadscale, desert shrub communities, 780-1880 m.

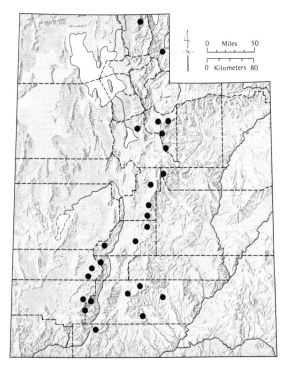

6. *Camissonia breviflora* (T. & G.) Raven July-Aug. Native perennial herb; streamside, pond and lake shores, moist to dry meadows in mountain brush to conifer communities, 1570-3300 m.

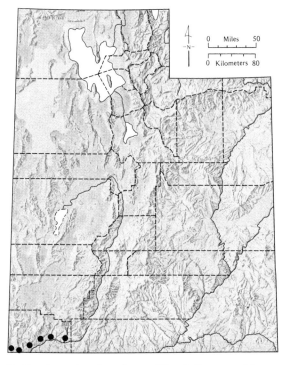

7. *Camissonia brevipes* (Gray) Raven Mar.-June. Native annual; creosote bush communities, 780-1060 m.

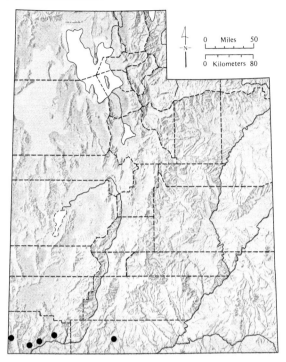

8. *Camissonia chamaenerioides* (Gray) Raven Apr.-May. Native annual; creosote bush, desert shrub communities, 910-1370 m.

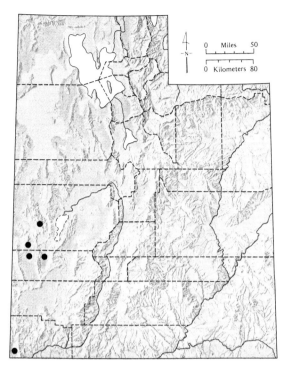

9. *Camissonia clavaeformis* (Torr. & Frem.) Raven May-July. Native annual; creosote bush, shadscale, desert shrub communities, 840-1760 m.

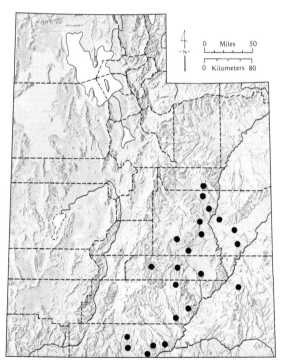

10. *Camissonia eastwoodiae* (Munz) Raven Apr.-June. Native annual; shadscale, mat saltbush, desert shrub communities, 1240-1790 m.

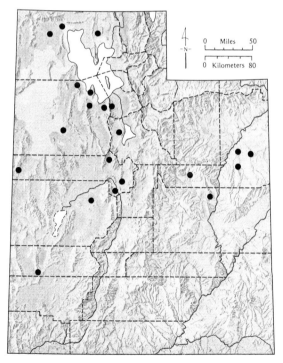

11. *Camissonia minor* (A. Nels.) Raven May-June. Native annual; shadscale, desert shrub communities, 1270-1730 m.

74. ONAGRACEAE

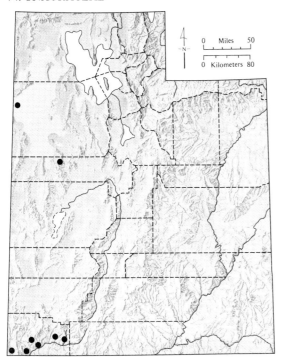

12. *Camissonia multijuga* (Wats.) Raven
Apr.-June. Native annual; creosote bush, shadscale,
desert shrub communities, 840-1640 m.

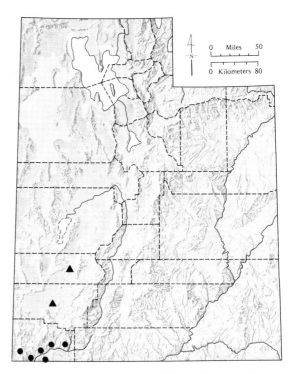

13. *Camissonia parryi* (Wats.) Raven   Apr.-
Sept. Native annual; creosote bush communities,
780-910 m.

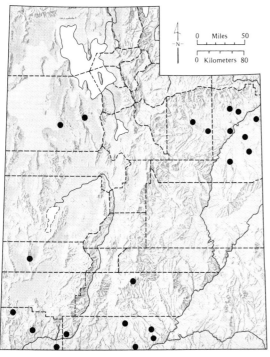

14. *Camissonia parvula* (Nutt.) Raven   May-
June. Native annual; desert shrub, pinyon-juniper
communities, usually on sandy sites, 1270-
2730 m.

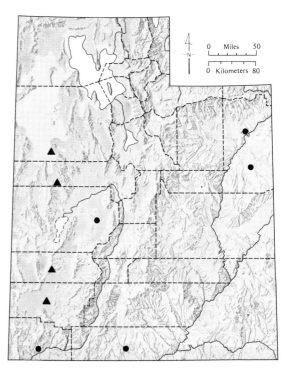

15. *Camissonia pterosperma* (Wats.) Raven
Apr.-May. Native annual; desert shrub, pinyon-
juniper communities, 1210-1820 m.

384

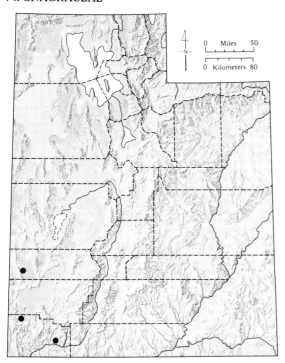

16. *Camissonia pusilla* Raven   Apr.-May.
Native annual; creosote bush, sagebrush, pinyon-
juniper communities, 910-1670 m.

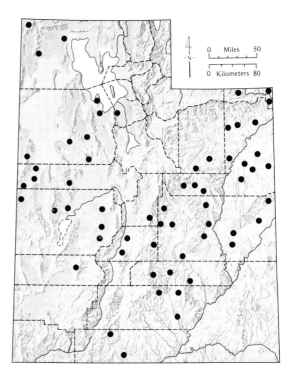

17. *Camissonia scapoidea* (T. & G.) Raven
May-June. Native annual; shadscale, desert shrub,
juniper communities, 1300-1970 m.

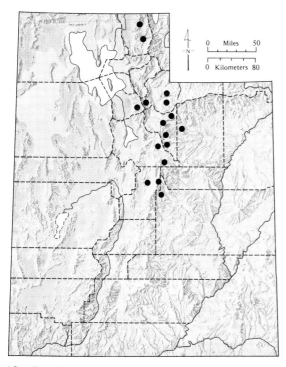

18. *Camissonia subacaulis* (Pursh) Raven
May-July. Native perennial herb; moist open sites
in mountain brush to aspen-fir communities, 1810-
2640 m.

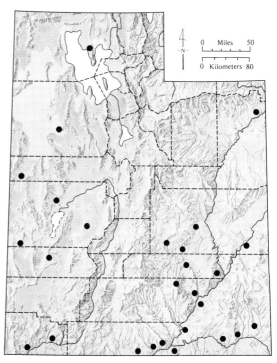

19. *Camissonia walkeri* (A. Nels.) Raven
May-June. Native annual; creosote bush, shadscale,
desert shrub communities, 910-1760 m.

385

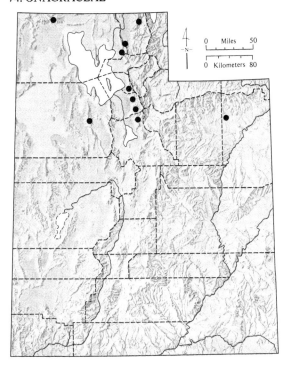

20. *Circaea alpina* L. Enchanters nightshade. June-Aug. Circumboreal perennial herb; shaded sites in mountain brush to conifer communities, 1600-2880 m.

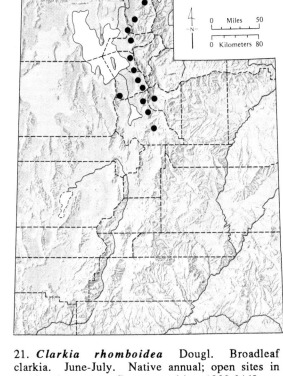

21. *Clarkia rhomboidea* Dougl. Broadleaf clarkia. June-July. Native annual; open sites in sagebrush to aspen-fir communities, 1300-2460 m.

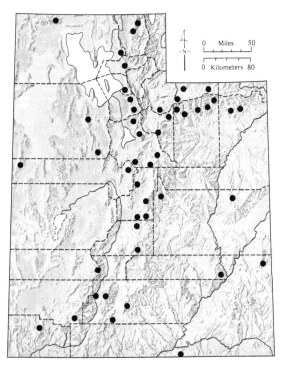

22. *Epilobium angustifolium* L. Fireweed. June-Aug. Circumboreal perennial herb; mesic sites in mountain brush to alpine meadow communities, 1510-3400 m.

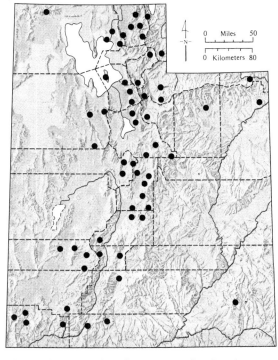

23. *Epilobium brachycarpum* Presl Autumn willowherb. May-Sept. Native annual; open sites in desert shrub to aspen-fir communities, 1270-2730 m.

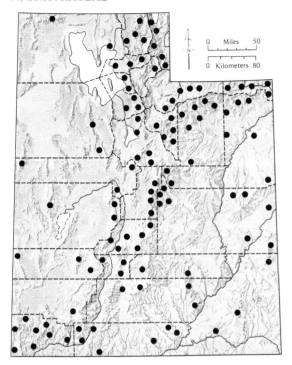

24. *Epilobium ciliatum* Raf. Northern willowherb. June-Sept. Native perennial herb; moist sites in creosote bush to conifer communities, 810-3180 m.

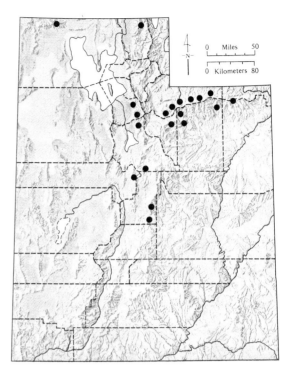

25. *Epilobium clavatum* Trel. Club willowherb. July-Sept. Native perennial herb; moist sites in ponderosa pine, aspen communities to above timberline, 2150-3610 m.

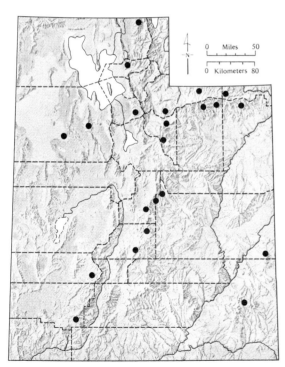

26. *Epilobium halleanum* Hausskn. Halls willowherb. July-Aug. Native perennial herb; moist sites in desert shrub communities to above timberline, 1300-3490 m.

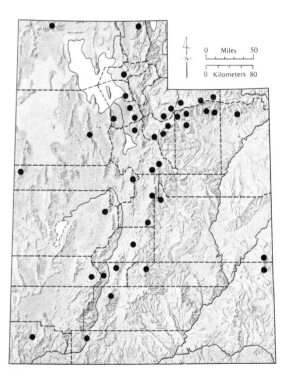

27. *Epilobium hornemannii* Rchb. Hornemann willowherb. June-Aug. Circumboreal perennial herb; moist sites in mountain brush communities to above timberline, 2000-3400 m.

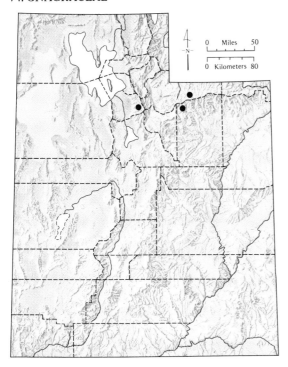

28. *Epilobium latifolium* L. Dwarf fireweed.
June-July. Circumboreal perennial herb; talus,
other rocky sites in aspen, conifer communities,
2270-3090 m.

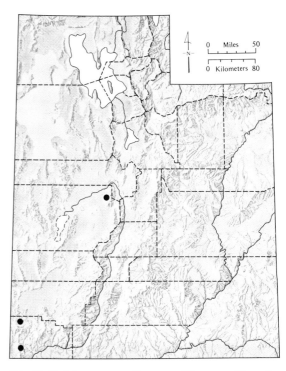

29. *Epilobium nevadense* Munz Nevada
willowherb. June-Sept. Native perennial herb;
cliffs and talus in creosote bush, pinyon-juniper
communities, 910-2430 m.

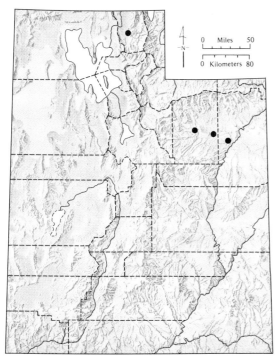

30. *Epilobium palustre* L. Marsh willowherb.
July-Aug. Circumboreal perennial herb; moist sites
in mountain brush communities, 1360-2310 m.

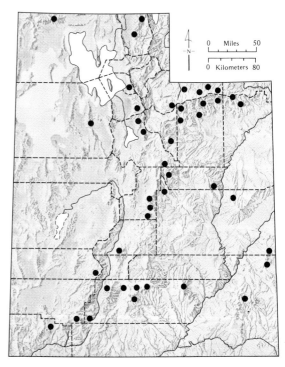

31. *Epilobium saximontanum* Hausskn.
Rocky Mountain willowherb. June-Aug. Native
perennial herb; moist sites in mountain brush
communities to above timberline, 1330-3700 m.

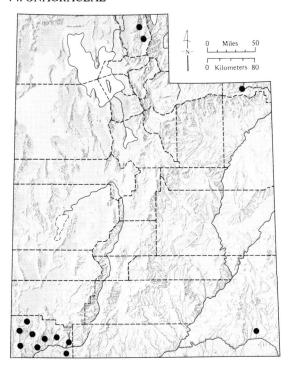

32. *Gaura coccinea* Pursh Scarlet lizardtail.
June-July. Native perennial herb; open sites in
creosote bush, pinyon-juniper, mountain brush
communities, 870-1790 m.

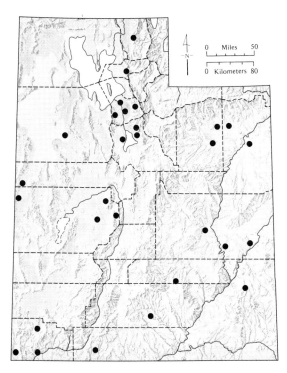

33. *Gaura parviflora* Lehm. Lizardtail. June-
July. Native annual or biennial; moist fields and
meadows, streamside, 870-1970 m.

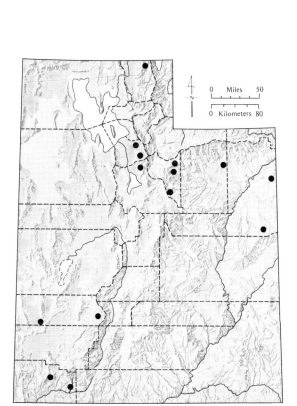

34. *Gayophytum decipiens* Lewis & Szweyk.
Deceptive groundsmoke. June-Aug. Native annual;
streamside, moist meadows, 1570-3030.

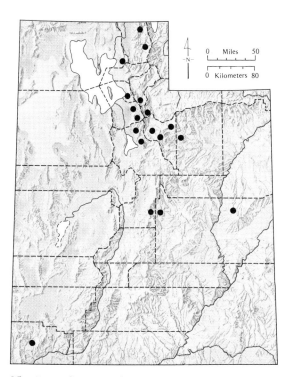

35. *Gayophytum diffusum* T. & G. Diffuse
groundsmoke. May-Sept. Native annual; dry open
sites in sagebrush to aspen-fir communities, 1450-
3120 m.

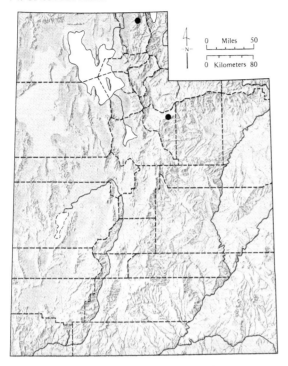

36. *Gayophytum humile* A. Juss. Low groundsmoke. June-Aug. Native annual; moist to dry, open sites in mountain brush communities, 2120-2430 m.

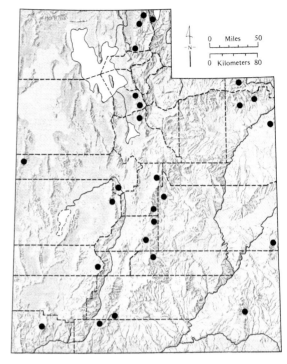

37. *Gayophytum racemosum* T. & G. Kitchen weed. June-Sept. Native annual; moist to dry meadows, streamside, open slopes, 1810-3150 m.

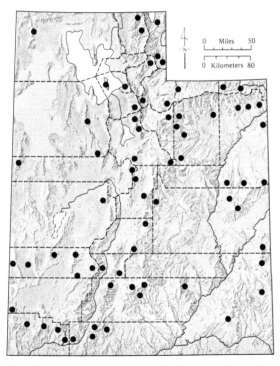

38. *Gayophytum ramosissimum* T. & G. Branchy groundsmoke. June-Aug. Native annual; dry open sites in sagebrush to aspen-fir communities, 1510-2910 m.

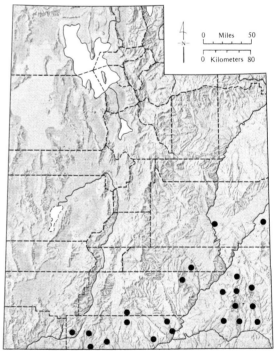

39. *Oenothera albicaulis* Pursh Whitestem evening primrose. May-July. Native annual; sandy sites in desert shrub to pinyon-juniper communities, 1210-2430 m.

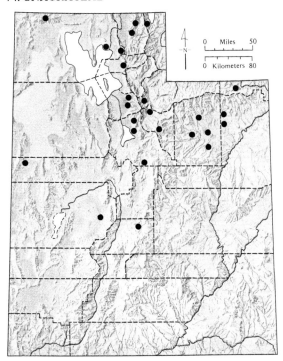

40. *Oenothera biennis* L. Biennial evening primrose. July-Sept. Native annual or biennial; roadsides, fields, streamside, open slopes, 1300-2550 m.

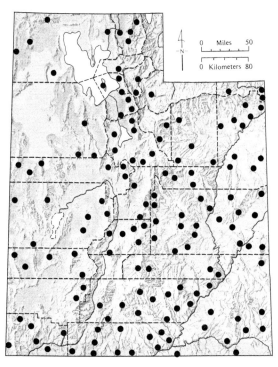

41. *Oenothera caespitosa* Nutt. Tufted evening primrose. Apr.-July. Native perennial herb; open dry sites in creosote bush to conifer communities, 910-2880 m.

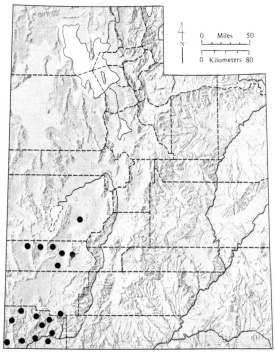

42. *Oenothera californica* (Wats.) Wats. Apr.-June. Native perennial herb; creosote bush to pinyon-juniper communities, 780-2120 m.

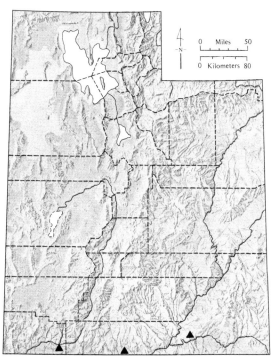

43. *Oenothera cavernae* Munz Apr.-May. Native annual; rocky sites in creosote bush to desert shrub communities, 840-1370 m.

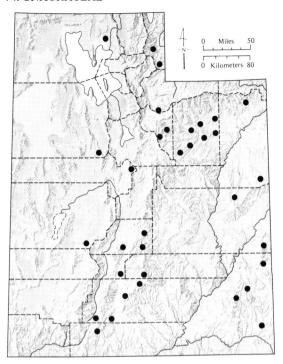

44. *Oenothera coronopifolia* T. & G.
Rootstock evening primrose. June-Aug. Native
perennial herb; open sites in mountain brush to
ponderosa pine, aspen communities, 1970-2730 m.

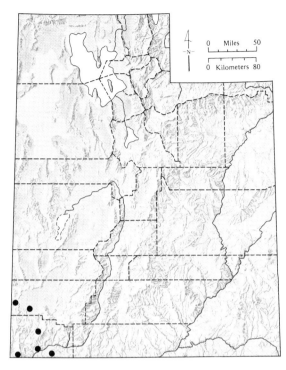

45. *Oenothera deltoides* Torr. & Frem.
Annual evening primrose. Apr.-May. Native
annual; creosote bush to pinyon-juniper
communities, often on dunes, 780-2430 m.

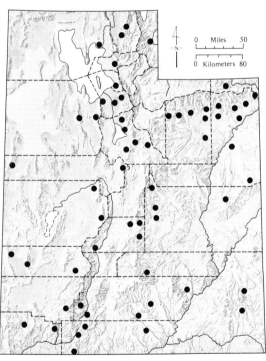

46. *Oenothera elata* H. B. K. Tall evening
primrose. July-Sept. Native biennial or perennial;
marshes, along waterways, in shade of oak-maple,
ponderosa pine, aspen-fir communities,
occasionally roadside, 1300-2820 m.

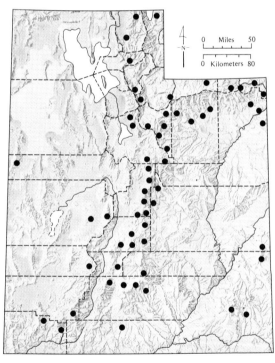

47. *Oenothera flava* (A. Nels.) Garrett Yellow
evening primrose. May-Aug. Native perennial
herb; wet to dry sites in mountain brush, ponderosa
pine, aspen, spruce-fir, meadow communities,
1240-3330 m.

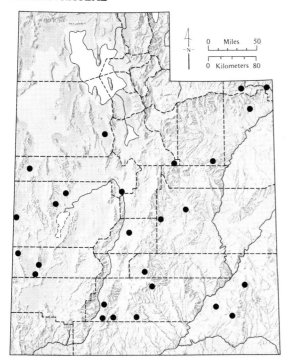

48. _Oenothera howardii_ (A. Nels.) W. L. Wagner   Bronze evening primrose.   May-Aug. Native perennial herb; rocky sites in desert shrub to ponderosa pine communities, 1510-2270 m.

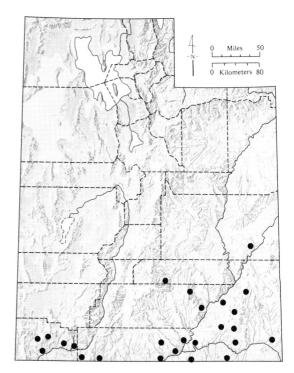

49. _Oenothera longissima_ Rydb.   July-Sept. Native perennial herb; hanging gardens, wet cliffs, moist canyon floors, 840-2490 m.

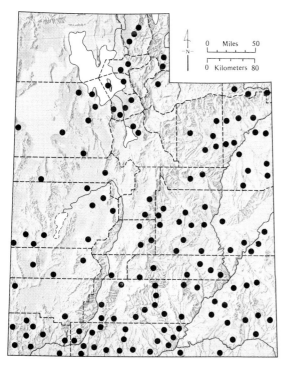

50. _Oenothera pallida_ Lindl.   Pale evening primrose.   May-Sept.   Native annual or perennial; sand dunes, disturbed sites in creosote bush to ponderosa pine communities, 910-2580 m.

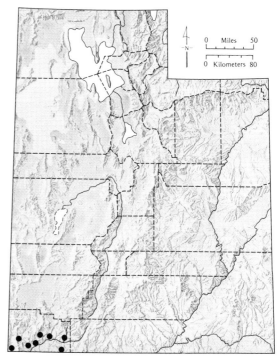

51. _Oenothera primiveris_ Gray   Early evening primrose.   Apr.-May.   Native annual; creosote bush, desert shrub communities, 780-1210 m.

74. ONAGRACEAE

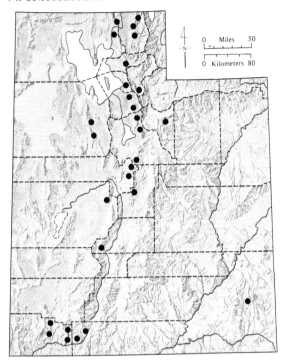

52. **Zauschneria latifolia** (Hook.) Greene Fire chalice. July-Sept. Native annual; dry open slopes in mountain brush to aspen-spruce-fir communities, often among rocks, 1510-3030 m.

75. OPHIOGLOSSACEAE

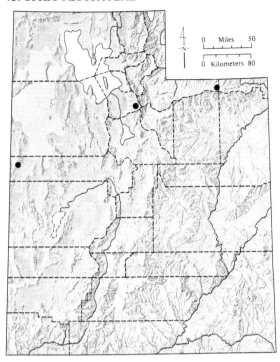

1. **Botrychium lanceolatum** (S. G. Gmel.) Ångström Lanceleaf grapefern. Circumboreal fern; wet meadows, 2420-3030 m.

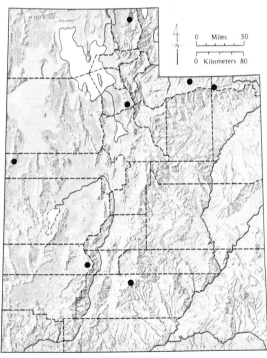

2. **Botrychium lunaria** (L.) Sw. Moonwort. Cosmopolitan fern; near springs, moist meadows, 2630-3030 m.

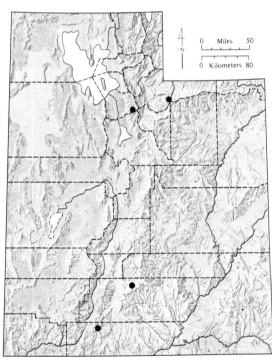

3. **Botrychium simplex** E. Hitchc. Little grapefern. Circumboreal fern; near springs, moist meadows, 3030-3180 m.

394

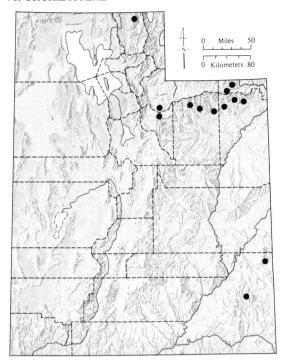

1. *Calypso bulbosa* (L.) Oakes Fairy slipper.
May-June. Native perennial herb; shaded sites in
lodgepole pine, spruce-fir communities, 1810-
2880 m.

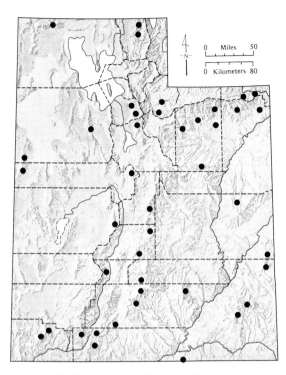

2. *Corallorhiza maculata* Raf. Spotted
coralroot. June-July. Native perennial herb;
shaded sites in aspen, conifer communities, 1510-
3030 m.

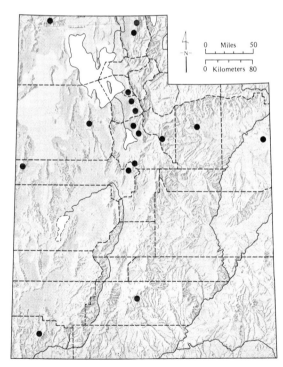

3. *Corallorhiza striata* Lindl. Striped
coralroot. June-July. Native perennial herb;
shaded sites in aspen, conifer communities, 1510-
2580 m.

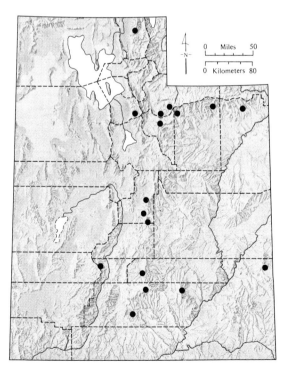

4. *Corallorhiza trifida* Chât. Northern
coralroot. July-Aug. Native perennial herb; shaded
sites in coniferous forests, 2240-3030 m.

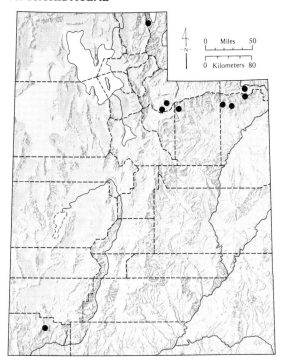

5. *Corallorhiza wisteriana* Conrad Spring coralroot. July-Aug. Native perennial herb; shaded sites in coniferous forests, 2720-2880 m.

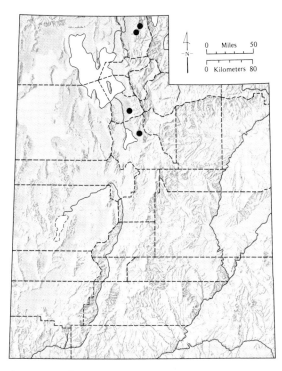

6. *Cypripedium calceolus* L. Lady's slipper. May-June. Circumboreal perennial herb; in shade along waterways, 1360-1610 m.

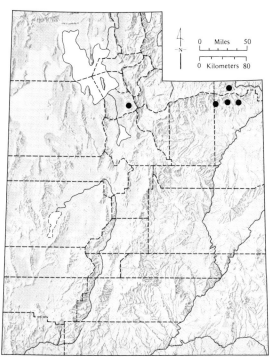

7. *Cypripedium fasciculatum* Wats. Brownie lady's slipper. June-July. Native perennial herb; dense shade in coniferous forests, 2420-2880 m.

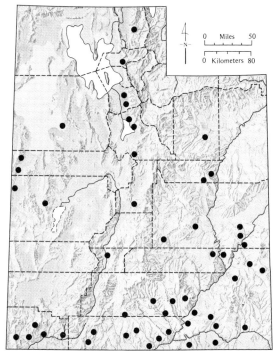

8. *Epipactis gigantea* Hook. Giant helleborine. May-July. Native perennial herb; hanging gardens, wet cliffs, near springs, 900-2120 m.

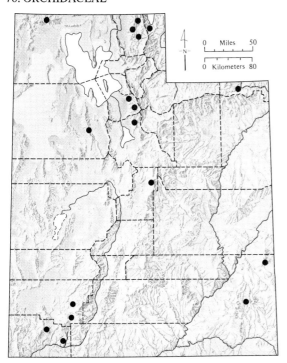

9. *Goodyera oblongifolia* Raf. Rattlesnake plantain. June-Aug. Native perennial herb; shaded sites in coniferous forests, 1360-2370 m.

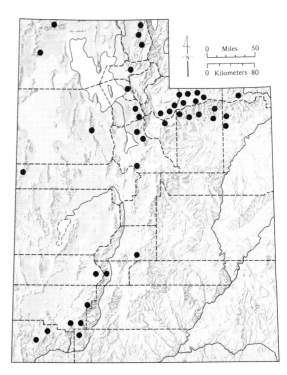

10. *Habenaria dilatata* (Pursh) Hook. White bog orchid. July-Aug. Native perennial herb; streamside, wet meadows, near seeps and springs, 1510-3180 m.

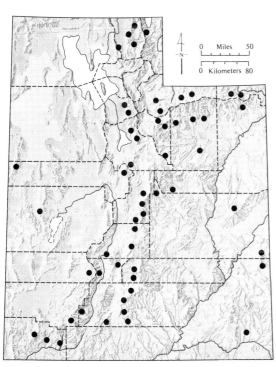

11. *Habenaria hyperborea* (L.) R. Br. Northern bog orchid. June-Aug. Native perennial herb; streamside, wet meadows, near seeps and springs, 1300-3340 m.

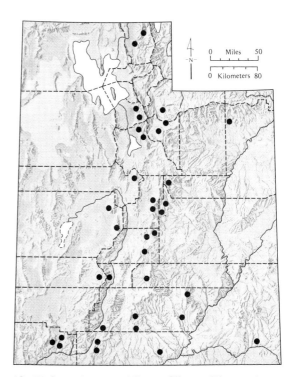

12. *Habenaria sparsiflora* Wats. Watson bog orchid. June-Aug. Native perennial herb; streamside, wet meadows, near seeps and springs, 1300-2490 m.

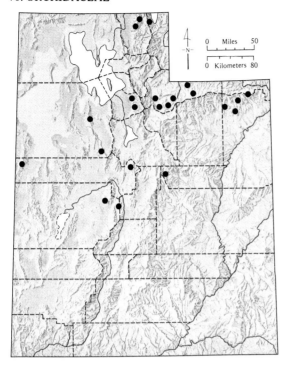

13. *Habenaria unalascensis* (Spreng.) Wats. Alaska rein orchid. June-Aug. Native perennial herb; moderately dry slopes in mountain brush, aspen, conifer communities, 1690-2940 m.

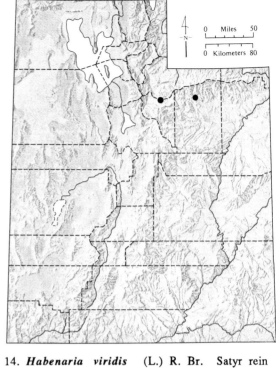

14. *Habenaria viridis* (L.) R. Br. Satyr rein orchid. July-Aug. Native perennial herb; moist to drying sites in aspen, conifer communities, 2420-2730 m.

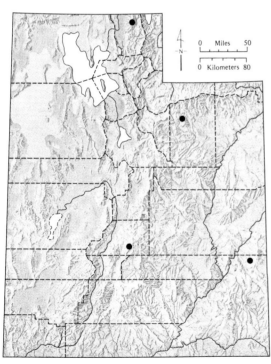

15. *Listera borealis* Morong Northern twayblade. June-July. Native perennial herb; shaded sites in coniferous forests, 2720-2880 m.

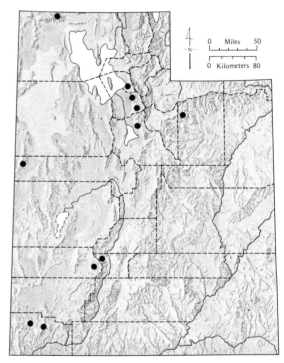

16. *Listera convallarioides* (Swartz) Torr. Broadleaf twayblade. June-Aug. Native perennial herb; shaded sites in coniferous forests, 1750-2550 m.

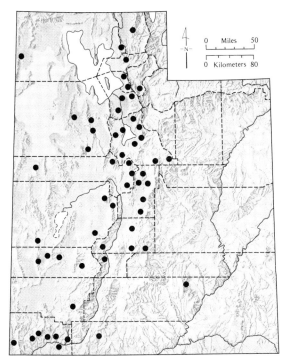

2. *Argemone munita* Dur. & Hilg.   Armed
prickly poppy. May-Sept. Native annual or
perennial; creosote bush to pinyon-juniper
communities, often in disturbed sites, 870-2490 m.

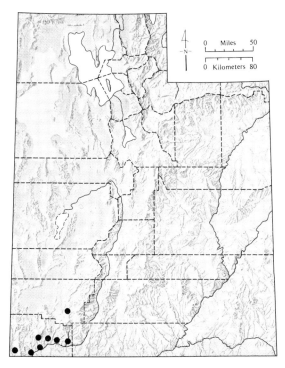

3. *Eschscholzia glytosperma* Greene   Desert
gold poppy. Mar.-May. Native annual; creosote
bush communities, 750-970 m.

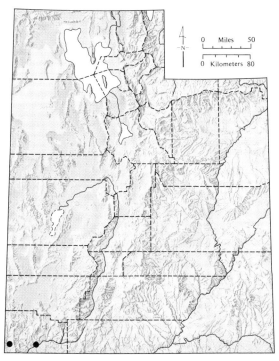

4. *Eschscholzia mexicana* Greene   Mexican
gold poppy. Apr.-May. Native annual; creosote
bush communities, 780-850 m.

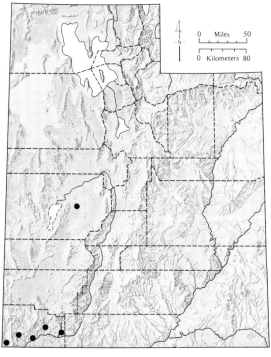

5. *Eschscholzia minutiflora* Wats. Little
gold poppy. Apr.-May. Native annual; creosote
bush communities, 810-970 m.

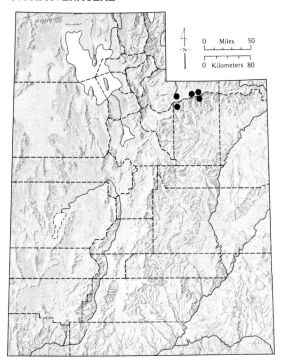

6. *Papaver radicatum* Rottb. July-Aug. Circumboreal perennial herb; exposed rocky slopes, chiefly above timberline, 3030-3940 m.

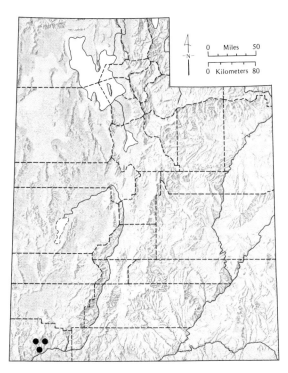

7. *Platystemon californicus* Benth. Creamcups. Apr.-May. Native annual; sandy sites in juniper communities, 1360-1520 m.

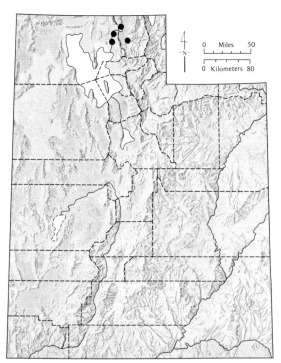

8. *Roemeria refracta* (Stev.) DC. Asian poppy. May-June. Introduced annual; roadsides, fields, along waterways, 1360-1520 m.

80. PINACEAE

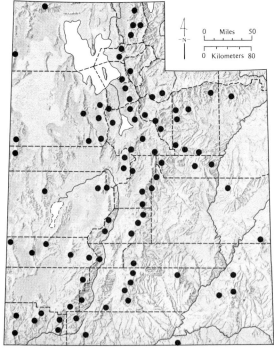

1. *Abies concolor* (Gord. & Glend.) Lindl. White fir. Native tree; a major component of the conifer forest, often codominant with *Picea pungens*, *Pseudotsuga menziesii*, and *Populus tremuloides*, 1810-2460 m.

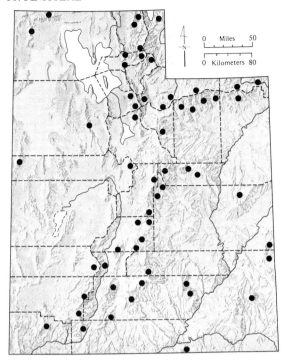

2. *Abies lasiocarpa* (Hook.) Nutt. Subalpine fir. Native tree; a major component of the conifer forest, often codominant with *Picea engelmannii*, 1970-3030 m.

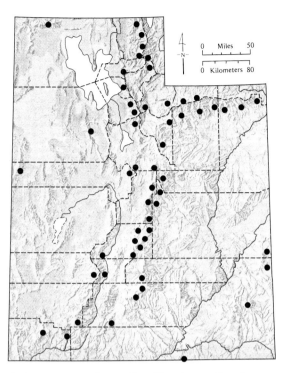

3. *Picea engelmannii* Engelm. Engelmann spruce. Native tree; a major component of the conifer forest, often codominant with *Abies lasiocarpa*, 2420-3180 m.

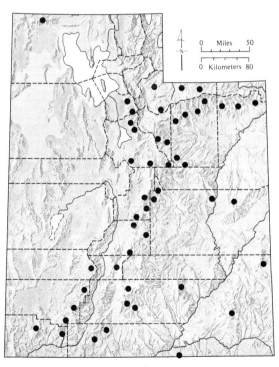

4. *Picea pungens* Engelm. Blue spruce. Native tree; often codominant with *Abies concolor* and *Populus tremuloides*, commonly streamside, 2120-2730 m.

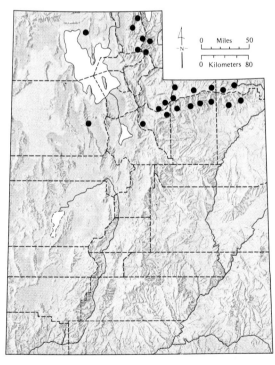

5. *Pinus contorta* Loud. Lodgepole pine. Native tree; dominant over large areas, 2270-3030 m.

403

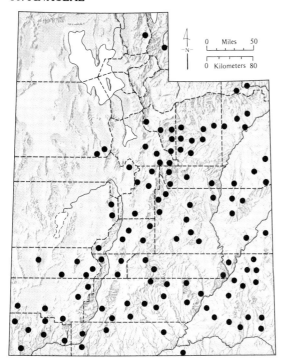

6. *Pinus edulis* Engelm. Two-needle pinyon. Native tree; often codominant with *Juniperus osteosperma*, 1660-2120 m.

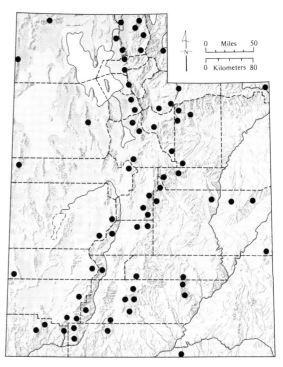

7. *Pinus flexilis* James Limber pine. Native tree; open rocky ridges, often with aspen, Douglas fir, bristlecone pine, ponderosa pine, or spruce-fir, 1840-3280 m.

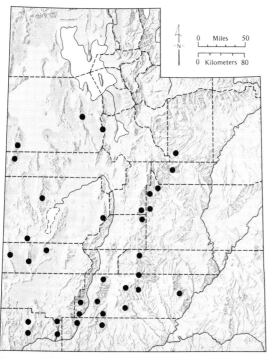

8. *Pinus longaeva* D. K. Bailey Bristlecone pine. Native tree; cliffs, windswept slopes and ridges, often with ponderosa pine, limber pine, or spruce-fir, 2120-3150 m.

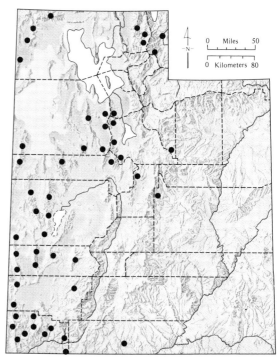

9. *Pinus monophylla* Torr. & Frem. Single-leaf pinyon. Native tree; often codominant with *Juniperus osteosperma*, 1270-2270 m.

80. PINACEAE

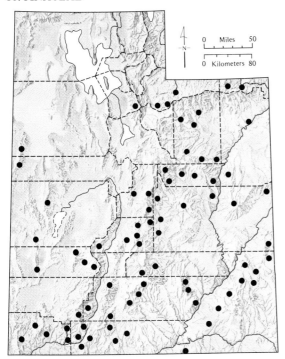

10. *Pinus ponderosa* Laws. Ponderosa or yellow pine. Native tree; dominant over large areas, and scattered in oak, aspen, and less commonly lodgepole, spruce-fir communities, 1660-2730 m.

11. *Pseudotsuga menziesii* (Mirb.) Franco Douglas fir. Native tree; a major component of the conifer forest, often codominant with *Abies concolor*, 1510-2730 m.

81. PLANTAGINACEAE

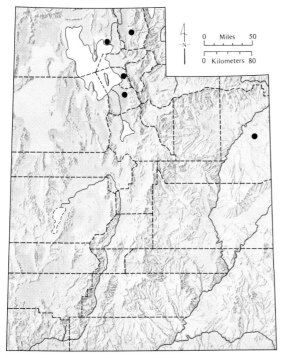

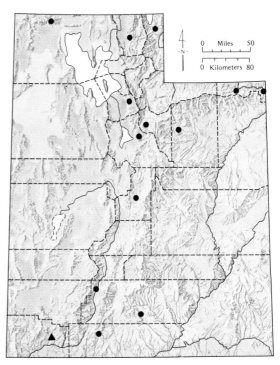

1. *Plantago elongata* Pursh Longleaf plantain. May-June. Native annual; moist sites in greasewood, shadscale communities, 1270-1400 m.

2. *Plantago eriopoda* Torr. Woolly-foot plantain. June-Aug. Native perennial herb; pond and lake shores, wet meadows, 1510-1910 m.

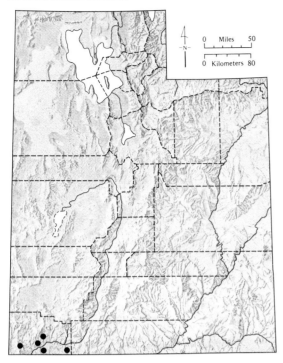

3. *Plantago insularis* Eastw. Mar.-May.
Native annual; Joshua tree, creosote bush
communities, 750-1210 m.

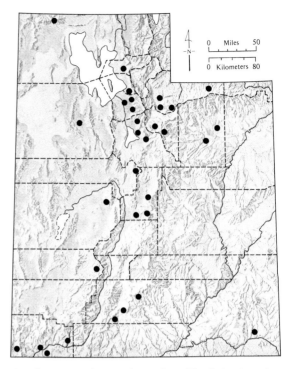

4. *Plantago lanceolata* L. English plantain.
May-Sept. Introduced perennial herb; disturbed
sites, 750-2670 m.

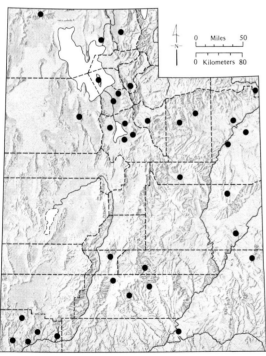

5. *Plantago major* L. Broadleaf plantain. May-
Aug. Introduced perennial herb; disturbed sites,
840-2030 m.

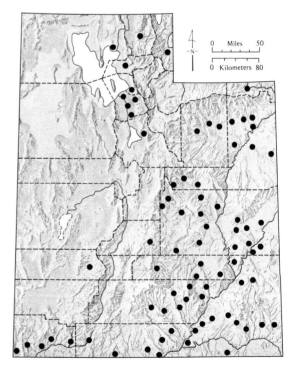

6. *Plantago patagonica* Jacq. Woolly
plantain. Mar.-Aug. Native annual; greasewood,
shadscale, sagebrush, juniper communities, salt
tolerant, 840-1980 m.

81. PLANTAGINACEAE

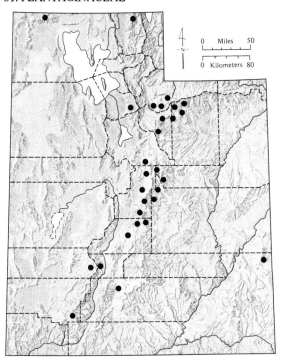

7. *Plantago tweedyi* Gray   Meadow plantain. May-Sept. Native annual; dry to wet meadows in aspen, spruce-fir communities, 2270-3180 m.

82. POACEAE

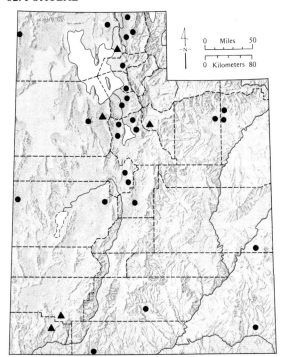

1. *Aegilops cylindrica* Host   Jointed goatgrass. May-Sept. Introduced annual; disturbed sites, 1070-2130 m.

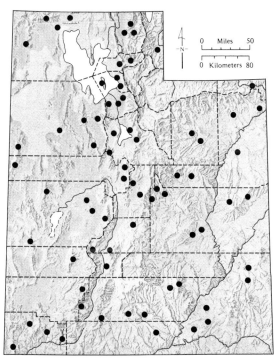

2. *Agropyron cristatum* (L.) Gaertn.   Fairway or crested wheatgrass.   May-Sept.   Introduced perennial; disturbed or revegetated sites along roads and on open slopes in salt desert shrub to ponderosa pine communities, 910-2740 m.

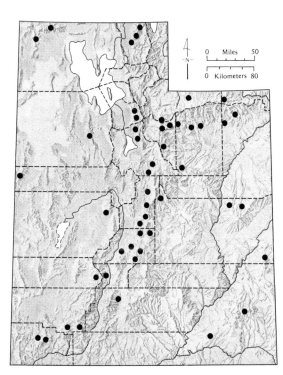

3. *Agrostis exarata* Trin.   Spike bentgrass. June-Sept. Native perennial; mesic to moist sites in pinyon-juniper to aspen-conifer communities, 1520-3200 m.

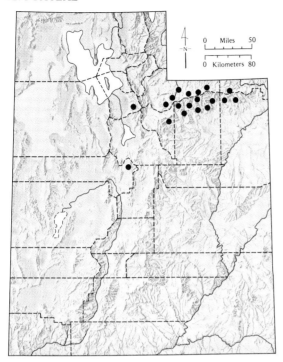

4. *Agrostis humilis* Vasey   Alpine bentgrass.
July-Sept. Native perennial; wet meadows, moist
open sites in conifer forests, 2740-3350 m.

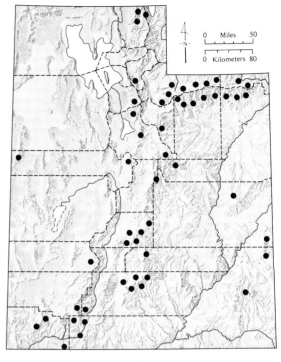

5. *Agrostis scabra* Willd. Ticklegrass. June-
Oct. Native perennial; meadows, open sites in
mountain brush, aspen, conifer communities, 2440-
3350 m.

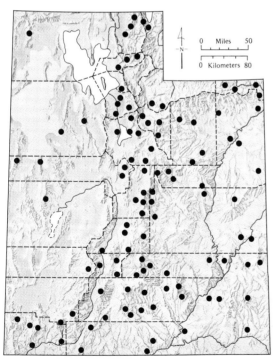

6. *Agrostis stolonifera* L. Redtop; carpet
bentgrass. June-Sept. Introduced perennial; along
waterways, in marshes and wet meadows,
greasewood to spruce-fir communities, 980-
3050 m.

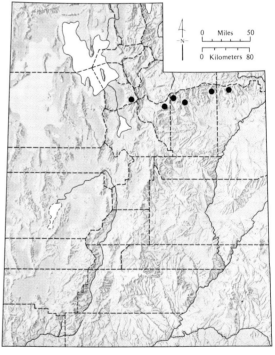

7. *Agrostis thurberiana* Hitchc. Thurber
bentgrass. July-Aug. Native perennial; wet
meadows, 2620-3340 m.

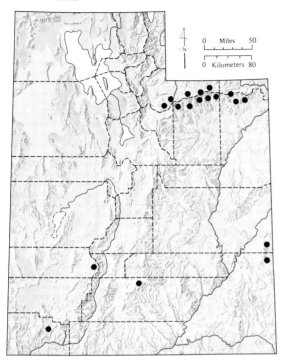

8. *Agrostis variabilis* Rydb. Mountain bentgrass. July-Sept. Native perennial; wet meadows, streamside, other moist sites in spruce-fir, lodgepole pine communities, 2930-3570 m.

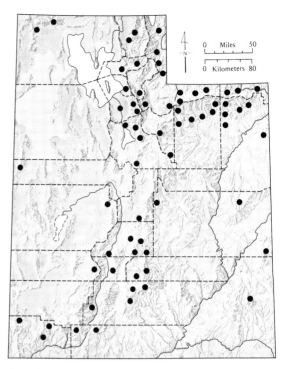

9. *Alopecurus aequalis* Sobol. Shortawn foxtail. June-Sept. Native perennial; along waterways, in wet, sometimes saline meadows, moist sites in aspen-conifer communities, 1280-3200 m.

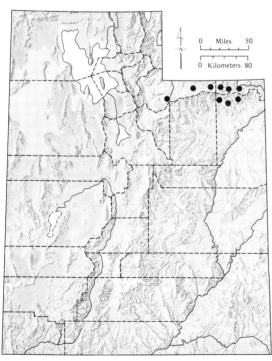

10. *Alopecurus alpinus* J. E. Sm. Alpine foxtail. June-Aug. Native perennial; along waterways, in mesic to moist sites in aspen, lodgepole pine, ponderosa pine, meadow communities, 2320-3230 m.

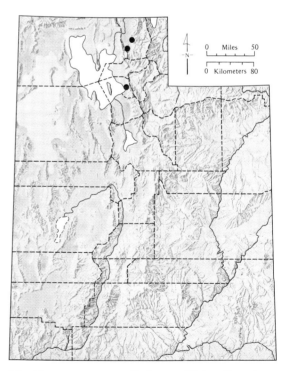

11. *Alopecurus carolinianus* Walt. Carolina foxtail. Apr.-May. Native annual; wet, often saline sites, 1270-1520 m.

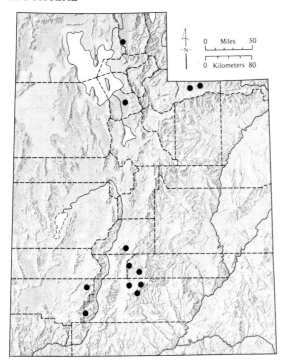

12. *Alopecurus geniculatus* L. Marsh or water foxtail. May-Sept. Introduced perennial; wet meadows, near springs and seeps, in aspen-spruce-fir communities, 1320-3200 m.

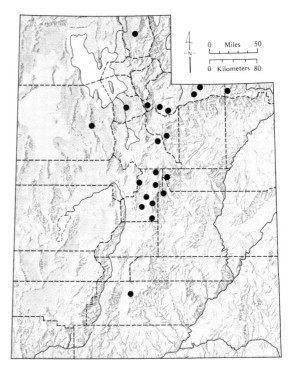

13. *Alopecurus pratensis* L. Meadow foxtail. May-Aug. Introduced perennial; chiefly where planted in pastures, meadows, and aspen-conifer communities, 1310-3230 m.

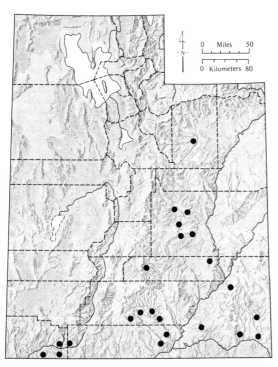

14. *Andropogon gerardii* Vit. Big bluestem. June-Sept. Native perennial; dry to moist sites in creosote bush to ponderosa pine communities, 850-1890 m.

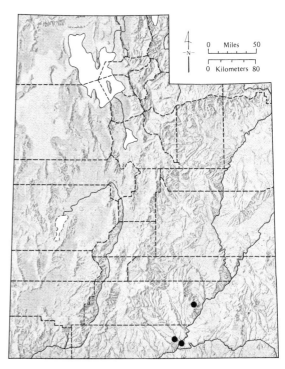

15. *Andropogon glomeratus* (Walt.) B. S. P. Bushy bluestem. Apr.-Oct. Native perennial; hanging gardens and along streams, 1120-1160 m.

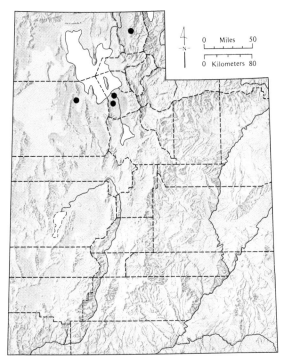

16. *Apera interrupta* (L.) Beauv. Italian windgrass. May-July. Introduced annual; greasewood communities, weed of lawns, 1300-1530 m.

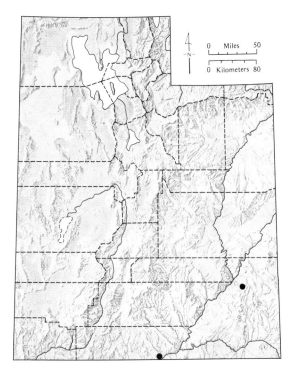

17. *Aristida arizonica* Vasey Arizona threeawn. July-Aug. Native perennial; desert shrub communities, 1300-1520 m.

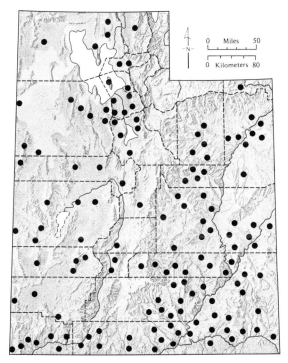

18. *Aristida purpurea* Nutt. Purple threeawn. Apr.-Sept. Native perennial, often the dominant grass; creosote bush, salt desert shrub, oak-sagebrush, pinyon-juniper communities, 820-2320 m.

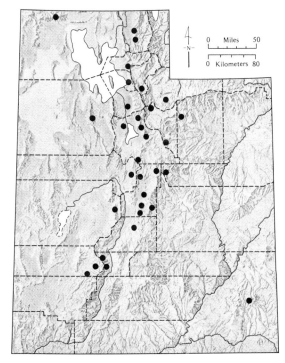

19. *Arrhenatherum elatius* (L.) J. & C. Presl Tall oatgrass. May-Sept. Introduced perennial; roadsides, streambanks, fields, and seeded sites in oak-sagebrush to aspen-conifer, meadow communities, 1310-3110 m.

82. POACEAE

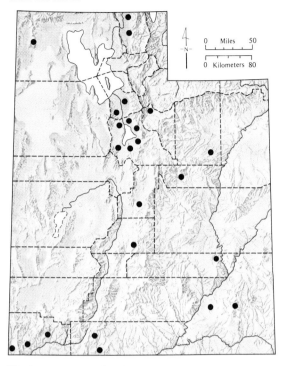

20. *Avena fatua* L. Oats. May-Oct. Introduced annual; cultivated and escaping, often a weed of other cereal crops, 850-2620 m.

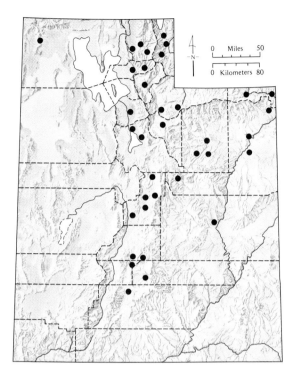

21. *Beckmannia syzigachne* (Steud.) Fern. June-Sept. Native annual; along waterways and in wet, rarely saline marshes, 1220-2740 m.

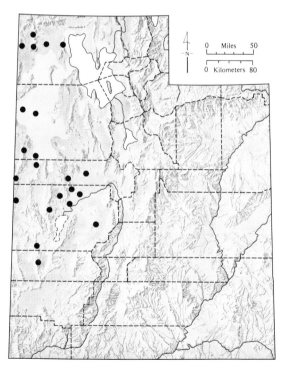

22. *Blepharidachne kingii* (Wats.) Hackel Desert grass. May-Aug. Native perennial; greasewood, desert shrub, sagebrush communities, 1070-1830 m.

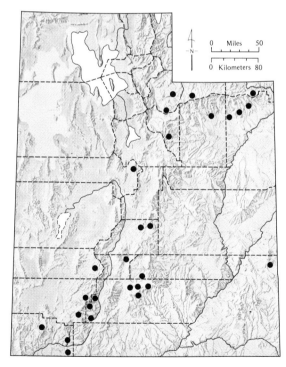

23. *Blepharoneuron tricholepis* (Torr.) Nash Hairy or pine dropseed. June-Oct. Native perennial; open sites in ponderosa pine, lodgepole pine communities, 1980-3200 m.

412

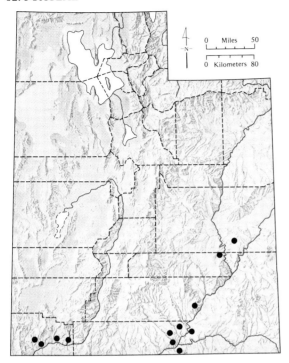

24. Bothriochloa barbinodis (Lag.) Herter
Cane bluestem. June-Dec. Native perennial; desert
shrub, pinyon-juniper, ponderosa pine
communities, 920-1830 m.

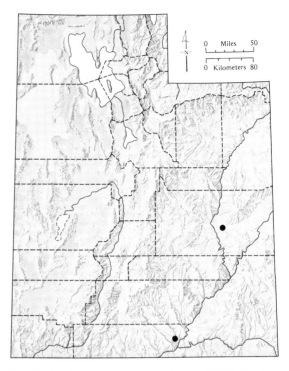

25. Bothriochloa laguroides (DC.) Herter
Silver bluestem. Aug.-Sept. Native perennial;
desert shrub communities, 1130-1520 m.

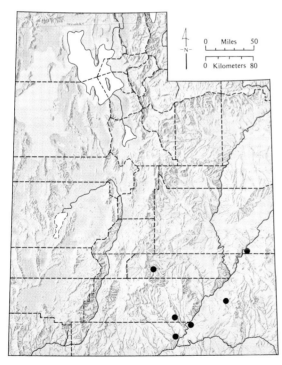

26. Bothriochloa springfieldii (Gould)
Parodi Springfield bluestem. June-Oct. Native
perennial; desert shrub communities, sandstone
cliffs, along waterways, 1130-1770 m.

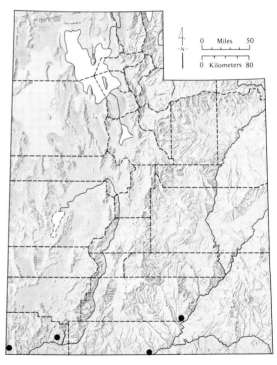

27. Bouteloua aristidoides (H. B. K.) Griseb.
Needle grama. July-Sept. Native annual; Joshua
tree, desert shrub communities, 910-1830 m.

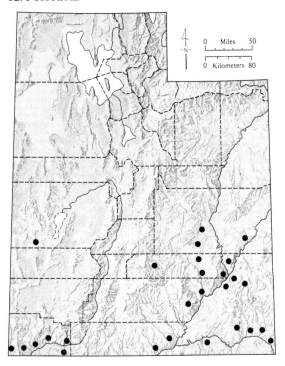

28. *Bouteloua barbata* Lag. Sixweeks grama.
Aug.-Oct. Native annual; creosote bush, desert
shrub communities, 850-1830 m.

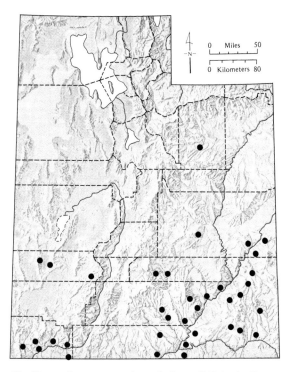

29. *Bouteloua curtipendula* (Michx.) Torr.
Sideoats grama. June-Oct. Native perennial; desert
shrub, sagebrush, pinyon-juniper, ponderosa pine
communities, 980-2240 m.

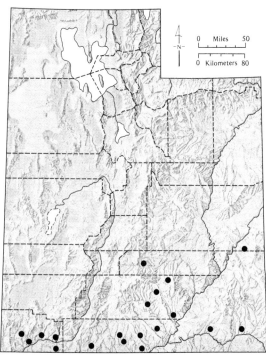

30. *Bouteloua eriopoda* (Torr.) Torr. Black
grama. Apr.-Oct. Native perennial; desert shrub,
pinyon-juniper communities, 850-2440 m.

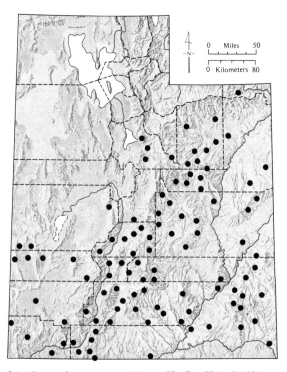

31. *Bouteloua gracilis* (H. B. K.) Griffiths
Blue grama. Apr.-Oct. Native perennial; salt desert
shrub to ponderosa pine communities, 980-2960 m.

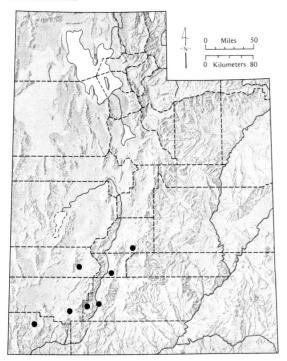

32. *Bouteloua simplex* Lag. Mat grama. Aug.-Oct. Native annual; roadsides, along waterways in greasewood, sagebrush communities, 1520-2440 m.

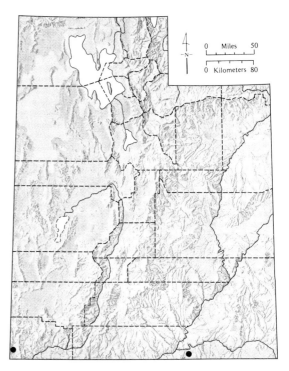

33. *Bouteloua trifida* Thurb. Red grama. May-July. Native perennial; cliffs and rocky hillsides, 920-1220 m.

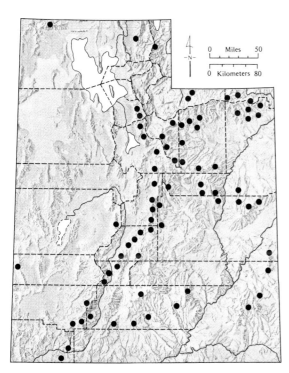

34. *Bromus anomalus* Fourn. Nodding brome. June-Sept. Native perennial; sagebrush, mountain brush, pinyon-juniper, ponderosa pine, aspen, spruce-fir, meadow communities, 1680-3350 m.

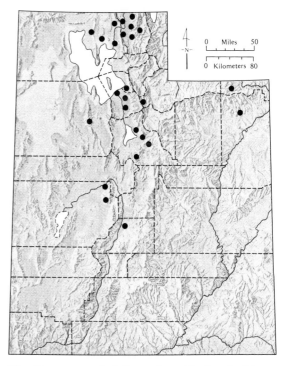

35. *Bromus briziformis* Fisch. & Mey. Rattlesnake chess. May-July. Introduced annual; salt desert shrub, sagebrush, mountain brush, juniper communities, 1280-1960 m.

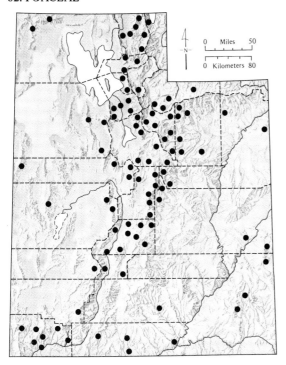

36. **Bromus carinatus** H. & A. Mountain or California brome. May-Sept. Native perennial, often the dominant grass; sagebrush, mountain brush, aspen, spruce-fir, subalpine meadow communities, 1830-3200 m.

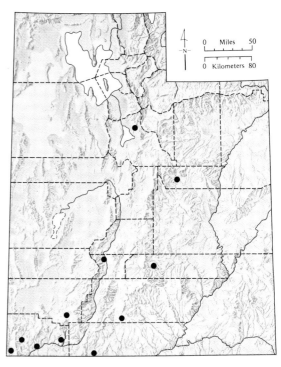

37. **Bromus catharticus** Vahl Rescue grass. Mar.-Nov. Introduced annual to perennial; along waterways, waste places, fallow fields, weed of cultivated sites, 850-1890 m.

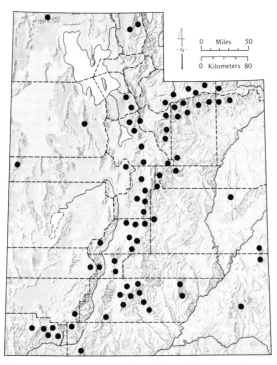

38. **Bromus ciliatus** L. Fringed brome. June-Sept. Native perennial; aspen-conifer communities, 1520-3510 m.

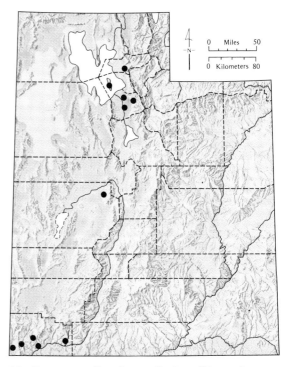

39. **Bromus diandrus** Roth Ripgut brome. Apr.-July. Introduced annual; disturbed sites in creosote bush, pinyon-juniper, mountain brush communities, 970-1990 m.

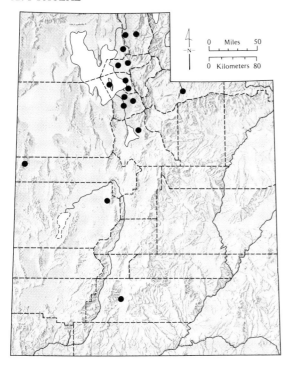

40. *Bromus hordeaceus* L. Soft chess. May-July. Introduced annual or biennial; salt desert shrub, sagebrush communities, 1280-2530 m.

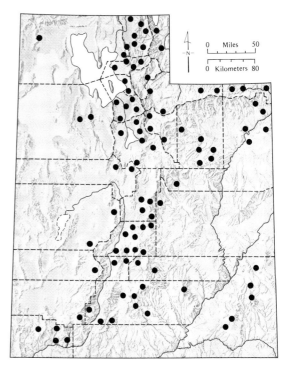

41. *Bromus inermis* Leyss. Smooth or Hungarian brome. June-Sept. Introduced perennial; along roads and waterways, fields and other waste places, openings in mountain brush to aspen-conifer and meadow communities, 1280-3240 m.

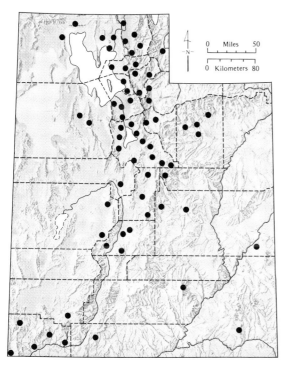

42. *Bromus japonicus* Murray Japanese or meadow chess. May-Sept. Introduced annual; greasewood to mountain brush, juniper, meadow communities, 760-2450 m.

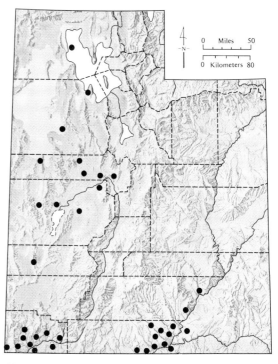

43. *Bromus rubens* L. Red or foxtail brome. Mar.-June. Introduced annual; creosote bush, desert shrub communities, 750-1710 m.

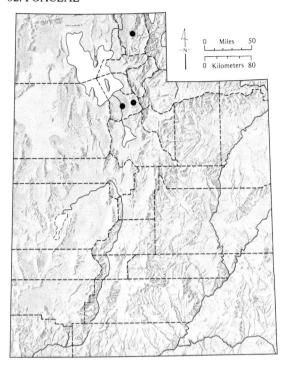

44. *Bromus secalinus* L. Rye chess. June-July. Introduced annual or biennial; waste places, cultivated fields, 1300-1530 m.

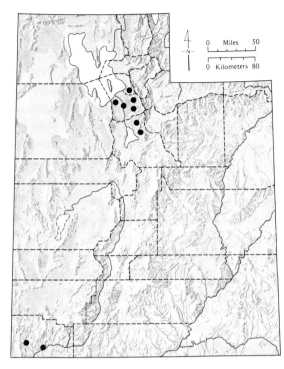

45. *Bromus sterilis* L. Poverty brome. Apr.-July. Introduced annual; waste places, 810-1830 m.

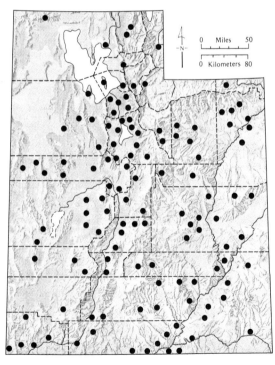

46. *Bromus tectorum* L. Cheatgrass; downy chess. Apr.-Aug. Introduced annual, dominant over large areas; salt desert shrub, sagebrush, pinyon-juniper communities, open slopes, 850-2590 m.

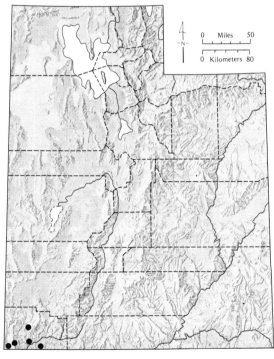

47. *Bromus trinii* Desv. Chilean chess. Apr.-Aug. Native annual; rock crevices, 940-1220 m.

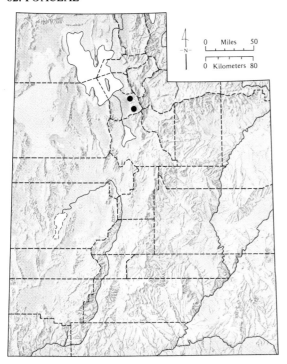

48. *Bromus vulgaris* (Hook.) Shear Columbia brome. July-Aug. Native perennial; aspen, spruce-fir communities, 1820-2300 m.

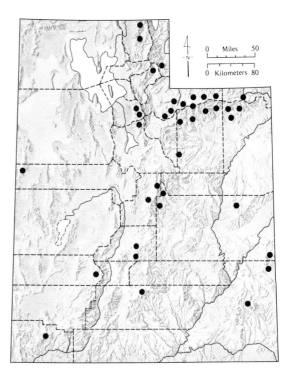

49. *Calamagrostis canadensis* (Michx.) Beauv. Bluejoint reedgrass. July-Sept. Circumboreal perennial; moist sites in meadows, aspen, spruce-fir, lodgepole pine, alpine communities, 1950-3360 m.

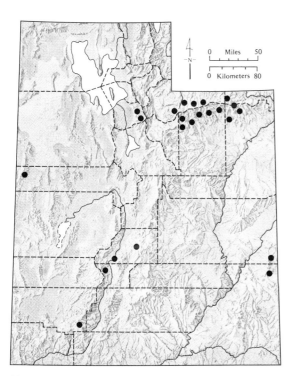

50. *Calamagrostis purpurascens* R. Br. Purple reedgrass. July-Sept. Native perennial; open rocky slopes, aspen, spruce-fir, lodgepole pine, meadow communities, 2290-3965 m.

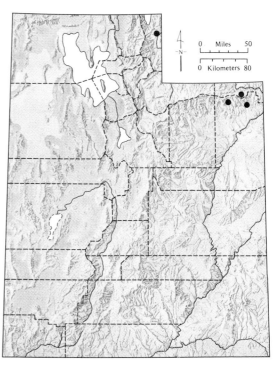

51. *Calamagrostis rubescens* Buckley Pinegrass. June-Aug. Native perennial; aspen, lodgepole pine, ponderosa pine communities, 2440-2750 m.

82. POACEAE

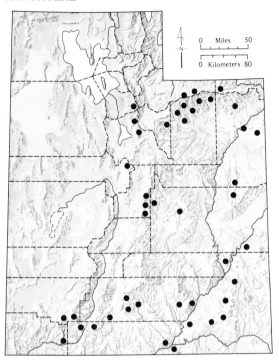

52. *Calamagrostis scopulorum* Jones Jones reedgrass. June-Nov. Native perennial; hanging gardens and other rocky sites, streamside, meadows, krummholz, 1070-3510 m.

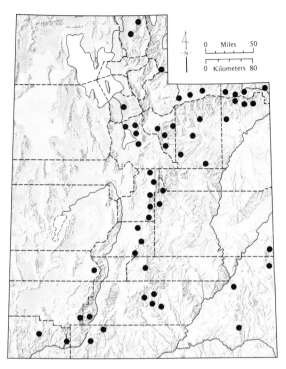

53. *Calamagrostis stricta* (Timm) Koel. Slimstem or northern reedgrass. June-Oct. Native perennial; streamside and other moist sites in ponderosa pine, spruce-fir, lodgepole pine, meadow communities, 1280-3230 m.

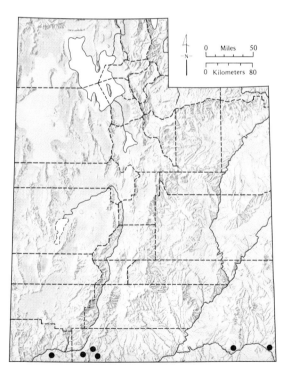

54. *Calamovilfa gigantea* (Nutt.) Scribn. & Merr. Big sandreed. June-Oct. Native perennial; dunes and other sandy sites in sagebrush, pinyon-juniper, ponderosa pine communities, 1330-1830 m.

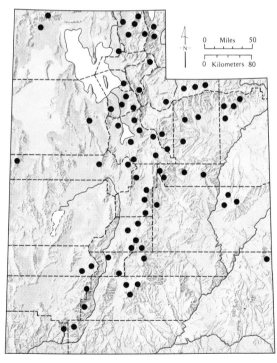

55. *Catabrosa aquatica* (L.) Beauv. Brookgrass. May-Sept. Native perennial; moist soil or shallow water of marshes, streams, springs, and meadows in mountain brush to conifer communities, 1300-3110 m.

420

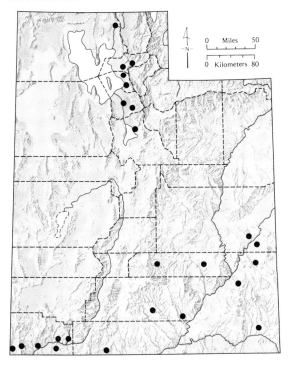

56. *Cenchrus longispinus* (Hack.) Fern. Field sandbur. July-Sept. Native annual; waste places, 840-1830 m.

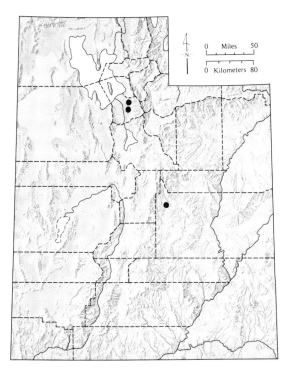

57. *Chloris verticillata* Nutt. Tumble windmillgrass. June-Aug. Native perennial; weed of cultivated sites, 1300-1830 m.

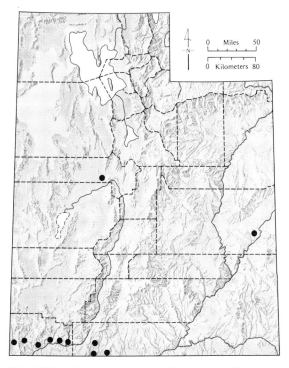

58. *Chloris virgata* Swartz Feather fingergrass. May-Oct. Native annual; along waterways and roadsides, weed of cultivated sites, 850-1830 m.

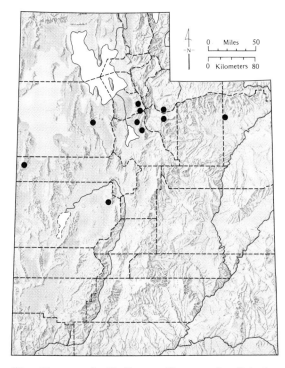

59. *Cinna latifolia* (Goeppert) Griseb. Drooping woodreed. June-Sept. Native perennial; streamside in mountain brush, aspen, spruce-fir communities, 1710-2600 m.

421

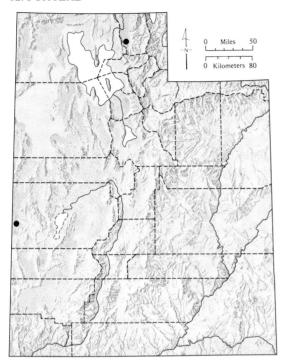

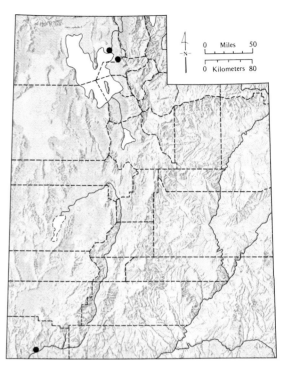

60. **Crypsis alopecuroides** (Pill. & Mitt.) Schrad. Pricklegrass. July-Oct. Introduced annual; margins of lakes, ponds, waterways, and in reservoir drawdown sites, 1360-1830 m.

61. **Crypsis schoenoides** (L.) Lam. Common pricklegrass. June-Sept. Introduced annual; margins of lakes, ponds, waterways, reservoir drawdown sites, 910-1530 m.

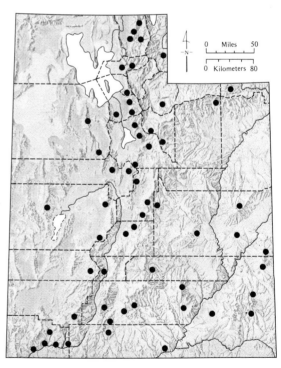

62. **Cynodon dactylon** (L.) Pers. Bermuda grass. May-Dec. Introduced perennial; weed of lawns, waste places, along waterways, 840-1530 m.

63. **Dactylis glomerata** L. Orchard grass. May-Oct. Introduced perennial; sagebrush, mountain brush, ponderosa pine, aspen, spruce-fir communities, 850-3235 m.

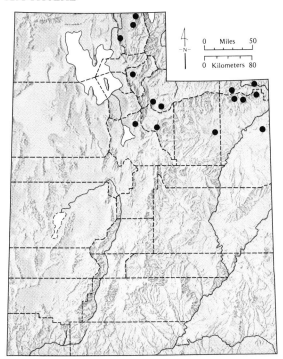

64. *Danthonia californica* Boland. California oatgrass. June-Aug. Native perennial; meadows, open grassy or rocky slopes, pinyon-juniper, ponderosa pine, aspen, spruce-fir communities, 1580-3050 m.

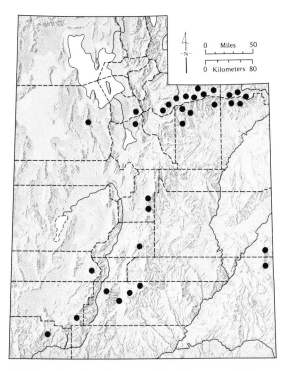

65. *Danthonia intermedia* Vasey Timber oatgrass. June-Sept. Native perennial; dry to moist meadows in spruce-fir, lodgepole pine communities, exposed rocky alpine ridges, 2440-3660 m.

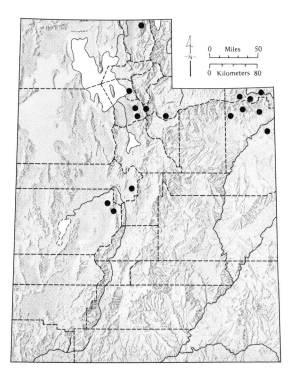

66. *Danthonia unispicata* (Thurb.) Macoun Oneside oatgrass. June-Sept. Native perennial; dry to wet sites in mountain brush, aspen-fir, ponderosa pine, lodgepole pine, meadow, alpine communities, 2130-3050 m.

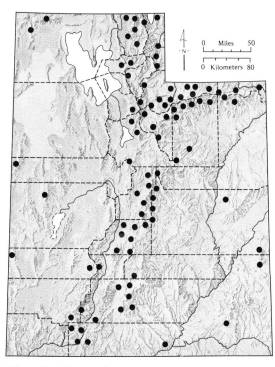

67. *Deschampsia cespitosa* (L.) Beauv. Tufted hairgrass. June-Oct. Native perennial; mesic to wet meadows, forest openings, shaded streamsides in conifer forests, 1370-3810 m.

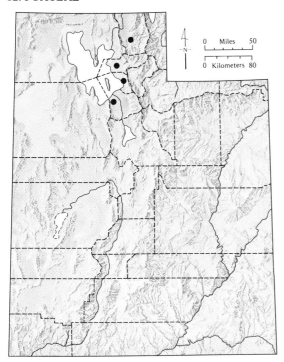

68. Deschampsia danthonioides (Trin.)
Benth. May-July. Native annual; salt desert shrub,
saline meadow communities, 1270-1530 m.

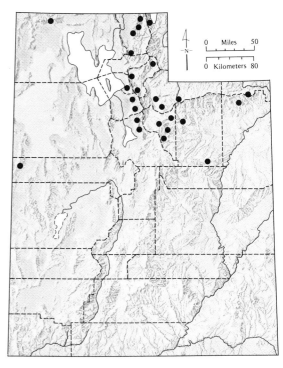

69. Deschampsia elongata (Hook.) Benth.
June-Sept. Native perennial; dry to moist sites,
streamside, mountain brush, aspen, lodgepole pine,
spruce-fir, meadow communities, 1830-3140 m.

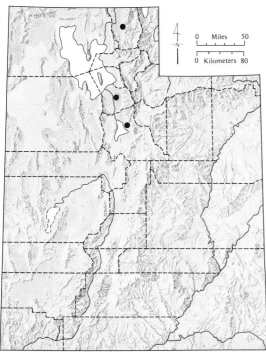

70. Digitaria ischaemum (Schreb.) Muhl.
Smooth crabgrass. Aug.-Sept. Introduced annual;
weed of lawns, waste places, 1360-1530 m.

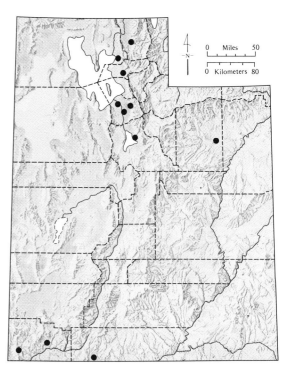

71. Digitaria sanguinalis (L.) Scop. Hairy
crabgrass. June-Oct. Introduced annual; weed of
lawns, gardens, waste places, 1030-1530 m.

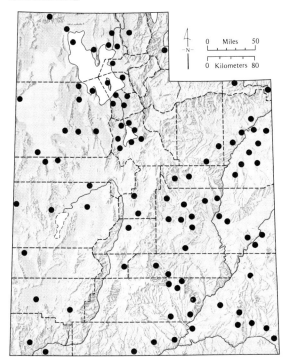

72. *Distichlis spicata* (L.) Greene Desert saltgrass. May-Sept. Native perennial; moist sites in salt desert shrub communities, often forming pure stands, occasionally invading neutral soils at higher elevations, 1020-2280 m.

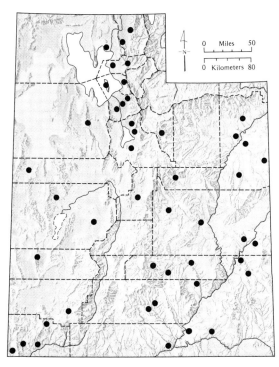

73. *Echinochloa crus-galli* (L.) Beauv. Barnyard grass. June-Oct. Native annual; weed of gardens, fields, other open sites, especially along waterways, 820-2140 m.

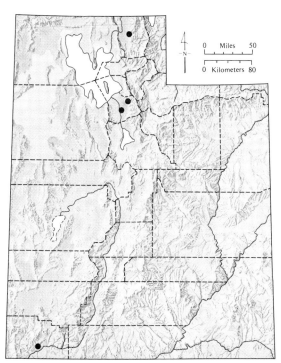

74. *Eleusine indica* (L.) Gaertn. Goosegrass. June-Oct. Introduced annual; weed of lawns, disturbed sites, 1300-1530 m.

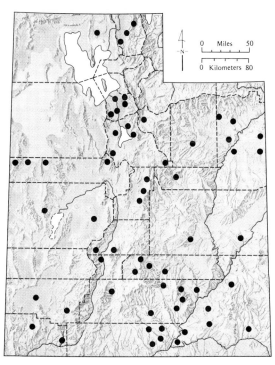

75. *Elymus canadensis* L. Canada wildrye. June-Sept. Native perennial; along waterways, moist, sometimes saline meadows, 1220-2440 m.

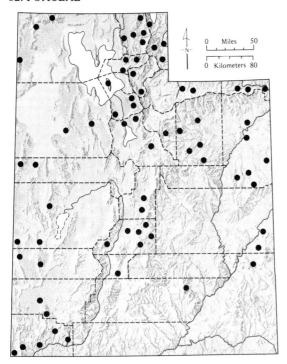

76. *Elymus cinereus* Scribn. & Merr. Great Basin wildrye. June-Sept. Native perennial; along waterways and roadsides, wet meadows, openings in sagebrush to conifer communities, 790-2900 m.

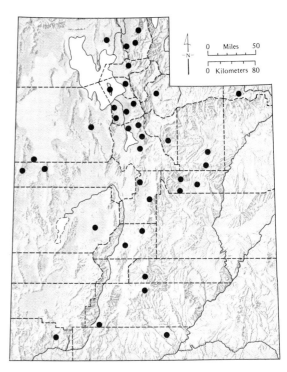

77. *Elymus elongatus* (Host) Runem. Tall wheatgrass. June-Aug. Introduced perennial; roadsides, salt desert shrub, sagebrush, aspen, lower montane grassland communities, 1220-2740 m.

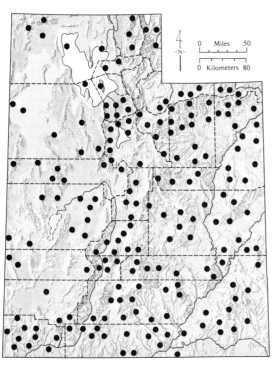

78. *Elymus elymoides* (Raf.) Swezey Squirreltail. Apr.-Oct. Native perennial; dry to moist sites, salt desert shrub to alpine grassland communities, 1070-3500 m.

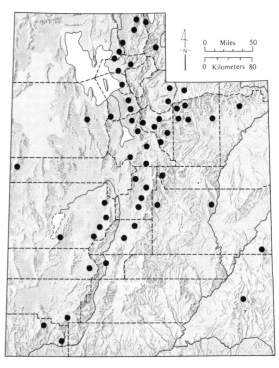

79. *Elymus glaucus* Buckl. Blue wildrye. June-Sept. Native perennial; mountain brush, aspen, ponderosa pine, lodgepole pine, spruce-fir communities, 1310-3200 m.

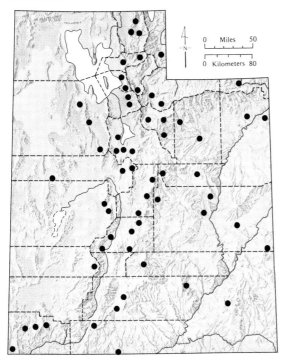

80. *Elymus hispidus* (Opiz) Meld. Intermediate wheatgrass. June-Aug. Introduced perennial; roadsides, other waste places in sagebrush to ponderosa pine, spruce-fir communities, 1280-3050 m.

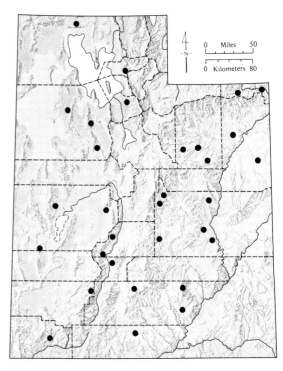

81. *Elymus junceus* Fisch. Russian wildrye. May-Aug. Introduced perennial; salt desert shrub to aspen, ponderosa pine communities, 1280-2870 m.

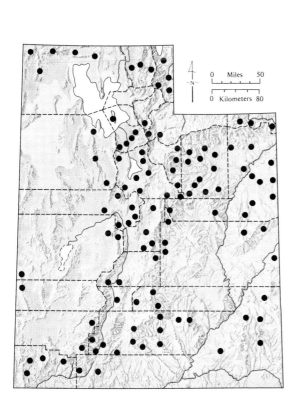

82. *Elymus lanceolatus* (Scribn. & Sm.) Gould Thickspike wheatgrass. May-Aug. Native perennial; roadsides and other disturbed sites, sagebrush to aspen, meadow communities, 1220-3350 m.

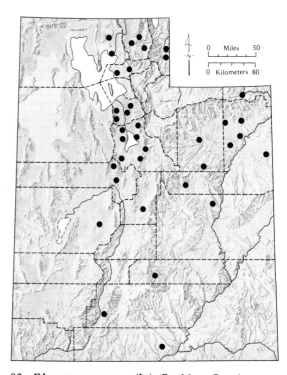

83. *Elymus repens* (L.) Gould Quackgrass; couchgrass. May-Sept. Introduced perennial; disturbed, mesic to moist sites, often as a weed of cultivated land, 1220-3050 m.

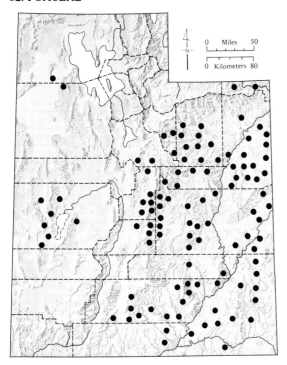

84. *Elymus salinus* Jones   Salina wildrye.
May-Aug.   Native perennial, often the dominant
grass; salt desert shrub, sagebrush-grass, pinyon-
juniper, ponderosa pine communities, 1520-
3050 m.

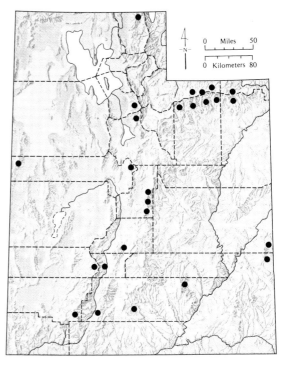

85. *Elymus scribneri* (Vasey) Jones   Scribner
or spreading wheatgrass.   June-Sept.   Native
perennial; open, often rocky slopes, exposed
alpine ridges, 2740-3810 m.

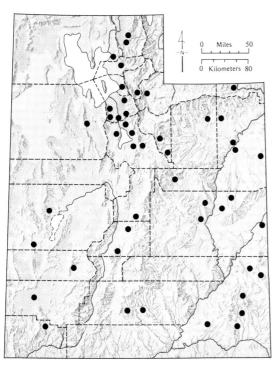

86. *Elymus smithii* (Rydb.) Gould   Western
wheatgrass.   June-Sept.   Native perennial; salt
desert shrub, sagebrush, mountain brush, pinyon-
juniper communities, 1220-2740 m.

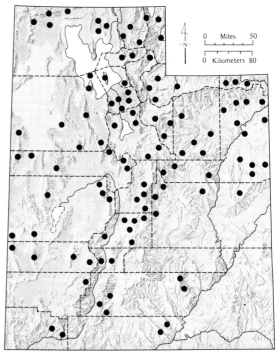

87. *Elymus spicatus* (Pursh) Gould   Bluebunch
wheatgrass.   May-Aug.   Native perennial, often the
dominant grass; sagebrush to ponderosa pine, open
sites in spruce-fir communities, 1370-2900 m.

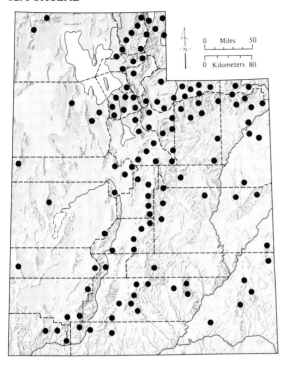

88. *Elymus trachycaulus* (Link) Shinners Slender wheatgrass. June-Sept. Native perennial, often the dominant grass; sagebrush-grass to conifer communities, alpine meadows, exposed rocky slopes, 1280-3660 m.

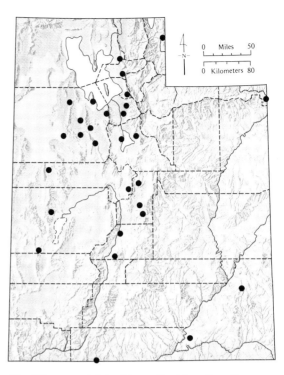

89. *Elymus triticoides* Buckl. Beardless or creeping wildrye. May-Sept. Native perennial; saline meadows, salt desert shrub, juniper communities, 1280-1830 m.

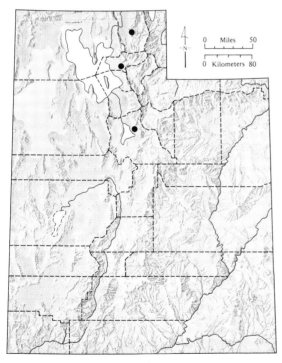

90. *Elymus virginicus* L. Virginia wildrye. July-Sept. Native perennial; weed of cultivated sites, 1360-1830 m.

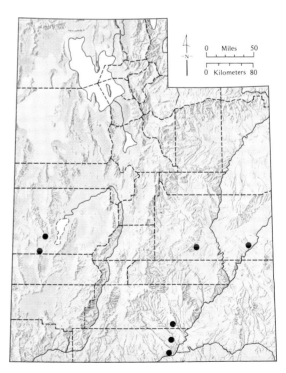

91. *Enneapogon desvauxii* Beauv. Spike pappusgrass. July-Oct. Native perennial; desert shrub communities, 1210-1800 m.

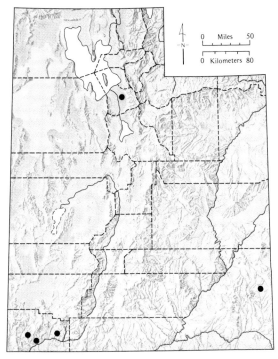

92. *Eragrostis barrelieri* Daveau
Mediterranean lovegrass. July-Nov. Introduced
annual; weed of gardens and disturbed, often sandy
sites, 1000-1520 m.

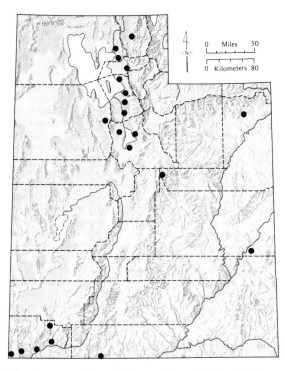

93. *Eragrostis cilianensis* (All.) Mosher
Stinkgrass. May-Oct. Introduced annual; waste
places, 850-2320 m.

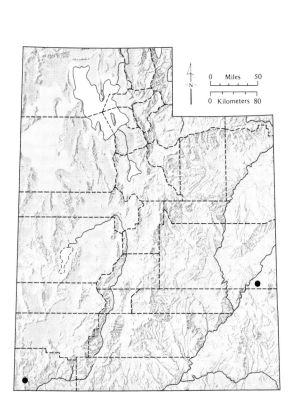

94. *Eragrostis curvula* (Schrad.) Nees
Weeping lovegrass. June-Aug. Introduced
perennial; disturbed sites in desert shrub, juniper
communities, 1330-1520 m.

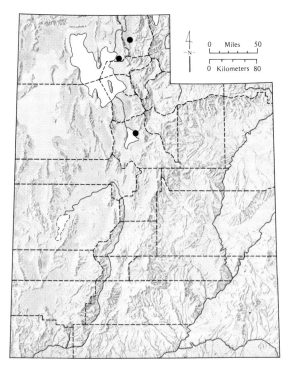

95. *Eragrostis hypnoides* (Lam.) B. S. P.
Teal or creeping lovegrass. June-Sept. Native
annual; along waterways, marshes, beds of drying
ponds, 1270-1520 m.

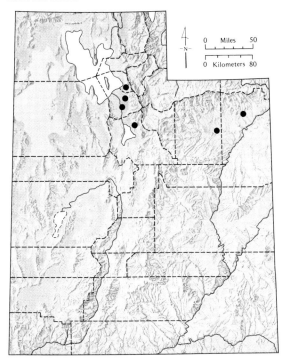

96. *Eragrostis mexicana* (Hornem.) Link Mexican lovegrass. July-Oct. Native annual; weed of gardens, waste places, 1360-1520 m.

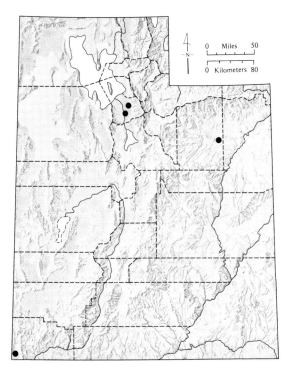

97. *Eragrostis minor* Host Minor lovegrass. Aug.-Oct. Introduced annual; weed of gardens, waste places, 800-1520 m.

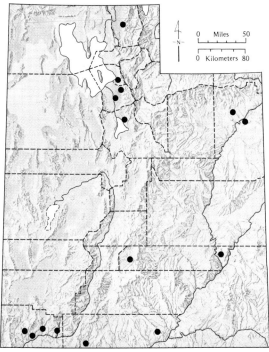

98. *Eragrostis pectinacea* (Michx.) Nees Tufted lovegrass. July-Nov. Native annual; along waterways, waste places, gardens, 910-1520 m.

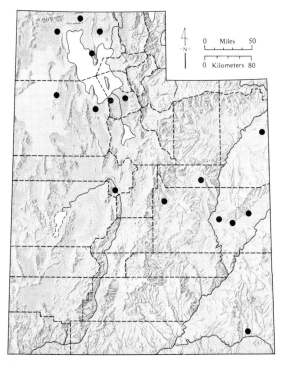

99. *Eremopyrum triticeum* (Gaertn.) Nevski Annual wheatgrass. Apr.-June. Introduced annual; disturbed sites in salt desert shrub, sagebrush, juniper communities, 1280-1520 m.

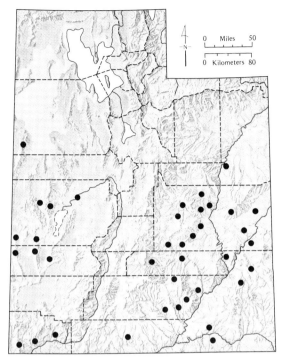

100. *Erioneuron pilosum* (Buckl.) Nash
Hairy tridens. Apr.-Aug. Native perennial;
creosote bush to pinyon-juniper communities, 910-
2130 m.

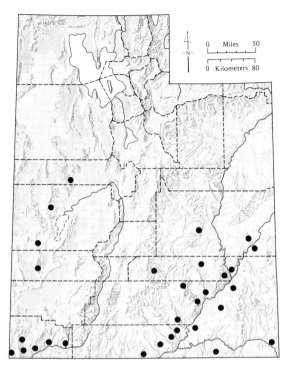

101. *Erioneuron pulchellum* (H. B. K.)
Tateoka Fluffgrass. Apr.-Oct. Native perennial;
creosote bush to pinyon-juniper communities, 820-
2130 m.

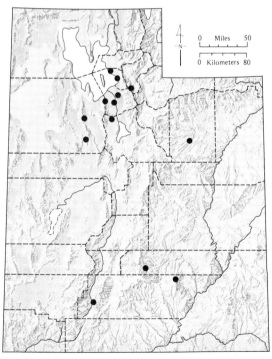

102. *Festuca arundinacea* Schreb. Tall fescue.
May-Sept. Introduced perennial; salt desert shrub,
sagebrush communities, roadsides, meadows, weed
of cultivated sites, 1280-1830 m.

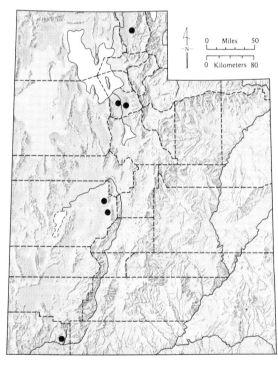

103. *Festuca bromoides* L. Annual fescue.
Apr.-June. Introduced annual; dry disturbed sites,
1310-1830 m.

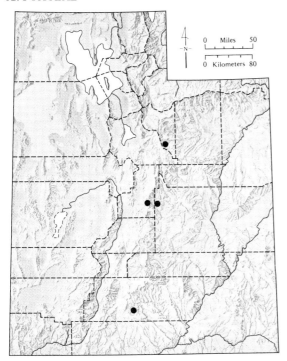

104. *Festuca dasyclada* Beal   Utah fescue.
June-Aug.   Native perennial; sagebrush, mountain
brush, juniper communities, 2130-3050 m.

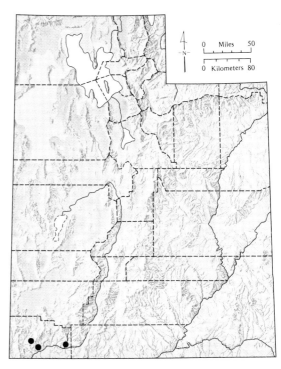

105. *Festuca microstachys* Nutt.   Small
fescue.   Apr.-June.   Native annual;   along
waterways, roadsides, dry open slopes, 1300-
1830 m.

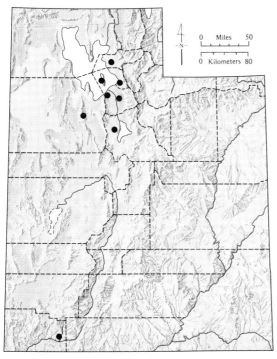

106. *Festuca myuros* L.   Myur fescue.   May-
June.   Introduced annual; saline meadows, salt
desert shrub communities, open slopes, roadsides,
1280-1830 m.

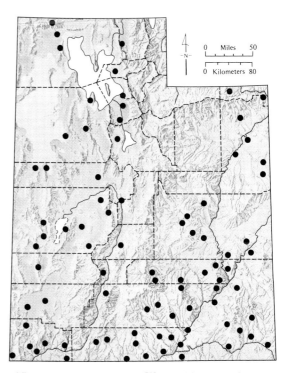

107. *Festuca octoflora* Walt.   Sixweeks fescue.
Mar.-July.   Native annual; creosote bush to pinyon-
juniper communities, 760-2290 m.

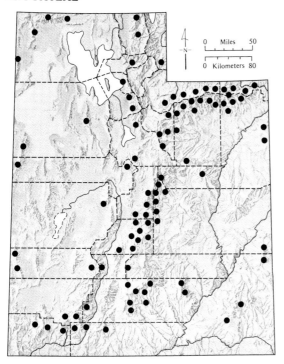

108. *Festuca ovina* L. Sheep fescue. June-Oct. Circumboreal perennial, often the dominant grass; sagebrush, openings in conifer communities, grassy and rocky alpine slopes, 1950-3960 m.

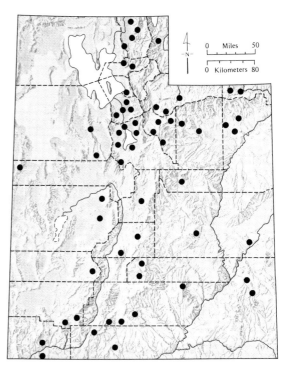

109. *Festuca pratensis* Huds. Meadow fescue. May-Sept. Introduced perennial; along waterways and roadsides, meadows, fallow fields, other disturbed sites, 1310-2900 m.

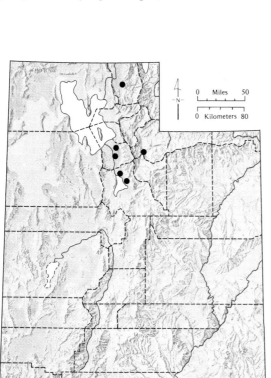

110. *Festuca rubra* L. Red fescue. May-Aug. Circumboreal perennial; in our area cultivated, escaping, possibly persistent, 1270-1370 m.

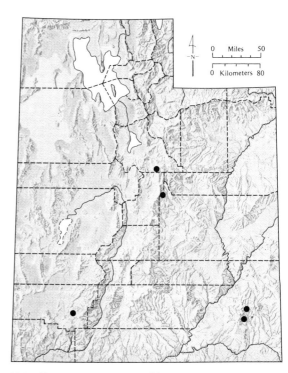

111. *Festuca sororia* Piper Ravine fescue. July-Aug. Native perennial; shaded sites in spruce-fir communities, 2440-3050 m.

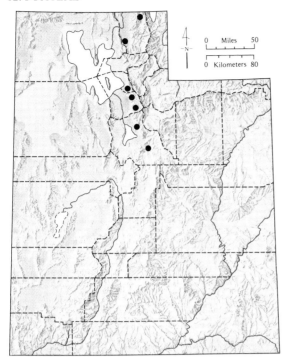

112. *Festuca subulata* Trin. Bearded fescue.
June-Aug. Native perennial; shaded sites in
mountain brush, aspen, spruce-fir communities,
1680-2320 m.

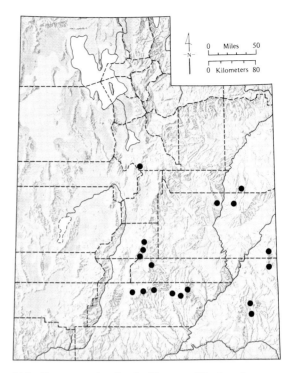

113. *Festuca thurberi* Vasey Thurber fescue.
June-Sept. Native perennial; shaded sites in aspen,
spruce-fir communities, 2130-3350 m.

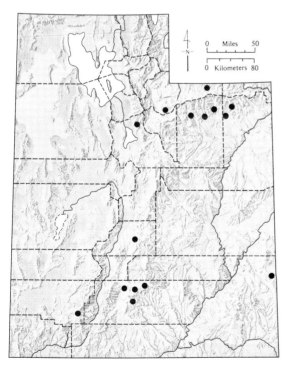

114. *Glyceria borealis* (Nash) Batch. Northern
mannagrass. June-Sept. Native perennial; wet
places in mountain brush to spruce-fir, lodgepole
pine, meadow communities, 1890-3140 m.

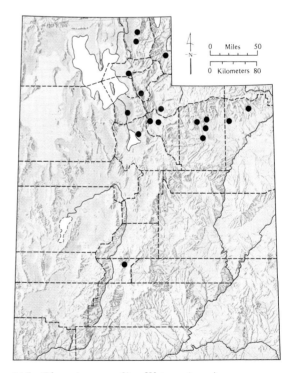

115. *Glyceria grandis* Wats. American mannagrass. June-Aug. Native perennial; along
waterways, wet meadows, 1310-2440 m.

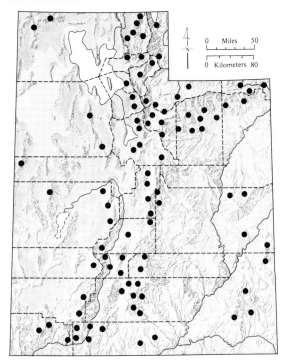

116. *Glyceria striata* (Lam.) Hitchc. Fowl mannagrass. May-Sept. Native perennial; wet sites in meadow, aspen-conifer communities, 1220-3200 m.

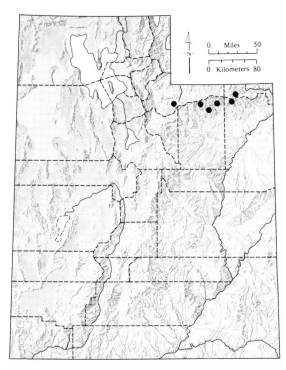

117. *Helictotrichon mortonianum* (Scribn.) Henr. Alpine oat. July-Sept. Native perennial; grass-sedge communities, along lake margins, open slopes above timberline, 3050-3720 m.

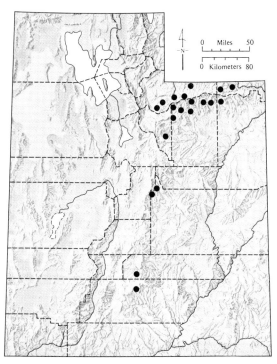

118. *Hierochlöe odorata* (L.) Beauv. Sweetgrass. May-Sept. Native perennial; wet meadows, streamside, lake shores, margins of spruce-fir and lodgepole pine communities, 2130-3500 m.

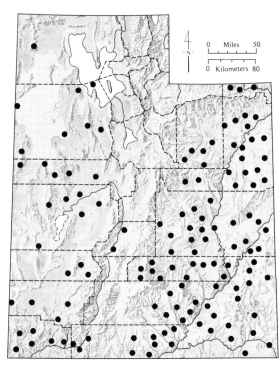

119. *Hilaria jamesii* (Torr.) Benth. Galleta; curlygrass. Apr.-Sept. Native perennial; creosote bush to pinyon-juniper communities, 1060-2130 m.

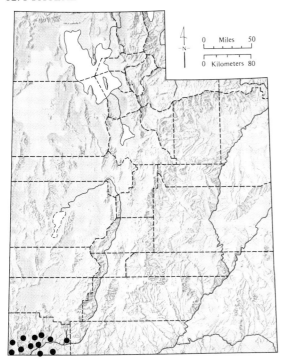

120. *Hilaria rigida* (Thurb.) Scribn. Big galleta. Apr.-Sept. Native perennial; creosote bush, shadscale communities, 760-1220 m.

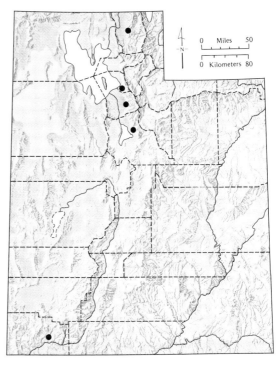

121. *Holcus lanatus* L. Yorkshirefog velvetgrass. June-Aug. Introduced perennial; disturbed sites, weed of lawns, 1210-1520 m.

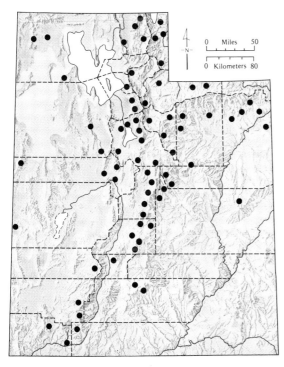

122. *Hordeum brachyantherum* Nevski Meadow barley. June-Sept. Introduced perennial; mesic to wet sites in spruce-fir communities, 1830-3200 m.

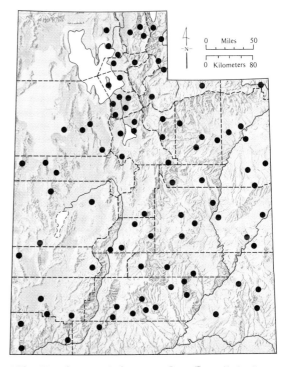

123. *Hordeum jubatum* L. Foxtail barley. May-Sept. Native perennial; roadsides, forming pure stands on moist saline sites, salt desert shrub to aspen-conifer communities, 1280-3200 m.

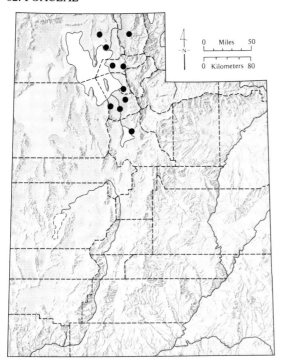

124. *Hordeum marinum* Huds. Mediterranean barley. May-July. Introduced annual; salt desert shrub, roadsides, dry waste places, 1200-1650 m.

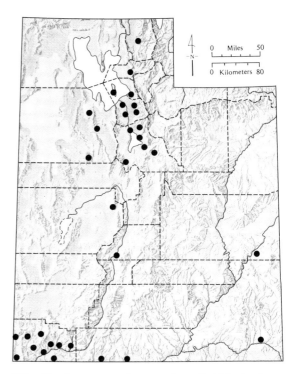

125. *Hordeum murinum* L. Rabbit barley. Apr.-Sept. Introduced annual; roadsides, weed of cultivated sites, waste places, 810-1830 m.

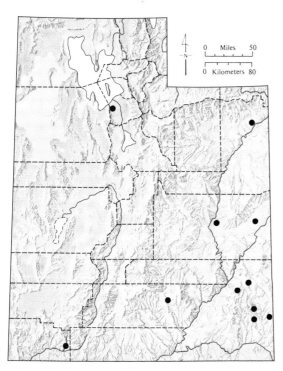

126. *Hordeum pusillum* Nutt. Little barley. Apr.-June. Native annual; salt desert shrub to pinyon-juniper communities, 1280-1980 m.

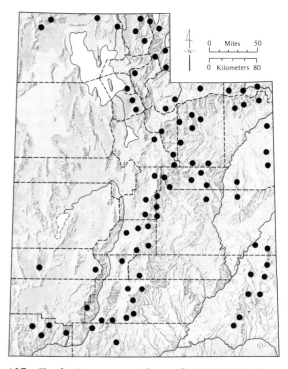

127. *Koeleria macrantha* (Ledeb.) Schultes Junegrass. May-Sept. Native perennial; sagebrush, mountain brush, pinyon-juniper communities, 1370-3480 m.

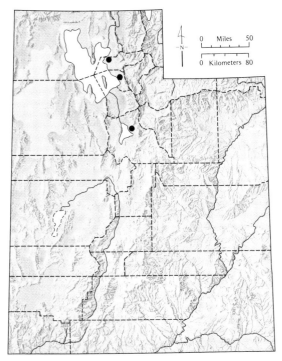

128. *Leersia oryzoides* (L.) Swartz Rice cutgrass. July-Oct. Native perennial; wet, heavily vegetated sites along waterways and in marshes, 1270-1400 m.

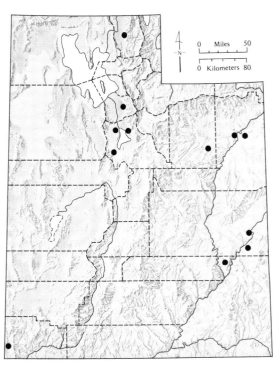

129. *Leptochloa fascicularis* (Lam.) Gray Bearded sprangletop. July-Oct. Native annual; wet or drying margins of waterways, lakes, ponds, 1310-2740 m.

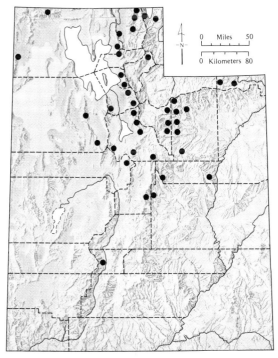

130. *Leucopoa kingii* (Wats.) W. A. Weber Spike fescue. May-Aug. Native perennial; open sites in oak-sagebrush, aspen, spruce-fir, alpine communities, 1370-3660 m.

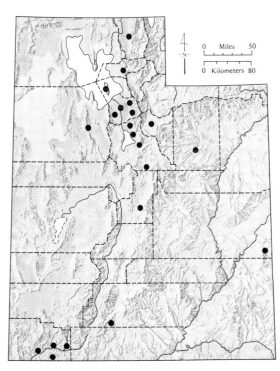

131. *Lolium perenne* L. Ryegrass. May-Sept. Introduced annual to perennial; cultivated, escaping and persistent in dry to moist sites, 770-2430 m.

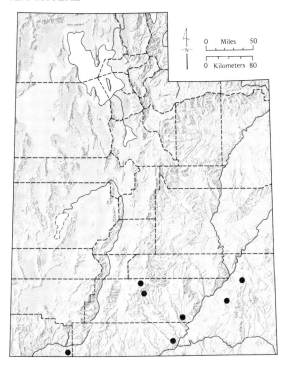

132. *Lycurus phleoides* H. B. K. Wolftail. June-Oct. Native perennial; open slopes and rock crevices in desert shrub, juniper communities, 1520-2130 m.

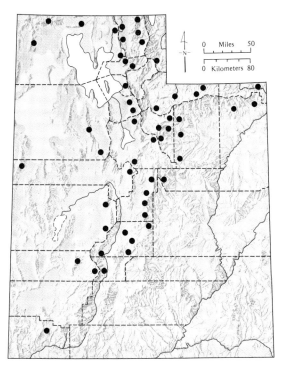

133. *Melica bulbosa* Port. & Coult. Oniongrass. May-Sept. Native perennial; open slopes in sagebrush to aspen, ponderosa pine communities, 1520-3200 m.

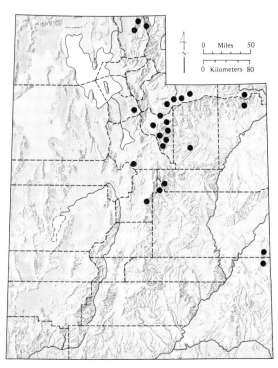

134. *Melica spectabilis* Scribn. Purple oniongrass. May-Aug. Native perennial; sagebrush to aspen, meadow communities, 1980-3200 m.

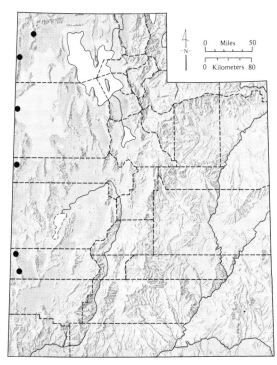

135. *Melica stricta* Bol. Rock melic. June-Aug. Native perennial; rocky slopes, open woods, 1520-2750 m.

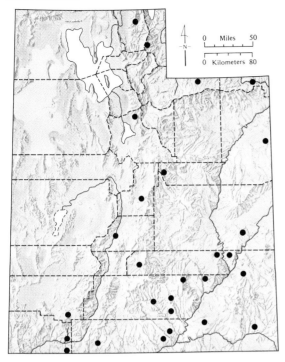

136. *Muhlenbergia andina* (Nutt.) Hitchc. Foxtail muhly. May-Sept. Native perennial; streamside, wet cliffs, 1370-2900 m.

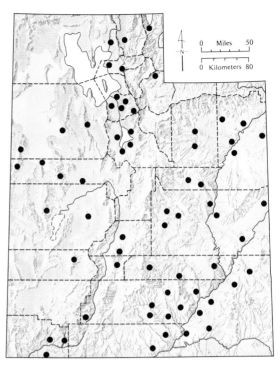

137. *Muhlenbergia asperifolia* (Nees & Mey.) Parodi Scratchgrass. May-Sept. Native perennial; along waterways, meadows in salt desert shrub to pinyon-juniper communities, often a weed of cultivated sites, 1000-2130 m.

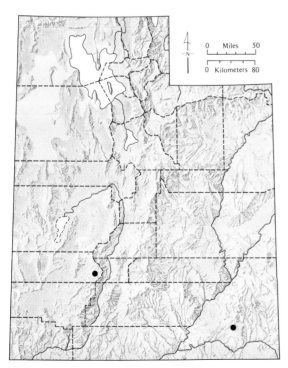

138. *Muhlenbergia depauperata* Scribn. Sixweeks muhly. July-Sept. Native annual; sagebrush, pinyon-juniper communities, 1370-2900 m.

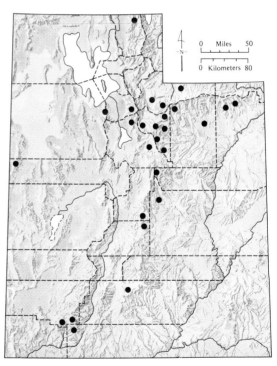

139. *Muhlenbergia filiformis* (Thurb.) Rydb. Pullup muhly. June-Oct. Native annual; wet meadows, wet to mesic sites in sagebrush, aspen, spruce-fir, lodgepole pine communities, 1280-3200 m.

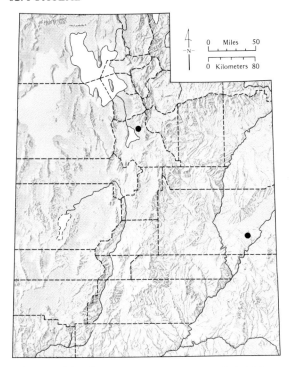

140. *Muhlenbergia mexicana* (L.) Trin. Mexican muhly. Aug.-Nov. Native perennial; along waterways and in other moist, often disturbed sites, 1390-1520 m.

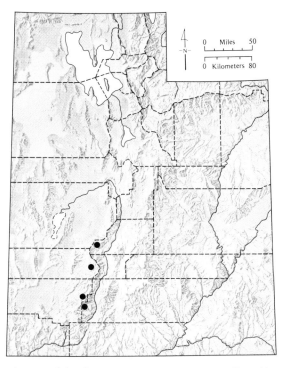

141. *Muhlenbergia minutissima* (Steud.) Swall. Annual muhly. June-Oct. Native annual; dry to mesic, open sites in sagebrush, pinyon-juniper, aspen, spruce communities, 1830-2740 m.

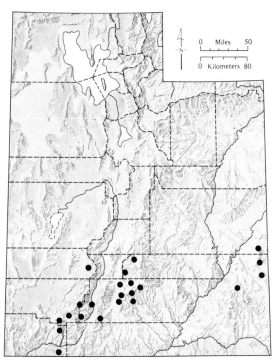

142. *Muhlenbergia montana* (Nutt.) Hitchc. Mountain muhly. July-Sept. Native perennial; grassy slopes, open sites in sagebrush, aspen, spruce-fir, ponderosa pine communities, 1820-3280 m.

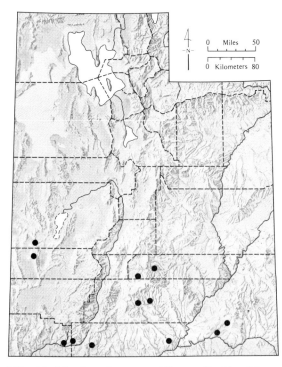

143. *Muhlenbergia pauciflora* Buckl. New Mexican muhly. Aug.-Oct. Native perennial; desert shrub to pinyon-juniper, ponderosa pine communities, 1520-2130 m.

442

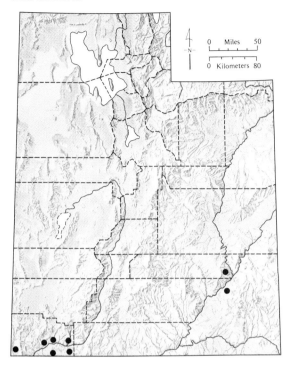

144. *Muhlenbergia porteri* Beal Bush muhly. Apr.-Dec. Native perennial; creosote bush, desert shrub communities, 760-1310 m.

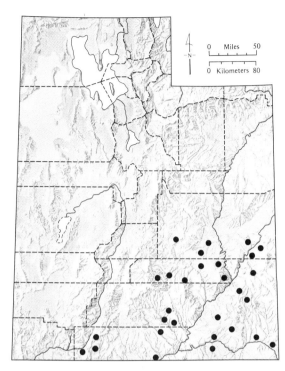

145. *Muhlenbergia pungens* Thurb. Sandhill muhly. June-Oct. Native perennial; desert shrub to pinyon-juniper communities, 1070-1980 m.

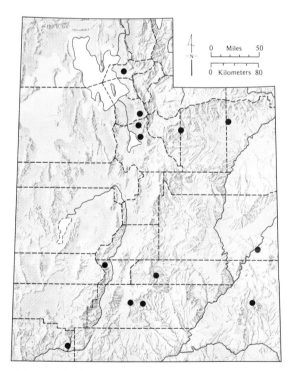

146. *Muhlenbergia racemosa* (Michx.) B.S.P. Green muhly. June-Oct. Native perennial; open slopes, hanging gardens, mountain brush, aspen, ponderosa pine, meadow communities, 1220-3050 m.

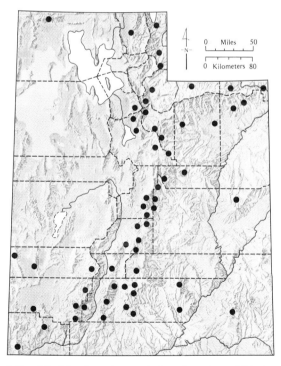

147. *Muhlenbergia richardsonis* (Trin.) Rydb. Mat muhly. June-Sept. Native perennial; sagebrush to aspen, spruce-fir, ponderosa pine, meadow communities, 1680-3200 m.

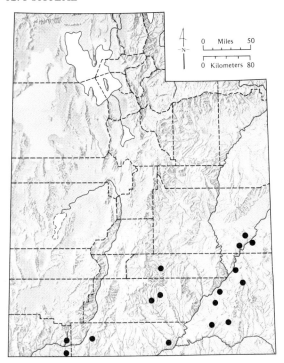

148. *Muhlenbergia thurberi* Rydb. Thurber muhly. May-Oct. Native perennial; hanging gardens, desert shrub, pinyon-juniper, ponderosa pine communities, 1130-2500 m.

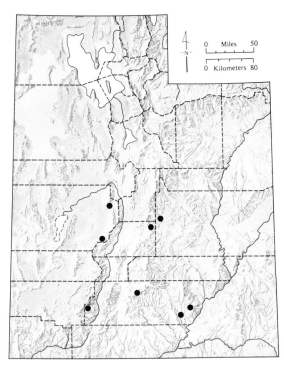

149. *Muhlenbergia wrightii* Coult. Spike muhly. June-Sept. Native perennial; desert shrub to pinyon-juniper, ponderosa pine communities, 1370-2740 m.

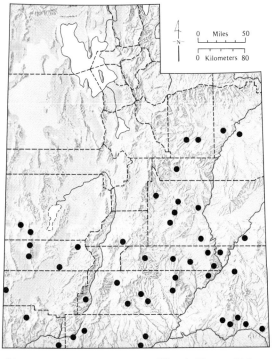

150. *Munroa squarrosa* (Nutt.) Torr. False buffalograss. July-Sept. Native annual; salt desert shrub to pinyon-juniper communities, 1280-2930 m.

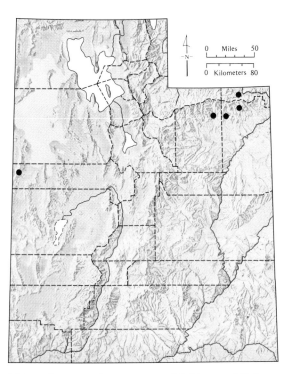

151. *Oryzopsis asperifolia* Michx. Roughleaf ricegrass. May-Aug. Native perennial; shaded sites in aspen, ponderosa pine, lodgepole pine communities, 2250-2770 m.

444

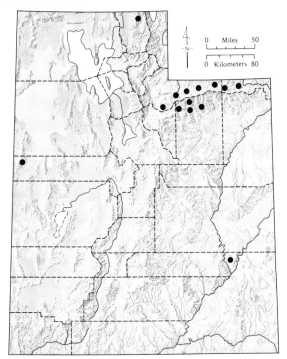

152. *Oryzopsis exigua* Thurb. Little ricegrass.
May-Aug. Native perennial; dry, open, often rocky
sites and aspen-fir, lodgepole pine communities,
1820-2900 m.

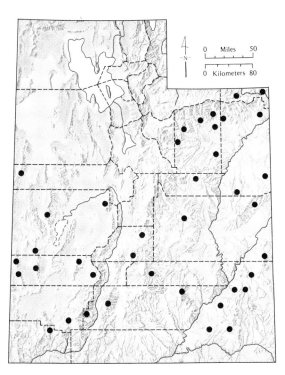

153. *Oryzopsis micrantha* (T. & R.) Thurb.
Littleseed ricegrass. May-Sept. Native perennial;
sagebrush, mountain brush, pinyon-juniper,
ponderosa pine communities, 1380-2930 m.

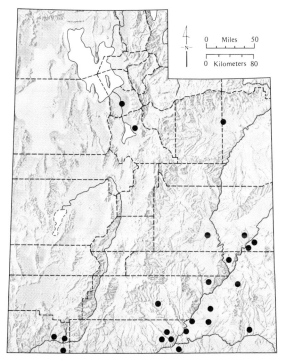

154. *Panicum acuminatum* Swartz Bundle
panicgrass. May-Oct. Native perennial; hanging
gardens, along waterways, 1070-2230 m.

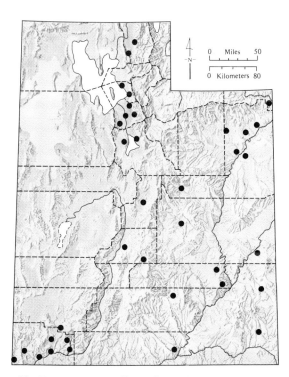

155. *Panicum capillare* L. Witchgrass. July-
Oct. Native annual; salt desert shrub, desert shrub,
along waterways, roadsides, other waste places,
850-1830 m.

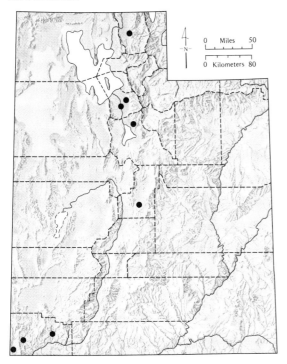

156. *Panicum miliaceum* L. Broomcorn panicgrass. July-Oct. Introduced annual; cultivated, escaping and persisting as a weed of gardens and waste places, 850-1830 m.

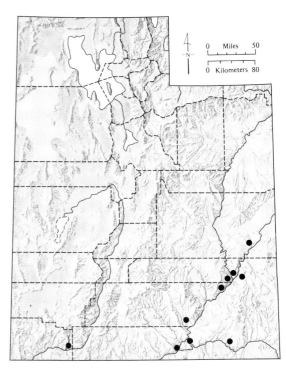

157. *Panicum obtusum* H. B. K. Vine mesquite. June-Oct. Native perennial; along waterways, open hillsides, sandstone ledges, 1010-1830 m.

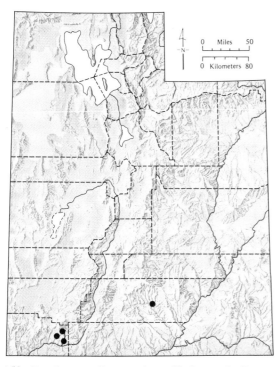

158. *Panicum oligosanthes* Shultes Scribner panicgrass. May-Aug. Native perennial; moist sandy soil or rock crevices in hanging garden, ponderosa pine communities, 850-2130 m.

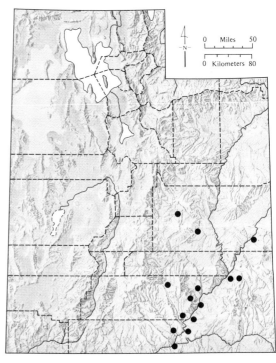

159. *Panicum virgatum* L. Switchgrass. June-Sept. Native perennial; along waterways, hanging gardens, 1030-1830 m.

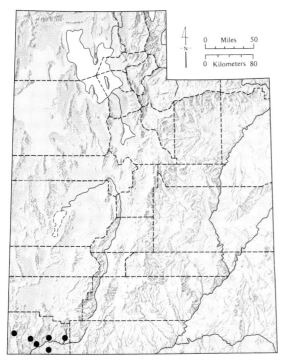

160. *Paspalum distichum* L. Knotgrass. July-Nov. Native perennial; along waterways, saline meadows, desert shrub communities, 820-1520 m.

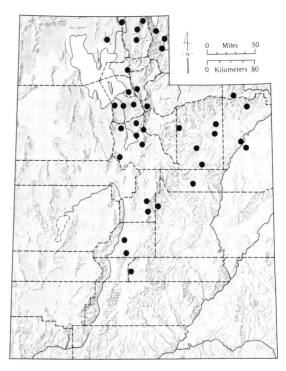

161. *Phalaris arundinacea* L. Reed canarygrass; ribbongrass. June-Oct. Circumboreal perennial; along waterways, wet meadows, 1290-2750 m.

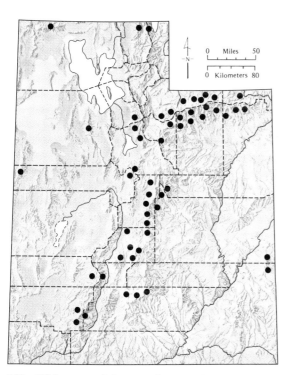

162. *Phleum alpinum* L. Alpine Timothy. June-Oct. Native perennial; streamside, mesic to wet meadows, openings in aspen, spruce-fir and ponderosa pine communities, 2130-3660 m.

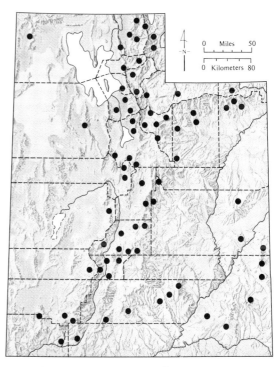

163. *Phleum pratense* L. Timothy. June-Sept. Introduced perennial; along roadsides and waterways, mountain brush and aspen, spruce-fir communities, 1310-3200 m.

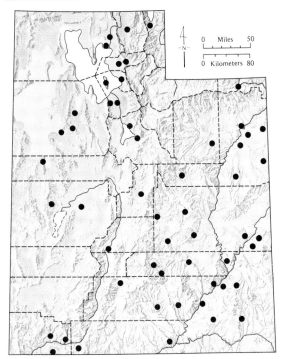

164. ***Phragmites australis*** (Cav.) Steud.
Common reed. June-Oct. Cosmopolitan perennial;
along waterways, fresh or salt water marshes, 970-
1980 m.

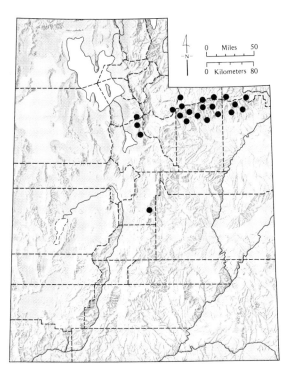

165. ***Poa alpina*** L. Alpine bluegrass. June-
Sept. Circumboreal perennial; meadows, along
streams and lake margins, conifer communities,
exposed rocky slopes above timberline, 2440-
3960 m.

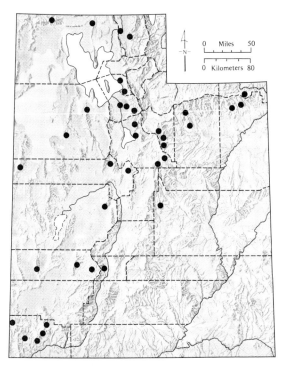

166. ***Poa annua*** L. Annual bluegrass. Apr.-Nov.
Annual to occasionally perennial; salt desert shrub
to montane meadow communities, invader of lawns
and other irrigated sites, 1220-2960 m.

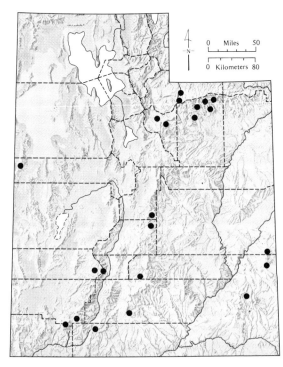

167. ***Poa arctica*** R. Br. Arctic bluegrass. July-
Aug. Circumboreal perennial; open slopes,
streamside, in aspen, spruce-fir, lodgepole pine,
meadow communities, 2560-3960 m.

448

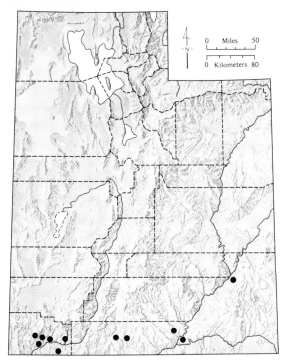

168. **Poa bigelovii** Vasey & Scribn. Bigelow
bluegrass. Mar.-May. Native annual; creosote
bush, desert shrub, juniper communities, 820-
1520 m.

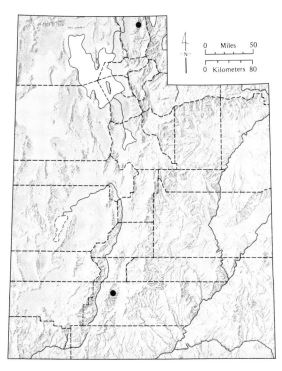

169. **Poa bolanderi** Vasey Bolander bluegrass.
July-Sept. Native annual; dry to moist, open or
wooded habitats, 1520-2620 m.

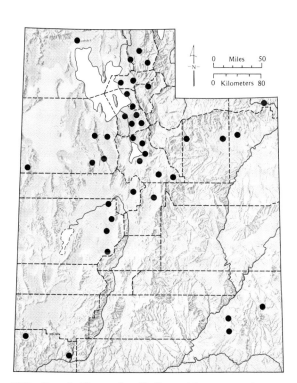

170. **Poa bulbosa** L. Bulbous bluegrass. Apr.-
July. Introduced perennial; weed of gardens and
waste places, streamside, sagebrush to conifer
communities, 1200-3000 m.

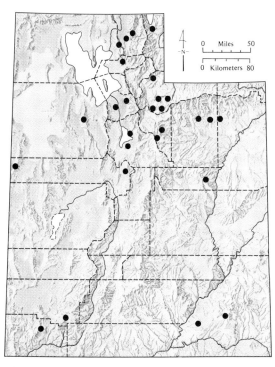

171. **Poa compressa** L. Canada bluegrass.
June-Sept. Introduced perennial; along waterways,
fallow fields and pastures, sagebrush to conifer
communities, often in the wake of disturbance,
1300-2600 m.

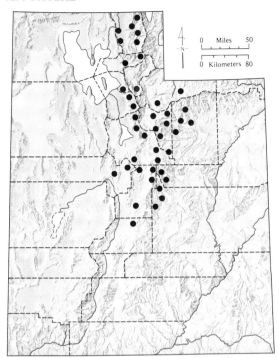

172. ***Poa curta*** Rydb. Wasatch bluegrass. May-Aug. Native perennial; shaded sites in oak-maple, aspen, spruce-fir communities, 1680-3200 m.

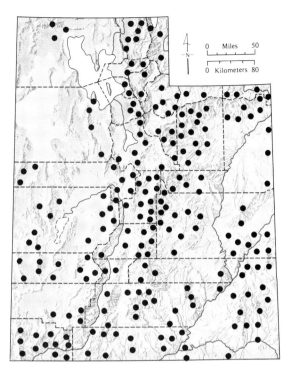

173. ***Poa fendleriana*** (Steud.) Vasey Muttongrass. Mar.-Aug. Native perennial; sagebrush, pinyon-juniper, mountain brush, ponderosa pine, openings in aspen-spruce-fir communities, exposed alpine slopes, 910-3660 m.

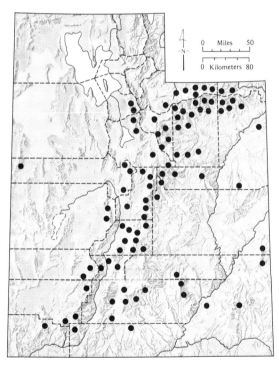

174. ***Poa glauca*** Vahl Greenland bluegrass. June-Sept. Circumboreal perennial; openings in aspen to conifer communities, alpine meadows, exposed rocky ridges, 2740-3740 m.

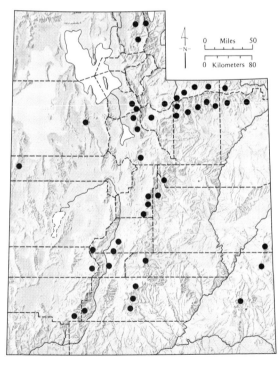

175. ***Poa leptocoma*** Trin. Bog bluegrass. June-Aug. Native perennial; shaded sites in aspen, spruce-fir, lodgepole pine communities, meadows, streamside, moist open slopes, 2130-3570 m.

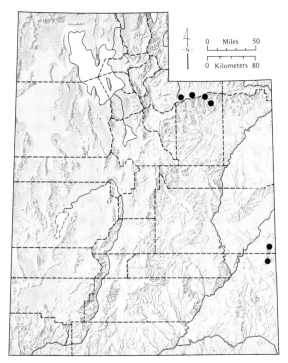

176. **Poa lettermanii** Vasey Letterman bluegrass. July-Aug. Native perennial; meadows, exposed, often rocky slopes, 3050-4000 m.

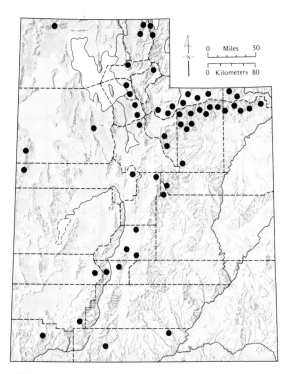

177. **Poa nervosa** (Hook.) Vasey Wheeler bluegrass. June-Sept. Native perennial; mountain brush, aspen, spruce-fir, lodgepole pine communities, krummholz, exposed rocky slopes, 1980-3660 m.

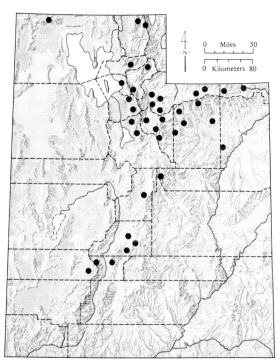

178. **Poa palustris** L. Fowl bluegrass. June-Sept. Circumboreal perennial; along waterways, moist meadows, damp woods, 1370-2900 m.

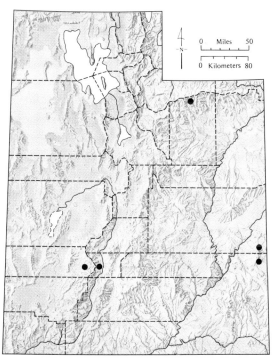

179. **Poa pattersonii** Vasey Patterson bluegrass. July-Aug. Native perennial; exposed rocky slopes at or above timberline, 3350-4000 m.

451

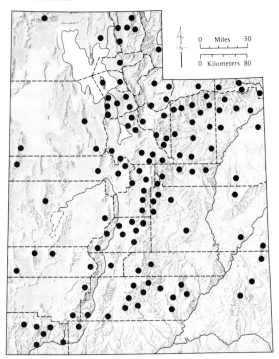

180. *Poa pratensis* L. Kentucky bluegrass. May-Aug. Circumboreal perennial; cultivated strains naturalized and occupying mesic to moist sites in greasewood to aspen-conifer communities, 1280-3290 m.

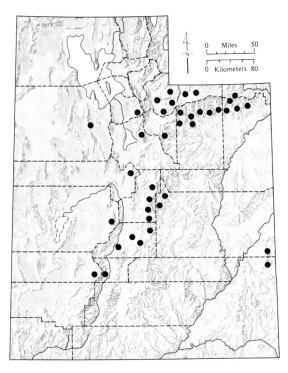

181. *Poa reflexa* Vasey & Scribn. Nodding bluegrass. June-Sept. Native perennial; spruce-fir communities, moist open slopes, 2550-3660 m.

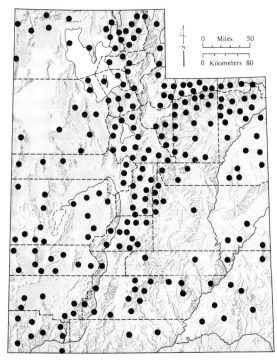

182. *Poa secunda* Presl Sandberg bluegrass. Apr.-Sept. Native perennial, often the dominant grass; salt desert shrub to aspen-conifer communities, meadows, exposed alpine slopes, 1280-3660 m.

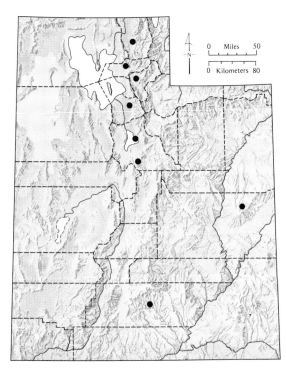

183. *Poa trivialis* L. Rough-stalked bluegrass. May-Aug. Introduced perennial; along waterways, wet meadows, moist woods, 1280-2440 m.

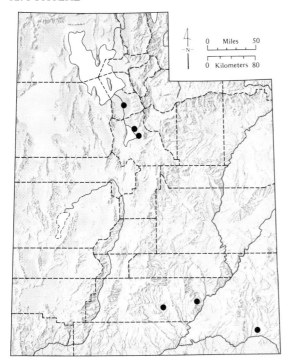

184. *Polypogon interruptus* H. B. K. Ditch polypogon. June-July. Native annual or perennial of hybrid origin; disturbed moist sites along waterways, pastures, 1270-1580 m.

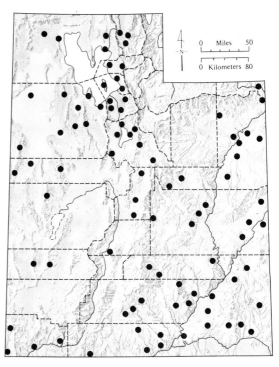

185. *Polypogon monspeliensis* (L.) Desf. Rabbitfoot grass. May-Aug. Introduced annual; along waterways, marshes, salt tolerant, 820-2130 m.

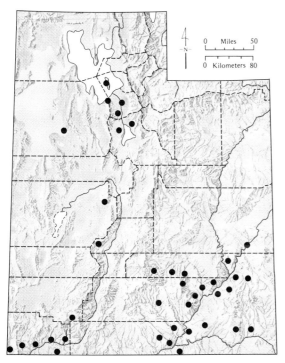

186. *Polypogon semiverticillatus* (Forsk.) Hylander Water polypogon. May-Oct. Introduced perennial; moist places, especially along waterways, 665-2130 m.

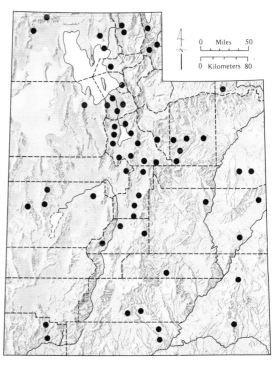

187. *Puccinellia distans* (L.) Parl. Weeping alkaligrass. May-Sept. Introduced perennial; moist sites in salt desert shrub communities, along waterways, in meadows, occasionally in conifer forests, 1070-2620 m.

453

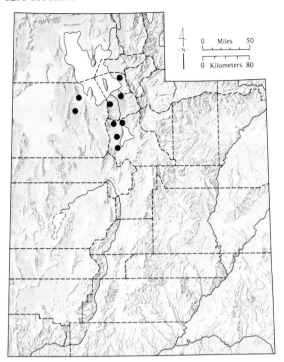

188. *Puccinellia fasciculata* (Torr.) Bickn. Torrey alkali grass. May-Sept. Introduced perennial; moist sites in salt desert shrub communities, 1280-1370 m.

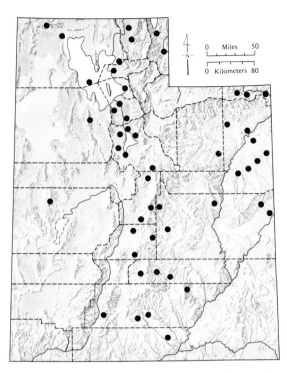

189. *Puccinellia nuttalliana* (Schultes) Hitchc. Nuttall alkaligrass. May-Sept. Native perennial; moist sites in salt desert shrub communities, meadows, along waterways, 1280-2620 m.

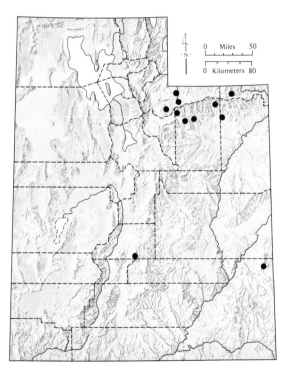

190. *Puccinellia pauciflora* (Presl) Munz Weak mannagrass. June-Sept. Native perennial; streamside in conifer forests, wet meadows, 2130-3230 m.

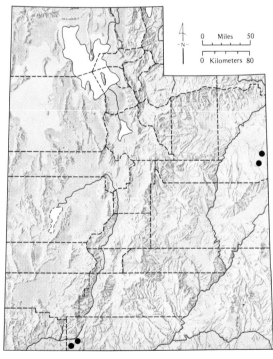

191. *Redfieldia flexuosa* (Thurb.) Vasey Blowout grass. July-Sept. Native perennial; sand dunes in desert shrub, pinyon-juniper communities, 1490-1830 m.

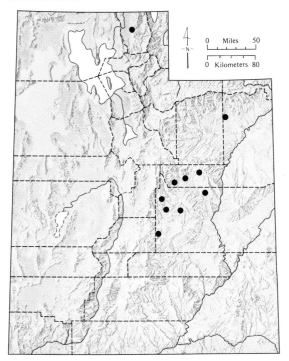

192. *Schedonnardus paniculatus* (Nutt.) Trel. Tumblegrass. May-Oct. Native perennial; disturbed sites, 1360-1830 m.

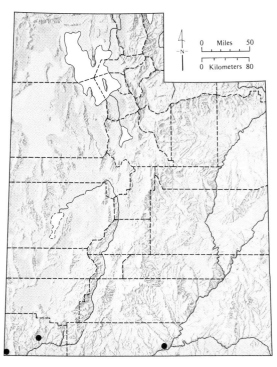

193. *Schismus arabicus* Nees Arabian Mediterranean grass. Mar.-May. Introduced annual; creosote bush, desert shrub communities, 910-1370 m.

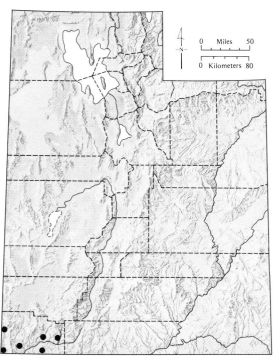

194. *Schismus barbatus* (L.) Thell. Mediterranean grass. Apr.-May. Introduced annual; creosote bush to pinyon-juniper communities, 760-1370 m.

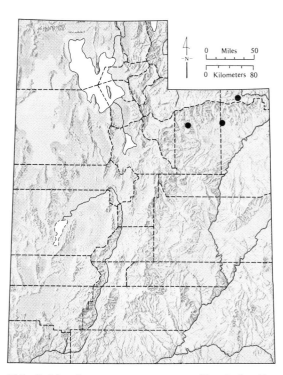

195. *Schizachne purpurascens* (Torr.) Swall. False medic. June-Aug. Native perennial; mesic to wet sites in aspen, lodgepole pine, ponderosa pine communities, 2030-2500 m.

82. POACEAE

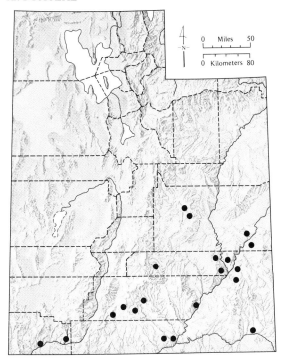

196. *Schizachyrium scoparium* (Michx.) Nash Little bluestem. Aug.-Oct. Native perennial; along waterways, hanging garden, desert shrub, pinyon-juniper, ponderosa pine communities, 1070-2290 m.

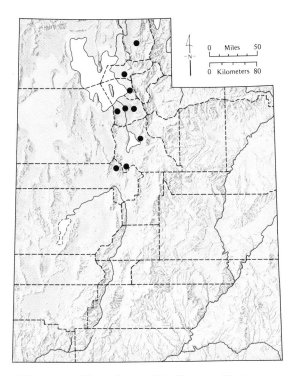

197. *Sclerochloa dura* (L.) Beauv. Hardgrass. Apr.-June. Introduced annual; dry waste places, 1300-1520 m.

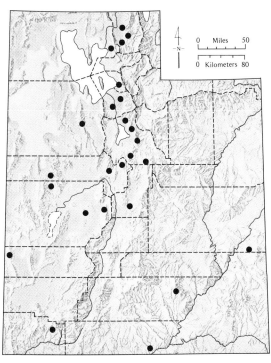

198. *Secale cereale* L. Rye. May-Sept. Introduced annual; cultivated, commonly escaping along roadsides, 1280-2900 m.

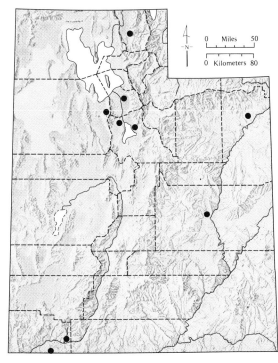

199. *Setaria glauca* (L.) Beauv. Yellow bristlegrass. Aug.-Sept. Introduced annual; dry waste places, 850-1520 m.

456

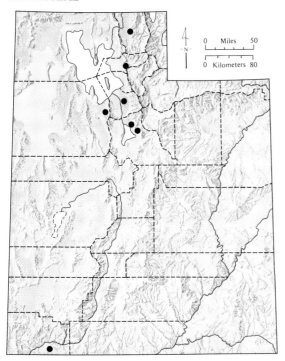

200. *Setaria verticillata* (L.) Beauv. Bur bristlegrass. July-Sept. Introduced annual; dry waste places, 850-1520 m.

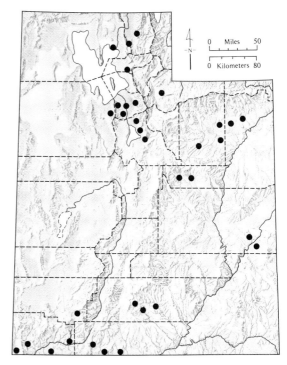

201. *Setaria viridis* (L.) Beauv. Green bristlegrass. July-Oct. Introduced annual; dry waste places, 1280-2130 m.

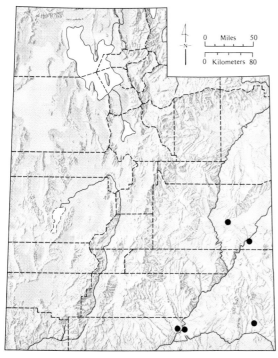

202. *Sorghastrum nutans* (L.) Nash Indiangrass. Aug.-Sept. Introduced perennial; hanging gardens, along washes, disturbed sites, 1200-2130 m.

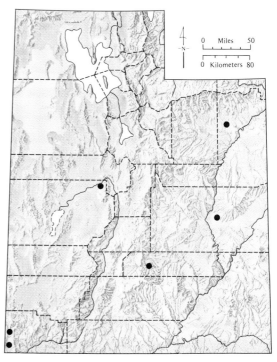

203. *Sorghum bicolor* (L.) Moench Milo; grain sorghum. July-Sept. Introduced annual; cultivated and escaping, 790-1500 m.

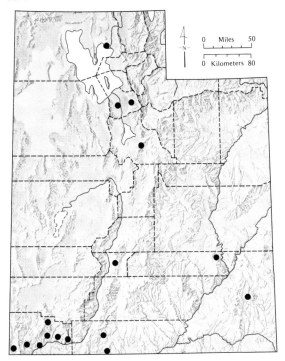

204. *Sorghum halepense* (L.) Pers. Johnson grass; millet. May-Oct. Introduced perennial; along waterways, moist waste places, 820-1500 m.

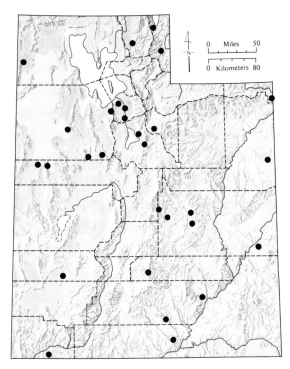

205. *Spartina gracilis* Trin. Alkali cordgrass. June-Sept. Native perennial; along waterways, wet meadows, hanging gardens, 1220-1980 m.

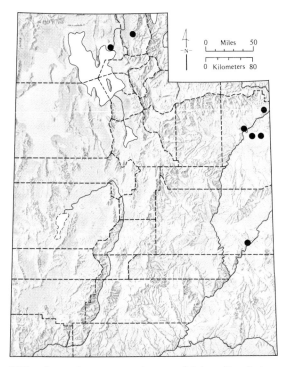

206. *Spartina pectinata* Link Prairie cordgrass; slough grass. June-Sept. Native perennial; wet, often saline sites along waterways and in wet meadows, 1210-1520 m.

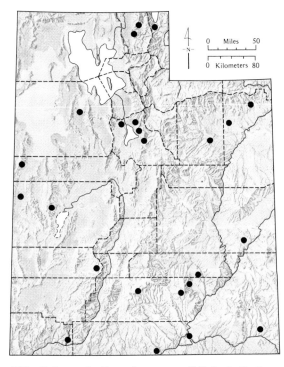

207. *Sphenopholis obtusata* (Michx.) Scribn. Prairie wedgegrass. June-Aug. Native annual to perennial; along waterways, in meadows, aspen, spruce-fir communities, 1220-2740 m.

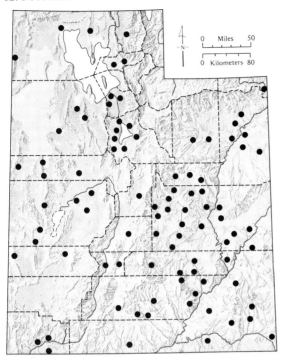

208. *Sporobolus airoides* (Torr.) Torr. Alkali sacaton. May-Oct. Native perennial; dry to moist sites in salt desert shrub, sagebrush, pinyon-juniper communities, 800-2350 m.

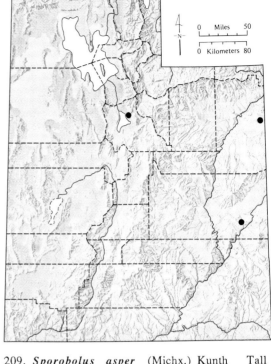

209. *Sporobolus asper* (Michx.) Kunth Tall dropseed. July-Sept. Native perennial; juniper communities, 1360-1530 m.

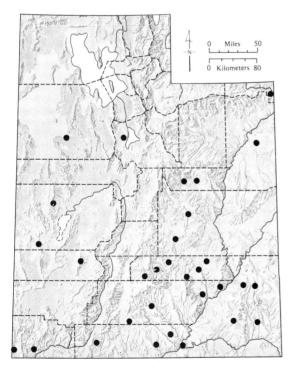

210. *Sporobolus contractus* Hitchc. Spike dropseed. May-Aug. Native perennial; salt desert shrub to pinyon-juniper communities, 1270-1980 m.

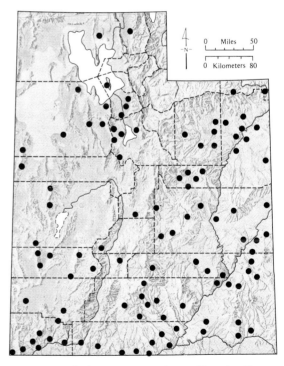

211. *Sporobolus cryptandrus* (Torr.) Gray Sand dropseed. Apr.-Oct. Native perennial; roadsides and other waste places in salt desert shrub to ponderosa pine communities, 850-2870 m.

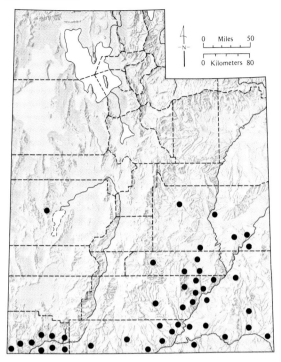

212. *Sporobolus flexuosus* (Thurb.) Rydb. Mesa dropseed. May-Nov. Native perennial; desert shrub, sagebrush, pinyon-juniper communities, 850-1710 m.

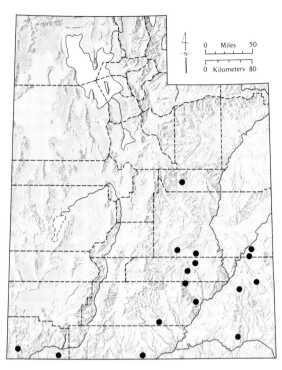

213. *Sporobolus giganteus* Nash Giant dropseed. May-Nov. Native perennial; desert shrub, juniper communities, often on sand dunes or roadsides, 1060-1830 m.

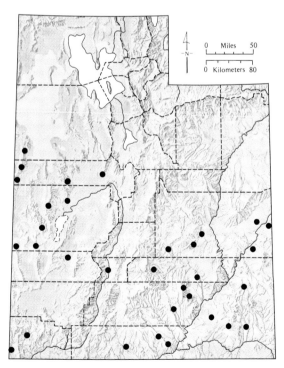

214. *Stipa arida* Jones Mormon needlegrass. May-July. Native perennial; shadscale, desert shrub, sagebrush, pinyon-juniper communities, 1050-2300 m.

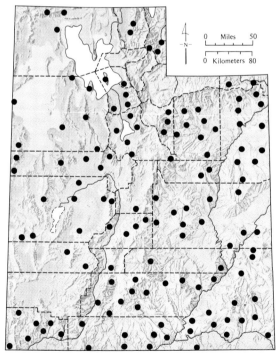

215. *Stipa comata* Trin. & Rupr. Needle-and-thread grass. Apr.-Sept. Native perennial, often the dominant grass; salt desert shrub to mountain brush communities, 1060-3050 m.

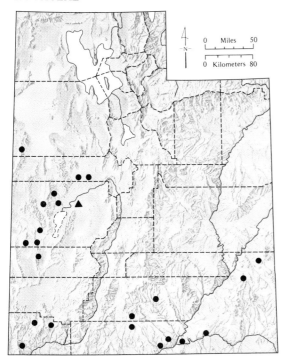

216. *Stipa coronata* Thurb. Crested needlegrass. May-Sept. Native perennial; salt desert shrub to pinyon-juniper communities, 1500-2700 m.

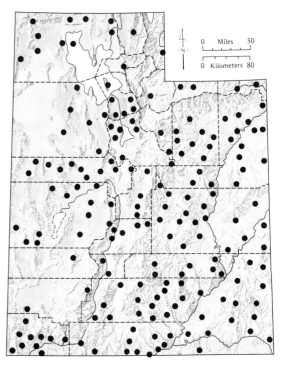

217. *Stipa hymenoides* R. & S. Indian ricegrass. May-Sept. Native perennial; creosote bush, salt desert shrub, sagebrush, mountain brush, pinyon-juniper, ponderosa pine communities, 750-2750 m.

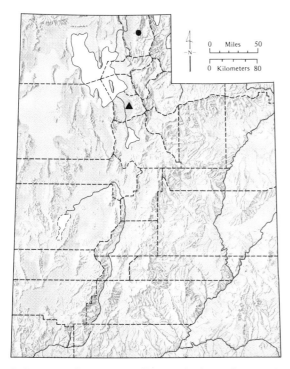

218. *Stipa lemmonii* (Vasey) Scribn. Lemmon needlegrass. June-July. Native perennial; sagebrush-grass communities, open woods, 1830-2280 m.

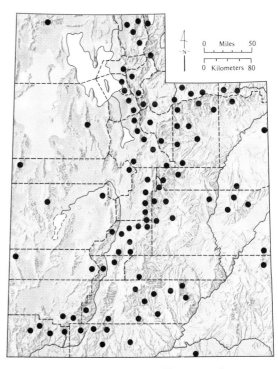

219. *Stipa lettermanii* Vasey Letterman needlegrass. June-Oct. Native perennial; sagebrush to pinyon-juniper, aspen-conifer communities, 1500-3570 m.

461

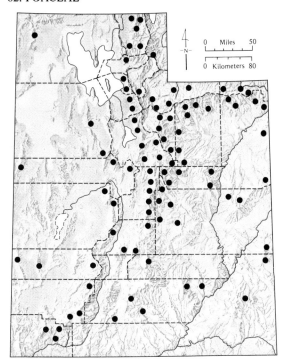

220. *Stipa nelsonii* Scribn. Nelson needlegrass. June-Sept. Native perennial; sagebrush to aspen-conifer communities, exposed alpine ridges, 1500-3350 m.

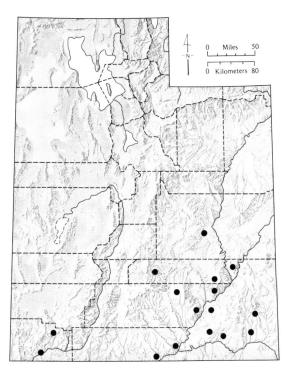

221. *Stipa neomexicana* (Thurb.) Scribn. New Mexico feathergrass. Apr.-June. Native perennial; desert shrub, pinyon-juniper communities, 910-2000 m.

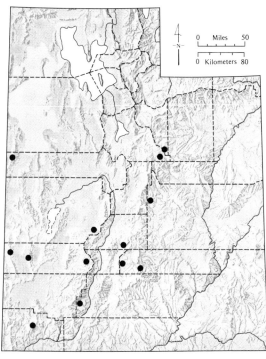

222. *Stipa pinetorum* Jones Pinewoods needlegrass. June-Aug. Native perennial; sagebrush to ponderosa pine communities, 2000-2900 m.

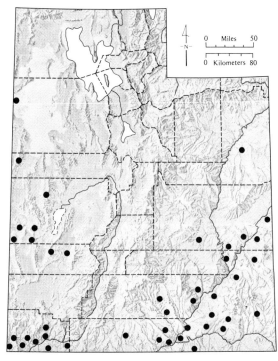

223. *Stipa speciosa* Trin. & Rupr. Desert needlegrass. Apr.-June. Native perennial; Joshua tree to pinyon-juniper communities, 800-1900 m.

462

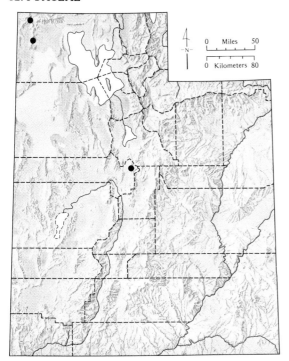

224. *Stipa thurberiana* Piper Thurber needlegrass. Apr.-July. Native perennial; sagebrush to pinyon-juniper communities, 1650-1980 m.

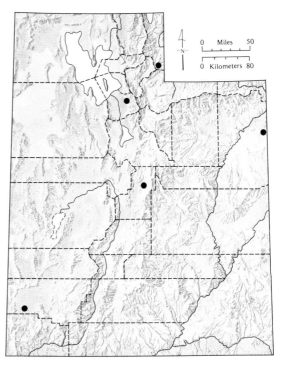

225. *Stipa viridula* Trin. Green needlegrass. June-July. Native perennial; roadsides, grass-sagebrush communities, 1370-2150 m.

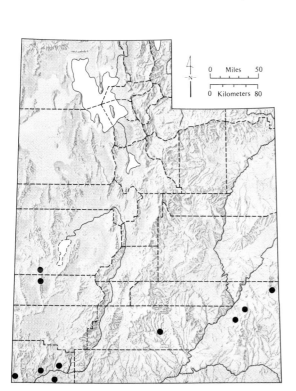

226. *Tridens muticus* (Torr.) Nash Slim tridens. May-Sept. Native perennial; creosote bush, desert shrub, sagebrush, pinyon-juniper communities, 665-1750 m.

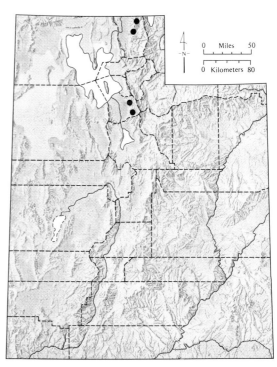

227. *Trisetum canescens* Buckl. Tall trisetum. July-Aug. Native perennial; shaded sites in maple, aspen, spruce-fir communities, on moist open slopes, 1980-2440 m.

82. POACEAE

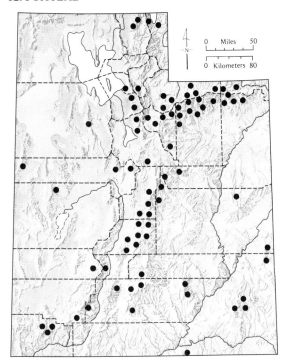

228. ***Trisetum spicatum*** (L.) Richt. Spike trisetum. June-Sept. Circumboreal perennial; dry to wet sites, aspen-conifer, meadow communities, exposed rocky slopes, 1830-4000 m.

229. ***Trisetum wolfii*** Vasey Wolf trisetum. June-Sept. Native perennial; aspen, spruce-fir communities, meadows, 2600-4000 m.

83. POLEMONIACEAE

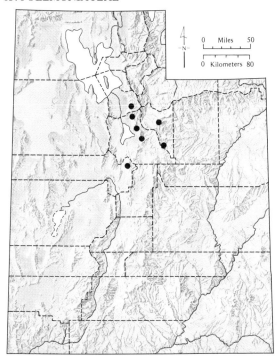

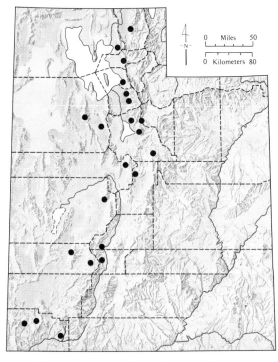

1. ***Collomia debilis*** (Wats.) Greene Alpine collomia. June-Aug. Native perennial herb; talus, rock crevices, 2570-3640 m.

2. ***Collomia grandiflora*** Lindl. June-Aug. Native annual; mountain brush to aspen-fir communities, 1450-2430 m.

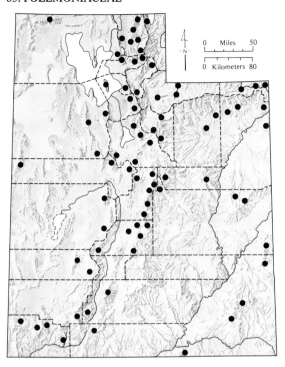

3. **Collomia linearis** Nutt. May-July. Native annual; sagebrush to aspen-fir communities, 1480-3250 m.

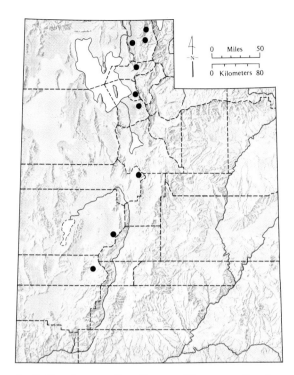

4. **Collomia tenella** Gray Mazama collomia. June-July. Native annual; sagebrush to aspen-fir communities, 1660-2730 m.

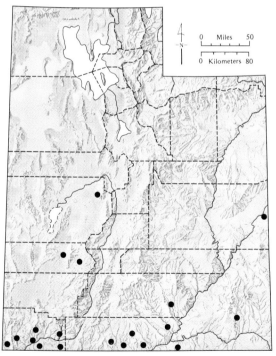

5. **Eriastrum diffusum** (Gray) Mason Spreading eriastrum. May-June. Native annual; creosote bush to pinyon-juniper communities, 1360-1820 m.

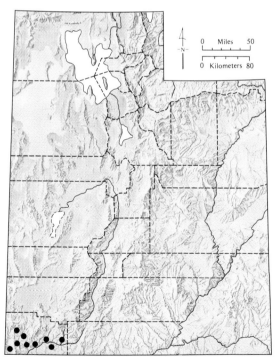

6. **Eriastrum eremicum** (Jeps.) Mason Desert eriastrum. May-June. Native annual; creosote bush, desert shrub communities, 840-1400 m.

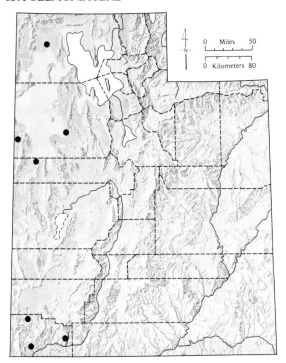

7. *Eriastrum sparsiflorum* (Eastw.) Mason Great Basin eriastrum. May-June. Native annual; desert shrub communities, 1300-1520 m.

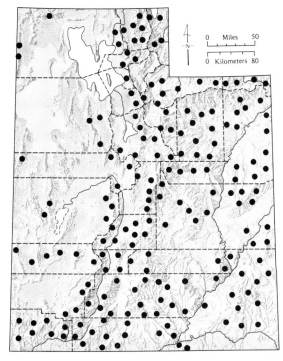

8. *Gilia aggregata* (Pursh) Spreng. Scarlet gilia; skyrocket. May-Aug. Native biennial or perennial; sagebrush to conifer communities, 1000-3330 m.

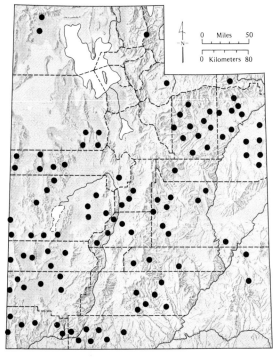

9. *Gilia congesta* Hook. Ballhead gilia. May-Sept. Native perennial herb; salt desert shrub, desert shrub, pinyon-juniper communities, 1060-2730 m.

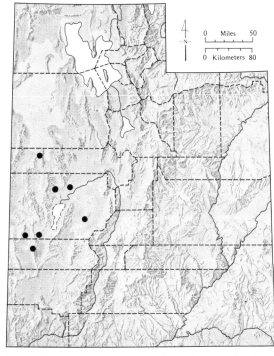

10. *Gilia depressa* Jones May-June. Native annual; salt desert shrub, desert shrub communities, 1360-1820 m.

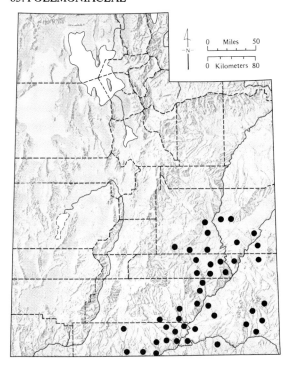

11. *Gilia gunnisonii* T. & G. Gunnison or sand-dune gilia. May-Nov. Native annual; desert shrub communities, 1090-1820 m.

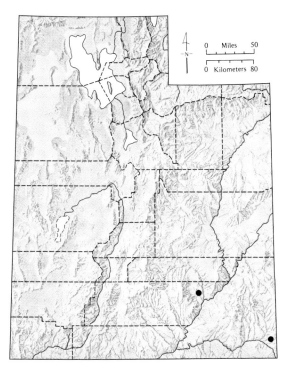

12. *Gilia haydenii* Gray San Juan gilia. May-July. Native biennial; desert shrub to ponderosa pine communities, 1210-1820 m.

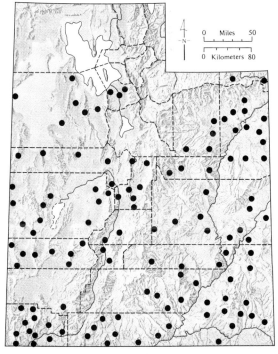

13. *Gilia inconspicua* (J. E. Sm.) Sweet Shy gilia. Mar.-July. Native annual; creosote bush to pinyon-juniper communities, 910-2120 m.

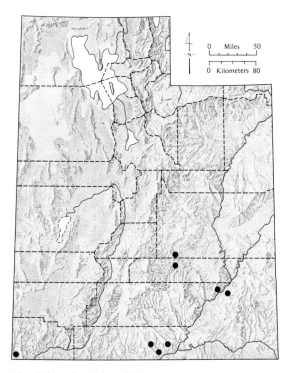

14. *Gilia latifolia* Wats. Spiny gilia. June-Sept. Native annual; creosote bush, shadscale, desert shrub communities, 1030-1580 m.

467

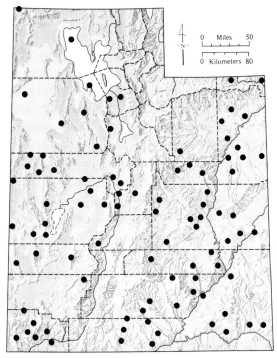

15. *Gilia leptomeria* Gray   Sand gilia.   May-July.   Native annual; creosote bush to pinyon-juniper communities, 910-1820 m.

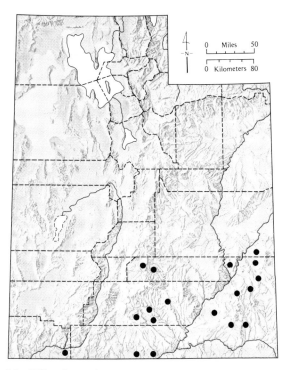

16. *Gilia longiflora* (Torr.) G. Don   May-Aug. Native annual or biennial; desert shrub to pinyon-juniper communities, 1360-2120 m.

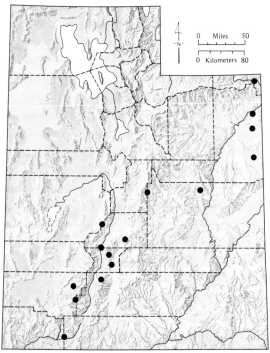

17. *Gilia pinnatifida* Nutt. Sticky gilia. June-July. Native annual or biennial; mountain brush, pinyon-juniper, fir communities, 1580-2880 m.

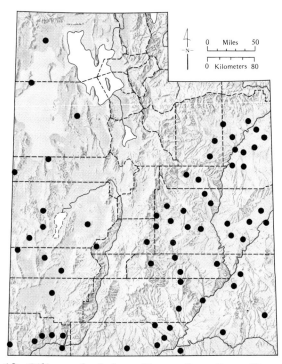

18. *Gilia polycladon* Torr.   Spreading gilia. Apr.-June. Native annual; salt desert shrub, desert shrub, juniper communities, 850-1970 m.

468

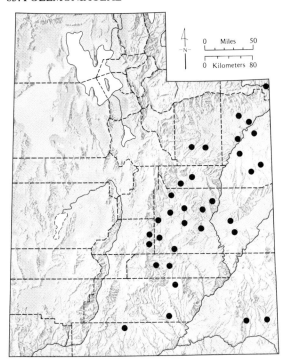

19. *Gilia pumila* Nutt. Dwarf gilia. May-July. Native annual; shadscale, mat saltbush, desert shrub communities, 1300-2120 m.

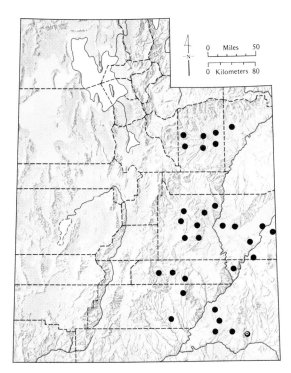

20. *Gilia roseata* Rydb. San Rafael gilia. May-July. Native perennial herb; desert shrub to pinyon-juniper communities, 1150-2180 m.

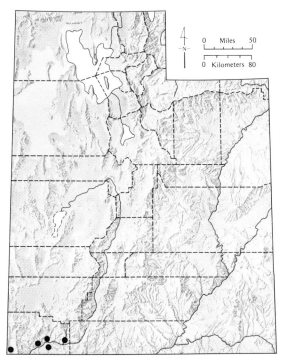

21. *Gilia scopulorum* Jones. Apr.-May. Native annual; creosote bush, Joshua tree communities, 720-910 m.

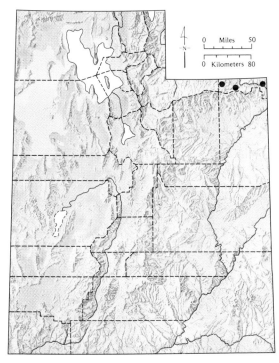

22. *Gilia spicata* Nutt. Spike gilia. May-July. Native perennial herb; sagebrush, juniper communities, 1510-2090 m.

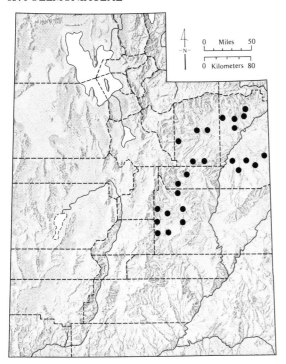

23. *Gilia stenothrysa* Gray Uinta gilia.
May-Sept. Native biennial; shadscale, mat
saltbush, desert shrub, pinyon-juniper
communities, 1540-2820 m.

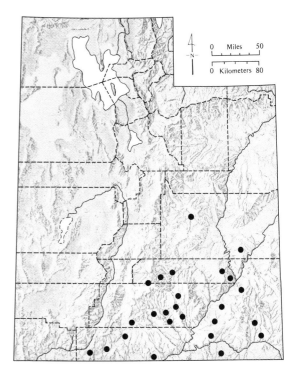

24. *Gilia subnuda* Gray Canyonlands gilia.
May-June. Native biennial or perennial; desert
shrub, pinyon-juniper communities, 1450-1970 m.

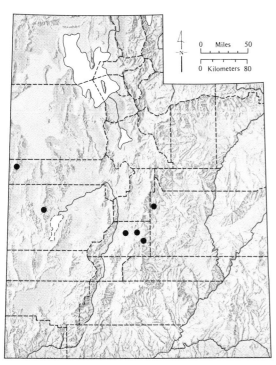

25. *Gilia tenerrima* Gray June-July. Native
annual; mountain brush to ponderosa pine
communities, 1970-2550 m.

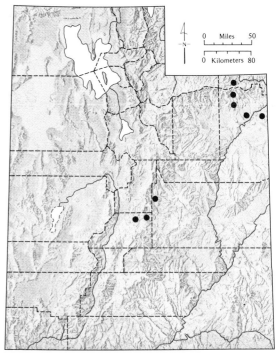

26. *Gymnosteris parvula* Heller June-July.
Native annual; mountain brush to ponderosa pine
communities, 2120-2550 m.

470

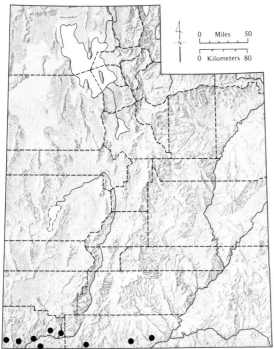

27. *Langloisia setosissima* (T. & G.) Greene
May-July. Native annual; Joshua tree, creosote
bush, desert shrub, pinyon-juniper communities,
730-1460 m.

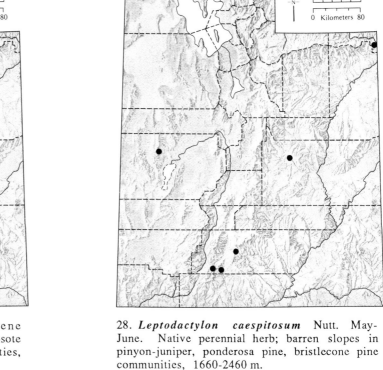

28. *Leptodactylon caespitosum* Nutt. May-
June. Native perennial herb; barren slopes in
pinyon-juniper, ponderosa pine, bristlecone pine
communities, 1660-2460 m.

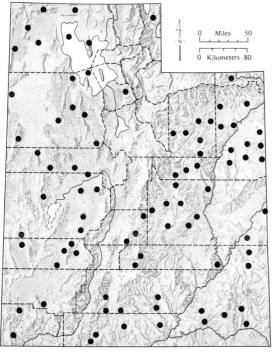

29. *Leptodactylon pungens* (Torr.) Nutt.
Apr.-July. Native shrub or subshrub; desert shrub
to pinyon-juniper communities, 1270-2180 m.

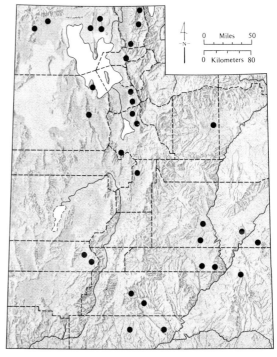

30. *Leptodactylon watsonii* (Gray) Rydb.
May-Aug. Native subshrub; juniper, mountain
brush to conifer communities, 1270-2730 m.

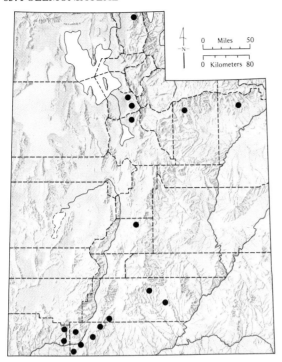

31. *Linanthastrum nuttallii* (Gray) Ewan
Nuttall flaxflower. Apr.-Aug. Native subshrub;
open slopes in pinyon-juniper to aspen-conifer
communities to above timberline, 1360-3180 m.

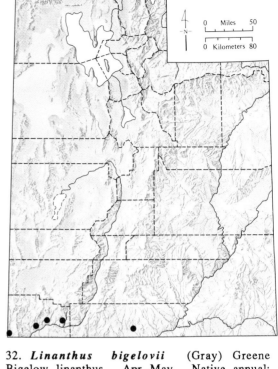

32. *Linanthus bigelovii* (Gray) Greene
Bigelow linanthus. Apr.-May. Native annual;
creosote bush to desert shrub communities, 810-
1210 m.

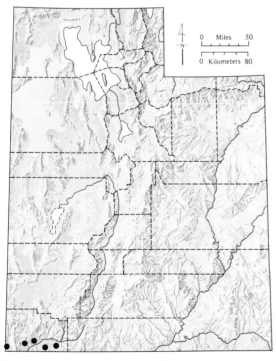

33. *Linanthus demissus* (Gray) Greene Mat
linanthus. Apr.-May. Native annual; creosote
bush communities, 790-970 m.

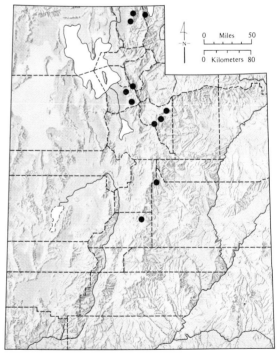

34. *Linanthus harknessii* (Curran) Greene
Three-seeded linanthus. June-Aug. Native annual;
meadows, mesic slopes in mountain brush, aspen
communities, 2060-2490 m.

472

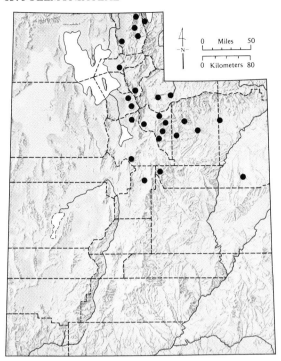

35. *Linanthus septentrionalis* Mason
Northern linanthus. May-July. Native annual;
mountain brush to conifer communities, 1810-
2670 m.

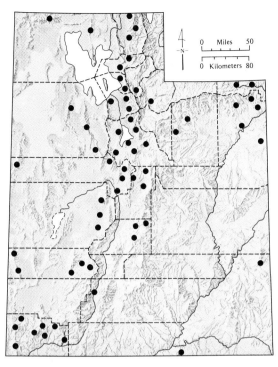

36. *Microsteris gracilis* (Hook.) Greene
Little polecat. Apr.-June. Native annual; salt
desert shrub, sagebrush, mountain brush, pinyon-
juniper communities, 1360-2580 m.

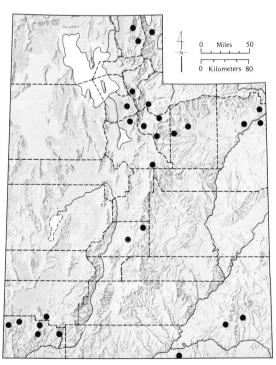

37. *Navarretia breweri* (Gray) Greene
Pincushion plant. June-Aug. Native annual;
mountain brush, pinyon-juniper to ponderosa pine,
aspen communities, 1780-3180 m.

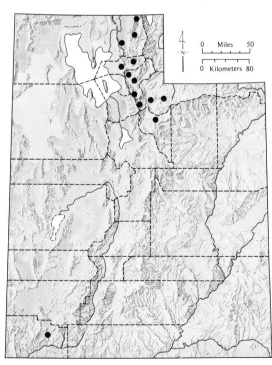

38. *Navarretia intertexta* (Benth.) Hook.
Great Basin navarettia. June-July. Native annual;
sagebrush, grass-forb, mountain brush
communities, often on disturbed sites, 1510-
2270 m.

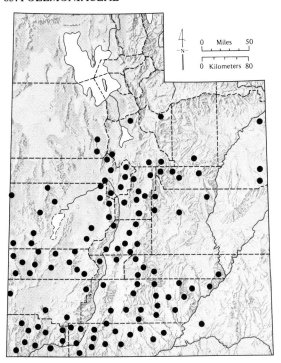

39. *Phlox austromontana* Cov. Desert phlox. Apr.-July. Native perennial herb; pinyon-juniper to ponderosa pine communities, 1400-3030 m.

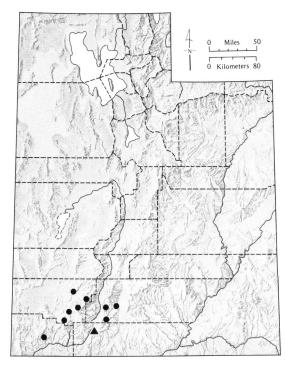

40. *Phlox gladiformis* (Jones) E. Nels. Cedar Canyon or daggerleaf phlox. May-June. Native perennial herb; cliffs, rocky slopes in pinyon-juniper, ponderosa pine, bristlecone pine communities, 1810-2430 m.

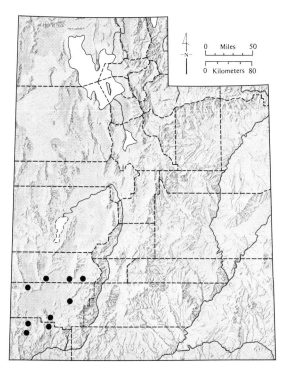

41. *Phlox griseola* Wherry Grayleaf phlox. May-June. Native perennial herb; desert shrub, pinyon-juniper communities, 1510-1970 m.

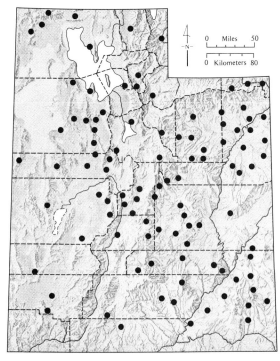

42. *Phlox hoodii* Richards. Carpet phlox. Apr.-July. Native perennial herb; salt desert shrub, desert shrub, pinyon-juniper communities, 1360-3180 m.

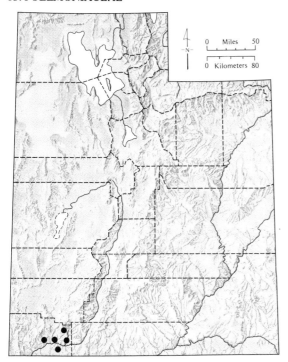

43. *Phlox jonesii* Wherry Zion Canyon phlox. Apr.-May. Native perennial herb; cliffs and rock ledges in oak, pinyon-juniper communities, 1210-1520 m.

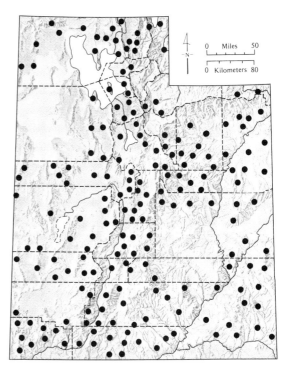

44. *Phlox longifolia* Nutt. Wild or longleaf phlox. Apr.-June. Native perennial herb; greasewood to mountain brush, pinyon-juniper communities, 1060-3030 m.

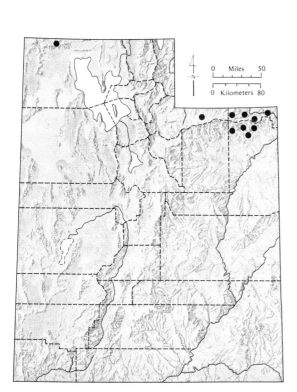

45. *Phlox multiflora* A. Nels. Rocky Mountain phlox. May-Aug. Native perennial herb; sagebrush to aspen-conifer communities, 2420-3030 m.

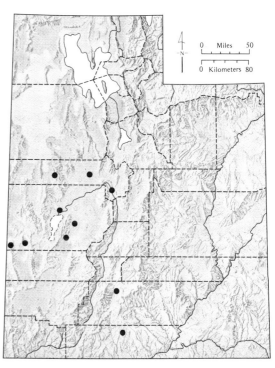

46. *Phlox muscoides* Nutt. Moss phlox. Mar.-June. Native perennial herb; salt desert shrub, desert shrub, pinyon-juniper communities, 1450-1670 m.

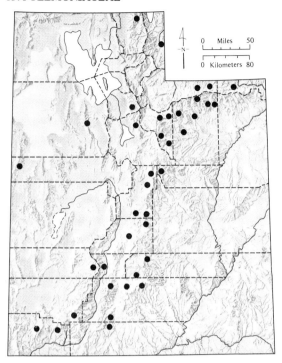

47. *Phlox pulvinata* (Wherry) Cronq. Cushion phlox. June-Aug. Native perennial herb; meadows, talus, openings in conifer forests, 2420-3490 m.

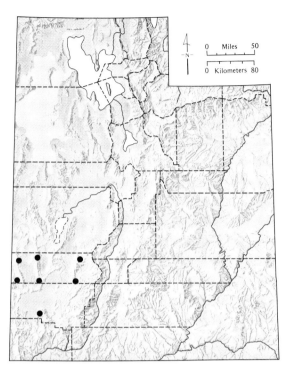

48. *Phlox tumulosa* Wherry Mound phlox. Apr.-June. Native perennial herb; salt desert shrub, desert shrub, pinyon-juniper communities, 1510-1970 m.

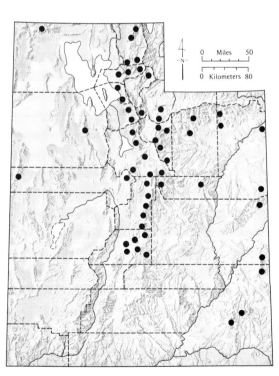

49. *Polemonium foliosissimum* Gray Leafy Jacobsladder. June-Aug. Native perennial herb; mountain brush to aspen-conifer communities, 1560-3270 m.

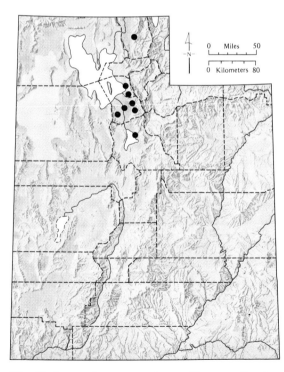

50. *Polemonium micranthum* Benth. Littlebells Jacobsladder. Apr.-June. Native annual; sagebrush-grass communities, 1300-1790 m.

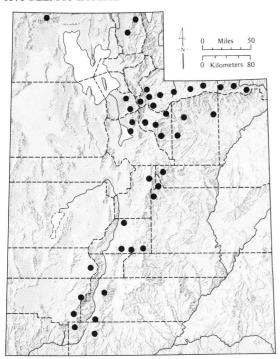

51. *Polemonium occidentale* Greene Western Jacobsladder; skunkweed. May-Aug. Native perennial herb; moist meadows, streamside in aspen-conifer communities, 1360-2970 m.

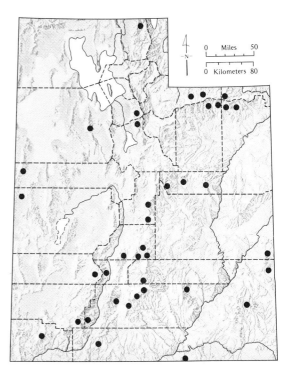

52. *Polemonium pulcherrimum* Hook. Pretty Jacobsladder; skunkleaf. June-Aug. Native perennial herb; shaded to open sites in conifer forests, exposed rocky sites, 2060-3640 m.

84. POLYGALACEAE

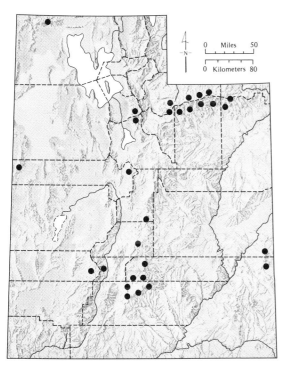

53. *Polemonium viscosum* Nutt. Sticky Jacobsladder; skypilot. June-Aug. Native perennial herb; exposed rocky ridges, often above timberline, 2780-3940 m.

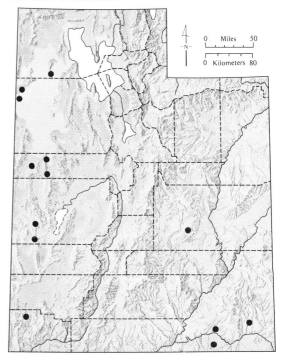

1. *Polygala intermontana* Wendt. Thorny milkwort. May-June. Native shrub; rocky sites in shadscale, desert shrub communities, 1210-2120 m.

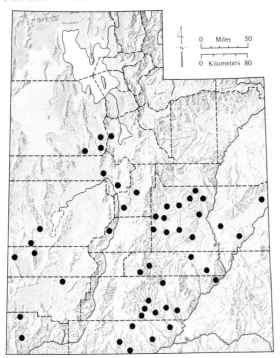

2. *Polygala subspinosa* Wats. Cushion milkwort. May-June. Native subshrub; desert shrub, pinyon-juniper communities, 1360-2270 m.

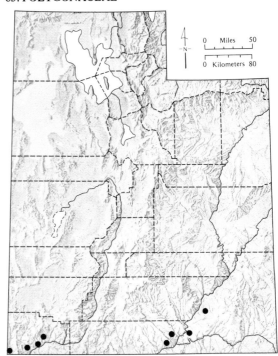

1. *Chorizanthe brevicornu* Torr. Short spineflower. Apr.-May. Native annual; creosote bush communities, 780-1220 m.

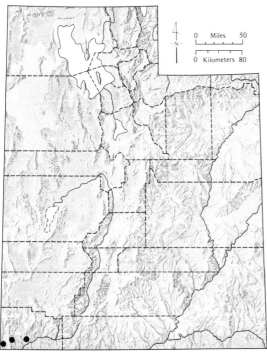

2. *Chorizanthe rigida* (Torr.) T. & G. Rigid spineflower. Apr.-May. Native annual; creosote bush communities, 760-1060 m.

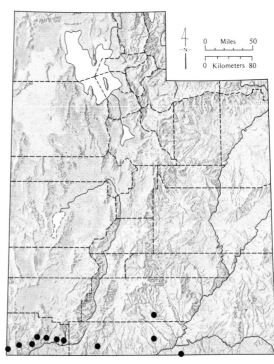

3. *Chorizanthe thurberi* (Gray) Wats. Thurber spineflower. Apr.-June. Native annual; creosote bush, desert shrub communities, 810-1670 m.

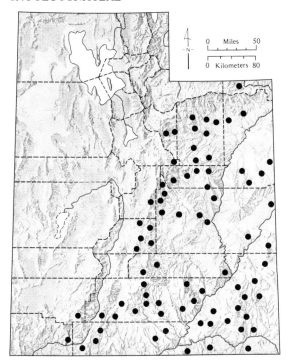

4. *Eriogonum alatum* Torr. Winged buckwheat. May-Aug. Native perennial herb; dry slopes, meadows, sagebrush to aspen-conifer communities, 1210-2880 m.

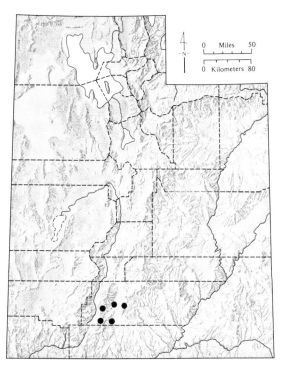

5. *Eriogonum aretioides* Barneby Widtsoe buckwheat. June-July. Native perennial herb; rocky slopes in pinyon-juniper, pine communities, 2240-2580 m.

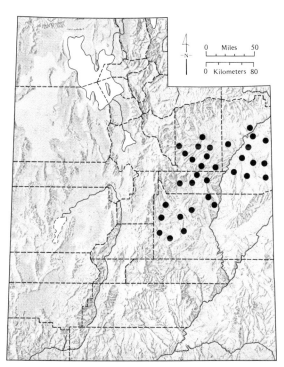

6. *Eriogonum batemanii* Jones Bateman buckwheat. July-Sept. Native perennial herb; shadscale, desert shrub to pinyon-juniper communities, 1510-2430 m.

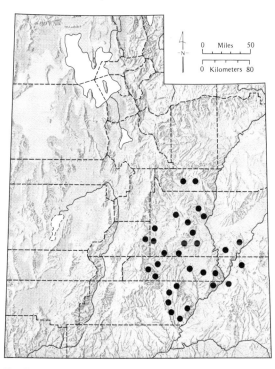

7. *Eriogonum bicolor* Jones Pretty buckwheat. Apr.-June. Native shrub; shadscale, desert shrub to pinyon-juniper communities, 1210-1970 m.

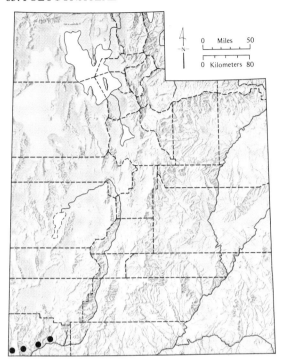

8. *Eriogonum brachypodum* T. & G. Parry buckwheat. Apr.-May. Native annual; creosote bush communities, 760-970 m.

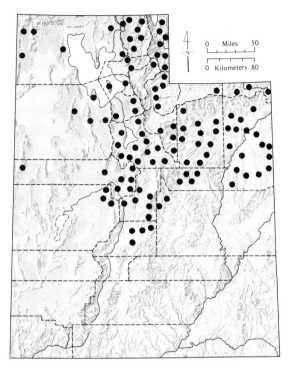

9. *Eriogonum brevicaule* Nutt. Shortstem buckwheat. July-Oct. Native perennial herb; dry open sites in mountain brush communities to above timberline, 1360-3490 m.

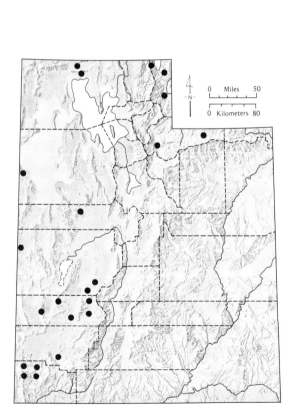

10. *Eriogonum caespitosum* Nutt. Mat buckwheat. May-June. Native perennial herb; desert shrub, mountain brush, pinyon-juniper communities, 1510-2430 m.

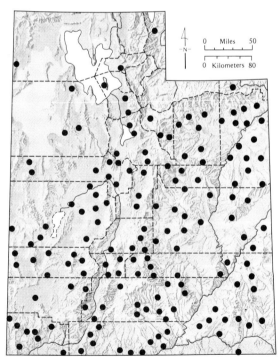

11. *Eriogonum cernuum* Nutt. Nodding buckwheat. May-Sept. Native annual; shadscale, desert shrub to conifer communities, 970-2890 m.

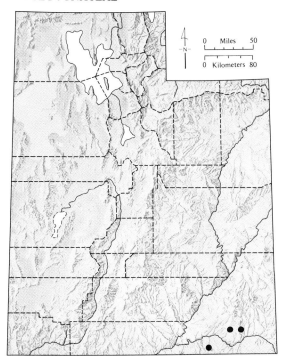

12. *Eriogonum clavellatum* Small Comb Wash buckwheat. May-June. Native shrub; desert shrub communities, 1300-1670 m.

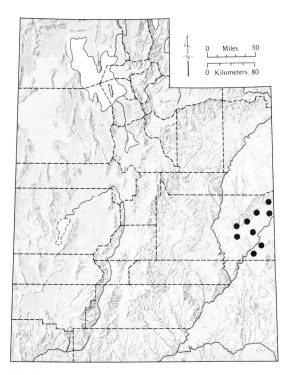

13. *Eriogonum contortum* Rydb. Grand buckwheat. June-Oct. Native shrub; shadscale, mat saltbush, desert shrub communities, 1270-1670 m.

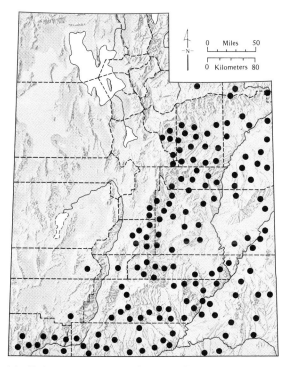

14. *Eriogonum corymbosum* Benth. Corymb buckwheat. June-Oct. Native shrub; shadscale, sagebrush, desert shrub to pinyon-juniper communities, 1060-2730 m.

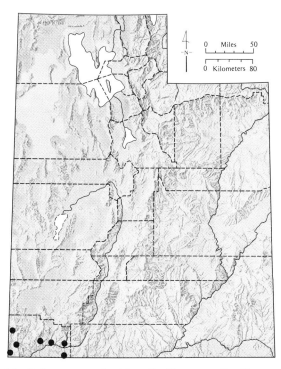

15. *Eriogonum davidsonii* Greene Davidson buckwheat. May-Oct. Native annual; creosote bush, desert shrub to pinyon-juniper communities, 780-1820 m.

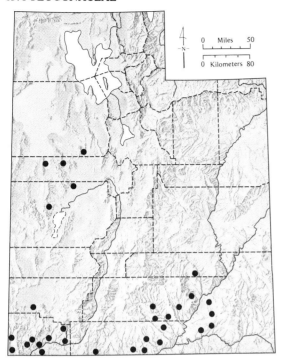

16. *Eriogonum deflexum* Torr. Skeletonweed buckwheat. May-Oct. Native annual; creosote bush, desert shrub, juniper communities, 760-1970 m.

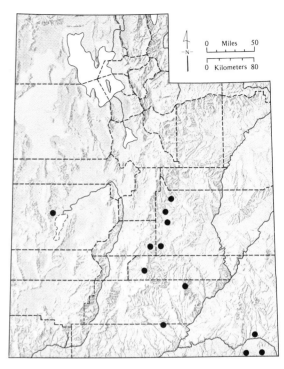

17. *Eriogonum divaricatum* Hook. Spreading buckwheat. May-July. Native annual; shadscale, mat saltbush, desert shrub communities, 1510-2000 m.

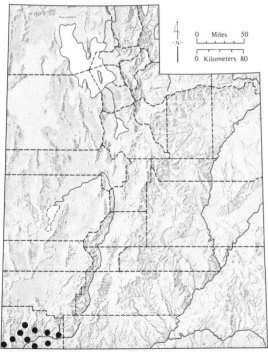

18. *Eriogonum fasciculatum* Benth. Mojave buckwheat. Apr.-June. Native shrub; creosote bush communities, 760-2120 m.

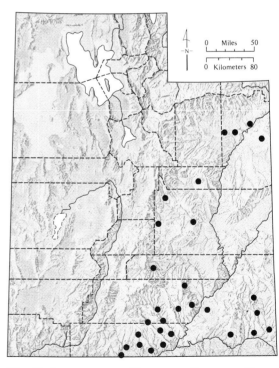

19. *Eriogonum flexum* Jones Bent buckwheat. May-June. Native annual; shadscale, desert shrub, pinyon-juniper communities, 1360-1970 m.

482

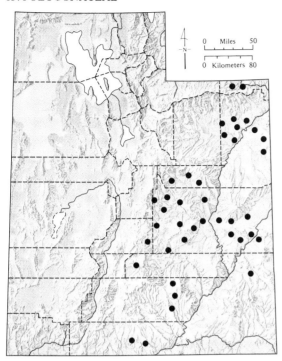

20. *Eriogonum gordonii* Benth. Gordon buckwheat. May-July. Native annual; shadscale, mat saltbush, pinyon-juniper communities, 1300-2180 m.

21. *Eriogonum heermannii* Dur. & Hilg. Heermann buckwheat. June-Oct. Native shrub; rock crevices in creosote bush, desert shrub communities, 960-1460 m.

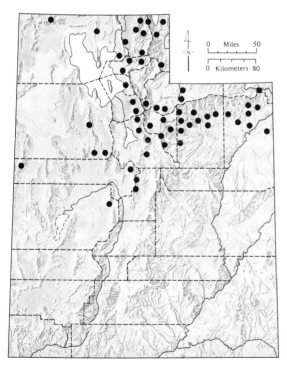

22. *Eriogonum heracleoides* Nutt. Whorled buckwheat. June-Aug. Native perennial herb; mountain brush to conifer communities, 1300-3270 m.

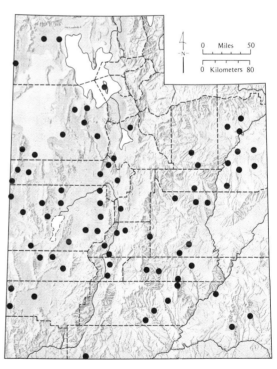

23. *Eriogonum hookeri* Wats. Watson buckwheat. June-Nov. Native annual; shadscale, desert shrub, pinyon-juniper communities, 1120-1970 m.

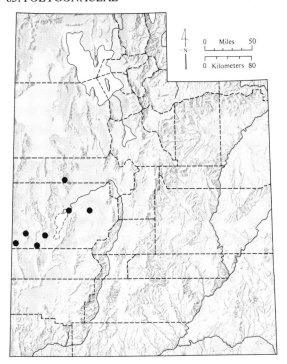

24. *Eriogonum howellianum* Reveal July-Sept. Native annual; rocky sites in shadscale, desert shrub communities, 1450-1730 m.

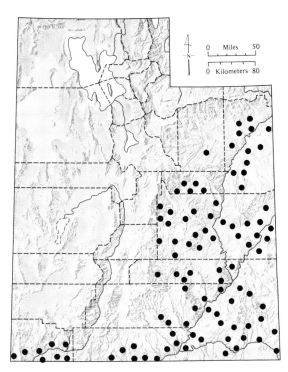

25. *Eriogonum inflatum* Torr. & Frem. Bottlestopper; desert trumpet. May-Aug. Native annual to perennial; creosote bush, mat saltbush, shadscale, pinyon-juniper communities, 760-1970 m.

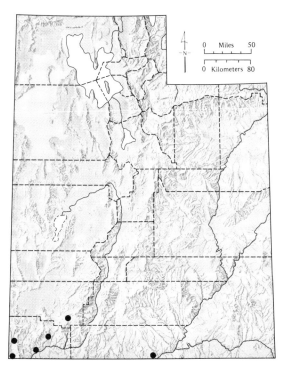

26. *Eriogonum insigne* Wats. Unique buckwheat. June-Nov. Native annual; creosote bush, desert shrub communities, 750-1150 m.

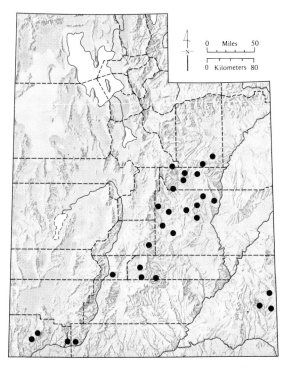

27. *Eriogonum jamesii* Benth. James buckwheat. June-Nov. Native perennial herb; creosote bush, desert shrub to ponderosa pine communities, 1000-2580 m.

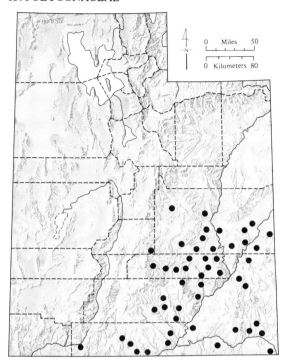

28. *Eriogonum leptocladon* T. & G. Sand buckwheat. June-Oct. Native shrub; desert shrub to pinyon-juniper communities, 1150-2000 m.

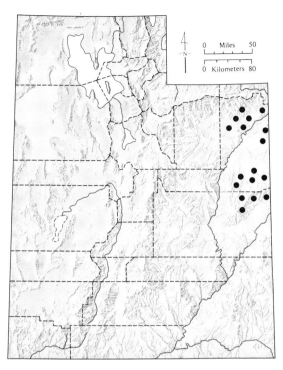

29. *Eriogonum lonchophyllum* T. & G. Longleaf buckwheat. July-Sept. Native shrub or subshrub; mountain brush, pinyon-juniper to conifer communities, 1510-2730 m.

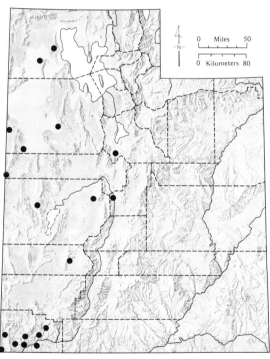

30. *Eriogonum maculatum* Heller Spotted buckwheat. Apr.-July. Native annual; sand dunes in creosote bush to desert shrub communities, 760-1820 m.

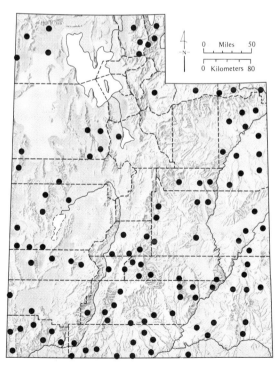

31. *Eriogonum microthecum* Nutt. Slender buckwheat. July-Sept. Native shrub; greasewood, shadscale, desert shrub to ponderosa pine communities, 970-2880 m.

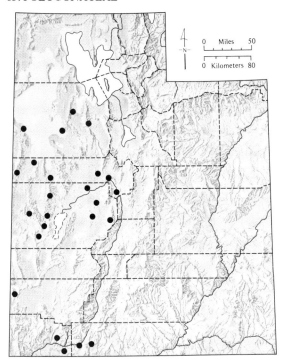

32. *Eriogonum nummulare* Jones Coin buckwheat. July-Nov. Native shrub or subshrub; desert shrub to pinyon-juniper communities, commonly on sand dunes, 1090-1970 m.

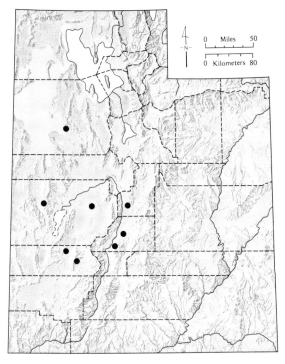

33. *Eriogonum nutans* T. & G. Dugway buckwheat. June-July. Native annual; shadscale, desert shrub communities, 1360-1880 m.

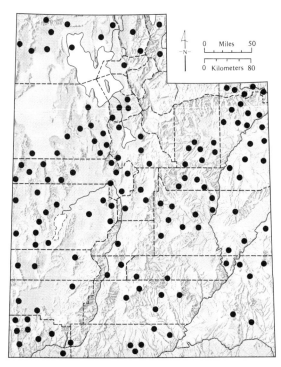

34. *Eriogonum ovalifolium* Nutt. Cushion buckwheat. May-Aug. Native perennial herb; shadscale, desert shrub communities to subalpine meadows, 1270-3640 m.

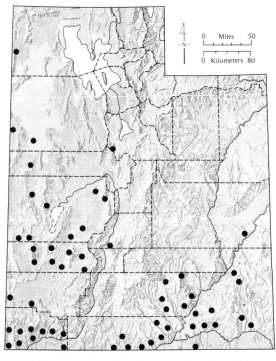

35. *Eriogonum palmerianum* Reveal Palmer buckwheat. May-Sept. Native annual; shadscale, desert shrub to pinyon-juniper communities, 970-1970 m.

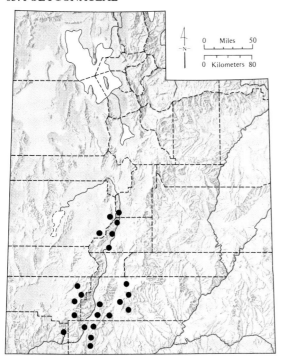

36. ***Eriogonum panguicense*** (Jones) Reveal Panguitch buckwheat. June-Aug. Native perennial herb; barren gravelly slopes in pinyon-juniper to alpine communities, 1660-3430 m.

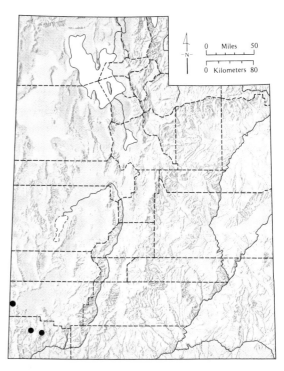

37. ***Eriogonum pharnaceoides*** Torr. Wirestem buckwheat. July-Aug. Native annual; pinyon-juniper to ponderosa pine communities, 1810-2640 m.

38. ***Eriogonum polycladon*** Benth. Leafy buckwheat. Aug.-Oct. Native annual; sagebrush to pinyon-juniper communities, 1660-1820 m.

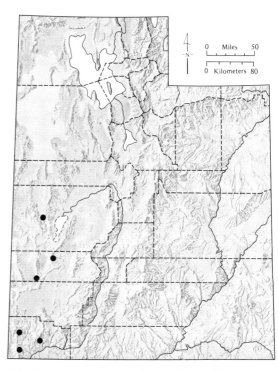

39. ***Eriogonum puberulum*** Wats. Red Creek buckwheat. June-July. Native annual; desert shrub to ponderosa pine communities, 1330-2730 m.

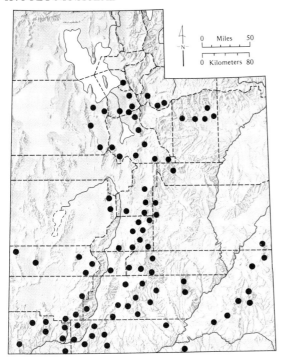

40. *Eriogonum racemosum* Nutt. Redroot buckwheat. June-Oct. Native perennial herb; mountain brush to ponderosa pine communities, 1330-2820 m.

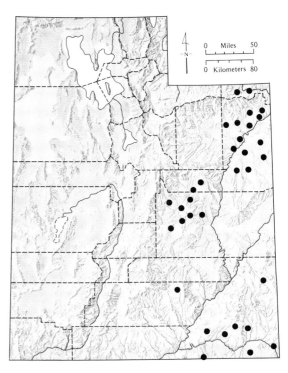

41. *Eriogonum salsuginosum* (Nutt.) Hook. Smooth buckwheat. May-July. Native annual; salt desert shrub to pinyon-juniper communities, 1300-2240 m.

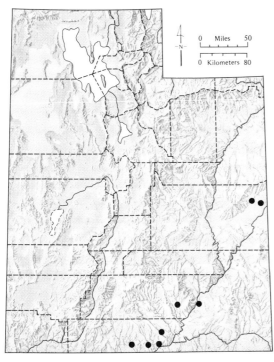

42. *Eriogonum scabrellum* Reveal Westwater buckwheat. July-Nov. Native annual; desert shrub communities, 1220-1700 m.

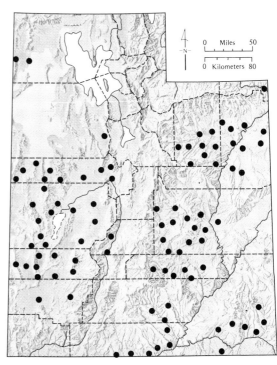

43. *Eriogonum shockleyi* Wats. Shockley buckwheat. May-July. Native perennial herb; shadscale, mat saltbush, desert shrub to pinyon-juniper communities, 1270-2120 m.

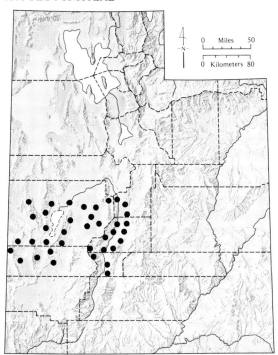

44. *Eriogonum spathulatum* Gray Sevier buckwheat. July-Sept. Native perennial herb; salt desert shrub to pinyon-juniper communities, 1390-2120 m.

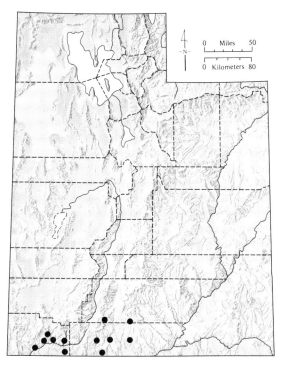

45. *Eriogonum subreniforme* Wats. Stokes buckwheat. May-Oct. Native annual; creosote bush to pinyon-juniper communities, 850-3000 m.

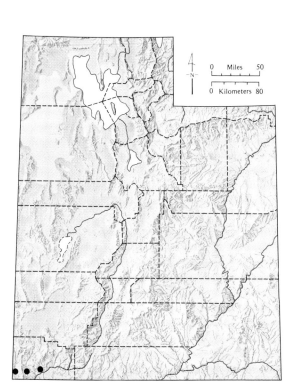

46. *Eriogonum thomasii* Torr. Thomas buckwheat. Apr.-May. Native annual; creosote bush communities, 780-910 m.

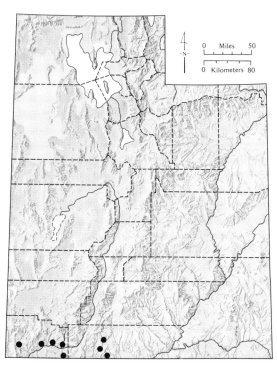

47. *Eriogonum thompsonae* Wats. Ellen buckwheat. Aug.-Sept. Native shrub or subshrub; creosote bush, desert shrub, pinyon-juniper communities, 1060-1520 m.

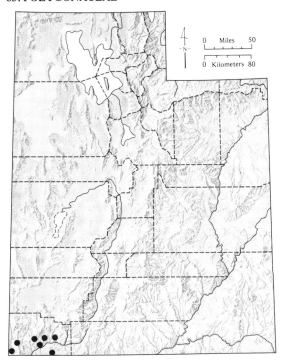

48. *Eriogonum trichopes* Torr. Slender-stipe buckwheat. Apr.-Oct. Native annual; creosote bush communities, 760-970 m.

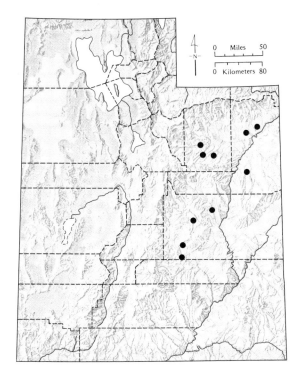

49. *Eriogonum tumulosum* (Barneby) Reveal Woodside buckwheat. May-July. Native perennial herb; pinyon-juniper communities, 1390-2150 m.

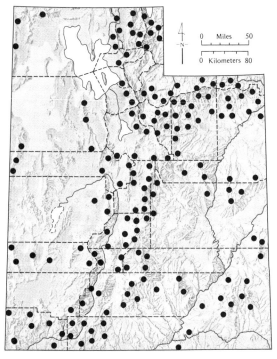

50. *Eriogonum umbellatum* Torr. Sulphur buckwheat. June-Oct. Native perennial herb or subshrub; sagebrush to spruce-fir communities, 1360-3640 m.

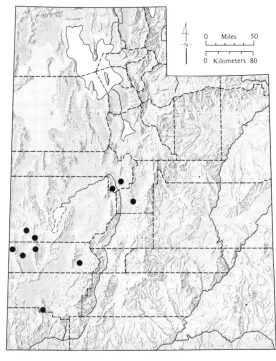

51. *Eriogonum villiflorum* Gray Gray buckwheat. May-July. Native perennial herb; sagebrush to pinyon-juniper communities, 1510-2340 m.

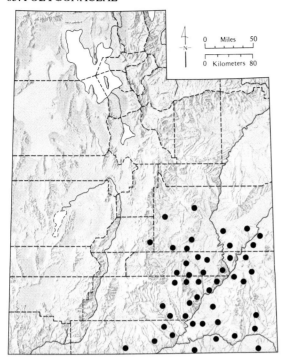

52. *Eriogonum wetherillii* Eastw. Wetherill buckwheat. June-Nov. Native annual; sagebrush to pinyon-juniper communities, 910-1120 m.

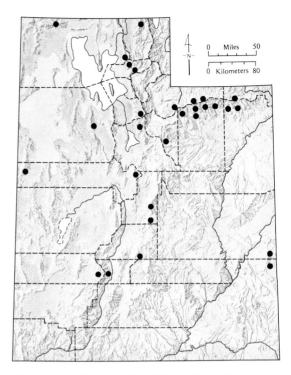

53. *Oxyria digyna* (L.) Hill Mountain sorrel. July-Aug. Circumboreal perennial herb; moist rocky slopes, 2550-3950 m.

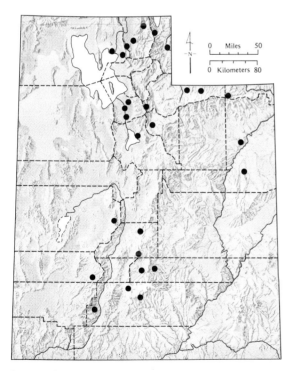

54. *Polygonum amphibium* L. Water smartweed. July-Aug. Cosmopolitan perennial herb; disturbed moist sites, marshes, shallow water, drying banks of ponds and waterways, 1270-3180 m.

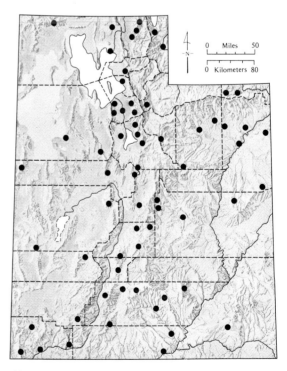

55. *Polygonum aviculare* L. Knotweed. May-Oct. Circumboreal annual; dry to moist, disturbed sites, 760-3180 m.

491

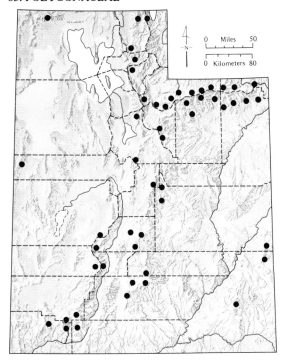

56. *Polygonum bistortoides* Pursh American bistort. May-Aug. Native perennial herb; moist meadows in aspen-conifer communities, 2120-3790 m.

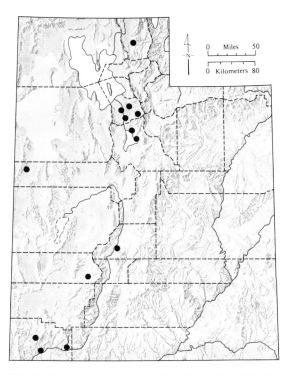

57. *Polygonum convolvulus* L. Black bindweed. July-Aug. Introduced annual; weed of gardens, fields, disturbed sites in mountain brush to conifer communities, 850-3030 m.

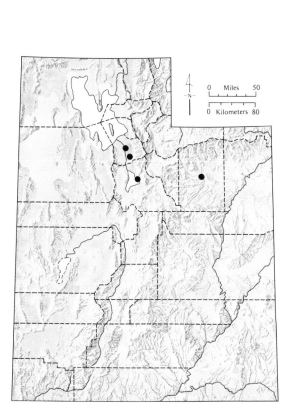

58. *Polygonum cuspidatum* Sieb. & Zucc. Fleece knotweed. July-Aug. Introduced perennial herb; cultivated and escaping, 1280-1520 m.

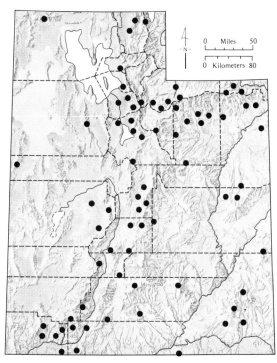

59. *Polygonum douglasii* Greene Douglas knotweed. May-Sept. Native annual; sagebrush to spruce-fir communities, 1300-3030 m.

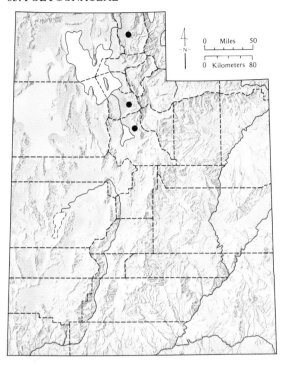

60. *Polygonum hydropiper* L. Waterpepper. July-Sept. Introduced annual to perennial; disturbed moist sites, marshes, shallow water, drying banks of ponds and waterways, 1300-1370 m.

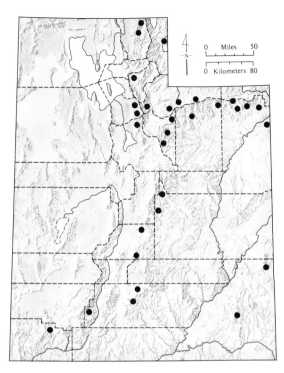

61. *Polygonum kelloggii* Greene Kellogg knotweed. June-Aug. Native annual; moist sites in sagebrush to aspen, spruce-fir communities, 1870-3270 m.

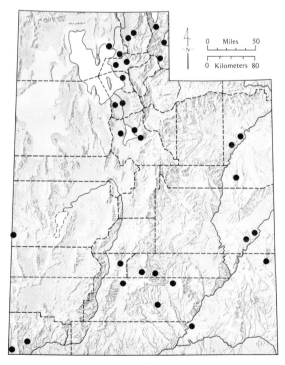

62. *Polygonum lapathifolium* L. Willow weed. June-Sept. Introduced annual; disturbed moist sites, marshes, shallow water and drying banks of ponds and waterways, 780-2120 m.

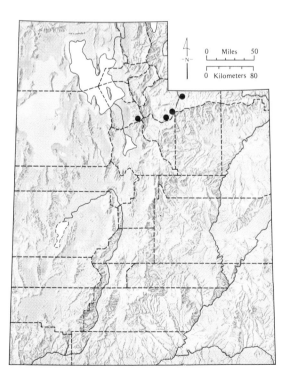

63. *Polygonum minimum* Wats. Broadleaf knotweed. Aug.-Sept. Native annual; open rocky sites in spruce-fir, alpine communities, 2420-3090 m.

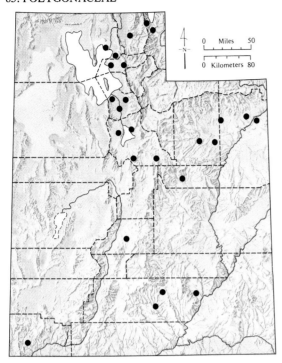

64. *Polygonum persicaria* L. Ladysthumb. June-Sept. Introduced annual; disturbed moist sites, marshes, shallow water and drying banks of ponds and waterways, 910-2120 m.

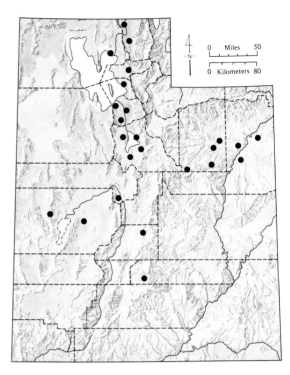

65. *Polygonum ramosissimum* Michx. Bushy knotweed. June-Sept. Native annual; disturbed, dry to moist sites, salt tolerant, 1300-1760 m.

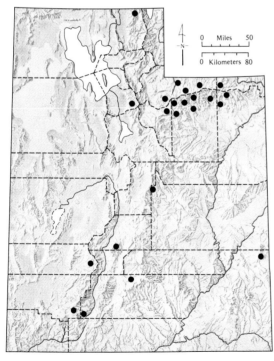

66. *Polygonum viviparum* L. Alpine bistort. July-Aug. Circumboreal perennial herb; wet meadows, streamside in conifer forests, 2420-3640 m.

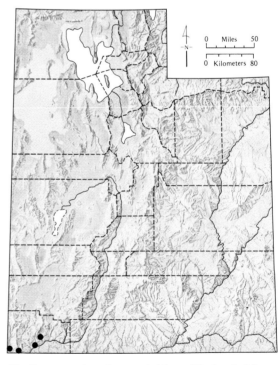

67. *Pterostegia drymarioides* Fisch. & Mey. Mar.-Apr. Native annual; rock crevices, 850-970 m.

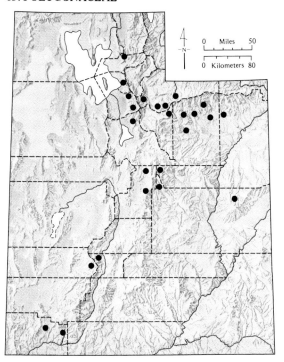

68. *Rumex acetosella* L. Sheep sorrel. June-Aug. Introduced perennial herb; roadsides, dry meadows, other open, usually disturbed sites, 1360-3030 m.

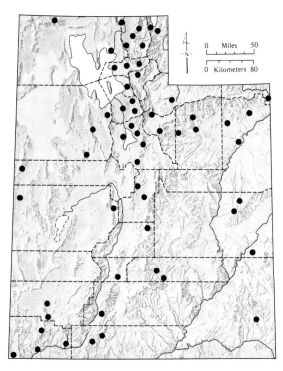

69. *Rumex crispus* L. Curly dock. May-Aug. Introduced perennial herb; dry to moist waste places, marshes, along waterways, wet meadows, 760-2730 m.

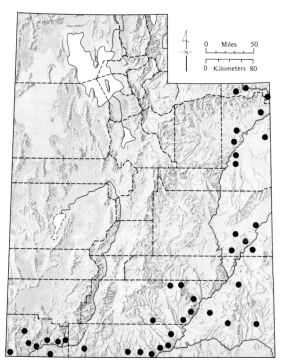

70. *Rumex hymenosepalus* Torr. Canaigre. Apr.-June. Native perennial herb; dry sandy sites, commonly on dunes, 960-1850 m.

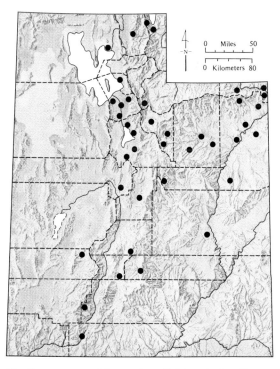

71. *Rumex maritimus* L. Golden dock. June-Oct. Circumboreal annual or biennial; marshes, along waterways, other moist, often disturbed sites, salt tolerant, 1210-2550 m.

495

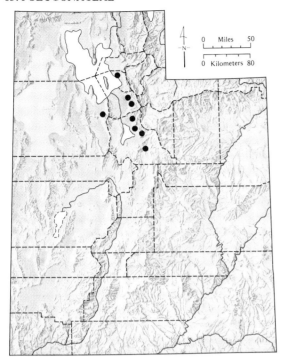

72. *Rumex obtusifolius* L. Bitter dock. July-Sept. Circumboreal perennial herb; marshes, along waterways, wet meadows, other moist, often disturbed sites, 1270-2360 m.

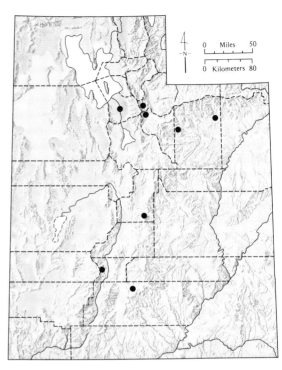

73. *Rumex occidentalis* Wats. Western dock. May-Aug. Native perennial herb; wet meadows, moist sites in aspen, spruce-fir communities, 1300-3030 m.

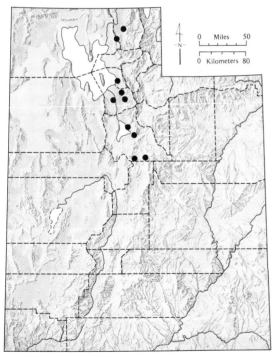

74. *Rumex patientia* L. Patience dock. June-Aug. Introduced perennial herb; moist to mesic, often disturbed sites, open slopes in sagebrush, mountain brush communities, 1300-2430 m.

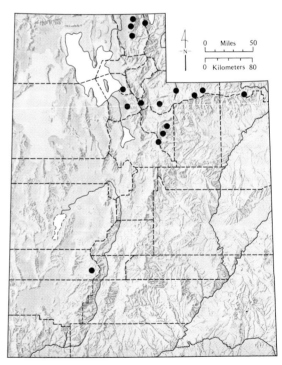

75. *Rumex paucifolius* Nutt. Alpine sorrel. June-Aug. Native perennial herb; open slopes in sagebrush, mountain brush communities, meadows in aspen, spruce-fir communities, 2000-3300 m.

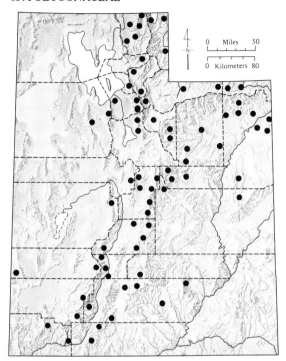

76. Rumex salicifolius Weinm. Beach dock. June-Sept. Native perennial herb; moist sites in greasewood to aspen-spruce-fir communities, often along margins of lakes and ponds, 1280-3180 m.

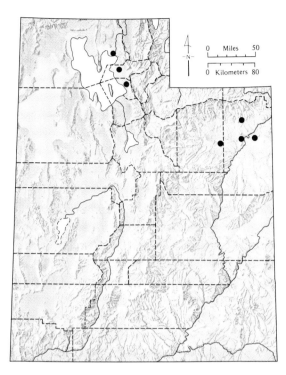

77. Rumex stenophyllus Ledeb. July-Sept. Introduced perennial herb; along waterways, other moist, often disturbed sites, 1300-1520 m.

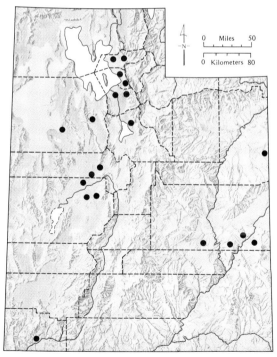

78. Rumex venosus Pursh Wild begonia; veiny dock. May-June. Native perennial herb; dry, disturbed, commonly sandy sites, often along railways, 870-1520 m.

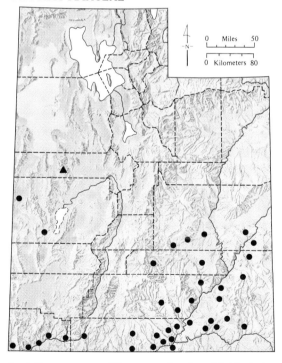

1. Adiantum capillus-veneris L. Maidenhair fern. Cosmopolitan; hanging gardens, near seeps and springs, 780-1670 m.

497

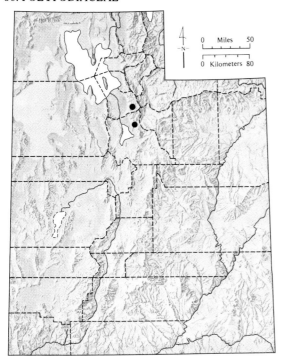

2. *Aspidotis densa* (Brack.) Lellinger Pod fern; Indian's dream. Native; moist to dry rock crevices, rocky slopes, 2570-2880 m.

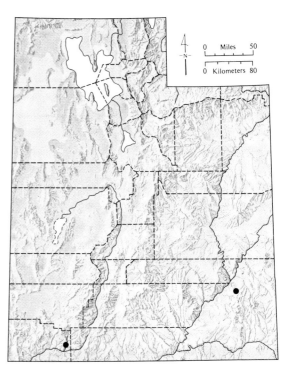

3. *Asplenium resiliens* Kunze Ebony spleenwort. Native; shaded rock crevices in desert shrub, pinyon-juniper, mountain brush communities, 1210-1520 m.

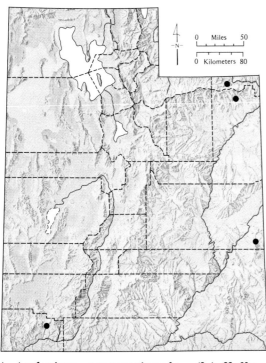

4. *Asplenium septentrionale* (L.) Hoffm. Grass fern. Circumboreal; rock crevices in sagebrush, mountain brush, pinyon-juniper, spruce-fir communities, 2240-2820 m.

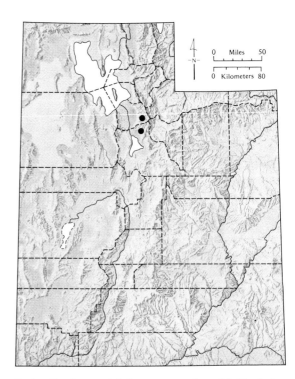

5. *Asplenium trichomanes* L. Maidenhair spleenwort. Circumboreal; rock crevices and talus in aspen, conifer communities, 2720-2880 m.

86. POLYPODIACEAE

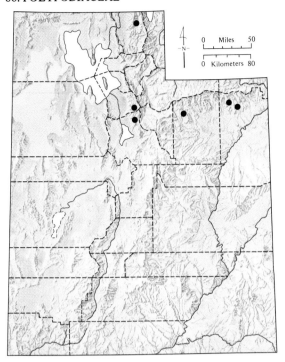

6. *Asplenium viride* Huds. Green spleenwort. Circumboreal; rock crevices in conifer and alpine communities, 2480-3180 m.

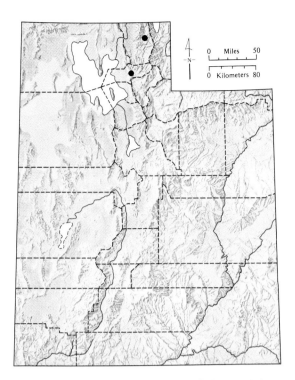

7. *Athyrium distentifolium* Opiz Alpine lady fern. Circumboreal; moist rocky sites, streamside, 2420-2580 m.

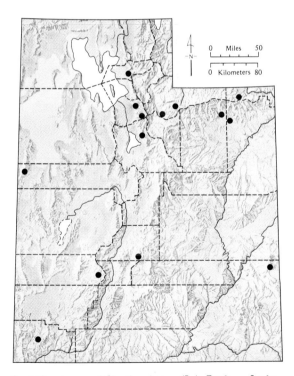

8. *Athyrium filix-femina* (L.) Roth Lady fern. Cosmopolitan; moist shaded sites in mountain brush to spruce-fir, ponderosa pine communities, 1810-2970 m.

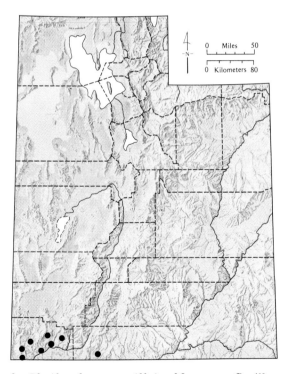

9. *Cheilanthes covillei* Maxon Coville lipfern. Native; rock crevices in creosote bush to pinyon-juniper communities, 970-1670 m.

499

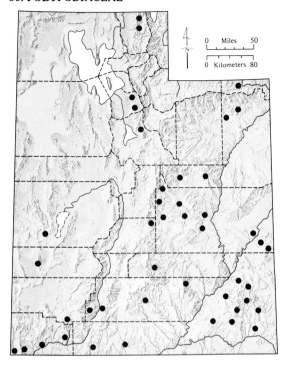

10. *Cheilanthes feei* Moore   Slender lipfern.
Native; hanging gardens, rock crevices in creosote
bush to conifer communities, 760-2910 m.

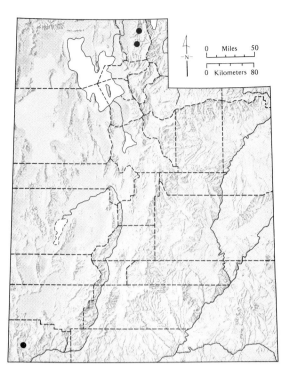

11. *Cheilanthes gracillima* D. C. Eat. Lace
fern. Native; rock crevices, 910-2430 m.

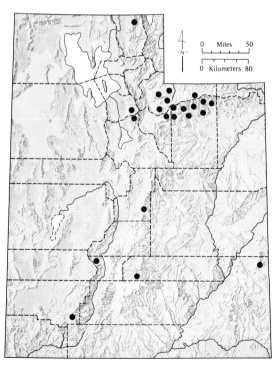

12. *Cryptogramma crispa* (L.) Hook.
American rockbrake; parsley fern. Circumboreal;
rock crevices and talus in conifer, alpine
communities, 2600-3330 m.

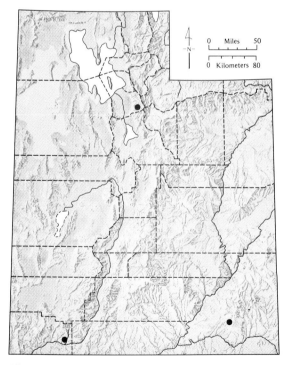

13. *Cystopteris bulbifera* (L.) Bernh.
Bulblet bladder fern. Native; from beneath rocks,
rock crevices, talus, 1210-2880 m.

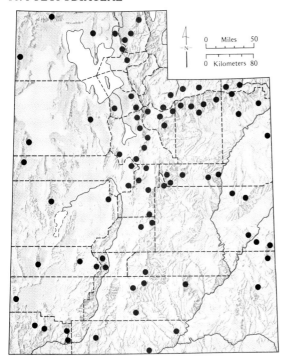

14. *Cystopteris fragilis* (L.) Bernh. Brittle fern. Native; from beneath rocks on shaded slopes, rock crevices, talus, streamside, 1450-3490 m.

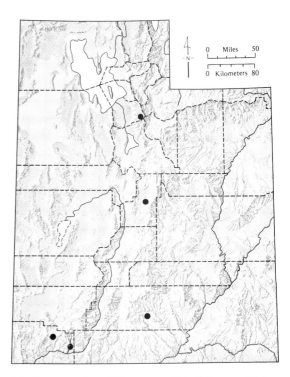

15. *Dryopteris filix-mas* (L.) Schott Male fern. Native; dense thickets, moist woods, streamside, 1360-2880 m.

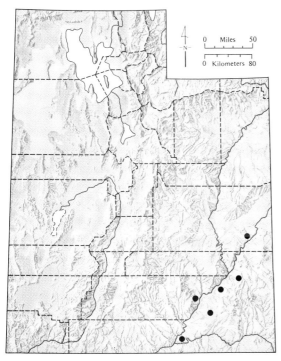

16. *Notholaena limitanea* Maxon Border cloak fern. Native; rock crevices in desert shrub communities, 1030-1520 m.

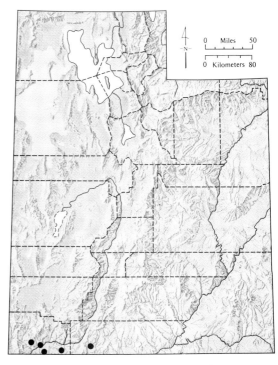

17. *Notholaena parryi* D. C. Eat. Parry cloak fern. Native; rock crevices in creosote bush, desert shrub communities, 780-1210 m.

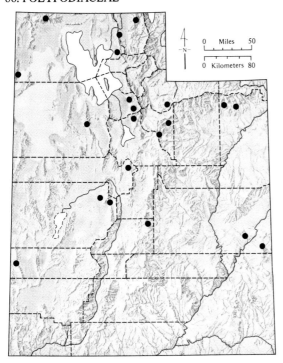

18. *Pellaea breweri* D. C. Eat. Brewer cliffbrake. Native; rocky slopes, dry to moist rock crevices and talus in sagebrush to spruce-fir communities, 1510-3330 m.

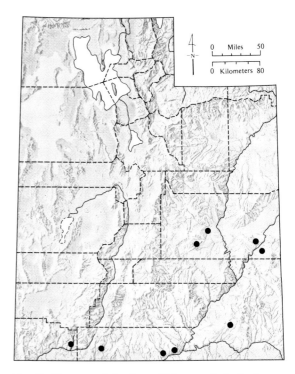

19. *Pellaea glabella* Kuhn Suksdorf or smooth cliffbrake. Native; rock crevices, hanging gardens, 1210-1580 m.

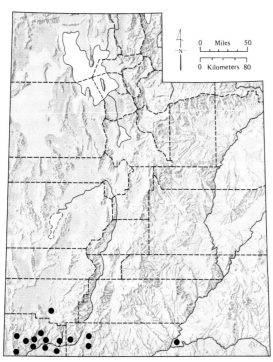

20. *Pellaea truncata* Goodding Spiny cliffbrake. Native; rock crevices in creosote bush to ponderosa pine communities, 970-2060 m.

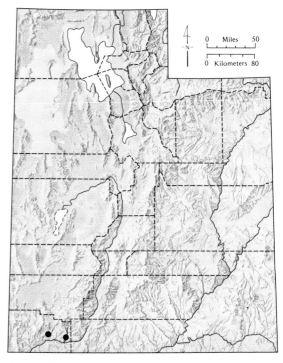

21. *Pellaea wrightiana* Hook. Wright cliffbrake. Native; rocky sites, especially along cliffs, 1660-2060 m.

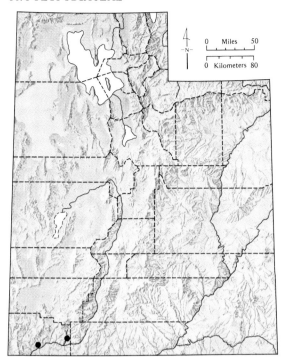

22. *Pityrogramma triangularis* (Kaulf.) Maxon Goldback fern. Native; rock crevices and from beneath rocks on shaded slopes in desert shrub to ponderosa pine communities, 910-1210 m.

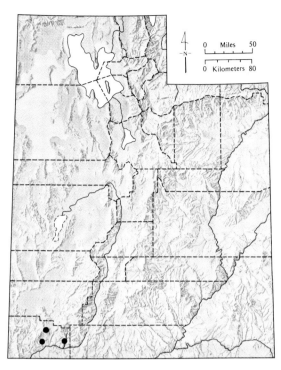

23. *Polypodium hesperium* Maxon Western polypody; licorice fern. Native; rock crevices, other mesic sites in ponderosa pine, mountain brush to spruce-fir communities, 1360-2880 m.

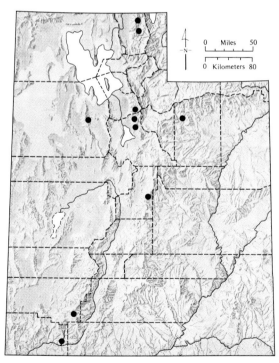

24. *Polystichum lonchitis* (L.) Roth Holly fern. Circumboreal; rock crevices in mountain brush to spruce-fir communities, 2240-3030 m.

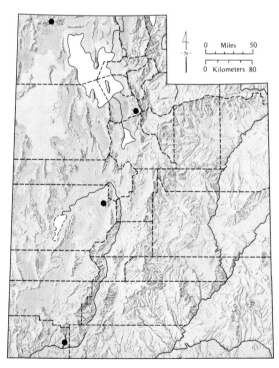

25. *Polystichum scopulinum* (D. C. Eat.) Maxon Rock or western holly fern. Native; rock crevices and from beneath rocks on open slopes, 1810-3150 m.

503

86. POLYPODIACEAE

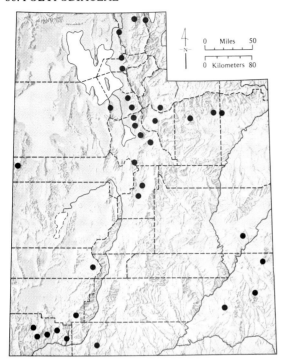

26. *Pteridium aquilinum* (L.) Kuhn Bracken
fern. Cosmopolitan; shaded to open sites in
mountain brush to spruce-fir communities, 1450-
2880 m.

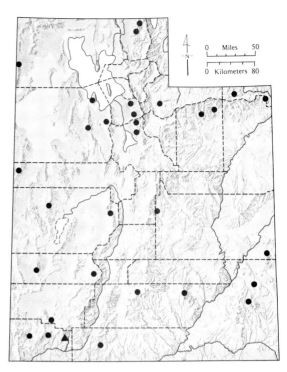

27. *Woodsia oregana* D. C. Eat. Oregon
woodsia; western cliff fern. Native; rock crevices,
talus, beneath rocks on dry open slopes in
sagebrush to white fir, pinyon-juniper, ponderosa
pine communities, 1810-2910 m.

87. PORTULACACEAE

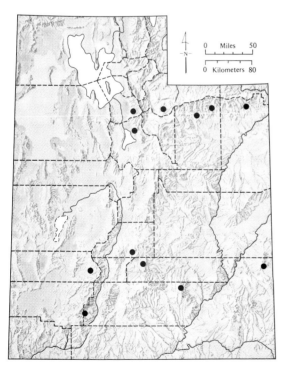

28. *Woodsia scopulina* D. C. Eat. Rocky
Mountain woodsia; mountain cliff fern. Native;
rock crevices and talus in mountain brush to alpine
communities, 2420-3330 m.

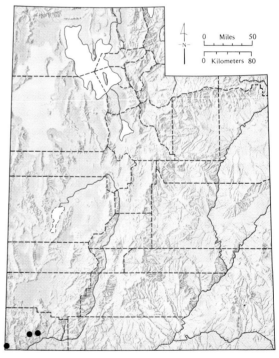

1. *Calyptridium monandrum* Nutt. Apr.-May.
Native annual; creosote bush communities, 760-
1060 m.

504

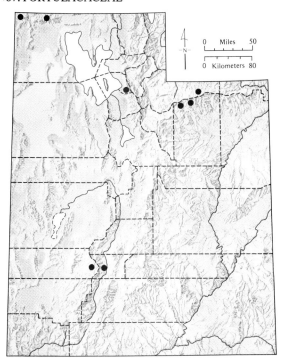

2. *Calyptridium umbellatum* (Torr.) Greene July-Sept. Native annual to perennnial; talus, rocky alpine slopes, 2970-3610 m.

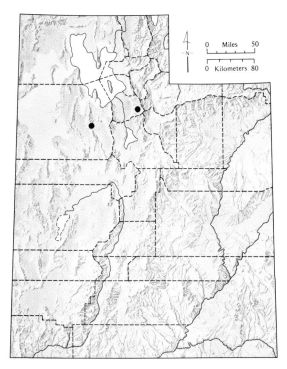

3. *Claytonia cordifolia* Wats. Heartleaf springbeauty. June-Aug. Native perennial herb; streamside, wet meadows, 2540-2880 m.

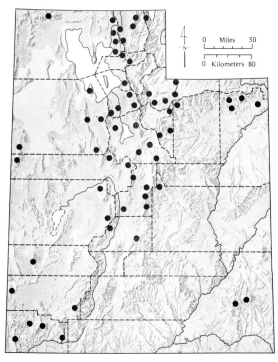

4. *Claytonia lanceolata* Pursh Lanceleaf springbeauty. Mar.-July. Native perennial herb; moist sites, sometimes in the wake of melting snow, in pinyon-juniper, mountain brush to aspen-conifer communities, 1510-3240 m.

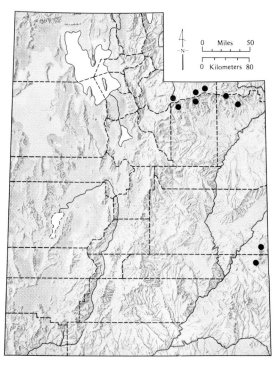

5. *Claytonia megarhiza* (Gray) Parry Alpine springbeauty. July-Sept. Native perennial herb; rock crevices, talus, 3030-3640 m.

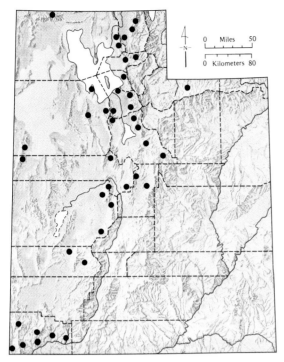

6. *Claytonia perfoliata* Donn Miner's lettuce. Mar.-June. Native annual; moist sites in creosote bush, pinyon-juniper to mountain brush communities, 760-3030 m.

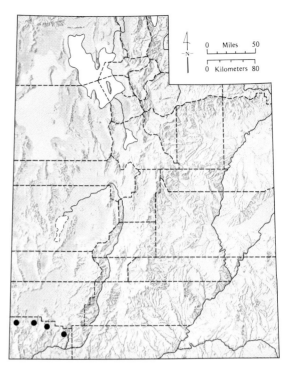

7. *Lewisia brachycalyx* Gray June-July. Native perennial herb; mountain brush, pinyon-juniper communities, 2180-2400 m.

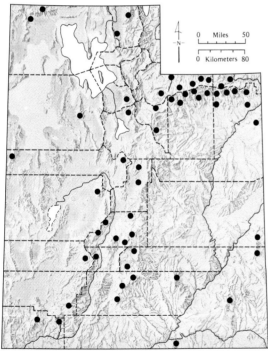

8. *Lewisia pygmaea* (Gray) Rob. Least lewisia. June-Aug. Native perennial herb; wet meadows, dry to moist sites in mountain brush to conifer communities, exposed rocky slopes, 1900-3490 m.

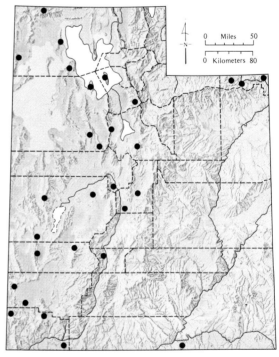

9. *Lewisia rediviva* Pursh Bitterroot. May-July. Native perennial herb; sagebrush to pinyon-juniper communities, commonly on open rocky sites, 1300-2940 m.

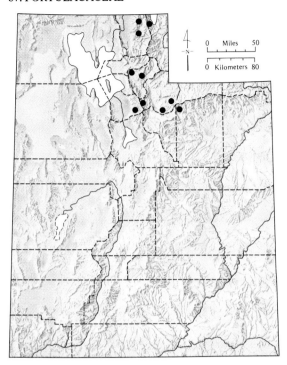

10. *Lewisia triphylla* (Wats.) Rob. Threeleaf lewisia. May-Aug. Native perennial herb; meadows, streamside, open, often rocky slopes, 1870-3210 m.

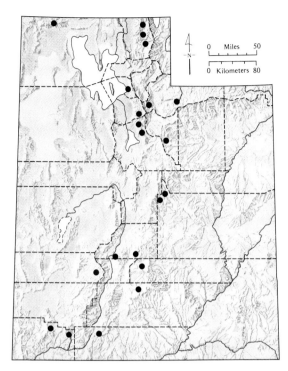

11. *Montia chamissoi* (Ledeb.) Rob. & Fern. Toadlily. June-Sept. Native perennial herb; shallow water, wet meadows, streambanks, other moist sites, often in the wake of snowmelt, 1810-3180 m.

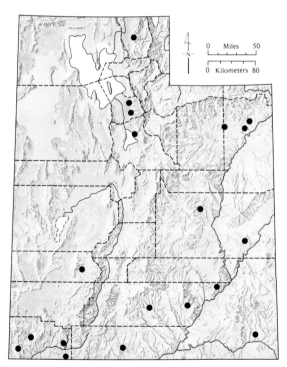

12. *Portulaca oleracea* L. Purslane. June-Aug. Cosmopolitan annual; waste places, 1330-2430 m.

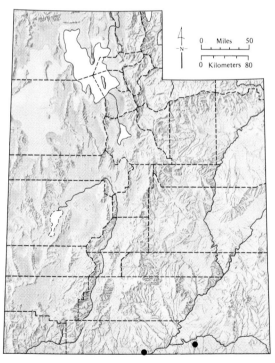

13. *Portulaca parvula* Gray Dwarf purslane. July-Aug. Native annual; desert shrub to pinyon-juniper communities, 1360-1880 m.

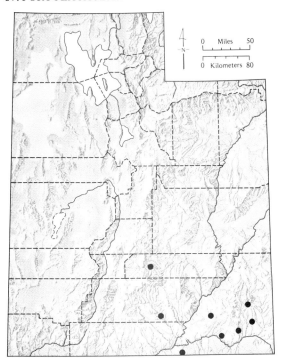

14. **Talinum brevifolium** Torr. Shortleaf flameflower. May-June. Native perennial herb; rocky sites in pinyon-juniper communities, 1510-1940 m.

15. **Talinum parviflorum** Nutt. Prairie flameflower. July-Aug. Native perennial herb; rocky sites in pinyon-juniper to ponderosa pine communities, 1510-2670 m.

88. POTAMOGETONACEAE

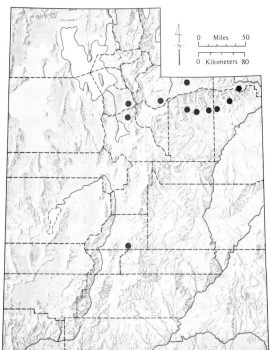

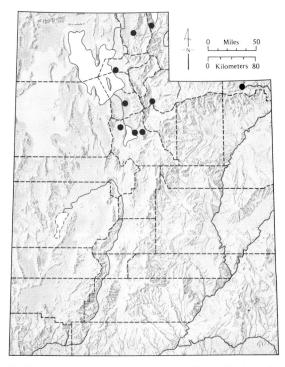

1. **Potamogeton alpinus** Balbis Northern pondweed. July-Aug. Circumboreal perennial; water of ponds, lakes, 2470-3030 m.

2. **Potamogeton crispus** L. Curlyleaf pondweed. July-Aug. Introduced perennial; fresh or brackish, quiet or slow-moving water of ponds, ditches, streams, 1360-1820 m.

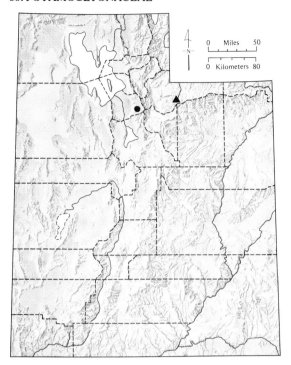

3. *Potamogeton epihydrus* Raf. Ribbonleaf pondweed. July-Aug. Native perennial; shallow to deep water of lakes, ponds, slow-moving streams, 2630-3030 m.

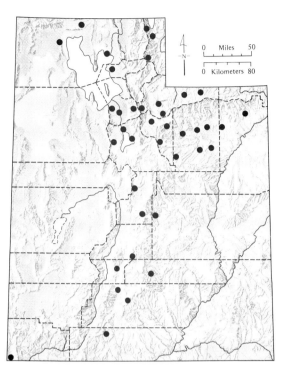

4. *Potamogeton filiformis* Pers. Fineleaf pondweed. July-Sept. Cosmopolitan perennial; in fresh or brackish, shallow water of ponds, lakes, slow-moving streams, 810-3030 m.

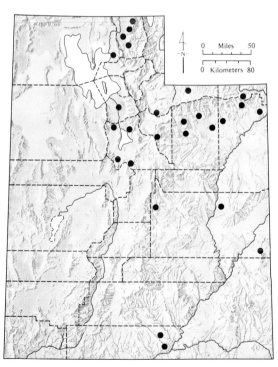

5. *Potamogeton foliosus* Raf. Leafy pondweed. July-Aug. Native perennial; shallow, often warm, quiet or slow-moving water of ponds, lakes, streams, 1300-2790 m.

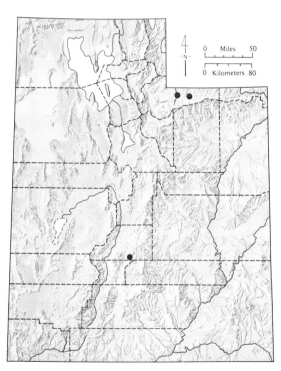

6. *Potamogeton friesii* Rupr. Fries pondweed. July-Aug. Circumboreal perennial; water of shallow ponds, lakes, 2570-3120 m.

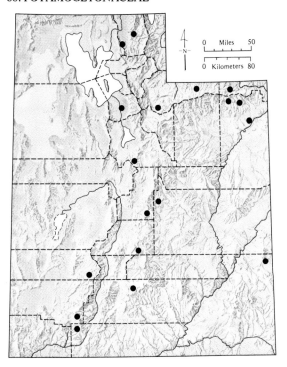

7. *Potamogeton gramineus* L. Grass pondweed. June-Aug. Circumboreal perennial; slow-moving or quiet water of ditches, marshes, ponds, lakes, 1300-3180 m.

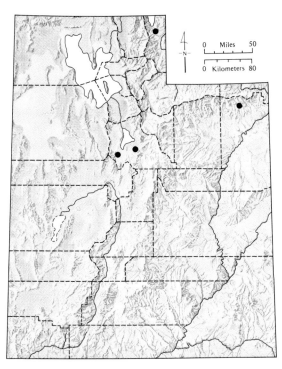

8. *Potamogeton natans* L. Floating pondweed. July-Aug. Circumboreal perennial; fresh or brackish water of slow-moving streams, shallow ponds and lakes, 1780-2730 m.

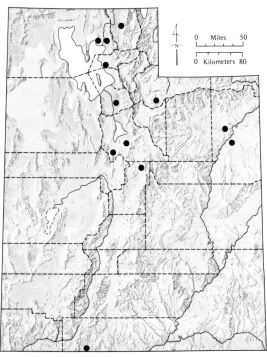

9. *Potamogeton nodosus* Poir. Longleaf pondweed. July-Aug. Cosmopolitan perennial; shallow to deep, quiet or slow-moving water of ponds, lakes, 1280-3030 m.

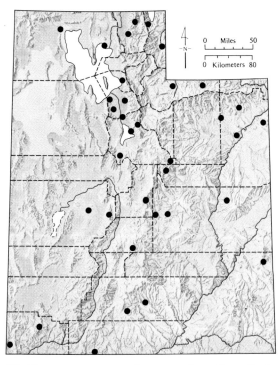

10. *Potamogeton pectinatus* L. Fennelleaf pondweed. July-Aug. Cosmopolitan perennial; fresh or brackish, shallow water of ditches, streams, ponds, lakes, 810-2580 m.

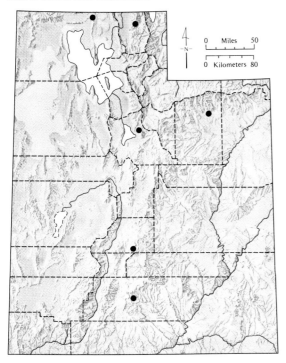

11. ***Potamogeton praelongus*** Wulf. Whitestem pondweed. June-Aug. Circumboreal perennial; deep cold water of lakes, 2620-2680 m.

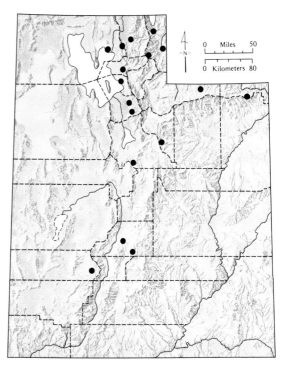

12. ***Potamogeton pusillus*** L. Dwarf pondweed. July-Aug. Circumboreal perennial; shallow slow-moving water of ponds, lakes, streams, 1280-3030 m.

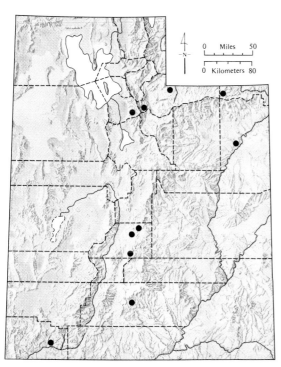

13. ***Potamogeton richardsonii*** (Benn.) Rydb. Richardson pondweed. June-Aug. Native perennial; shallow water of ponds, lakes, slow-moving streams, 1280-2730 m.

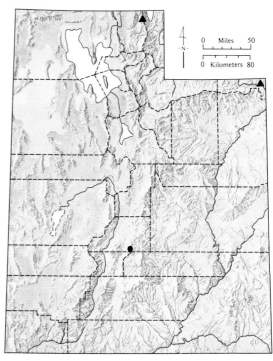

14. ***Potamogeton robbinsii*** Oakes Robbins pondweed. Aug.-Sept. Native perennial; slow-moving deep water of lakes, ponds, 2700-2900 m.

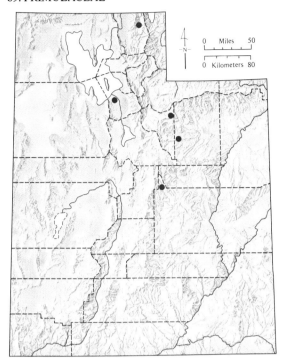

1. *Androsace filiformis* Retz. Slenderleaf rockjasmine. July-Aug. Native perennial herb; marshes, meadows, lake shores, 1280-3030 m.

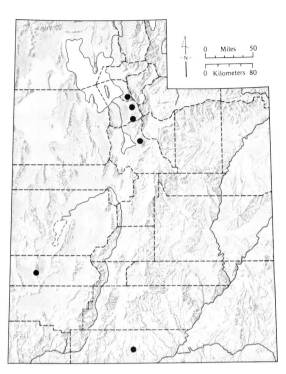

2. *Androsace occidentalis* Pursh Western rockjasmine. May-June. Native annual; dry open slopes in sagebrush communities, 1420-1580 m.

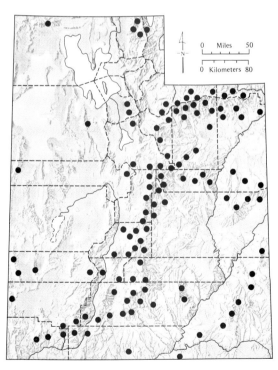

3. *Androsace septentrionalis* L. Pygmy-flower rockjasmine. May-Aug. Circumboreal annual; dry to moist sites in mountain brush to aspen-conifer, alpine communities, often on open rocky slopes, 1810-3580 m.

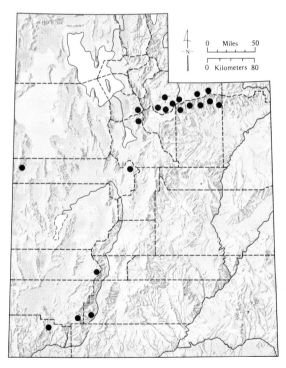

4. *Dodecatheon alpinum* (Gray) Greene Alpine shooting star. June-Aug. Native perennial herb; streamside, meadows, alpine communities, 2570-3490 m.

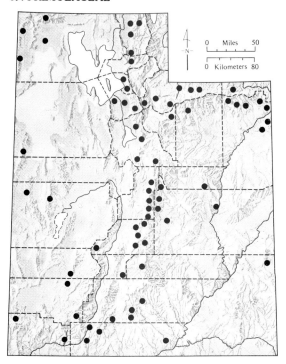

5. *Dodecatheon pulchellum* (Raf.) Merr. Pretty shooting star. Apr.-Aug. Native perennial herb; wet cliffs, moist meadows, shaded sites in conifer forests, 1360-3330 m.

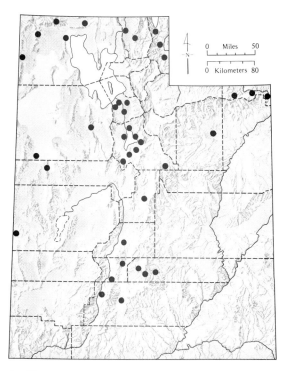

6. *Glaux maritima* L. Sea milkwort. June-July. Circumboreal perennial herb; wet meadows, near seeps and springs, salt tolerant, 1300-2180 m.

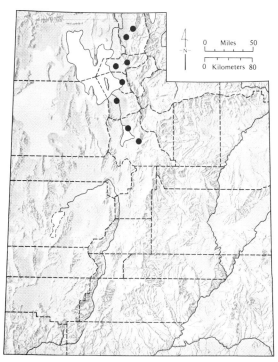

7. *Lysimachia ciliata* L. Fringed loosestrife. June-July. Native perennial herb; wet meadows, along waterways, 1360-1820 m.

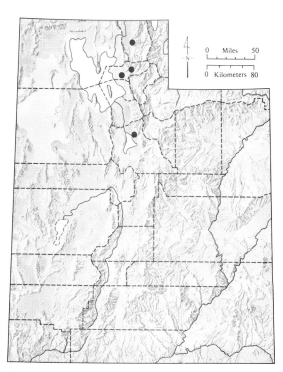

8. *Lysimachia thrysiflora* L. Tufted loosestrife. June-July. Circumboreal perennial herb; wet meadows, 1360-1820 m.

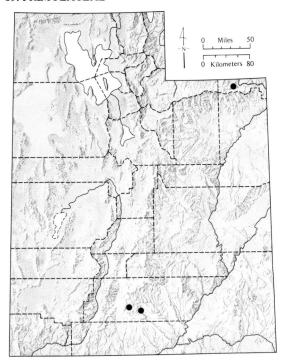

9. *Primula incana* Jones   Silvery primrose.
June-July.   Native perennial herb; marshes, wet
meadows, 1970-2640 m.

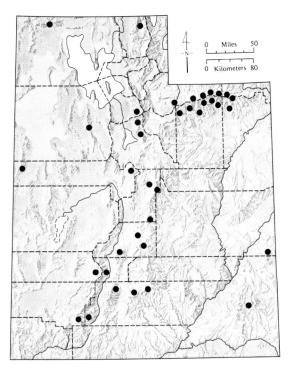

10. *Primula parryi* Gray   Parry primrose.
June-Aug.   Native perennial herb; rock crevices,
talus, alpine communities, 2450-3940 m.

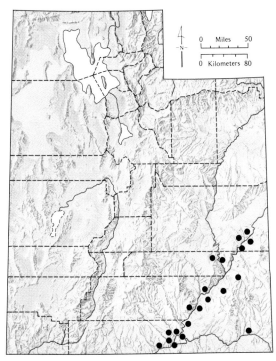

11. *Primula specuicola* Rydb.   Cave primrose.
Mar.-June.   Native perennial herb; hanging
gardens, wet cliffs, 1210-1520 m.

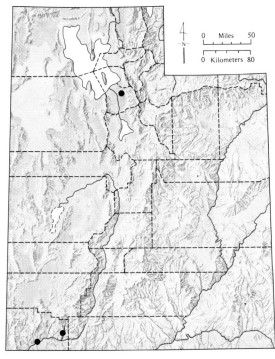

12. *Samolus   parviflorus*   Raf.   Water
pimpernell; brookweed.   May-Aug.   Native
perennial herb; along waterways, wet meadows,
840-1300 m.

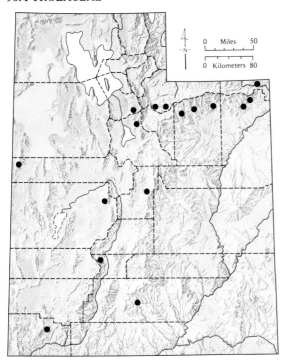

1. *Chimaphila umbellata* (L.) Barton
Pipsissewa; prince's pine. June-Aug. Circumboreal
perennial herb; dense shade in conifer forests,
1800-2730 m.

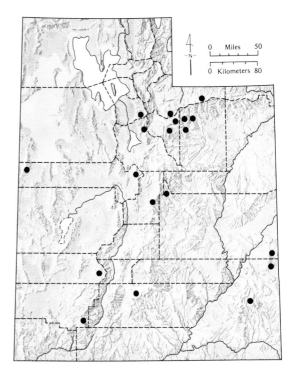

2. *Moneses uniflora* (L.) Gray   Wax flower;
wood nymph. July-Aug. Circumboreal perennial
herb; shaded sites in conifer forests, 2480-3330 m.

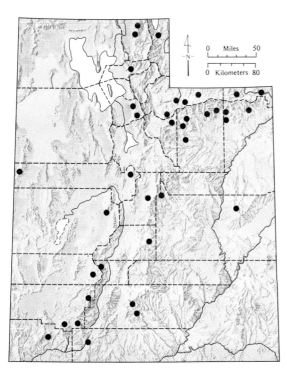

3. *Pyrola asarifolia* Michx.   Swamp or
liverleaf wintergreen. June-Aug. Native perennial
herb; shaded, usually wet sites in mountain brush,
aspen-spruce-fir, lodgepole pine communities,
1820-3180 m.

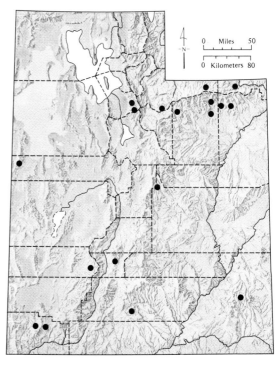

4. *Pyrola chlorantha* Swartz   Green
wintergreen. July-Aug. Native perennial herb;
shaded sites in conifer forests, 2600-3030 m.

90. PYROLACEAE

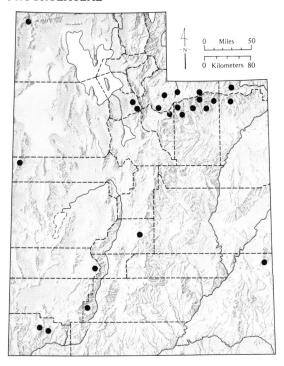

5. *Pyrola minor* L. Lesser wintergreen. July-Aug. Circumboreal perennial herb; moist shaded sites in conifer forests, 2270-3400 m.

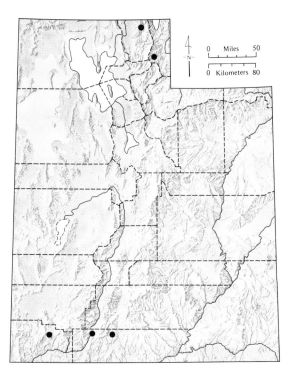

6. *Pyrola picta* J. E. Sm. Pictureleaf wintergreen. July-Aug. Native perennial herb; shaded sites in ponderosa pine, lodgepole pine, fir communities, 2420-2580 m.

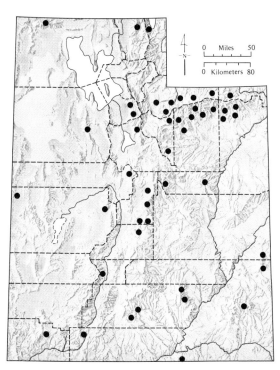

7. *Pyrola secunda* L. Sidebells wintergreen; shinleaf. June-Aug. Circumboreal perennial herb; shaded sites in aspen, spruce-fir communities, 2000-3400 m.

91. RANUNCULACEAE

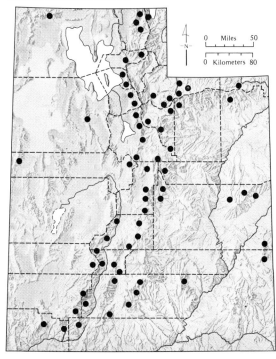

1. *Aconitum columbianum* Nutt. Monkshood. June-Aug. Native perennial herb; shaded sites in mountain brush to conifer communities, 1750-3350 m.

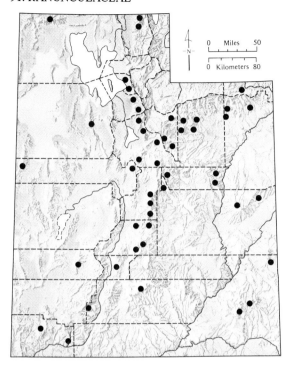

2. *Actaea rubra* (Ait.) Willd. Baneberry. May-Aug. Native perennial herb; shaded sites in mountain brush to conifer communities, 1570-2970 m.

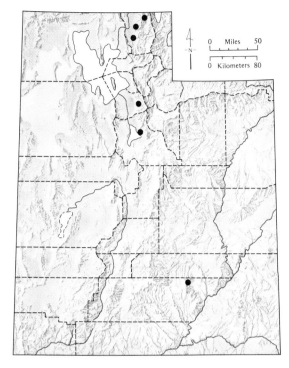

3. *Adonis aestivalis* L. Pheasant-eye. May-June. Introduced annual; cultivated, escaping and persistent, 1330-2030 m.

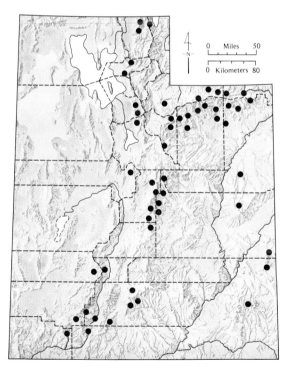

4. *Anemone multifida* Poir. Globeflower; cutleaf anemone. June-Aug. Native perennial herb; sagebrush to spruce-fir, ponderosa pine forests, moist meadows, open rocky slopes, often above timberline, 2180-3490 m.

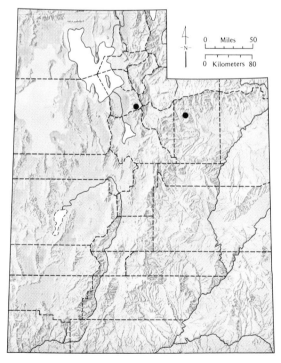

5. *Anemone parviflora* Michx. Arctic windflower. July-Aug. Native perennial herb; lake shores in spruce-fir communities, 3030-3180 m.

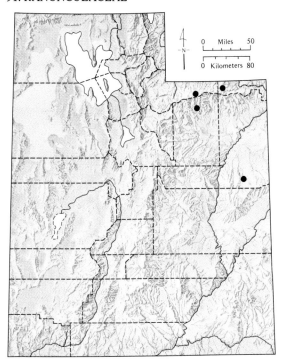

6. *Anemone patens* L. Pasque flower. July-Aug. Native perennial herb; aspen, lodgepole pine, ponderosa pine communities, 2040-2800 m.

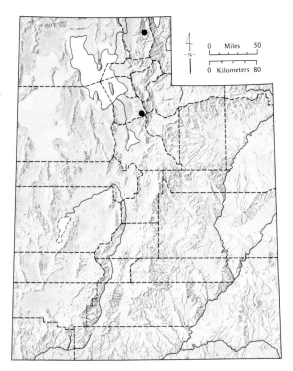

7. *Anemone quinquefolia* L. American wood anemone. May-July. Native perennial herb; openings in spruce-fir communities, 2030-2880 m.

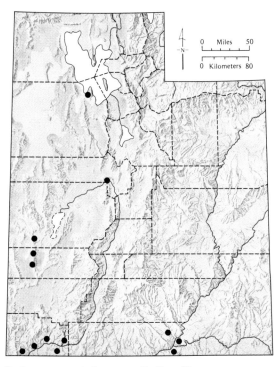

8. *Anemone tuberosa* Rydb. Desert anemone. Mar.-May. Native perennial herb; rocky sites in creosote bush to desert shrub communities, 840-1640 m.

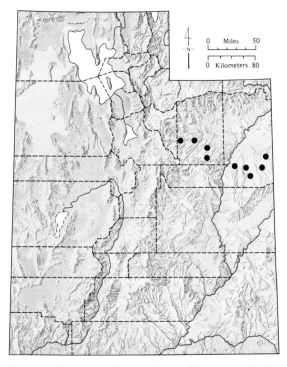

9. *Aquilegia barnebyi* Munz Shale columbine. June-July. Native perennial herb; moist to dry sites in desert shrub to pinyon-juniper communities, 1750-2120 m.

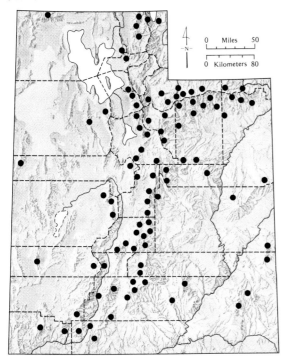

10. *Aquilegia caerulea* James Colorado columbine. June-Aug. Native perennial herb; shaded sites in mountain brush to conifer communities, 1660-3640 m.

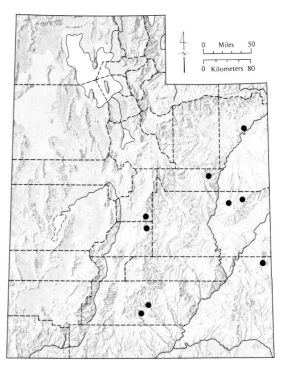

11. *Aquilegia elegantula* Greene Elegant columbine. June-July. Native perennial herb; mountain brush to conifer communities, often in rock crevices, 1660-3180 m.

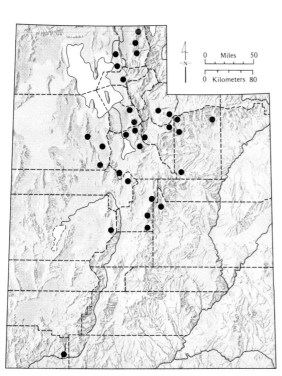

12. *Aquilegia flavescens* Wats. Yellow columbine. June-Aug. Native perennial herb; mountain brush to conifer communities, 1360-3250 m.

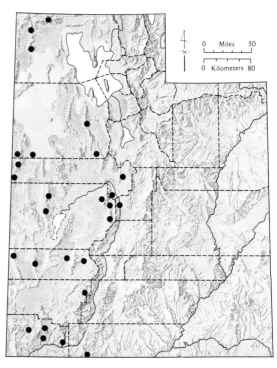

13. *Aquilegia formosa* Fisch. Western columbine. May-Sept. Native perennial herb; streamside, near seeps and springs in desert shrub to conifer communities, 1360-3030 m.

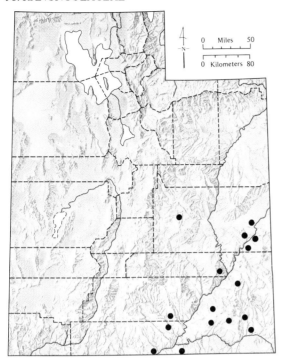

14. *Aquilegia micrantha* Eastw. Alcove columbine. May-June. Native perennial herb; hanging gardens, near seeps and springs in desert shrub communities, 1270-2330 m.

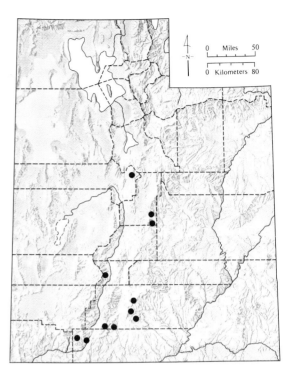

15. *Aquilegia scopulorum* Tides. Rock columbine. June-Aug. Native perennial herb; pinyon-juniper, ponderosa pine, bristlecone pine, spruce-fir communities, usually among rocks, 2120-3330 m.

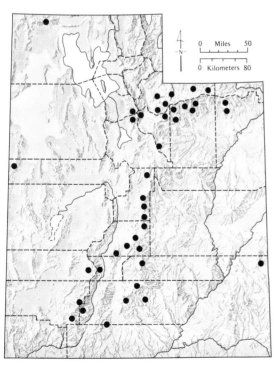

16. *Caltha leptosepala* DC. Marsh marigold. May-July. Native perennial herb; streamside, wet meadows, near seeps and springs in aspen-conifer communities to above timberline, 2270-3490 m.

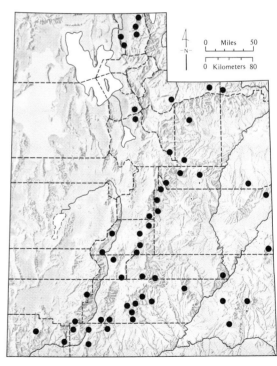

17. *Clematis columbiana* (Nutt.) T. & G. Rocky Mountain clematis. May-Sept. Native perennial herb; open slopes or in shade, mountain brush to conifer communities, 1450-3300 m.

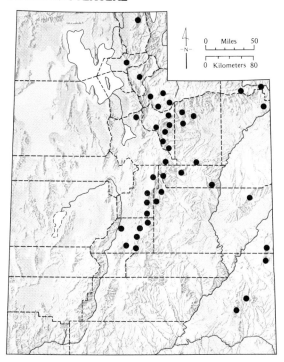

18. *Clematis hirsutissima* Pursh Lion's beard. May-Aug. Native perennial herb; meadows, mountain brush, aspen, spruce-fir, ponderosa pine communities, 2030-3330 m.

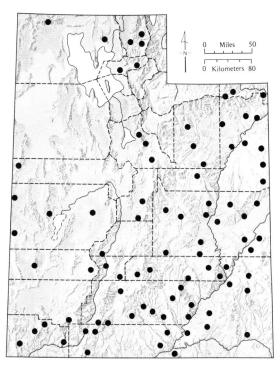

19. *Clematis ligusticifolia* Nutt. White virgin's bower. July-Aug. Native perennial vine; meadows, along waterways and fences in creosote bush to pinyon-juniper communities, 940-2430 m.

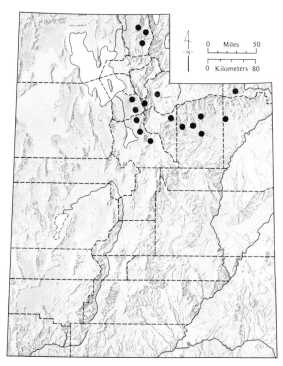

20. *Clematis occidentalis* (Hornem.) DC. Blue clematis. May-Aug. Native perennial vine; shaded sites in mountain brush to spruce-fir communities, 1660-2640 m.

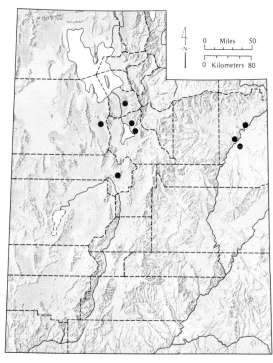

21. *Clematis orientalis* L. Oriental clematis. July-Sept. Introduced perennial vine; streamside, waste places, 1360-2270 m.

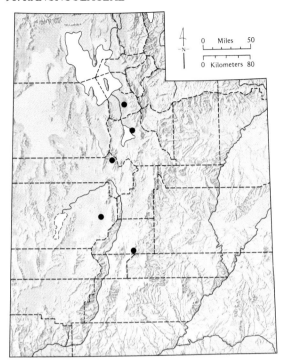

22. **Delphinium ajacis** L. Rocket larkspur. June-Aug. Introduced annual; cultivated, escaping, possibly persistent, 1300-2120 m.

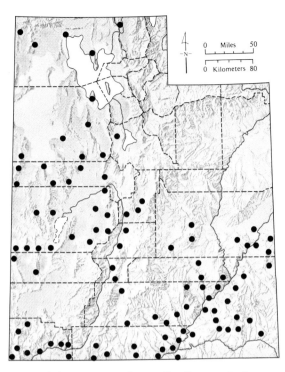

23. **Delphinium andersonii** Gray Anderson larkspur. Apr.-June. Native perennial herb; creosote bush to pinyon-juniper and mountain brush communities, 780-2730 m.

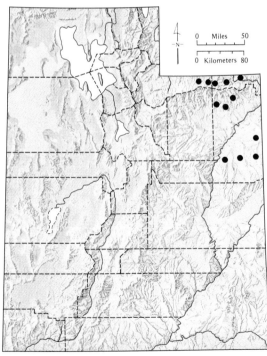

24. **Delphinium geyeri** Greene Geyer larkspur. May-Aug. Native perennial herb; desert shrub to aspen communities, 1690-2700 m.

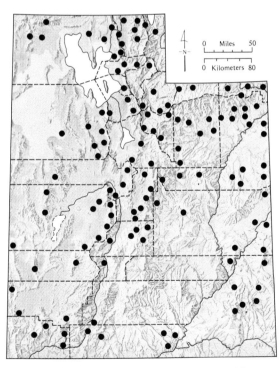

25. **Delphinium nuttallianum** Pritz. Nelson or low larkspur. Apr.-July. Native perennial herb; desert shrub to meadow, conifer communities, 1210-3270 m.

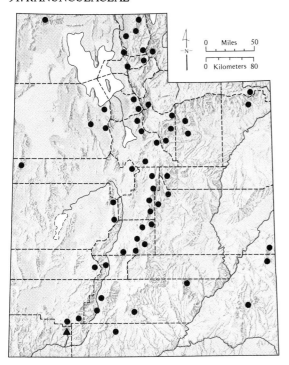

26. *Delphinium occidentale* (Wats.) Wats. Western larkspur. July-Aug. Native perennial herb; sagebrush to aspen, spruce-fir, ponderosa pine, meadow communities, 1570-3330 m.

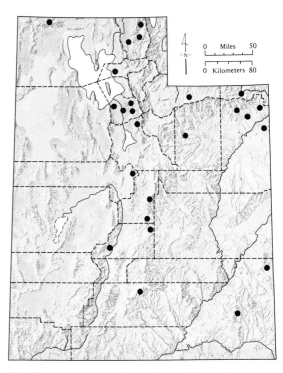

27. *Myosurus apetalus* Gay Mousetail. Apr.-Aug. Native annual; moist sites in salt desert shrub communities, pond and lake margins, meadows, 1280-3030 m.

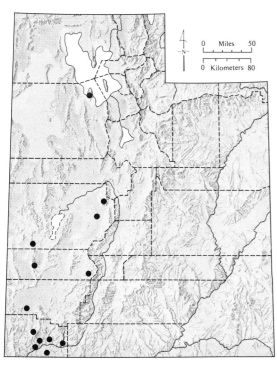

28. *Myosurus cupulatus* Wats. Horseshoe mousetail. Apr.-May. Native annual; desert shrub to mountain brush, usually among rocks or in mud of ephemeral pools, 1060-2120 m.

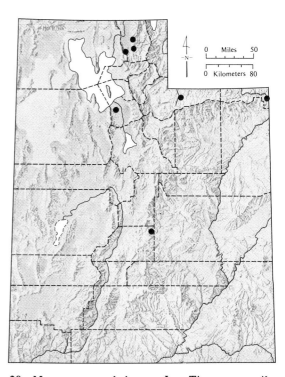

29. *Myosurus minimus* L. Tiny mousetail. Apr.-July. Circumboreal annual; moist sites, salt desert shrub to mountain brush communities, 1280-2520 m.

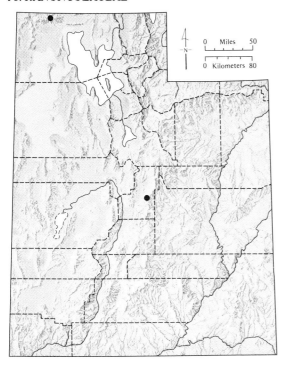

30. *Paeonia brownii* Hook. Peony. May-June. Native perennial herb; sagebrush, mountain brush communities, 1510-1820 m.

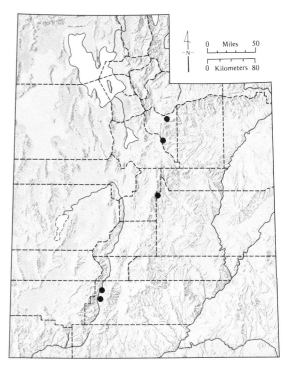

31. *Ranunculus acriformis* Gray Sharpseed buttercup. July-Aug. Native perennial herb; wet meadows, 1940-2840 m.

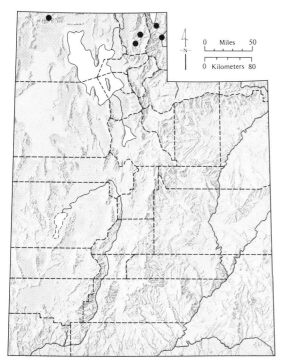

32. *Ranunculus acris* L. Tall buttercup. June-Sept. Introduced perennial herb; streamside, wet meadows, 1970-2120 m.

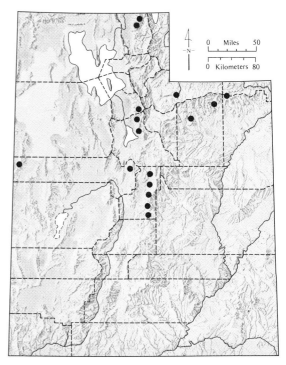

33. *Ranunculus adoneus* Gray Alpine buttercup. June-Aug. Native perennial herb; open, often rocky slopes, meadow, spruce-fir communities, often in the wake of melting snow, 2480-3330 m.

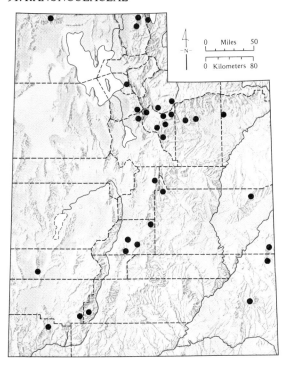

34. *Ranunculus alismaefolius* Benth. Plantainleaf buttercup. May-July. Native perennial herb; sagebrush-mountain brush to spruce-fir, wet meadow communities, 2240-3640 m.

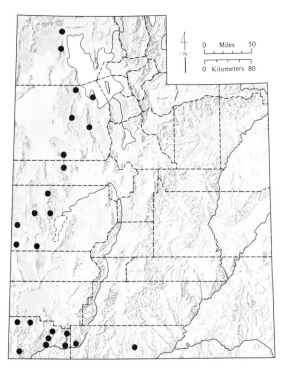

35. *Ranunculus andersonii* Gray Violet buttercup. Apr.-May. Native perennial herb; creosote bush to ponderosa pine, aspen-fir communities, commonly in rock crevices, 970-2400 m.

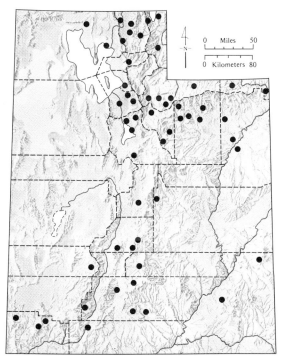

36. *Ranunculus aquatilis* L. Water crowfoot. May-Sept. Circumboreal perennial herb; in water of streams, ponds, lakes, 1270-3270 m.

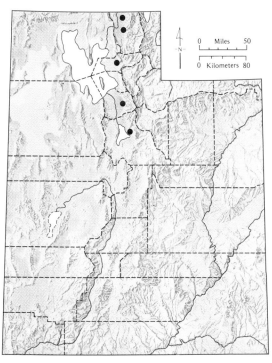

37. *Ranunculus arvensis* L. Field or corn buttercup. May-June. Introduced annual; open waste places, 1360-1670 m.

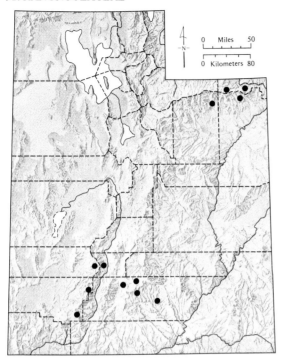

38. *Ranunculus cardiophyllus* Hook. Showy
buttercup. June-Aug. Native perennial herb;
meadows in aspen-conifer communities, 2300-
3580 m.

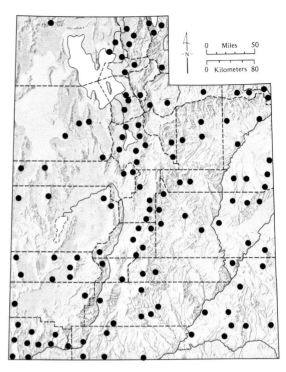

39. *Ranunculus cymbalaria* Pursh Marsh
buttercup. May-Sept. Native perennial herb;
streamside, marshes, pond and lake margins, 780-
2730 m.

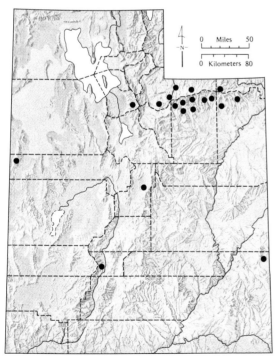

40. *Ranunculus eschscholtzii* Schlecht.
Eschscholtz buttercup. July-Aug. Native perennial
herb; meadows, openings in spruce-fir forests, open
rocky slopes, often in the wake of melting snow,
2720-3490 m.

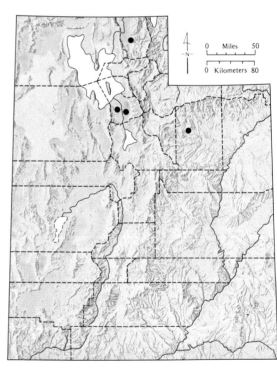

41. *Ranunculus flabellaris* Raf. Yellow-water
crowfoot. Apr.-May. Native perennial herb;
marshes, along waterways, other wet sites, 1300-
2300 m.

526

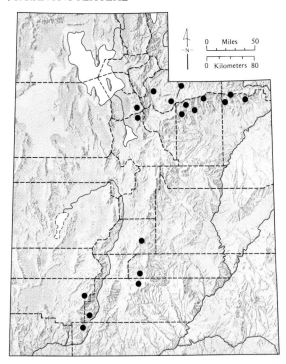

42. ***Ranunculus flammula*** L. Spearwort. July-
Aug. Circumboreal perennial herb; wet to drying
mud along margins of lakes and ponds, wet sites or
shallow water in meadows in aspen-conifer
communities, 2330-3330 m.

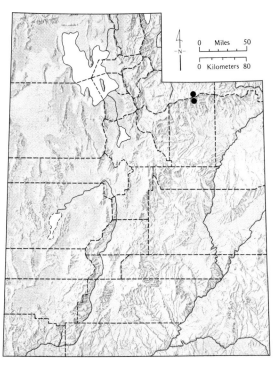

43. ***Ranunculus gelidus*** Kar. & Kir. Gel
buttercup. July-Aug. Native perennial herb; rocky
slopes and meadows above timberline, 3480-
3790 m.

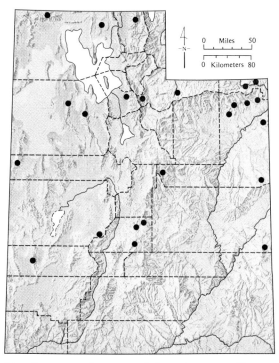

44. ***Ranunculus glaberrimus*** Hook.
Sagebrush buttercup. Apr.-June. Native perennial
herb; open slopes, streamside, meadows in
sagebrush to aspen-conifer communities, 1450-
3030 m.

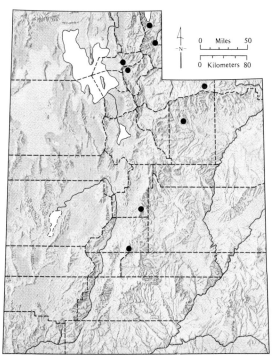

45. ***Ranunculus gmelinii*** DC. Gmelin
buttercup. June-Aug. Native perennial herb; water
or drying mud of streams and ponds, 1690-2910 m.

527

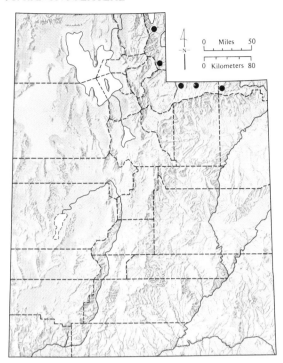

46. *Ranunculus hyperboreus* Rottb. Arctic buttercup. July-Aug. Circumboreal perennial herb; marshes, wet meadows, 1910-2880 m.

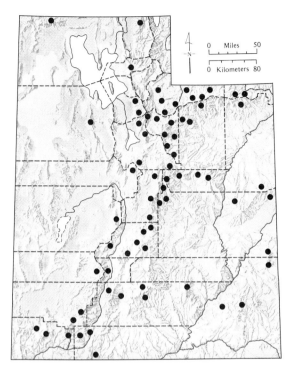

47. *Ranunculus inamoenus* Greene Drab buttercup. June-Sept. Native perennial herb; open slopes, streamside, wet meadows in sagebrush to aspen-conifer communities, 1360-3490 m.

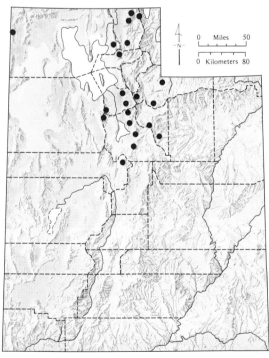

48. *Ranunculus jovis* A. Nels. Jupiter buttercup. Feb.-July. Native perennial herb; moist sites in sagebrush to aspen, spruce-fir communities, often in the wake of melting snow, 1660-2730 m.

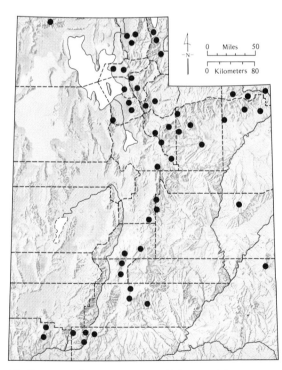

49. *Ranunculus macounii* Britton Macoun or bristly crowfoot. May-July. Native annual to perennial; streamside, pond margins, wet meadows, 1390-2880 m.

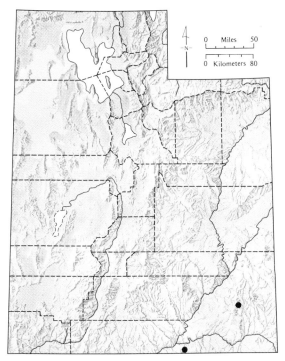

50. *Ranunculus oreogenes* Greene Mountain buttercup. Apr.-June. Native perennial herb; pinyon-juniper, ponderosa pine communities, 2270-2520 m.

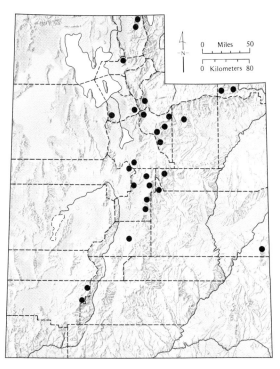

51. *Ranunculus orthorhynchus* Hook. Straightbeak buttercup. May-Aug. Native perennial herb; along waterways, wet meadows, near seeps and springs in sagebrush-grass, pinyon-juniper, aspen-spruce-fir communities, 2120-3030 m.

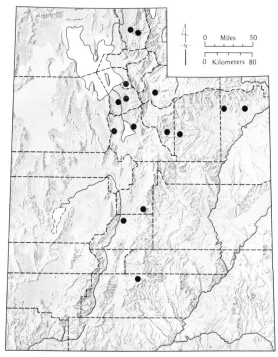

52. *Ranunculus repens* L. Creeping buttercup. May-June. Introduced perennial herb; along waterways, wet meadows, weed of cultivated and disturbed moist places, 1300-2340 m.

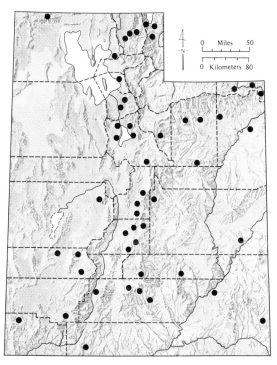

53. *Ranunculus sceleratus* L. Blister buttercup. May-Sept. Circumboreal annual; along waterways, pond margins, marshes, near seeps and springs, wet meadows, 1280-3120 m.

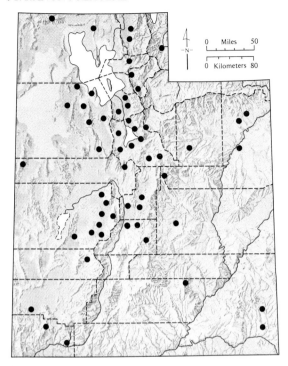

54. *Ranunculus testiculatus* Crantz Bur buttercup. Apr.-June. Introduced annual; disturbed sites in salt desert shrub to mountain brush communities, 1150-3030 m.

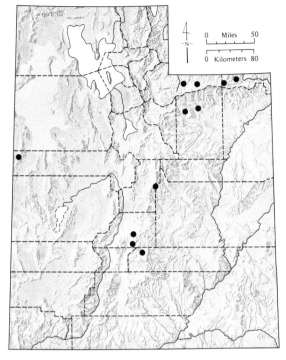

55. *Thalictrum alpinum* L. Arctic meadowrue. July-Aug. Circumboreal perennial herb; wet meadows, 2570-3090 m.

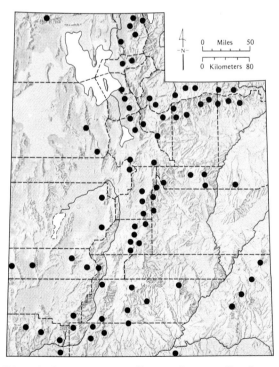

56. *Thalictrum fendleri* Gray Fendler meadowrue. June-Aug. Native perennial herb; open to shaded sites in mountain brush to aspen-conifer communities, 1360-3430 m.

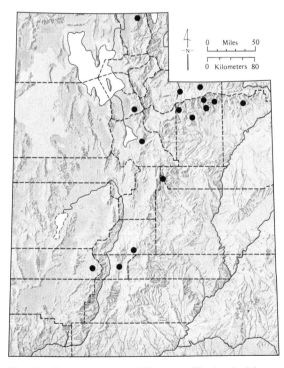

57. *Thalictrum sparsiflorum* Fisch. & Mey. Fewleaf meadowrue. June-Aug. Native perennial herb; open to shaded sites in aspen-conifer communities, 1840-3330 m.

91. RANUNCULACEAE

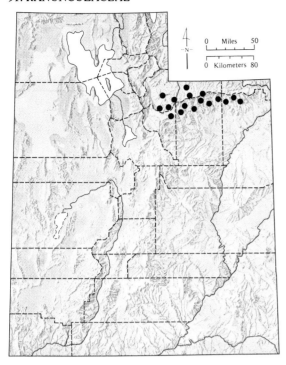

58. **Trollius laxus** Salisb. American globe-flower. June-Aug. Native perennial herb; wet meadows, other moist sites in aspen-conifer communities, 2620-3490 m.

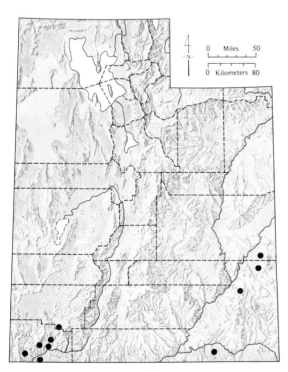

2. **Ceanothus greggii** Gray Desert mountain lilac. Apr.-May. Native perennial herb; creosote bush to pinyon-juniper communities, 910-1370 m.

92. RHAMNACEAE

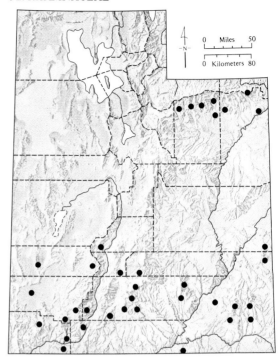

1. **Ceanothus fendleri** Gray Fendler mountain lilac. June-July. Native perennial herb; ponderosa pine communities, dry, often rocky slopes, 1060-2580 m.

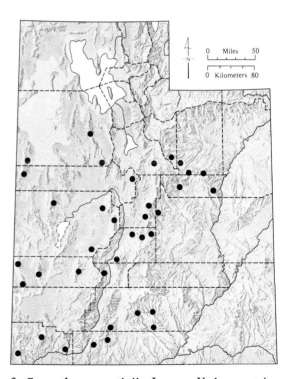

3. **Ceanothus martinii** Jones Utah mountain lilac. June-July. Native perennial herb; pinyon-juniper, mountain brush to conifer communities, 2030-2910 m.

92. RHAMNACEAE

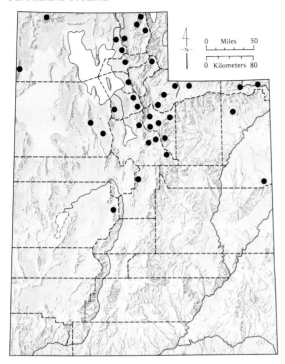

4. *Ceanothus velutinus* Dougl. Deerbrush. June-Aug. Native perennial herb; mountain brush to conifer communities, 1810-2880 m.

5. *Rhamnus betulaefolia* Greene Birchleaf buckthorn. May-June. Native perennial herb; hanging gardens, rock crevices in desert shrub communities, 970-1880 m.

93. ROSACEAE

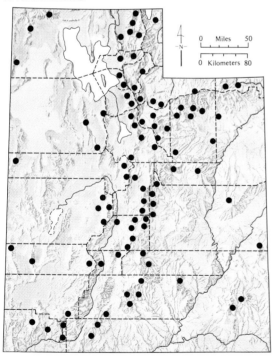

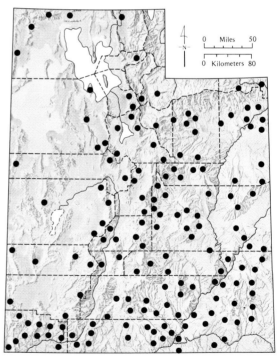

1. *Amelanchier alnifolia* Nutt. Serviceberry; saskatoon. May-Aug. Native shrub, a major component of the mountain brush community; streamside, meadows, mesic slopes in sagebrush to aspen-conifer communities, 1210-2880 m.

2. *Amelanchier utahensis* Koehne Utah serviceberry. May-Aug. Native shrub, a major component of the mountain brush community; streamside, dry slopes in creosote bush to mountain brush, pinyon-juniper, ponderosa pine communities, 970-2730 m.

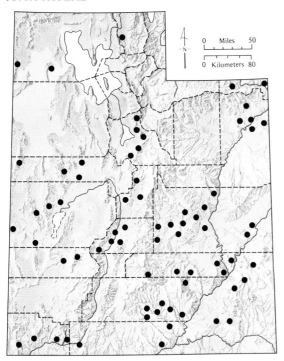

3. *Cercocarpus intricatus* Wats. Dwarf mountain mahogany. Mar.-Apr. Native shrub, a major component of the mountain brush community; rock crevices, dry slopes, desert shrub to mountain brush communities, 1360-2880 m.

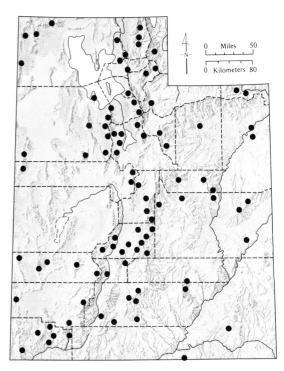

4. *Cercocarpus ledifolius* Nutt. Curlleaf mountain mahogany. May-June. Native shrub, a major component of the mountain brush community; dry open slopes and rocky ridges in mountain brush, pinyon-juniper to conifer communities, 1360-2900 m.

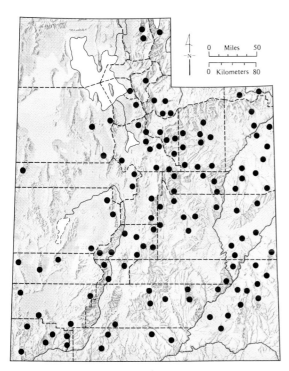

5. *Cercocarpus montanus* Raf. Alder leaf mountain mahogany. Apr.-June. Native shrub, a major component of the mountain brush community; dry, often rocky slopes, sagebrush to ponderosa pine communities, 1330-2730 m.

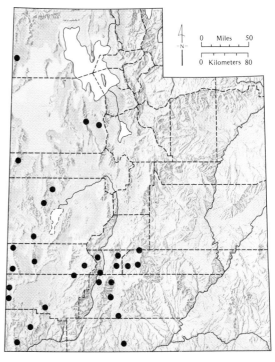

6. *Chamaebatiaria millefolium* (Torr.) Maxim. Fern bush. June-Sept. Native shrub; dry, often rocky slopes, rock crevices in cliffs in desert shrub, sagebrush, pinyon-juniper communities, 1510-2880 m.

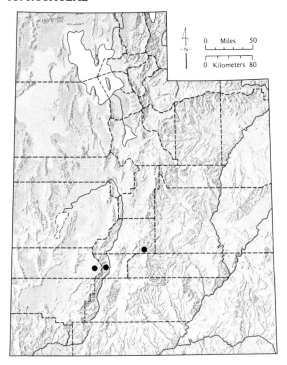

7. *Chamaerhodos erecta* (L.) Bunge June-Aug. Native biennial or perennial; sagebrush to alpine communities, 2720-3400 m.

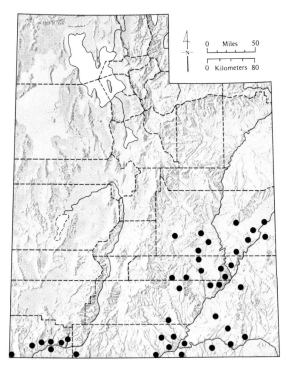

8. *Coleogyne ramosissima* Torr. Blackbrush. Apr.-June. Native shrub, a major component of the desert shrub community, often forming pure stands; creosote bush, desert shrub communities, 910-2000 m.

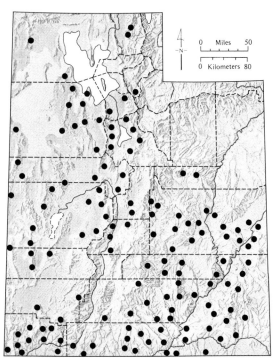

9. *Cowania mexicana* D. Don Cliffrose. Apr.-June. Native shrub; a major component of the desert shrub community; dry hillsides, cliffs in creosote bush to pinyon-juniper communities, 810-2180 m.

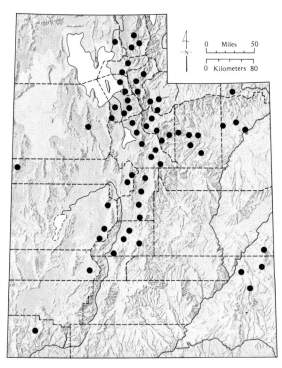

10. *Crataegus douglasii* Lindl. Douglas or river hawthorn. May-June. Native shrub or small tree; along waterways and other moist sites, 1300-2550 m.

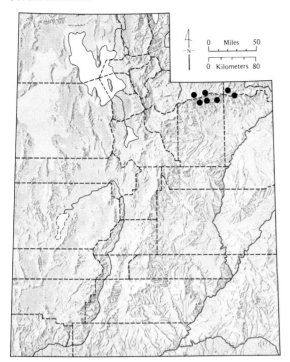

11. *Dryas octopetala* L. Mountain avens.
July-Aug. Circumboreal shrub; talus, rocky ridges
and meadows above timberline, 3330-3940 m.

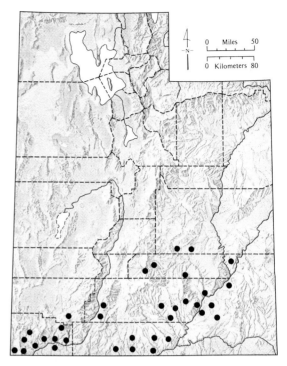

12. *Fallugia paradoxa* (D. Don) Endl. Apache
plume. May-June. Native shrub; dry washes in
desert shrub to pinyon-juniper communities, 780-
2120 m.

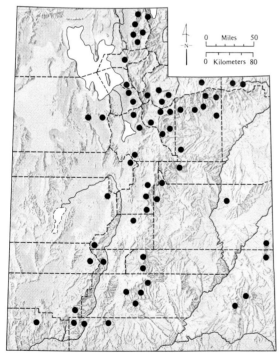

13. *Fragaria vesca* L. Woodland strawberry.
May-July. Native perennial herb; mountain brush
to aspen-conifer, alpine communities, 1360-
3520 m.

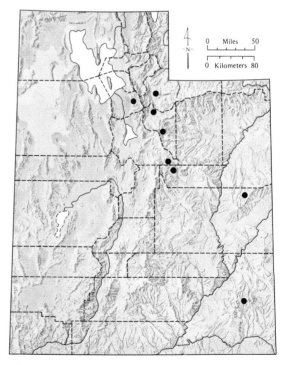

14. *Geum aleppicum* Jacq. Erect avens. June-
July. Circumboreal perennial herb; streamside,
moist meadows, 1360-2880 m.

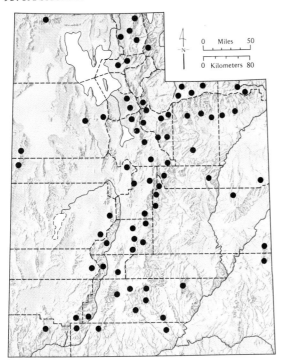

15. *Geum macrophyllum* Willd. Largeleaf
avens. May-Aug. Native perennial herb; marshes,
streamside, moist meadows in mountain brush to
aspen, spruce-fir communities, 1510-3030 m.

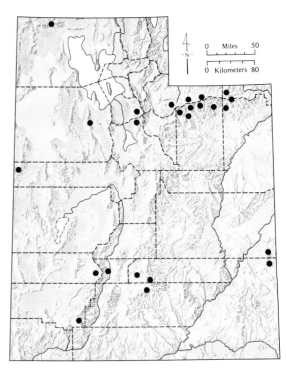

16. *Geum rossii* (R. Br.) Ser. Ross or alpine
avens. June-Aug. Native perennial herb; open
slopes, meadows, rocky ridges, often above
timberline, 2790-3940 m.

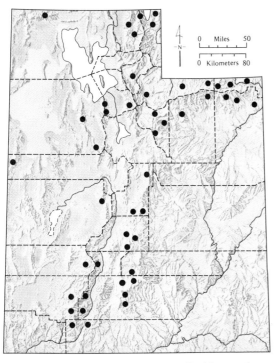

17. *Geum triflorum* Pursh   Prairie smoke.
May-July. Native perennial herb; open rocky to
grassy slopes, meadows, streamside in sagebrush to
aspen, spruce-fir, alpine communities, 1510-3490
m.

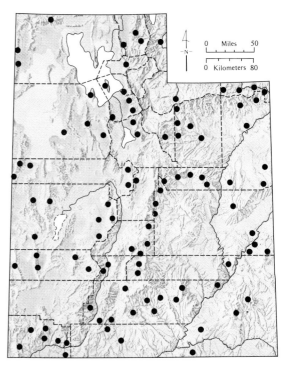

18. *Holodiscus dumosus* (Nutt.) Heller   Bush
ocean spray. June-July. Native shrub; cliffs, talus,
rock crevices from desert shrub to alpine
communities, 1210-3330 m.

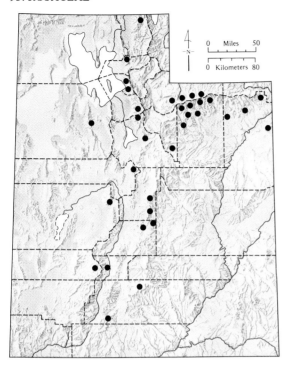

19. *Ivesia gordonii* (Hook.) T. & G. Gordon ivesia. July-Aug. Native perennial herb; open rocky or grassy slopes and exposed ridges in sagebrush to alpine communities, 2010-3330 m.

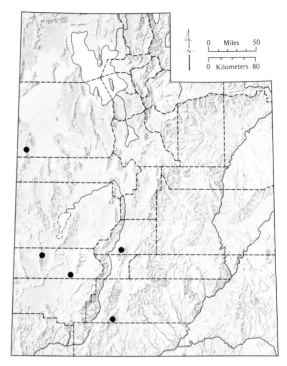

20. *Ivesia kingii* Wats. King ivesia. June-Aug. Native perennial herb; salt desert shrub communities, near hot springs, 1510-2430 m.

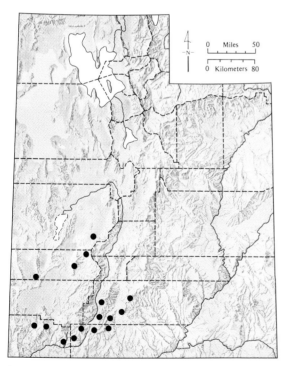

21. *Ivesia sabulosa* (Jones) Jones Sevier ivesia. June-July. Native perennial herb; sagebrush to ponderosa pine, bristlecone pine-spruce communities, 1510-2880 m.

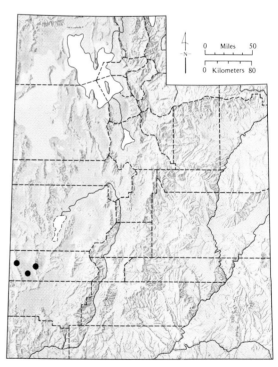

22. *Ivesia shockleyi* Wats. Shockley ivesia. June-July. Native perennial herb; rock crevices, gravelly slopes in pinyon-juniper to ponderosa pine communities, 2000-2800 m.

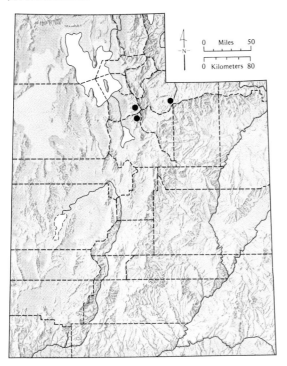

23. *Ivesia utahensis* Wats. Utah ivesia. July-Aug. Native perennial herb; open, rocky slopes in spruce-fir communities to above timberline, 3030-3330 m.

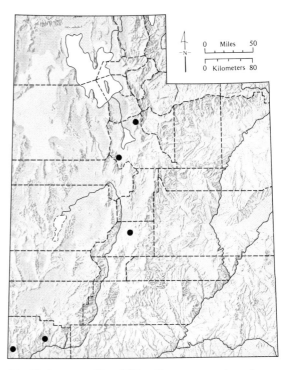

24. *Malus pumila* Mill. Common apple. Apr.-May. Introduced tree; cultivated and escaping, 780-1520 m.

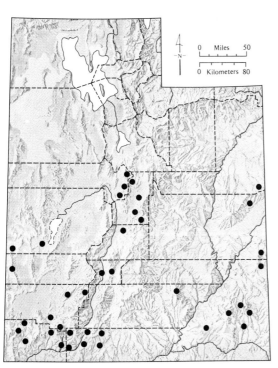

25. *Peraphyllum ramosissimum* Nutt. Squaw-apple. Apr.-May. Native perennial herb; sagebrush to ponderosa pine communities, 1360-2580 m.

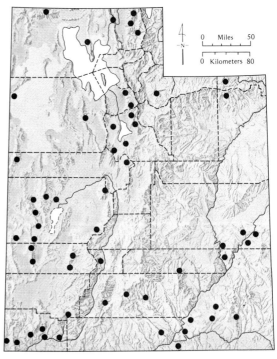

26. *Petrophytum caespitosum* (Nutt.) Rydb. Rock spiraea. June-Sept. Native mat-forming shrub; hanging gardens, rock outcrops in sagebrush to spruce-fir communities, 1210-3030 m.

538

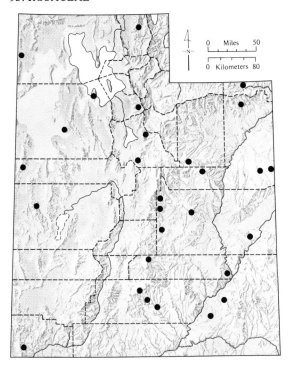

27. *Physocarpus alternans* (Jones) J. T. Howell Dwarf ninebark. May-Aug. Native shrub; rocky sites in desert shrub to ponderosa pine communities, 1300-2580 m.

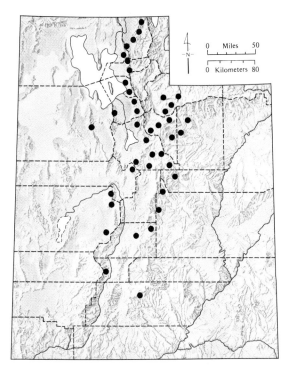

28. *Physocarpus malvaceus* (Greene) Kuntze Mallowleaf ninebark. May-July. Native shrub; a major component of the mountain brush community; streamside, moist slopes in mountain brush to conifer communities, 1510-2880 m.

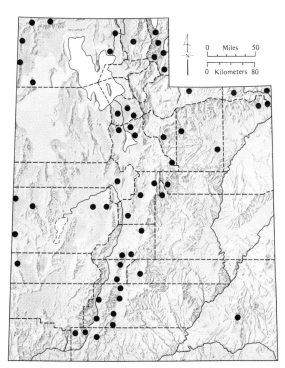

29. *Potentilla anserina* L. Silverweed cinquefoil. May-Sept. Circumboreal perennial herb; streamside, wet meadows, lake shores, 1300-2580 m.

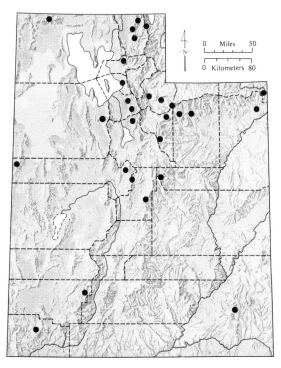

30. *Potentilla arguta* Pursh Sharptoothed cinquefoil. May-Aug. Native perennial herb; streamside, meadows, mountain brush to conifer communities, often in shaded sites, 1390-3030 m.

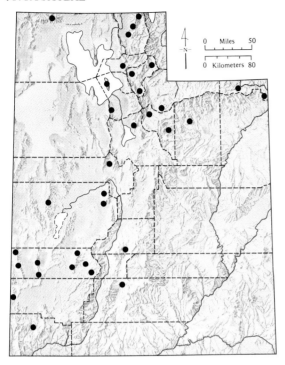

31. *Potentilla biennis* Greene Biennial cinquefoil. June-July. Native annual or biennial; along waterways, meadows, near seeps and springs, 1330-2610 m.

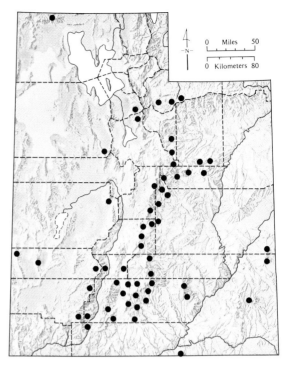

32. *Potentilla concinna* Richards. Pretty cinquefoil. May-July. Native perennial herb; sagebrush, pinyon-juniper, ponderosa pine, spruce-fir communities to above timberline, 1970-3490 m.

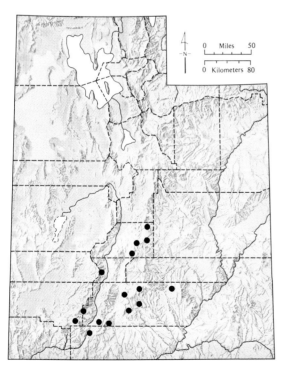

33. *Potentilla crinita* Gray Bearded cinquefoil. July-Aug. Native perennial herb; open, often rocky sites in mountain brush to aspen, ponderosa pine communities, 2270-2730 m.

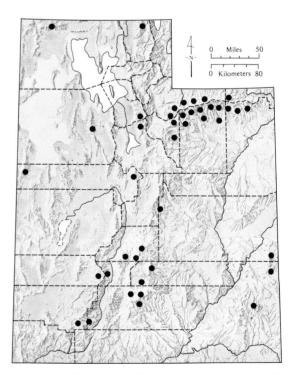

34. *Potentilla diversifolia* Lehm. Wedgeleaf cinquefoil. June-Aug. Native perennial herb; moist to dry sites in mountain brush, ponderosa pine, spruce-fir, alpine communities, 2120-3580 m.

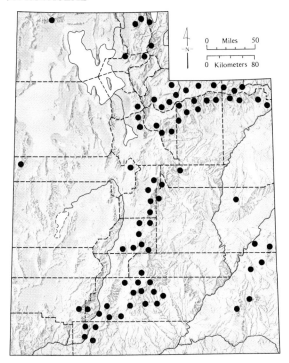

35. *Potentilla fruticosa* L. Shrubby cinquefoil. May-Sept. Circumboreal shrub; meadows, sagebrush to ponderosa pine, aspen, spruce-fir, alpine communities, 1880-3580 m.

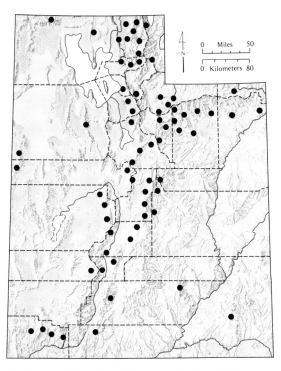

36. *Potentilla glandulosa* Lindl. Sticky or glandular cinquefoil. May-Aug. Native perennial herb; meadows, mountain brush to aspen-conifer communities, 1390-3180 m.

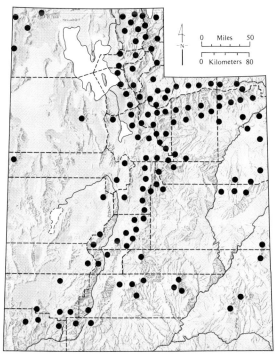

37. *Potentilla gracilis* Hook. Slender cinquefoil. May-Sept. Native perennial herb; meadows, sagebrush to aspen, spruce-fir, alpine communities, 1360-3490 m.

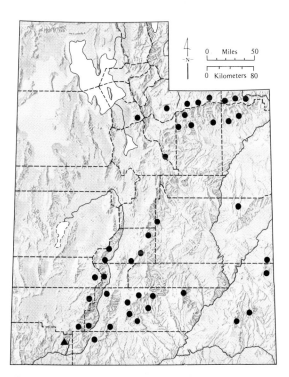

38. *Potentilla hippiana* Lehm. Horse cinquefoil. July-Aug. Native perennial herb; dry, often rocky sites in aspen, spruce-fir, alpine communities, 2420-3640 m.

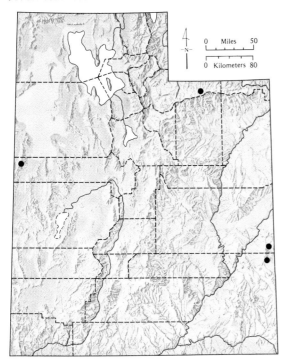

39. *Potentilla nivea* L. Snowy cinquefoil. July-Aug. Circumboreal perennial herb; open sites in conifer to alpine communities, 3300-3940 m.

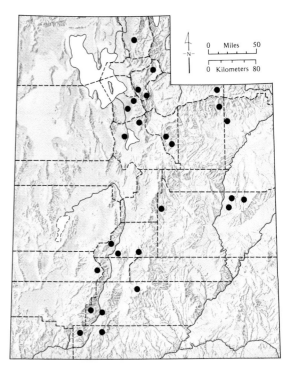

40. *Potentilla norvegica* L. Norwegian cinquefoil. June-Aug. Circumboreal annual or biennial; wet meadows, near seeps and springs, pond margins, shaded sites in mountain brush communities, 1300-2900 m.

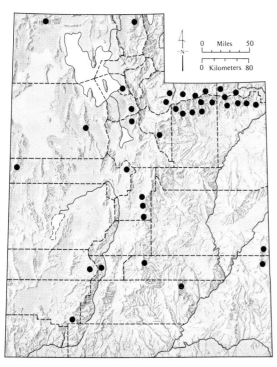

41. *Potentilla ovina* Macoun Sheep cinquefoil. June-Aug. Native perennial herb; meadows, rocky ridges in aspen-conifer to alpine communities, 2420-3490 m.

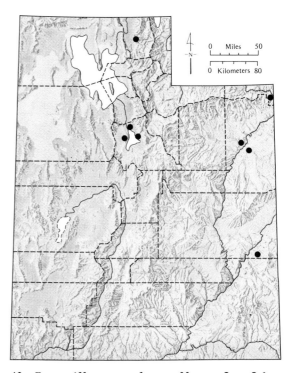

42. *Potentilla paradoxa* Nutt. June-July. Native annual to perennial; marshes, lake shores, 1360-1660 m.

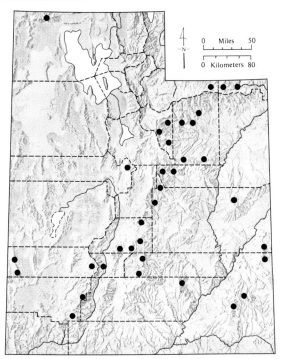

43. *Potentilla pensylvanica* L. July-Aug. Native perennial herb; open, often rocky sites in sagebrush communities to above timberline, 2240-3490 m.

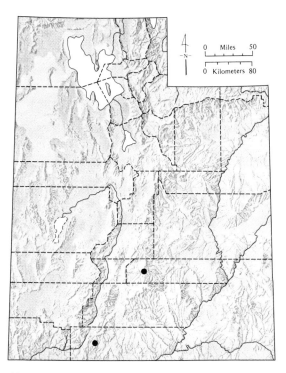

44. *Potentilla plattensis* Nutt. July-Aug. Native perennial herb; wet meadows, other moist sites, 1810-2120 m.

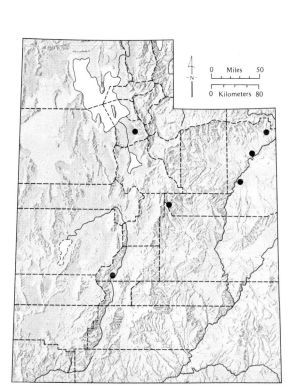

45. *Potentilla rivalis* Nutt. Brook cinquefoil. June-July. Native annual or biennial; moist sites, 1390-2300 m.

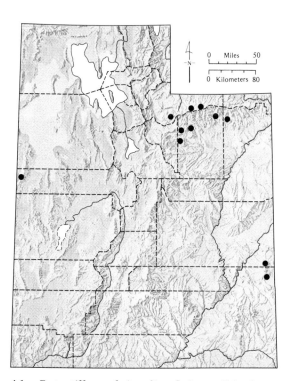

46. *Potentilla rubricaulis* Lehm. July-Aug. Native perennial herb; open sites in aspen to alpine communities, 2390-3790 m.

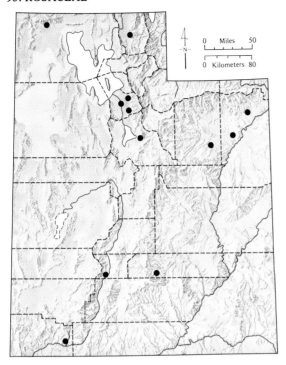

47. *Prunus americana* Marsh. American plum. May-June. Native shrub or small tree; cultivated, escaping and persistent, 1330-1940 m.

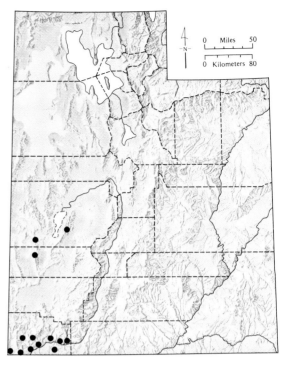

48. *Prunus fasciculata* (Torr.) Gray Desert peach. Mar.-May. Native shrub; creosote bush, desert shrub communities, 780-1520 m.

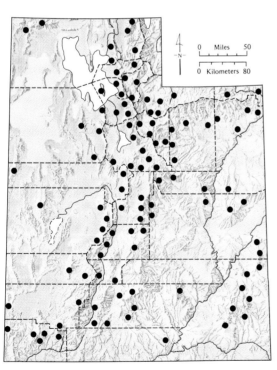

49. *Prunus virginiana* L. Chokecherry. May-July. Native shrub or small tree, an important component of the mountain brush community; sagebrush, pinyon-juniper, mountain brush, aspen communities, 1360-3030 m.

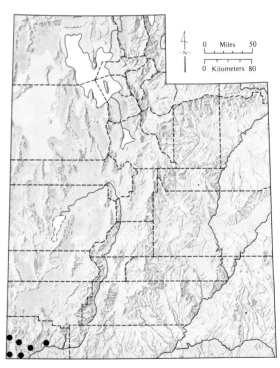

50. *Purshia glandulosa* Curran Desert bitterbrush. Apr.-May. Native shrub; creosote bush, desert shrub, pinyon-juniper communities, 970-1370 m.

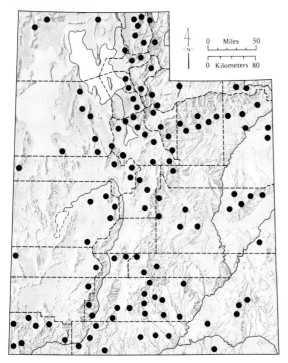

51. *Purshia tridentata* (Pursh) DC.
Bitterbrush. May-June. Native shrub; sagebrush,
mountain brush, pinyon-juniper, ponderosa pine
communities, 1210-2730 m.

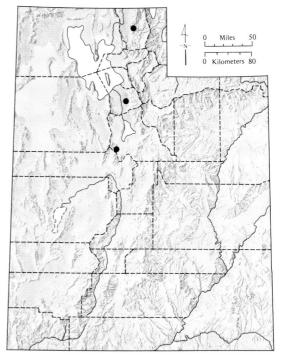

52. *Rosa canina* L. Dog rose. May-June.
Introduced shrub; cultivated, escaping and
persistent, 1330-1400 m.

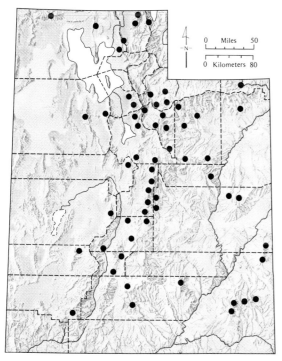

53. *Rosa nutkana* Presl Nutka rose. June-Aug.
Native shrub; mountain brush to conifer
communities, 1660-3150 m.

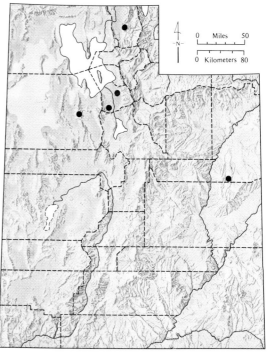

54. *Rosa rubiginosa* L. June-July. Introduced
shrub; cultivated, escaping and persistent, 1360-
2730 m.

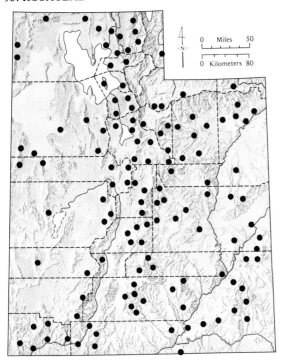

55. *Rosa woodsii* Lindl. Woods rose. June-Aug. Native shrub; marshes, along waterways, mountain brush to conifer communities, 840-3330 m.

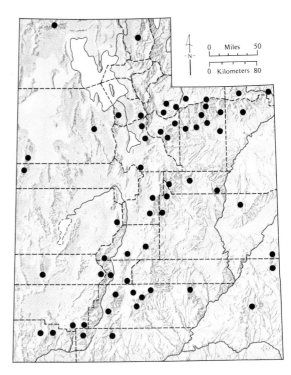

56. *Rubus idaeus* L. Raspberry. July-Aug. Circumboreal shrub; streamside, mountain brush to conifer communities, talus, 1780-3330 m.

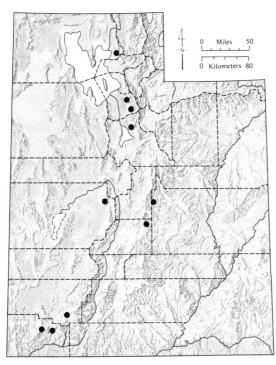

57. *Rubus leucodermis* T. & G. Black raspberry. June-July. Native shrub; streamside, rock crevices in sagebrush to ponderosa pine communities, 1450-2280 m.

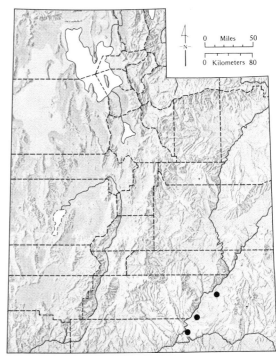

58. *Rubus neomexicanus* Gray New Mexican raspberry. Apr.-May. Native shrub; hanging gardens, 1150-1580 m.

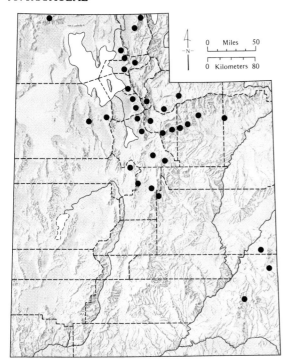

59. *Rubus parviflorus* Nutt. Thimbleberry. June-Aug. Native shrub; shaded sites, streamside in mountain brush to spruce-fir communities, 1630-2880 m.

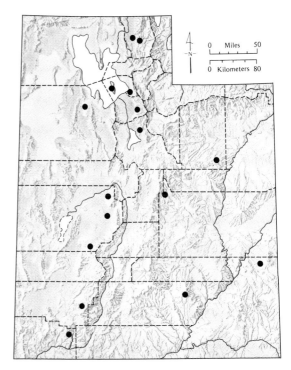

60. *Sanguisorba minor* Scop. Burnet. May-Aug. Introduced perennial herb; roadsides, disturbed or revegetated slopes, 1330-2300 m.

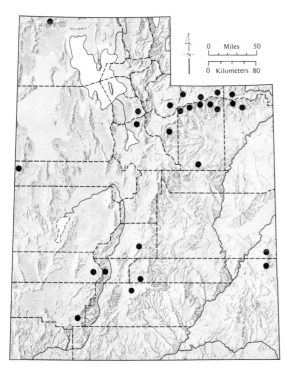

61. *Sibbaldia procumbens* L. July-Aug. Circumboreal perennial herb; meadows, open slopes in spruce-fir, lodgepole pine, krummholz, alpine communities, 2690-3790 m.

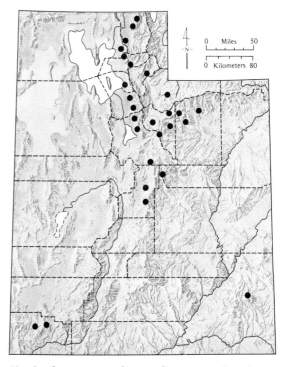

62. *Sorbus scopulina* Greene American mountain ash. May-July. Native shrub or small tree; open to shaded sites in mountain brush, aspen-conifer communities, 1510-2880 m.

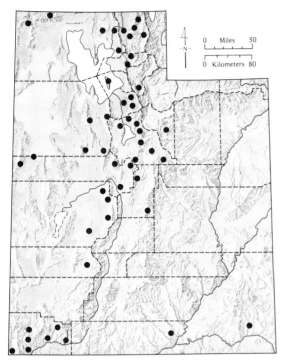

1. *Galium aparine* L. Cleavers; catchweed bedstraw. May-June. Circumboreal annual; meadows, shaded sites in mountain brush to spruce-fir communities, occasionally invading cultivated sites, 1300-3030 m.

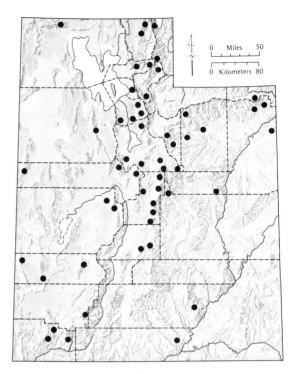

2. *Galium bifolium* Wats. Twinleaf bedstraw. May-Aug. Native annual; shaded sites in mountain brush to conifer communities, exposed rocky slopes at higher elevations, 1960-3180 m.

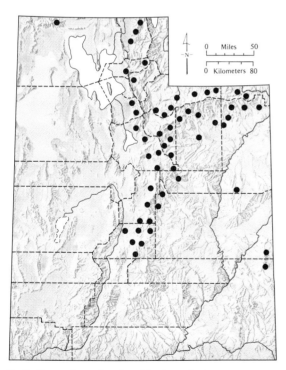

3. *Galium boreale* L. Northern bedstraw. July-Aug. Circumboreal perennial herb; shaded sites in mountain brush to conifer communities, 1630-3030 m.

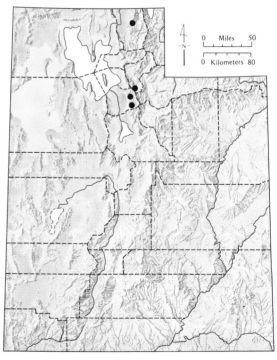

4. *Galium mexicanum* Kunth Rough bedstraw. June-Aug. Native perennial herb; streamside, shaded sites in mountain brush to aspen, spruce-fir communities, 1660-3030 m.

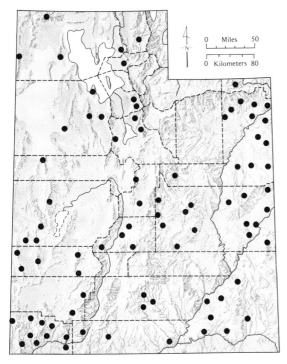

5. *Galium multiflorum* Kell. Shrubby bedstraw. May-July. Native perennial herb or subshrub; desert shrub, pinyon-juniper, mountain brush, fir, spruce communities, chiefly in dry rocky sites, 910-2820 m.

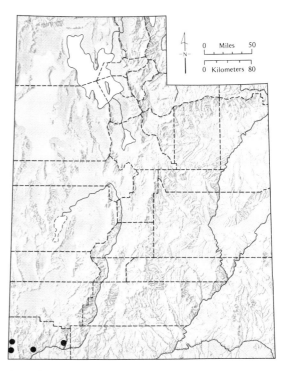

6. *Galium proliferum* Gray Bear bedstraw. Mar.-May. Native annual; creosote bush communities, 910-1120 m.

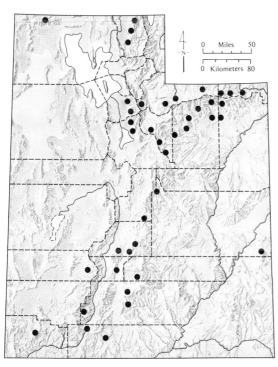

7. *Galium trifidum* L. Small bedstraw. July-Aug. Circumboreal perennial herb; streamside, wet meadows, pond margins in mountain brush to aspen-conifer, alpine communities, 1360-3330 m.

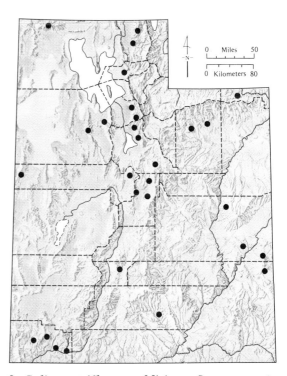

8. *Galium triflorum* Michx. Sweet-scented bedstraw. June-Aug. Circumboreal perennial herb; streamside, other moist sites, in mountain brush, aspen-fir communities, 1210-2670 m.

94. RUBIACEAE

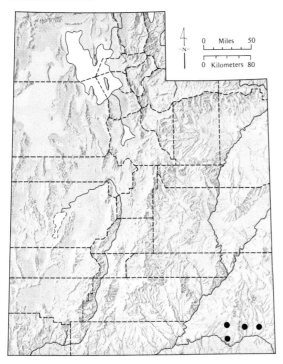

9. *Houstonia rubra* Cav. Bluets. May-Aug. Native perennial herb; desert shrub communities, 1210-1370 m.

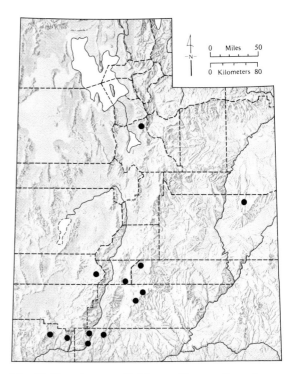

10. *Kelloggia galioides* Torr. June-Aug. Native perennial herb; sagebrush, pinyon-juniper, ponderosa pine communities, 2090-2670 m.

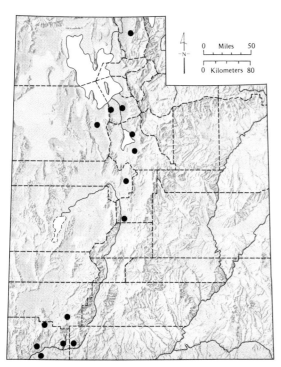

11. *Rubia tinctorum* L. Madder. July-Sept. Introduced perennial herb; along waterways, 910-1580 m.

95. RUPPIACEAE

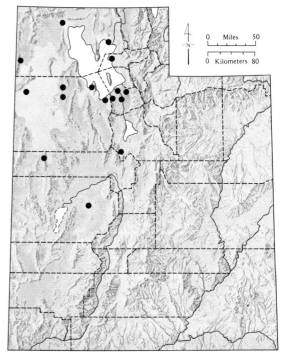

1. *Ruppia maritima* L. Ditchgrass. Apr.-Sept. Cosmopolitan perennial herb; brackish water of ditches, ponds, marshes, 1270-1520 m.

96. RUTACEAE

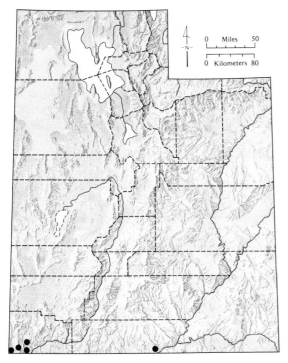

1. ***Thamnosma montana*** Torr. & Frem.
Turpentine bush. Mar.-May. Native shrub; Joshua
tree, creosote bush communities, 750-1060 m.

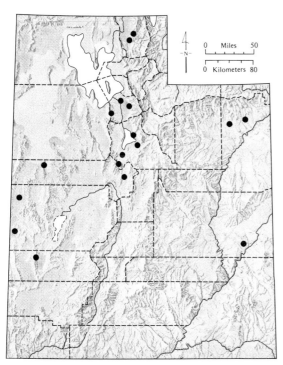

2. ***Populus alba*** L. White poplar. Apr.-May.
Introduced tree; cultivated, escaping and persistent,
1270-1980 m.

97. SALICACEAE

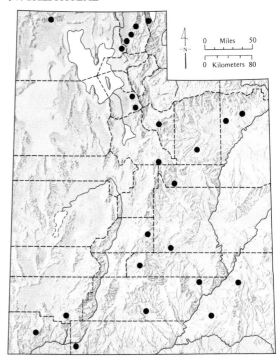

1. ***Populus* x *acuminata*** Rydb. Lanceleaf
cottonwood. Apr.-May. Native tree, a hybrid
between *P. angustifolia* and *P. fremontii* ; along
rivers and streams, pond and lake margins, 1360-
2120 m.

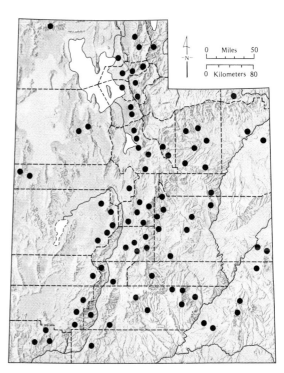

3. ***Populus angustifolia*** James Narrowleaf
cottonwood. Apr.-May. Native tree; along rivers
and streams, 1360-2440 m.

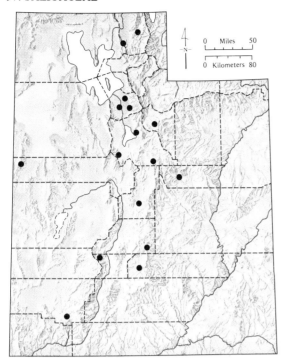

4. *Populus balsamifera* L. Balsam poplar; black cottonwood. Mar.-May. Introduced tree; cultivated, escaping and persistent, 1360-2350 m.

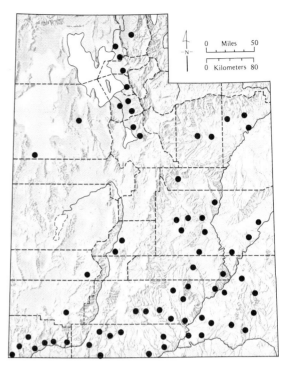

5. *Populus fremontii* Wats. Fremont cottonwood. Apr.-June. Native tree; along rivers and streams, dry washes, 760-2120 m.

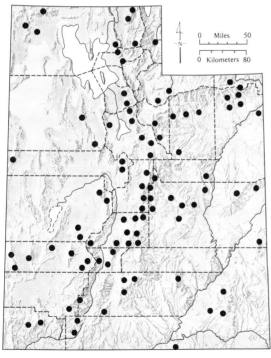

6. *Populus tremuloides* Michx. Quaking aspen. Apr.-May. Native tree; streamside, montane slopes, dominant or codominant with conifers over large areas, 1400-3200 m.

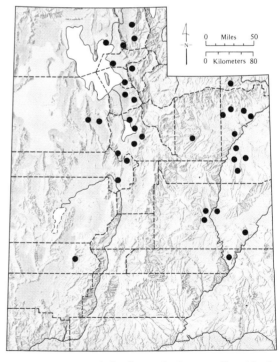

7. *Salix amygdaloides* Anderss. Peachleaf willow. Apr.-June. Native tree; along waterways, pond and lake margins, other moist sites, 1070-1710 m.

97. SALICACEAE

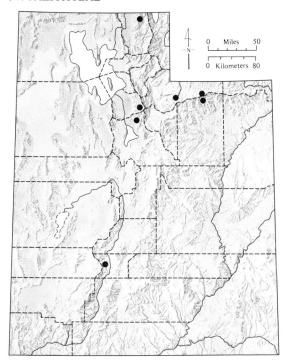

8. *Salix arctica* Pall. Arctic willow. July-Aug. Native shrub; wet meadows or moist open slopes, 2720-3600 m.

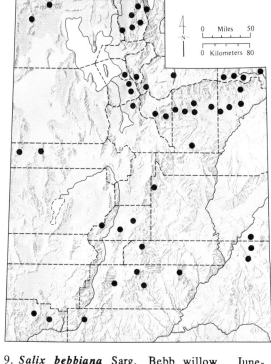

9. *Salix bebbiana* Sarg. Bebb willow. June-July. Native shrub; marshes, streamside, near seeps and springs, lakeshores, 1370-2790 m.

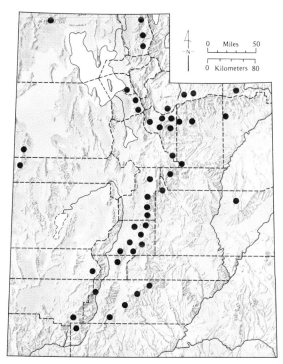

10. *Salix boothii* Dorn Booth willow. June-July. Native shrub; streamside, wet meadows, 2070-3050 m.

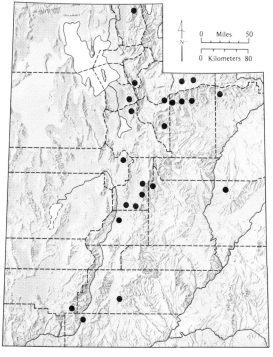

11. *Salix brachycarpa* Nutt. Barrenground willow. July-Aug. Native shrub; streamside, wet meadows, open rocky slopes, talus, 2070-3430 m.

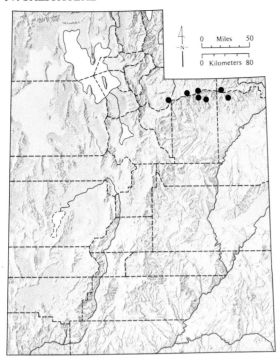

12. *Salix cascadensis* Ckll. Cascade willow. Aug.-Sept. Native shrub; above timberline, 3350-3930 m.

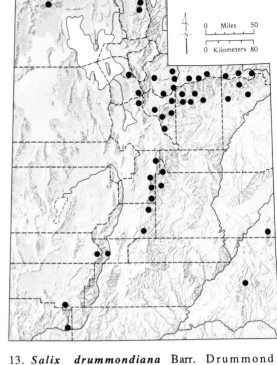

13. *Salix drummondiana* Barr. Drummond willow. June-Aug. Native shrub; streamside, wet meadows, near seeps and springs, 2120-3330 m.

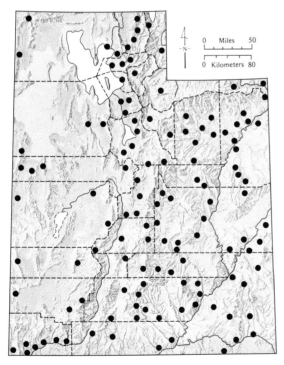

14. *Salix exigua* Nutt. Sandbar or coyote willow. Apr.-July. Native shrub; along waterways, marshes, near seeps and springs, wet pastures and fields, salt tolerant, 820-2570 m.

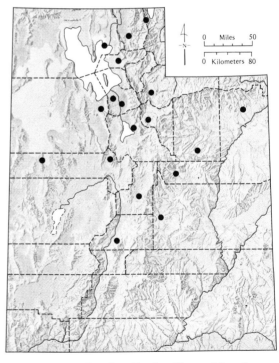

15. *Salix fragilis* L. Crack willow. May-June. Introduced tree; cultivated, escaping and persistent along waterways, other moist sites, 1270-2080 m.

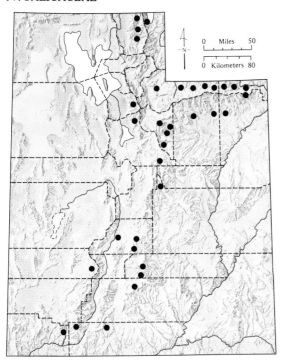

16. *Salix geyeriana* Anderss. Geyer willow. June-July. Native shrub; along rivers and streams, other moist sites, 1820-2900 m.

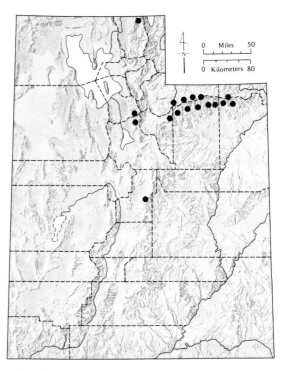

17. *Salix glauca* L. Grayleaf willow. July-Aug. Circumboreal shrub; streamside, wet meadows, talus, alpine communities, often in the wake of snowmelt, 2720-3340 m.

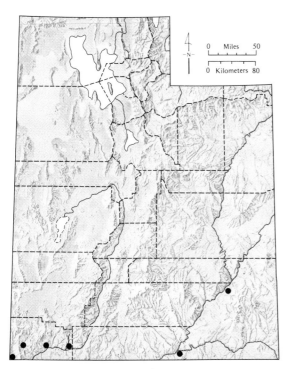

18. *Salix laevigata* Bebb Red willow. Mar.-Apr. Native shrub or small tree; along waterways in creosote bush to desert shrub communities, 750-1370 m.

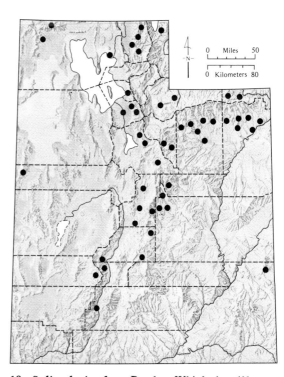

19. *Salix lasiandra* Benth. Whiplash willow. May-July. Native shrub or small tree; marshes, floodplains, pond margins, streamside, wet meadows, 1360-2580 m.

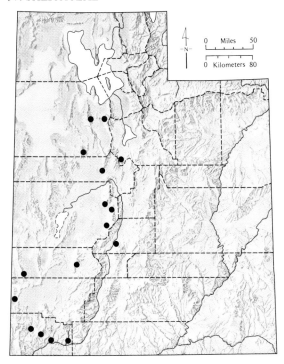

20. *Salix lasiolepis* Benth. Arroyo willow.
May-June. Native shrub or small tree; along
washes and waterways, 1450-2300 m.

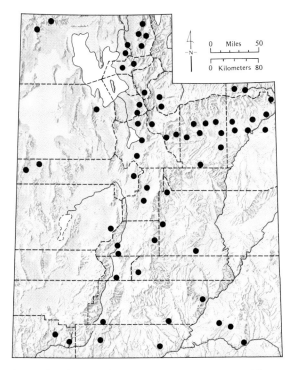

21. *Salix lutea* Nutt. Yellow willow. Apr.-May.
Native shrub; along waterways, 1300-2370 m.

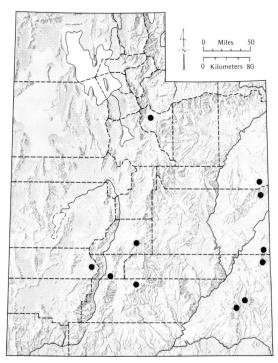

22. *Salix monticola* Bebb Mountain willow.
June-July. Native shrub; streamside, near seeps and
springs, 1910-3180 m.

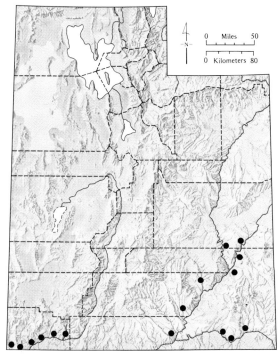

23. *Salix nigra* Marsh. Black willow. Apr.-
June. Native shrub or small tree; along waterways
in creosote bush, desert shrub communities, 750-
1590 m.

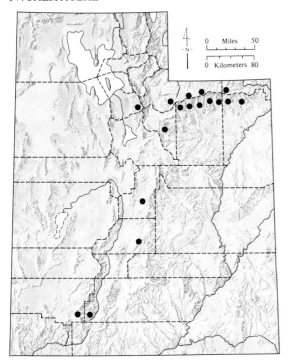

24. *Salix planifolia* Pursh Planeleaf willow.
July-Aug. Native shrub; streamside, pond and lake
margins, wet meadows, 2250-3660 m.

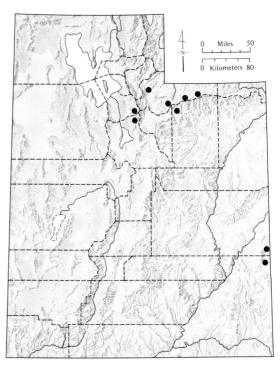

25. *Salix reticulata* L. Snow willow. June-
Aug. Circumboreal dwarf shrub; lake margins,
moist slopes, rocky ridges above timberline, 2970-
3970 m.

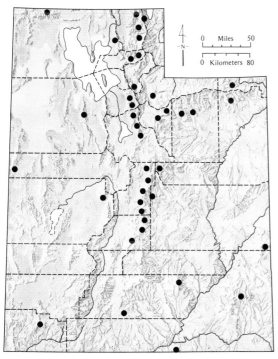

26. *Salix scouleriana* Barr. Scouler willow.
Apr.-June. Native shrub or small tree; streamside;
mesic slopes in aspen and conifer communities,
1400-3360 m.

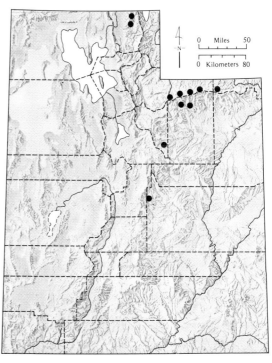

27. *Salix wolfii* Bebb Wolf willow. July-
Aug. Native shrub; streamside, pond and lake
margins, 2470-3290 m.

98. SALVINIACEAE

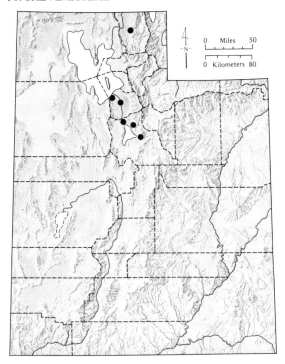

1. *Azolla mexicana* Presl Mexican waterfern. Native herb; in water of ditches or ponds, occasionally in mud, 1300-1360 m.

99. SANTALACEAE

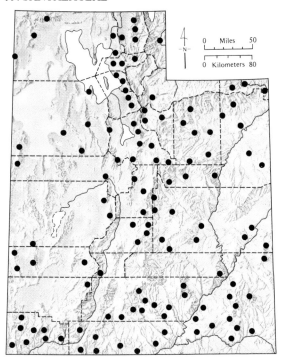

1. *Comandra umbellata* (L.) Nutt. Bastard toadflax. Apr.-Aug. Native perennial herb; open sites in desert shrub to conifer communities, 1300-2580 m.

100. SAURURACEAE

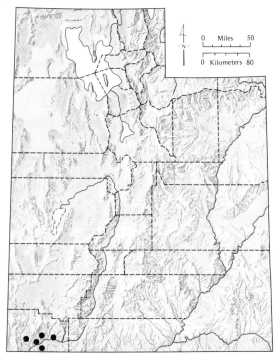

1. *Anemopsis californica* (Nutt.) H. & A. Yerba mansa. Apr.-May. Native perennial herb; along waterways, near seeps and springs, salt tolerant, 840-1210 m.

101. SAXIFRAGACEAE

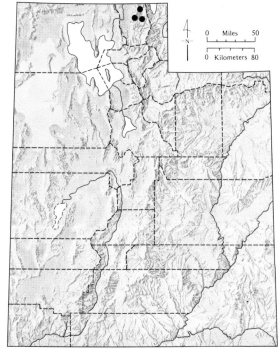

1. *Boykinia jamesii* (Torr.) Engl. James saxifrage. July-Sept. Native perennial herb; rock crevices, 2680-3000 m.

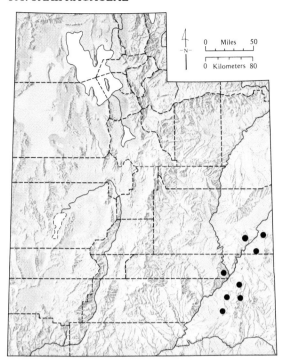

2. *Fendlera rupicola* Gray Fendlerbush. May-July. Native shrub; desert shrub to pinyon-juniper communities, 1370-1730 m.

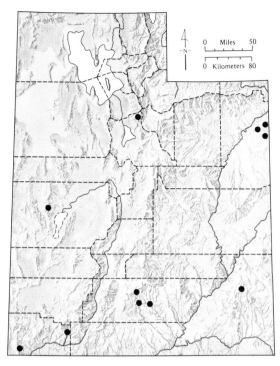

3. *Fendlerella utahensis* (Wats.) Heller Utah fendlerella. June-July. Native shrub; sagebrush, pinyon-juniper, mountain brush communities, 1480-2730 m.

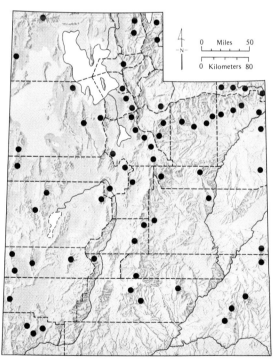

4. *Heuchera parvifolia* Nutt. Littleleaf alumroot. May-Aug. Native perennial herb; sagebrush, pinyon-juniper, mountain brush, ponderosa pine, aspen-fir communities, often in rocky sites, 1670-3200 m.

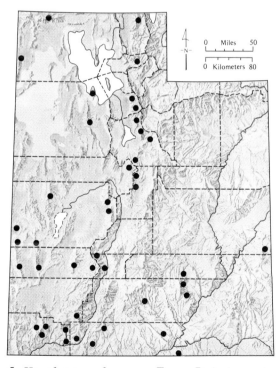

5. *Heuchera rubescens* Torr. Red alumroot; wild coralbells. June-Aug. Native perennial herb; rocky crevices in sagebrush to aspen-conifer communities, 1370-3360 m.

559

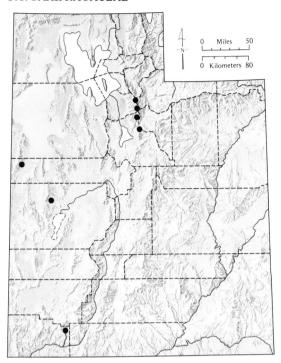

6. *Jamesia americana* T. & G. Cliff jamesia. June-Aug. Native shrub; on cliffs, other rocky sites in mountain brush to spruce-fir communities, 1220-3200 m.

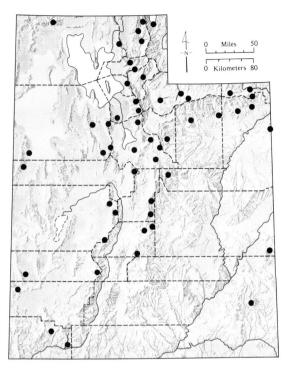

7. *Lithophragma glabra* Nutt. Fringecup woodland star. Apr.-June. Native perennial herb; greasewood to aspen-conifer communities, 1310-3050 m.

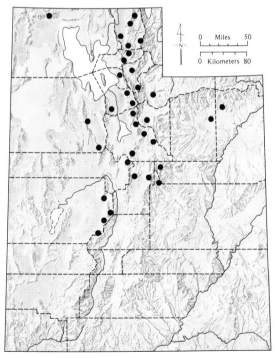

8. *Lithophragma parviflora* (Hook.) T. & G. Smallflower woodland star. Apr.-July. Native perennial herb; shaded to open sites in sagebrush, oak, aspen-conifer communities, 1420-2580 m.

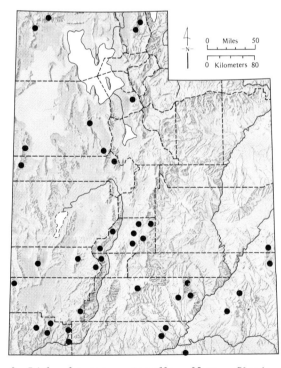

9. *Lithophragma tenella* Nutt. Slender woodland star. Apr.-May. Native perennial herb; open to shaded sites, sagebrush to aspen-conifer communities, 1310-3050 m.

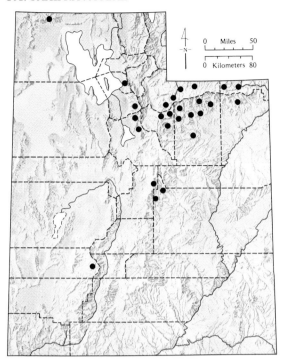

10. *Mitella pentandra* Hook. Fivestar
miterwort. June-Aug. Native perennial herb; moist
shaded sites in aspen-conifer, alpine communities,
1740-3650 m.

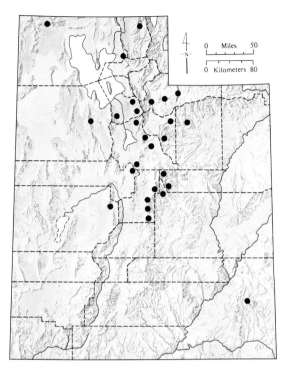

11. *Mitella stauropetala* Piper Smallflower
miterwort. May-Aug. Native perennial herb;
streamside, shaded sites in mountain brush to
aspen-conifer communities, 1610-3050 m.

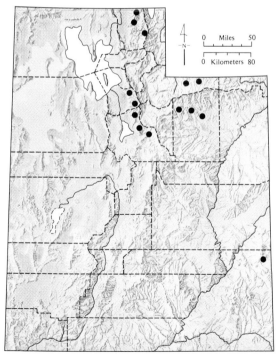

12. *Parnassia fimbriata* Koenig Fringed
grass-of-Parnassus. July-Aug. Native perennial
herb; streamside, near seeps and springs, pond and
lake margins in mountain brush to aspen, spruce-fir
communities, 2010-3360 m.

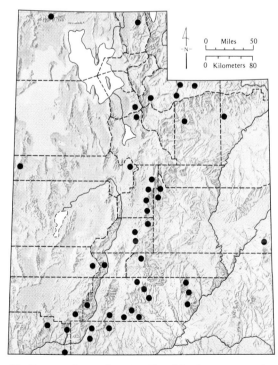

13. *Parnassia palustris* L. Northern grass-of-
Parnassus. July-Aug. Circumboreal perennial herb;
streamside, wet meadows, near seeps and springs,
shaded sites in aspen, spruce-fir communities,
1370-3420 m.

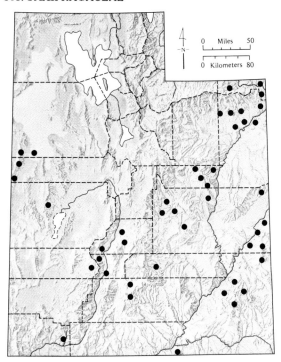

14. *Philadelphus microphyllus* Gray Littleleaf mockorange. May-July. Native shrub; mountain brush, pinyon-juniper, ponderosa pine, aspen-fir communities, 1220-2640 m.

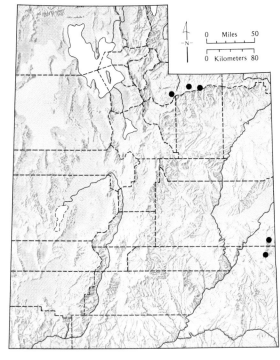

15. *Saxifraga adscendens* L. Wedgeleaf saxifrage. July-Aug. Native perennial herb; rocky slopes, mostly above timberline, 2880-3940 m.

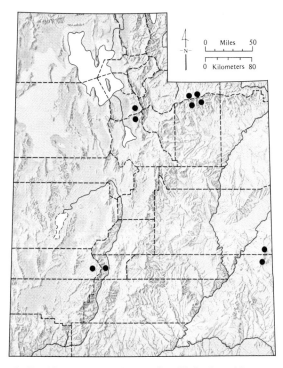

16. *Saxifraga caespitosa* L. Tufted saxifrage. July-Aug. Circumboreal perennial herb; spruce forests, exposed rocky ridges above timberline, 2980-3990 m.

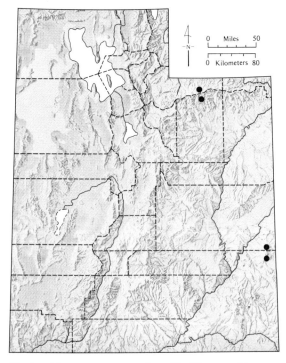

17. *Saxifraga cernua* L. Nodding saxifrage. July-Aug. Circumboreal perennial herb; rocky sites above timberline, 3330-3960 m.

562

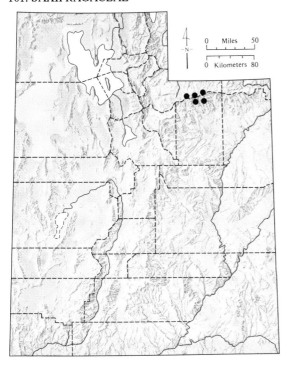

18. **Saxifraga chrysantha** Gray Golden saxifrage. July-Aug. Native perennial herb; meadows, rocky sites above timberline, 3330-3960 m.

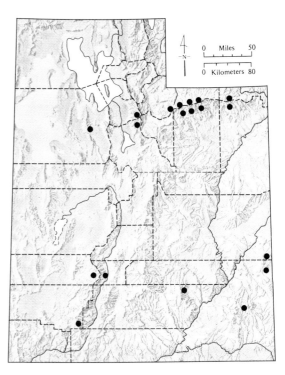

19. **Saxifraga debilis** Engelm. Pygmy saxifrage. July-Aug. Native perennial herb; spruce communities, rocky sites above timberline, 2730-3960 m.

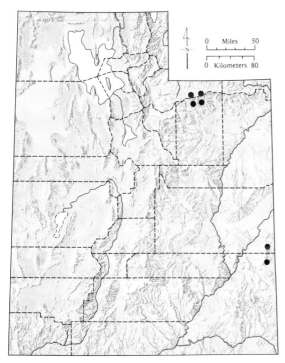

20. **Saxifraga flagellaris** Willd. Whiplash saxifrage. July-Aug. Circumboreal perennial herb; conifer forests to above timberline, 3030-3960 m.

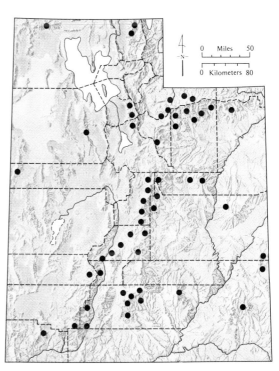

21. **Saxifraga odontoloma** Piper Brook saxifrage. May-Aug. Native perennial herb; streamsides, near seeps and springs, pond and lake margins in mountain brush to conifer communities, 1820-3390 m.

563

101. SAXIFRAGACEAE

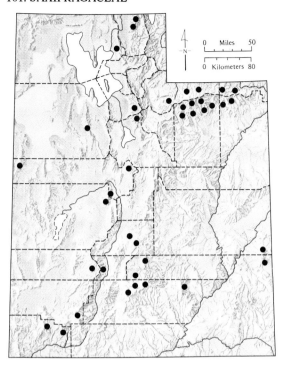

22. *Saxifraga rhomboidea* Greene
Diamondleaf saxifrage. June-July. Native
perennial herb; conifer forests, alpine meadows,
2070-3960 m.

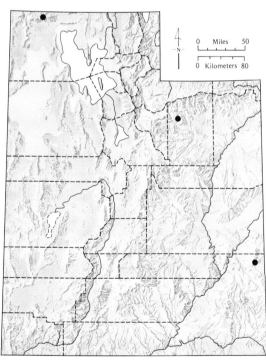

2. *Besseya wyomingensis* (A. Nels.) Rydb.
Wyoming kittentails. May-Aug. Native perennial
herb; meadows, moist sites on rocky ridges, 2390-
3580 m.

102. SCROPHULARIACEAE

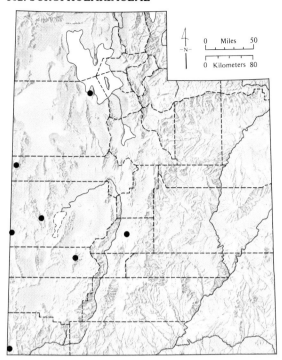

1. *Antirrhinum kingii* Wats. King
snapdragon. Apr.-June. Native annual; creosote
bush to desert shrub communities, 1000-2000 m.

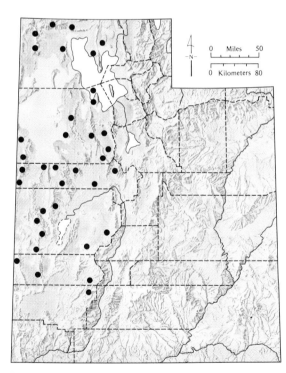

3. *Castilleja angustifolia* (Nutt.) G. Don
May-July. Native perennial herb; desert shrub to
pinyon-juniper communities, 1240-2580 m.

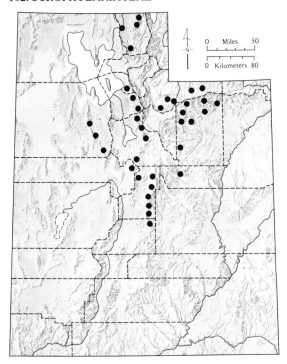

4. *Castilleja applegatei* Fern. Wavyleaf paintbrush. June-Aug. Native perennial herb; dry, mostly rocky slopes and exposed ridges, sagebrush to conifer, krummholz, alpine communities, 1810-3430 m.

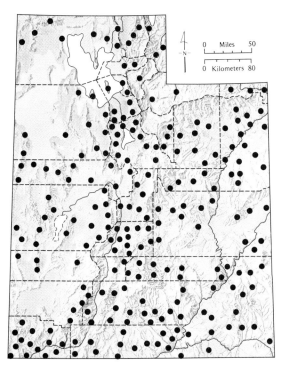

5. *Castilleja chromosa* A. Nels. Desert paintbrush. Apr.-June. Native perennial herb; creosote bush to ponderosa pine communities, 810-2730 m.

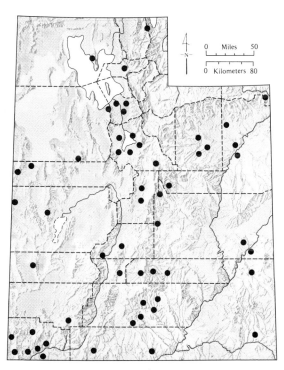

6. *Castilleja exilis* A. Nels. Marsh or annual paintbrush. June-Aug. Native annual; marshes, near seeps and springs, moist meadows, other wet places in salt desert shrub to mountain brush communities, 840-2790 m.

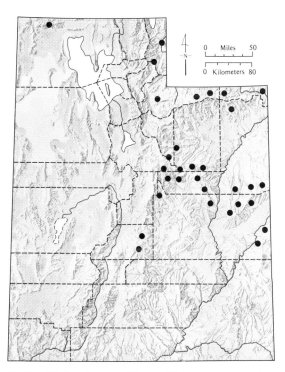

7. *Castilleja flava* Wats. Yellow paintbrush. June-Aug. Native perennial herb; sagebrush to ponderosa pine communities, 1790-3050 m.

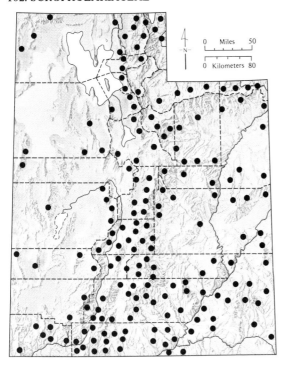

8. *Castilleja linariifolia* Benth. Narrowleaf or Wyoming paintbrush. June-Aug. Native perennial herb; desert shrub to aspen-conifer communities, 1150-3340 m.

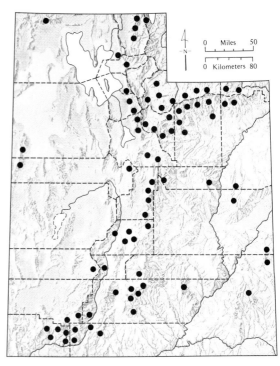

9. *Castilleja miniata* Hook. Scarlet paintbrush. July-Sept. Native perennial herb; dry to wet sites, open slopes, meadows, mountain brush to aspen, spruce-fir communities, often among rocks, 1510-3430 m.

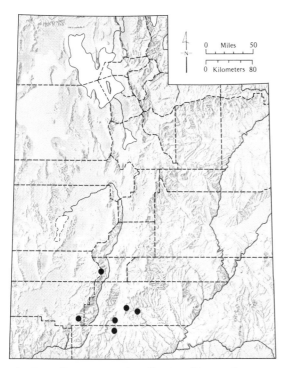

10. *Castilleja parvula* Rydb. Tushar Plateau paintbrush. June-July. Native perennial herb; bristlecone pine, ponderosa pine communities, talus, exposed alpine ridges, 2270-3050 m.

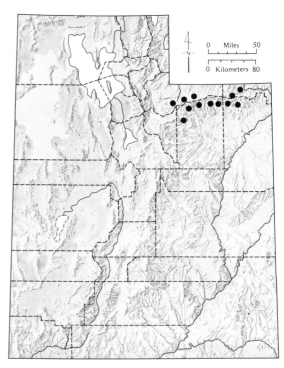

11. *Castilleja pulchella* Rydb. Pretty paintbrush. July-Aug. Native perennial herb; subalpine conifer communities, rocky sites above timberline, 3030-3730 m.

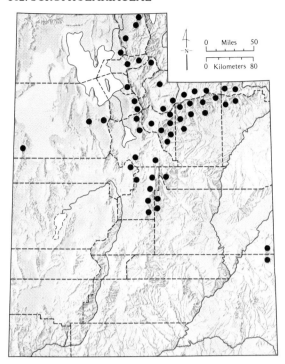

12. *Castilleja rhexifolia* Rydb. Rhexia-leaf
paintbrush. June-Aug. Native perennial herb;
moist, open, rocky to well-vegetated slopes in
mountain brush to aspen-conifer, meadow
communities, occasionally above timberline, 2000-
3490 m.

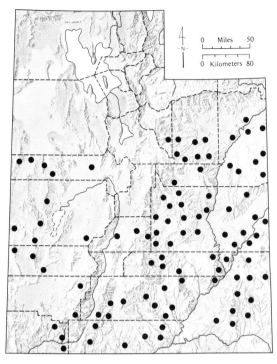

13. *Castilleja scabrida* Eastw. Eastwood
paintbrush. Apr.-June. Native perennial herb; dry,
often rocky sites in greasewood to pinyon-juniper
communities, 1210-2610 m.

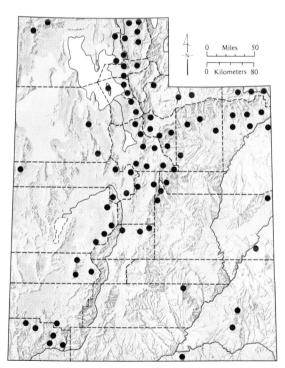

14. *Collinsia parviflora* Lindl. Blue-eyed
Mary. Apr.-Aug. Native annual; open or shaded
sites in sagebrush to conifer communities, 910-
2730 m.

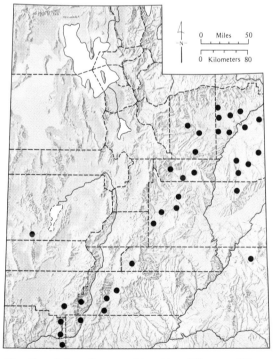

15. *Cordylanthus kingii* Wats. King
birdsbeak. June-Oct. Native annual; mat saltbush,
desert shrub, pinyon-juniper, ponderosa pine
communities, 1510-2580 m.

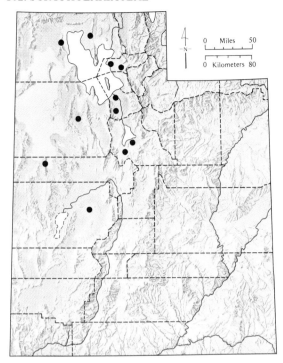

16. *Cordylanthus maritimus* Benth. Alkali birdsbeak. July-Sept. Native annual; moist saline sites, 840-1370 m.

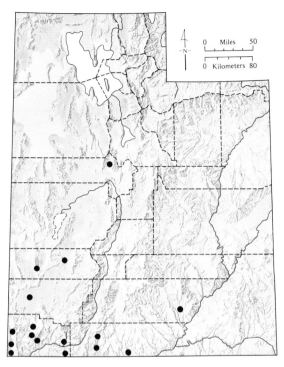

17. *Cordylanthus parviflorus* (Ferris) Wiggins Smallflower birdsbeak. July-Oct. Native annual; creosote bush to pinyon-juniper communities, 820-2120 m.

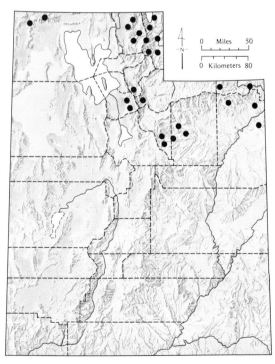

18. *Cordylanthus ramosus* Benth. Branched birdsbeak. June-Aug. Native annual; sagebrush to pinyon-juniper communities, 1670-2490 m.

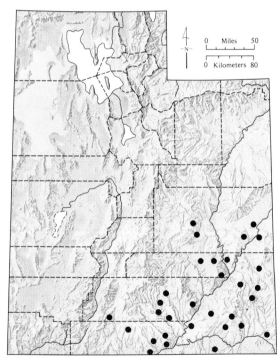

19. *Cordylanthus wrightii* Gray Wright birdsbeak. June-Oct. Native annual; desert shrub to ponderosa pine communities, 1150-2120 m.

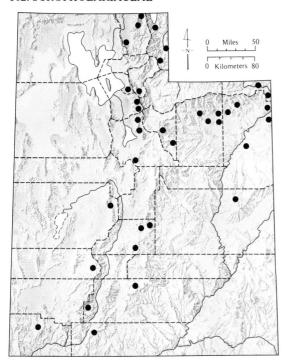

20. *Limosella aquatica* L. Mudwort. June-Sept. Circumboreal perennial; shallow water and drying margins of ponds and marshes in mountain brush to conifer communities, 1450-3050 m.

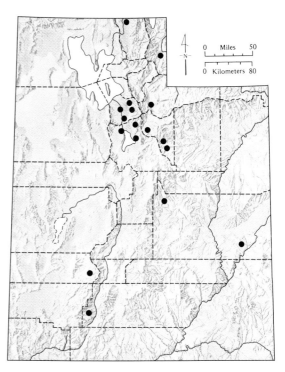

21. *Linaria dalmatica* (L.) Miller Dalmation toadflax. May-Aug. Introduced perennial herb; dry, open, usually rocky sites in sagebrush to aspen communities, 1300-2460 m.

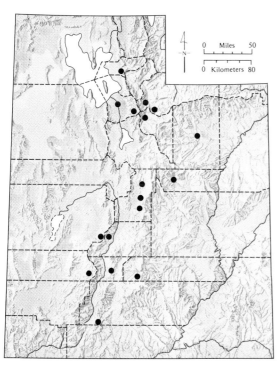

22. *Linaria vulgaris* Hill Butter-and-eggs. July-Aug. Introduced perennial herb; disturbed sites in sagebrush to aspen-conifer communities, 1270-3050 m.

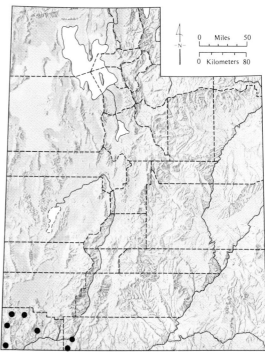

23. *Mimetanthe pilosa* (Benth.) Greene Downy mimetanthe. June-Aug. Native annual; moist sites in creosote bush, desert shrub communities, 810-1880 m.

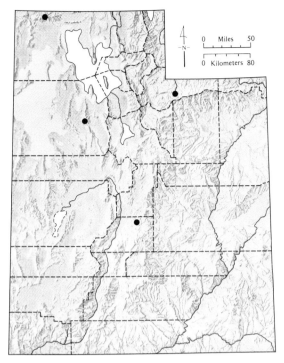

24. *Mimulus breweri* (Greene) Cov. Brewer monkeyflower. June-Aug. Native annual; moist sites in ponderosa pine, aspen-fir communities, 2540-2730 m.

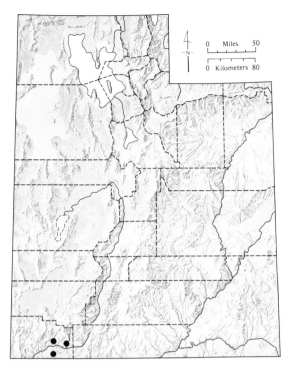

25. *Mimulus cardinalis* Benth. Cardinal monkeyflower. May-June. Native perennial herb; hanging gardens, streamside, near seeps and springs, 1000-1520 m.

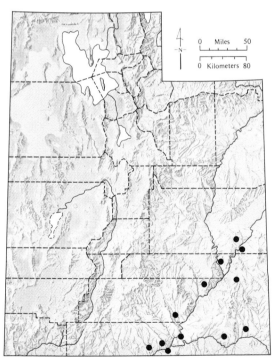

26. *Mimulus eastwoodiae* Rydb. July-Sept. Native perennial herb; hanging gardens, near seeps and springs, 940-1370 m.

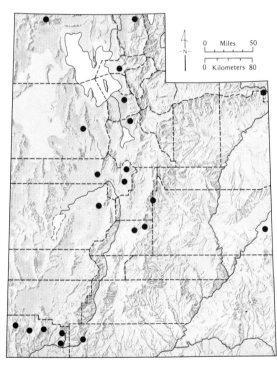

27. *Mimulus floribundus* Lindl. Floriferous monkeyflower. June-Sept. Native annual; crevices of shaded cliffs and ledges, moist canyon floors, seeps, wet streambanks in pinyon-juniper, ponderosa pine, aspen-conifer communities, 1360-2970 m.

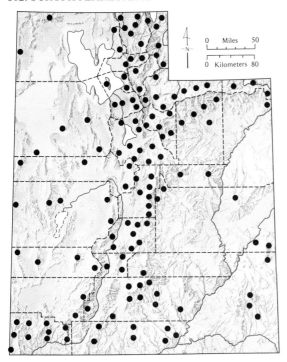

28. *Mimulus guttatus* DC. Common or yellow monkeyflower. May-Sept. Circumboreal annual or perennial herb; marshes, along waterways, wet meadows, near seeps and springs in desert shrub to aspen-conifer communities, 910-3150 m.

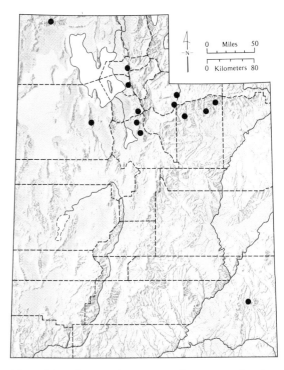

29. *Mimulus lewisii* Pursh Lewis monkeyflower. June-Aug. Native perennial herb; streamside in mountain brush to aspen-conifer communities, 1400-3490 m.

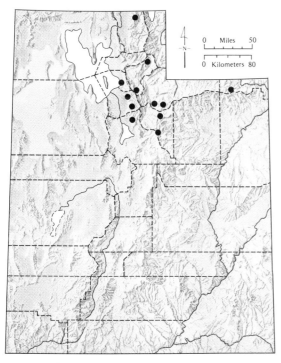

30. *Mimulus moschatus* Lindl. Musk monkeyflower. June-Sept. Native perennial herb; wet meadows, streamside, near seeps and springs in sagebrush to aspen-conifer communities, 1660-3050 m.

31. *Mimulus parryi* Gray Parry monkeyflower. Apr.-May. Native annual; washes and gravel slopes in creosote bush, desert shrub communities, 790-1220 m.

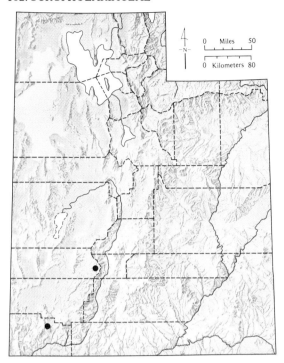

32. *Mimulus primuloides* Benth. Primrose or meadow monkeyflower. July-Aug. Native perennial herb; streamside, wet meadows, in aspen, spruce-fir communities, 2600-2790 m.

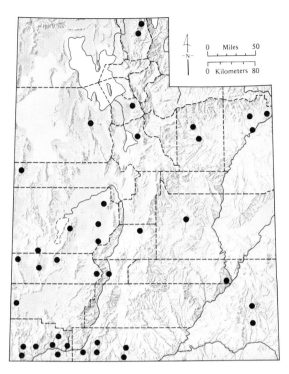

33. *Mimulus rubellus* Gray Apr.-July. Native annual; dry to more often moist sites in sagebrush to conifer communities, 1210-2730 m.

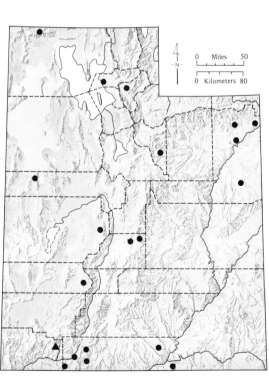

34. *Mimulus suksdorfii* Gray Suksdorf monkeyflower. May-July. Native annual; mesic to moist, often sandy sites in greasewood, sagebrush, pinyon-juniper, mountain brush, aspen, ponderosa pine communities, 1300-2610 m.

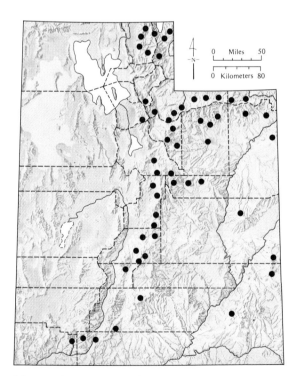

35. *Orthocarpus luteus* Nutt. Yellow owlclover. July-Sept. Native annual; meadows, open slopes in sagebrush, ponderosa pine, aspen-fir communities, 1450-2940 m.

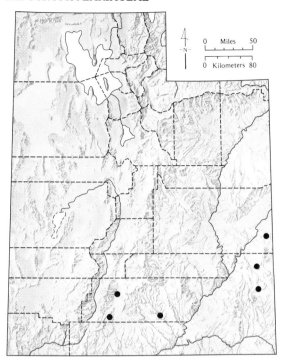

36. *Orthocarpus purpureo-albus* Gray
Purple-white owlclover. July-Aug. Native annual;
dry open slopes in sagebrush to ponderosa pine
communities, 1360-2550 m.

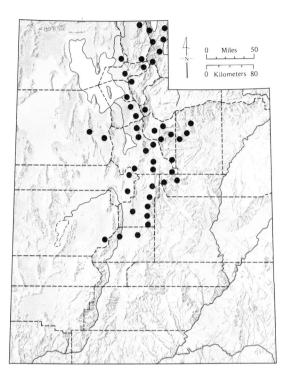

37. *Orthocarpus tolmiei* H. & A. Tolmie
owlclover. July-Aug. Native annual; open slopes
in sagebrush to aspen, spruce-fir communities,
1720-3180 m.

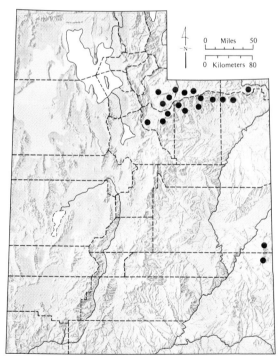

38. *Pedicularis bracteosa* Benth. Bracteate
lousewort. July-Aug. Native perennial herb;
aspen-conifer communities, 2480-3490 m.

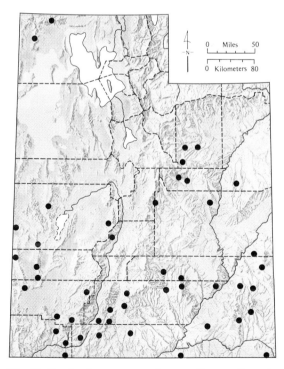

39. *Pedicularis centranthera* Gray Dwarf
lousewort. Apr.-July. Native perennial herb;
pinyon-juniper to ponderosa pine communities,
1360-2670 m.

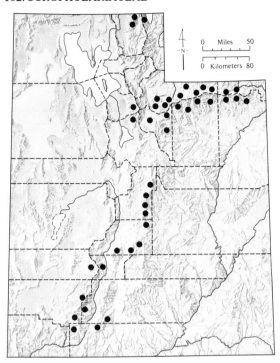

40. *Pedicularis groenlandica* Retz. Elephant head; pink elephants. June-Aug. Native perennial herb; wet montane to alpine meadows, occasionally other moist sites in conifer communities, 2570-3640 m.

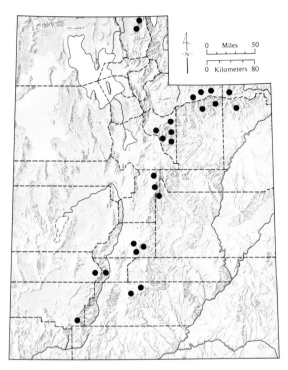

41. *Pedicularis parryi* Gray   Parry lousewort. June-July. Native perennial herb; open slopes, mesic to wet meadows in sagebrush, aspen-conifer communities to above timberline, 2300-3580 m.

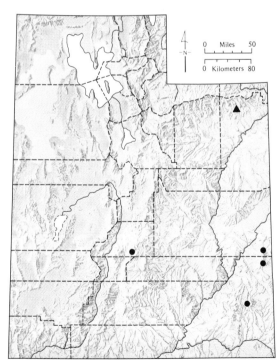

42. *Pedicularis procera* Gray   Gray lousewort. July-Aug. Native perennial herb; aspen, spruce-fir communities, 2570-3180 m.

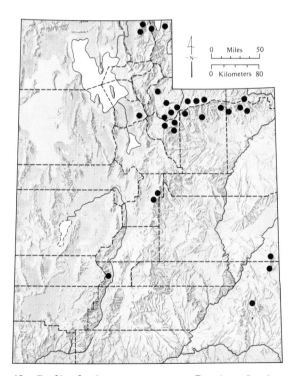

43. *Pedicularis racemosa* Benth. Leafy lousewort. June-Aug. Native perennial herb; meadows, shaded sites in aspen-conifer communities, 2240-3340 m.

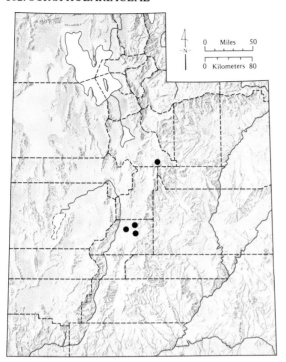

44. *Penstemon abietinus* Pennell Firleaf penstemon. June-Aug. Native perennial herb or subshrub; mountain brush, pinyon-juniper communities, 1750-2300 m.

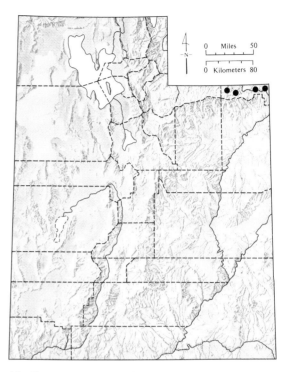

45. *Penstemon acaulis* L. Williams June-July. Native perennial herb; dry sites in sagebrush, pinyon-juniper communities, 1780-2220 m.

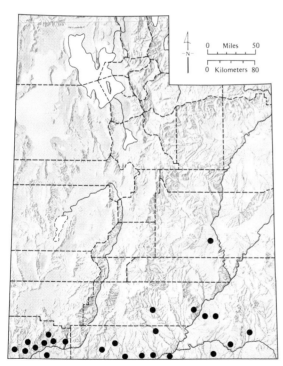

46. *Penstemon ambiguus* Torr. Bush penstemon. May-July. Native shrub; creosote bush, desert shrub to juniper communities, typically in sandy soil, 760-1950 m.

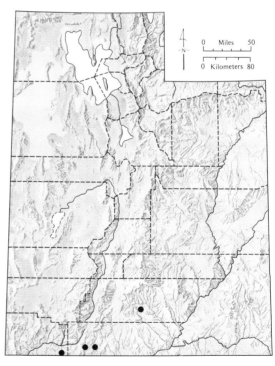

47. *Penstemon ammophilus* N. Holmgren & L. Shultz Sand-loving penstemon. May-June. Native perennial herb; sandy soil in desert shrub to ponderosa pine communities, 1540-2200 m.

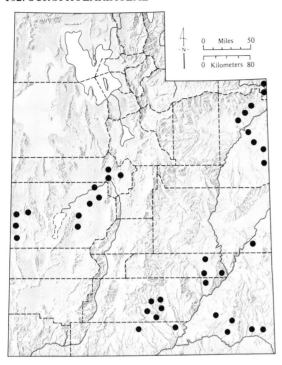

48. *Penstemon angustifolius* Pursh Narrowleaf penstemon. Apr.-June. Native perennial herb; desert shrub to pinyon-juniper communities, 1200-2280 m.

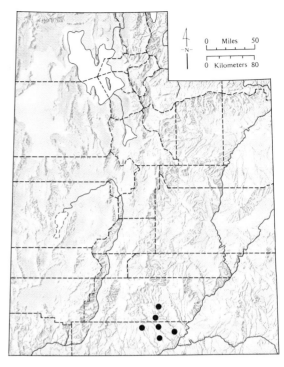

49. *Penstemon atwoodii* Welsh Atwood penstemon. May-June. Native perennial herb; pinyon-juniper communities, 1650-2100 m.

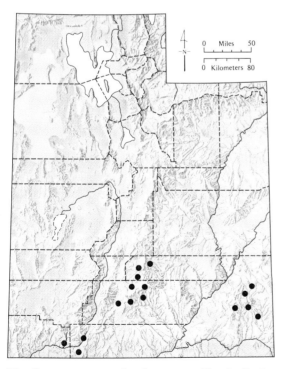

50. *Penstemon barbatus* (Cav.) Roth Beardlip penstemon. June-Aug. Native perennial herb; desert shrub to ponderosa pine communities, 1360-2660 m.

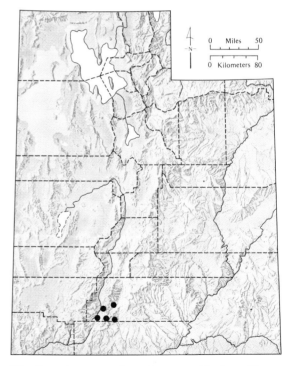

51. *Penstemon bracteatus* Keck Platy penstemon. May-July. Native perennial herb; talus in ponderosa pine, limber pine, bristlecone pine communities, 2180-2430 m.

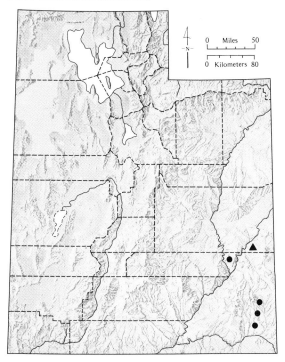

52. *Penstemon breviculus* (Keck) Nisbet & R. Jackson   Shortstem penstemon.   May-June. Native perennial herb; desert shrub to pinyon-juniper communities, 1600-2000 m.

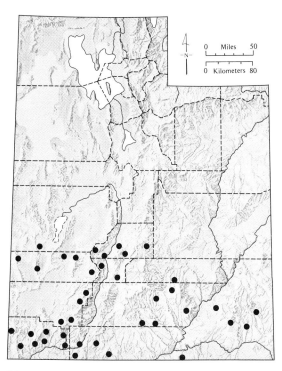

53. *Penstemon bridgesii* Gray   Bridges or beaked penstemon.   June-Sept.   Native perennial herb; creosote bush to conifer communities, 1000-3340 m.

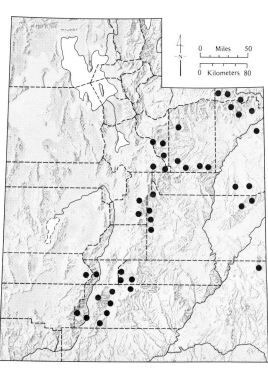

54. *Penstemon caespitosus* Gray   Mat penstemon.   May-Aug.   Native perennial herb; sagebrush to aspen-conifer communities, 1970-3250 m.

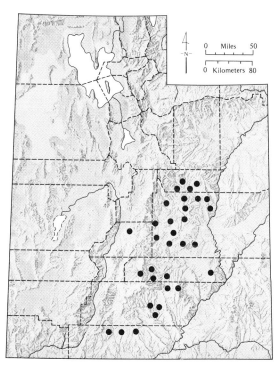

55. *Penstemon carnosus* Pennell   Fleshy penstemon.   May-June.   Native perennial herb; shadscale, desert shrub to pinyon-juniper communities, 1500-2500 m.

577

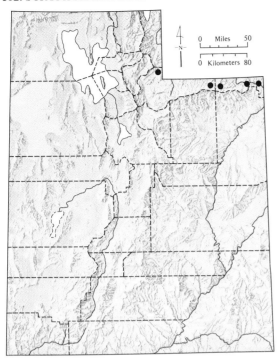

56. *Penstemon cleburnei* Jones   Cleburne penstemon.   May-July.   Native perennial herb; sagebrush-grass communities, 1800-2730 m.

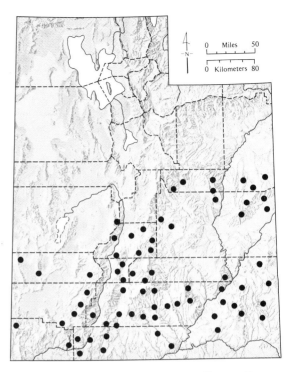

57. *Penstemon comarrhenus* Gray   Dusty penstemon.   June-Aug.   Native perennial herb; desert shrub, sagebrush-grass, pinyon-juniper, ponderosa pine, aspen-fir communities, 1480-3000 m.

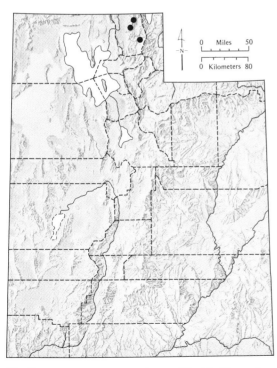

58. *Penstemon compactus* (Keck) Crosswh. Bear River Range penstemon.   June-Aug.   Native perennial herb; open rocky sites in aspen-conifer communities, 2120-2880 m.

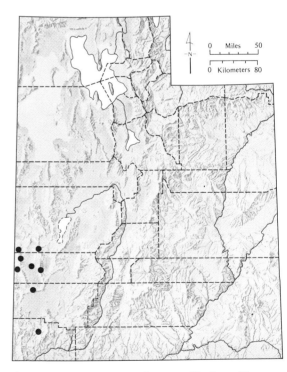

59. *Penstemon concinnus* Keck   Elegant penstemon.   May-July.   Native perennial herb; pinyon-juniper communities, 1510-2300 m.

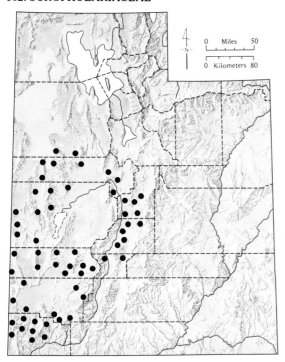

60. *Penstemon confusus* Jones   Apr.-June.
Native perennial herb; creosote bush, shadscale,
desert shrub, pinyon-juniper communities, 1000-
2200 m.

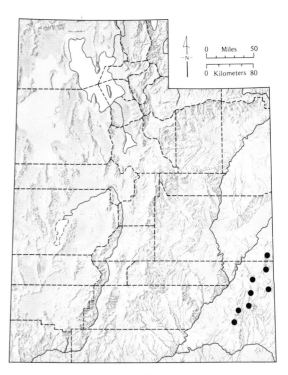

61. *Penstemon crandallii* A. Nels. Crandall
penstemon. June-July. Native perennial herb;
sagebrush, oak, pinyon-juniper communities,
2000-2700 m.

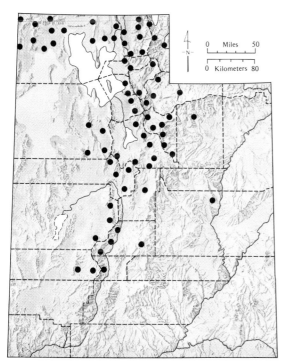

62. *Penstemon cyananthus* Hook. Wasatch
penstemon. May-Aug. Native perennial herb;
open slopes in mountain brush, meadows, open to
shaded sites in aspen-conifer communities, 1510-
3300 m.

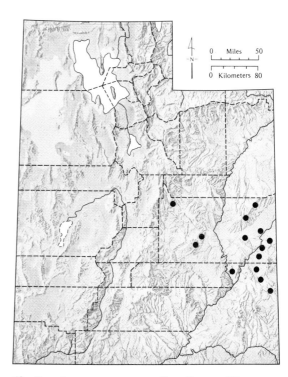

63. *Penstemon cyanocaulis* Pays. Bluestem
penstemon. May-June. Native perennial herb;
desert shrub to pinyon-juniper communities, 1300-
2300 m.

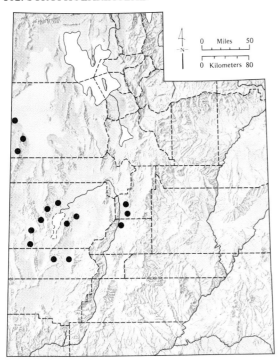

64. **Penstemon dolius** Pennell Jones penstemon. May-June. Native perennial herb; shadscale, desert shrub to pinyon-juniper communities, 1370-2350 m.

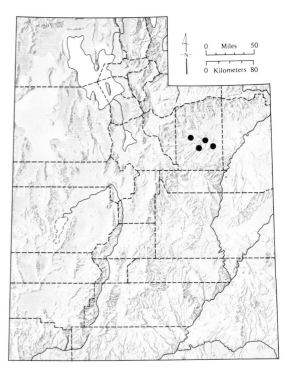

65. **Penstemon duchesnensis** (N. Holmgren) Neese Duchesne penstemon. May-June. Native perennial herb; pinyon-juniper communities, 1510-1670 m.

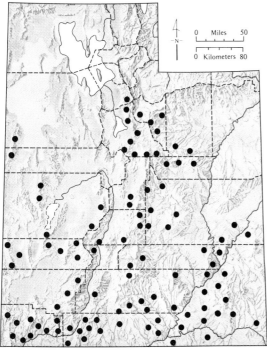

66. **Penstemon eatonii** Gray Eaton or firecracker penstemon. Apr.-July. Native perennial herb; creosote bush to aspen-conifer communities, 840-3400 m.

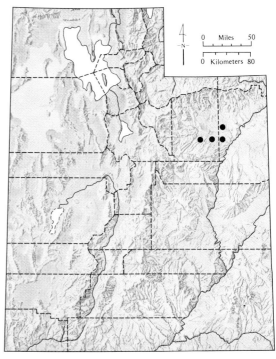

67. **Penstemon flowersii** Neese & Welsh Flowers penstemon. May-June. Native perennial herb; shadscale, desert shrub communities, 1490-1520 m.

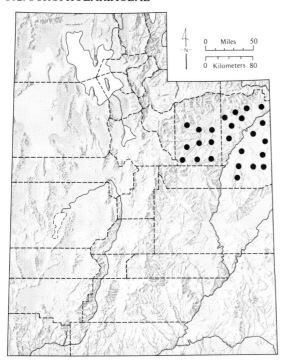

68. *Penstemon fremontii* T. & G. Fremont penstemon. May-July. Native perennial herb; shadscale, desert shrub to pinyon-juniper communities, 1510-2400 m.

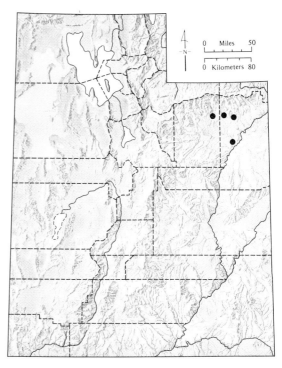

69. *Penstemon goodrichii* N. Holmgren Goodrich penstemon. May-June. Native perennial herb; shadscale, desert shrub communities, 1700-1800 m.

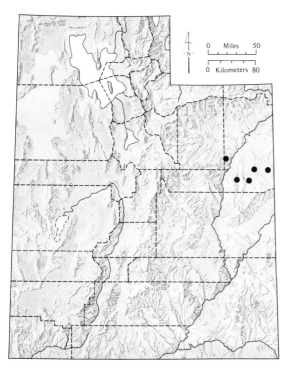

70. *Penstemon grahamii* Keck Uinta Basin penstemon. May-June. Native perennial herb; shadscale, pinyon-juniper communities, on usually rocky sites, 1720-1970 m.

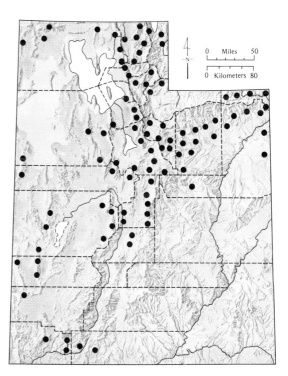

71. *Penstemon humilis* Gray Low penstemon. Apr.-Aug. Native perennial herb; sagebrush communities to above timberline, often on open rocky slopes, 1600-3340 m.

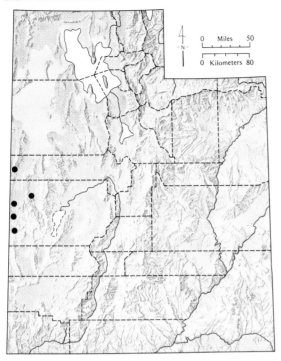

72. *Penstemon immanifestus* N. Holmgren
May-July. Native perennial herb; greasewood,
shadscale communities, 1500-1640 m.

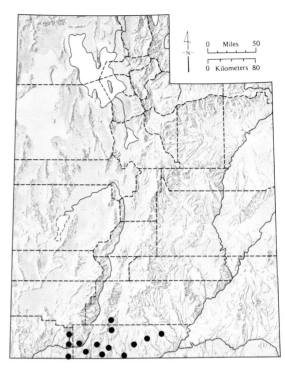

73. *Penstemon laevis* Pennell May-June.
Smooth penstemon. Native perennial herb;
sagebrush, pinyon-juniper, ponderosa pine
communities, usually in sandy soil, 1500-2150 m.

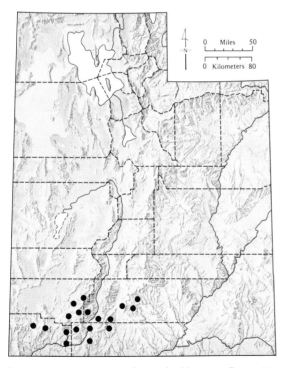

74. *Penstemon leiophyllus* Pennell
Markagunt penstemon. June-Aug. Native
perennial herb; mountain brush to aspen-conifer
communities, 1820-3500 m.

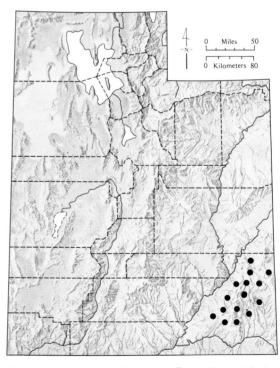

75. *Penstemon lentus* Pennell Abajo
penstemon. May-June. Native perennial herb;
shadscale, desert shrub to ponderosa pine
communities, 1500-2600 m.

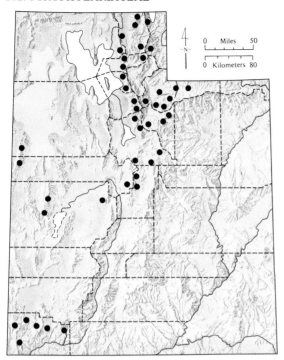

76. _Penstemon leonardii_ Rydb. Leonard penstemon. May-Aug. Native perennial herb or subshrub; sagebrush, pinyon-juniper, mountain brush to aspen-conifer communities, often on rocky sites, 1830-3050 m.

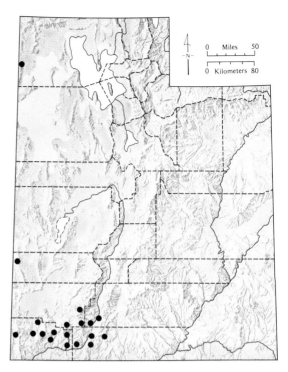

77. _Penstemon linarioides_ Gray Siler penstemon. May-Aug. Native perennial herb or subshrub; sagebrush to ponderosa pine communities, 1810-3050 m.

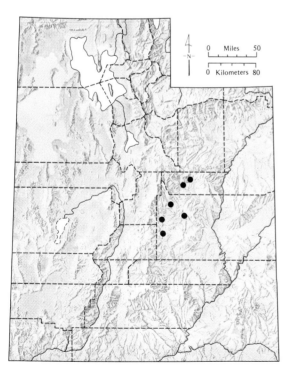

78. _Penstemon marcusii_ (Keck) N. Holmgren Price penstemon. May-June. Native perennial herb; shadscale, desert shrub communities, 1370-1970 m.

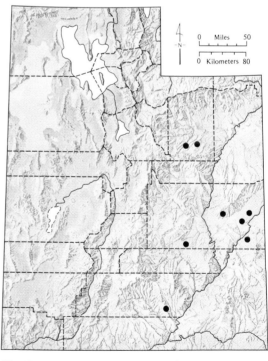

79. _Penstemon moffattii_ Eastw. Moffatt penstemon. May-June. Native perennial herb; desert shrub to pinyon-juniper communities, 1300-1900 m.

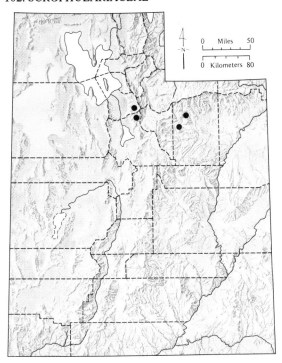

80. **Penstemon montanus** Greene Cordroot penstemon. July-Aug. Native perennial herb; talus and rock crevices in aspen, spruce-fir communities to above timberline, 2280-3600 m.

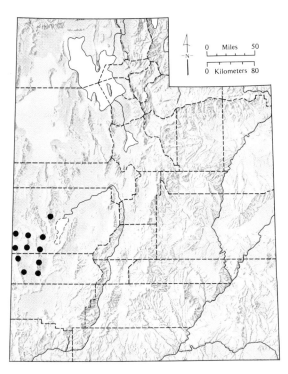

81. **Penstemon nanus** Keck Dwarf penstemon. May-June. Native perennial herb; shadscale, desert shrub to pinyon-juniper communities, 1580-2140 m.

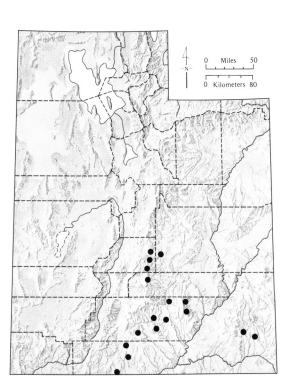

82. **Penstemon ophianthus** Pennell May-June. Native perennial herb; shadscale, desert shrub to ponderosa pine communities, 1510-2400 m.

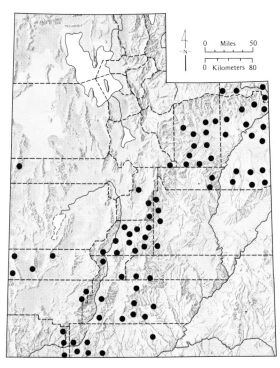

83. **Penstemon pachyphyllus** Rydb. Thickleaf penstemon. May-July. Native perennial herb; desert shrub to aspen-conifer communities, 1370-3200 m.

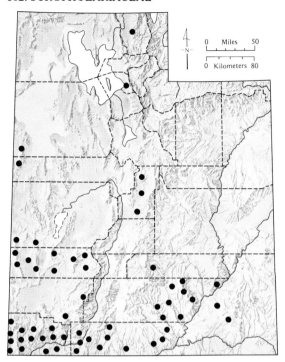

84. *Penstemon palmeri* Gray Palmer penstemon. May-Aug. Native perennial herb; creosote bush to ponderosa pine communities, 800-2730 m.

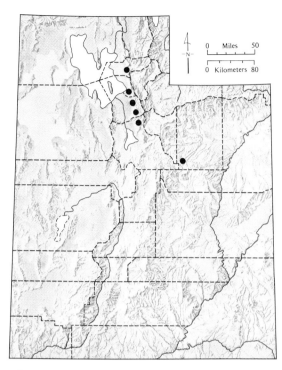

85. *Penstemon platyphyllus* Rydb. Broadleaf penstemon. May-Aug. Native perennial herb; open rocky sites in mountain brush communities, 1480-2700 m.

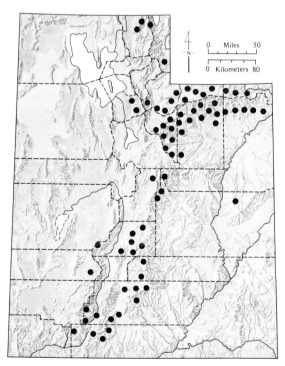

86. *Penstemon procerus* Graham Littleflower penstemon. June-Aug. Native perennial herb; mostly moist sites in mountain brush communities to above timberline, 1970-3580 m.

87. *Penstemon radicosus* A. Nels. Matroot penstemon. June-July. Native perennial herb; dry slopes in sagebrush, pinyon-juniper, mountain mahogany communities, 1360-3030 m.

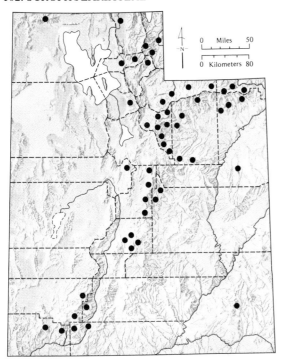

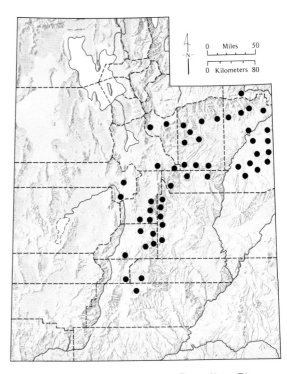

88. *Penstemon rydbergii* A. Nels. Rydberg penstemon. June-Aug. Native perennial herb; open to wooded slopes in mountain brush to alpine communities, 1760-3490 m.

89. *Penstemon scariosus* Pennell Plateau penstemon. June-Aug. Native perennial herb; desert shrub to aspen-conifer communities, 1510-3180 m.

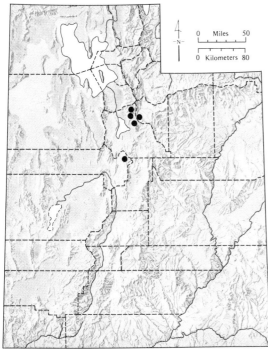

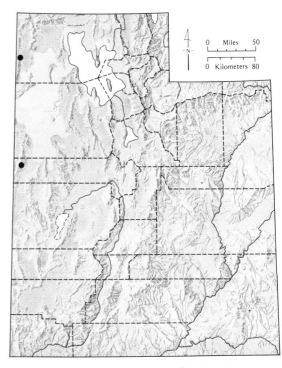

90. *Penstemon sepalulus* A. Nels. Littlecup penstemon. June-July. Native perennial herb; sagebrush to aspen-fir communities, 1510-2580 m.

91. *Penstemon speciosus* Lindl. Showy or royal penstemon. June-July. Native perennial herb; sagebrush, mountain mahogany, pinyon-juniper communities, 1970-2940 m.

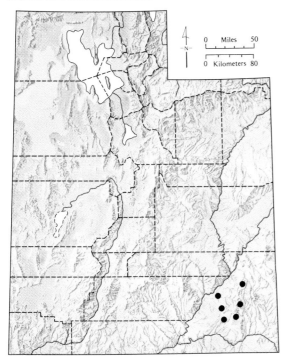

92. **Penstemon strictiformis** Rydb. May-June. Native perennial herb; desert shrub to pinyon-juniper communities, 1630-2060 m.

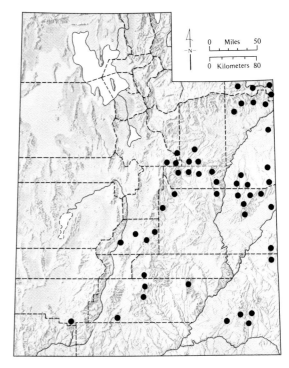

93. **Penstemon strictus** Benth. Rocky Mountain penstemon. June-Aug. Native perennial herb; mountain brush to aspen-conifer communities, 2060-3280 m.

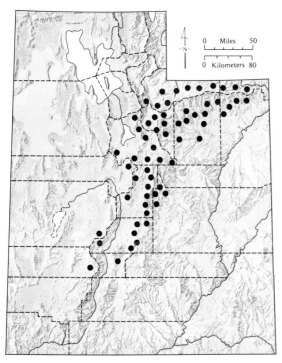

94. **Penstemon subglaber** Rydb. June-Sept. Native perennial herb; open sites in sagebrush to conifer communities, 1630-3440 m.

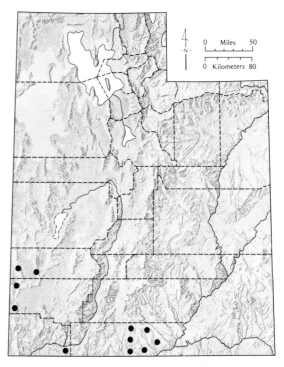

95. **Penstemon thompsoniae** (Gray) Rydb. Thompson penstemon. May-June. Native perennial herb or subshrub; desert shrub to pinyon-juniper communities, 1660-2060 m.

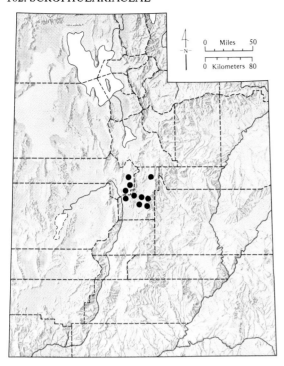

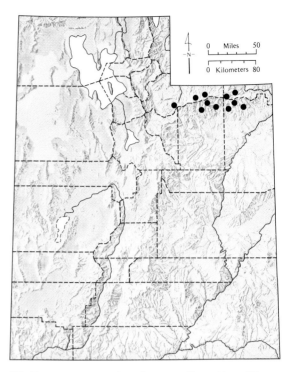

96. *Penstemon tidestromii* Pennell
Tidestrom penstemon. May-June. Native perennial
herb; desert shrub to pinyon-juniper communities,
1700-2490 m.

97. *Penstemon uintahensis* Pennell Uinta
Mountain penstemon. July-Aug. Native perennial
herb; meadows, open rocky ridges in conifer
forests to above timberline, 3030-3640 m.

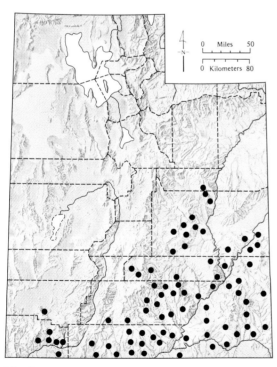

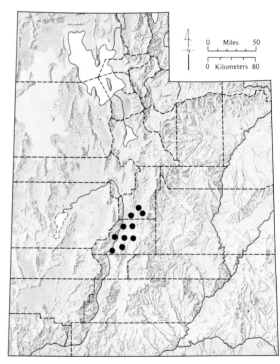

98. *Penstemon utahensis* Eastw. Utah
penstemon. Apr.-June. Native perennial herb;
desert shrub, mountain brush, pinyon-juniper
communities, 1300-2300 m.

99. *Penstemon wardii* Gray Ward penstemon.
June-July. Native perennial herb; shadscale, desert
shrub, pinyon-juniper communities, 1540-2060 m.

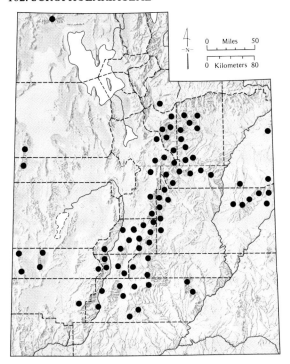

100. *Penstemon watsonii* Gray Watson penstemon. June-Aug. Native perennial herb; sagebrush to conifer communities, 1870-3180 m.

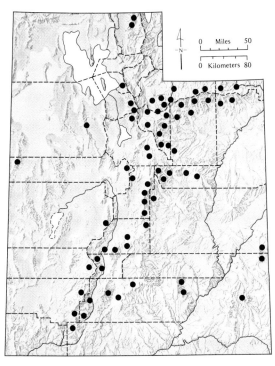

101. *Penstemon whippleanus* Gray Whipple penstemon. May-Aug. Native perennial herb; open to shaded sites in aspen-conifer communities to above timberline, 1780-3550 m.

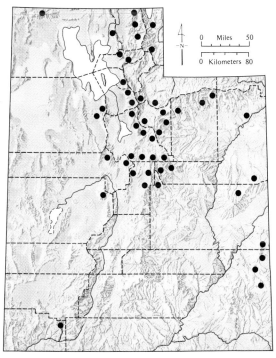

102. *Scrophularia lanceolata* Pursh Lanceleaf figwort. June-Aug. Native perennial herb; streamside, open to shaded sites in mountain brush to conifer communities, 1510-3250 m.

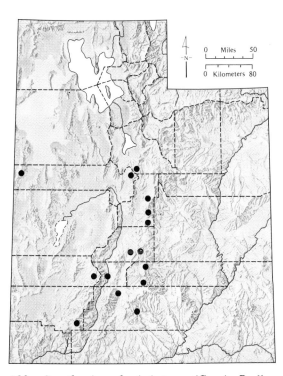

103. *Synthyris laciniata* (Gray) Rydb. Kittentails. May-July. Native perennial herb; conifer communities to above timberline, often in the wake of snowmelt, 2570-3490 m.

589

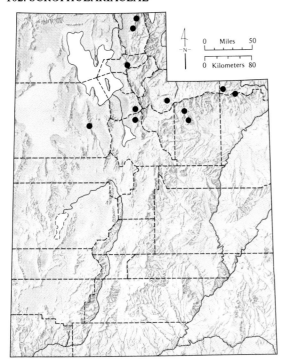

104. *Synthyris pinnatifida* Wats. Cutleaf kittentails. June-Aug. Native perennial herb; wet meadows, conifer forests to above timberline, often on exposed rocky slopes, 2420-3340 m.

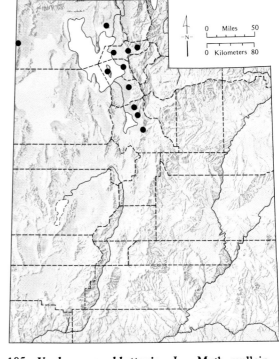

105. *Verbascum blattaria* L. Moth mullein. June-Sept. Introduced biennial; dry to mesic, disturbed sites, 1360-1670 m.

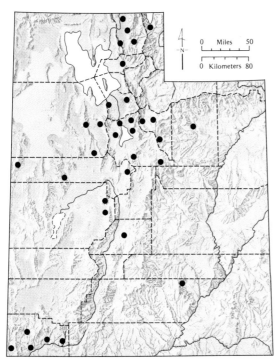

106. *Verbascum thapsus* L. Flannel or woolly mullein. July-Aug. Introduced biennial; moist to dry, disturbed sites, 800-2610 m.

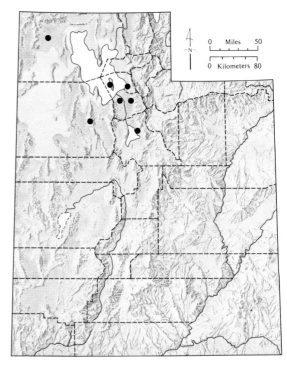

107. *Verbascum virgatum* Stokes Wand mullein. June-Aug. Introduced biennial; dry to mesic, disturbed sites, 1280-1700 m.

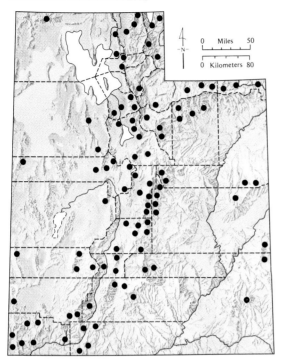

108. *Veronica americana* Benth. American brooklime. May-Sept. Native perennial herb; in shallow water or wet sites associated with streams, meadows, ponds, seeps, springs, 800-3150 m.

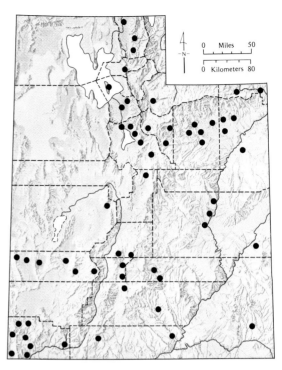

109. *Veronica anagallis-aquatica* L. Water speedwell. May-Aug. Introduced perennial herb; in shallow water or wet sites associated with streams, meadows, ponds, seeps, springs, 800-2250 m.

110. *Veronica arvensis* L. Corn speedwell. Apr.-May. Introduced annual; disturbed, often cultivated sites, 1360-1820 m.

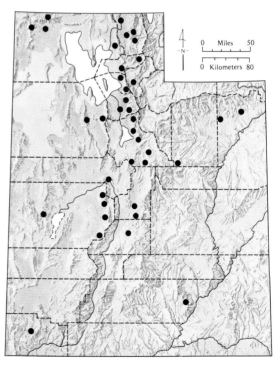

111. *Veronica biloba* L. Snow speedwell. Apr.-June. Introduced annual; dry to mesic, disturbed sites, 1300-3050 m.

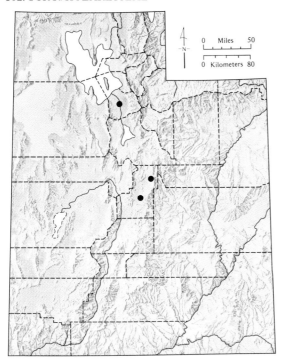

112. *Veronica catenata* Pennell Chain speedwell. June-July. Native perennial herb; in shallow water or wet sites associated with streams, meadows, ponds, seeps, springs, 1300-2490 m.

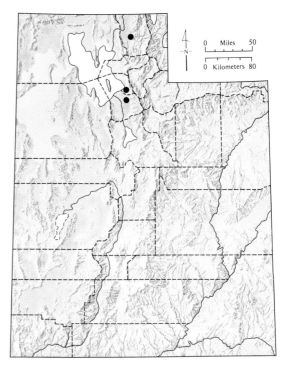

113. *Veronica hederaefolia* L. Ivyleaf speedwell. Apr.-May. Introduced annual; dry to mesic, disturbed sites, 1300-1610 m.

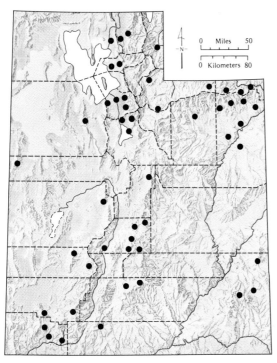

114. *Veronica peregrina* L. Purslane speedwell. June-Aug. Circumboreal annual; wet sites associated with waterways, meadows, ponds, lakes, moist slopes, weed of cultivated sites, 1300-3050 m.

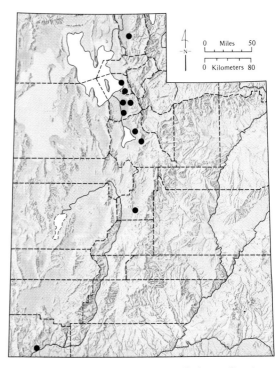

115. *Veronica persica* Poir. Persian speedwell. Apr.-May. Introduced annual; weed of lawns, other cultivated sites, disturbed areas, 840-1400 m.

102. SCROPHULARIACEAE

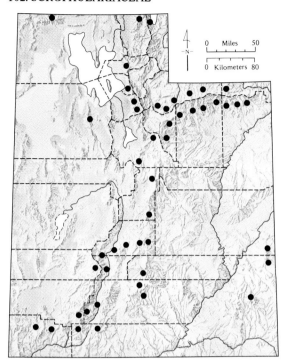

116. *Veronica serpyllifolia* L. Thymeleaf speedwell. June-Aug. Native perennial herb; along waterways, moist meadows, 1970-3190 m.

117. *Veronica wormskjoldii* R. & S. Wormskjold or American alpine speedwell. July-Aug. Native perennial herb; moist slopes, wet meadows, streamside, 2820-3490 m.

103. SELAGINELLACEAE

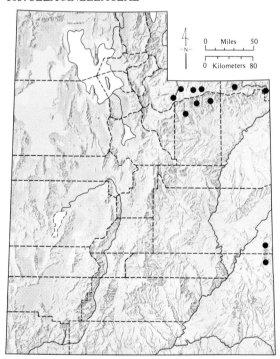

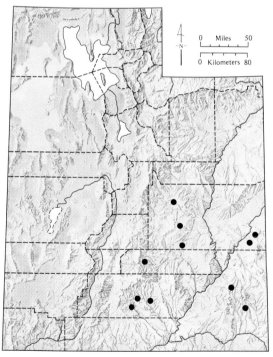

1. *Selaginella densa* Rydb. Rydberg spikemoss. Native; rock crevices, talus, 1810-3760 m.

2. *Selaginella mutica* Underw. Awnless spikemoss. Native; rock crevices in desert shrub communities, 1210-1790 m.

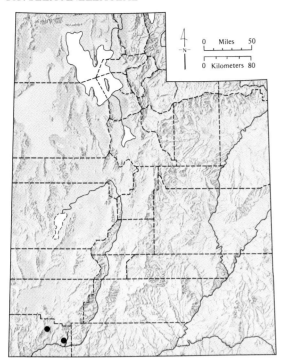

3. Selaginella underwoodii Hieron. Underwood spikemoss. Native; rock crevices in desert shrub to ponderosa pine communities, 1690-1820 m.

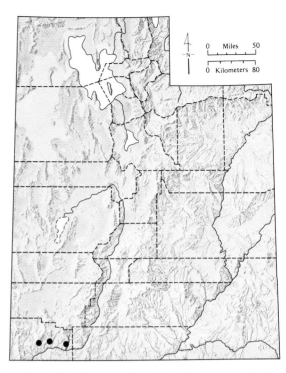

4. Selaginella utahensis Flowers Utah spikemoss. Native; protected rock crevices in oak, pinyon-juniper communities, 970-1970 m.

104. SIMAROUBACEAE

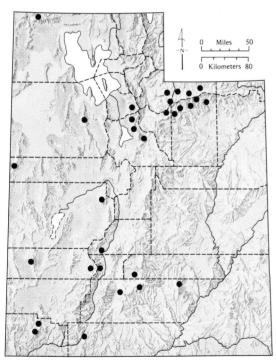

5. Selaginella watsonii Underw. Watson spikemoss. Native; exposed rock crevices, talus, 1970-3940 m.

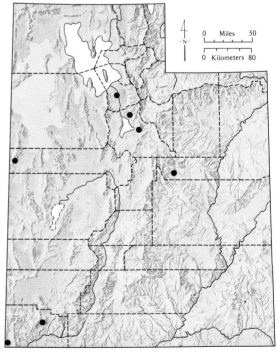

1. Ailanthus altissima (Mill.) Swingle Tree-of-heaven. June-July. Introduced tree; cultivated, escaping and persistent, 850-1370 m.

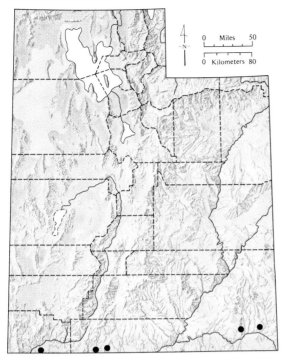

1. *Chamaesaracha coronopus* (Dunal) Gray False nightshade. June-Sept. Native perennial herb; desert shrub communities, 1360-1610 m.

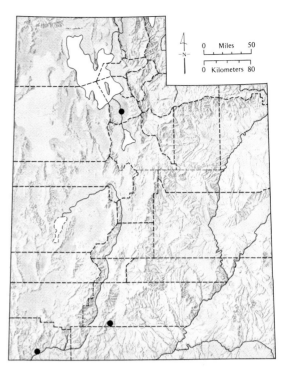

2. *Datura stramonium* L. Jimson weed. Aug.-Sept. Introduced annual; disturbed sites in creosote bush to desert shrub communities, 910-1670 m.

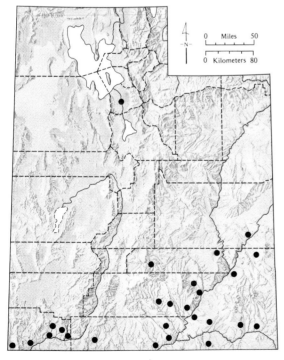

3. *Datura wrightii* Regel Indian apple; tolguacha. May-July. Native perennial herb; creosote bush to sagebrush communities, 840-1520 m.

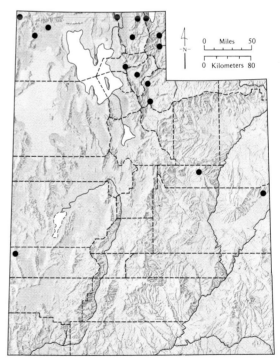

4. *Hyoscyamus niger* L. Black henbane. June-July. Introduced annual or biennial; waste places, 1660-2370 m.

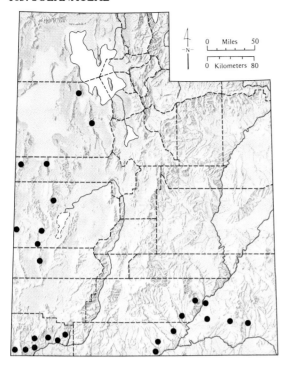

5. *Lycium andersonii* Gray Anderson wolfberry; waterjacket. Mar.-May. Native shrub; creosote bush to desert shrub communities, 840-1700 m.

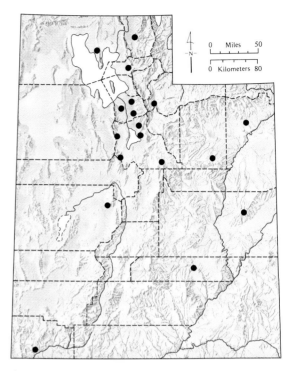

6. *Lycium barbarum* L. Matrimony vine. May-Sept. Introduced perennial shrub or vine; cultivated, escaping and persistent, 1270-1910 m.

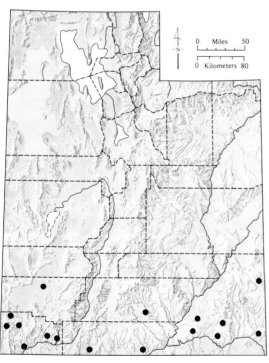

7. *Lycium pallidum* Miers Pale wolfberry. May-June. Native shrub; desert shrub to pinyon-juniper communities, 910-1820 m.

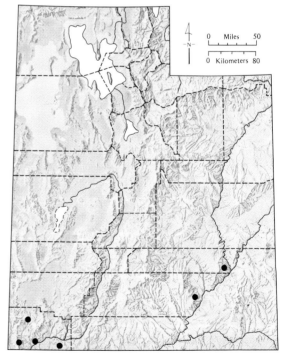

8. *Lycium torreyi* Gray Torrey wolfberry; squaw desertthorn. Mar.-May. Native shrub; creosote bush to pinyon-juniper communities, 840-2120 m.

596

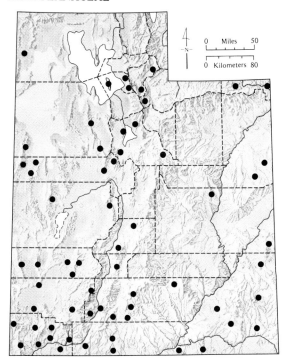

9. Nicotiana attenuata Wats. Coyote tobacco. June-Sept. Native annual; creosote bush to ponderosa pine communities, 910-2430 m.

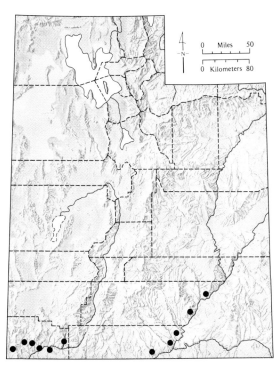

10. Nicotiana trigonophylla Dunal Desert tobacco. Apr.-May. Native annual or perennial herb; creosote bush, desert shrub communities, 750-1060 m.

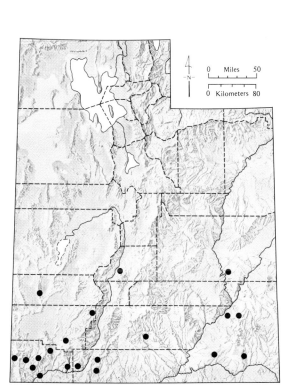

11. Physalis hederaefolia Gray Ivyleaf groundcherry. May-June. Native perennial herb; desert shrub to pinyon-juniper communities, 1060-2280 m.

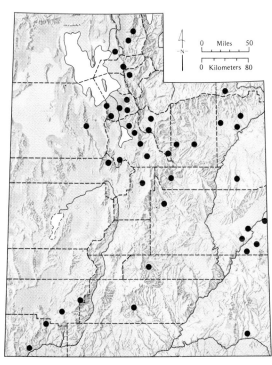

12. Physalis longifolia Nutt. Longleaf groundcherry. June-Aug. Native perennial herb; desert shrub to aspen communities, often invading cultivated and otherwise disturbed sites, 910-2500 m.

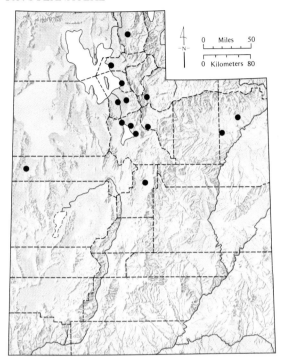

13. *Solanum dulcamara* L. European bittersweet. June-Aug. Introduced shrub or vine; irrigated or otherwise disturbed moist sites, 1330-1600 m.

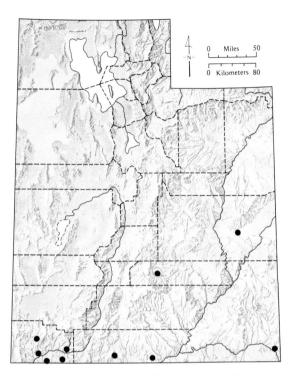

14. *Solanum elaeagnifolium* Cav. Silverleaf nightshade; bull nettle. May-Aug. Native perennial herb; disturbed sites, 910-1300 m.

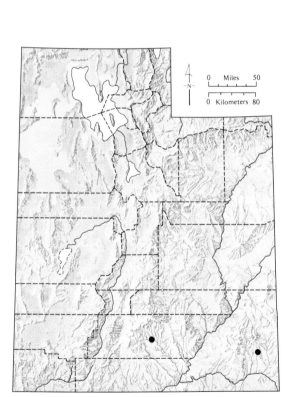

15. *Solanum jamesii* Torr. James potato. June-July. Native perennial herb; desert shrub communities, 1630-1790 m.

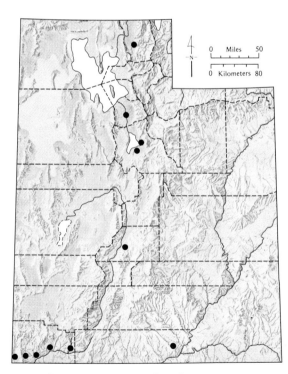

16. *Solanum nigrum* L. Black nightshade. June-Aug. Introduced annual; waste places, 780-1370 m.

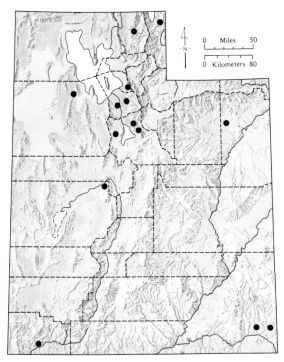

17. *Solanum rostratum* Dunal Buffalobur; Kansas thistle. July-Aug. Native annual; waste places, occasionally invading cultivated sites, 1300-1520 m.

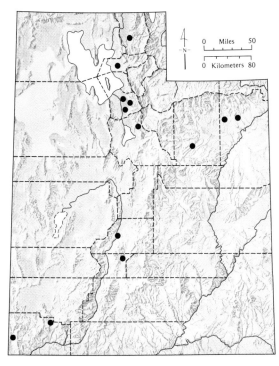

18. *Solanum sarrachoides* Mart. Hairy nightshade. July-Sept. Introduced annual; disturbed sites, 1300-1730 m.

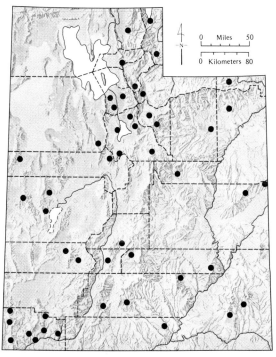

19. *Solanum triflorum* Nutt. Cutleaf nightshade. June-Aug. Native annual; disturbed sites, 1270-2670 m.

106. SPARGANIACEAE

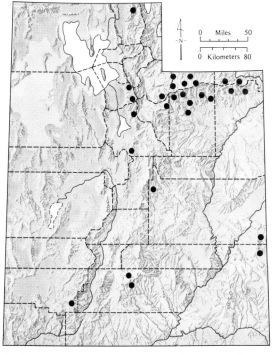

1. *Sparganium angustifolium* Michx. Narrowleaf burreed. June-Aug. Circumboreal perennial herb; ponds, lakes, 1420-3340 m.

106. SPARGANIACEAE

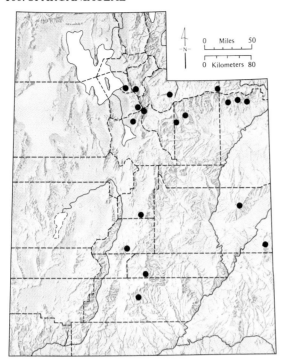

2. *Sparganium emersum* Rehmann Emersed burreed. June-Sept. Native perennial herb; wet meadows, water of ponds, lakes, 2420-3030 m.

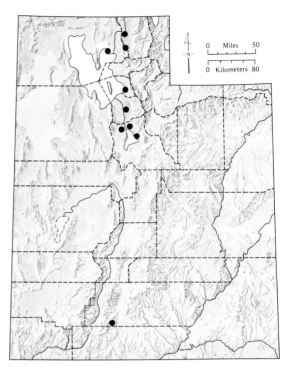

3. *Sparganium eurycarpum* Engelm. Giant burreed. June-Oct. Native perennial herb; wet meadows, streamside, ponds, 1300-2120 m.

107. TAMARICACEAE

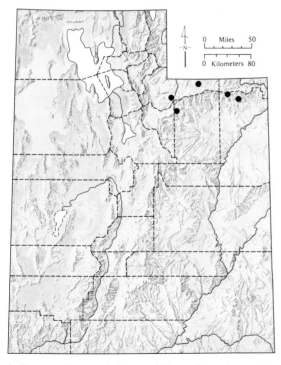

4. *Sparganium minimum* Fries Least burreed. July-Aug. Native perennial herb; water of ponds, lakes, 2880-3030 m.

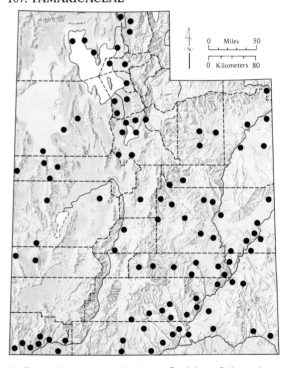

1. *Tamarix ramosissima* Ledeb. Salt cedar tamarisk. May-July. Introduced shrub or small tree; cultivated, invading marshes, banks of streams and rivers, salt tolerant, 910-1850 m.

107. TAMARICACEAE

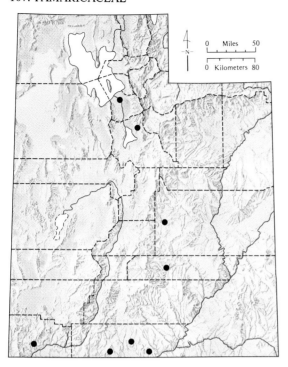

2. *Tamarix tetrandra* Pall. Fourstamen tamarisk. May-June. Introduced shrub or small tree; cultivated, invading marshes, banks of streams and rivers, salt tolerant, 970-1520 m.

108. TYPHACEAE

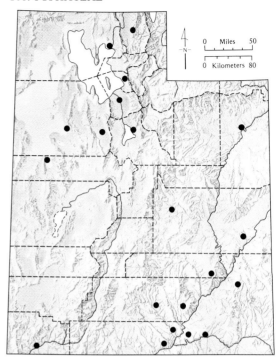

1. *Typha domingensis* Pers. Southern cattail. June-Aug. Native perennial; shallow or quiet, often saline water, 910-1370 m.

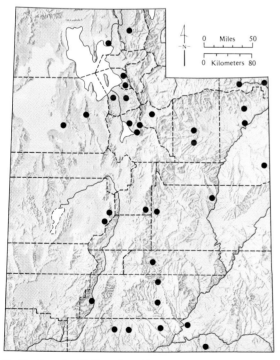

2. *Typha latifolia* L. Common cattail. June-Aug. Cosmopolitan perennial; shallow water of marshes, other quiet or slow-moving waters, seepage areas, 1270-2610 m.

109. ULMACEAE

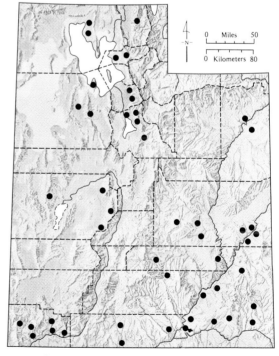

1. *Celtis reticulata* Torr. Netleaf hackberry. Apr.-May. Native tree; desert shrub to mountain brush communities; 910-1520 m.

109. ULMACEAE

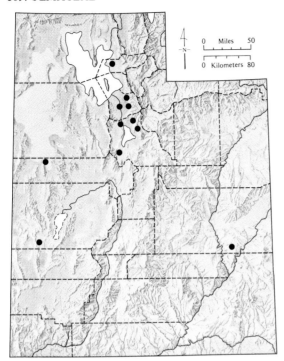

2. ***Ulmus pumila*** L. Siberian elm. Apr.-May. Introduced tree; cultivated, invading waste places, 1300-1520 m.

110. URTICACEAE

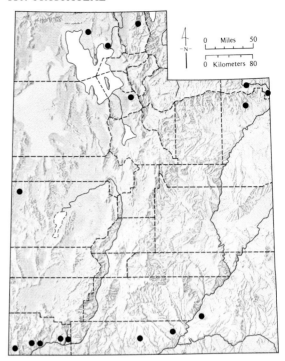

1. ***Parietaria pensylvanica*** Willd. Hammerwort. Mar.-Aug. Native annual; protected rock crevices in creosote bush, desert shrub communities, 750-1730 m.

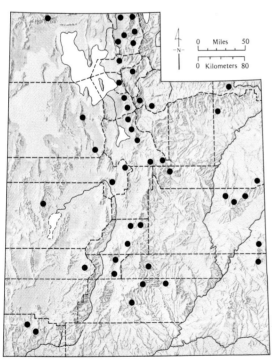

2. ***Urtica dioica*** L. Stinging nettle. July-Aug. Cosmopolitan perennial herb; streamside, moist to mesic meadows, margins of ponds and lakes, mostly shaded sites in mountain brush to spruce-fir communities, 1510-3180 m.

111. VALERIANACEAE

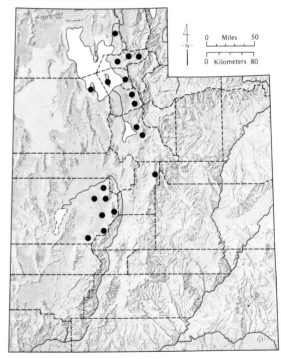

1. ***Plectritis macrocera*** T. & G. Apr.-May. Native annual; open moist slopes in desert shrub, mountain brush communities, 1360-2120 m.

111. VALERIANACEAE

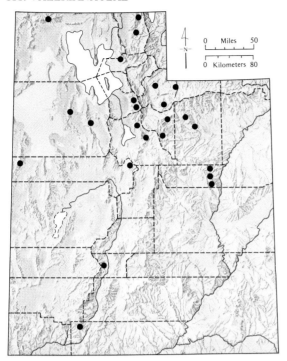

2. *Valeriana acutiloba* Rydb. Cordilleran valerian. June-Aug. Native perennial herb; open moist sites in aspen to krummholz communities, 1970-3580 m.

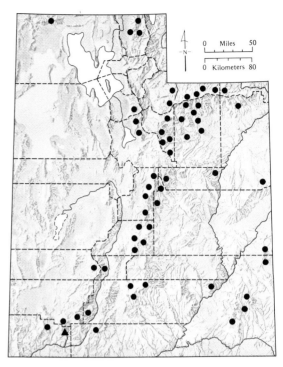

3. *Valeriana edulis* T. & G. Taprooted valerian. June-Aug. Native perennial herb; moist meadows, open sites in mountain brush to conifer communities, 1360-3490 m.

112. VERBENACEAE

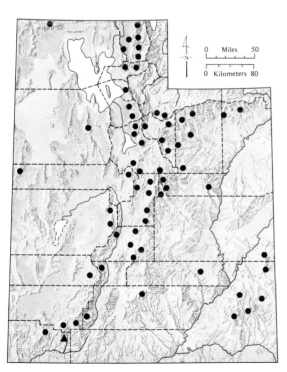

4. *Valeriana occidentalis* Heller Western valerian. May-July. Native perennial herb; streamside, moist, mostly shaded sites in mountain brush to spruce-fir communities, 1600-3460 m.

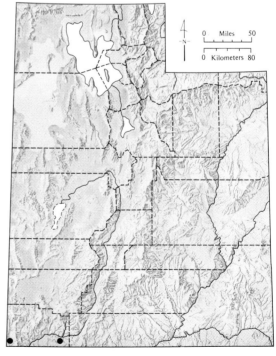

1. *Aloysia wrightii* (Gray) Heller Oreganillo. Aug.-Oct. Native shrub; creosote bush, desert shrub communities, 840-1060 m.

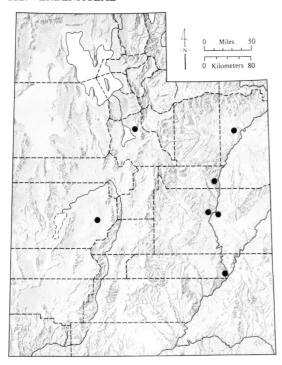

2. *Phyla cuneifolia* (Torr.) Greene Wedgeleaf frogfruit. June-July. Native perennial herb; streamside, moist meadows, 1570-1670 m.

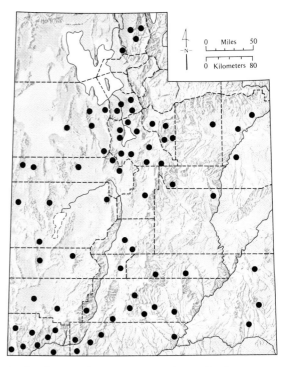

3. *Verbena bracteata* Lag. & Rodr. Prostrate vervain. May-Oct. Native annual to perennial; roadsides, fields, other disturbed sites, 780-2700 m.

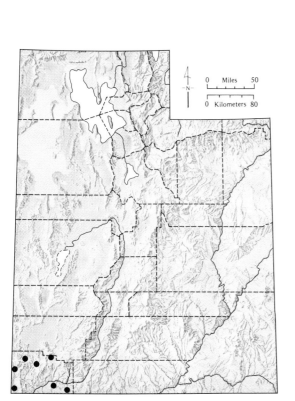

4. *Verbena gooddingii* Briq. Goodding vervain. May-June. Native perennial herb; creosote bush to pinyon-juniper communities, 780-1550 m.

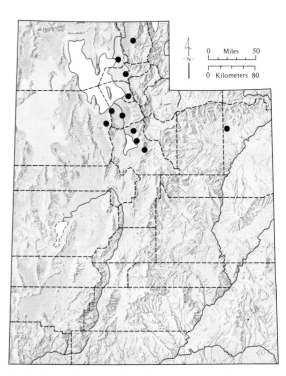

5. *Verbena hastata* L. Blue vervain. June-Aug. Native perennial herb; moist meadows, along waterways, other moist, often disturbed sites, 1270-1520 m.

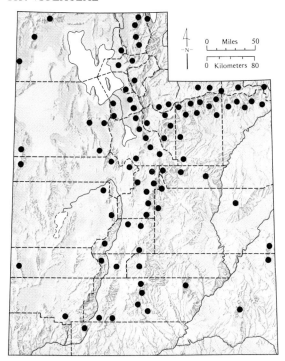

1. *Viola adunca* J. E. Sm. Blue violet.
Apr.-July. Native perennial herb; shaded sites
in mountain brush to conifer communities,
1510-3490 m.

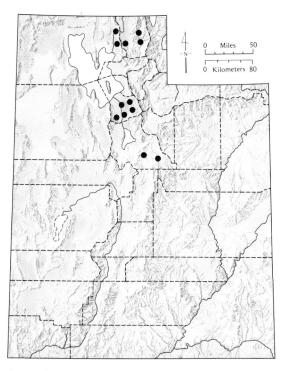

2. *Viola beckwithii* T. & G. Beckwith
violet. Apr.-May. Native perennial herb;
sagebrush communities, 1330-1460 m.

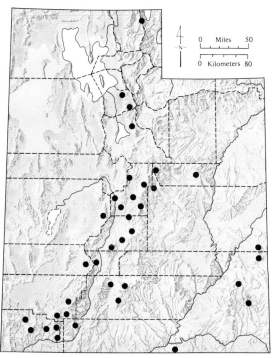

3. *Viola canadensis* L. Canada violet.
Apr.-Sept. Native perennial herb; shaded sites
in mountain brush to conifer communities,
1360-3180 m.

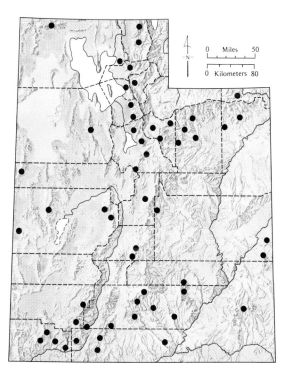

4. *Viola nephrophylla* Greene Bog
violet. Apr.-June. Native perennial herb;
marshes, streamside, near seeps and springs in
desert shrub to conifer communities, 1210-
3150 m.

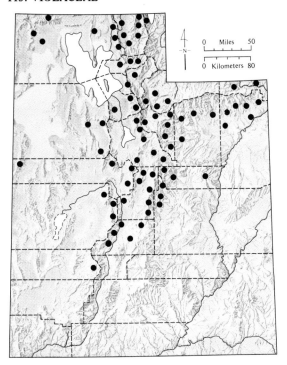

5. *Viola nuttallii* Pursh Nuttall violet.
Apr.-Aug. Native perennial herb; open or
shaded sites in sagebrush to aspen
communities, 1500-3500 m.

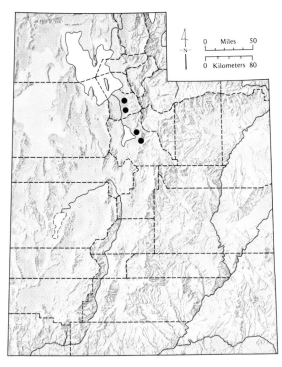

6. *Viola odorata* L. Sweet or English
violet. Mar.-Oct. Introduced perennial herb;
cultivated, escaping, invading lawns and
gardens, 1330-1430 m.

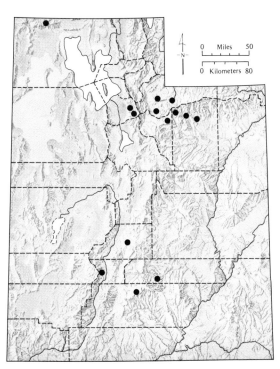

7. *Viola palustris* L. Marsh violet. June-
July. Native perennial herb; wet meadows or
streamside in aspen-conifer communities, 2420-
3030 m.

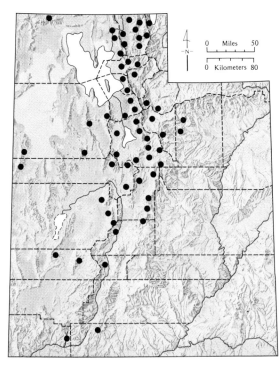

8. *Viola purpurea* Kell. Pine violet. Apr.-
July. Native perennial herb; open or shaded sites
in sagebrush to aspen communities, 1510-3030 m.

113. VIOLACEAE

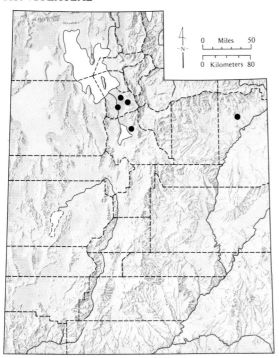

9. *Viola tricolor* L. Pansy. May-July. Introduced annual to perennial; disturbed mesic sites, 1510-2070 m.

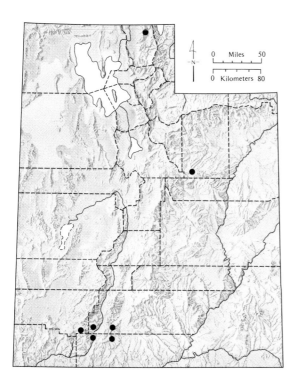

2. *Arceuthobium cyanocarpum* Coult. & Nels. Limber pine dwarf mistletoe. July-Aug. Native; parasitic on *Pinus flexilis* and *Pinus longaeva*, 2480-2730 m.

114. VISCACEAE

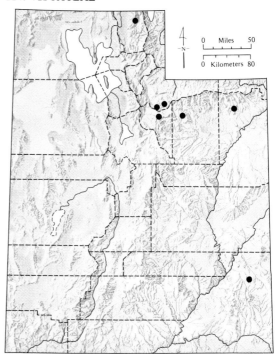

1. *Arceuthobium americanum* Engelm. Dwarf mistletoe. Apr.-July. Native; parasitic on *Pinus contorta* and *Pinus ponderosa*, 2120-2730 m.

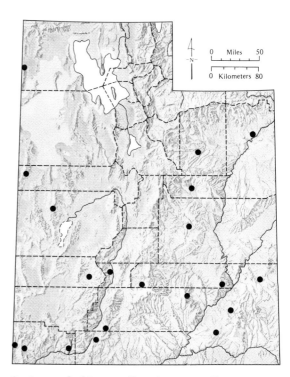

3. *Arceuthobium divaricatum* Engelm. Pinyon dwarf mistletoe. Aug.-Sept. Native; parasitic on *Pinus edulis* and *Pinus monophylla*., 1180-2120 m.

607

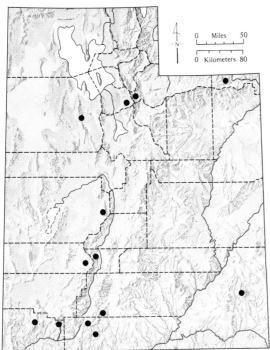

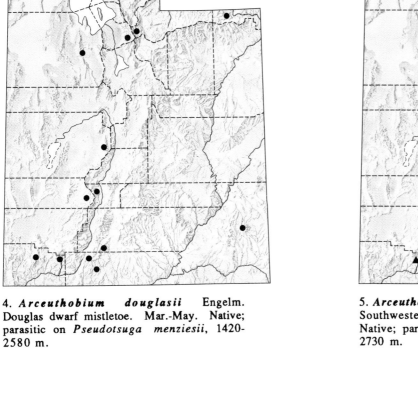

4. *Arceuthobium douglasii* Engelm.
Douglas dwarf mistletoe. Mar.-May. Native;
parasitic on *Pseudotsuga menziesii*, 1420-
2580 m.

5. *Arceuthobium vaginatum* (Willd.) Presl
Southwestern dwarf mistletoe. May-July.
Native; parasitic on *Pinus ponderosa*, 1810-
2730 m.

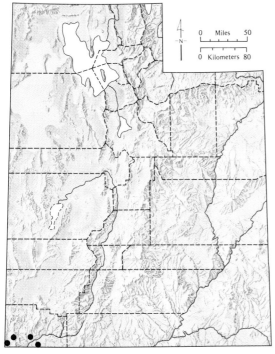

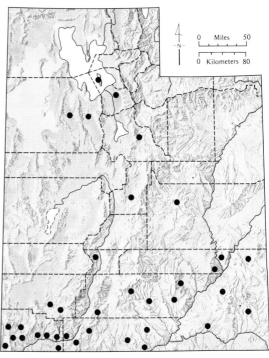

6. *Phoradendron californicum* Nutt.
Acacia mistletoe. Apr.-June. Native; parasitic
on *Acacia greggii*, 750-910 m.

7. *Phoradendron juniperinum* Gray
Juniper mistletoe. Apr.-Aug. Native; parasitic
on *Juniperus* species, 1120-2280 m.

115. VITACEAE

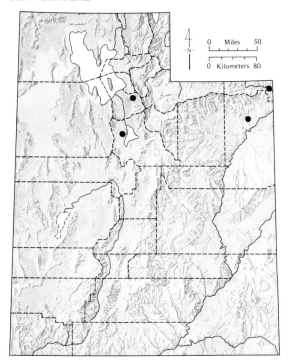

1. ***Parthenocissus quinquefolia*** (L.)
Planch. Virginia creeper. June-July.
Introduced perennial vine; cultivated, escaping
and persistent, 1360-1520 m.

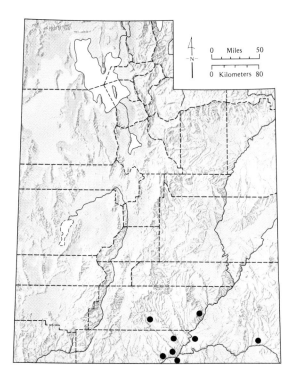

2. ***Parthenocissus vitacea*** (Knerr) Hitchc.
Thicket creeper. June-July. Native perennial
vine; hanging gardens, 1210-1370 m.

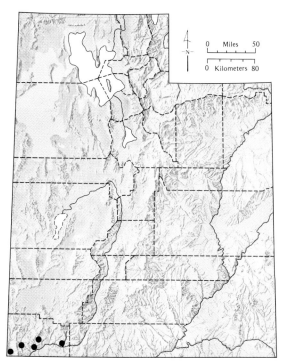

3. ***Vitus arizonica*** Engelm. Canyon grape.
June-July. Native perennial vine; streamside,
near seeps and springs, 910-1820 m.

116. ZANNICHELLIACEAE

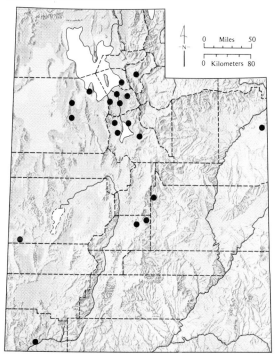

1. ***Zanichellia palustris*** L. June-Oct.
Horned pondweed. Cosmopolitan perennial;
fresh or brackish water, 1300-2580 m.

609

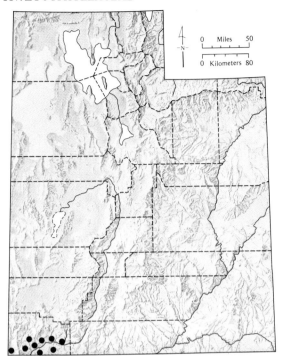

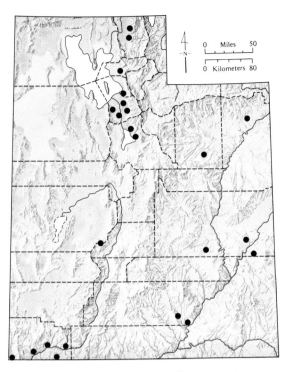

1. *Larrea tridentata* (DC.) Cov. Creosote bush. May-Aug. Native shrub; dominant locally, 840-1160 m.

2. *Tribulus terrestris* L. Puncture vine. July-Sept. Introduced annual; open, waste places, 840-2120 m.

APPENDIX

PLANTS RESTRICTED IN DISTRIBUTION

The following list of 384 taxa originally included only those plants collected from a single location or from an area small enough to have been represented by a solitary dot on a map. Plant collections obtained subsequent to the preparation of the main body of the text, however, revealed that a few species occur in two more or less distant populations.

Unless referenced, the species included here are based exclusively on specimens examined by the authors in the various herbaria. Entries for plants not previously reported from Utah in the literature are followed by the acronym of the herbarium or herbaria in which specimens of such plants are held: BRY (Brigham Young University), UTC (Utah State University), and UT (University of Utah).

Names preceded by an asterisk are those of taxa currently listed by the U.S. Fish and Wildlife Service (1987; addendum, 1988) as endangered or threatened.

1. ADOXACEAE
   Adoxa moschatellina L.; circumboreal perennial herb; moist shady sites along streams, San Juan Co.

2. AGAVACEAE
   Nolina microcarpa Wats., native perennial herb, rocky slopes in canyons, Washington Co.
   Yucca schidigera Ortega, native shrublike to arborescent plant, creosote bush communities, Washington Co.

3. AIZOACEAE
   Trianthema portulacastrum L., native annual, disturbed sites, Washington Co.

4. ALISMATACEAE
   Sagittaria latifolia Willd., native perennial aquatic, wet meadow, San Pete Co.

5. AMARANTHACEAE
   Acanthochiton wrightii Torr., native annual, desert shrub community, Kane Co.
   Amaranthus californicus (Moq.) Wats.; native annual; mudflats; Dry Lake, Cache Co.
   A. fimbriatus (Torr.) Benth., native annual, Joshua tree-creosote bush community, Washington Co.
   A. lividus L.; introduced annual; moist sites near Utah Lake, Utah Co.

6. APIACEAE
   Angelica kingii (Wats.) C. & R.; native perennial herb; streamside in aspen-fir communities; Deep Creek Range, Juab Co.
   Cymopterus evertii Hartman & Kirkpatrick, native perennial herb, rocky ledges in spruce-limber pine communities, Uintah Co. (UT).
   Foeniculum vulgare Miller, introduced perennial herb, disturbed sites, Utah and Washington counties.
   Ligusticum grayi C. & R.; native perennial herb; conifer-forb communities; Raft River Mtns., Box Elder Co.
   Musineon lineare (Rydb.) Math.; native perennial herb; limestone cliffs; Bear River Range, Cache Co.
   Oreoxis bakeri C. & R.; native perennial herb; alpine communities; La Sal Mtns., Grand-San Juan counties.
   O. trotteri Welsh & Goodrich, native perennial herb, juniper-desert shrub community, Grand Co. (Welsh et al., 1987).
   Podistera eastwoodiae (C. & R.) Math. & Const.; native perennial herb; alpine slopes; La Sal Mtns., Grand-San Juan counties.
   Torilis arvensis (Huds.) Link; introduced annual invading a cultivated site; La Verkin, Washington Co.

7. APOCYNACEAE
   Amsonia tomentosa Torr. & Frem., native perennial herb, Joshua tree-creosote bush community, Washington Co. (Cronquist et al., 1984).

8. ARALIACEAE
   Aralia racemosa L.; native perennial herb; rock crevices; Zion National Park, Washington Co.

9. ASCLEPIADACEAE
   Asclepias involucrata Engelm., native perennial herb; sagebrush, desert shrub, pinyon-juniper communities; San Juan Co. (Welsh et al., 1987).
   *A. welshii N. Holmgren & P. Holmgren; native perennial herb; Coral Pink Sand Dunes, Kane Co.
   Cynanchum utahense (Engelm.) Woodson, native perennial herb, creosote bush community, Washington Co.

10. ASTERACEAE

Adenophyllum cooperi (Gray) Strother, native perennial herb, creosote bush community, Washington Co.

Amphipappus fremontii T. & G., native shrub, creosote bush community, Washington Co.

Arctium lappa L., introduced biennial, disturbed site, Salt Lake Co.

Arnica nevadensis Gray; native perennial herb; alpine slopes, meadows; La Sal Mtns., San Juan Co. (UTC).

Artemisia abrotanum L., introduced perennial herb, escaped from cultivation, Washington Co.

A. annua L., introduced annual, disturbed sites, Washington Co.

Aster campestris Nutt., native perennial herb, moist saline meadows, Beaver Co. (C. L. Hitchcock, 1955).

A. sibiricus L.; interruptedly circumboreal perennial herb; spruce community; Uinta Mtns., Summit Co.

Atrichoseris platyphylla Gray; native annual; Joshua tree, desert shrub communities; Washington Co.

Bebbia juncea (Benth.) Greene; native shrub; gravelly sites; Beaver Dam Wash, Washington Co.

Bellis perennis L., introduced perennial herb, cultivated, escaping and invading lawns, Salt Lake Co.

Bidens tenuisecta Gray, native annual, disturbed sites, Garfield Co. (UTC).

Calycoseris parryi Gray, native annual, creosote bush community, Washington Co.

C. wrightii Gray, native annual, creosote bush community, Washington Co.

Carthamnus tinctorius L., introduced annual, escaped from cultivation, Cache Co. (UTC).

Centaurea jacea L., introduced perennial, disturbed sites, Salt Lake Co.

Cirsium centaureae (Rydb.) Schum.; native perennial herb; mountain brush communities; Abajo Mtns., San Juan Co.

C. virginensis Welsh, native perennial herb, moist saline sites, Washington Co.

Cnicus benedictus L., introduced annual, disturbed sites, Washington Co.

Conyza coulteri Gray; native annual; Joshua tree-creosote bush community; Beaver Dam Wash, Washington Co.

Encelia farinosa (ay, native shrub, desert shrub community, Washington Co. (Welsh et al., 1987).

Erigeron canaani Welsh; native perennial herb; crevices in sandstone in a ponderosa pine community; Canaan Mtn., Washington Co.

E. corymbosus Nutt., native perennial herb, grass-sagebrush community, Rich Co. (Welsh et al., 1987).

E. cronquistii Maguire; native perennial herb; limestone cliffs; Bear River Range, Cache Co.

E. filifolius Nutt., native perennial herb, aspen-conifer community, Cache Co.

E. humilis Grah.; circumboreal perennial herb; alpine meadows; La Sal Mtns., Grand-San Juan counties (BRY).

E. linearis (Hook.) Piper, native perennial herb, sagebrush-juniper communities, Box Elder Co.

E. mancus Rydb.; native perennial herb; alpine grass-forb communities; La Sal Mtns., Grand-San Juan counties.

E. melanocephalus (A. Nels.) A. Nels.; native perennial herb; alpine grass-forb communites; La Sal Mtns., Grand-San Juan counties.

E. sionis Cronq.; native perennial herb; seeps and hanging gardens in ponderosa pine communities; Zion National Park, Washington Co.

E. untermannii Welsh & Goodrich, native perennial herb, openings in pinyon-juniper communities, Uintah and Duchesne counties.

E. zothecinus Welsh, native perennial herb, saline seeps in vertical cliff walls, Kane Co. (Welsh et al., 1987).

Filago californica Nutt., native annual, creosote bush community, Washington Co.

Gaillardia arizonica Gray, native annual, creosote bush community, Washington Co.

Geraea canescens T. & G.; native annual; desert wash in creosote bush community; Beaver Dam Wash, Washington Co.

Gnaphalium luteo-album L.; introduced annual; moist sites in ponderosa pine communities; Canaan Mtn., Washington Co.

G. microcephalum Nutt., native perennial herb, open rocky hillside, Weber Co.

Grindelia aphanactis Rydb., native biennial, disturbed sites, Kane and San Juan counties (Welsh et al., 1987).

G. laciniata Rydb., native perennial herb, sandy washes, San Juan Co. (Welsh et al., 1987).

Haplopappus apargioides Gray; native perennial herb; alpine slope; Tushar Mtns., Piute Co. (Welsh et al., 1987).

H. croceus Rydb.; native perennial herb; mountain brush community; La Sal Mtns., San Juan Co.

H. laricifolius Gray, native shrub, turbinella live oak community, Washington Co.

H. spinulosus (Pursh) DC., native perennial herb, desert shrub communities, San Juan and Washington counties.

Helianthus ciliaris DC.; native perennial herb, disturbed sites, Sevier and Washington counties (BRY, UTC).

Heterotheca grandiflora Nutt., native annual-biennial herb, disturbed sandy site, Washington Co.

H. psammophila Wagenkn., native annual-biennial herb, sandy roadside, Washington Co. (Meyer, 1976).

H. zionensis Semple; native shrub; ponderosa pine, spruce-fir communities; Kane and Washington counties (Semple, 1987).

Hieracium fendleri Sch.-Bip., native perennial herb, ponderosa pine community, Washington Co.

Hymenoxys lapidicola Welsh & Neese, native perennial herb, ponderosa pine community, Uintah Co.

H. lemmonii (Greene) Ckll., native perennial herb, saline meadows, Tooele and Millard counties (Welsh et al., 1987).

Kuhnia chlorolepis Woot. & Standl., native perennial herb, wash in rabbitbrush community, Uintah Co.

Lactuca biennis (Moench) Fern., native annual-biennial herb, streamside in oak-maple community, Salt Lake Co.

L. canadensis L., native annual-biennial herb, moist sites, Kane Co.

L. ludoviciana (Nutt.) Riddell, native biennial-perennial herb, disturbed site, Salt Lake Co.

Lapsana communis L., introduced annual, shaded site in maple community, Salt Lake Co.

Lepidospartum latisquamum Wats., native shrub, wash in rabbitbrush community, Millard Co.

Lygodesmia doloresensis Tomb, native perennial herb, desert shrub-juniper community, Grand Co.

L. entrada Welsh & Goodrich, native perennial herb, desert shrub-juniper community, Grand Co.

L. juncea (Pursh) D. Don, native perennial herb, sand dunes, Juab Co.

Malacothrix coulteri Harv. & Gray, native annual, creosote bush community, Washington Co.

Monoptilon bellidiforme T. & G., native annual, Joshua tree-creosote bush community, Washington Co.

Parthenium incanum H. B. K., native shrub, creosote bush community, Washington Co.

Perityle emoryi Torr., native annual, desert shrub community, Washington Co.

P. specuicola Welsh & Neese, native perennial herb, hanging garden communities, Grand Co.

Petasites sagittatus (Banks) Gray; native perennial herb; streamside; Little Cottonwood Canyon, Wasatch Range, Salt Lake Co. (UT).

Peucephyllum schottii (Gray) Gray, native shrub, creosote bush community, Washington Co.

Psilostrophe tagetina (Nutt.) Greene; native perennial herb; desert shrub community; Grand, San Juan counties.

Rafinesquia californica Nutt., native annual, creosote bush community, Washington Co. (Welsh et al., 1987).

Rudbeckia laciniata L.; native perennial herb; moist meadows; La Sal Mtns., San Juan Co.

Solidago spectabilis (D. C. Eat.) Gray; native perennial herb; saline seeps; Millard, Washington counties (Welsh et al., 1987).

Sphaeromeria capitata Nutt., native perennial herb, bristlecone pine community, Garfield Co.

Stephanomeria parryi Gray, native perennial herb, desert shrub community, Kane Co.

Tanacetum douglasii DC., native perennial herb, disturbed site, Salt Lake Co. (UTC).

Thelesperma megapotamicum (Spreng.) Kuntze, native perennial herb, desert shrub community, San Juan Co.

Townsendia aprica Welsh & Reveal; native perennial herb; shadscale, other desert shrub, pinyon-juniper communities; Emery and Sevier counties.

T. condensata D. C. Eat.; native perennial herb; alpine slopes; Tushar Mtns., Piute Co.

T. scapigera D. C. Eat., native biennial-perennial herb, sagebrush communities to alpine slopes, Millard Co.

Xanthium spinosum L., introduced annual herb, Utah Co. (Welsh et al., 1987).

Xylorhiza cronquistii Welsh & Atwood, native perennial herb, pinyon-juniper community, Kane Co.

11. BORAGINACEAE

Cryptantha angustifolia (Torr.) Greene, native annual, creosote bush community, Washington Co.

C. elata (Eastw.) Pays., native biennial-perennial herb, shadscale-desert shrub community, Grand Co.

C. flaccida (Dougl.) Greene, native annual, creosote bush community, Washington Co. (BRY).

C. interrupta (Greene) Pays.; native perennial herb; salt desert shrub, sagebrush, pinyon-juniper communities; Box Elder Co. (Welsh et al., 1987).

C. racemosa (Wats.) Greene, native annual, Joshua tree-creosote bush community, Washington Co. (Welsh et al., 1987).

C. semiglabra Barneby, native perennial herb, desert shrub, Washington Co. (Cronquist et al., 1984).

Echium vulgare L., introduced biennial, disturbed sites, Summit Co.

Hackelia ibapensis L. Shultz & J. Shultz; native perennial herb; granite outcrops; Deep Creek Mtns., Juab Co.

Myosotis micrantha Pallas, introduced annual, ponderosa pine communities, Daggett Co.

Pectocarya platycarpa M. & J., native annual, creosote bush community, Washington Co.

P. recurvata Jtn.; native annual; Joshua tree, creosote bush communities; Washington Co. (Welsh et al., 1987).

Plagiobothrys kingii (Wats.) Gray; native annual, shadscale, sagebrush, juniper communities; Box Elder Co. (Cronquist et al., 1984).

Tiquilia canescens (DC.) A. Richardson, native perennial herb, Joshua tree-creosote bush community, Washington Co.

12. BRASSICACEAE

Alliaria officinalis Andrz., introduced biennial, disturbed sites, Summit Co.

Arabis schistacea Roll., native perennial herb, sagebrush community, Garfield Co. (Welsh et al., 1987).

A. vivariensis Welsh; native perennial herb; desert shrub, pinyon-juniper communities; Uintah Co. (Welsh et al., 1987).

Athysanus pusillus (Hook.) Greene, native annual, shaded sites, Washington Co. (Welsh et al., 1987).

Berteroa incana (L.) DC., introduced annual, disturbed sites, Daggett Co.

Brassica hirta Moench, introduced annual, escaped from cultivation, Utah Co.

Cardamine oligosperma Nutt.; native annual-biennial; moist sites streamside; Uinta Mtns., Summit Co.

Caulanthus cooperi (Wats.) Pays., native annual, Joshua tree-creosote bush community, Washington Co.

Draba brachystylis Rydb.; native annual-biennial; aspen-fir communities; Wasatch Range, Salt Lake-Utah counties.

D. crassa Rydb.; native perennial herb; alpine meadows, typically in talus; Uinta Mtns., Duchesne-Summit counties.

D. douglasii Gray, native perennial herb, open montane slopes, Box Elder Co.

D. kassii Welsh; native perennial herb; pinyon, mountain brush, white fir communities; Deep Creek Mtns., Tooele Co. (Welsh et al., 1987).

D. sobolifera Rydb.; native perennial herb; spruce-fir communities, talus; Tushar Mtns., Beaver-Piute-Sevier counties.

Lepidium barnebyanum Reveal, native perennial herb, pinyon-juniper community, Duchesne Co.

L. ostleri Welsh & Goodrich; native perennial herb; pinyon-juniper communities; San Francisco Mtns., Beaver Co.

Lesquerella fendleri (Gray) Wats., native perennial herb, desert shrub community, San Juan Co.

L. prostrata A. Nels., native perennial herb, sagebrush-juniper community, Rich Co.

L. tumulosa (Barneby) Reveal, native perennial herb, desert grass-juniper community, Kane Co.

Rorippa sylvestris (L.) Besser, introduced perennial herb, drying mud of ponds, Wasatch Co.

Schoenocrambe argillacea (Welsh & Atwood) Roll., native perennial herb, desert shrub community, Uintah Co.

S. barnebyi (Welsh & Atwood) Roll.; native perennial herb; shadscale, other desert shrub communities; Emery Co.

Thelypodiopsis ambigua (Wats.) Al-Shehbaz, native biennial-perennial, pinyon-juniper community, Kane Co.

Thelypodium milleflorum A. Nels., native biennial, sagebrush-juniper community, Box Elder Co.

13. BUDDLEJACEAE

Buddleja utahensis Cov.; native shrub; creosote bush, desert shrub communities; Beaver Dam Mtns., Washington Co.

14. CACTACEAE

Echinocactus polycephalus Engelm. & Bigel.; native perennial; creosote bush, pinyon-juniper, desert shrub communities; Washington Co. (Meyer, 1976) and Kane Co. (Benson, 1982).

Ferocactus acanthodes (Lem.) Britt. & Rose; native perennial; rocky sites; Beaver Dam Mtns., Washington Co.

Mammillaria tetrancistra Engelm., native perennial, creosote bush community, Washington Co.

Opuntia littoralis (Engelm.) Ckll., native perennial, pinyon-juniper community, Washington Co.

Pediocactus despainii Welsh & Goodrich, native perennial, pinyon-juniper community, Emery Co.

*P. sileri (Engelm.) L. Benson, native perennial, desert shrub community, Washington Co.

P. winkleri Heil, native perennial, shadscale-desert shrub community, Wayne Co.

15. CAMPANULACEAE

Nemacladus rubescens Greene; native annual; Joshua tree, creosote bush communities; Washington Co. (Cronquist et al., 1984).

Triodanus perfoliata (L.) Nieuwl., introduced annual, disturbed sites, Kane and Washington counties.

16. CARYOPHYLLACEAE

Loeflingia squarrosa Nutt., native annual, mountain brush community, Washington Co. (Welsh et al., 1987).

Sagina procumbens L., circumboreal biennial-perennial herb, disturbed sites, Salt Lake Co.

Spergularia media (L.) Presl, introduced annual-perennial herb, saline sites, Davis Co.

17. CELASTRACEAE

Mortonia scabrella Gray, native shrub, creosote bush community, Washington Co.

18. CHENOPODIACEAE

Atriplex elegans (Moq.) D. Dietr., native annual, disturbed sites, Washington Co.

A. hymenelytra (Torr.) Wats., native shrub, Joshua tree-creosote bush community, Washington Co.

A. lentiformis (Torr.) Wats., native shrub, saline sites along waterways, Washington Co.

A. pleiantha W. A. Weber, native annual, saline sites, San Juan Co.
A. semibaccata R. Br., introduced subshrub, disturbed sites, Washington Co.
A. torreyi (Wats.) Wats., native shrub, creosote bush community, Washington Co.
Monolepis pusilla Wats.; native annual; shadscale, other desert shrub communities; Uintah Co.

19. CONVOLVULACEAE

Calystegia longipes (Wats.) Brummitt, native perennial herb, desert shrub communities, Washington Co. (Cronquist et al., 1984).
Convolvulus equitans Benth.; native perennial herb; Joshua tree, creosote bush communities; Washington Co.

20. CRASSULACEAE

Dudleya pulverulenta (Nutt.) Britt. & Rose; native perennial herb; limestone cliffs; Beaver Dam Mtns., Washington Co.
Tillaea aquatica L., circumboreal annual, wet meadow, Daggett Co.

21. CUCURBITACEAE

Cucurbita palmata Wats., native perennial herb, creosote bush community, Washington Co.

22. CUPRESSACEAE

Juniperus monosperma (Engelm.) Sarg., native shrub or small tree, in association with *Juniperus osteosperma*, San Juan Co. (Cronquist et al., 1972).

23. CUSCUTACEAE

Cuscuta applanata Engelm., native annual, disturbed site, Washington Co.
C. warneri Yunck., native annual, disturbed site, Millard Co.

24. CYPERACEAE

Carex arapahoensis Clokey; native perennial; alpine slopes; La Sal Mtns., Grand-San Juan counties.
C. bebbii Olney; native perennial; along waterways; Uinta Mtns., Uintah Co.
C. capitata L.; circumboreal perennial; alpine slopes; Uinta Mtns., Duchesne Co.
C. crawei Dewey, native perennial, wet meadow, Kane Co.
C. foetida All.; native perennial; wet meadow; Uinta Mtns., Wasatch Co.
C. lasiocarpa Ehrh.; native perennial; wet meadows, pond margins; Uinta Mtns., Daggett-Uintah counties.
C. perglobosa Mack.; native perennial; alpine slopes; La Sal Mtns., Grand-San Juan counties.
C. pyrenaica Wahl.; native perennial; moist alpine sites; Uinta Mtns., Duchesne Co.
Cyperus acuminatus Torr. & Hook., native annual, mud flats, Millard Co.
Eleocharis bella (Piper) Svens., native annual, wet sites in pinyon-juniper communities, Washington Co.
E. flavescens (Poir.) Urban, native perennial, moist montane sites, Cache Co.
E. ovata (Roth) R. & S., interruptedly circumboreal annual, shore of Utah Lake, Utah Co.
Scirpus nevadensis Wats., native perennial, saline meadows, Juab Co.

25. ELATINACEAE

Elatine californica Gray, native annual, mud flats along Dry Lake, Cache Co.

26. EUPHORBIACEAE

Eremocarpus setigerus (Hook.) Benth., native annual, creosote bush community, Washington Co.
Euphorbia cyathophora Murr., native annual, along waterways, Washington Co. (Welsh et al., 1987).
E. setiloba Engelm., native annual, Joshua tree-creosote bush community, Washington Co.

27. FABACEAE

Acacia greggii Gray; native shrub or small tree; desert shrub community; Beaver Dam Wash, Washington Co.
Astragalus anserinus Atwood, Goodrich, & Welsh; native perennial herb; sagebrush-juniper community; Goose Creek Mtns., Box Elder Co.
A. aretioides (Jones) Barneby, native perennial herb, rock outcrops, Daggett Co.
A. desereticus Barneby, native perennial herb, sagebrush-juniper community, Utah Co.
A. emoryanus (Rydb.) Cory, native annual, pinyon-juniper community, Kane Co.
A. filipes Torr., native perennial herb, sagebrush-juniper community, Box Elder Co.
A. holmgreniorum Barneby, native perennial herb, creosote bush community, Washington Co.
A. iodanthus Wats., native perennial herb, sagebrush-juniper community, Box Elder Co.
A. loanus Barneby, native perennial herb, pinyon-juniper community, Sevier Co.
*A. montii Welsh, native perennial herb, limestone talus, San Pete Co.
A. nelsonianus Barneby, native perennial herb, desert shrub community, Daggett Co.
A. robbinsii (Oakes) Gray; native perennial herb; willow community; Uinta Mtns., Summit Co.

A. uncialus Barneby, native perennial herb, shadscale community, Millard Co.

A. wetherillii Jones, native perennial herb, pinyon-juniper community, Grand Co.

Desmanthus illinoensis (Michx.) MacM., perennial herb native to the eastern U.S., escaped from cultivation, Washington Co.

Lupinus arbustus Lindl.; native perennial herb; sagebrush, pinyon-juniper communities; Deep Creek Mtns., Juab-Tooele counties.

L. latifolius Agardh, native perennial herb, oakbrush community, Washington Co.

Melilotus indica (L.) All., introduced annual, disturbed sites, Washington Co.

Psoralea epipsila Barneby, native perennial herb, pinyon-juniper community, Kane Co.

Psorothamnus arborescens (Torr.) Barneby, native shrub, desert shrub communities, Kane Co.

Sphaerophysa salsula (Pallas) DC., introduced perennial herb, disturbed sites, Uinta Basin (Welsh et al., 1987).

Trifolium beckwithii Wats., native perennial herb, montane meadows, Sevier Co.

28. GENTIANACEAE

Frasera gypsicola (Barneby) Post; native perennial herb; greasewood, shadscale communities; Millard Co.

Lomatogonium rotatum (L.) Fries, circumboreal annual, wet meadows, Daggett Co. (BRY, UT).

29. GROSSULARIACEAE

Ribes laxiflorum Pursh; native shrub; wet sites in aspen-spruce community; Deep Creek Mtns., Juab Co.

30. HYDROCHARITACEAE

Elodea longivaginata St. John, native perennial aquatic, ponds, Wasatch Co.

31. HYDROPHYLLACEAE

Hesperochiron californicus (Benth.) Wats., native perennial herb, saline meadows, Summit Co. (Cronquist et al., 1984).

Hydrophyllum fendleri (Gray) Heller; native perennial herb; shaded sites in mountain brush, ponderosa pine communities; Abajo Mtns., San Juan Co.

*Phacelia argillacea Atwood, native annual, pinyon-juniper community, Utah Co.

P. austromontana J. T. Howell, native annual, ponderosa pine community, Washington Co.

P. coerulea Greene, native annual, creosote bush community, Washington Co.

P. cryptantha Greene, native annual, creosote bush community, Washington Co. (Cronquist et al., 1984).

P. glandulifera Piper; native annual; juniper community; Raft River Mtns., Box Elder Co.

P. laxiflora J. T. Howell; native perennial herb; limestone cliffs; Virgin River Gorge, Washington Co. (Welsh et al., 1987).

P. lutea (H. & A.) J. T. Howell; native annual; shadscale, other desert shrub communities; San Pete Co.

P. peirsoniana J. T. Howell; native annual; sagebrush-pinyon-juniper community; Beaver Dam Wash, Washington Co. (Welsh et al., 1987).

P. tetramera J. T. Howell, native annual, saline sites, Weber Co.

32. IRIDACEAE

Iris pariensis Welsh, native perennial herb, grass-shrub community, Kane Co. (Welsh et al., 1987).

Sisyrinchium douglasii A. Dietr., native perennial herb, sagebrush community, Tooele Co.

33. ISOETACEAE

Isoetes echinospora Durieu; circumboreal perennial aquatic; ponds, lakes; Uinta Mtns. (Cronquist et al., 1972).

I. howellii Engelm.; native perennial aquatic; ponds, lakes; Cache Co.

I. lacustris L., interruptedly circumboreal perennial aquatic, lakes, Uinta Mtns. (Cronquist et al., 1972).

34. JUNCACEAE

Juncus gerardii Lois., native perennial, hot springs, Salt Lake Co.

J. tweedyi Rydb., native perennial, hot springs, Box Elder Co.

35. KRAMERIACEAE

Krameria grayi Rose & Painter; native shrub; creosote bush, desert shrub communities; Washington Co.

36. LAMIACEAE

Dracocephalum thymiflorum L., introduced annual, sagebrush-pinyon-juniper community, Sevier Co.

Satureja vulgaris (L.) Fritsch; native perennial herb; sagebrush, ponderosa pine communities; Washington Co.

Scutellaria nana Gray; native perennial herb; sagebrush, pinyon-juniper communities; Washington Co.

Stachys rothrockii Gray; native perennial herb; salt desert shrub, pinyon-juniper communities; Kane Co.

37. LEMNACEAE
Lemna obscura (Austin) Daubs, native floating aquatic, sluggish streams and ponds, Beaver Co.

38. LILIACEAE
Allium passeyi N. Holmgren & A. Holmgren, native perennial herb, sagebrush communities, Box Elder Co.
Calochortus kennedyi Porter, native perennial herb, desert shrub communities, Kane Co.

39. LOASACEAE
Eucnide urens (Gray) Parry, native perennial herb, creosote bush community, Washington Co.
Mentzelia shultziorum Prigge, native shrublike herb, shadscale community, Grand Co.
M. tricuspis Gray, native annual, creosote bush community, Washington Co.
Petalonyx nitidus Wats., native perennial herb, desert shrub community, Washington Co.

40. LYTHRACEAE
Didiplis diandra (Nutt.) Wood; native annual aquatic; shallow water; Fish Lake, Sevier Co.

41. MALVACEAE
Abutilon parvulum Gray, native perennial herb, desert shrub, Washington Co. (Meyer, 1976).
Sphaeralcea digitata (Greene) Rydb., native perennial herb, pinyon-juniper community, San Juan Co.

42. NAJADACEAE
Najas caespitosa (Maguire) Reveal; native perennial aquatic; shallow water; Fish Lake, Sevier Co.

43. NYCTAGINACEAE
Mirabilis nyctaginea (Michx.) MacM., native perennial herb, disturbed sites, Utah Co.

44. NYMPHAEACEAE
Nymphaea odorata Ait., native perennial aquatic, ponds and springs, Kane Co.

45. OLEACEAE
Menodora spinescens Gray, native shrub, desert shrub community, Washington Co.

46. ONAGRACEAE
Camissonia atwoodii Cronq.; native annual; shadscale community; Smoky Mtn., Kane Co.
C. gouldii Raven, native annual, desert shrub community, Washington Co.
C. refracta (Wats.) Raven, native annual, desert shrub community, Washington Co.
Epilobium glaberrimum Barbey; native perennial herb; subalpine-alpine talus; Wasatch Range, Salt Lake Co.
E. oregonense Hausskn.; native perennial herb; aspen-spruce-fir community; Uinta Mtns., Summit Co. (UTC).

47. OPHIOGLOSSACEAE
Botrychium boreale Milde; circumboreal fern; high wet meadows; Uinta Mtns., Summit Co.
B. crenulatum Wagner; native fern; wet meadows; Uinta Mtns., Wasatch Co. (pers. comm., W. H. Wagner, 1987).
B. echo Wagner; native fern; grassy slopes, lake margins; Summit Co. (Wagner and Wagner, 1983).
B. hesperium (Maxon & Clausen) Wagner & Lellinger; native fern; rocky roadsides to wet meadows; Deep Creek Mtns., Juab Co. (pers. comm., W. H. Wagner, 1987).
B. minganense Vict.; native fern; wet streamside under *Salix* sp.; Deep Creek Mtns., Juab Co. (pers. comm., W. H. Wagner, 1987).
B. paradoxum Wagner, native fern, meadow, Garfield Co. (pers. comm., W. H. Wagner, 1987).
B. pinnatum H. St. John; native fern; rocky roadsides to wet meadows; Uinta Mtns., Summit Co. (pers. comm., W. H. Wagner, 1987).

48. ORCHIDACEAE
Habenaria obtusata (Banks) Richards., native perennial herb, streamside in spruce-fir communities, Duchesne Co.
Listera cordata (L.) R. Br., native perennial herb, shaded sites in conifer forests, Duchesne Co.

49. PAPAVERACEAE
Arctomecon humilis Cov., native perennial herb, gypsum soil, creosote bush community, Washington Co.

50. PINACEAE
Larix occidentalis Nutt.; introduced tree; escaped from cultivation; Wasatch Range, Salt Lake Co.

Pinus monticola D. Don; introduced tree; escaped from cultivation; Wasatch Range, Salt Lake Co.

51. PLANTAGINACEAE

Plantago virginica L., native annual, disturbed site, Salt Lake Co. (UT).

52. POACEAE

Aristida adscensionis L., native annual, desert shrub community, Kane Co.

Arundo donax L., introduced perennial, escaped from cultivation, Washington Co.

Bothriochloa ischaemum (L.) H. Keng, introduced perennial, escaped from cultivation, Utah Co.

Bouteloua hirsuta Lag.; native perennial; open gravelly site; Zion National Park, Washington Co.

Buchloë dactyloides (Nutt.) Engelm., native perennial, disturbed grassy site, Daggett Co.

Elymus simplex Scribn. & Will., native perennial, along Green River, Daggett Co.

Eragrostis lehmanniana Nees, introduced perennial, creosote bush community, Washington Co.

Eriochloa contracta Hitchc., native annual, disturbed site, creosote bush community, Washington Co.

E. gracilis (Fourn.) Hitchc., native annual, disturbed sites, Washington Co. (pers. comm., L. Higgins, 1988, BRY).

Imperata brevifolia Vasey, native perennial, streamside, San Juan Co.

Leptochloa filiformis (Lam.) Beauv., native annual, near spring in creosote bush community, Washington Co.

L. uninervia (Presl) Hitchc. & Chase, native annual, moist site in grass community, Utah Co.

Melica porteri Scribn., native perennial, mountain brush-aspen community, San Juan Co.

Muhlenbergia microsperma (DC.) Kunth, native annual, creosote bush community, Washington Co.

M. repens (Presl) Hitchc., native perennial, sagebrush community, Kane Co.

M. schreberi J. F. Gmel., native perennial, dry hillside, Washington Co.

Panicum antidotale Retz., introduced perennial, creosote bush-desert shrub community, Washington Co.

P. dichotomiflorum Michx., native annual, cracks in curbing and along waterways, Salt Lake Co.

P. hallii Vasey, native perennial, juniper-grass community, Beaver Co.

Puccinellia simplex Scribn., native annual, sheep-grazed greasewood community, Weber Co.

Saccharum ravennae (L.) Murr., introduced perennial, escaped from cultivation, Washington Co.

Sporobolus pulvinatus Swallen, native annual-perennial, desert shrub community, San Juan Co.

S. texanus Vasey, native perennial, desert shrub community, Grand Co. (BRY).

Taeniatherum caput-medusae (L.) Nevski, introduced annual, disturbed site, Box Elder Co. (pers. comm., L. M. Schultz, 1988, UTC).

53. POLEMONIACEAE

Collomia tinctoria Gray, native annual, wet meadow, Sevier Co. (Welsh et al., 1987).

Gilia caespitosa Gray, native perennial herb, gypsum soils on open slopes and cliff faces in pinyon-juniper communities, Wayne Co.

G. capillaris Kellogg; native annual; disturbed sites along valley drainages; Bear River Range, Cache Co. (Cronquist et al., 1984).

G. filiformis Gray, native annual, creosote bush community, Washington Co.

G. flavocincta A. Nels., native annual, salt desert shrub, Kane Co. (Welsh et al., 1987).

G. gilioides (Benth.) Greene; native annual; sagebrush, pinyon-juniper communities; Washington Co.

G. stellata Heller; native annual; Joshua tree, creosote bush communities; Washington Co.

G. tridactyla Rydb.; native perennial herb; spruce-fir communities, wet meadows, talus; Iron and Piute counties.

Langloisia schottii (Torr.) Greene, native annual, Joshua tree-creosote bush community, Washington Co.

Linanthus aureus (Nutt.) Greene, native annual, ponderosa pine community, Washington Co.

L. dichotomus Benth., native annual, mountain brush community, Washington Co.

Phlox cluteana A. Nels.; native perennial herb; ponderosa pine community; Navajo Mtn., San Juan Co.

Polemonium brandegei (Gray) Greene; native perennial herb; montane meadow; Tushar Mtns., Piute Co.

54. POLYGALACEAE

Polygala verticillata L., native annual herb, meadow, Uintah Co. (Welsh et al., 1987).

55. POLYGONACEAE

Eriogonum baileyi Wats.; native annual; sagebrush, mountain brush communities; Beaver Co.

E. cronquistii Reveal; native perennial shrub or subshrub; rocky sites in pinyon, mountain brush communities; Henry Mtns., Garfield Co.

E. darrovii Kearn., native annual, pinyon-juniper community, Kane Co.

E. nidularium Cov., native annual, desert shrub communities, Washington Co.

E. plumatella Dur. & Hilg.; native shrub; creosote bush community; Beaver Dam Mtns., Washington Co. (Welsh et al., 1987).

E. pusillum T. & G., native annual, Joshua tree-creosote bush community, Washington Co.

E. soredium Reveal; native perennial herb; sagebrush, pinyon-juniper communities; San Francisco Mtns., Beaver Co.

E. wrightii Torr.; native shrub; pinyon-juniper, mountain brush communities; Washington Co.

Oxytheca perfoliata T. & G., native annual, Joshua tree-creosote bush community, Washington Co.

Rumex dentatus L., introduced annual-biennial, disturbed site along stream, Salt Lake Co.

56. POLYPODIACEAE

Adiantum pedatum L.; native fern; crevices of shaded cliffs; Wasatch Range, Salt Lake Co.; Washington Co.

Asplenium adiantum-nigrum L., native fern, shaded sandstone cliffs, Washington Co.

Cryptogramma stelleri (Gmel.) Prantl, native fern, moist shaded rock outcrops, Utah Co.

Notholaena jonesii Maxon, native fern, rock crevices, Washington Co.

Pellaea atropurpurea (L.) Link, native fern, rock crevices, Washington Co. (BRY).

Polystichum kruckebergii Wagner; native fern; rock crevices; Raft River Mtns., Box Elder Co.

57. PORTULACACEAE

Calyptridium parryi Gray, native annual, disturbed site in ponderosa pine community, Sevier Co.

Montia linearis (Dougl.) Greene, native annual, moist meadow, Morgan Co.

Talinum thompsonii Atwood & Welsh, native perennial herb, pinyon-juniper community, Emery Co.

58. POTAMOGETONACEAE

Potamogeton illinoensis Morong; native perennial aquatic; ponds, lakes; Cache Co. (Welsh et al., 1987).

P. strictifolius Benn.; native perennial aquatic; slow-moving water; Bear River, northern Utah (Cronquist et al., 1977).

P. vaginatus Turcz.; native perennial aquatic; ponds, lakes; Utah Co.

P. zosteriformis Fern.; native perennial aquatic; ponds, lakes; Fish Lake, Sevier Co.

59. PRIMULACEAE

Anagallis arvensis L., introduced annual, disturbed sites, Salt Lake Co.

Androsace carinata Torr.; native perennial herb; alpine meadows and slopes; La Sal Mtns., San Juan Co.

Dodecatheon dentatum Hook., native perennial herb, wet rock crevices, Salt Lake Co.

D. redolens (Hall) H. J. Thomps.; native perennial herb; wet montane meadows; Deep Creek Mtns., Juab Co.

Primula domensis Kass & Welsh; native perennial herb; limestone crevices; House Range, Millard Co.

*P. maguirei L. Williams, native perennial herb, limestone crevices, Cache Co.

60. PYROLACEAE

Chimaphila menziesii (R. Br.) Spreng.; native shrub; juniper-mountain brush community; Zion National Park, Washington Co. (Welsh et al., 1987).

61. RANUNCULACEAE

Aquilegia chrysantha Gray; native perennial herb; hanging gardens, streamside and seeps; Zion Canyon, Washington Co.

Ranunculus aestivalis L. Benson, native perennial herb, moist meadow, Garfield Co.

R. pedatifidus J. E. Sm.; circumboreal perennial herb; alpine slopes; Uinta Mtns., Summit Co.

R. ranunculinus (Nutt.) Rydb.; native perennial herb; rock outcrops in mountain brush, aspen, spruce-fir communities; Cache Co.

Trautvetteria caroliniensis (Walt.) Vail; native perennial herb; wet streamside; Abajo Mtns., San Juan Co.

62. RHAMNACEAE

Rhamnus alnifolia L'Her., native shrub, mountain brush community, Salt Lake Co.

63. ROSACEAE

Crataegus chrysocarpa Ashe, native shrub, along waterways, Cache Co.

C. succulenta Link.; native shrub or small tree; streamside; Provo Canyon, Utah Co.

Ivesia setosa (Wats.) Rydb.; native perennial herb; rock outcrops; Deep Creek Mtns., Juab-Tooele counties.

Potentilla angelliae N. Holmgren; native perennial herb; rocky subalpine meadow; Aquarius Plateau, Wayne Co. (N. H. Holmgren, 1987).

P. cottamii N. Holmgren; native perennial herb; crevices of quartzite outcrop; Pilot Range and Raft River Mtns., Box Elder Co. (N. H. Holmgren, 1987).

P. palustris (L.) Scop.; circumboreal perennial herb; wet meadows; Uinta Mtns., Uintah Co.

Prunus emarginata (Dougl.) Walp.; native shrub or small tree; desert shrub, pinyon-juniper communities; Washington Co. (Welsh et al., 1987).

Purpusia saxosa Brandeg.; native perennial herb; meadow near Kolob Reservoir; Washington Co. (Meyer, 1976).

64. RUBIACEAE
Galium wrightii Gray; native perennial herb; pinyon-juniper communities; Zion National Park, Washington Co. (BRY).

65. SAXIFRAGACEAE
Peltiphyllum peltatum (Torr.) Engl.; native perennial herb; streamside; Mt. Timpanogos, Wasatch Range, Utah Co.
Saxifraga bronchialis L.; native perennial herb; rocky slopes; La Sal Mtns., Grand-San Juan counties.
S. hirculus L.; circumboreal perennial herb; wet meadows; Uinta Mtns., Daggett Co.
S. integrifolia Hook.; native perennial herb; open rocky site in conifer community; Franklin Basin, Cache Co.

66. SCROPHULARIACEAE
Antirrhinum filipes Gray, native annual, Joshua tree-creosote bush community, Washington Co.
Besseya alpina (Gray) Rydb.; native perennial herb; moist rocky alpine meadows; La Sal Mtns., San Juan Co.
Castilleja aquariensis N. Holmgren; native perennial herb; grass-sagebrush communities; Aquarius Plateau, Garfield Co.
C. nana Eastw.; native perennial herb; alpine meadows; Deep Creek Mtns., Juab-Tooele counties.
C. occidentalis Torr.; native perennial herb; alpine meadows, slopes; La Sal Mtns., Grand-San Juan counties.
Cymbalaria muralis Gaert., Mey., & Scherb., introduced perennial herb, sidewalk crevice, Salt Lake Co. (UT).
Gratiola neglecta Torr.; native annual; moist places; Cache Valley, Cache Co. (Cronquist et al., 1984).
Maurandya antirrhiniflora Willd., native perennial vine, creosote bush community, Washington Co. (Cronquist et al., 1984).
Mimulus bigelovii (Gray) Gray; native annual; Joshua tree, creosote bush communities; Washington Co.
M. spissus Grant; native annual; gravelly slopes; Beaver Dam Wash, Washington Co.
Mohavea breviflora Cov., native annual, Joshua tree-creosote bush community, Washington Co.
Pedicularis contorta Benth.; native perennial herb; sagebrush-forb community; Raft River Mtns., Box Elder Co.
Penstemon deustus Lindl., native perennial herb or subshrub, pinyon-juniper community, Box Elder Co.
P. navajoa N. Holmgren; native perennial herb; aspen-conifer communities; Navajo Mt., San Juan Co.
P. parvus Pennell; native perennial herb; grass-sagebrush community; Aquarius Plateau, Garfield Co.
P. petiolatus Brandeg., native perennial subshrub, rock outcrops in Joshua tree-creosote bush community, Washington Co.
P. pinorum L. Shultz & J. Shultz, native perennial herb, pinyon-juniper community, Iron Co.

67. SOLANACEAE
Lycium cooperi Gray, native shrub, creosote bush-desert shrub community, Washington Co.
Petunia parviflora Juss.; native annual herb; moist site; Beaver Dam Wash, Washington Co.
Physalis crassifolia Benth., native perennial herb, creosote bush communities, Washington Co.
P. heterophylla Nees, native perennial herb, disturbed site, Salt Lake Co.
P. lobata Torr.; native perennial herb; pinyon-juniper communities; La Sal Mtns., Grand-San Juan counties.
P. pubescens L., native annual, disturbed site, Washington Co.
Solanum carolinense L., native perennial herb, waste places, Salt Lake Co.

68. VALERIANACEAE
Valeriana arizonica Gray; native perennial herb; moist canyon; Zion National Park, Washington Co.
Valerianella locusta (L.) Betcke, introduced annual-biennial, disturbed site, Salt Lake Co. (Cronquist et al., 1984).

69. VERBENACEAE
Phyla nodiflora (L.) Greene, introduced perennial herb, escaped from cultivation, Washington Co.
Verbena macdougalii Heller, native perennial herb, ponderosa pine community, Garfield Co.

70. VIOLACEAE
Viola arvensis Murr., introduced annual, escaped from cultivation, Cache Co.

71. VISCACEAE
Arceuthobium abietinum Munz, native mistletoe, parasitic on *Abies concolor*, Kane Co.

72. ZYGOPHYLLACEAE
Fagonia laevis Standl., native perennial herb, creosote bush community, Washington Co.
Kallstroemia californica (Wats.) Vail, native annual, desert shrub community, Kane Co.

BIBLIOGRAPHY

Aiken, S. G. 1981. A conspectus of *Myriophyllum* (Haloragaceae) in North America. Brittonia 33: 57-69.

Allen, G. A. 1984. Morphological and cytological variation in the western North American *Aster occidentalis* complex (Asteraceae). Syst. Bot. 9: 175-191.

_____ . 1985. The hybrid origin of *Aster ascendens* (Asteraceae). Amer. J. Bot. 72: 268-277.

Allred, K. W. 1976. The plant family Gentianaceae in Utah. Great Basin Nat. 36: 483-495.

Al-Shehbaz, A. 1973. The biosystematics of the genus *Thelypodium* (Cruciferae). Contr. Gray Herb. 204: 3-148.

Anderson, L. C. 1986. An overview of the genus *Chrysothamnus*. In: Biology of *Artemisia* and *Chrysothamnus*, E. D. McArthur and B. L. Welch, eds., pp. 29-54. U.S. Forest Service, Intermtn. Research Sta., Ogden, Utah.

Arnow, L. A. 1987. Gramineae. In: A Utah flora, S. L. Welsh, N. D. Atwood, S. Goodrich, and L. C. Higgins, pp. 684-788. Great Basin Nat. Mem. 9.

Arnow, L. A.; B. J. Albee; A. M. Wyckoff. 1980. Flora of the Central Wasatch Front, Utah. Utah Mus. Nat. Hist., University of Utah, Salt Lake City. 663 pp.

Atwood, N. D. 1975. A revision of the *Phacelia crenulatae* group (Hydrophyllaceae) for North America. Great Basin Nat. 35: 127-190.

_____ . 1976. The Hydrophyllaceae of Utah. Great Basin Nat. 36: 1-55.

Bailey, D. K. 1970. Phytogeography and taxonomy of *Pinus* subsection *balfourianae*. Ann. Missouri Bot. Gard. 57: 210-249.

Bailey, L. H. 1951. Manual of cultivated plants. Macmillan Co., New York. 1116 pp.

Barkley, T. M. 1978. *Senecio*. North American flora, ser. 2, part 10: 50-139.

Barneby, R. C. 1964. Atlas of North American *Astragalus*. Mem. New York Bot. Gard. 13: 1-1188.

_____ . 1966. New sorts of *Lesquerella*, *Euphorbia*, and *Viguiera* from Kane Co., Utah. Leafl. W. Bot. 10: 313-317.

_____ . 1977. *Daleae imagines*. Mem. New York Bot. Gard. 27: 1-891.

Baum, B. R. 1967. Introduced and naturalized tamarisks in the United States and Canada (Tamaricaceae). Baileya 15: 19-25

_____ . 1978. The genus *Tamarix*. Israel Acad. Sci. & Hum., Jerusalem. 179 pp.

Beaman, J. L. 1957. The systematics and evolution of *Townsendia* (Compositae). Contr. Gray Herb. 183: 1-151.

Beatley, J. C. 1973. Russian thistle (*Salsola*) species in western United States. J. Range Mangm. 26: 225-226.

Benson, L. 1948. A treatise on the North American Ranunculi . Amer. Midl. Nat. 40: 1-264.

_____ . 1954. Supplement to a treatise on the North American Ranunculi. Amer. Midl. Nat. 52: 328-369.

_____ . 1982. The cacti of the United States and Canada. Stanford University Press, Stanford. 1044 pp.

Benson, L.; R. A. Darrow. 1981. Trees and shrubs of the southwestern deserts. University of Arizona Press, Tucson. 416 pp.

Berger, A. 1924. A taxonomic review of currants and gooseberries. New York Agric. Exp. Sta. Tech. Bull. 109: 1-118.

Bierner, M. W. 1972. Taxonomy of *Helenium* sect. *Tetrodus* and a conspectus of North American *Helenium* (Compositae). Brittonia 24: 331-355.

_____ . 1974. A systematic study of *Dugaldia* (Compositae). Brittonia 26: 385-392.

Blackwell, W. H., Jr.; M. D. Baechle; G. Williamson. 1978. Synopsis of *Kochia* (Chenopodiaceae) in North America. Sida 7: 248-254.

Burch, D. 1966. The application of the Linnaean names of some New World species of *Euphorbia* subgenus *Chamaesyce* . Rhodora 68: 155-166.

Campbell, G. 1952. The genus *Myosurus* L. (Ranunculaceae) in North America. Aliso 2: 398-403.

Chambers, K. L. 1964. The nomenclature of *Microseris* Lindleyi (DC.) Gray. Leafl. W. Bot. 10: 106-108.

Chuang, T. I.; L. R. Heckard. 1973. Taxonomy of *Cordylanthus* subgenus *Hemistegia* (Scrophulariaceae). Brittonia 25: 135-158.

Collins, L. T. 1973. "Systematics of *Orobanche* section *Myzorrhiza* (Orobanchaceae) with emphasis on *O. ludoviciana* ." University of Wisconsin, Milwaukee. 219 pp. Dissertation.

Constance, L.; R. C. Rollins. 1936. A revision of *Gilia congesta* and its allies. Amer. J. Bot. 23: 433-440.

Correll, D. S.; M. C. Johnston. 1970. Manual of the vascular plants of Texas. Texas Research Foundation, Renner. 1881 pp.

Crampton, B. 1954. Morphological and ecological considerations in the classification of *Navarretia* (Polemoniaceae). Madroño 12: 225-238.

Cronquist, A. 1943. Revision of the western North American species of *Aster* centering about *Aster foliaceus* Lindl. Amer. Midl. Nat. 29: 429-468.

_____ . 1981. An integrated system of classification of flowering plants. Columbia University Press, New York. 1262 pp.

Cronquist, A.; A. H. Holmgren; N. H. Holmgren; J. L. Reveal. 1972. Intermountain flora. Vol. 1. Hafner Publishing Co., New York. 270 pp.

Cronquist, A.; A. H. Holmgren; N. H. Holmgren; J. L. Reveal; P. K. Holmgren. 1977. Intermountain flora. Vol. 6. Columbia University Press, New York. 584 pp.

621

_____. 1984. Intermountain flora. Vol. 4. New York Botanical Garden, Bronx. 573 pp.

Cronquist, A.; D. D. Keck. 1957. A reconstruction of the genus *Machaeranthera*. Brittonia 9: 231-239.

Darlington, J. 1934. A monograph of the genus *Mentzelia*. Ann. Missouri Bot. Gard. 21: 103-227.

Davidson, J. F. 1950. The genus *Polemonium* (Tournefort) L. Univ. Calif. Publ. Bot. 23: 209-282.

Dempster, L. T. 1976. *Galium mexicanum* (Rubiaceae) of Central America and western North America. Madroño 23: 378-386.

Dempster, L. T.; F. Ehrendorfer. 1965. Evolution of the *Galium multiflorum* complex in western North America 2. Critical taxonomic revision. Brittonia 17: 289-334.

Dietrich, W.; P. H. Raven. 1976. An earlier name for *Oenothera strigosa* (Onagraceae). Ann. Missouri Bot. Gard. 63: 382-383.

Dorn, R. D. 1977. Manual of the vascular plants of Wyoming. Garland Publishing, New York. 2 vols.

_____. 1978. A new species of *Draba* (Cruciferae) from Wyoming and Utah. Madroño 25: 101-103.

_____. 1988. *Chenopodium simplex*, an older name for *C. gigantospermum* (Chenopodiaceae). Madroño 35: 162.

Dorn, R. D.; R. L. Hartman. 1988. Nomenclature of *Lomatium nuttallii*, *L. kingii*, and *L. megarrhizum* (Apiaceae). Madrono 35: 70-71.

Douglas, G. W.; K. E. Denford; I. Karas. 1977. A contribution to the taxonomy of *Antennaria alpina* var. *media*, *A. microphylla*, and *A. umbrinella* in western North America. Can. J. Bot. 55: 925-933.

Ediger, R. I. 1970. A revision of section *Suffruticosi* of the genus *Senecio* (Compositae). Sida 3: 504-524.

Ediger, R. I.; T. M. Barkley. 1978. *Arnica*. North American flora, ser. 2, part 10: 16-44.

Ellison, W. L. 1971. Taxonomy of *Platyschkuhria* (Compositae). Brittonia 23: 269-279.

England, J. L. 1982. A new species of *Penstemon* (Scrophulariaceae) from the Uinta Basin of Utah and Colorado. Great Basin Nat. 42: 367-368.

Ewan, J. 1945. A synopsis of the North American species of *Delphinium* . Univ. Colorado Stud., ser. D, 2: 55-244.

Flowers, S. 1944. Ferns of Utah. Bull. Univ. Utah 35: 1-87.

Fowler, B. A.; B. L. Turner. 1977. *Selinocarpus* and *Ammocodon*. Phytologia 37: 177-208.

Fryxell, P. A. 1974. The North American malvellas (Malvaceae). Southw. Nat. 19: 97-103.

Galloway, L. A. 1975. Systematics of the North American desert species of *Abronia* and *Tripterocalyx* (Nyctaginaceae). Brittonia 27: 328-347.

Gardner, R. C. 1974. Systematics of *Cirsium* (Compositae) in Wyoming. Madroño 22: 239-265.

Gillett, J. M. 1957. A revision of the North American species of *Gentianella* Moench. Ann. Missouri Bot. Gard. 44: 195-269.

Glad, J. B. 1976. Taxonomy of *Mentzelia mollis* and allied species (Loasaceae). Madroño 23: 283-292.

Gleason, H. A.; A. Cronquist. 1963. Manual of the vascular plants of the northeastern United States and adjacent Canada. Van Nostrand Reinhold Co., New York. 810 pp.

Goodrich, S. 1987. Cyperaceae, Juncaceae, *Ribes*, Saxifragaceae, Salicaceae, Saxifragaceae, Umbelliferae. In: A Utah flora, S. L. Welsh, N. D. Atwood, S. Goodrich, and L. C. Higgins. Great Basin Nat. Mem. 9.

Grant, A.; V. Grant. 1956. Genetic and taxonomic studies in *Gilia* 8. The cobwebby gilias. Aliso 3: 203-287.

Grant, V. 1956. A synopsis of *Ipomopsis*. Aliso 3: 351-362.

Haber, E. 1972. Priority of the binomial *Pyrola chlorantha*. Rhodora 74: 396-397.

Hall, H. M. 1928. The genus *Haplopappus*, a phylogenetic study in the Compositae. Publ. Carnegie Inst. Wash. 389. 391 pp.

Hall, H. M; F. E. Clements. 1923. The phylogenetic method in taxonomy; the North American species of *Artemisia, Chrysothamnus, and Atriplex*. Publ. Carnegie Inst. Wash. 326. 355 pp.

Hanson, C. A. 1962. "Perennial *Atriplex* of Utah and the northern deserts." Brigham Young University, Provo, Utah. 133 pp. Thesis.

Harms, V. L. 1974. A preliminary conspectus of *Heterotheca* sect. *Chrysopsis* (Compositae). Castanea 39: 155-166.

Harrington, H. D. 1954. Manual of the plants of Colorado. Sage Books, Denver. 666 pp.

Harrison, H. K. 1972. Contributions to the study of the genus *Eriastrum*. 2. Notes concerning the type specimens and descriptions of the species. Brigham Young Univ. Sci. Bull., Biol. ser. 16: 1-26.

Hartman, R. L. 1976. "A conspectus of *Machaeranthera* (Compositae: Asteraceae) and a biosystematic study of *Machaeranthera*." University of Texas, Austin. University Microfilms Intenational, Ann Arbor, Michigan. 181 pp. Dissertation.

Hartman, R. L.; R. S. Kirkpatrick. 1986. A new species of *Cymopterus* (Umbelliferae) from northwestern Wyoming. Brittonia 38: 420-426.

Hawksworth, F. G.; D. Wiens. 1972. Biology and classification of dwarf mistletoes (*Arceuthobium*). USDA, Agriculture Handbook 401. U.S. Government Printing Office, Washington, D.C. 234 pp.

Heckard, L. R. 1973. A taxonomic re-interpretation of the *Orobanche californica* complex. Madroño 22: 41-70.

Heiser, C. B., Jr. 1969. The North American sunflowers (*Helianthus*). Mem. Torrey Bot. Club 22: 1-218.

Henderson, D. M. 1976. A biosystematic study of Pacific Northwestern blue-eyed grasses (*Sisyrinchium*, Iridaceae). Brittonia 28: 149-176.

Higgins, L. C. 1971. A revision of *Cryptantha* subgenus *Oreocarya*. Brigham Young Univ. Sci. Bull., Biol. ser. 13: 1-63.

_____. 1972. The Boraginaceae of Utah. Brigham Young Univ. Sci. Bull., Biol. ser. 16: 1-83.

Hill, S. R. 1982. A Monograph of the genus *Malvastrum* 3. Rhodora 84: 317-409.

Hinton, W. F. 1975. Systematics of the *Calyptridium umbellatum* complex (Portulacaceae). Brittonia 27: 197- 208.

Hitchcock, C. L. 1941. A revision of the drabas of western North America. Univ. Wash. Publ. Biol. 2: 1-132.

Hitchcock, C. L.; A. Cronquist; M. Ownbey; J. W. Thompson. 1955-1969. Vascular plants of the Pacific Northwest. University of Washington Press, Seattle. 5 parts.

Hitchcock, C. L.; B. Maguire. 1947. A revision of the North American species of *Silene*. Univ. Wash. Publ. Biol. 13: 1-73.

Hoch, P. C. 1978. "Systematics and evolution of the *Epilobium ciliatum* complex in North America (Onagraceae)." Washington University, St. Louis, Missouri. University Microfilms International, Ann Arbor, Michigan. 176 pp. Dissertation.

Holmgren, A. H.; L. M. Shultz; T. K. Lowrey. 1976. *Sphaeromeria*, a genus closer to *Artemisia* than to *Tanacetum* (Asteraceae: Anthemideae). Brittonia 28: 252-262.

Holmgren, N. H. 1987. Two new species of *Potentilla* (Rosaceae) from the Intermountain Region of western U.S.A. Brittonia 39: 340-344.

Hopkins, C. O.; W. H. Blackwell, Jr. 1977. Synopsis of *Suaeda* (Chenopodiaceae) in North America. Sida 7: 147-173.

Houle, F.; L. Brouillet. 1985. Chromosome number determinations in *Aster* section *Conyzopsis* (Asteraceae). Brittonia 37: 369-372.

Howell, J. T. 1971. A new name for "winter fat". Wasmann J. Biol. 29: 105.

Iltis, H. H. 1965. The genus *Gentianopsis* (Gentianaceae): Transfers and phytogeographic comments. Sida 2: 129-154.

Johnson, D. E. 1978. "Systematics of Eriophyllinae." University of California, Berkeley. 186 pp. Dissertation.

Johnston, B. C. 1980. "Studies of population variability leading to a new classification of *Potentilla* sect. *multijugae* (Rosaceae)." University of Colorado, Boulder. University Microfilms International, Ann Arbor, Michigan. 217 pp. Dissertation.

Jones, A. G. 1980. A classification of the New World species of *Aster* (Asteraceae). Brittonia 32: 230-239.

_____. 1984. Nomenclatural notes on *Aster* (Asteraceae) 2. New combinations and some transfers. Phytologia 55: 373-388.

Jones, M. E. 1898. *Ceanothus martinii*. Contr. W. Bot. 8: 41-42.

Kearney, T. H. 1935. The North American species of *Sphaeralcea* subgenus *Eusphaeralcea*. Univ. Calif. Publ. Bot. 19: 1-128.

Kearney, T. H.; R. H. Peebles; collaborators. 1969. Arizona flora, 2d ed. University of California Press, Berkeley. 1085 pp.

Keck, D. D. 1938. Revision of *Hackelia* and *Ivesia*. Lloydia 1: 75-142.

Klein, W. M. 1962. New taxa and recombinations in *Oenothera* (*Anogra*). Aliso 5: 179-180.

Krapovickas, A. 1970. El genero *Malvella* Jaub. & Spach (Malvaceae) en la Republica Argentina. Bonplandia 3: 53-62.

Landolt, E. 1986. The family of Lemnaceae—a monographic study. Veröffentlichungen Des Geobotanischen Institutes Der Eidg. Techn. Hochschule Stiftung Rübel, Zurich. 566 pp.

Lane, M. A. 1982. Generic limitation of *Xanthocephalum, Gutierrezia, Amphiachyris, Gymnosperma, Greenella,* and *Thurovia* (Compositae: Astereae). Syst. Bot. 7: 405-416.

Lellinger, D. B. 1985. Ferns and fern allies of the United States and Canada. Smithsonian Institution Press. Washington, D.C. 389 pp.

Lewis, H.; J. Szweykowski. 1964. The genus *Gayophytum* (Onagraceae). Brittonia 16: 343-391.

Maguire, B. 1946. Studies in the Caryophyllaceae 2. *Arenaria nuttallii* and *A. filiorum* , section *Alsine*. Madroño 8: 258-263.

_____. 1947. Studies in the Caryophllaceae 3. A synopsis of the North American species of *Arenaria*, section *Eremogone* Fenzl. Bull. Torrey Bot. Club 74: 38-56.

_____. 1950. Studies in the Caryophyllaceae 4. A synopsis of the North American species of the subfamily Silenoideae. Rhodora 52: 233-245.

_____. 1951. Studies in the Caryophyllaceae 5. *Arenaria* in America North of Mexico. A conspectus. Amer. Midl. Nat. 46: 493-511.

_____. 1958. *Arenaria rossii* and some of its relatives in America. Rhodora 60: 44-58.

Martin, W. C.; C. R. Hutchins. 1980. A flora of New Mexico. Strauss & Cramer, Hirschberg, Germany. 2 vols.

Mason, H. L. 1945. The genus *Eriastrum* and the influence of Bentham and Gray upon the problem of generic confusion in Polemoniaceae. Madroño 8: 65-91.

Mathias, M. E. 1930. Studies in the Umbelliferae 3. A monograph of *Cymopterus*, including a critical study of related genera. Ann. Missouri Bot. Gard. 17: 213-477.

_____. 1938. A revision of the genus *Lomatium*. Ann. Missouri Bot. Gard. 25: 225-297.

Mathias, M. E.; L. Constance. 1944-1945. Umbelliferae. North American flora 28 B: 43-297.

Matthews, J. F.; P. A. Levins. 1985. *Portulaca pilosa* L., *P. mundula* I. M. Johnst., and *P. parvula* Gray in the southwest. Sida 11: 45-61.

Mayes, R. L. 1976. "A cytotaxonomic and chemosystematic study of the genus *Pyrrocoma*." University of Texas, Austin. 216 pp. Dissertation.

McClintock, E. 1951. Studies in California ornamental plants 3. The tamarisks. J. Calif. Hort. Soc. 12: 76-82.

McDougall, W. B. 1973. Seed plants of northern Arizona. Museum of Northern Arizona, Flagstaff. 594 pp.

McLaughlin, S. P. 1982. A revision of the southwestern species of *Amsonia* (Apocynaceae). Ann. Missouri Bot. Gard. 69: 336-350.

McNeill, J. 1975. A generic revision of Portulacaceae tribe Montieae using techniques of numerical taxonomy. Can. J. Bot. 53: 789-809.

_____. 1978. *Silene alba* and *S. dioica* in North America and the generic delimitation of *Lychnis, Melandrium*, and *Silene* (Caryophyllaceae). Can. J. Bot. 56: 279-308.

McNeill, J.; H. C. Prentice. 1981. The correct name for white campion or white cockle. Taxon 30: 27-31.

Meyer, S. E. 1976. "Annotated checklist of the vascular plants of Washington County, Utah." University of Nevada, Las Vegas. 276 pp. Thesis.

Moore, R. J.; C. Franklin. 1974. The *Cirsium arizonicum* complex of the southeastern United States. Can. J. Bot. 52: 543-551.

Mulligan, G. A. 1971. Cytotaxonomic studies of the closely allied *Draba cana, D. lanceolata, D. cinerea*, and *D. groenlandica* in Canada and Alaska. Can. J. Bot. 49: 89-93.

_____. 1980. The genus *Cicuta* in North America. Can. J. Bot. 58: 1755-1767.

Munz, P. A. 1968. A California flora. University of California Press, Berkeley. 1681 pp.

_____. 1968. Supplement to a California flora. University of California Press, Berkeley. 224 pp.

_____. 1974. A flora of southern California. University of California Press, Berkeley. 1086 pp.

Nesom, G. L. 1982. Systematics of the *Erigeron rusbyi* group (Asteraceae) and delimitation of sect. *Peregrinus*. Syst. Bot. 7: 457-470.

Niehaus, T. 1980. The *Brodiaea* complex. Four Seasons 6: 11-21.

Niles, W. E. 1970. Taxonomic investigations in the genera *Perityle* and *Laphamia* (Compositae). Mem. New York Bot. Gard. 21: 1-82.

Nuttall, T. 1840. Descriptions of new species and genera of plants in the natural order of the Compositae. Trans. Amer. Philos. Soc. II, 7: 283-453.

Patterson, R. 1977. A revision of *Linanthus* sect. *Siphonella* (Polemoniaceae). Madroño 24: 36-48.

_____. 1977. The generic status of perennial species of *Linanthus* (Polemoniaceae). Taxon 26: 507-511.

Payne, W. W. 1964. A re-evaluation of the genus *Ambrosia* (Compositae). J. Arnold Arbor. 45: 401-430.

Payson, E. B. 1922. A synoptical revision of the genus *Cleomella*. Univ. Wyoming Publ. Sci., Bot. 1: 29-46.

Pilz, G. E. 1978. Systematics of *Mirabilis* subgenus *Quamoclidion* (Nyctaginaceae). Madroño 25: 113-132.

Pray, T. R. Notes on the distribution of some American cheilanthoid ferns. Amer. Fern. J. 57: 52-58.

Prigge, B. A. 1986. New species of *Mentzelia* (Loasaceae) from Grand County, Utah. Great Basin Nat. 46: 361-363.

Rauschert, S. 1974. Nomenklatorische probleme in der Gattung *Matricaria* L. Folia Geobot. Phytotax. 9: 249-260.

Raven, P. H. 1969. A revison of the genus *Camissonia* (Onagraceae). Contr. U.S. Natl. Herb. 37: 161-396.

Raven, P. H.; W. Dietrich; W. Stubbe. 1979. An outline of the systematics of *Oenothera* subsect. *Euoenothera* (Onagraceae). Syst. Bot. 4: 242-252.

Reveal, J. L. 1970. A revision of the Utah species of *Townsendia* (Compositae). Great Basin Nat. 30: 23-52.

_____. 1973. *Eriogonum* (Polygonaceae) of Utah. Phytologia 25: 169-217.

Reveal, J. L.; B. J. Ertter. 1976. Re-establishment of *Stenogonum* Nutt. (Polygonaceae). Great Basin Nat. 36: 272-280.

Reveal, J. L.; N. H. Holmgren. 1972. *Ceratoides*, an older generic name for *Krascheninikovia* and *Eurotia*. Taxon 21: 209.

Richards, E. L. 1968. A monograph of the genus *Ratibida*. Rhodora 70: 348-393.

Richardson, A. 1976. Reinstatement of the genus *Tiquilia* (Boraginaceae, Ehretioideae) and description of four new species. Sida 6: 235-240.

_____. 1977. Monograph of the genus *Tiquilia* (*Coldenia*, sensu lato), Boraginaceae: Ehretioideae. Rhodora 79: 467-572.

Robbins, G. T. 1944. North American species of *Androsace*. Amer. Midl. Nat. 32: 137-163.

Rogers, C. M. 1968. Yellow-flowered species of *Linum* in Central America and western North America. Brittonia 20: 107-135.

Rollins, R. 1979. *Dithyrea* and a related genus (Cruciferae). Bussey Inst., Harvard University Press, Cambridge, 32 pp.

_____. 1981. Studies on *Arabis* (Cruciferae) of western North America. Syst. Bot. 6: 55-64.

_____. 1981. Studies in the genus *Physaria* (Cruciferae). Brittonia 33: 332-341.

_____. 1981. Weeds of the Cruciferae (Brassicaceae) in North America. J. Arnold Arbor. 62: 517-540.

_____. 1982. *Thelypodiopsis* and *Schoenocrambe* (Cruciferae). Contr. Gray Herb. 212: 71-102.

_____. 1982. Studies on *Arabis* (Cruciferae) of western North America 2. Contr. Gray Herb. 212: 103-114.

_____. 1983. Studies in the Cruciferae of western North America. J. Arnold Arbor. 64: 491-510.

Rollins, R.; E. A. Shaw. 1973. The genus *Lesquerella* (Cruciferae) in North America. Harvard University Press, Cambridge. 288 pp.

Rosendahl, C. O.; F. K. Butters; O. Lakela. 1936. A monograph on the genus *Heuchera*. Minnesota Stud. Pl. Sci. 2: 1-180.

Rydberg, P. A. 1922. Flora of the Rocky Mountains and adjacent Plains. 2d ed. Published by the author, New York. 1143 pp.

Scoggan, H. J. 1978. The flora of Canada. Parts 2, 3, and 4. National Museum of Canada, Ottawa. 545 pp.

Semple, J. C. 1977. Cytotaxonomy of *Chrysopsis* and *Heterotheca* (Compositae-Astereae): a new interpretation of phylogeny. Can. J. Bot. 55: 2503-2513.

_____. 1987. New names, combinations, and lectotypifications in *Heterotheca* (Compositae: Astereae). Brittonia 39: 379-386.

Shaw, R. J. 1952. Cytotaxonomic study of the genus *Geranium* in the Wasatch region of Idaho and Utah. Madroño 11: 297-304.

Sheviak, C. J. 1984. *Spiranthes diluvialis* (Orchidaceae), a new species from the western United States. Brittonia 36: 8-14.

Shinners, L. H. 1950. Notes on Texas Compositae 5. Field and Lab. 17: 32-42.

Shultz, L. M. 1983. "Systematics and anatomical studies of *Artemisia* subgenus *Tridentatae*." Claremont Graduate School, Claremont, California. 182 pp. Dissertation.

_____. 1986. Taxonomic and geographic limits of *Artemisia* subgenus *Tridentatae* (Beetle) McArthur. In: The biology of *Artemisia* and *Chrysothamnus*, E. D. McArthur and B. L. Welch, eds., pp. 20-28. U.S. Forest Service, Intermtn. Research Sta., Ogden, Utah.

Shultz, L. M.; J. S. Shultz. 1981. A new species of *Hackelia* (Boraginaceae) from Utah. Brittonia 33: 159-161.

_____. 1985. *Penstemon pinorum* (Scrophulariaceae), a new species from Utah. Brittonia 37: 98-101.

Sieren, D. J. 1981. The taxonomy of the genus *Euthamia*. Rhodora 83: 551-579.

Standley, P. C. 1934. Rubiaceae. North American Flora 32: 159-258.

St. John, H. 1941. Revision of the genus *Swertia* (Gentianaceae) of the Americas and the reduction of *Frasera*. Amer. Midl. Nat. 26: 1-24.

Strother, J. L. 1969. Systematics of *Dyssodia* Canavilles. Univ. Calif. Publ. Bot. 48: 1-88.

_____. 1974. Taxonomy of *Tetradymia* (Compositae: Senecioneae). Brittonia 26: 177-202.

_____. 1986. Renovation of *Dyssodia* (Compositae: Tageteae). Sida 11: 371-378.

Strother, J. L.; G. Pilz. 1975. Taxonomy of *Psathyrotes* (Compositae: Senecioneae). Madroño 23:24-40.

Sutherland, D. M. 1967. "A taxonomic revision of the low larkspurs of the Pacific Northwest." University of Washington, Seattle. 178 pp. Dissertation.

Taylor, R. L. 1965. The genus *Lithophragma* (Saxifragaceae). Univ. Calif. Publ. Bot. 37: 1-122.

Thompson, H. J. 1963. Cytotaxonomic observations on *Mentzelia* sect. *Bartonia* (Loasaceae). Madroño 17: 16-22.

Thompson, H. J.; J. Roberts. 1971. Observations on *Mentzelia* in southern California. Phytologia 21: 279-288.

Tidestrom, I. 1925. Flora of Utah and Nevada. Contrib. U.S. Natl. Herb. 25: 1-665.

Tomb, A. S. 1980. Taxonomy of *Lygodesmia* (Asteraceae). Syst. Bot. Monogr. 1: 1-51.

Towner, H. F. 1977. The biosystematics of *Calylophus* (Onagraceae). Ann. Missouri Bot. Gard. 64: 48-120.

Towner, H. F.; P. H. Raven. 1970. A new species and some new combinations in *Calylophus* (Onagraceae). Madroño 20: 241-245.

Tucker, J. M. 1970. Studies in the *Quercus undulata* complex 4. The contribution of *Quercus havardii*. Amer. J. Bot. 57: 71-84.

_____. 1971. Studies in the *Quercus undulata* complex 5. The type of *Quercus undulata*. Amer. J. Bot. 58: 329-341.

Turner, B. L.; M. I. Morris. 1976. Systematics of *Palafoxia* (Asteraceae: Heleneae). Rhodora 78: 567-628.

Tutin, T. G.; V. H. Heywood; N. A. Burges; D. M. Moore; D. H. Valentine; S. M. Walters; D. A. Webb. 1968-1980. Flora Europaea. Cambridge University Press, Cambridge. 5 vol.

Ugborogho, R. E. 1973. North American *Cerastium arvense* L. Cytologia 38: 559-566.

Urbatsch, L. E. 1976. Systematics of the *Ericameria cuneata* complex (Compositae: Astereae). Madroño 23: 338-343.

Urbatsch, L. E.; J. R. Wussow. 1979. The taxonomic affinities of *Happlopappus linearifolius* (Asteraceae–Astereae). Brittonia 31: 265-275.

U.S. Fish and Wildlife Service. 1987. Endangered and threatened wildlife and plants. U.S. Government Printing Office, Washington, D.C. 32 pp.

U.S. Soil Conservation Service. 1982. National list of scientific plant names. U.S. Government Printing Office, Washington, D.C. 2 vols.

_____. 1986. Utah list of scientific and common plant names. Salt Lake City. 169 pp.

Veno, B. A. 1979. "A revision of the genus *Pectocarya* (Boraginaceae) including reduction to synonymy of the genus *Harpagonella* (Boraginaceae)." University of California, Los Angeles. 201 pp. Dissertation.

Wagner, W. H., Jr.; F. S. Wagner. 1983. Two moonworts of the Rocky Mountains: *Botrychium hesperium* and a new species formerly confused with it. Amer. Fern J. 73: 53-62.

Wagner, W. L. 1981. *Oenothera acutissima* (Onagraceae), a new species from northwestern Colorado and adjacent Utah. Syst. Bot. 6: 153-158.

_____. 1983. New species and combinations in the genus *Oenothera* (Onagraceae). Ann. Missouri Bot. Gard. 70: 194-196.

Watson, T. J. 1977. Taxonomy of *Xylorhiza* (Asteraceae-Astereae). Brittonia 29: 199-216.

Weber, W. A. 1946. A taxonomic and cytological study of the genus *Wyethia* with notes on the related genus *Balsamorhiza*. Amer. Midl. Nat. 35: 400-452.

_____ . 1950. A new species and subgenus of *Atriplex* from southwestern Colorado. Madroño 10: 187.

_____ . 1952. The genus *Helianthella* (Compositae). Amer. Midl. Nat. 48: 1-35.

_____ . 1973. Additions to the Colorado flora 5, with nomenclature revisions. Southw. Nat. 18: 317-329.

_____ . 1976. Rocky Mountain flora. Colorado Associated University Press, Boulder. 479 pp.

_____ . 1979. Additions to the flora of Colorado 6. Phytologia 41: 486.

_____ . 1987. Colorado flora: western slope. Colorado Associated Press, Boulder. 530 pp.

Welsh, S. L. 1975. Utah plant novelties in *Cymopterus* and *Penstemon*. Great Basin Nat. 35: 377-378.

_____ . 1978. Utah flora: Fabaceae. Great Basin Nat. 38: 225-367.

_____ . 1980. Utah flora: Malvaceae. Great Basin Nat. 40: 27-37.

_____ . 1980. Utah flora: Miscellaneous families. Great Basin Nat. 40: 38-58.

_____ . 1982. Utah flora: Rosaceae. Great Basin Nat. 42: 1-44.

_____ . 1982. New taxa of thistles (*Cirsium*, Asteraceae) in Utah. Great Basin Nat. 42: 199-202.

_____ . 1984. Utah flora: Cactaceae. Great Basin Nat. 44: 52-69.

_____ . 1984. Utah flora: Chenopodiaceae. Great Basin Nat. 44: 183-209.

_____ . 1984. Utah flora: Polygonaceae. Great Basin Nat. 44: 519-557.

Welsh, S. L.; N. D. Atwood; S. Goodrich; L. C. Higgins. 1987. A Utah flora. Great Basin Nat. Mem. 9: 1-894.

Welsh, S. L.; J. Reveal. 1977. Utah flora: Brassicaceae. Great Basin Nat. 37: 279-365.

Wendt, T. 1979. Notes on the genus *Polygala* in the United States and Mexico. J. Arnold Arbor. 60: 504-514.

Wheeler, L. C. 1941. *Euphorbia* subgenus *Chamaesyce* in Canada and the United States exclusive of southern Florida. Rhodora 43: 97-154, 168-205, 223-286.

Wherry, E. T. 1955. The genus *Phlox*. Morris Arbor. Monogr. 3. Philadelphia. 174 pp.

Wiens, D. 1964. Revision of the acataphyllous species of *Phoradendron*. Brittonia 16: 11-54.

Wilken, D. H. 1975. A systematic study of the genus *Hulsea*. Brittonia 27: 228-244.

Woodson, R. E., Jr. 1941. The North American Asclepiadaceae 1. Perspective of the genera. Ann. Missouri Bot. Gard. 28: 193-244.

Yates, W. F., Jr.; C. B. Heiser, Jr. 1979. Synopsis of *Heliomeris*. Proc. Indiana Acad. Sci. 88: 364-372.

Yuncker, T. G. 1965. *Cuscuta*. North American flora, ser. 2, part 4: 1-51.

INDEX

The first number following species or colloquial names is the family number, the second is the map number (a page index to families is provided on the inside back cover).

Species with restricted distribution (see preface) are followed by "App." (Appendix) and the family number assigned in the appendix.

Synonyms and names preferred by other authors are italicized and have an = sign between the family and map number of the plant to which these alternate names have been applied. In a few instances, where multiple colloquial names are in current use, one name is given in the text; additional names are provided in the index.

Family names appear in boldface or, if they are alternate names, in bold italics.

C. Chr., 82=186
stolonifera, 82-6
thurberiana, 82-7
variabilis, 82-8
Ailanthus
altissima, 104-1
Aizoaceae, 3; App. 3
Alcea
rosea L., 66=2
alder
mountain, 12-1
white, 12-1
Aletes
latiloba Rydb., 7=42
macdougalii, 7-1
alfalfa, 41-138
yellow, 41-136
Alisma
gramineum, 4-1
plantago-aquatica, 4-2
triviale Pursh, 4=2
Alismataceae, 4; App. 4
alkaligrass
Nuttall, 82-189
Torrey, 82-188
weeping, 82-187
alkali heath family, 43
alkali weed, 27-3
alkanet
blue, 14-5
bugloss, 14-6
Allenrolfea
occidentalis, 25-1
Alliaceae = 61 in part
Alliaria
officinalis, App. 12
petiolata (Bieb.) Cavara &
Grande, App. 12 =
A. officinalis
Allionia
incarnata, 71-5
Allium
acuminatum, 61-1
atrorubens, 61-2
bisceptrum, 61-3
brandegei, 61-4
brevistylum, 61-5
campanulatum, 61-6
cernuum, 61-7
geyeri, 61-8
macropetalum, 61-9
nevadense, 61-10
parvum, 61-11
passeyi, App. 38
textile, 61-12
Allophyllum
gilioides (Benth.) A. D.
Grant & V. Grant, App. 53
= Gilia gilioides
Alnus
incana, 12-1
tenuifolia Nutt., 12=1
Alopecurus
aequalis, 82-9

alpinus, 82-10
carolinianus, 82-11
geniculatus, 82-12
pratensis, 82-13
Aloysia
wrightii, 112-1
Alsinaceae = 22 in part
Alsine
media L., 22=39
Althaea
rosea, 66-2
alumroot
littleleaf, 101-4
red, 101-5
Alyssum, 15-1
alyssoides, 15-1
desert, 15-2
desertorum, 15-2
lesser, 15-3
minus, 15-3
sweet, 15-103
Szowits, 15-4
szowitsianum, 15-4
amaranth family, 5
Amaranthaceae, 5; App. 5
Amaranthus
acanthochiton (Torr.) Sauer,
App. 5 = Acanthochiton
wrightii
albus, 5-1
blitoides, 5-2
californicus, App. 5
fimbriatus, App. 5
graecizans auct. non L., 5=2
hybridus L., 5=4
lividus, App. 5
powellii, 5-3
retroflexus, 5-4
Ambrosia
acanthicarpa, 10-8
artemisiifolia, 10-9
dumosa, 10-10
elatior L., 10=9
eriocentra, 10-11
psilostachya, 10-12
tomentosa, 10-13
trifida, 10-14
Amelanchier
alnifolia, 93-1
utahensis, 93-2
Amerosedum
lanceolatum (Torr.) Löve &
Löve, 29=2
Ammannia
coccinea Rottb., 65=1
purple, 65-1
robusta, 65-1
Amphipappus
fremontii, App. 10
Amphiscirpus
nevadensis (Wats.) Yeboah,
App. 24 = Scirpus
nevadensis
Amsinckia

intermedia, 14-1
menziesii, 14-2
retrorsa, 14-3
tessellata, 14-4
Amsonia
brevifolia Gray, App. 7 =
A. tomentosa
eastwoodiana, 8-1
jonesii, 8-2
tomentosa, App. 7
Anacardiaceae, 6
Anagallis
arvensis, App. 59
Anaphalis
margaritacea, 10-15
Anchusa
azurea, 14-5
officinalis, 14-6
Andropogon
barbinodis Lag., 82=24
chrysocomus Nash, 82=14
gerardii, 82-14
glomeratus, 82-15
hallii Hack., 82=14
ischaemum L., App. 52 =
Bothriochloa ischaemum
laguroides DC., 82=25
saccharoides auct. non
Swartz, 82=25
scoparius Michx., 82=196
springfieldii Gould, 82=26
Androsace
carinata, App. 59
chamaejasme auct. non Host,
App. 59 = A. carinata
filiformis, 89-1
occidentalis, 89-2
septentrionalis, 89-3
Androstephium
breviflorum, 61-13
Anemone
American wood, 91-7
cutleaf, 91-4
desert, 91-8
multifida, 91-4
parviflora, 91-5
patens, 91-6
quinquefolia, 91-7
tuberosa, 91-8
Anemopsis
californica, 100-1
Angelica
kingii, App. 6
pinnata, 7-2
rock, 7-3
roseana, 7-3
small-leaf, 7-2
Utah, 7-4
Wheeler, 7-4
wheeleri, 7-4
Anisantha
diandra (Roth) Tutin, 82=39
sterilis (L.) Nevski, 82=45
tectorum (L.) Nevski, 82=46

633

Convallariaceae = 61 in part
Convolvulaceae, 27; App. 19
Convolvulus
    arvensis, 27-2
    equitans, App. 19
    sepium L., 27=1
Conyza
    canadensis, 10-147
    coulteri, App. 10
copperweed, 10-306
coralbells, wild, 101-5
Corallorhiza
    maculata, 76-2
    striata, 76-3
    trifida, 76-4
    wisteriana, 76-5
coralroot
    northern, 76-4
    spotted, 76-2
    spring, 76-5
    striped, 76-3
cordgrass
    alkali, 82-205
    prairie, 82-206
Cordylanthus
    kingii, 102-15
    maritimus, 102-16
    parviflorus, 102-17
    ramosus, 102-18
    wrightii, 102-19
Coriflora
    hirsutissima (Pursh) W. A.
      Weber, 91=18
Corispermum
    hyssopifolium auct. non L.,
      25=29
    nitidum auct. non Kit., 25=29
    villosum, 25-29
Cornaceae, 28
Cornus
    sericea, 28-1
    stolonifera Michx., 28=1
Coronilla
    varia, 41-101
Corydalis
    aurea, 44-1
    caseana, 44-2
    fitweed, 44-2
    golden, 44-1
Coryphantha
    Missouri, 16-1
    missouriensis, 16-1
    vivipara, 16-2
    viviparous, 16-2
costmary, 10-85
cottonsedge
    many-spike, 33-93
    Scheuchzeri, 33-94
cottonthistle, Scotch, 10-305
cottonwood
    black, 97-4
    Fremont, 97-5
    lanceleaf, 97-1
    narrowleaf, 97-3

couchgrass, 82-83
cow cabbage, 9-2
cow parsnip, 7-28
Cowania
    mexicana, 93-9
cowbane, Fendler, 7-55
cowcockle, 22-43
crabgrass
    hairy, 82-71
    smooth, 82-70
cranesbill
    Bicknell, 46-3
    Carolina, 46-5
    slender, 46-6
Crassipes
    annuus Swallen, 82=197
Crassula
    aquatica (L.) Schoenl., App.
      20 = Tillaea aquatica
Crassulaceae, 29; App. 20
Crataegus
    chrysocarpa, App. 63
    douglasii, 93-10
    rivularis Nutt., 93=10
    succulenta, App. 63
creamcups, 79-7
creeper
    thicket, 115-2
    Virginia, 115-1
creeping Jenny, 27-2
creosote bush, 117-1
Crepis
    acuminata, 10-148
    atrabarba, 10-149
    barbigera Coville, 10=151
    capillaris, 10-150
    glauca (Nutt.) T. & G., 10=155
    intermedia, 10-151
    modocensis, 10-152
    nana, 10-153
    occidentalis, 10-154
    runcinata, 10-155
cress
    mouse-ear, 15-5
    toadflax, 15-72
Cressa
    truxillensis, 27-3
Critesion
    brachyantherum (Nevski)
      Barkworth & D. Dewey,
      82=122
    glaucum (Steud.) Löve,
      82=125
    jubatum (L.) Nevski, 82=123
    marinum (Hudson) Löve,
      82=124
    murinum (L.) Löve, 82=125
    pusillum (Nutt.) Löve,
      82=126
Crossosomataceae = 23 in
    part
Croton
    californicus, 40-1
    texensis, 40-2

crowfoot
    bristly, 91-49
    Macoun, 91-49
    water, 91-36
    yellow-water, 91-41
crownbeard, golden, 10-398
crownvetch, 41-101
Cruciferae = 15
Crunocallis
    chamissoi (Ledeb.) Ckll.,
      87=11
Crypsis
    alopecuroides, 82-60
    schoenoides, 82-61
cryptanth
    Baker, 14-11
    Barneby, 14-13
    bearded, 14-12
    beguiling, 14-23
    bent-nut, 14-43
    bramble, 14-24
    bristly, 14-48
    broom, 14-46
    canyon, 14-50
    carbon, 14-36
    compact, 14-19
    cushion, 14-18
    dwarf, 14-31
    erect, 14-49
    fragrant, 14-30
    golden, 14-20
    gray, 14-17
    head, 14-16
    Johnston, 14-32
    Jones, 14-33
    Kelsey, 14-34
    low, 14-8
    matted, 14-18
    mound, 14-19
    Nevada, 14-38
    Osterhout, 14-39
    plains, 14-21
    plateau, 14-28
    redroot, 14-37
    Rollins, 14-44
    San Juan, 14-42
    San Rafael, 14-33
    scrambling, 14-24
    silky, 14-47
    slender, 14-29
    smallflower, 14-14
    spreading, 14-15
    tawny, 14-28
    Torrey, 14-51
    tufted, 14-15
    Uinta Basin, 14-14
    Utah, 14-52
    Virgin River, 14-53
    Watson, 14-54
    Wilkes, 14-10
    winged-nut, 14-41
    yellow, 14-26
    yelloweye, 14-27
Cryptantha

abata, 14-8
affinis, 14-9
ambigua, 14-10
angustifolia, App. 11
bakeri, 14-11
barbigera, 14-12
barnebyi, 14-13
breviflora, 14-14
caespitosa, 14-15
capitata, 14-16
cinerea, 14-17
circumscissa, 14-18
compacta, 14-19
confertiflora, 14-20
crassisepala, 14-21
creutzfeldtii, 14-22
decipiens, 14-23
dumetorum, 14-24
elata, App. 11
fendleri, 14-25
flaccida, App. 11
flava, 14-26
flavoculata, 14-27
fulvocanescens, 14-28
gracilis, 14-29
grahamii, 14-30
humilis, 14-31
inaequata Johnston, not in
    Utah (Cronquist et al.,
    1964)
interrupta, App. 11
jamesii (Torr.) Pays., 14=17
johnstonii, 14-32
jonesiana, 14-33
kelseyana, 14-34
longiflora, 14-35
mensana, 14-36
micrantha, 14-37
nana (Eastw.) Pays., 14=31
nevadensis, 14-38
ochroleuca Higgins, 14=19
osterhoutii, 14-39
paradoxa, 14-40
pterocarya, 14-41
pustulosa, 14-42
racemosa, App. 11
recurvata, 14-43
rollinsii, 14-44
rugulosa, 14-45
scoparia, 14-46
semiglabra, App. 11
sericea, 14-47
setosissima, 14-48
stricta, 14-49
suffruticosa (Torr.) Greene,
    14=17
tenuis, 14-50
torreyana, 14-51
utahensis, 14-52
virginensis, 14-53
watsonii, 14-54
wetherillii, 14-55
Cryptogramma
    acrostichoides R. Br., 86=12

crispa, 86-12
stelleri, App. 56
Cryptogrammaceae = 86 in
    part
cucumber
    root, 61-30
    wild mock, 30-3
Cucurbita
    foetidissima, 30-2
    palmata, App. 21
Cucurbitaceae, 30; App. 21
cudweed
    hoary, 10-223
    lowland, 10-224
    marsh, 226
    sticky, 10-227
    straw, 10-225
Cupressaceae, 31; App. 22
curlygrass, 82-119
currant family, 47
currant
    alpine prickly, 47-7
    golden, 47-1
    Rothrock, 47-11
    squaw, 47-2
    sticky, 47-10
    wax, 47-2
    western, 47-3
    wild black, 47-3
    wolf, 47-11
Cuscuta
    applanata, App. 23
    approximata, 32-1
    campestris Yunck., 32=8
    cephalanthii, 32-2
    cuspidata, 32-3
    denticulata, 32-4
    indecora, 32-5
    megalocarpa, 32-6
    nevadensis J. R. Johnst.,
        32=9
    occidentalis, 32-7
    pentagona, 32-8
    salina, 32-9
    umbrosa Hook., 32=6
    warneri, App. 23
Cuscutaceae, 32; App. 23
cutgrass, rice, 82-128
Cyclachaena
    xanthifolia (Nutt.) Fresen.,
        10=281
Cycladenia
    humilis, 8-5
    low, 8-5
Cycloloma
    atriplicifolium, 25-30
Cylindropuntia
    whipplei (Engelm. & Bigel.)
        Knuth, 16=16
Cylindropyrum
    cylindrica (Host) Löve, 82=1
Cymbalaria
    muralis, App. 66
Cymopterus

acaulis, 7-10
basalticus, 7-11
beckii, 7-12
bulbosus, 7-13
coulteri, 7-14
duchesnensis, 7-15
evertii, App. 6
fendleri Gray, 7=10
globosus, 7-16
hendersonii, 7-17
higginsii Welsh, 7=10
ibapensis, 7-18
jonesii Coult. & Rose, 7=25
lemmonii, 7-19
longipes, 7-20
minimus, 7-21
multinervatus, 7-22
newberryi, 7-23
petraeus Jones, 7=26
purpurascens, 7-24
purpureus, 7-25
rosei (Jones) Jones, 7=25
terebinthinus, 7-26
Cynanchum
    utahense, App. 9
Cynodon
    dactylon, 82-62
Cynoglossum
    officinale, 14-56
Cyperaceae, 33; App. 24
Cyperus
    acuminatus, App. 24
    aristatus, 33-82
    erythrorhizos, 33-83
    esculentus, 33-84
    schweinitzii, 33-85
cypress family, 31
cypress, summer, 25-34
Cypripediaceae = 76 in part
Cypripedium
    calceolus, 76-6
    fasciculatum, 76-7
Cyrtorhyncha
    ranunculina Nutt., App. 60 =
        Ranunculus ranunculinus
Cystopteris
    bulbifera, 86-13
    fragilis, 86-14
Dactylis
    glomerata, 82-63
daisy, see fleabane
daisy, ox-eye, 10-285
Dalea
    arborescens Gray, App. 27 =
        Psorothamnus arborescens
    candida Willd., 41=104
    epica Welsh, 41=102
    flavescens, 41-102
    fremontii Gray, 41=161
    lanata, 41-103
    oligophylla, 41-104
    Searls, 41-105
    searlsiae, 41-105
    woolly, 41-103

644

647

651

albicaulis, 74-39
avita (Klein) Klein, 74=42
biennis, 74-40
caespitosa, 74-41
californica, 74-42
cavernae, 74-43
coronopifolia, 74-44
deltoides, 74-45
elata, 74-46
flava, 74-47
hookeri T. & G., 74=46
howardii, 74-48
lavandulaefolia T. & G., 74=3
longissima, 74-49
pallida, 74-50
primiveris, 74-51
strigosa (Rydb.) Mkze. &
  Bush, 74=40
trichocalyx Nutt., 74=50
villosa Thunb., 74=40
Oleaceae, 73; App. 45
oleaster family, 35
Oligosporus
  campestris (L.) Cassini,
    10=44
  dracunculus (L.) Poljakov,
    10=47
olive family, 73
olive
  desert, 73-1
  Russian, 35-1
Onagraceae, 74; App. 46
onion
  Brandegee, 61-4
  dusky, 61-6
  Geyer, 61-8
  largeflower, 61-9
  Nevada, 61-10
  nodding, 61-7
  shortstyle, 61-5
  small, 61-11
  tapertip, 61-1
  textile, 61-12
  twincrest, 61-3
oniongrass, 82-133
  purple, 82-134
Onobrychis
  viciifolia, 41-141
Onopordum
  acanthium, 10-305
Ophioglossaceae, 75; App.
  47
Opuntia
  acanthocarpa, 16-6
  aurea Baxter, 16=10
  basilaris, 16-7
  chlorotica, 16-8
  echinocarpa, 16-9
  erinacea, 16-10
  fragilis, 16-11
  littoralis, App. 14
  macrorhiza, 16-12
  phaeacantha, 16-13
  polyacantha, 16-14

pulchella, 16-15
whipplei, 16-16
orach
  Blue Valley, 25-8
  fat-hen, 25-12
  garden, 25-10
  Powell, 25-13
  silver, 25-2
  spear, 25-12
  stalked, 25-15
  tumbling, 25-14
  wolf, 25-16
Orchidaceae, 76; App. 48
orchid family, 76
oreganillo, 112-1
Oregon grape, 11-3
Oreobroma
  nevadensis (Gray) Howell,
    87=8
  pygmaea (Gray) Howell, 87=8
Oreocarya
  bakeri Greene, 14=11
  breviflora Osterh., 14=14
  caespitosa A. Nels., 14=15
  elata Eastw., App. 11 =
    Cryptantha elata
  flava A. Nels., 14=26
  flavoculata A. Nels., 14=27
  fulvocanescens (Gray) Greene,
    14=28
  humilis Greene, 14=31
  longiflora A. Nels., 14=35
  mensana Jones, 14=36
  osterhoutii Pays., 14=39
  paradoxa A. Nels., 14=40
  pustulosa Rydb., 14=42
  rollinsii (Johnston) W. A.
    Weber, 14=44
  sericea (Gray) Greene, 14=47
  stricta Osterh., 14=49
  suffruticosa (Torr.) Greene,
    14=17
Oreochrysum
  parryi (Gray) Rydb., 10=244
Oreoxis
  alpina, 7-50
  alpine, 7-50
  bakeri, App. 6
  trotteri, App. 6
Orobanchaceae, 77
Orobanche
  californica auct. non Cham. &
    Schlecht., 77=1
  cooperi (Gray) Heller, 77=3
  corymbosa, 77-1
  fasciculata, 77-2
  ludoviciana, 77-3
  multiflora Nutt., 77=3
  uniflora, 77-4
Orogenia
  linearifolia, 7-51
Orthilia
  secunda (L.) House, 90=7
Orthocarpus

luteus, 102-35
purpureo-albus, 102-36
tolmiei, 102-37
Oryzopsis
  asperifolia, 82-151
  exigua, 82-152
  hymenoides (R. & S.) Ricker,
    82=217
  micrantha, 82-153
Osmorhiza
  chilensis, 7-52
  depauperata, 7-53
  occidentalis, 7-54
Ostrya
  knowltonii, 12-4
owlclover
  purple-white, 102-36
  Tolmie, 102-37
  yellow, 102-35
Oxalidaceae, 78
Oxalis
  corniculata, 78-1
ox-eye daisy, 10-285
Oxybaphus
  linearis (Pursh) Rob., 71=9
  multiflorus Torr., 71=10
Oxypolis
  fendleri, 7-55
Oxyria
  digyna, 85-53
Oxytenia
  acerosa, 10-306
Oxytheca
  perfoliata, App. 55
Oxytropis
  besseyi, 41, 142
  deflexa, 41-143
  jonesii Barneby, 41=146
  lambertii, 41-144
  multiceps, 41-145
  obnapiformis C. L. Porter,
    41=142
  oreophila, 41-146
  parryi, 41-147
  sericea, 41-148
  viscida, 41-149
oyster plant, 10-395
Pachistima, see Paxistima
Pachystima, see Paxistima
Packera
  cana (Hook.) Weber & Löve,
    10=329
  crocata (Rydb.) Weber &
    Löve, 10=331
  dimorphophylla (Greene)
    Weber & Löve, 10=332
  fendleri (Gray) Weber &
    Löve, 10=334
  multilobata (T. & G.) Weber &
    Löve, 10=341
  neomexicana (Gray) Weber &
    Löve, 10=342
  oodes (Rydb.) W. A. Weber,
    10=348

657

Howell, App. 31 = P. lutea
sericea, 51-35
tetramera, App. 31
threadleaf, 51-31
Utah, 51-36
utahensis, 51-36
vallis-mortae, 51-37
white, 51-14
Phalaris
arundinacea, 82-161
Phalaroides
arundinacea (L.) Raüschert,
82=161
pheasant-eye, 91-3
Philadelphus
microphyllus, 101-14
Phleum
alpinum, 82-162
pratense, 82-163
phlox family, 83
Phlox
austromontana, 83-39
carpet, 83-42
Cedar Canyon, 83-40
cluteana, App. 53
cushion, 83-47
daggerleaf, 83-40
desert, 83-39
gladiformis, 83-40
grayleaf, 83-41
griseola, 83-41
hoodii, 83-42
jonesii, 83-43
longifolia, 83-44
longleaf, 83-44
moss, 83-46
mound, 83-48
multiflora, 83-45
muscoides, 83-46
pulvinata, 83-47
Rocky Mountain, 83-45
tumulosa, 83-48
wild, 83-44
Zion Canyon, 83-43
Phoradendron
californicum, 114-6
juniperinum, 114-7
Phragmites
australis, 82-164
communis Trin., 82=164
Phyla
cuneifolia, 112-2
nodiflora, App. 69
Physalis
crassifolia, App. 67
fendleri Gray, 105=11
hederaefolia, 105-11
heterophylla, App. 67
lobata, App. 67
longifolia, 105-12
pubescens, App. 67
virginiana Mill., 105=12
Physaria
acutifolia, 15-108

chambersii, 15-109
floribunda, 15-110
grahamii Morton, 15=110
lepidota Roll., 15=109
newberryi, 15-111
rollinsii Mulligan, 15=108
Physocarpus
alternans, 93-27
malvaceus, 93-28
monogynus (Torr.) Coult.,
93=28
Physostegia
parviflora, 58-20
Picea
engelmannii, 80-3
pungens, 80-4
pickleweed, 25-1
Picradenia
helenioides Rydb., 10=273
lemmonii Greene, App. 10 =
Hymenoxys lemmonii
richardsonii Hook., 10=275
Picrothamnus
desertorum Nutt., 10=57
pigweed
Powell, 5-3
prostrate, 5-2
redroot, 5-4
tumbling, 5-1
winged, 25 30
pimpernell, water, 89-12
Pinaceae, 80; App. 50
pincushion plant, 83-37
pine family, 80
pine
bristlecone, 80-8
limber, 80-7
lodgepole, 80-5
ponderosa, 80-10
yellow, 80-10
pineapple weed, 10-302
pinedrops, 39-8
pinegrass, 82-51
pingue, 10-275
pink elephants, 102-40
pink family, 22
Pinus
contorta, 80-5
edulis, 80-6
flexilis, 80-7
longaeva, 80-8
monophylla, 80-9
monticola, App. 50
ponderosa, 80-10
pinyon
single-leaf, 80-9
two-needle, 80-6
Piperia
unalascensis (Spreng.) Rydb.,
76=13
pipsissewa, 90-1
Pityrogramma
triangularis, 86-22
Plagiobothrys

arizonicus, 14-79
jonesii, 14-80
kingii, App. 11
leptocladus, 14-81
scouleri, 14-82
tenellus, 14-83
plant
obedient, 58-20
pincusion, 83-37
Plantaginaceae, 81; App. 51
Plantago
elongata, 81-1
eriopoda, 81-2
insularis, 81-3
lanceolata, 81-4
major, 81-5
patagonica, 81-6
purshii R. & S., 81=6
tweedyi, 81-7
virginica, App. 51
plantain family, 81
plantain
broadleaf, 81-5
English, 81-4
longleaf, 81-1
meadow, 81-7
rattlesnake, 76-9
woolly, 81-6
woolly-foot, 81-2
Platanthera
dilatata (Pursh) L. C. Beck,
76=10
hyperborea (L.) Lindl., 76=11
obtusata (Banks) Lindl., App.
48 = Habenaria obtusata
sparsiflora (Wats.) Schlecht.,
76=12
Platyschkuhria
integrifolia, 10-314
Platystemon
californicus, 79-7
Plectritis
macrocera, 111-1
Pluchea
camphorata, 10-315
sericea, 10-316
plum, American, 93-47
plume, Apache, 93-12
Pneumonanthe
affinis (Griseb.) Greene, 45=6
parryi (Engelm.) Greene, 45=9
Poa
abbreviata auct. non R. Br.,
82=179
aggassizensis J. Boivin & D.
Löve, 82=180
alpina, 82-165
ampla Merr., 82=182
annua, 82-166
arctica, 82-167
bigelovii, 82-168
bolanderi, 82-169
bulbosa, 82-170
canbyi (Scribn.) Howell,

658

undulata, 42-3
quillwort family, 54
rabbitbrush
  alkali, 10-119
  desert, 10-124
  dwarf, 10-120
  Greene, 10-121
  mountain, 10-128
  Parry, 10-125
  rubber, 10-123
  southwest, 10-126
  spreading, 10-122
  Vasey, 10-127
Rafinesquia
  californica, App. 10
  neomexicana, 10-323
ragged rustlers, 10-270
ragweed, 10-12
  bur, 10-8
  common, 10-9
  giant, 10-14
  low, 10-13
  western, 10-12
Ranunculaceae, 91; App. 61
Ranunculus
  acriformis, 91-312
  acris, 91-32
  adoneus, 91-33
  alismaefolius, 91-34
  andersonii, 91-35
  aquatilis, 91-36
  arvensis, 91-37
  cardiophyllus, 91-38
  circinatus Sibth., 91=36
  cymbalaria, 91-39
  eschscholtzii, 91-40
  flabellaris, 91-41
  flammula, 91-42
  gelidus, 91-43
  glaberrimus, 91-44
  gmelinii, 91-45
  hyperboreus, 91-46
  inamoenus, 91-47
  jovis, 91-48
  juniperinus Jones, 91=35
  longirostris Godron, 91=36
  macounii, 91-49
  natans C. A. Mey., 91=46
  oreogenes, 91-50
  orthorhynchus, 91-51
  pedatifidus, App. 61
  ranunculinus, App. 61
  repens, 91-52
  sceleratus, 91-53
  testiculatus, 91-54
raspberry, 93-56
  black, 93-57
  New Mexican, 93-58
ratany family, 57
ratany, range, 57-1
Ratibida
  columnaris (Sims) D. Don,
    10=324
  columnifera, 10-324

redbud, western, 41-99
Redfieldia
  flexuosa, 82-191
redtop, 82-6
reed, common, 82-164
reedgrass
  bluejoint, 82-49
  Jones, 82-52
  northern, 82-53
  purple, 82-50
  slimstem, 82-53
rein orchid
  Alaska, 76-13
  satyr, 76-14
Reverchonia
  arenaria, 40-23
Reynoutria
  japonica Houtt., 85=58
Rhamnaceae, 92; App. 62
Rhamnus
  alnifolia, App. 62
  betulaefolia, 92-5
Rhodiola
  integrifolia Raf., 29=4
Rhus
  aromatica Ait., 6=2
  cismontana Greene, 6=1
  glabra, 6-1
  radicans L., 6=3
  trilobata, 6-2
ribbongrass, reed, 82-161
Ribes
  aureum, 47-1
  cereum, 47-2
  hudsonianum, 74-3
  inerme, 47-4
  lacustre, 47-5
  laxiflorum, App. 29
  leptanthum, 47-6
  mogollonicum Greene, 47=11
  montigenum, 47-7
  petiolare Dougl., 47=3
  setosum, 47-8
  velutinum, 47-9
  viscosissimum, 47-10
  wolfii, 47-11
ricegrass
  Indian, 82-217
  little, 82-152
  littleseed, 82-153
  roughleaf, 82-151
Robinia
  neomexicana, 41-164
  pseudoacacia, 41-165
rockbrake, American, 86-12
rockcress
  common, 15-16
  Drummond, 15-7
  hairy, 15-9
  hoary, 15-17
  Holboell, 15-10
  Lemmon, 15-11
  littleleaf, 15-14
  Lyall, 15-13

Munz, 15-20
Nuttall, 15-15
pretty, 15-18
Selby, 15-19
sicklepod, 15-21
tower, 15-8
rockdaisy
  Jones, 10-312
  Stansbury, 10-311
rocket
  dame's, 15-74
  London, 15-118
rockjasmine
  pygmy-flower, 89-3
  slenderleaf, 89-1
  western, 89-2
rockparsley, mountain, 7-17
Roemeria
  refracta, 79-8
root, cucumber, 61-30
Rorippa
  curvipes, 15-112
  islandica auct. non (Oeder)
    Borb., 15=113
  nasturtium-aquaticum (L.)
    Schinz & Thell., 15=106
  palustris, 15-113
  sinuata, 15-114
  sphaerocarpa (Gray) Britt.,
    15=113
  sylvestris, App. 12
  tenerrima, 15-115
Rosa
  canina, 93-52
  eglanteria L., 93=54
  manca Greene, 93=53
  neomexicana Ckll., 93=55
  nutkana, 93-53
  rubiginosa, 93-54
  woodsii, 93-55
Rosaceae, 93; App. 63
rose family, 93
rose
  dog, 93-52
  nutka, 93-53
  woods, 93-55
Rubacer
  parviflorum (Nutt.) Rydb.,
    93=59
rubberplant, Colorado, 10-275
Rubia
  tinctorum, 94-11
Rubiaceae, 94; App. 64
Rubus
  idaeus, 93-56
  leucodermis, 93-57
  neomexicanus, 93-58
  parviflorus, 93-59
Rudbeckia
  ampla A. Nels., App. 10 =
    R. laciniata
  laciniata, App. 10
  montana Gray, 10=325
  occidentalis, 10-325

selfheal, 58-22
Selinocarpus
  diffusus Gray, 71=13
  nevadensis, 71-13
Senecio
  amplectens, 10-326
  atratus, 10-327
  aureus L., 10=351
  bigelovii, 10-328
  blitoides Greene, 10=335
  canus, 10-329
  crassulus, 10-330
  crocatus, 10-331
  dimorphophyllus, 10-332
  douglasii DC., 10=339, 340
  eremophilus, 10-333
  fendleri, 10-334
  fremontii, 10-335
  hartianus, 10-336
  hydrophilus, 10-337
  integerrimus, 10-338
  kingii Rydb., 10=333
  longilobus, 10-339
  monoensis, 10-340
  multilobatus, 10-341
  mutabilis Greene, 10=342
  neomexicanus, 10-342
  pauperculus, 10-343
  pudicus, 10-344
  purshianus Nutt., 10=329
  saxosus Klatt, 10=351
  serra, 10-345
  spartioides, 10-346
  sphaerocephalus, 10-347
  streptanthifolius, 10-348
  triangularis, 10-349
  uintahensis (A. Nels.)
    Greenm., 10=341
  vulgaris, 10-350
  werneriaefolius, 10-351
senna, bladder, 41-100
Seriphidium
  arbusculum (Nutt.) W. A.
    Weber, 10=41
  canum (Pursh) W. A. Weber,
    10=45
  novum A. Nels., 10=53
  pygmaeum (Gray) W. A.
    Weber, 10=54
  tridentatum (Nutt.) W. A.
    Weber, 10=58
  vaseyanum (Rydb.) W. A.
    Weber, 10=58
serviceberry, 93-1
  Utah, 93-2
Sesuvium
  verrucosum, 3-2
Setaria
  glauca, 82-199
  lutescens (Weigel) Hubb.,
    82=199
  verticillata, 82-200
  viridis, 82-201
shadscale, 25-4

shellflower, 58-15
Shepherdia
  argentea, 35-3
  canadensis, 35-4
  rotundifolia, 35-5
shepherd's purse, 15-29
shooting star
  alpine, 89-4
  pretty, 89-5
Sibbaldia
  procumbens, 93-61
Sida
  hederacea (Dougl.) Torr., 66=7
  leprosa (Ort.) K. Schum, 66=7
Sidalcea
  candida, 66-8
  neomexicana, 66-9
  oregana, 66-10
Silene
  acaulis, 22-26
  alba (Miller) Krause, 22=19
  antirrhina, 22-27
  douglasii, 22-28
  menziesii, 22-29
  petersonii, 22-30
  pratensis (Rafn.) Gren. &
    Godr., 22=19
  scouleri, 22-31
  verecunda, 22-32
silktassel, yellowleaf, 28-2
silverberry, 35-2
Simaroubaceae, 104
Sinapsis
  alba L., App. 12 = Brassica
    hirta
  arvensis L., 15=26
Sinopteridaceae = 86 in part
Sisymbrium
  altissimum, 15-117
  irio, 15-118
  linifolium Nutt., 15=116
  officinale, 15-119
Sisyrinchium
  angustifolium auct non Mill.
    53=5
  demissum, 53-4
  douglasii, App. 32
  idahoense, 53-5
  montanum auct. non Greene,
    53=5
  radicatum Bickn., 53=4
Sitanion
  breviaristatum J. G. Sm.,
    82=78
  hystrix (Nutt.) J. G. Sm.,
    82=78
  jubatum J. G. Sm., 82=78
  longifolium J. G. Sm., 82=78
Sium
  suave, 7-59
skeletonweed
  Arizona, 10-287
  largeflower, 10-289
  smoothseed, 10-288

skullcap, 58-28
  littlecap, 58-29
skunkbush, 6-2
skunkleaf, 83-52
skunkweed, 83-54
skypilot, 83-53
skyrocket, 83-8
slipper, fairy, 76-1
sloughgrass, American, 82-21
smartweed, water, 85-54
Smelowskia
  calycina, 15-120
Smilacina
  racemosa, 61-28
  stellata, 61-29
smotherweed, 25-17
snakeweed
  broom, 10-232
  golden, 10-231
  threadleaf, 10-230
snapdragon family, 102
snapdragon, king, 102-1
sneezeweed
  autumn, 10-249
  orange, 10-158
snowball, 71-2
snowberry
  longflower, 21-6
  mountain, 21-8
  western, 21-7
Solanaceae, 105; App. 67
Solanum
  carolinense, App. 67
  dulcamara, 105-13
  elaeagnifolium, 105-14
  jamesii, 105-15
  nigrum, 105-16
  rostratum, 105-17
  sarrachoides, 105-18
  triflorum, 105-19
Solidago
  canadensis, 10-352
  elongata Nutt., 10=352
  lepida DC., 10=352
  missouriensis, 10-353
  multiradiata, 10-354
  nana, 10-355
  occidentalis (Nutt.) T. & G.,
    10=214
  parryi (Gray) Greene, 10=244
  petradoria Blake, 10=313
  sparsiflora, 10-356
  spathulata, 10-357
  spectabilis, App. 10
  trinervata Greene, 10=356
  velutina DC., 10=356
solomon seal
  false, 61-28
  starry false, 61-29
Sonchus
  arvensis, 10-358
  asper, 10-359
  oleraceus, 10-360
  uliginosus Bieb., 10=358

667

61=34
Tradescantia
  occidentalis, 26-1
Tragia
  ramosa, 40-24
  stylaris Muell.-Arg., 40=24
Tragopogon
  dubius, 10-394
  major Jacq., 10=394
  porrifolius, 10-395
  pratensis, 10-396
Trautvetteria
  caroliniensis, App. 61
tree-of-heaven, 104-1
trefoil
  bush, 41-121
  common, 41-120
  foothill, 41-119
  Mojave, 41-118
  slender, 41-122
  Utah, 41-123
  Wright, 41-124
Trianthema
  portulacastrum, App. 3
Tribulus
  terrestris, 117-2
Tricardia
  Watson, 51-38
  watsonii, 51-38
Tridens
  hairy, 82-100
  muticus, 82-226
  pilosus Hitchc., 82=100
  pulchellus (H.B.K.) Hitchc.,
    82=101
  slim, 82-226
Trifolium
  andersonii, 41-169
  andinum, 41-170
  beckwithii, App. 27
  dasyphyllum, 41-171
  eriocephalum, 41-171
  fragiferum, 41-173
  gymnocarpon, 41-174
  hybridum, 41-175
  kingii, 41-176
  longipes, 41-177
  macilentum, 41-178
  nanum, 41-179
  parryi, 41-180
  pratense, 41-181
  repens, 41-182
  variegatum, 41-183
  wormskjoldii, 41-184
Triglochin
  concinna, 56-1
  maritima, 56-2
  palustris, 56-3
Triodanus
  perfoliata, App. 15
Tripterocalyx
  carneus, 71-14
  cyclopterus (Gray) Standl.,
    71=14

micranthus, 71-15
Trisetum
  canescens, 82-227
  montanum Vasey, 82=228
  spicatum, 82-228
  spike, 82-228
  tall, 82-227
  Wolf, 82-229
  wolfii, 82-229
Triteleia
  grandiflora, 61-31
Triticum
  cylindricum (Host) Cesati,
    82=1
Trollius
  albiflorus (Gray) Rydb., 91=58
  laxus, 91-58
Tryphane
  rubella (Wahl.) Reichb., 22=10
tule, 33-98
tumblegrass, 82-192
tumbleweed, 25-39
turpentine bush, 96-1
Turritis
  glabra L., 15=8
twayblade
  broadleaf, 76-16
  northern, 76-15
twinflower, Linnaeus, 21-1
twinpod
  chamber, 15-109
  Newberry, 15-111
  Rydberg, 15-108
twisted-stalk, 61-30
twistflower, 15-124
Typha
  angustifolia auct. non L.,
    108=1
  domingensis, 108-1
  latifolia, 108-2
Typhaceae, 108
Ulmaceae, 109
Ulmus
  pumila, 109-2
Umbelliferae = 7
unicorn plant family, 68
unicorn plant, small-flowered,
  68-1
Urtica
  dioica, 110-2
  gracilis Ait., 110=2
Urticaceae, 110
Utricularia
  intermedia, 60-1
  macrorhiza Le Conte, 60=3
  minor, 60-2
  vulgaris, 60-3
Uvulariaceae = 61 in part
Vaccaria
  pyramidata, 22-43
Vaccinium
  caespitosum, 39-9
  globulare Rydb., 39=10
  membranaceum, 39-10

myrtillus, 39-11
occidentale, 39-12
scoparium, 39-13
valerian family, 111
valerian
  cordilleran, 111-2
  taprooted, 111-3
  western, 111-4
Valeriana
  acutiloba, 111-2
  arizonica, App. 68
  edulis, 111-3
  occidentalis, 111-4
Valerianaceae, 111; App. 68
Valerianella
  locusta, App. 68
Vanclevea
  pillar, 10-397
  stylosa, 10-397
velvetgrass, Yorkshirefog,
  82-121
velvetleaf, 66-1
Veratrum
  californicum, 61-32
  tenuipetalum Heller, 61=32
Verbascum
  blattaria, 102-105
  thapsus, 102-106
  virgatum, 102-107
Verbena
  bracteata, 112-3
  clay, 71-1
  goodingii, 112-4
  hastata, 112-5
  macdougalli, App. 69
Verbenaceae, 112; App. 69
Verbesina
  encelioides, 10-398
Veronica
  americana, 102-108
  anagallis-aquatica, 102-109
  arvensis, 102-110
  biloba, 102-111
  catenata, 102-112
  hederifolia, 102-113
  nutans Bong., 102=117
  peregrina, 102-114
  persica, 102-115
  serpyllifolia, 102-116
  wormskjoldii, 102-117
Veronicastrum
  serpyllifolium (L.) Fourr.,
    102=116
vervain family, 112
vervain
  blue, 112-5
  Goodding, 112-4
  prostrate, 112-3
vetch
  American, 41-185
  hairy, 41-187
  Louisiana, 41-186
Vexibia
  nuttalliana (Turner) W. A.

670

PAGE INDEX TO FAMILIES